Best and Promising Practices
in Developmental Disabilities

Best and Promising Practices in Developmental Disabilities

Edited by
Alan Hilton
and
Ravic Ringlaben

pro·ed
An International Publisher

8700 Shoal Creek Boulevard
Austin, Texas 78757-6897

© 1998 by PRO-ED, Inc.
8700 Shoal Creek Boulevard
Austin, Texas 78757-6897

Library of Congress Cataloging–in–Publication Data

Best and promising practices in developmental disabilities/edited by
  Alan Hilton and Ravic Ringlaben.
        p.   cm.
    Includes bibliographical references (p.   ) and index.
    ISBN 0-89079-720-X (paperback : alk. paper)
    1. Developmentally disabled—Education—United States.
  2. Developmentally disabled—Services for—United States.
  3. Developmentally disabled—United States—Psychology.   4. Social
  skills—Study and teaching—United States.   5. Special education
  teachers—Training of—United States.   I. Hilton, Alan (Alan L.)
  II. Ringlaben, Ravic.
HV1570.5.U65B47   1998
362.1'968—dc21   97-18844
                                                  CIP

This book is designed in Goudy.

Production Manager: Alan Grimes
Production Coordinator: Karen Swain
Managing Editor: Chris Olson
Art Director: Thomas Barkley
Designer: Lee Anne Landry
Staff Copyeditor: Suzi Hunn
Reprints Buyer: Alicia Woods
Preproduction Coordinator: Chris Anne Worsham
Project Editor: Debra Berman
Production Assistant: Claudette Landry
Production Assistant: Dolly Fisk Jackson

Printed in the United States of America

3   4   5   6   7   8   9   10   02   01   00

Dedicated to
Tyson Hilton (1981–1991)
and
Rachal Beth Ringlaben

Contents

Contributors

Shauna M. Adams, EdD
University of Dayton
300 College Park Drive
Dayton, OH 45469

Diane E. Berkell Zager, PhD
Long Island University
Department of Special Education
C. W. Post Campus
Brookville, NY 11548

Felix F. Billingsley, PhD
University of Washington
Area of Special Education
Box 353600
Seattle, WA 98115

Arlene Bloom, EdD
Jersey City State College
Administration, Curriculum and
    Instruction Department
2039 Kennedy Boulevard
Jersey City, NJ 07305-1597

James M. Brown, PhD
University of Minnesota
Vocational Education Building, Room 460
St. Paul, MN 55108

Pat Brown, MEd
University of Washington
Center for Transition Services
EEU WJ-10
Seattle, WA 98195

Dale Dahmen-Jones, MEd
University of Arkansas at Little Rock
33rd and University
Little Rock, AR 72204

MaryAnn Demchak, PhD
University of Nevada, Reno
Department of Curriculum and Instruction
Mail Stop 282
Reno, NV 89557

Patricia J. Edelen-Smith, EdD
University of Hawaii at Manoa
Department of Special Education
120 Wist Hall
Honolulu, HI 96822

Steven R. Forness, EdD
*University of California at Los Angeles,
    Neuropsychiatric Hospital*
Psychiatry and Biobehavioral Sciences
760 Westwood Plaza
Los Angeles, CA 90024

Yvonne Bullock Fryberger, MS
*Cincinnati Center for Developmental
    Disorders*
3300 Elland Avenue, Room 379
Cincinnati, OH 45229

Kent Gerlach, EdD
Pacific Lutheran University
School of Education
Department of Special Education
Tacoma, WA 98447-0003

Steven Goodman, MA
Ottawa Area Intermediate School District
13565 Port Sheldon Road
Holland, MI 49423

Alan Hilton, EdD
440 12th Avenue
Santa Cruz, CA 95062

Ann Horwath, MS
University of Hawaii at Manoa
1776 University Avenue, UA 4–6
Honolulu, HI 96822

Deborah Huntington, EdD
3829 Dakota Court
Du, GA 30136

Kenneth A. Kavale, PhD
University of Iowa
Special Education
N 259 Lindquist Center
Iowa City, IA 52242

Earle Knowlton, EdD
University of Kansas
Department of Special Education
3001 Robert Dole Human Development
    Center
Lawrence, KS 66045

Mary F. Landers, EdD
University of Dayton
300 College Park Drive
Dayton, OH 45469

Christine A. Macfarlane, PhD
University of Northern Iowa
Department of Special Education
150A Schindler Education Center
Cedar Falls, IA 50614-0601

James E. Martin, PhD
University of Colorado at Colorado Springs
Department of Special Education
1861 Austin Bluffs Parkway
Colorado Springs, CO 80933

Dennis D. Munk, EdD
Carthage College
Education Department
2001 Alford Park Drive
Kenosha, WI 53140-1994

Howard P. Parette, Jr., EdD
Southeast Missouri State University
Department of Elementary, Early, and
    Special Education
One University Plaza
Cape Girardeau, MO 63701

Darlene E. Perner, EdD
Department of Education
P.O. Box 6000
Fredericton, New Brunswick
Canada E3B 5H1

Anna Lou Pickett, BA
City University of New York
National Resource Center for
 Paraprofessionals in Education
 and Related Services
Center for Advanced Study in Education
25 West 43rd Street, Room 620N
New York, NY 10036

Gordon L. Porter, LLD
School District 12
P.O. Box 40
138 Chapel Street
Woodstock, New Brunswick
Canada E0J 2B0

Linda Price, MA
University of Washington
Center for Transition Services
EEU WJ-10
Seattle, WA 98195

Alan C. Repp, PhD
Northern Illinois University
Department of Educational Psychology,
 Counseling, and Special Education
DeKalb, IL 60115

Ravic Ringlaben, EdD
University of Arkansas at Little Rock
Department of Teacher Education
33rd & University
Little Rock, AR 72204

Andrea Rosenthal-Malek, PhD
Monmouth College
8 Kimberly Drive
Wayside, NJ 07712

Deanna J. Sands, EdD
University of Colorado at Denver
Division of Technology and Support
 Services
Campus Box 106
Denver, CO 80217-3364

J. David Smith, EdD
Longwood College
School of Education and Human Services
201 High Street
Farmville, VA 23909

Garnett J. Smith, EdD
University of Hawaii at Manoa
Hawaii University Affiliated Program
1776 University Avenue UA 4–6
Honolulu, HI 96822

Tom E. C. Smith, EdD
University of Arkansas at Little Rock
Department of Teacher Education
33rd & University
Little Rock, AR 72204

Scott Sparks, PhD
Ohio University
Box 86, McCracken Hall
Athens, OH 45701

Robert A. Stodden, PhD
University of Hawaii at Manoa
Hawaii University Affiliated Program
1776 University Avenue UA 4–6
Honolulu, HI 96822

Toni Van Laarhoven, EdD
Northern Illinois University
Department of Educational Psychology,
 Counseling, and Special Education
DeKalb, IL 60115

H. Roberta Weaver, EdD
University of Dayton
Teacher Education
300 College Park Drive
Dayton, OH 45469

Michael L. Wehmeyer, PhD
The Arc National Headquarters
Department of Research and Program
 Services
500 East Border Street, Suite 300
Arlington, TX 76010

John J. Wheeler, PhD
Tennessee Technological University
Box 5074
Cookeville, TN 38505

Introduction

CHAPTER 1

Alan Hilton and Ravic Ringlaben

Learning Outcomes

After reading this chapter, you should be able to

■ Discuss the origin of best practices in the field of developmental disabilities.

■ Differentiate between best and effective practices.

■ Understand the rationale for the setup of the rest of the book.

TERMS

The following terms are important for the understanding of this chapter:

Best practices: Those overriding practices that direct service provision to individuals with developmental disabilities.

Effective practices: Those approaches that have been effective in practice and have been validated through research.

Promising practices: Those approaches that have been effective in practice.

Goal and Purpose of this Text

The goal of this text is to provide a description of current effective practices within a framework of the existing and established best practices. It is hoped that this compilation of thought and practice will provide guidance and direction for the training of professionals and the direct service to students with developmental disabilities.

Best Practices and Promising Practice

Various authors (e.g., Peters & Heron, 1993; Salisbury, 1991) have argued that the term *best practices* in the field of special education is misused, misunderstood, and a misnomer. In one of the most rational discussions of this issue, Peters and Heron (1993) pointed out a number of problems associated with use of the term in the literature: Similar terms are used interchangeably; attachment of the term to a practice is often based on value rather than effectiveness; the term is

applied to a wide range of practices, from innovative ideas to value-driven imperatives; and use of the term *best* does not identify which practices are truly best. Peters and Heron proposed criteria for establishing best practices based on five questions: Is there a sound theoretical base? Is there methodological integrity of the research? Is there consensus with existing literature? Is there evidence of consistently desired outcomes? Is there evidence of social validity? Although we agree with Peters and Heron that the current use of the term has led to confusion and lack of clarity of what are best practices, we feel that the five component criteria they proposed do not help either because it is exceedingly difficult or impossible to place any practice on the list of best practices.

Therefore, the planning of this book was based on two simple premises. The first is that best practices in the field of developmental disabilities have been established by the professional community. These practices possess affirmative answers to part or most of the questions asked above. These best practices are overriding principles upon which promising practices for service and instruction are based. Promising and effective practices exist that have been validated through professional practice and/or research.

The second premise is that the best, effective, and promising practices are guiding practices in any setting where the individual with disabilities is served. Although this book was not started with an intent to focus on the inclusion movement and its impact on educating students with developmental disabilities, as the chapters were developed, this underlying emphasis became evident. This is a recognition of the fact that inclusion of individuals with developmental disabilities in schools and the larger community is a reality of the last decade of this century. Further, it is a recognition that best and promising practices should be implemented in all settings serving individuals with developmental disabilities. These practices, along with program development, allocation and use of resources, and training for service providers and parents, should influence direct services for individuals with developmental disabilities.

Defining *Best Practices*

There is no clear origin of the use of the term best practices in the field of developmental disabilities or special education (Peters & Heron, 1993). In fact, the early discussions of what later became known as best practices did not include the term best but used other terms, such as "program qualities" (Bellamy & Wilcox, 1980), "appropriate characteristics" (Bates, Renzaglia, & Wehman, 1981), and "components of effective and appropriate education" (Hilton, Faught, & Hagen, 1984).

Bellamy and Wilcox in 1980 made one of the early attempts to define best practices. They presented a set of criteria or program qualities that should be present in secondary programs for autistic and other students who have severe disabilities. Their purpose was to stimulate discussion and research concerning these emerging services. Bellamy and Wilcox included the following program characteristics as representing best practices: integrated, age appropriate, community referenced, future oriented, noncategorical, comprehensive, parental involvement, and effective.

Bates et al. developed a list of characteristics in 1981 to help teachers evaluate the appropriateness of programs for students with severe and profound disabilities. They delineated 12 practices: age-appropriate curriculum and materials, specific objectives, functional activities, consistent cue hierarchy, data collection and charting, periodic revision of the Individualized Education Program (IEP), classroom schedule, instruction outside of the classroom, integrated therapy, instruction in small groups, interaction with students without disabilities, and family involvement. Bates et al. suggested that these characteristics would help teachers to decide on critical parameters of their programs and would "promote better service delivery for students" (p. 148) with severe and profound disabilities.

In 1984 Hilton et al. discussed practices that principals could use to evaluate the quality of self-contained special education classrooms. Their practices were based on the earlier work of Bellamy and Wilcox (1980) and Bates et al. (1981), along with experience in evaluating and supervising self-contained settings. Hilton et al. recommended the following best practices: classroom schedule, instruction in small groups, integrated therapy, functional curriculum, specific individual programs, data collection and charting, specific objectives, periodic review, integration with students without disabilities, age-appropriate curriculum and materials, instruction outside the classroom, and family involvement.

In 1986, as part of a Vermont statewide change project, Fox and his colleagues developed a set of "best education practice" statements and accompanying indicators. These statements included age-appropriate placement, integrated delivery of related service, social integration, transition planning, community-based training, curricular expectations, systematic data-based instruction, home–school partnership, and systematic program evaluation.

In 1988 Snell provided a statement concerning best practices of the day and the future. This description of best practices provided a curricular focus, but woven into the content of the article was a well–thought out rationale for integrating students with severe disabilities into instructional settings with other students. Snell included the following best practices: promoting generalization, improving attitudes toward people with disabilities, daily interaction with peers who do not have disabilities, partial participation, teaching academics, integrating instruction into natural routine, integrating therapy, making instructional decisions to improve teaching, analyzing the functions of maladaptive behavior, and integration of students with severe disabilities with other students.

Also in 1988 McDonnell and Hardman provided a synthesis of best practices associated with the development of exemplary early childhood special education programs. They included these characteristics: integrated, comprehensive, normalized, adaptable, peer and family referenced, and outcome based.

Williams, Fox, Thousand, and Fox (1990) attempted to identify and validate best practices for the field of severe disabilities through the use of an expert panel and a questionnaire sent to practitioners, administrators, and parents. This research identified nine best practices: age-appropriate placement, integrated delivery of services, social integration, transition planning, community-based training, curricular expectations based on adult needs, systematic data-based instruction, home–school partnership, and systematic program evaluation. Although this study was limited to the state of Vermont, their findings conceptually paralleled the other literature but with updated terminology.

There have been other discussions of best practices, most notably in the field of behavioral disorders. For several decades the field of emotional and behavioral disorders has examined best practices in relationship to programs. To effectively evaluate programs for youth with emotional and behavioral disorders, a professional must define what it takes for effective functioning of such programs. Grosenick and Huntze (1983) attempted to define program elements through an analysis of literature because they found very little in the way of quality information regarding existing programs and evaluation of programs. In an attempt to find what did, in fact, exist in the literature in the way of program descriptions and descriptions of program evaluation, they surveyed 365 sources in the following categories: philosophy or ideational context; program goals; population definition; program entry; methods, curriculum, and materials; exit procedures; evaluation; and program operation.

Grosenick and others have consistently investigated program practices (e.g., Grosenick, George, & George, 1987, 1988). In 1988, for example, they identified eight essential components: philosophy, goals, student needs and identification, instructional methods and curriculum, community involvement, program design and operation, exit procedures, and evaluation.

In 1991 the Peacock Hill Working Group reported on successful strategies and practices in the field of emotional or behavioral disorders. They identified seven strategies that were effective with the population: systematic, data-based interventions; continuous assessment and monitoring of progress; provision for practice of new skills; treatment matched to the problem; multicomponent treatment; programming for transfer and maintenance; and commitment to sustained intervention.

The Division on Mental Retardation of the Council for Exceptional Children published a book titled *Best Practices in Mild Mental Retardation* (Robinson, Patton, Polloway, & Sargent, 1989). However, this text was actually a discussion of *promising*, not best, practices.

Although there have been other discussions of best practices for use with other populations (e.g., Wallace, Cohen, & Polloway, 1987) or topics (e.g., McLean, 1992) on the fringes of developmental disabilities, they do little but reinforce the fact that there is an overriding set of principles that should guide practice. Perhaps for the lack of a better term, we have decided to continue the use of the term best practice, but we use the term to refer to the overriding principles—that is, we recommend the use of the best practices as categories for effective practices.

Format of the Text

The format of this book then follows the above logic; that is, sections are based on best practices that are accepted by the field, as noted in the references cited previously. The chapters within these sections are based on effective or promising practices in working with the population.

Acknowledgments

This project was undertaken as a service to the members of the Division on Mental Retardation and Developmental Disabilities of the International Council for Exceptional Children and professionals in the field of developmental disabilities in general. The development of this book was funded by the Division. It is the intent of the Division to provide an up-to-date discussion of best and effective practices in the field of developmental disorders.

The chapter authors and book's editors were not paid for writing or editing any portion of this book and will not receive income from the sales of the book. Profits from sales of the book will go to the Division, but the individual contributors receive nothing. These authors have donated their efforts as a service to those in the field, with the intent of improving services to persons with developmental disabilities.

We wish to thank David Finn for early input and editing assistance; Tom E. C. Smith for his assistance and input during proposal, development, and publication phases of this book; and the individual members of the Board of Directors of the Division on Mental Retardation and Developmental Disabilities who served during the 2-plus years this work has taken. Finally, we wish to thank the numerous chapter authors and co-authors for their expertise and the timely development of their chapters. It is this group of professionals who provided the content to the framework we provide. Without them this book would not exist.

References

Bates, P., Renzaglia, A., & Wehman, P. (1981). Characteristics of appropriate education for severely and profoundly handicapped students. *Education and Training of the Mentally Retarded, 4*, 142–149.

Bellamy, G. T., & Wilcox, B. (1980). Secondary education for severely handicapped students: Guidelines for quality services. In B. Wilcox & A. Thompson (Eds.), *Critical issues in educating autistic children and youth* (pp. 241–261). Washington, DC: U.S. Department of Education.

Fox, W., Thousand, J., Williams, W., Fox, T., Towne, P., Reid, R., Conn-Powers, C., & Calcagnie, L. (1986). *Best education practices '86: Educating learners with severe handicaps*. Burlington: University of Vermont Center for Developmental Disabilities.

Grosenick, J. K., George, M. P., & George, N. L. (1987). A profile of school programs for the behaviorally disordered: Twenty years after Morse, Cutler, and Fink. *Behavioral Disorders, 12*, 159–168.

Grosenick, J. K., George, N. L., & George, M. P. (1988). The availability of program descriptions among programs for seriously emotionally disturbed students. *Behavioral Disorders, 13*, 108–115.

Grosenick, J. K., & Huntze, S. (1983). *More questions than answers: Review and analysis of programs for behaviorally disordered children and youth.* Columbia: National Needs Analysis Project in Behavior Disorders: University of Missouri–Columbia, Department of Special Education.

Hilton, A., Faught, K. K., & Hagen, M. (1984). A yardstick for special education. *Principal, 64*(2), 34–36.

McDonnell, A., & Hardman, M. (1988). A syntheses of "best practice" guidelines for early childhood services. *Journal for Division of Early Childhood, 12,* 328–341.

McLean, J. (1992). *Assuring best practices in communication for child and youth with severe disabilities.* Keynote Address, Second National Symposium on Effective Communication, McLean, VA. (ERIC Document Reproduction Service No. ED 359 693)

Peacock Hill Working Group. (1991). Problems and promises in special education and related services for children and youth with emotional or behavioral disorders. *Behavioral Disorders, 16,* 299–313.

Peters, M. T., & Heron, T. E. (1993). When the best is not good enough: An examination of best practice. *The Journal of Special Education, 26,* 371–385.

Robinson, G. A., Patton, J. R., Polloway, E. A., & Sargent, L. R. (1989). *Best practices in mild mental disabilities.* Reston, VA: The Division on Mental Retardation of the Council for Exceptional Children.

Salisbury, C. L. (1991). Mainstreaming during the early childhood years. *Exceptional Children, 57,* 146–153.

Snell, M. E. (1988). Curriculum and methodology for individuals with severe disabilities. *Education and Training in Mental Retardation, 23,* 302–314.

Wallace, G., Cohen, S. B., & Polloway, E. A. (1987). *Language arts.* Austin, TX: PRO-ED.

Williams, W., Fox, T. J., Thousand, J., & Fox, W. (1990). Level of acceptance and implementation of best practices in the education of students with severe handicaps in Vermont. *Education and Training in Mental Retardation, 25,* 120–131.

Definition and Placement

SECTION I

Best Practices

There is strong agreement in the field and in the best practices literature that appropriate placement of students with disabilities should be based on three critical concepts. The first is *noncategorical placement*. Although this concept is changing with the inclusion movement, it has clearly been established that noncategorical placement means that the student is placed in a setting based on his or her needs for services and curriculum rather than on the category of his or her disability.

The second critical concept is that students with developmental disabilities should have a high level of *inclusion* in settings with students who do not have disabilities. Although much discussion has appeared in the literature concerning the inclusion of students with developmental disabilities into general education classrooms, the data on the success of programs, which would support the benefit to all students of these practices, are mixed. The inclusionary practices that have been demonstrated as effective ways of serving students, for the purposes of this section, are viewed as promising and/or effective practices.

The third critical concept found in the best practices literature is that students with disabilities should be placed in settings that provide *age-appropriate placement*. The age-

appropriate concept, however, is not limited to age-mates, but should include all aspects of the educational process, such as furniture, recreational equipment, curriculum orientation, community interaction, and leisure activities. Age appropriateness is not a concept that is worked toward, but a concept that drives decision making concerning these aspects of an individual's life.

This Section of the Book

Section I frames the orientation of the book. It provides a clear perspective to the concept and definition of developmental disabilities (Chapter 2) and of mental retardation (Chapter 3), the largest category of developmental disabilities. Both of these chapters provide a historical perspective and discuss current trends in the field of special education. Chapter 4 points out the problems of definition and the categories to which definitions lead by providing a discussion of syndromes that contain characteristics found in the definition of mental retardation. Brought to light in these initial chapters is that service needs of students should be defined by their functional skills and individual needs, not by categories.

Developmental Disabilities: Definition, Description, and Directions

CHAPTER 2

Tom E. C. Smith

Learning Outcomes

After reading this chapter, you should be able to

■ Define developmental disabilities and describe the characteristics and needs of individuals with developmental disabilities.

■ Describe the reasons why services for persons with disabilities have been moving to a noncategorical, more functional service model.

■ Discuss legislation that has affected services for persons with developmental disabilities.

TERMS

The following terms are important for the understanding of this chapter:

Assistive technology: A variety of devices and aids that can assist persons with disabilities to achieve success in different environments.

Developmental disabilities: A broad group of disabilities that occur between birth and 22 years of age that have lifelong implications for persons and that substantially limit numerous life functions.

Functional services: Services that are designed to assist persons with disabilities to develop useful, functional skills.

Generic services: Services that are based on needs of persons rather than categorical classification systems.

Individual supports: Services that are designed to support individuals with disabilities in natural settings.

Background

Although individuals with disabilities have received a variety of services for many years, the nature of these services has not remained static, but has been changing almost constantly as new developments and new philosophies have become dominant. One example of change is in the way individuals with disabilities are classified and categorized for intervention purposes. The field of special education has become more and more generic over the past decade. Originally, schools served only students with certain types of disabilities (e.g., mental retardation, cerebral palsy, learning disabilities). As services have evolved, the orientation toward providing interventions to students with disabilities has moved toward a more generic, or generalized, approach.

Many teacher training programs currently train teachers to work with students with various functional abilities, not children with certain clinical labels. Likewise, many states, such as Arkansas, Tennessee, and Alabama, no longer certify teachers to work with children who are designated by a particular label. Rather, certification also has moved to a more generic, functional model, resulting in teachers being trained and certified to teach children with *mild* disabilities or children with *severe* disabilities. There are many reasons why special education and other services for individuals with disabilities have moved to a more generic service model. These include the movement to functional services, the inclusion movement, provision of individual supports, and the current approach to defining mental retardation by the American Association on Mental Retardation (AAMR).

Movement to Functional Services

Although states continue to determine student eligibility for services under the Individuals with Disabilities Act of 1990 (IDEA) by category, such as mental retardation and learning disabilities, many have eliminated categorical special education services in favor of services based on more functional skill levels of students. For example, many states provide services to students based on their having *mild* or *severe* disabilities rather than their being clinically classified as having mental retardation, learning disabilities, or emotional problems (Smith, Finn, & Dowdy, 1993). This generic classification and service model has partly eroded the distinction once held by programs that provided services only to students classified as having mental retardation, learning disabilities, or some other specific type of disability.

The changing model of providing special education for students with mental retardation, learning disabilities, or other specific categories of disabilities is also shown by the changes in teacher training programs. Whereas there used to be many categorical training programs for teachers of students with mental retardation and teachers of students with learning disabilities, more and more teacher preparation programs are now generic in nature, focusing on functional ability levels, such as mild or severe disabilities. One only has to look at the decline in the number of college textbooks focusing on teaching students with mental retardation and the increase in those that emphasize teaching students with mild disabilities to realize the change of focus in special education.

In many public schools no teachers are designated specifically to teach students with mental retardation, learning disabilities, or other categorical disabilities, and no classrooms are specifically for students with these clinical descriptions. Many schools also have eliminated the classrooms that had been designated for students classified as *educable mentally retarded* or *trainable mentally retarded*. In place of these classrooms designated by categories of disabilities and staffed by categorically trained and certified teachers are resource rooms and resource room teachers (MacMillan, 1989).

The Inclusion Movement

The inclusion movement also has contributed to the generic trend of services and teacher training. Proponents of inclusion of students with disabilities emphasize the functionality of each child over categorical labels of any kind. The aim is to provide appropriate services to children in settings with their nondisabled, chronological-age peers, as much as possible without regard to clinical label. The student receives services and supports, for the most part, in the general education classroom rather than in separate rooms. This represents a major shift from the traditional categorical services provided students with mental retardation, learning disabilities, and other categorical disabilities during the early period of special education (Smith, Polloway, Patton, & Dowdy, 1998). The result of this loss of program identity has added to the absorption of students with categorical labels into the general special education service system and broader educational system.

Provision of Individual Supports

Concomitant with the inclusion trend in schools is the national movement to include individuals with all types of disabilities in *normalized* community settings (Clees, 1992). The provision of supports for families and individuals to facilitate community inclusion has helped professionals and adult service agencies move away from the idea of providing services only to persons with a single label, such as mental retardation, to providing services to individuals who need specific interventions (Walker, 1994). For example, rather than working primarily with individuals with physical disabilities, vocational rehabilitation counselors are finding themselves working with a variety of people with different disabilities in community settings. The result is that programs for adults, similar to programs for children, have lost their identity as serving only individuals with mental retardation or other specific disability categories.

AAMR Definition of Mental Retardation

The American Association on Mental Retardation (AAMR) has consistently supplied the field of disabilities with the definition of mental retardation that has been the most widely accepted and used. The most recent revision of the definition, published in 1992 (Luckasson et al., 1992), represents a significant shift from previous AAMR definitions and is compatible with many of the other trends in the field of disabilities. It suggests that it is very difficult to classify an individual based on test scores or other predetermined criteria. Rather, the definition places an emphasis on the levels of supports (e.g., intermittent or limited) needed by individuals to achieve success rather than on degrees of deficits (e.g., mild, moderate, severe, profound) exhibited. This shift in focus places an emphasis on providing the appropriate level of supports to enable the individual to live successfully in a normalized community setting, as opposed to the level of disability presented by the person with mental retardation.

Defining Developmental Disabilities

Developmental disabilities is an umbrella category encompassing problems that begin affecting individuals during their development, generally defined as age 5 to the 22nd birthday. The category has a functional orientation, identifying individuals whose disabilities will create needs in specific activities. In 1993 Congress noted that there were over 3 million individuals in the United States with developmental disabilities (President's Committee on Mental Retardation, 1995). Unlike conditions that are short term in duration, developmental disabilities are chronic disabilities that will likely continue indefinitely. Therefore, the long-term impact of developmental disabilities is extensive. Individuals with developmental disabilities, because of the lifelong nature of their conditions, will likely require some level of supports and services during their lifetime.

The developmental disabilities category, unlike the category of mental retardation and other specific, clinical categories of disabilities, includes a wide variety of specific conditions that impact on people's lives. The 1994 amendments to the Developmental Disabilities Assistance and Bill of Rights Act of 1987 defines developmental disabilities as

> a severe, chronic disability of an individual 5 years of age or older that
>
> (A) is attributable to a mental or physical impairment or combination of mental and physical impairments;
>
> (B) is manifested before the individual attains the age of 22;
>
> (C) is likely to continue indefinitely;
>
> (D) results in substantial functional limitations in three or more of the following areas of major life activity—
>
> > (i)   self care;
> >
> > (ii) receptive and expressive language;
> >
> > (iii) learning;
> >
> > (iv) mobility;
> >
> > (v)   self-direction;
> >
> > (vi) capacity for independent living; and
> >
> > (vii) economic self-sufficiency; and
>
> (E) reflects the individual's need for a combination and sequence of special, interdisciplinary, or generic services, supports, or other assistance that is of lifelong or extended duration and is individually planned and coordinated, except that such term, when applied to infants and young children means individuals from birth to age 5, inclusive, who have substantial developmental delay or specific congenital or acquired conditions with a high probability of resulting in developmental disabilities if services are not provided. [§ 102(7)]

The definition included in the Developmental Disabilities Assistance and Bill of Rights Act of 1987 focuses much more on functional than on categorical issues, and encompasses a wide variety of possible disabling conditions (Wolfe, 1992). It goes well beyond the single category of mental retardation or any other single disability group in scope. For example, the category of developmental disabilities includes the following conditions:

- Mental retardation
- Epilepsy
- Spina bifida
- Cerebral palsy (Omgee, 1992)
- Emotional problems (Clark, Reavis, & Jenson, 1992)
- Autism (Eaves, 1992)
- Deaf–blindness (Marchant, 1992)
- Prader Willi syndrome
- Fragile x syndrome
- Sickle cell anemia

These are only a few of the many conditions that can be classified as developmental disabilities. Even learning disabilities can be considered developmental disabilities (Bender, 1992), which enlarges the population significantly due to the large numbers of individuals classified as having learning disabilities.

Although children with many of these conditions have generally been provided appropriate educational programs, the categorical special education system that has been in place under IDEA has required schools to categorize children into a specific disability group in order to make them eligible for services. In most cases, the requirement of categorical labels has not had a negative impact on the appropriateness of services; however, the mandated categorical system fails to meet the needs of some children. For example, for children with Prader Willi syndrome to be served, they usually have to be classified as having mental retardation. Although mental retardation is a frequent characteristic of Prader Willi syndrome, the fact remains that, by serving a child on the basis of mental retardation, the overall needs related to Prader Willi syndrome, concerning weight and diet management, may go unnoticed. It is hoped that the more functional, generic category of developmental disabilities increases the likelihood that school personnel and others providing services to children will focus their interventions based on individual strengths, weaknesses, and needs, rather than on preconceived notions related to any categorical disability group.

Characteristics and Needs of Individuals with Developmental Disabilities

As a result of the heterogeneity of the category of developmental disabilities, it is difficult to establish universal characteristics and needs for this group of individuals. However, some characteristics and needs are fairly common among individuals considered to have developmental disabilities. By definition, individuals with developmental disabilities manifest a severe, *chronic* disability that will likely exist throughout the individual's life. The result will likely be the need for lifelong specialized services and assistance, provided in a coordinated and culturally competent manner, by many different agencies, professionals, advocates, community representatives, and others (Developmental Disabilities Assistance and Bill of Rights Act, 1994).

Another characteristic of individuals with developmental disabilities, by definition, is that these disabilities result in substantial limitations in a variety of functional, life activities. These include self-care, language and communication, learning, mobility, self-direction, and economic self-sufficiency. The category of developmental disabilities is thus characterized by *functional* limitations and impact. If the disability does not result in limitations in at least three of the noted life activities, then the person, by definition, does not have a developmental disability.

Depending on the specific characteristics of persons with developmental disabilities, direct individualized services or environmental supports might be needed. Direct individualized services include such things as attendant care, educational intervention, and counseling. Environmental supports encompass the many different interventions that can modify the person's environment (e.g., making a particular apartment physically accessible for a person in a wheelchair). Often, individuals with developmental disabilities need both direct individualized services and environmental modifications. However, some individuals may require actions in only one of these areas.

Self-Care Needs

Self-care is directly related to independent living. Individuals with developmental disabilities, while varying a great deal in their self-care needs, frequently require assistance in daily living activities (Langone, 1992). The nature of their chronic, severe disabilities frequently affects their ability to live independently. Many individuals with developmental needs may require, for instance, personal assistance services, which are "a range of services, provided by one or more individuals, designed to assist an individual with a disability to perform daily living activities on or off a job that such individual would typically perform if such individual did not have a disability" (Developmental Disabilities Assistance and Bill of Rights Act of 1994).

Self-care skills are generally grouped into two major categories: (a) eating and (b) dressing and grooming (Langone, 1992). Although the services provided by personal assistants vary greatly, depending on the specific needs of each individual with a disability, these services typically focus in these two areas.

Language and Communication Needs

Individuals with developmental disabilities frequently display deficits in both receptive and expressive language. Language problems range from mild expressive speech problems to profound dysfunction in both receptive and expressive language abilities (Talbott, 1992). Regardless of the degree of language and communication problems, interventions are almost always warranted because of the critical role that language plays in society (Polloway & Smith, 1992).

Numerous interventions are related to communication problems, depending on the specific nature of the problem. For example, interventions might be as simple as the development of a language-enriching environment by the teacher or as complex as the use of cochlear implants to facilitate communication skills (Polloway & Smith, 1992). Depending on the complexity of the intervention, a variety of individuals could be involved in providing services. Speech–language specialists may need to be involved with persons who have severe language and communication problems, whereas positive role models may be the only individuals needed by persons with mild language and communication problems.

Learning Needs

Of all needs exhibited by individuals with developmental disabilities, learning is probably the most often addressed. "Perhaps nowhere has service provision for individuals with developmental disabilities been more comprehensive than in the educational setting" (Wolfe, 1992, p. 126). Special education services for students with developmental disabilities have expanded rapidly during the past 20 years. With the beginning of federal mandates to provide a free appropriate public education to children with disabilities in 1975 (Education for All Handicapped Children Act) came a widespread increase in the number and types of children served in special education programs. Indeed, the *Sixteenth Annual Report to Congress on the Implementation of the Individuals with Disabilities Education Act* (IDEA) reveals that nearly 1.5 million more children with disabilities were served in special education programs in the 1992–1993 than in the 1976–1977 school year (U.S. Department of Education, 1994).

Special education is directly related to the learning needs of children with developmental disabilities. Through the Individualized Education Program (IEP) process, school personnel develop intervention programs that target the learning needs of each child (Smith et al., 1998). The learning needs of adults are also addressed through various service models. Vocational rehabilitation agencies, adult day-care programs, and adult education programs are all involved in assisting adults with learning problems to develop skills necessary for independent living.

Mobility Needs

Orientation and mobility training has long been a service provided for individuals with visual disabilities. However, recently it has become clear that such services are also needed by some individuals with other disabilities. Many persons with developmental disabilities require training in these areas, especially mobility (Clees, 1992). For example, individuals with cerebral palsy, because of their impairments in posture and movement, frequently require mobility assistance (Inge, 1992). Also, persons with mental retardation may need assistance in using public transportation resources. Among the numerous barriers to mobility for persons with developmental disabilities are the following: *physical barriers* (e.g., stairs without a ramp), *social barriers* (e.g., not allowing some children to participate in certain physical activities), and *transportation barriers* (e.g., lack of accessible transportation) (Clees, 1992).

Mobility needs for individuals with developmental disabilities can take several different forms, including (a) ambulation within or between settings (walking, running, sliding, pulling, crawling, transferring to/from wheelchair), and (b) conveyance within or between settings (adapted or nonadapted cars and vans, manual or electric wheelchairs, scooters, bicycles, tricycles, public transportation) (Clees, 1992).

Self-Direction Needs

A significant need for persons with developmental disabilities is self-direction—the taking charge of the events that affect one's life and, furthermore, believing that such control is possible (Langone, 1992). Too often, service providers and family members encourage persons with disabilities to be dependent by not respecting their choices in various decisions. This *denial of choice* keeps individuals with disabilities "in a position of having all aspects of their lives determined through an outer locus of control, thereby denying the person the opportunity to internalize control, which is essential to learning and growth" (Brawner-Jones, 1994, p. 505). Often, the result of such overcontrol is *learned helplessness*, in which individuals actually learn to believe that they are not capable of participating in the decision-making activities affecting their own life, and are thus not capable of independent living.

Self-advocacy is the process whereby individuals literally advocate for themselves. With training, individuals with developmental disabilities not only make decisions about issues affecting their lives, but understand their role in managing and controlling their own lives. "As we move more toward the reality of an inclusive society, it seems inconceivable that such an ideal could ever be fully reached without people with severe disabilities being able to participate in the choices that affect their lives" (McDonnell, Hardman, McDonnell, & Kiefer-O'Donnell, 1995, p. 68).

Economic Self-Sufficiency Needs

Economic self-sufficiency is a problem for many Americans; the presence of a developmental disability compounds this problem. Data indicate that unemployment and underemployment are common problems among adults with developmental disabilities. However, a great deal of literature exists that suggests that economic self-sufficiency for many persons with developmental disabilities is attainable (Langone, 1992). Unfortunately, economic self-sufficiency for these individuals is not automatic; certain services need to be available to assist individuals in attaining this life goal. Therefore, a primary service need for many of these individuals is work-related supports.

Transition services to assist individuals with disabilities in moving from school environments to work environments is now mandated by federal law. One of the primary goals of transition programming is to ensure uninterrupted services and supports for individuals with disabilities and their families (McDonnell et al., 1995). Schools must develop transition plans and work with adult service agencies to implement those plans (Smith et al., 1998). These transition programs should not only focus on the development of job skills and interests but also include goals and objectives related to independent adult functioning, in general (Smith & Dowdy, 1992).

Once transition has been completed from school to postschool environments, various programs need to be in place to assist individuals in getting and keeping jobs. Supported employment is a program for persons with disabilities that facilitates their inclusion into *normalized* society through employment opportunities. An important concept of supported employment is that the individual with a disability is placed in a regular, competitive job in a community setting instead of a sheltered employment situation.

Supported employment can be described as paid employment for individuals with disabilities whose employment at normal pay rates is unlikely because of their disabilities, and who need ongoing support services (McDonnell et al., 1995). The support services are provided on the job site with a job coach, who works alongside the individual with a disability, slowly decreasing the amount of intervention required for the employee to successfully complete the task. Another possible component of supported employment includes training other workers at the work site about a person's disability and ways they can provide various supports.

In addition to supported employment and other employment assistance programs, federal and state policies need to be changed to end the disincentive for working by individuals with disabilities. The loss of benefits due to working should be reexamined in order to modify current policies to avoid the presence of incentives not to work.

General Needs

In addition to the needs described above, some general needs of individuals with developmental disabilities must be addressed. Foremost is the need for service coordination, which is defined in the Developmental Disabilities Act as

> activities that assist and enable individuals with developmental disabilities and their families to access services, supports and other assistance, and includes:
>
> (A) the provision of information to individuals with developmental disabilities and their families about the availability of services, supports, and other assistance;
>
> (B) assistance in obtaining appropriate services, supports, and other assistance, which may include facilitating and organizing such assistance;
>
> (C) coordination and monitoring of services, supports, and other assistance provided singly or in combination to individuals with developmental disabilities and their families to ensure accessibility, continuity, and accountability of such assistance; and
>
> (D) follow-along services that ensure, through a continuing relationship, that the changing needs of individuals with developmental disabilities and their families are recognized and appropriately met. (p. 10)

Without service coordination, individuals with developmental disabilities and their families are often at a loss about what services are available, how to access services, and how to ensure coordinated intervention efforts related to the disability.

Still another general need is in the area of technology. Assistive technology can be defined as a large group of aids, tools, and equipment that can enhance functioning for persons with disabilities in classrooms, worksites, home settings, and community locations. Assistive technology includes a variety of equipment and materials, including simple technologies, such as adapted spoons and switch-adapted, battery-operated toys, as well as complex computerized systems (Parette, Hofmann, & VanBiervliet, 1994). Assistive technology can be a major asset for professionals, family members, and individuals with developmental disabilities. For further information on this topic, see Chapter 17 in this text.

Legislation and Needs of Individuals with Developmental Disabilities

As noted above, individuals with developmental disabilities exhibit significant needs, many of which are being addressed by schools and other service agencies. There are several reasons for the array of services available for persons with developmental disabilities. These include parental advocacy, self-advocacy, litigation, and research that has revealed the efficacy of various services. However, the most important reason that services become available for individuals with developmental disabilities is legislation. Without laws requiring that certain services be made available to persons with disabilities, it is unlikely that the services would be as widespread as they are.

Although state and local governments have made laws and policies affecting individuals with disabilities, the federal government's legislation has had the most impact. Many landmark federal legislative acts have had significant impact on services for persons with developmental disabilities. These include the following (see Wolfe, 1992):

- *The Developmental Disabilities Services and Facilities Construction Act of 1970*—This act first introduced the concept of *developmental disabilities*.

- *Title XIX of the Social Security Act (1971)*—This law required intermediate care facilities for individuals with mental retardation to provide "active treatment" to residents.

- *Education for All Handicapped Children Act of 1975*—This law resulted in mandates for schools to provide appropriate educational services to children with disabilities.

- *Rehabilitation, Comprehensive Services, and Developmental Disabilities Amendment (1978)*—This law redefined the term developmental disability to focus more on functionality.

- *Developmental Disabilities Act Amendment (1984)*—This law included employment-related activities as a focus.

- *Developmental Disabilities Assistance and Bill of Rights Act (1990)*—This act reauthorized the Developmental Disabilities Act of 1984 and put a great deal of emphasis on protection and advocacy.

- *Education of the Handicapped Act Amendments of 1990*—These amendments renamed the act to the Individuals with Disabilities Education Act (IDEA), added autism and traumatic brain injury as disability categories, and required transition planning for students with disabilities.

- *The Americans with Disabilities Act of 1990*—This law is a massive civil rights act for individuals with disabilities and affects most of U.S. society.

Although legislation alone has not resulted in improved services for persons with developmental disabilities, it has created an environment in which professionals, legislators, family members, and individuals with disabilities have begun working together to improve the quality and quantity of services available.

Summary

This chapter has presented information that focused on the broad umbrella category called developmental disabilities. A rationale was presented for more generic terms describing individuals with disabilities. As pointed out, several trends are supportive of more generic, functional classification groups. The movement toward generic services is one reason for more functional disability groups. In addition to this movement, the current AAMR definition, which focuses more on functional descriptions of individuals with mental retardation than did previous definitions, and inclusion have supported the trend toward more generic services based on functional needs of persons with disabilities. Further, the chapter provided a definition of developmental disabilities and some general characteristics of individuals classified as having developmental disabilities. Needs and services for individuals with developmental disabilities, as well as legislation that affects individuals with developmental disabilities, were discussed.

QUESTIONS

1. What are three reasons why services for persons with developmental disabilities have been moving toward a more functional orientation?

2. What role has the current AAMR definition of mental retardation played in the trend toward more generic, functional service models?

3. What is the definition of developmental disabilities and how does the term relate to the category of mental retardation?

4. Describe some of the characteristics and needs of persons with developmental disabilities.

5. What laws have had impacts on services to people with developmental disabilities since 1970?

References

Americans with Disabilities Act of 1990, 42 U.S.C. § 12101 *et seq.*

Bender, W. N. (1992). Learning disabilities. In P. J. McLaughlin & P. Wehman (Eds.), *Developmental disabilities* (pp. 82–95). Boston: Andover Medical.

Brawner-Jones, N. (1994). Support needs and strategies for adults with profound disabilities. In L. Sternberg (Ed.), *Individuals with profound disabilities* (pp. 485–511). Austin, TX: PRO-ED.

Clark, E., Reavis, H. K., & Jenson, W. R. (1992). Emotional impairments. In P. J. McLaughlin & P. Wehman (Eds.), *Developmental disabilities* (pp. 54–66). Boston: Andover Medical.

Clees, T. (1992). Community living. In P. J. McLaughlin & P. Wehman (Eds.), *Developmental disabilities* (pp. 228–266). Boston: Andover Medical.

Developmental Disabilities Assistance and Bill of Rights Act of 1994. Administration on Developmental Disabilities, U.S. Department of Health and Human Services. Washington, DC: U.S. Printing Office.

Developmental Disabilities Services and Facilities Construction Act of 1970, 84 Stat. 1316, 1325.

Eaves, R. C. (1992). Autism. In P. J. McLaughlin & P. Wehman (Eds.), *Developmental disabilities* (pp. 68–80). Boston: Andover Medical.

Education for All Handicapped Children Act of 1975, 20 U.S.C. § 1400 *et seq.*

Individuals with Disabilities Education Act of 1990, 20 U.S.C. § 1400 *et seq.*

Inge, K. J. (1992). Cerebral palsy. In P. J. McLaughlin & P. Wehman (Eds.), *Developmental disabilities* (pp. 30–52). Boston: Andover Medical.

Langone, J. (1992). Mild to moderate mental retardation. In P. J. McLaughlin & P. Wehman (Eds.), *Developmental disabilities* (pp. 1–15). Boston: Andover Medical.

Luckasson, R., Coulter, D. L., Polloway, E. A., Reiss, S., Schalock, R. L., Snell, M. E., Spitalnik, D. M., & Stark, J. A. (1992). *Mental retardation: Definition, classification, and systems of supports.* Washington, DC: American Association on Mental Retardation.

MacMillan, D. L. (1989). Mild mental retardation: Emerging issues. In G. A. Robinson, J. R. Patton, E. A. Polloway, & S. R. Sargent (Eds.), *Best practices in mild mental retardation* (pp. 1–19). Reston, VA: Council for Exceptional Children, Division on Mental Retardation.

Marchant, J. M. (1992). Deaf–blind handicapping conditions. In P. J. McLaughlin & P. Wehman (Eds.), *Developmental disabilities* (pp. 113–122). Boston: Andover Medical.

McDonnell, J. J., Hardman, M. L., McDonnell, A. P., & Kiefer-O'Donnell, R. (1995). *An introduction to persons with severe disabilities.* Needham Heights, MA: Allyn & Bacon.

Omgee, P. L. (1992). Cerebral palsy. In P. J. McLaughlin & P. Wehman (Eds.), *Developmental disabilities* (pp. 30–52). Boston: Andover Medical.

Parette, H. P., Hofmann, A., & VanBiervliet, A. (1994). The professional's role in obtaining funding for assistive technology for infants and toddlers with disabilities. *Teaching Exceptional Children, 26,* 22–28.

Polloway, E. A., & Smith, T. E. C. (1992). *Language instruction for students with disabilities.* Denver: Love.

President's Committee on Mental Retardation. (1995). *State collaboration for community membership*. Washington, DC: Author.

Rehabilitation, Comprehensive Services, and Developmental Disabilities Amendment of 1978, 92 Stat. 2955.

Smith, T. E. C., & Dowdy, C. A. (1992). Future-based assessment and intervention and mental retardation. *Education and Training in Mental Retardation, 27*, 23–31.

Smith, T. E. C., Finn, D. M., & Dowdy, C. A. (1993). *Teaching students with mild disabilities*. Ft. Worth: Harcourt & Brace.

Smith, T. E. C., Polloway, E. A., Patton, J. R., & Dowdy, C. A. (1998). *Teaching students with special needs in inclusive settings* (2nd ed.). Needham Heights, MA: Allyn & Bacon.

Talbott, R. E. (1992). Communication disorders. In P. J. McLaughlin & P. Wehman (Eds.), *Developmental disabilities* (pp. 96–111). Boston: Andover Medical.

U.S. Department of Education. (1994). *Sixteenth annual report to Congress on the implementation of the Individuals with Disabilities Education Act*. Washington, DC: Author.

Walker, P. (1994). Housing and support services: Expanding options for people with severe disabilities. *NARIC Quarterly, 4*, 1–4.

Wolfe, P. S. (1992). Challenges for service providers. In P. J. McLaughlin & P. Wehman (Eds.), *Developmental disabilities* (pp. 124–140). Boston: Andover Medical.

Defining Mental Retardation: The Natural History of a Concept[1]

CHAPTER 3

J. David Smith

Learning Outcomes

After reading this chapter, you should be able to

■ Understand the history of attempts to define mental retardation.

■ Describe the major features of the most recent American Association on Mental Retardation definition.

■ Identify and explain the implications of the new definition of mental retardation for special educators and for students with mental retardation and their families.

TERMS

The following terms are important for the understanding of this chapter:

Adaptive behavior: This term refers to the quality of a person's everyday performance in coping with the demands of the environment.

American Association on Mental Retardation: A multidisciplinary organization formerly known as the American Association on Mental Deficiency. It has been the organization that has developed definitions and classification systems for mental retardation throughout the 20th century.

Developmental period: The developmental period for the purpose of defining mental retardation extends from conception to age 18.

Subaverage general intellectual functioning: This term generally refers to poor performance on an intelligence test. The exact score for a cutoff point between retarded and nonretarded performance has differed in various revisions of the definition of mental retardation.

Historical Conceptions of Mental Retardation

People with mental retardation have been described in many ways over the centuries and decades. The words used to label them have ranged from pejorative terms, such as dumb and stupid, to words that were originally used for medical classification, such as idiot (used as a description for severe retardation) and imbecile (a term used to describe less severe retardation).

The American psychologist Henry Goddard coined the term moron from a Greek word meaning foolish. This label came to be widely applied during the first half of the 20th century to people who were considered to be "high grade defectives"—that is, individuals who were characterized as not being retarded severely enough to be obvious to a casual observer and who had not been brain damaged by disease or injury. These were people whose retardation was considered to be hereditary (Smith, 1985).

Generic terms such as feebleminded, mentally defective, mentally deficient, and mentally retarded have been used until

---

[1]Major portions of this chapter were published earlier in "The Revised AAMR Definition of Mental Retardation: The MRDD Position," by J. David Smith, 1994, *Education and Training in Mental Retardation and Developmental Disabilities, 29,* pp. 179–183.

the stigma associated with them becomes great. A new term is then created. A current trend, for example, is to use the term *developmental disability* in the place of mental retardation.

As the provision of educational services for students with mental retardation expanded during the 1950s and 1960s, special educators increasingly used terms to describe their students according to educational classifications. These classifications were used to describe both the anticipated level of educational achievement of these students and the corresponding educational placements to which they were assigned. Students who were labeled educable mentally retarded were expected to be able to learn to read and write at the elementary level but at a much slower pace. Students described as trainable mentally retarded were considered capable of learning only a few isolated words and very limited counting skills. They were considered capable of becoming semi-independent at best. Children and adults who were perceived to be unable to function even at the trainable level were often referred to as "subtrainable" or "custodial." They were thought of as being below a level that made them the true responsibility of schools and special educators.

Another classification system has been used more frequently by psychologists and physicians. These professionals classify individuals, according to their performance on IQ tests, as having mild, moderate, severe, or profound mental retardation. Although these classifications and the tests on which they are based have been criticized for many years, they have remained in widespread use. This is primarily because of the relative ease and efficiency of IQ testing, and the structured system of categorization that these scores provide. Although criticism of IQ tests led to an increasing emphasis on the assessment of social, self-care, communication, and vocational skills and other adaptive behavior, IQ measures have continued to be dominant in the classification of mental retardation (Smith & Polloway, 1979).

The passage of the Education for All Handicapped Children Act of 1975 (EHA; Public Law [P.L.] 94-142) has long been hailed as a landmark event in special education and in the overall movement to secure the rights of people with disabilities. This designation is well deserved. It is an irony, however, that since the enactment of that law there has been a marked decrease in the number of children with mental retardation receiving the benefits of its provisions. Over the last 20 years, there has been a dramatic decline in the number of students with mental retardation being served in public schools (Polloway & Smith, 1988).

One of the reasons for the decreasing numbers of students with mental retardation in public school programs is that many children who would have been classified as mildly mentally retarded in the past are now diagnosed as having learning disabilities and are served on that basis. Other students are not classified as retarded because professionals and parents are reluctant to use that term because of the stigma associated with it. Unfortunately, many of these children,

although not classified, are not receiving the services they need to succeed in school. Many end up in the ranks of children who are considered "slow learners." Unfortunately, they are not eligible for help on that basis. This trend has also contributed to the fact that students who remain in special education classes for those with mild mental retardation tend to have greater needs than those who were in those classes 20 years ago (Polloway & Smith, 1988).

The fact that changes in attitudes and policies can determine to such a large extent the numbers of people considered to have mental retardation illustrates the degree to which mental retardation is a social construct. As the eminent U.S. psychologist Seymour Sarason observed, "Mental retardation is never a thing or a characteristic of an individual, but rather a social invention stemming from time-bound societal values and ideology that make diagnosis and management seem both necessary and socially desirable" (Sarason, 1985, p. 233). Given the social meaning of the term mental retardation and the many applications it has been given to people with varied physical, social, and personal circumstances in their lives, it is important to review some of the definitions of mental retardation that have been used for identifying people as having the condition. It is also important to understand how definitions have been used as a basis for intervening in the lives of these people.

The American Association for Mental Retardation's Attempts at Defining Mental Retardation

Early Definition of Mental Retardation

Several formal definitions of mental retardation were developed during the first half of the 20th century. The most important of these, and the one that continues to influence the defining of mental retardation, was authored by Edgar Doll. His definition included six criteria he considered essential to the concept of mental retardation. These were "(1) social incompetence, (2) due to mental subnormality, (3) which has been developmentally arrested, (4) which obtains at maturity, (5) is of constitutional origin, and (6) is essentially incurable" (Doll, 1941, p. 215). The first four of these factors have continued to be central to the concept of mental retardation. The association of social incompetencies and deficits in mental ability is a thread that runs from Doll's definition through the most current definitions. The same is true for the emphasis on mental retardation as a disability that originates during the developmental period.

The last two elements of Doll's definition, however, have not continued to be operative in contemporary definitions of mental retardation. Retardation is no longer viewed as always the result of "constitutional" (physiological) factors. It has long been recognized that there are environmental variables that are important as causes of mental retardation. Much retardation, for example, is still associated with the depriving effects of poverty. Mental retardation is also no longer considered to be an "incurable" condition. The goals of educational services for some students, in fact, may be to help those students achieve a level of competence at which it would no longer be appropriate to describe them as having mental retardation.

The legacy of Doll's conceptualization of mental retardation can be seen most clearly in definitions that have been developed during the second half of the 20th century by the American Association on Mental Retardation (AAMR). The definitions published by this professional organization, formally called the American Association on Mental Deficiency, have always included the criteria of lower measured intelligence and deficits in social competence. They have also consistently referred to mental retardation as a developmental disability.

In 1959 an AAMR committee published a definition of mental retardation that read, "Mental retardation refers to subaverage general intellectual functioning which originates during the developmental period and is associated with impairment in adaptive behavior" (Heber, 1959). This definition was revised in 1961. The revision specified the meaning of the term subaverage general intellectual functioning in a manner that was to have a considerable impact on the field of mental retardation. One standard deviation below the mean on an intelligence test was specified as the point at which intellectual functioning should be considered subnormal. This specification meant that on an IQ test with a mean of 100 and a standard deviation of 15, any score below 85 would be diagnostic of mental retardation. If the total population was tested and classified on this basis, almost 16% would be diagnosed as having mental retardation. Even higher percentages would be expected to result in subpopulations where minority status, language factors, or socioeconomic background might depress intelligence test scores. It was also argued that many children and adolescents with marginal IQ scores (the large number with scores between 70 and 85) functioned very efficiently in their homes and communities. Their retarded performance was evident only in school settings (Heber, 1961).

There were also criticisms of the concept of adaptive behavior as it was presented in the 1961 definition. The argument was made that adaptive behavior, as it was included in the definition, was not actually functional for the diagnosis of mental retardation. It was argued that the determination of retardation continued to be based on intelligence tests and that intelligence was not significantly "associated" with adaptive behavior in this process (Clausen, 1972).

In 1973 an AAMR committee constructed another revised definition of mental retardation. The committee, chaired by Herbert Grossman, developed this revision with criticisms of the 1961 definition in mind. The definition read, "Mental retardation refers to significantly subaverage general intellectual functioning existing concurrently with deficits in adaptive behavior and manifested during the development period" (Grossman, 1973). This revision specified that significantly subaverage general intellectual functioning was to be determined by a score of at least two standard deviations below the mean on an intelligence test. This meant that the cutoff point for mental retardation was essentially moved downward from 85 to 70. This change lowered the percentage of the population that might be identified as having mental retardation from 16% to approximately 2.25%. This revision meant that fewer people would be labeled retarded because of language differences, socioeconomic factors, or minority status. It also meant, however, that fewer students were eligible for special education services. This is a particularly important consideration since the 1973 AAMR definition was adopted for defining mental retardation under EHA.

The 1973 definition also strengthened the importance of adaptive behavior in the determination of mental retardation. It stated that deficits in adaptive behavior must exist concurrently with subaverage intellectual functioning instead of being associated with them. The definition extended the developmental period from 16 to 18 years of age. It also changed the wording from "originates during" to "manifested during" in reference to the developmental aspect of mental retardation.

In 1977 the AAMR published a new manual on mental retardation terminology and classification. There were no substantive changes to the definition. The role of clinical judgment, however, was emphasized in the manual. Allowance was made as well for diagnosing people with IQs up to 10 points above the 70 cutoff score as having mental retardation if they also showed marked deficits in adaptive behavior (Grossman, 1977).

The 1983 AAMR definition further expanded the developmental period from conception (instead of birth) to age 18. This change officially made persons with mental retardation resulting from prenatal factors eligible to be classified. This AAMR definition also cautioned against the strict adherence to standard deviations and emphasized that measurement errors could result in false-positive or false-negative identifications of mental retardation.

The revisions that have been made during the last three decades in the definition of mental retardation have been accompanied by changes in the numbers of people thought to have the condition. In particular, the number of children identified as having mental retardation has decreased significantly. During the 1976–1977 school years, approximately 820,000 students were classified as having mental retardation. In the 1992–1993 school year, that number had dropped to less than 534,000 (U.S. Department of Education, 1994). As indicated earlier, the decline in the number of students identified as having mild levels of retardation and the rise of the number of students identified as having learning disabilities have been associated with this overall reduction in the category of retardation (Baumeister, 1987; Forness & Polloway, 1987).

The decrease in the numbers of children identified as having mental retardation is complex, however, with a number of other contributing factors. Polloway and Smith (1988) examined these factors in detail. In addition to the increasing sensitivity of parents and school personnel to the stigma associated with retardation as a classification, among the most important reasons that they discuss for the changes in the numbers of students considered to have mental retardation are (a) the impact of changes in the AAMR definition; (b) the effect of legislation challenging the use of IQ tests and increasing the caution that is necessary before identifying minority children as having mental retardation; and (c) the positive effect of early childhood intervention programs.

The 1992 Revision of the Definition

In 1992 the AAMR published a revision of its manual on the definition and classification of mental retardation. The definition itself includes dramatic changes:

> Mental retardation refers to substantial limitations in present functioning. It is characterized by significantly subaverage intellectual functioning, existing concurrently with related limitations in two or more of the following applicable adaptive skill areas: communication, self-care, home living, social skills, community use, self-direction, health and safety, functional academics, leisure, and work. Mental retardation manifests before age 18. (Luckasson et al., 1992, p. 1)

The 1992 AAMR definition has a functional perspective on retardation. It defines mental retardation according to how a person functions in daily life, through conceptual, practical, and social intelligence (Luckasson et al., 1992, p. 5). The definition focuses on the relations among capabilities (cognition, learning, and adaptive skills), environments (the characteristics and expectations of a person's life situation), and functioning (the functional match between capabilities and environments) (Luckasson et al., 1992, pp. 9–10). It defines mental retardation as the outcome of disabling circumstances. This conception of mental retardation is presented by AAMR as a paradigm shift. Retardation is no longer viewed as being the characteristic of an individual; instead, it is the product of interactions between a person and the nature and demands of that person's environment.

The phrase "limitations in present functioning" indicates that mental retardation is a current state, rather than a permanent trait. This change emphasizes that mental retardation may be a transitory state.

There are a number of other distinctly different elements in the manual's perspective on mental retardation. These changes include the following: (a) the global term adaptive behavior has been extended to the 10 specific adaptive skill areas, and each of these skill areas is discussed at some length in the manual; (b) four assumptions for the application of the definition are asserted along with the definition; and (c) rather than a subclassification into four levels of mental retardation, the new system subclassifies the intensities and patterns of support systems required by individuals. The levels of need that require supports are *intermittent needs*, which are episodic in nature and do not always require support; *limited needs*, which are consistent over time but are limited in intensity; *extensive needs*, which are long term and serious; and *pervasive needs*, which are constant and intense throughout life (Luckasson et al., 1992).

The following four assumptions are presented as being essential to the application of the definition. First, valid assessment considers cultural and linguistic diversity as well as differences in communication and behavioral factors. Second, the existence of limitations in adaptive skills occurs within the context of community environments typical of the individual's age-peers and is indexed to the person's individualized needs for support. Third, specific adaptive limitations often coexist with strengths in other adaptive skills or other person capabilities. Fourth, with appropriate supports over a sustained period, the life functioning of the person with mental retardation will generally improve.

Implications of the AAMR Definition

Shortly after the publication of the 1992 AAMR definition, the Board of Directors of the Mental Retardation and Developmental Disabilities Division (MRDD) of the Council for Exceptional Children reviewed the definition. As a result of that review, the MRDD Critical Issues Committee was asked to examine the definition more carefully in terms of its implications for special educators and their students. This group recognized the positive efforts and the resulting improvements in the definition made by AAMR; however, it felt that there were important potential implications of the new definition for the education of children and adults with mental retardation. These observations and concerns were published in *MR Express* (Smith, 1993a, 1993b), and input from the membership of MRDD was invited. The following paragraphs describe some of the concerns and questions raised by members of the board of MRDD, the Critical Issues Committee, and the membership.

1. What are the ramifications of the changes for teacher training? Many teacher training programs provide specialized instruction for teachers expected to teach students with mild, moderate, severe, or profound disabilities. In fact, many do so under grants allocated for the purpose of training

teachers who work with students having disabilities. If there are no distinctions (e.g., severe or mild), will there be differentiated training? Is there enough time in teacher training programs to sufficiently prepare teachers to teach students who fall along the whole continuum of mental retardation, from those having extensive need for support to those who have only intermittent needs for support? It is recognized that the AAMR goal was to formulate a definition that focuses on the needs of persons with mental retardation and to look beyond current professional practices. The revised definition, however, must be viewed in terms of its impact on the preparation of teachers who will be able to help people with mental retardation achieve a more positive life in society. The question of how teachers and other helping professionals are to be prepared for meeting the spectrum of needs defined in the new manual has not been raised elsewhere in the literature concerning the revision. This is an issue that is deserving of the best scrutiny of the membership of MRDD.

2. In what ways will the AAMR definitional changes affect teacher certification requirements? Some states and provinces have significantly revised their certification requirements to ensure that teachers have appropriate training to work with students with disabilities at specific levels of severity. What will be the implications of the definitional changes for teacher certification standards that have been developed over several decades in an effort to ensure that teachers have appropriate preparation to teach children in disability categories that no longer exist with the adoption of the 1992 AAMR revisions?

3. How will these changes impact special education funding? Some states and provinces fund special education using weighted formulas whereby programs for students classified as having severe disabilities receive larger allocations of funds than those for students having mild disabilities. States and provinces using unit funding procedures also often provide for smaller class sizes when students are classified as having severe disabilities. How will the changes in the AAMR definition be interpreted in the equations of support for those students who have the varying levels of need addressed by the definitional changes? Will the political and bureaucratic structures that control the flow of resources to assist people with mental retardation be quick to respond to these changes? What can be done to facilitate their responsiveness?

4. Will the four levels of mental retardation no longer recognized in the definition be supplanted by the new equivalents? For practical reasons related to teacher training, certification, and funding, will the levels profound, severe, moderate, and mild be substituted with the new terms? It is possible that the new terms may carry the same practical meaning: "pervasive need for support" (profound); "extensive need for support" (severe); "limited need for support" (moderate); and "intermittent need for support" (mild). If

this happens, will anything have actually been gained by changing this aspect of the definition?

5. The movement away from severity levels to levels of needed support may become very cumbersome in placement and individual educational program conferences where classification on the basis of severity of disability still occurs due to child count requirements. School districts may use the support system described and the associated intensity of need levels, but may still need to use severity of disability levels of retardation for legal and economic reasons. The most important questions about this issue seem to be whether the new definition, without levels of severity, will encumber professional communication or will indeed facilitate new thought and improved educational services to children and adults with mental retardation.

6. Although the increased specificity of the domains of adaptive behavior in the new definition is a conceptual improvement, the tools for measuring these domains are simply not available as yet. This fact increases the danger that uninformed or irresponsible clinical judgment could prove very damaging in the mental retardation diagnostic process. MacMillan, Gresham, and Siperstein (1993) raised and explored in some detail the concern that a lack of consideration for developmental factors is evident in the adaptive behavior domains defined in the AAMR definition revisions. This concern was also raised by the membership of MRDD. Again, the question of assessment, this time in relation to developmentally adaptive behavior, was a concern.

7. Among MRDD respondents, a concern was raised about the expanded proportion of the population that is eligible for classification as mentally retarded because of the IQ cutoff of 75 adopted in the definition. A related concern was the impact this might have on children and adolescents from minority backgrounds. This is consistent with the conclusion of MacMillan et al. (1993) that the IQ criterion of 75 recommended in the revised AAMR definition will increase the number of people eligible to be classified as having mental retardation. This claim is refuted by Reiss (1994), who posits that the new definition does not, in fact, raise the IQ cutoff from the AAMR definition adopted in 1983. Reiss also asserts that AAMR has been criticized unfairly for not making greater use of firm IQ cutoffs in redefining mental retardation. Some of these same critics, according to Reiss, point out the cultural bias of intelligence tests yet misunderstand that cultural bias is an argument for flexibility in the use of IQ instruments rather than against it.

8. Group differences between children and adolescents in the mild mental retardation category and those in the other categorical levels of mental retardation have long been recognized. The differentiation of this group has been important for the advocacy for children within the group and for the protection of children who should not be diagnosed as having mild retardation. Some members of MRDD believe that the abrupt change in classification included in

the definition may jeopardize both the advocacy and the protection that has been afforded those who are touched by the complexities of mild mental retardation.

Additionally, MRDD members made the following positive observations on the adaptive behavior features of the new AAMR definition: First, the qualification of two or more adaptive behavior skill areas is positive since it will make evaluators address adaptive behavior by relevant skill areas rather than as a global skill. Second, the listing of the subskills of adaptive behavior in the definition itself is also positive since it will guide evaluators to develop subskill profiles within the areas of adaptive behavior, as is already done for academic and vocational areas; it may cause school districts to develop curricular designs for specific skills rather than the concept of general adaptive behavior. It will encourage teams to develop goals and objectives within the subskill areas, making need areas and the evaluation of them more concrete. Third, several of the subskills of adaptive behavior (home living, social skills, community use, functional academics, leisure, and work) relate to the revised definition of mandated transitional areas in the Individuals with Disabilities Education Act of 1990.

The Position of MRDD on the Definition

These concerns and observations of the membership of MRDD were published, along with a position statement that was adopted by the MRDD Board of Directors. That position statement declared the following:

> The Board of Directors of the Mental Retardation and Developmental Disabilities Division of the Council for Exceptional Children resolves that the American Association on Mental Retardation (AAMR) made a significant contribution to the field through its 1992 revision of the manual on definition and classification of mental retardation. The Board acknowledges in particular the effort that the AAMR has made to focus greater attention on the needs of individuals rather than on degrees of deficits residing within persons with retardation.
>
> The Board notes also that this redefinition is encouraging a vigorous evaluation within the field of the issues of identification, classification, educational programming and placement, and the training of teachers. The Board urges the membership of the Division to study the AAMR definition and classification system, to consider the statements of critics of the changes it embodies and to examine its implications for themselves in their roles as educators, scholars and advocates in the field of mental retardation.
>
> It is the position of the Board of Directors that the revised definition and classification system of mental retardation offered to the field by the AAMR is serving as a positive stimulus for debate in the field on issues of critical importance to persons with mental retardation, their

families and to professionals. It is recognized, however, that the changes and their implications are so profound that they require the most careful consideration before they are implemented in special education practices. The Board encourages member of MRDD to be participants in the process of analyzing these implications and to be actively engaged in representing the best interests of persons with mental retardation in this regard. (Adopted by the Board of Directors, MRDD, October 16, 1993; cited in Smith, 1994, p. 179)

Mental Retardation: The Future of a Concept

A great deal of professional and academic heat has been generated by the revisions in the AAMR definition and classification on guidelines of mental retardation. The revisions have been characterized as reflecting a professional tug-of-war between differing factions in the field. Even within AAMR there have been sharp differences of opinion concerning the revised definition. John Jacobson, president of the AAMR Psychology Division, has been quoted as saying, "The new AAMR manual is a political manifesto, not a clinical document" (Michaelson, 1993, p. 34). He described the changes in IQ range and adaptive behavior criteria for diagnosing mental retardation as being politically motivated rather than based on research. This position and other criticisms of the revisions have appeared elsewhere in professional literature (Jacobson & Mulick, 1993; MacMillan et al., 1993).

The authors of the new AAMR manual have described their revisions as reflecting a paradigm shift in the field of mental retardation. This paradigm shift is seen as consisting of two elements. The first is a change in the conception of mental retardation from a trait existing in an individual to an expression of the interaction between an individual with limited intellectual and adaptive skills, and that individual's environment. The second element of the paradigm shift is the emphasis on the pattern of the individual's needs rather than a focus on deficits (Schalock et al., 1994).

Paradigm shifts may be critical to growth, change, and improvement in any field. Thomas Kuhn (1962), in his classic book *The Structure of Scientific Revolutions*, defined paradigms as the shared worldviews of scientists, as shared ways of viewing certain realities. Kuhn argued that these shared views become so strong and institutionalized that only a sudden and dramatic break from these views can bring on a positive revolution in thinking.

On the other hand, Stephen Jay Gould (1994) has pointed out that nothing is more dangerous and constraining than a dogmatic worldview that is imposed on other people and their futures. Some of the people who have criticized the AAMR revisions have come very close to accusing its authors of producing dogma.

It must be remembered that, unlike physics, for example, where a paradigm shift from the worldview of Newton to that of Einstein did nothing to change the reality of the physical universe, a paradigm shift in the field of mental retardation may have profound implications for the education, care, and treatment of millions of human beings.

The effort to define mental retardation in a way that is as scientifically accurate as possible continues. The effort to define it in a way that promotes greater sensitivity to the needs of people with mental retardation also continues. The successful resolution of the tension between meeting these two goals will determine the future of a concept.

QUESTIONS

1. What are some of the reasons that the number of students with mental retardation has declined in recent years?

2. What aspects of Edgar Doll's definition of mental retardation have not continued to be operative in the way mental retardation is viewed?

3. How did the 1961 definition differ from the 1959 definition of mental retardation? What impact does it have on the field?

4. What are the major new features of the 1992 AAMR definition of mental retardation?

5. What are some possible implications of the deletion of levels of severity from the definition of mental retardation?

References

Baumeister, A. (1987). Mental retardation: Some conceptions and dilemmas. *American Psychologist, 42,* 796–800.

Clausen, J. A. (1972). The continuing problem of defining mental deficiency. *Journal of Special Education, 6,* 97–106.

Doll, E. A. (1941). The essentials of an inclusive concept of mental deficiency. *American Journal of Mental Deficiency, 46,* 214–229.

Education for All Handicapped Children Act of 1975, 20 U.S.C. § 1400 *et seq.*

Forness, S., & Polloway, E. (1987). Physical and psychiatric diagnoses of pupils with mild mental retardation. *Education and Training in Mental Retardation, 22,* 221–227.

Gould, S. J. (1994). In the mind of the beholder. *Natural History, 103*(2), 14–23.

Grossman, H. J. (Ed.). (1973). *Manual on terminology and classification in mental retardation.* Washington, DC: American Association on Mental Deficiency.

Grossman, H. J. (Ed.). (1977). *Manual on terminology and classification in mental retardation.* Washington, DC: American Association on Mental Deficiency.

Heber, R. F. (1959). A manual on terminology and classification in mental retardation. *Monograph Supplement American Journal of Mental Deficiency, 62.*

Heber, R. F. (1961). A manual on terminology and classification in mental retardation (rev. ed.). *Monograph Supplement American Journal of Mental Deficiency, 64.*

Individuals with Disabilities Education Act of 1990, 20 U.S.C. § 1400 *et seq.*

Jacobson, J., & Mulick, J. (1993). APA takes a step forward in professional practice. *Psychology in Mental Retardation and Developmental Disabilities, 19,* 4–8.

Kuhn, J. (1962). *The structure of scientific revolutions.* Chicago: The University of Chicago Press.

Luckasson, R., Coulter, D. L., Polloway, E. A., Reiss, S., Schalock, L. L., Snell, M. E., Spitalnik, D. M., & Stark, J. A. (1992). *Mental retardation: Definition, classification, and systems of supports.* Washington, DC: American Association on Mental Retardation.

MacMillan, D., Gresham, F., & Siperstein, G. (1993). Conceptual and psychometric concerns about the 1992 AAMR definition of mental retardation. *American Journal on Mental Retardation, 98,* 325–335.

Michaelson, R. (1993). Tug-of-war is developing over defining retardation. *APA Monitor, 24*(5), 34.

Polloway, E. A., & Smith, J. D. (1988). Current status of the mild mental retardation construct: Identification, placement, and programs. In M. Wang, M. Reynolds, & H. Walberg (Eds.), *The handbook of special education: Research and practice* (pp. 1–22). Oxford, England: Pergamon Press.

Reiss, S. (1994). Issues in defining mental retardation. *American Journal on Mental Retardation, 99,* 201–206.

Sarason, S. (1985). *Psychology and mental retardation: Perspectives in change.* Austin, TX: PRO-ED.

Schalock, R., Coulter, D., Polloway, E., Reiss, S., Snell, M., Spitalnik, D., & Stark, J. (1994). The changing conception of mental retardation: Implications for the field. *Mental Retardation, 32,* 181–193.

Smith, J. D. (1985). *Minds made feeble: The myth and legacy of the Kallikaks.* Rockville, MD: Aspen.

Smith, J. D. (1993a). The AAMR manual revisions: Assessment of the changes and their implications for special educators. *MRDD Express, 3*(2), 3, 14.

Smith, J. D. (1993b). New AAMR definition serving as a positive stimulus for debate. *MRDD Express, 4*(2), 3, 11, 12.

Smith, J. D. (1994). The revised AAMR definition of mental retardation: The MRDD position. *Education and Training in Mental Retardation and Developmental Disabilities, 29,* 179–183.

Smith, J. D., & Polloway, E. (1979). The dimension of adaptive behavior in mental retardation research: An analysis of recent practices. *American Journal of Mental Deficiency, 84,* 203–206.

U.S. Department of Education. (1994). *Sixteenth annual report to Congress on the implementation of the Individuals with Disabilities Act.* Washington, DC: U.S. Government Printing Office.

Syndromes on the Margins of Mental Retardation: Dual Diagnosis and Balkanization

CHAPTER 4

Steven R. Forness and Kenneth A. Kavale

Learning Outcomes

After reading this chapter, you should be able to

■ Identify the basic diagnostic features of children with traumatic brain injury, fetal alcohol syndrome, prenatal substance abuse, and fragile X syndrome.

■ Describe the types of learning or behavioral disorders that are prominent in each of these syndromes.

■ Identify the special education needs that these children may have in common.

TERMS

The following terms are important for the understanding of this chapter:

Balkanization: The breaking up of geographical regions or, in this sense, "special education categories" into smaller independent units or entities.

Dual diagnosis: Occurrence of emotional or behavioral disorders in children with mental retardation or other cognitive disorders.

Fetal alcohol syndrome: Disorder caused by mother's excessive use of alcohol during pregnancy, resulting in a child with impaired cognitive functioning, distinctive physical or facial features, and possible behavioral difficulties. (*Fetal alcohol effect* refers to a child without all of the physical features but with cognitive and behavioral impairments that may be similar to those of fetal alcohol syndrome.)

Fragile-X syndrome: Disorder caused by a defect in the X chromosome, resulting in a child with impaired cognitive functioning, distinctive physical or facial features, and a variety of learning or behavioral abnormalities.

Prenatal substance abuse: Disorder caused by mother's excessive use of illicit drugs (usually cocaine) during pregnancy, resulting in a child with relatively mild cognitive impairments but a range of possible behavioral and attentional difficulties.

Traumatic brain injury: Damage to the brain that results in a variety of attentional, memory, and learning difficulties that may be complicated by behavioral or emotional difficulties.

Introduction

The field of mental retardation has presumably entered a new era with publication of the American Association on Mental Retardation's (AAMR's) ninth edition of its official classification manual (Luckasson et al., 1992). This new diagnostic scheme purports not only to broaden the concept of adaptive behavior but also to extend the notion of mental retardation as at least partially dependent on availability of social supports. It further underlines the importance of con-

text in which mental retardation occurs and notes the possibility of specific areas of strength coexisting with observed limitations. Finally, it eliminates the four classifications previously used to denote degrees of severity and introduces classification by intensity of supports needed. Thus, the new relationship of mental retardation to the field of developmental disabilities may be less clear.

MacMillan, Gresham, and Siperstein (1993) criticized this scheme. Their objections focused on the 75 IQ cutoff point for eligibility, failure to differentiate among the

10 adaptive skill areas, and imprecision of classification by levels of supports. They demonstrated that more than twice the number of individuals could become eligible for the diagnosis of mental retardation than under the 70 IQ cutoff used in the old definition and considerably more than this when one considers toughening of test norms in recently revised intelligence tests. They noted, on the other hand, that reliabilities for individual domains of adaptive skills are considerably less satisfactory than the global scores for adaptive behavior used under the previous definition and that developmental considerations might prevent some younger children from being found eligible because many of the 10 adaptive skill areas may be less relevant to infancy or early childhood. Finally, they suggested that classification by four levels of support not only is imprecise and unreliable but also ignores well-established differentiation between organic and familial mental retardation. They suggested that the AAMR could lose credibility with such a flawed definition, a sentiment echoed by Borthwick-Duffy (1994).

It is not entirely clear, at this point, whether this new definition will indeed be more or less restrictive than the previous definition (i.e., will identify a greater or lesser number of persons as having mental retardation). Under current procedures only two of 10 adaptive skill areas need to be deficient in order for a person to qualify as having mental retardation. This is, in fact, much less restrictive than the current federal definition of developmental disabilities, which requires substantial limitations in three or more areas of life activity (Kiernan, Smith, & Ostrowsky, 1986). This and the more liberal upper limits of IQ noted by Macmillan and his colleagues would suggest that developmental problems in certain adaptive skill areas might argue for fewer children being identified, particularly in the early years, as noted above. Moreover, AAMR itself acknowledges the risk that integral consideration of social supports in the definition might disenfranchise certain persons from diagnostic eligibility, in that it might require "that individuals with mental retardation repeatedly 're-prove' the disability, thereby discouraging applicants and cutting back on the number of recipients of services" (Luckasson et al., 1992, p. 148).

The issue of definition has been particularly critical in the field of special education in that there has been a marked decline in the percentage of children found eligible under the categorical definition of mental retardation (MR) used in public schools in recent years (Forness & MacMillan, 1989; MacMillan & Forness, 1993). The categorical designations of learning disabilities (LD) and serious emotional disturbance (SED) have also been particularly prominent in terms of definitional issues because of similar questions about restrictiveness of these two categories (Forness & Knitzer, 1992; Kavale, Forness, & Lorsbach, 1991). There is yet additional confusion inherent in the potential for dual diagnosis, that is, co-occurrence of emotional or behavioral problems with learning disabilities and mental retardation

(Forness, Kavale, & Lopez, 1993; Forness & Polloway, 1987; Forness & Sinclair, 1990).

These three categories (MR, LD, and SED) have also figured prominently in regard to regular classroom inclusion, at least partly because of the perceived arbitrariness of definitional boundaries for such categories. This leads in turn to the belief that, because little of significance separates eligible children from their nonidentified counterparts, there can be little benefit to extensive segregation or highly specialized programs, especially for children at the margins of one definition or another.

The failure to resolve these interrelated issues seems recently to have led to yet another trend in the field. This trend, while not entirely new, seems nonetheless to have become rather pervasive in the past several years. It involves the propensity to consider certain discrete disorders as not only uniquely eligible for special education but also distinctly deserving of their own unique category for eligibility. An early forerunner of this trend toward proliferation of categories involved the disorder of autism. This disorder was removed from the serious emotional disturbance category in the initial years after passage and implementation of the Education for All Handicapped Children Act of 1975 (EHA; P.L. 94-142) and was made a subcategory under the existing category of other health impairments (OHI). The rationale espoused by parents and advocates, at the time, involved the then newly recognized biomedical etiology of autism, which was presumed to separate it from the majority of other emotional and behavioral disorders that were believed to have primarily psychosocial origins (Forness & Kavale, 1984). In actual fact, this enabled concerned advocates and professionals in many states to create a separate category of autism along with classrooms specifically for children with autism, although nearly four of five children with autism function in the range of mental retardation and most have social or behavioral disorders. They would thus qualify for existing categories of either mental retardation or severe emotional disturbance. As of the 1992–1993 school year, however, autism became a completely separate category for purposes of reporting the annual count of children served in special education, as mandated by the Individuals with Disabilities Education Act of 1990 (P.L. 101-476) (Kincaid, 1993).

There also has been a relatively recent movement to create an entirely separate category of attention-deficit disorders (ADD) in special education (Parker, 1989). Many children with ADD have been found not to qualify under the SED or LD definitions in special education (Forness, Youpa, Hanna, Cantwell, & Swanson, 1992). Both professional and parent advocates petitioned Congress for ADD as a separate category in 1990 and even went so far as to develop a school definition of ADD (Swanson, 1990). Although a new ADD category has not yet been created, the U.S. Department of Education conducted a notice of inquiry to survey the need in this area. The department subsequently issued a memorandum clarifying that existing regulations for LD, SED, or OHI categories could be used to qualify some children with ADD for special education (Davila, Williams, & MacDonald, 1991). The memorandum also noted that federal regulations under Section 504 of the Rehabilitation Act of 1973 could be applied to ensure accommodations in the regular classroom for yet other children with ADD who might not qualify for special education (Davila et al., 1991). Although ADD is not strictly a separate category of special education at present, there has been grant support from the U.S. Office of Special Education Programs to develop centers for further study of school-related aspects of ADD (Council for Exceptional Children, 1992). The preliminary findings of these centers have recently been reported (Hocutt, McKinney, & Montague, 1993) and may indeed renew interest in creating a separate category. It is of interest to note that children with both ADD and MR are being found and treated in increasing numbers (Gadow & Poling, 1988) and that attentional difficulties have long been considered a key problem in classroom functioning of children with mental retardation (Forness & Kavale, 1993; Kavale & Forness, 1992).

Balkanization in Special Education

Such a process of proliferation of categories appears to have the same effect on special education that Balkanization has on the geopolitical scene—that is, the breaking up of a region into small (and often antagonistic) units. Balkanization, generally beginning with recognition of the presumably separate cultural–ethnic identity of a people, is followed by a movement to create a separate government to accommodate the needs of this group. Unfortunately, this is often accompanied by "ethnic cleansing" to ensure that only a select people are included in this newly created state or nation. The parallel process in special education begins with recognition of a specific disorder presumed to have unique needs not being met by established eligibility categories. This engenders a movement to create a separate category complete with its own rules for diagnostic eligibility and its own separate educational programs.

In some cases, this unfortunately is accompanied by a cleansing or limitation of the category to only very specific types of children with the disorder. A recent example of cleansing involves attempts by the Child and Adolescent Network of the National Alliance for the Mentally Ill (NAMI) to restrict the special education category for children with emotional or behavioral disorders to only those children having one of 16 "neurobiologic disorders," previously termed "biologically based brain diseases" (Peschel, Peschel,

Howe, & Howe, 1992). These disorders (e.g., schizophrenia, bipolar disorder, obsessive–compulsive disorder, attention-deficit disorder) are sanctioned by NAMI because they are considered to have distinct biomedical etiologies and are treated with specific psychopharmacologic agents. As such, they are presumably considered as less stigmatizing than other forms of mental illness in that they are seen as essentially no different from other medical diseases. However, certain children, such as those suffering serious and often chronic symptoms of posttraumatic stress disorder secondary to sustained physical or sexual abuse, are thereby purged from this category because etiology and treatment needs (analogous to "ethnic identity") are presumably different. A similar cleansing issue occurs in the proposed new category of attention-deficit disorders in the controversy as to whether attention-deficit disorders without hyperactivity should be included (Garfinkel, 1990; Silver, 1990).

The potential effect of the Balkanization process on special education is not only to tie up administrative and diagnostic resources in determining separate eligibility for each disorder but also to create increasingly more numerous types of special programs. Each program is seen as distinct from other categorical programs and is viewed as the only means wherein children so identified can receive intervention appropriate to their unique disorder. It is interesting to note that, prior to the passage of EHA, there were seven special education categories—mental retardation, speech or language disorders, learning disabilities, serious emotional disturbance, physical handicaps, visual impairments, and hearing impairments. Multiple handicaps, other health impairments, and deaf–blindness were since added to the original seven; and autism and traumatic brain injury have been added more recently (U.S. Department of Education, 1993). This brings the total to 12 categories.

Four selected disorders are described very briefly herein as examples of this process. These disorders are traumatic brain injury, fetal alcohol syndrome, prenatal substance abuse, and fragile X syndrome. Other disorders could indeed have been selected, and several other examples of new morbidity have been suggested (Baumeister, Kupstas, & Klindworth, 1990). These four disorders were selected, however, because one has recently become a category and the others have been seriously proposed as categories in special education. They also have been selected because they have traditionally been considered as major contributing etiologies to mental retardation (President's Committee on Mental Retardation, 1993). Descriptions of the four disorders are followed by a comparison of these disorders across various learning and behavioral dimensions of special education needs.

It should be noted at the outset, as will be evident from review of intellectual or IQ data on these four disorders, that Balkanization may ultimately affect the categories of LD and SED more than the category of MR. It is further possible that the SED category may be the most affected in that LD eligibility criteria have been rendered considerably more restrictive over recent years because of increasingly rigorous IQ–achievement discrepancy criteria (Mercer, King-Sears, & Mercer, 1990). Thus, there may be a shift of children with these disorders out of the MR and LD categories and into the SED category in that their social or behavioral symptoms may be seen as more pertinent than their cognitive deficits to special education needs (Fad & Ryser, 1993).

Traumatic Brain Injury

The movement to create a separate category for traumatic brain injury has indeed been successful in that traumatic brain injury is now a separate category in the federal count of children receiving special education services. The federal government issued guidelines on the diagnostic criteria for traumatic brain injury (Kincaid, 1993), and discussions of special education issues have begun to appear (e.g., Gerring & Carney, 1992; Mira & Tyler, 1991). History of head trauma with loss of consciousness appears to be the primary diagnostic indicator, and traumatic brain injury can be classified as potentially severe if loss of consciousness exceeds 5 minutes. Prevalence of the disorder has been estimated at approximately 0.5% to 1% of school enrollment but understandably increases with age. As many as 3% of adolescents may have experienced head trauma serious enough to have had school-related sequellae. Many of these cases, however, may be mild to moderate with only momentary loss of consciousness and relatively rapid recovery. The path of recovery in the first year after head trauma is considered to be a critical indicator of future progress. Primary educational symptoms involve problems in organizing sensory input that are often expressed as attention and memory disorders. Underachievement and slowed response are thus common. Word finding difficulties are particularly disabling in reference to a wide variety of academic tasks. Return of IQ to premorbid levels within the first few months seems to be characteristic in all but the most severe cases (Mira & Tyler, 1991). Although learning difficulties are still likely to be a substantial handicap, a wide variety of potential emotional or behavioral disorders nonetheless are associated with the disorder (Hadders-Algra & Touwen, 1992). These may include inattention or impulsivity, irritability or temper outburst, and social isolation or depression. Occasional outbursts of silliness, involuntary yawning responses, and other such mannerisms associated with traumatic brain injury may contribute to social difficulties. Seizures also may be present in up to 20% of cases.

Advocacy for traumatic brain injury as a separate special education category has come not only from parents of affected children but also from professionals in local rehabilitation hospitals and agencies. This movement has been successful, at least in part, because traumatic brain injury is less controversial in terms of diagnostic indications and severity

of need for school supports than other potentially new categories, such as attention-deficit disorders. Current federal criteria for child count and clarification of eligibility by the U.S. Department of Education may begin to suggest the nature and extent of disability associated with this latest of special education categories.

Fetal Alcohol Syndrome

Advocacy efforts for fetal alcohol syndrome and prenatal substance abuse have not enjoyed as much success as those for traumatic brain injury. The reason for this is possibly that calls for separate special programs have come primarily from medical professionals treating these two disorders and not directly from parents. Prenatal stigma associated with these disorders may be at least comparable to that previously associated with mental illness, which has rendered it quite difficult to enlist parents in such public causes (Forness, 1988). A significant difference between the two disorders in terms of movement toward separate special education categories is that fetal alcohol syndrome has traditionally been more closely associated with the category of mental retardation than has prenatal substance abuse. More recent evidence, however, has suggested that the mean IQ of children with fetal alcohol syndrome averages just above 70 (Streissguth, Randels, & Smith, 1991). Children with fetal alcohol effects, who have history of exposure in utero, but only partial fetal alcohol syndrome phenotype or less obvious central nervous system dysfunction, have an average IQ of approximately 82. Given the potential of the new mental retardation definition to restrict special education for young children with mild mental retardation, noted earlier, it is possible that well more than half of children with fetal alcohol syndrome will not be candidates for this category and may need programs more typical of children with learning disabilities or severe emotional disturbance.

Diagnostic features of fetal alcohol syndrome include pre- or postnatal growth retardation, particularly in length and head circumference, evidence of central nervous system involvement, and a variety of head or facial anomalies including microcephaly, droopy eyelids, short palpebral fissures, indistinct philtrum, or thin upper lip (Streissguth, Aase, Clarren, Randels, LaDue, & Smith, 1991). Prevalence has been estimated at .2% to .5% of school enrollment (West, 1986), but this is primarily extrapolation from incidence figures, and definitive studies on exact extent of affected school children have not been done. In regard to school-related symptoms, concentration and memory deficits are primary. Underachievement may well be present and is likely to be somewhat more pronounced in math than in reading. Pragmatic language difficulties are also prominent. A variety of emotional or behavioral problems also have been documented, including impulsivity, hyperactivity, sullenness, social withdrawal, surges of anxiety, immaturity, and conduct disorders.

As noted above, although there have been calls for special education programs for such children, these have not been as pronounced as those for children with attention-deficit disorder or traumatic brain injury, nor have they been as clearly directed at *separate* special education programs (Streissguth, 1990). Also as noted above, an important aspect of these efforts has been increasing recognition of the potential similarity of the needs of children with fetal alcohol syndrome or fetal alcohol effects to those of children in LD or SED rather than MR categories of special education (Bauer, 1991).

Prenatal Substance Abuse

There has been somewhat more success for special school programs for children with prenatal substance abuse than for children with fetal alcohol syndrome. This is at least partly because of more recent public concern over this problem in the general context of the fight against illegal drug abuse. The most prominent diagnostic features of prenatal substance abuse involve prenatal growth retardation and neurobehavioral abnormalities. Infants or very young children may suffer from jitteriness or tremors, are difficult to soothe, have poor social interaction, and display poorly organized play (Howard, Beckwith, Rodning, & Kropenski, 1989; Sparks, 1992). Microcephaly and some limb malformations, including missing digits or missing bones in the forearm, may also be present. As for fetal alcohol syndrome, careful prevalence studies have not been done in relation to school enrollment, but estimates from incidence figures suggest that .2% to .5% may not be unusual. It is important to note that some inner-city hospitals commonly report 10% or more of live births to have been exposed to illicit drugs (Kropenski et al., 1992), but it is not yet clear what percentage of these infants will be affected as they reach school years.

A variety of school-related symptoms, however, may be present as these children reach preschool or kindergarten (Bauer, 1991; Sparks, 1992). These include visual–motor deficits, underachievement, and either unresponsive or poorly organized behavior. IQ has generally been reported in the 75 to 90 range. A variety of emotional or behavioral difficulties may also be present, including deficits in social cognition and inattentive or impulsive behavior. It is important to note that in both fetal alcohol syndrome and prenatal substance abuse social or emotional difficulties may also arise as a response to unstable or chaotic early living environments, including multiple foster home placements. It is also important to note the possible overlap between these two disorders in that prenatal maternal behavior may have involved polysubstance abuse.

Although a separate special education category has not been formally proposed, there have been special programs funded by the U.S. Department of Education for specific training of preschool personnel in this area, as well as two preschool demonstration classrooms in Los Angeles City Schools specifically for children with prenatal substance abuse (Kropenski et al., 1992). There may be more significant needs for special education as prospective follow-up studies begin to produce findings on children with prenatal substance abuse during school years.

Fragile X Syndrome

The final disorder discussed in this chapter has also been more highly associated with the mental retardation category, but it is clear that significant numbers of children with fragile X syndrome not only fall into the normal IQ range but also display a number of specific behavioral and learning disabilities (Hagerman & Sobersky, 1989). This has raised concern in regard to special education eligibility. Prevalence of the disorder has actually been estimated at 1% to 5% in the general population (Simensen & Rogers, 1989), but estimates of school-age children needing special assistance may be no greater than .3%. Diagnostic symptoms include an elongated face, large ears, prominent forehead, large jaw, hypertension in finger joints, and enlarged testicles in males (Schopmeyer & Lowe, 1992).

There are multiple learning and behavioral problems associated with fragile X syndrome outside the realm of those cases with mental retardation (Santos, 1992). Prominent are sequential language deficits in which vocabulary may be relatively unimpaired but grammatical sequencing or other language processes are affected. Speech may be rapid, tangential, or perseverative. Overlap between cases of autism and fragile X syndrome has indeed been noted. Math disabilities are sometimes common. It should be noted that, whereas as many as 20% of males with fragile X syndrome have IQs above 70, some 60% or more of females with the syndrome may have IQs above 70. Some IQ decline in later school years may occur. Emotional or behavioral problems include inattention, hyperactivity, social anxiety, and a variety of autistic spectrum disorders. It should be pointed out that many children with fragile X syndrome, as is the case with other disorders discussed in this chapter, are nonetheless sensitive, personable, and engaging even when learning difficulties are present.

Psychoeducational characteristics in fragile X syndrome are a prominent feature of research by Hagerman and her associates (Brainard, Schreiner, & Hagerman, 1991; Hagerman et al., 1989). Use of computers to attenuate some learning or language processing difficulties and particular attention to minimizing sociobehavioral problems have been the focus of some classroom demonstration efforts by Hagerman's group in the Denver Public Schools. A national fragile X syndrome newsletter developed with her assistance also focuses on separate special education needs. These advocacy efforts, while not yet focused on a separate special education category, have nonetheless enjoyed substantial cooperation from parents. The overlap of this disorder with autism and with attention-deficit disorder has thus led some parents of children with fragile X syndrome to focus instead on these as separate categories, although the case has been made that etiology-based educational approaches may be particularly relevant in fragile X syndrome (Dykens, Hodapp, & Leckman, 1993; Hodapp & Dykens, 1992).

Special Education Needs in the Four Disorders

Throughout the discussion of these four disorders, several common themes occur: There is considerable overlap in IQ distributions, language problems, underachievement or learning difficulties, inattention or impulsiveness, and emotional or behavioral problems in conduct, depressive, or anxiety disorder spectra. In regard to special education needs, these are depicted in Table 4.1 using a numerical scheme to denote the extent of each symptom within each of the four disorders and the extent to which symptoms appear characteristic of children with each disorder across studies.

As noted in Table 4.1, there is considerable evidence that mean IQ, as generally reported across studies, would produce an IQ distribution that could overlap considerably across the four disorders. Primary language disorders are not necessarily found in common, but underachievement or learning disabilities, inattention or impulsiveness, and conduct disorders are seen in significant numbers of children within each of the four disorders. A case can also be made

Table 4.1
Commonality of School or Behavioral Symptoms in Four Disorders: Traumatic Brain Injury (TBI), Fetal Alcohol Syndrome (FAS), Prenatal Substance Abuse (PSA), and Fragile X Syndrome (FXS)

Problem Area	TBI	FAS	PSA	FXS
IQ above 70 or 75	1	1	1	2
Language impairments	2	2	3	1
Underachievement or LD	1	1	1	1
Inattention, impulsiveness	1	2	1	1
Conduct spectrum disorders	2	1	1	2
Depressive spectrum disorders	2	2	3	3
Anxiety spectrum disorders	3	2	3	2

Note. 1 indicates that this feature is probably characteristic of most children having this disorder, 2 indicates that this feature is probably characteristic of many children having this disorder, and 3 indicates that this feature is characteristic of at least some children having this disorder, as reported in literature on each disorder.

that depressive and anxiety disorders are present in at least some children in each of the disorders.

In all, these four disorders not only seem to have a surprising amount of variability of symptoms within disorders (vertical columns) but also a striking amount of commonality across disorders (horizontal rows). The argument can thus be made that these disorders not only have a great deal in common with one another, but also have a great deal in common with existing categories of learning disability and severe emotional disturbance. The pending change in severe emotional disturbance terminology to "emotional or behavioral disorders" (Forness & Knitzer, 1992) may even enhance this commonality in regard to the sociobehavioral variables depicted in Table 4.1.

Conclusion

The relevance of special education Balkanization for the field of mental retardation seems particularly acute. There has been a continuing downward trend in identification of school children in the category of mental retardation since passage of EHA (Forness, 1990). Recent figures indicate that only 1.14% of schoolchildren are identified in the mental retardation category and that more than half of all states continue to show a decline in this identification rate in the 1991–1992 school year (U.S. Department of Education, 1993). The four disorders reviewed in this chapter have been largely associated in the past with the category of mental retardation, as noted earlier. There may well be a potential marginalization of these disorders within the category of mental retardation as this category shrinks in size, although it seems as yet unclear what effect the new mental retardation definition might have on identification rates. This marginalization may not necessarily lead to a diagnostic exchange with the category of learning disabilities in that IQ of children with these four disorders generally seems to be in the 70 to 90 range. This is unfortunately the range, as noted above, in which children may have an IQ too high to qualify for mental retardation and too low to meet discrepancy criteria for learning disabilities. The dual-diagnostic features of these disorders, in which social or behavioral symptoms occur across several psychiatric spectra, may increasingly lead to consideration of these children for placement in the severe emotional disturbance category. This might occur, ironically, just as recognition of the significance of dual diagnosis increases within the field of mental retardation (Einfeld, 1992; Singh, Sood, Sonenklar, & Ellis, 1991).

The possibility remains, however, that children with such marginal disorders might not qualify for any of the major categories of special education. Thus, the movement to Balkanize by creating new categories may not abate. This potential proliferation of categories or Balkanization of special education is not entirely disadvantageous. In many instances, identity as a separate disorder enhances potential for effective collaborative treatments, as in the case of stimulant medication for children with attention-deficit disorder (Gadow & Poling, 1988) or supportive rehabilitation therapy for traumatic brain injury (Mira & Tyler, 1991). Primary or secondary prevention may also be more likely, as in the case of genetic counseling for fragile X syndrome (Santos, 1992) or social welfare interventions for children with alcohol or substance abuse (Bauer, 1991). Such opportunities may be missed when school staff is unaware of the presence of specific disorders. There is also little doubt that professional and parent cooperation tends to be enhanced when these biomedical disorders are accorded full recognition in special education of their presumably unique needs for specific treatment approaches.

The disadvantages of Balkanization are also manifest. Foremost among them are the probable waste of diagnostic and administrative resources in determining eligibility for special education in more and more circumscribed categories. As the information in Table 4.1 suggests, this circumscription may be largely unnecessary for special education, as opposed to biomedical, needs. As the trend toward regular class integration increases, Balkanization tends also to accentuate differences at the same time that inclusion seeks to minimize them. Indeed, the cleansing problem suggests that,

once a disorder is determined to be present, additional time and energy may have to be spent in determining that other disorders are not present, in that these might call for consideration of yet other categories. This becomes a particular problem in cases of co-morbidity in which dilemmas may arise over which category should determine primary special education placement. Particularly problematic is the potential for separate classroom programs for each and every disorder.

A middle ground may be possible, however, in which school professionals in mental retardation, learning disabilities, and serious emotional disturbance become familiar with individual features and symptoms of each disorder while maintaining adherence to traditional categorical or noncategorical programs. In such a system, professionals and parents might be assured that certain standards for effective collaboration with biomedical treatments would be met at the same time that relevant special needs are determined. The professionalism of special education demands a categorical system that reflects its own effective standards of care in a time of limited resources. A proliferation of categories may not be in this interest. A "common market" approach may thus be more feasible than a process of Balkanization in the current economic and political climate of special education.

QUESTIONS

1. Which of the following is not currently an official federal category of special education eligibility: (a) autism, (b) traumatic brain injury, (c) attention deficit disorder, or (d) other health impairments.

2. In traumatic brain injury, the disorder is considered potentially severe if loss of consciousness exceeds (a) 30 seconds, (b) 1 minute, (c) 2 minutes, or (d) 5 minutes.

3. Children with fetal alcohol syndrome and fetal alcohol effects (a) invariably have mental retardation, (b) do not have mental retardation but do have learning disabilities, (c) now have their own exclusive diagnostic special education category, or (d) may qualify for special education in the LD, MR, or SED categories or not qualify at all.

4. Children with prenatal substance abuse (a) generally have IQs in the 75 to 90 range, (b) have cognitive difficulties but not behavioral abnormalities, (c) are not likely to have mothers who drank alcohol as well as abused drugs, or (d) are never eligible for special education but only for preventive measures in the regular classroom.

5. Children with fragile X syndrome are not likely to (a) have autism or autistic features, (b) be exclusively female, (c) have an IQ in the normal range, or (d) have large or prominent ears.

References

Bauer, A. M. (1991). Drug and alcohol exposed children: Implications for special education for students identified as behaviorally disordered. *Behavioral Disorders, 17,* 72–79.

Baumeister, A. A., Kupstas, F., & Klindworth, L. M. (1990). New morbidity: Implications for prevention of children's disabilities. *Exceptionality, 1,* 1–16.

Borthwick-Duffy, S. (1994). Review of *Mental retardation: Definition, classification and systems of support. American Journal of Mental Retardation, 98,* 541–544.

Brainard, S. S., Schreiner, R. A., & Hagerman, R. J. (1991). Cognitive profiles of adult carrier fragile X females. *American Journal of Medical Genetics, 38,* 505–508.

Council for Exceptional Children. (1992). *Children with ADD: A shared responsibility.* Reston, VA: Author.

Davila, R. R., Williams, M. L., & MacDonald, J. T. (1991). *Clarification of policy to address the needs of children with attention deficit disorders within general and/or special education*. Washington, DC: U.S. Department of Education, Office of Special Education and Rehabilitation Services.

Dykens, E. M., Hodapp, R. M., & Leckman, J. F. (1993). *Development and psychopathology in fragile X syndrome*. Newbury Park, CA: Sage.

Education for All Handicapped Children Act of 1975, 20 U.S.C. § 1400 *et seq.*

Einfeld, S. L. (1992). Clinical assessment of psychiatric symptoms in mentally retarded individuals. *Australia and New Zealand Journal of Psychiatry, 26*, 48–63.

Fad, K. S., & Ryser, G. R. (1993). Social/behavioral variables related to success in general education. *Remedial and Special Education, 14*(1), 25–35.

Forness, S. (1988). Planning for the needs of children with serious emotional disturbance: The National Special Education and Mental Health Coalition. *Behavioral Disorders, 13*, 127–133.

Forness, S. (1990). Summary of Symposium on Epidemiology: Educational aspects of epidemiology. *Academy on Mental Retardation Newsletter, 10*(2), 9–11.

Forness, S. R., & Kavale, K. A. (1984). Autistic children in school: The role of the pediatrician. *Pediatric Annals, 13*, 319–328.

Forness, S. R., & Kavale, K. A. (1993). Strategies to improve basic learning and memory deficits in mental retardation: A meta-analysis of experimental studies. *Education and Training in Mental Retardation, 28*, 99–110.

Forness, S., Kavale, K. A., & Lopez, M. (1993). Conduct disorders in school: Special education eligibility and co-morbidity. *Journal of Emotional and Behavioral Disorders, 1*, 101–108.

Forness, S. R., & Knitzer, J. (1992). A new proposed definition and terminology to replace "serious emotional disturbance" in the Individuals with Disabilities Education Act. *School Psychology Review, 21*, 12–20.

Forness, S. R., & MacMillan, D. L. (1989). Mental retardation and the special education system. *Annals of Psychiatry, 19*, 190–196.

Forness, S. R., & Polloway, E. (1987). Physical and psychiatric diagnoses of pupils with mild mental retardation currently being referred by schools for related services. *Education and Training of the Mentally Retarded, 22*, 221–228.

Forness, S., & Sinclair, E. (1990). Learning disabilities in clinical depression. In H. L. Swanson & B. Keogh (Eds.), *Learning disabilities: Theoretical and research issues* (pp. 315–332). Hillsdale, NJ: Erlbaum.

Forness, S. R., Youpa, D., Hanna, G. L., Cantwell, D. P., & Swanson, J. N. (1992). Classroom instructional characteristic in attention deficit hyperactivity disorder: Comparison of pure and mixed subgroups. *Behavioral Disorders, 17*, 115–120.

Gadow, K. D., & Poling, E. (1988). *Pharmacotherapy and mental retardation*. Austin, TX: PRO-ED.

Garfinkel, B. D. (1990). *Attention deficit disorders: Report of the DSM–IV work group*. (Available from Division of Child and Adolescent Psychiatry, University of Minnesota Medical School, Minneapolis, MN 55455)

Gerring, J. P., & Carney, J. M. (1992). *Head trauma: Strategies for educational reintegration* (2nd ed.). San Diego: Singular.

Hadders-Algra, M., & Touwen, B. C. L. (1992). Minor neurological dysfunction is more closely related to learning difficulties than to behavioral problems. *Journal of Learning Disabilities, 25*, 649–657.

Hagerman, R. J., Schreiner, R. A., Kemper, M. B., Wittenberger, M. D., Zahn, B., & Habicht, K. (1989). Longitudinal IQ changes in fragile X males. *American Journal of Medical Genetics, 33*, 513–518.

Hagerman, R. J., & Sobersky, W. E. (1989). Psychopathology in fragile X syndrome. *American Journal of Orthopsychiatry, 59*, 142–152.

Hocutt, A. M., McKinney, J. D., & Montague, M. (1993). Issues in the education of students with attention deficit disorder: Introduction to the special issue. *Exceptional Children, 60*, 103–106.

Hodapp, R. M., & Dykens, E. M. (1992). The role of etiology in education of children with mental retardation. *McGill Journal of Education, 27*, 165–173.

Howard, J., Beckwith, L., Rodning, C., & Kropenski, V. (1989). The development of young children of substance-abusing parents: Insights from seven years of intervention and research. *Zero to Three: Bulletin of National Center for Clinical Infant Programs, 9*(5), 8–16.

Individuals with Disabilities Education Act of 1990, 20 U.S.C. § 1400 *et seq.*

Kavale, K. A., & Forness, S. R. (1992). Learning difficulties and memory problems in mental retardation: A meta-analysis of theoretical perspectives. In T. Scruggs & M. Mastropieri (Eds.), *Advances in learning and behavioral disabilities* (Vol. 7, pp. 177–219). Greenwich, CT: JAI Press.

Kavale, K. A., Forness, S. R., & Lorsbach, T. (1991). Definition for definitions of learning disabilities. *Learning Disability Quarterly, 14*, 257–266.

Kiernan, W. E., Smith, B. C., & Ostrowsky, M. B. (1986). Developmental disabilities: Definitional issues. In W. E. Kiernan & J. A. Stark (Eds.), *Pathways to employment for adults with developmental disabilities* (pp. 11–20). Baltimore: Brookes.

Kincaid, J. (1993). New federal regulations add disabilities and expand service. *Special Edge, 7*(3), 4.

Kropenski, V., Howard, J., Edelstein, S. B., Sorenson, M. D., Tyler, R., & Moore, A. (1992). Interdisciplinary–interagency training for professionals serving chemically dependent families. *OSERS News in Print, 4*(3), 18–22.

Luckasson, R., Coulter, D. L., Polloway, E. A., Reiss, S., Schalock, R. L., Snell, M. E., Spitalnik, D. M., & Stark, J. A. (1992). *Mental retardation: Definition, classifications, and systems of supports* (9th ed.). Washington, DC: American Association on Mental Retardation.

MacMillan, D. L., & Forness, S. R. (1993). Mental retardation. In M. C. Alkin (Ed.), *Encyclopedia of educational research* (pp. 825–830). New York: McGraw-Hill.

MacMillan, D. L., Gresham, F. M., & Siperstein, G. N. (1993). Conceptual and psychometric concerns about the 1992 AAMR definition of mental retardation. *American Journal on Mental Retardation, 98*, 325–335.

Mercer, C. D., King-Sears, P., & Mercer, A. R. (1990). Learning disability definitions and criteria used by state education departments. *Learning Disability Quarterly, 13*, 141–152.

Mira, M. P., & Tyler, J. S. (1991). Students with traumatic brain injury: Making the transition from hospital to school. *Focus on Exceptional Children, 23*(5), 1–12.

Parker, H. C. (1989). *Children with attention deficit disorder: Education position paper*. (Available from Children with Attention Deficit Disorder, CH.A.D.D., 1989 N. Pine Island Road, Plantation, FL 33322)

Peschel, E., Peschel, R., Howe, C., & Howe, J. (Eds.). (1992). *Neurobiological disorders in children and adolescents*. San Francisco: Jossey-Bass.

President's Committee on Mental Retardation. (1993). *The new morbidity: Recommendations for action and an updated guide to state planning for the prevention of mental retardation and related disabilities associated with socioeconomic conditions*. Washington, DC: U.S. Department of Health and Human Services.

Rehabilitation Act of 1973, Section 504, 29 U.S.C. § 706 *et seq.* (Codified at 34 C.F.R. 6 104 *et seq.*)

Santos, K. E. (1992). Fragile X syndrome: An educator's role in identification, prevention, and intervention. *Remedial and Special Education, 13*(2), 32–39.

Schopmeyer, B. B., & Lowe, F. H. (Eds.). (1992). *The fragile X child*. San Diego: Singular.

Silver, L. B. (1990). Attention deficit hyperactivity: Is it a learning disability or related disorder? *Journal of Learning Disabilities, 23*, 394–397.

Simensen, R. J., & Rogers, R. C. (1989). School psychology and medical diagnosis: The fragile X syndrome. *Psychology in the Schools, 26*, 380–389.

Singh, N. N., Sood, A., Sonenklar, N., & Ellis, C. R. (1991). Assessment and diagnosis of mental illness in persons with mental retardation: Methods and measures. *Behavior Modification, 15*, 419–443.

Sparks, S. N. (1992). *Children of prenatal substance abuse*. San Diego: Singular.

Streissguth, A. P. (1990). Fetal alcohol syndrome and the teratogenicity of alcohol: Policy implications. *King County Medical Society Bulletin, 69*, 32–39.

Streissguth, A. P., Aase, J. M., Clarren, S. K., Randels, S. P., LaDue, R. A., & Smith, D. F. (1991). Fetal alcohol syndrome in adolescents and adults. *Journal of American Medical Association, 265*(15), 1961–1966.

Streissguth, A. P., Randels, S. P., & Smith, D. F. (1991). A test–retest study of intelligence in patients with fetal alcohol syndrome: Implications for care. *Journal of American Academy and Child Adolescent Psychiatry, 30*, 584–587.

Swanson, J. M. (1990). *Report of the steering committee on the ADD amendment to EHA*. (Available from Professional Group for Attention and Related Disorders, Child Development Center, University of California, 19262 Jamboree, Irvine, CA 92715)

U.S. Department of Education. (1993). *Fifteenth annual report to Congress on the implementation of the Education of Individuals with Disabilities Act*. Washington, DC: U.S. Office of Special Education.

West, J. R. (1986). *Alcohol and brain development*. New York: Oxford University Press.

Appropriate Assessment and Curriculum

SECTION II

Best Practices

The best practices literature describes appropriate assessment and curriculum as essential components for the education of students with developmental disabilities. Defining appropriate curriculum for students with developmental disabilities rests primarily on the individual needs of the student. Individual needs must be defined through well-developed assessment; however, the assessment that is used to determine eligibility (i.e., norm-referenced and other standardized measures) for the most part falls short in defining the specific curriculum needs of an individual with developmental disabilities. Practices in this area are evolving; promising and effective practices are found in criterion-referenced and curriculum-based assessment approaches.

The identification of specific curricular goals and objectives should follow from assessment. Effective professionals ensure that curriculum and material used for instruction are age appropriate and reflect a future (adult) functioning orientation. Other philosophical underpinnings of appropriate curriculum include community-referenced curriculum objectives to reflect the local realities, academics taught with a functional focus, and expectations (criteria) reflecting adult realities.

The best practice of using appropriate curriculum does not imply a disability-specific approach but does hinge on the future functioning, age, and severity of the disability. Higher functioning students with developmental disabilities normally need a greater percentage of traditional academics (taught with a functional focus), whereas lower functioning students often need an increased focus on social and self-help skills, vocational skills, and independent living activities.

Age considerations should be a factor in prioritizing curricular skills selected for an individual. Students need to be taught in age-appropriate settings, using age-appropriate materials, and the curriculum decisions should not be made based on developmental or mental age considerations.

Severity of disability is useful as a consideration only when it is employed to describe the impact of the disability on current and future demands, learning rate, and/or service needs based on current skills. It then may be said that what defines appropriate curriculum may vary for lower functioning individuals (i.e., those with more severe disabilities) and higher functioning individuals (i.e., those with less severe disabilities). For the more severely involved population, a future-oriented functional skills curriculum has been shown to be appropriate. On the other hand, students with what have been termed mild disabilities may well benefit from a more traditional academic curriculum.

Adaptations, modifications, and additions to curriculum again are dictated by individual needs, age (years left before exiting formal programming), present functioning, and the ultimate placement of the student. These changes to curriculum (as well as total curriculums) are often accomplished through specific instructional practices that fit the individual. Once again, assessment plays a major role in determining such changes.

This Section of the Book

Chapters 5 and 6 provide a comprehensive overview of assessment of students with developmental disabilities as that assessment leads to placement of a student into services and into the curriculum. Chapter 7 provides a discussion on determining and developing appropriate curriculum, and on the elements essential to establishing appropriate curriculum for students with developmental disabilities. Chapters 8 and 9 address areas that have been shown to be promising practices in leading to successful inclusion of individuals with developmental disabilities in schools and society. Although life skills, friendships, and social competence are not the only areas of curriculum essential to students with developmental disabilities, these chapters exemplify how modifications and additions to the traditional curriculum need to be made, depending on the individual's needs.

The chapters in this section move from broader, more general to more specific concepts. The chapters are full of both promising and proven effective practices in the areas of curriculum and assessment.

Assessment: The Key to Appropriate Curriculum and Instruction

CHAPTER 5

Christine A. Macfarlane

Learning Outcomes

After reading this chapter, you should be able to

- Understand the difference between formative and summative evaluation.

- Describe the various components of the assessment cycle.

- Describe the various types of assessment used during initial assessment.

- Describe the various types of assessment models used for ongoing assessment.

TERMS

The following terms are important for the understanding of this chapter:

Aim: Rate-based performance standards for fair pairs.

Assessment: The total process of measurement and evaluation.

Critical effect: The natural outcome of completing a routine (e.g., hunger is satisfied because a sandwich was fixed and eaten).

Discrepancy analysis: Comparing the individual's performance against the performance of peers without disabilities.

Distributed trials: An instructional format in which a predetermined number of opportunities to respond are taught with other instructional skills across a session or school day.

Equal-interval graph: An arithmetic chart in which the distance between each of the number lines and each of the day lines is the same.

Evaluation: A data-based decision-making process.

Expert system: A computer program incorporating aspects of artificial intelligence that has been designed to emulate the human decision making needed to solve a real-world problem.

Fair pair: Data collected simultaneously for the appropriate and inappropriate response.

Formative evaluation: An ongoing, dynamic process to continually or frequently gather information during instruction or the development of an educational product.

Learning channels: The ways in which the learner receives information, processes it, and responds.

Massed trials: An instructional format that uses multiple opportunities to respond during an instructional session.

Measurement: The process of gathering information, that is, collecting data.

Movement cycle: The length of time from the observable beginning of a response to the observable end of a response. The response can then be repeated.

Natural cue: A stimulus (e.g., sight, sound, smell) that occurs within the environment and serves as a prompt or cue to perform a task or routine.

Natural routine: A sequence that begins with a natural cue and ends when the learner achieves the critical effect.

(continues)

Norm-referenced test: A test designed to compare the learner's performance to the performance of same-age peers.

Pinpoint: A specific behavior that is the target of instruction and measurement.

Skill analysis: A logical sequence of instructional skills designed to guide the learner from the acquisition stage of learning to the maintenance stage of learning.

Social validity: The value of behavior change for an individual as evaluated by important others in that person's life or by the individual.

Spaced trials: An instructional format that incorporates a waiting period or "down time" between each opportunity to respond.

Standard celeration chart: A semi-logarithmic chart which accurately displays frequency of behavior in terms of rate of learning.

Standardized test: A test designed to evaluate each learner's performance against the same established criterion.

Summative evaluation: An assessment process that documents the effectiveness of instruction, a specific program, or an educational product upon completion by conducting assessment at two points in time, the beginning and the end.

Task analysis: A step-by-step chain of specific responses necessary to complete a motoric behavior.

Therbligs: A strategy developed by Frank and Lillian Gilbreth for classifying 17 efficient and nonefficient human movements according to the industrial engineering principle known as motion study. *Note: Therbligs* is *Gilbreth* spelled backwards with the last two letters reversed.

Tool skill: Any prerequisite skill required to perform a task.

Introduction

A hallmark of best practices for persons with developmental disabilities is the effective and judicious use of measurement and evaluation. The Education for All Handicapped Children Act of 1975 (P.L. 94-142) mandated assessment procedures throughout the process of identifying, placing, and teaching persons with developmental disabilities because gathering salient information followed by careful analysis leads to effective decision making, all of which ensure optimal delivery of services. To work with persons with disabilities without engaging in the assessment process wastes valuable time and resources. Only through assessment can professionals document individual progress, determine program quality, and hold programs accountable.

In a generic sense, measurement is the process of gathering information (i.e., collecting data), whereas evaluation is a decision-making process. Together, the processes are called assessment. Depending on the frequency and timing of measurement, evaluation may be thought of as formative (Fuchs & Fuchs, 1986) or summative. *Formative evaluation* is an ongoing process in which information is continually or frequently gathered during instruction. During formative evaluation professionals repeatedly ask the question, "Is this working?" If the answer is maybe or no, then one asks, "What can I do to make it better or to make it work?" The intent is to systematically mark progress, make decisions, and then make changes, if needed, to assure that learners reach objectives in an effective and efficient manner. *Summative evaluation,* on the other hand, documents the effec-

tiveness of instruction or a specific program upon completion. Measurement occurs at the beginning and at the end. Summative evaluation then answers the questions, "Did this work?" and "How well did it work?" Both formative and summative types of evaluation are important tools, but each serves a different purpose. It appears that, in practice, regular educators have traditionally relied more on summative evaluation procedures whereas special educators have found it necessary to concentrate on formative evaluation procedures.

The focus of measurement and the outcome of evaluation depend on where the learner with a disability is on the educational continuum (Browder, 1991). Thus, the purpose for measurement and evaluation varies depending on the targeted outcome. Early assessments may be conducted in order to screen for potential problems. Other assessments may be conducted during the prereferral stage to determine whether assistance can be provided to the learner within regular education settings rather than through referral for special education. If special education appears necessary, educators, parents, and the learner then focus on assessments to diagnose, place, and determine broad, long-range goals. At this point, an Individualized Education Program (IEP) is developed based on the information gathered. The focus then narrows to instructional assessment. From then on, the focus ebbs and flows in a cyclic manner depending on the learner and current demands of the environment. Extensive assessments are conducted infrequently (e.g., every 1 to 3 years), whereas instructional assessments are likely conducted on a daily basis. Figure 5.1 contains a flowchart that describes the assessment process.

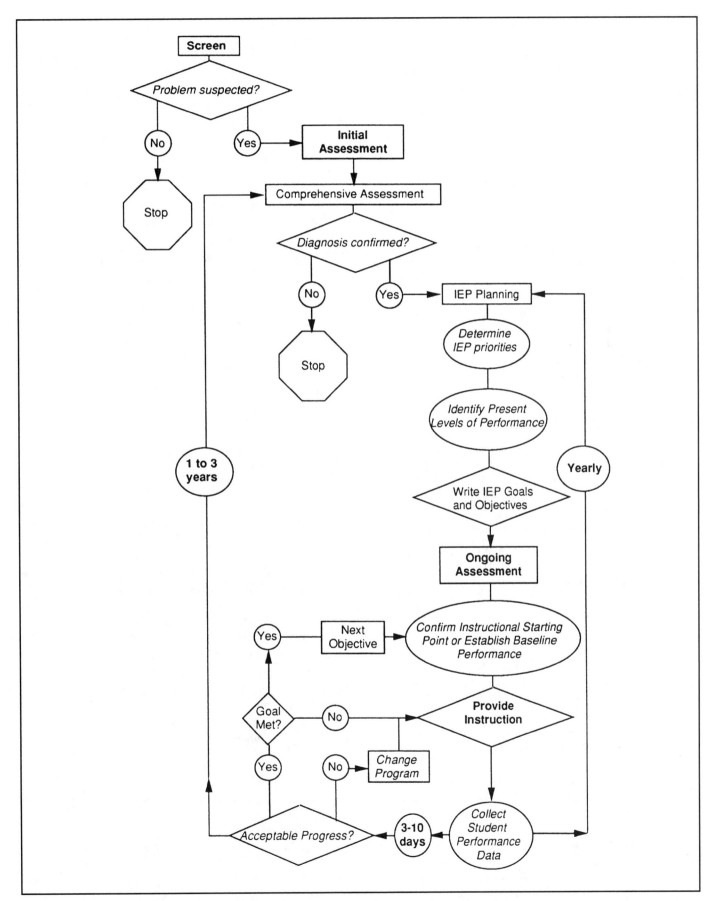

Figure 5.1. A flowchart depicting the ebb and flow of the assessment process from screening through ongoing assessment.

One of the most exciting improvements in the process of measurement and evaluation has been the use of technology to augment and support human expertise. From computer-administered tests and computer-assisted data-collection systems to applications in artificial intelligence (e.g., expert systems), technology has affected the quality and accuracy of assessments. Other computer applications have simply made measurement faster and more efficient.

Initial Assessment

Each successive step or phase in the assessment process builds upon information gathered during the previous phase and guides the next phase. Browder (1991) identified two major assessment phases. Initial assessment, the first major link in this chain of events, is composed of comprehensive and annual assessment. Later, ongoing assessments determine the beginning point for instruction and document progress or lack of progress toward IEP goals. The cumulative effect of initial and ongoing assessment supports an annual reevaluation of the learner's goals.

Comprehensive Assessment

Comprehensive assessment is needed when the learner is referred for diagnosis, to determine the extent of the disability, or to assist in long-range planning. Historically, standardized or norm-referenced tests have been emphasized in the assessment of persons with disabilities. The use of these tests allows professionals to document the extent of a learner's variance from the normal population and to identify major strengths and weaknesses. Ultimately, this assessment determines eligibility and leads to specialized services or confirms the need for continued services. An extensive discussion on the classification of mental retardation can be found in the ninth edition of *Mental Retardation: Definition, Classification, and Systems of Supports* (American Association on Mental Retardation [AAMR], 1992). Although standardized tests may be needed to diagnose, determine eligibility, reevaluate, and assist in long-range planning, they are not always appropriate for curriculum planning or documenting acquisition of specific instructional objectives. In those cases, assessment must focus specifically on individual characteristics and instructional targets.

Norm-referenced tests are generally used to determine levels of intelligence, such as the *Stanford–Binet Intelligence Scale: Fourth Edition* (Thorndike, Hagen, & Sattler, 1986) or *Wechsler Intelligence Scale for Children–Third Edition* (Wechsler, 1991). The test administrator, usually a school psychologist, must be well trained in order to maintain the test's reliability and validity. Information from these tests generates an IQ score or mental age. Specialized tests are available to measure intelligence in persons with sensory impairments (Hiskey, 1966), physical impairments (Burgemeister, Blum, & Lorge, 1972), severe and profound mental retardation, or limited English proficiency (Mercer & Lewis, 1978), as well as young learners (Bayley, 1993).

Norm-referenced tests also are available to determine grade level of academic performance (e.g., *Peabody Individual Achievement Test–Revised*, Markwardt, 1989). Achievement tests also are available in single-subject areas, such as the *Woodcock Reading Mastery Tests–Revised* (Woodcock, 1987) and the *KeyMath Revised: A Diagnostic Inventory of Essential Mathematics* (Connolly, 1988). To determine comparable educational needs of children under age 6, developmental milestones can be assessed by means of norm-referenced instruments such as the *Early Learning Accomplishment Profile* (Glover, Preminger, & Sanford, 1988).

Norm-referenced tests, such as the *Vineland Adaptive Behavior Scale* (Sparrow, Balla, & Cicchetti, 1985), determine adaptive behavior correlated with chronological age. Administering tests that measure academic performance and adaptive skills does not usually require the same level of training as does administering tests of intelligence, and these tests are often administered by teachers or other professionals who are very familiar with the learner. Because tests that measure adaptive skills require first-hand knowledge of the learner, the teacher may need to set up analog situations in some instances to determine whether the learner can perform a certain skill and/or to what level.

A disability such as mental retardation must be thought of as multidimensional. In addition to assessment of intellectual functioning and adaptive behavior, AAMR (1992) supports a broader approach that includes identifying the types of support needed by a person and the level or intensity of support needed. Additional assessments should be given to evaluate psychological functioning and behavior, physical and health considerations, the etiology of the disability, and environmental considerations. Observing the learner in natural settings (e.g., home, school) and interviewing significant others enhances the assessment process and provides significant information (Waterman, 1994). The total breadth of information gathered impacts substantially on future decisions.

Cultural and Linguistic Diversity

Even though comprehensive assessment is mandated for persons with disabilities, assessments to diagnose a disability and place a person in an appropriate special education setting can be fraught with problems. Regardless of the format of or orientation (e.g., developmental, environmental) to comprehensive assessment, it is vital that professionals respect and take into account the learner's culture (AAMR, 1992). Only then will measurement yield accurate information and thus facilitate appropriate decision making. In the past, unacknowledged cultural and linguistic differences (i.e., lack of English proficiency) have sometimes led to misdiagnosed disabilities and overplacement in special education programs. Sections 300.530 through 300.534 of the Education of the Handicapped Act regulate the process of "nondiscriminatory testing." The outcomes of several legal cases have confirmed the need to consider, respect, and accommodate for these differences during the assessment process (Turnbull, 1990). Overrepresentation of minorities in special education is still a problem that cannot be ignored.

Dynamic assessment may be a solution to the problems encountered in testing learners with minority backgrounds (Waterman, 1994). Lack of exposure to the problems or tasks on a standardized test may be alleviated by allowing interaction with the learner during the assessment process. This planned-for interaction focuses on gathering anecdotal information throughout the test to assist in determining how the child learns. In this approach, professionals engage in a dialogue with the learner, providing prompts, models, explanations of why a particular task is relevant, and praise or encouragement. Learners are encouraged to verbalize their problem-solving strategies before and after each question. Although difficult to administer and interpret, dynamic assessment may provide detailed information on how a child learns, which could be very helpful in instructional planning.

Other potential difficulties in a multifactorial assessment are limitations due to an individual's sensory, motor, or communication impairments (AAMR, 1992). The presence of one or more of these impairments can seriously affect the assessment process and the outcome. If available, specialized instruments designed for persons with a specific impairment should be selected. Otherwise, traditional methods for questioning and responding must be modified.

Finally, some persons with disabilities simply may not sit still long enough to take any type of test (Browder & Snell, 1988). Unfortunately, the occurrence of any of these problems seriously jeopardizes the reliability and validity of the outcome.

Applications of Technology

Perhaps an even more important consideration is the potential for inconsistency by the professional and the fallacy of human judgment (AAMR, 1992). Like the learner, test administrators can have good days and bad days and/or be influenced by extraneous factors. One solution to this problem is the use of expert systems to augment human judgment and verify the accuracy of the assessment process. Expert systems, an application of the computer science subdomain of artificial intelligence, emulate human expertise necessary to solve specific problems. In this case the problem is the correctness of classification as a result of the assessment process. For example, CLASS.IH (Ferrara, Williams, & Giere, 1987)

contains Utah rules and regulations that govern the classification of a learner with a mild or moderate mental disability. The expert system systematically checks to see that nothing has been overlooked, verifies information and conclusions as correct, and confirms that classification was arrived at correctly. Other expert systems developed at Utah State University by Ferrara and his colleagues include CLASS.BD (Baer, Ferrara, Althouse, & Reavis, 1988), to assist in the classification of learners with behavior disorders, and CLASS.LD2 (Ferrara & Hofmeister, 1986), to assist in the classification of learners with learning disabilities.

Another application of computer programs is the administration and/or scoring of standardized tests (Hasselbring & Moore, 1990). When assessment takes place at a computer terminal, the learner can use alternative input devices (e.g., adapted keyboard) and/or specific adaptations (e.g., screen reader for visually impaired). As the learner takes the test, the program automatically scores it. Other programs are available to simply score standardized tests. In all instances, the potential for human error is reduced or eliminated and time is saved. The computer accurately and efficiently does what it has been programmed to do without ever getting tired, without ever being judgmental, without ever forgetting to ask a question, and without ever forgetting a step. The use of technology has tremendous potential to assist both the learner and the professional during the comprehensive assessment process.

The results of comprehensive assessments are critical in helping to establish the presence of a disability and to document the level of severity. Theoretically, equal consideration should be given to all test results. However, in practice, professionals have relied heavily on the results of IQ tests (AAMR, 1992). Current thinking suggests that emphasis must shift away from IQ tests to results of tests measuring adaptive behavior.

If the results of an initial assessment indicate that a learner has a disability and thus qualifies for special education services, two types of comprehensive assessments are mandated. A comprehensive reevaluation assessment needs to occur at least every 3 years to update the file and confirm the need for continued special education services. For younger children this reevaluation may occur more frequently. Second, IEPs are developed, reviewed, or updated by conducting at least annually a comprehensive assessment that focuses on instructional goals.

Annual IEP Assessment

Once qualification for special education has been established (or confirmed), and on an annual basis, the assessment process shifts gears to gather information to develop an IEP. For school-aged learners with mild disabilities, assessment will reflect the traditional public school curriculum of reading, mathematics, written expression, and other academic skills, along with social skills, motor and perceptual skills, and career education (for older learners). Young learners and learners with moderate, severe, or profound disabilities will need an alternative approach to assessment.

Developmental Approach

One approach for determining appropriate curriculum placement for young learners (i.e., birth to age 6) with disabilities is to use developmental assessment. This strategy focuses on determining whether the learner has achieved developmental milestones that children would normally achieve by a certain age. Typically, this is done with a standardized criterion-referenced test, such as the *Brigance Diagnostic Inventory of Early Development–Revised* (Brigance, 1991). Some tests use a rating scale to assess quality or level of development. Recent refinements have extended the assessment process to include the needs of the entire family (i.e., parents, siblings, extended family) (Venn, 1994). A transdisciplinary team that includes parents as key participants conducts the assessment. Each professional must have excellent observational skills, access to work samples (i.e., portfolio) or records, and the option of setting up analog situations. Difficulties in developmental assessment may occur if the child experiences certain impairments (e.g., physical) and/or has a moderate, severe, or profound disability. In some cases early assessment and intervention may prevent at-risk children from developing a disability or reduce the severity or the impact of the disability on the learner.

Initially, assessment and curriculum are geared to gross and fine motor skills, communication skills, social skills, cognitive skills, and self-help skills. Later, the emphasis broadens to include preacademic skills and eventually academic skills. Goals are selected sequentially, with acquisition of one skill serving as the prerequisite for advancing to the next higher skill or step.

Early efforts in educating persons with moderate, severe, and profound disabilities relied on developmental assessment to guide instruction regardless of the individual's age (Browder, 1991). If a learner with developmental disabilities tested out at a 3-year-old level, curriculum goals would then be aimed at skill acquisition normal for a nondisabled 3-year-old. F. Brown and Snell (1993a) noted several problems or dangers with this approach. It assumes that typical behavior of children is an appropriate yardstick for children with disabilities. In reality, curriculum based on developmental milestones can quickly become age inappropriate (e.g., playing with a doll) or nonfunctional. Isolated skills (e.g., grasping) may not generalize across curricular or environmental domains (e.g., holding a pencil, holding a spoon). Also, the rationale for including particular skills may have merit in a testing situation but fail to carry over in a realistic way to the instructional environment.

Life Skills Approach

The increasing emphasis on the need for functional, age-appropriate assessment and curriculum that examines a person's ability to live as independently as possible within the community has led to the development and implementation of several assessment tools with a life skills orientation (Browder, 1991). Ecological inventories, adaptive behavior scales, and/or curriculum-based assessment are three tools used to look at the real-world demands, both academic and nonacademic, of functioning within home, school, and community. Although this form of assessment has been used more frequently with persons who have severe disabilities, it is appropriate for learners of all ages and disability (Cronin & Patton, 1993).

Regardless of the approach to assessment, educators, parents, and the learner must work together to establish priorities, determine present levels of performance, and set reasonable timelines for the acquisition of future goals and objectives. This provides the transition from comprehensive assessment to ongoing, instructional assessment. The outcome of this process is an instructional road map for the coming year.

Establishing Priorities

Any approach to assessment is certain to generate a long list of deficits. Rather than tackle the unwieldy task of assessing the entire list, it is advantageous to establish priorities before further assessment takes place (Browder, 1991). The establishment of priorities closely correlates with the philosophical orientation used during the comprehensive assessment process. With the standard approach, priorities parallel the regular education curriculum with modifications as necessary. With a developmental approach, priorities support the acquisition of normal developmental milestones. A life skills approach concentrates on helping the learner become as independent as possible. Once established, priorities become the goals and objectives for an IEP.

One widespread method for establishing priorities is curriculum-based assessment (Choate, Enright, Miller, Poteet, & Rakes, 1992). In this context, curriculum-based assessment provides an extensive database from which to target skills and identify priorities. Assessment can be conducted using indirect assessment methods (e.g., teacher interview, questionnaires, rating scales, school records) and/or direct assessment methods. Thus, curriculum-based assessment helps the professional identify areas of need and document learner strengths.

For learners with severe disabilities, Browder (1991) suggested a life skills approach for prioritizing assessment and instruction that considers information from several sources. Potential skills are rated for preference by the learner, caregivers, and significant others (e.g., potential employers). A skill's value is also judged on (a) societal expectations, including the learner's ethnicity and culture; (b) skill utility and other practical issues (e.g., time constraints); and (c) whether partial participation is a legitimate option. As a practical measure, the use of a prioritization checklist facilitates simultaneous consideration of all these factors. The use of environmental or ecological inventories can also guide the process of prioritizing goals and objectives. This assessment strategy is discussed in a later section of this chapter.

For learners with moderate, severe, or profound disabilities in inclusive settings, COACH (*Choosing Options and Accommodations for Children*) (Giangreco, Cloninger, & Iverson, 1993) offers an extensive guide for determining priorities. Prioritization begins with an in-depth parental interview to select one to three "valued life outcomes." Parents then target from one to nine curricular areas "designed to augment or extend general education curriculum" (p. 35). Within each curricular area (e.g., communication, socialization, personal management, leisure/recreation, applied academics, home, school, community, vocational school), parents have the option of rating the activity listed, delaying assessment until the educational team meets, or skipping it for a period of time. Ratings reflect current level of proficiency, note resistance to assistance, and target emerging skills. Parents decide whether a skill needs work and rank their top five choices. Given the top five priorities in each curriculum area, a total of eight top priorities is determined during cross-prioritization. Later, the entire educational team meets to translate these priorities into goals and objectives.

Present Levels of Educational Performance

Documentation of present levels of educational performance is one of the major components in an IEP. Long-term goals and short-term objectives are selected specifically to build on noted strengths and acquired skills, as well as to target identified weaknesses and deficit skills. The information gathered at this point serves as a summation of previous work and as a starting point for future instruction. Data from either summative or formative evaluation methods may be presented to document a learner's progress. The assessment instruments may be either formal or informal (i.e., teacher made). In most instances assessment is direct rather than indirect.

Deciding what to teach is an important task that must be based on accurate and complete information. The term assessment-based instruction implies that an appropriate analysis of learning-related behaviors leads to sound instruction (Polloway, Patton, Payne, & Payne, 1989, p. 41). As the process for finalizing annual IEP goals and objectives takes place, close attention must be paid to measurement and evaluation formats that are to be used later for ongoing assessment. In some instances the information gathered to

support selection of annual goals provides a starting point for instruction or confirms current performance. However, in most instances, additional, more specific information must be gathered during initial assessment. Therefore, careful attention must be paid to methods used to gather information. The following methods are effective in determining what to teach and have supportive linkages with later methods of assessment-based instruction.

Criterion-Referenced Tests

Perhaps more than any other diagnostic–prescriptive form of assessment, criterion-referenced tests have been the workhorse of assessment-based instruction. Since teachers first wondered whether students learned what was taught, criterion-referenced tests have been used to discover the answer to that question. Professionals may choose to use commercially available tests or construct their own. Commercial tests may focus on broad, typical skills or measure specific skills that correspond to a published curriculum. A problem arises if teachers narrow their instructional focus to only what is on the test. In that case they may lose "the richness and variety that characterize good instruction" (Witt, Elliott, Kramer, & Gresham, 1994, p. 31). Teacher-constructed tests have the advantage of being more learner specific, but care must be given that they are properly constructed.

In either scenario the purpose of this direct form of assessment is to compare learner performance to established criteria rather than the performance of other learners. A hierarchical sequence of skills broken down into small and discreet units is the hallmark of a criterion-referenced test. A major advantage is that criterion-referenced tests can be used for formative evaluation; that is, the learner can be frequently assessed, often daily, as instruction occurs. This affords the opportunity to document progress, determine instructional effectiveness, and prepare for the next instructional phase (Witt et al., 1994). All of this presumes that appropriate criteria have been established, and that failure to acquire skills is a result of lack of exposure to the material rather than the myriad of other factors that influence instruction.

Ecological Assessment

The recognition that numerous environmental factors have an impact on a learner during instruction created a need for ecological assessment. This type of assessment, regardless of format (e.g., norm referenced, criterion referenced, informal), must be framed within the context of ecological factors (Witt et al., 1994). However, few tools exist to help educators through this complex process. *The Instructional Environment Scale* (Ysseldyke & Christenson, 1987) contains a qualitative observation scale that covers 12 variables in the instructional environment that can affect learner performance (e.g., instructional presentation, academic engaged time, motivational strategies). For the most part, though, educators must self-identify salient indicators and assess the learner and environment concurrently to determine the effects on instruction.

Ecological Inventories

The purpose of an ecological or environmental inventory is to gather highly individualized information about specific demands in a learner's natural environment related to all aspects of that person's life—that is, the need to live a quality lifestyle as independently as possible and to work and recreate within the community. L. Brown and colleagues (1979) conceptualized this need as "domains of adult functioning" (e.g., community, domestic, leisure, and vocational). F. Brown and Snell (1993a) suggested adding a school domain to address specific skills needed for school (e.g., riding a school bus) and the needs of young learners. Related skills, such as communication, motor, social, and functional academics, are then embedded within the natural context of a domain.

Redundancy across domains leads to prioritization. First, all current and future environments are identified. Then, each environment is divided into subenvironments. Next, the teacher lists the activities that can happen in each subenvironment. Finally, skills needed to accomplish those activities are noted. Figure 5.2 provides an example of this strategy, using a format suggested by L. Brown et al. (1979).

Underlying the ecological inventory is the philosophy that persons with disabilities have the right to and should access the same environments available to persons without disabilities. The difference between what a peer can do within a specific environment (e.g., bowling alley) and what the person with a developmental disability can currently do becomes a discrepancy analysis. Although specific formats or strategies for conducting an ecological inventory can be identified and replicated, questions are often open ended and likely answers are frequently not predetermined. The teacher must interview and observe the person with a disability and peers, access samples of the learner's work (i.e., portfolio), or set up analog situations. Results may differ based on age; disability; level of disability; communities in which the person lives, works, and plays; and/or assessment bias. A major advantage of this approach is that the community reference increases the probability of obtaining social validity (Kazdin, 1977; Wolf, 1978); that is, members of the learner's community will approve of (a) the selection of goals, (b) the methods for teaching those goals, and (c) the instructional outcome.

The major disadvantages in using an ecological inventory are time requirements and difficulty in establishing reliability. The IMPACT Curriculum (Neel & Billingsley, 1989) is one example of a systematic, formal ecological inventory that overcomes these disadvantages. Two comprehensive inventories, one for home and community and one for school and community, guide the initial assessment in identifying (a) how much supervision the learner requires, (b) the form and function of the learner's communicative behavior, and (c) the different environments the learner accesses. Figure 5.3 contains a section of the IMPACT Environmental Inventory for Home and Community. When compared with Figure 5.2, the content (i.e., leisure skills) appears similar, but the process is notably different. The final instructional outcome may be very similar or may differ markedly.

Outcome-Based Assessment

The outcome-based approach to assessment reflects concern that education should be meaningful and result in acquisition of skills important for real-world situations (Waterman, 1994). Educational outcomes are selected based on what the learner needs to know to function as an effective adult. Competencies necessary to achieve the outcomes are delineated in a sequential order and then further divided into subskills. Then, much like a criterion-referenced test, teachers determine which subskills the learner has mastered and which ones they have not.

Functional Analysis

A functional analysis is a complex, multifaceted, specialized ecological inventory designed to assess behaviors (Young, Kemblowski, Blair, & Macfarlane, 1992). The intent is to identify the variable(s) within the environment that maintain appropriate and inappropriate behavior and then design an intervention strategy that reduces or eliminates the effect of the variable(s) on the inappropriate behavior. The process begins with indirect assessment. Significant people in the student's environment (e.g., caregivers, siblings, teachers, friends) are interviewed to obtain essential information about the behavior(s) and the individual. The object is to try to accurately predict when the behavior(s) will and will not occur and hypothesize the probable function of the behavior(s). Functional analysis is based on behavioral philosophy and it is assumed that all behavior has as its goal either positive reinforcement (i.e., the aquisiton of something positive) or negative reinforcement (i.e., the removal of something undesirable). Within that context four behavioral functions further describe the motivation for the problem behavior. People use behavior to (a) escape or avoid, (b) obtain material or tangible resources, (c) obtain sensory stimulation, and/or (d) obtain attention. Student records are reviewed and analyzed for behavioral patterns and to gather information on past successful and unsuccessful interventions. The probable

Ben Jones Age: 12   Domain: Leisure

Current Environment	School gymnasium		Future Environment	Community wellness center	
Subenvironment(s)	Activities	Skills	Subenvironment(s)	Activities	Skills
Locker room	• Changing clothes	-Undress -Dress -Tie shoes	*Reception area*	• Checking in	-Show ID -Obtain towel
	• Locker	-Use locker -Open door -Shut door -Use lock	*Locker room*	• Checking out • Changing clothes	-Leave towel -Undress -Dress -Tie shoes
	• Showering	-Wash body -Dry off -Be modest		• Locker	-Use locker -Open door -Shut door -Use lock
Bleachers	• Roll call	-Sitting -Answer here -Spectator		• Showering	-Wash body -Shampoo -Dry off -Be modest
Gym floor	• Basketball	-Dribble -Shoot -Pass		• Grooming	-Deodorant -Comb hair
	• Line dancing	-Imitate steps	*Equipment room*	• Use treadmill	-Walk -Wait turn
			Sauna	• Steam bath	-Open door -Close door -Sit -Watch time
			Running/jogging track	• Fast walk	-Lane courtesy -Walking -Count laps
			Swimming pool	• Swim laps	-Swimsuit -Enter pool -Freestyle -Turns -Exit pool
			Basketball court	• Basketball	-Dribble -Shoot -Pass

Current Environment	Little league ballpark		Future Environment	University stadium	
Subenvironment(s)	Activities	Skills	Subenvironment(s)	Activities	Skills
Bleachers	• Spectator	-Climb stairs -Sit -Cheer -Watch game	*Bleachers*	• Spectator	-Climb stairs -Sit -Cheer -Watch game

Current Environment	Bedroom (Family Home)		Future Environment	Bedroom (Group Home)	
Subenvironment(s)	Activities	Skills	Subenvironment(s)	Activities	Skills
Bed	• Read book	-Turn pages -Read -Use bookmark	*Easy chair*	• Read book	-Turn pages -Read -Use bookmark

Current Environment	Back yard (Family Home)		Future Environment	Deck (Group Home)	
Subenvironment(s)	Activities	Skills	Subenvironment(s)	Activities	Skills
Swing set	• Push sibling	-Place on seat -Push carefully -Help down	*Glider*	• Swing	-Sit -Push with foot -Conversation

Figure 5.2. Example of an ecological inventory following the format suggested by L. Brown et al. (1979) to determine current and future environments in the leisure domain, subenvironments, activities within each subenvironment, and skills needed to complete each activity.

Where Does Your Student Go?

One of the main parts of your student's program is to increase the number of places where he or she can go. This part of the questionnaire tells us about the places you and your class visit and how well your student does in different places with different people and gives you an opportunity to list specific problems your student has in various situations.

How often does your child play outside?

_X_ Frequently   ____ Occasionally   ____ Never

Where does your student usually play when outside? If your student plays in more than one place on a regular basis, please tell us about how much time is spent in each place.

In protected courtyard? _X_ Hrs. _6 hours /week_

Is your yard or playground fenced? _X_ Yes   ____ No _parts are fenced, but not all_

In areas outside playground or courtyard? _X_ Hrs. _3 hours/week_

In a park or neighborhood area near school? _X_ Hrs. _10 hours/week_

When your student does play outside, how much supervision does he or she require? (*Check all that apply.*)

_X_ My student can play independently

   _X_ Alone

   _X_ With other children

____ My student will play with help from aides or teachers

____ My student will play with help from other children in my class

_X_ My student will play with help from other children in the school

_X_ My student will play outside with help from family members

_X_ My student will play outside with help from friends or neighbors

What types of problems, if any, does your student present when playing outside (e.g., runs away, tears at plants and eats them, hits other children, runs out into traffic)?

Doesn't always pay attention to what the other kids are doing. Will try to join games already in progress. Sometimes he gets in the way of their games and could get hurt.

Figure 5.3. Example of the school and community inventory using open-ended questions with some preselected answers to guide the ecological assessment. Adapted from *IMPACT: A Functional Curriculum Handbook for Students with Moderate to Severe Disabilities* [pp. 167–169], by R. S. Neel and F. F. Billingsley, 1989, Baltimore: Brookes. Copyright 1989 by Paul H. Brookes Publishing Co. Adapted with permission.

Which community/recreation settings does your student use?

Plays Little League baseball. Goes to the public swimming pool in the summer. Goes on various field trips with his class (e.g., bowling alley, fast food restaurants, movie theater, mall).

When your student goes to a community recreation setting, what amount of direct supervision is required? (*Check all that apply.*)

____ None (independent)

_X_ With other students in the class

_X_ With teacher or aide

_X_ With family members

_X_ With friends or neighbors

Do you regularly use these environments as part of the regular school day?

_X_ Yes   ____ No

If you do not use these places on a regular basis, how often does your class frequent these places ?

____ Almost never   ____ Once a quarter   ____ Once a month

What community services (e.g., restaurants, stores, house of worship) does your student use?

Walmart, McDonald's, Shakey's Pizza, Musicland, Scheel's Sporting Goods, Hy-Vee grocery store, First Presbyterian Church, Donutland

When your student does use community services, what level of direct supervision is required? (*Check all that apply.*)

____ None (independent)

_X_ With other members of the class

_X_ Teachers and/or aides

_X_ With family members

_X_ With friends or neighbors

Do you use these places regularly as part of the school day?

_X_ Yes   ____ No

(continues)

Figure 5.3. Continued.

If you do not use these places on a regular basis, how often does your class frequent these places?

_____ Almost never   _____ Once a quarter   _____ Once a month

Are there places that you or other members of your class go where you usually would not take your student?

_____ Yes   _X_ No

If yes, where? _____

_____

_____

What problems are created when he or she does go along?

He won't eat meat because it's difficult for him to chew. Likes to talk to strangers and can disappear quickly. Has trouble serving self from buffet at Shakey's.

What skills does your student need to learn before you would feel comfortable letting him or her go with you on a regular basis? If the problems are different in different situations, please list each separately. (*Attach a separate sheet if you need more space.*)

Is able to go on a regular basis, but needs to learn to (a) identify nonmeat items at the fast food restaurants, (b) serve himself at Shakey's, and (c) confine conversations to friends or only say "hi" to strangers.

What skills would your student have to learn to be able to go to these places alone? If the skills needed are different in different situations, please list each separately. (*Attach a separate sheet if you need more space.*)

He would definitely have to understand the dangers of talking to any stranger. Money skills, survival reading skills, and time-telling skills. Needs to learn to maintain an "inside" voice in restaurants.

Figure 5.3. Continued.

function of the behavior (e.g., to escape a difficult task) is then hypothesized. Systematic manipulation of the pertinent variables is then conducted to confirm or disaffirm the hypothesis. For example, the professional might set up sev-

eral short observational sessions involving a repetitive cycle of 5 minutes of easy task followed by 5 minutes of hard task. A higher frequency of behavioral problems during the hard task would confirm the hypothesis that escape–avoidance is

Does your student like to ride on the bus? __X__ Yes _____ No

What problems occur, if any, when he or she has to ride:

   5-15 minutes *no problems occur* _____

   _____

   15 minutes or more *will fidget in seat, turn around and look at other passengers, may talk "silly"* _____

Figure 5.3. Continued.

the function of the behavior. Once function is confirmed, the next step is to determine communicative intent, or motivation, for the behavior. Questions that might be asked by the professional include the following: Why does the person want to escape this difficult task? Is it because of insufficient instruction? Does the person need help, a break, or more incentive? Once identified, this information leads to an appropriate intervention (e.g., teach the person to request help).

The complexity of a functional analysis and the intensity of some problem behaviors can make this type of analysis difficult for teachers to administer alone. Behavioral consultants frequently assist by conducting observations, analyzing data, and providing an intervention plan. *DECEL* (Young et al., 1992), an expert database system, was designed to assist with the functional analysis process. A series of components guides the user through the entire process, from functional analysis to development and evaluation of an appropriate intervention. Comprehensive guides, such as *Functional Analysis of Problem Behavior: A Practical Assessment Guide* (O'Neill, Horner, Albin, Storey, & Sprague, 1990) and *Severe Behavior Problems: A Functional Communication Training Approach* (Durand, 1990), are also available to walk professionals through the process.

Reinforcer Surveys

Reinforcer surveys to determine learner preferences are another form of ecological assessment. What motivates a person to learn, or what will reinforce correct behavior, is an important question to answer. For learners who can state their preferences by a vocal or nonvocal strategy, it may simply be a matter of asking. For others it may mean setting up analog situations to field-test a variety of potential primary and secondary reinforcers (Blair, Macfarlane, & Young, 1991). The professional gauges the level of interest and, thus, the potential reinforcing value by measuring time spent with the item, number of requests for the same item, and positive body language.

Quality Indicators

Assessment that considers the learner's social and educational environments leads to more viable instructional outcomes. Consideration of qualitative indicators can further enhance the assessment process.

Social Validity

Determining social validity is a matter of documenting the significance of assessment-based instruction on a person's life (Kazdin, 1977; Wolf, 1978). Professionals may want to pose the following questions: As an educational team, did we select the correct priorities? Did instruction help the person meet the goals and objectives? Is the community satisfied with the results? Without social validity there is no confirmation; there are no answers. Social comparison is one strategy for social validation (Kazdin, 1980). These questions are considered: What is expected of nondisabled peers in similar settings? Is the learner's behavior within acceptable limits? Subjective evaluation relies on the judgment of important people within the learner's environment or experts to evaluate acceptability of his or her behavior. These questions are considered: Does that person see a change? Does that person approve? When educators pay attention to the questions inherent in establishing social validity, the probability that people with disabilities will truly benefit from instructional programs should increase.

Educational Validity

Educational validity (Voeltz & Evans, 1983) is a strategy for evaluating the quality of instructional programs according to three criteria. To meet the *internal validity* criterion, change must have occurred as a direct result of the instructional program. The *educational integrity* criterion is met when instruction took place as outlined in the IEP. The third criterion, *qualitative significance*, depends on whether instruction actually benefited the person and the extent to which it is seen as valuable in the judgment of significant others within the community. Thus, Jose's instructional program to learn how to open his locker meets the criteria of internal validity. Baseline data supported that he did not have the skill prior to instruction. The teacher gathered data throughout the instructional process to document his progress as he acquired the skill. The objectives and evaluation procedures were carefully thought out during the IEP meeting and later followed during the instructional process. The criterion of educational integrity was met. Finally, the other students in Jose's school think it is "cool" that Jose can open his own locker; that is qualitative significance.

Qualify of Life Indicators

Meyer and Evans (1989) urged educators to look beyond the immediate effects of instruction to long-term significance. Besides improvement in the target skill and acquisition of alternative skills and positive behaviors, instructional programs should (a) produce positive collateral effects and reduce side effects; (b) reduce medical and crisis management; (c) result in more community integration and less restrictive placements; (d) increase individual choice, happiness, and satisfaction; (e) improve perceptions of others; and (f) expand social relationships and support networks.

Ongoing Assessment

The product of initial assessment is an IEP, which guides the learner's yearly instructional program. As stated, linkages exist between methods of prioritizing IEP goals and objectives and methods to guide ongoing assessment. Effective teachers' methods of choice for ongoing assessment depend on several factors, such as the instructional program, the target skill, extraneous demands on teacher time, and the information needed to make instructional decisions (Browder, 1991). Each situation, comprised of learner, teacher, and classroom environment, is unique. Appropriate selections must be determined for each individual based on need and effective practices.

The principle that assessment should reflect the natural environment raises the question of whether to use formal, commercially available materials or to rely on informal, teacher-made materials. The advantages of formal assessment instruments are availability, ease of use, completeness, and standardization. Teachers simply give the formal test, score it, and report the results. Teacher-made assessments require substantial investments of time to develop and may not be reliable or valid (Fuchs & Fuchs, 1990). There is a possibility that information will be overlooked, collected incorrectly, or not collected at all. The value, though, is that if well done, a teacher-made instrument reflects the culture and individual preferences of the learner, characteristics

within the learner's community, specific demands of the natural environment, and most important, what is being taught.

Within the natural context, professionals must also remember to measure what is important. For persons with severe disabilities, F. Brown and Snell (1993b) raised one additional qualitative issue. If "meaningful measurement" is going to take place, then learning must be evaluated within the context of life quality. Qualitative "yardsticks" such as social validity (Wolf, 1978), educational validity (Voeltz & Evans, 1983), and quality of life indicators (Meyer & Evans, 1989) assist professionals to look beyond numbers to what matters most: the impact on a person's life. It is not enough to know that a learner correctly selected a toy to play with or the prompt level required; it is more important to know the learner enjoyed playing with it.

Assessment Models

The following models represent effective practices in assessment-based instruction. Two critical factors drive the selection of the appropriate method. First, the method of measurement and evaluation must correlate with the criterion set forth in the IEP goal or objective. Table 5.1 suggests some typical formats of measurement to evaluate various criteria. Second, just as instruction must match the student's stage of learning, assessment also must be appropriate to that stage.

Stages of Learning

One approach to learning suggests that learning occurs in three to four stages (Young, West, & Macfarlane, 1994). Emphasis on the accuracy or quality of response characterizes the acquisition stage of learning. Responses generally occur at low rates and may require extensive learner effort or teacher prompts to perform. The fluency-building stage of learning is characterized by more accurate performance at a higher rate. This suggests that the skill is becoming automatic. A high level of proficiency marks the end of the fluency-building stage. In the generalization stage of learning, the skill is used in more than one setting and under different conditions. The maintenance stage of learning implies that the behavior will continue to occur without further training or supervision. Depending on the stage of learning, teachers select different instructional techniques; thus, stage of learning also affects choice of appropriate assessment techniques.

Task Analytic Assessment

The identification of a sequence of skills or behavioral components of a task provides the framework for task analytic assessment. The term *task analysis* has become a catch-all phrase for several different concepts. Although similar, the strategy for determining skill sequences is not the same as identifying steps to complete a single task. A *skill analysis* provides a road map for teaching and measuring a series of

Table 5.1

Measurement Formats That Assist in Documenting Various Types of Criteria

If you want to evaluate:	Then measure:	Use:
Accuracy	Number of occurrences Number right/wrong Correct/incorrect Approximation of model (e.g., handwriting)	Permanent products (e.g., worksheets) Event frequency recording
Level of independence	Number of prompts Type of prompts (e.g., indirect verbal, direct verbal, model, physical) Number of supervisor contacts	Discrete categorization recording (e.g., task analysis, checklist)
Endurance	Length of time Distance	Duration recording (e.g., seconds, minutes, hours) Interval recording Momentary time sampling Feet, yards, miles
Quickness	Number completed Correct/errors Length of time How soon started	Rate/frequency (e.g., probe sheets) Duration recording Latency (e.g., seconds, minutes)
Generalization	Number of different people Number of different settings Number of different exemplars	Permanent products Behavioral observation Interview
Maintenance	Accuracy over time	Permanent products Behavioral observation Self-management
Quality	Level of satisfaction Anecdotal behavior	Permanent products (e.g., products) Portfolios Discrete categorization recording Ratings (e.g., Likert scale) Field notes
Behavioral States	Sleep cycle Wake cycle	Interval recording Behavioral observation
Behavioral patterns	Time of occurrence Ecological variables Behavior	Interval recording Antecedent–Behavior–Consequence recording Field notes Event frequency recording Duration recording

skills. A task analysis is a step-by-step breakdown of the responses required to complete a task. For example, a simple task analysis for writing sentences could involve the following steps: (a) begin sentence with capital letter, (b) write words in sequence, (c) maintain spacing between words, and (d) end sentence with punctuation mark. The skill analysis might be structured as follows: (a) write sentence with partial physical assistance and model, (b) write sentence with model, (c) write sentence with verbal cue, and (d) write sentence independently. Another skill analysis might focus on placement of the model (i.e., on the learner's paper, in a workbook, on the blackboard) or the ability to write between smaller and smaller lines. Later task analyses could identify the steps in writing a personal letter, writing a business letter, and addressing an envelope.

Most task analytic assessments are designed to measure an individual's ability to independently perform complex, motoric chains of behaviors such as shoe-tying, loading a dishwasher, or getting a drink of milk (see Figure 5.4). Learner behavior may be continuous (e.g., brushing teeth) or noncontinuous (e.g., taking a bath during which the caregiver shampoos the child's hair) (Browder, 1991). Task analyses can also be developed within the context of activity-based routines. Neel and Billingsley (1989) structured the

1. Obtain glass
   a. Go to cupboard.
   b. Open cupboard door.
   c. Remove glass from cupboard with nondominant hand.
   d. Shut cupboard door.
   e. Set glass down on counter by refrigerator.

2. Obtain milk
   a. Open refrigerator door.
   b. Grasp milk jug by handle.
   c. Remove milk jug from refrigerator.
   d. Shut refrigerator door.
   e. Set milk jug on counter.

3. Pour milk
   a. Remove cap from milk jug.
   b. Set cap on counter.
   c. Grasp milk jug by handle with dominant hand.
   d. Hold glass steady with nondominant hand.
   e. Center mouth of milk jug over glass about 1" above the rim.
   f. Pour until milk is within 1" of top of glass.

4. Put milk away
   a. Return milk jug to upright position and set on counter.
   b. Replace cap.
   c. Open refrigerator.
   d. Grasp milk jug by handle.
   e. Return to refrigerator.
   f. Shut refrigerator door.

Figure 5.4. A task analysis for getting a drink of milk.

IMPACT Curriculum to reflect natural routines within a person's environment (e.g., getting ready for school, eating lunch in the school cafeteria). A routine begins with a natural cue and ends with the critical effect. Thirst is the natural cue to get a drink. The critical effect is the satisfaction of thirst. With this model, the task analysis in Figure 5.4 would include drinking the milk. Choosing the drink could be a mini-routine. Various beverages (e.g., milk, juice) in the refrigerator would serve as natural cues, and making the choice is the critical effect. Getting a drink can be a sub-routine within a routine for eating a meal or an independent routine at other times during the day.

Assessment of a learner's ability to know when to perform a task is as important as measuring how well the learner does the task. Including additional components can enhance task analytic assessment. F. Brown, Evans, Week, and Owen (1987) identified functional competencies that lead to increased independence. In addition to the core, the learner needs to (a) identify thirst and move to the kitchen (task initiation); (b) wash hands, locate the correct cupboard, and get a glass (task preparation); (c) determine what to do if a clean glass is not available (problem solve); (d) avoid spilling the milk while pouring (monitor quality); (e) maintain a normal pace (monitor tempo); and (f) put the milk away and put the glass in the dishwasher when finished (task termination). Communication skills, choice making, and social skills provide enrichment and should also be assessed. In the real world getting a drink is often part of meal preparation. Asking family members or other diners what they would like to drink, choosing between milk and other available beverages, and making requests or responding to requests are all important skills that improve quality of life.

As with any form of assessment, task analytic assessment requires planning and advance preparation (Browder, 1991). When developing a task analysis, it is important to first consider the learner's current performance. Second, it is important to identify the best and most appropriate way to complete a task. For example, refrigerated beverage containers should always be put away closed, capped, or sealed with some type of lid. Failure to do so could result in the beverage's absorbing odors from the refrigerator that could alter the taste. Open beverages may also lose nutritional value or become contaminated with bacteria. After identifying the motoric responses, it may be necessary to adapt the task. Younger children or persons with poor fine motor skills might encounter difficulty manipulating a gallon milk jug. Purchasing milk in smaller containers or using a plastic holder could simplify the task. Another option could be to use the principle of partial participation and assign responsibility for completing designated steps within the task analysis to another person. Finally, a permanent line on a special glass could mark the full point and serve as a stimulus to stop pouring milk.

Writing a task analysis is in itself a task analysis. One begins by writing the steps in sequence using definitive terms. Observing a person without disabilities or another family member performing the task, doing the task oneself, or recalling one's own performance will help in the process. It is important to exclude personal idiosyncratic behavior and to include family and learner preferences for doing a task (e.g., wetting the toothbrush before putting toothpaste on vs. putting the toothpaste on and then wetting it). Determining the size of the step requires practice (Young et al., 1994). Generally, learners who have a higher functioning level can successfully complete a task with fairly broad steps (e.g., the numbered steps in Figure 5.4). Learners with lower levels of functioning may require that a task be broken down into smaller steps (i.e., the lettered steps in Figure 5.4). At times step size may be influenced by task difficulty (e.g., tying shoes vs. using Velcro fasteners) and/or previous experience. An appropriate-sized step provides the right amount of information during assessment. A series of small steps may create difficulty for the professional in recording the learner's performance, particularly if the learner is able to complete the task quickly. Steps that are too large may not provide enough information if the learner makes an error or might incorrectly indicate lack of independent performance. If the learner could not obtain the milk, was it because he or she could not open the door, was unable to identify the milk jug, could not lift the milk off the shelf, or became frustrated? Within a routine, learned subroutines may be collapsed into large steps whereas unknown subroutines require a greater degree of specificity.

For vocational tasks, frequently performed tasks, or tasks that require quick responses, it may be necessary to determine the most efficient way to perform a task. Browder (1991) described the origin of therbligs and how to apply them to the development of task analyses. Therbligs incorporate an industrial engineering principle called motion study to define eight efficient motor movements—grasp, reach, move, release, pre-position, assemble, disassemble, and use—and nine inefficient motor movements—search, select, hold, position, inspect, unavoidable delay, avoidable delay, plan, and rest to overcome fatigue. Thus, "reach for milk jug" is efficient, whereas "search for milk jug" is not. Simultaneous or sequential movements are defined for each hand (i.e., dominant and nondominant) to enhance coordination, save time, and reduce or eliminate nonessential movement. The end result is a concise and efficient task analysis that can be completed quickly and with fluid motor movements.

After writing the steps, one should ask someone else to try to complete the task exactly as outlined. Next, one should revise the task analysis: Add missing steps, delete unnecessary steps, and clarify questionable steps. The last step before proceeding with assessment is a final check to assure an accurate task analysis. Implementing a task analytic assessment involves further planning. Figure 5.5 is an example of a task analytic assessment.

Discreet Trial or Opportunity Assessment

When the professional does not need to measure chains of behavior, but instead needs to focus on single, specific responses, then measuring repeated trials or opportunities to respond becomes the ongoing assessment tool of choice (Browder, 1991). For example, some educators must wait for a "teaching opportunity" to occur (e.g., new person walks into the room). They depend on incidental or coincidental teaching formats to provide instruction (e.g., teach greeting

others). Thus, assessment is opportunity bound. Effective early childhood special educators frequently use incidental or coincidental formats to assess young learners within play contexts. Repeated trials assessment correlates with instruction that uses massed, distributed, or spaced trials. Some professionals have viewed the use of massed trials for instructional purposes as inappropriate. From their perspective, concentrated, repetitive practice on isolated skills has limited application. However, there are times when this type of instruction, and thus this type of assessment, is appropriate. For example, when the learner is in the acquisition stage of learning, it is critical to determine whether the correct response is emerging—that is, whether the learner is beginning to acquire the target skill. The learner will need many opportunities to respond in order to demonstrate this. Functional skills, such as coin identification, color identification, answering "what" questions, or number recognition, are appropriate for repeated trials assessment.

A matrix can provide the professional with a planning tool to structure a repeated trials assessment to include functional items and reflect natural contexts. Careful planning will reduce redundancy, eliminate gaps, and maximize efficiency. In the example shown in Figure 5.6, the teacher first identified all the measuring utensils in the learner's current environment (e.g., set of measuring spoons from a local discount store, plastic measuring cups). Next, the teacher identified various wet and dry ingredients with dissimilar consistencies (e.g., peanut butter, mayonnaise) or textures (e.g., flour, chocolate chips) and unique methods of measuring (e.g., frozen juice concentrate, stick margarine) in the learner's environment. The last step was to mark off measures commonly associated with the use of an ingredient. Now the teacher can design a concise, practical assessment by discriminatively sampling from the matrix rather than assessing all combinations.

Although the motoric skill of filling a measuring cup (see Figure 5.5) could be framed within a task analytic assessment, the teacher may want to combine the two types of assessment and expeditiously gather additional information on number of correct responses or variety of responses as well as on the learner's use of the skill within a chain of behaviors. Figure 5.7 provides an example of a repeated trials assessment that gathers information about multiple responses when selecting measuring utensils but also incorporates an abbreviated task analytic assessment. This is both efficient and appropriate. Recipes frequently call for various measurements of different ingredients. In the real world (e.g., vocational settings, home), the cook must identify the specific measure and use it correctly. Thus, the need for a combined approach to assessment is justified. The natural context has also been considered. Therefore, assessment has been structured within the natural context of making salt dough to gather the most information.

ON-GOING ASSESSMENT WORKSHEET

Learner **Cathy Cook** Age **8** Domain **Domestic**

Long-term Objective **Measures dry and liquid ingredients for use in simple recipes.**

Assessor **Beth Johnson** Number of trials **2** Date of Assessment **10-7-94** Time start 10:00 am Time stop 10:15 am

Setting **Kitchen Center** **10-8-94** Time start 10:00 am Time stop 10:20 am

SPECIFIC DIRECTIONS FOR CONDUCTING ASSESSMENT

Cue

"We're going to measure some flour so that we can make pancakes. I want you to do your very best. Pancakes are going to taste really good this morning."

"Find the 1 cup measure."

"Fill it."

"Find the 1/2 cup measure."

"Fill it."

"Find the 1/4 cup measure."

"Fill it."

Initial Assessment task/skill analysis

Step	1	1/2	1/4	1	1/2	1/4
1. Select correct measuring cup.	3	3	3	3	3	3
2. Grasp measuring cup in dominant hand.	4	4	3	4	4	4
3. Grasp knife in non dominant hand.	4	4	4	4	4	4
4. Move measuring cup to canister.	4	4	4	4	4	4
5. Use measuring cup to dip dry ingredient into cup. Overfill.	2	3	3	2	3	3
6. Hold measuring cup over canister.	4	4	4	4	4	4
7. Position straight edge of knife at rim of measuring cup.	1	1	1	1	1	1
8. Move knife across rim of cup pushing excess dry ingredient into the canister.	1	1	1	1	1	1
9. Move measuring cup to cooking/mixing container.	4	4	4	4	4	4
	27	28	27	28	28	28

82/108 = 76% Trial 1   84/108 = 78% Trial 2

Materials

flour cannister, blue 1/4 cup measure, green 1/2 cup measure, red 1 cup measure, table knife, mixing bowl

Definition of Correct Response

Independent response on each step.

Definition of Incorrect Response

Needs verbal cue, model, or physical assistance on individual step.

Reinforcer(s) and schedule

Verbal Praise VI 1:3 steps, as needed to stay on task. Will make pancakes when finished.

Error correction procedure

None. If Cathy cannot perform step independently, will use system of least prompts until Cathy completes step.

(Mark changes in different color pen based on initial assessment performance)

Summary of initial assessment results   Cathy could identify the correct measuring cup by color only. She demonstrated independent grasping skills. Cathy needed a verbal cue ("fill it clear full") with the 1/2 c. & 1/4 c. She needed a model to fill the larger 1 c. Cathy required minimal hand-over-hand assistance to use the knife as a level. She did not appear frustrated and seemed to enjoy it.

Legend for Data Collection

4 = independent
3 = with verbal cue
2 = with model
1 = with partial physical assistance

Instructional Objective #1 Given color-coded 1 (red), 1/2 (green), & 1/4 (blue) cup measures overfilled with flour, a table knife, and a model. Cathy will move the table knife across the rim of the measuring cup, scraping the excess flour into the cannister for 4/5 trials to the satisfaction of the teacher for 2 consecutive cooking periods.

List of instructional objectives and short term objective is attached.

Figure 5.5. An example of a completed task analytic assessment designed to measure a person's ability to use graduated measuring cups with dry ingredients.

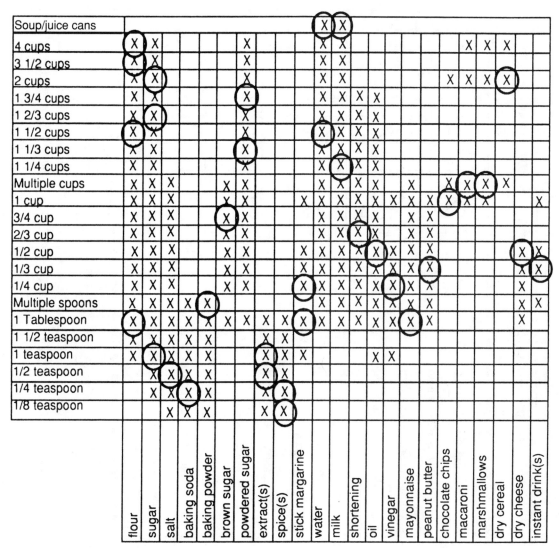

Figure 5.6. An example of a matrix for planning a repeated trials assessment of measurement for cooking. The Xs represent potential combinations; the circles indicate selected combinations for assessment.

Curriculum-Based Measurement

Curriculum-based measurement provides a tool to repeatedly measure basic skills or academic behavior. In a review of alternative assessment devices, Fuchs and Fuchs (1990) described curriculum-based measurement as

> a set of measurement and evaluation procedures developed by Deno and colleagues . . . for the purpose of evaluating student progress in reading, spelling, written expression, and math. These procedures . . . incorporate the following dimensions: (a) selection of one long-term goal, instead of a series of short-term curricular steps, for monitoring student growth; (b) measurement of standard behaviors, which have documented reliability, validity, and sensitivity to student growth . . . ; (c) use of prescribed measurement methods (e.g., test duration, frequency, administration, and scoring) that have acceptable reliability, validity, and sensitivity to student

change . . . ; (d) incorporation of rules that prescribe systematic procedures for summarizing and evaluating the assessment information; and (e) accommodation of any instructional paradigm (e.g., behavior, cognitive). (p. 10)

To use curriculum-based measurement, a teacher determines a long-term goal and appropriate criterion, such as reading fourth-grade level material at a proficiency of 90 correct words per minute with fewer than six errors. The teacher selects criteria that will demonstrate mastery based on experience, expectation, or average class scores. The teacher develops a systematic method for administering the assessment and follows that format precisely at least twice a week for the entire school year. In order to measure the above goal, the teacher might randomly select passages from the fourth-grade reading curriculum, provide the learner with the predetermined directions, listen to the student read for 1 minute, and note the errors. The correct score and error

ONGOING ASSESSMENT WORKSHEET

Learner __Cathy Cook__   Age __8__   Domain __Domestic__

Long-term Objective __Measures dry and liquid ingredients for use in simple recipes.__

Assessor __Beth Johnson__   Number of trials __2__   Date(s) of Assessment __10-9-94__

Setting __Kitchen Center__   SPECIFIC DIRECTIONS FOR CONDUCTING ASSESSMENT __10-10-94__

Initial assessment task/skill analysis		Trial 1 Time start 10:00 am Time stop 10:30 am	Trial 2 Time start 10:05 am Time stop 10:30 am WITH MODEL	Trial 2 WITH PARTIAL PHYSICAL ASSISTANCE
*Measure 1 cup flour.	1 cup	+ / +	- / +	
Measure 1/2 cup flour.	1/2 cup	+ / +	+ / +	
Measure 1/4 cup flour.	1/4 cup	- / +	- / +	
Measure 1/3 cup salt.	1/3 cup	- / +	- / +	
Measure 1 cup water.	1 cup (L)*	+ / -	+ / -	
Measure 1 1/2 cup water.	1 1/2 cup (L)*	- / +	- / -	
Measure 1 T. salt.	1 T.	- / +	- / +	+
Measure 1 t. cream of tartar.	1 t.	+ / +	- / -	+
Measure 1/2 t. cream of tartar.	1/2 t.	- / -	- / -	+
Measure 1/4 t. cream of tartar.	1/4 t.	- / -	- / -	+
Measure 1/8 t. cream of tartar.	1/8 t.	- / -	- / -	+
		4/11 = 36% 2/11 = 18%	2/11 = 18%	

Materials
1 cup, 1/2 cup, 1/3 cup, 1/4 cup, 2 cup liquid measure, 1 T., 1t., 1/2 t., 1/4 t., 1/8 t. flour, salt water, cream of tartar, flash cards with measures

Cue
"We're going to make salt dough. Here's the ____ (flour). [Show card with measure.] Find the correct measuring utensil and measure the right amount."

Definition of Correct Response
Uses correct measure.
*Measure is level & full.

Definition of Incorrect Response
Uses wrong measure.
*Spills over, less than full, heaped.

Reinforcer(s) and schedule
Verbal praise VI 30 secs. as needed to stay on task. Can work with dough when finished.

Error correction procedure
None. If spill occurs, wipe up mess and proceed.

(Mark changes in different color pen based on initial assessment performance)

Summary of initial assessment results When Cathy got to the part where she needed to use measuring spoons, she could not level them correctly. I tried giving her a model and then partical physical assistance at the wrist. She could measure liquids, but was unable to get the correct amount. She can measure dry ingredients into all sizes of cups. Her only problem is underfilling the cup.

Legend for Data Collection
+ = correct
- = incorrect
*L = liquid measuring cup

Instructional Objective #1 Given a model, measuring spoons of 1/2, 1/4, and 1/8 teaspoons, and assorted spices in boxes with a flip top lid; Cathy will fill the measuring spoons and scrape them off against the inner edge of the spice container for 4/5 trials for 3 consecutive days.

Figure 5.7. An example of a repeated trials assessment combined with an abbreviated task analytic assessment designed to measure a person's ability to match a written stimulus with various dry, liquid, and spoon measuring utensils and fill those measuring utensils correctly.

score would then be plotted on an equal-interval graph for future analysis and decision making.

One of the disadvantages of curriculum-based measurement is that, despite its demonstrated effectiveness, teachers are reluctant to collect, graph, and analyze the data because they view the method as time consuming (Fuchs, Fuchs, Hamlett, & Hasselbring, 1987; Fuchs, Hamlett, Fuchs, Stecker, & Ferguson, 1988). To address that problem, a computer-based monitoring program was developed to assist teachers. However, teachers found using the computer to store and graph the data more time consuming than traditional paper-and-pencil approaches (Fuchs et al., 1987), although this approach did prove effective for analyzing learner data. Further development has led to increased efficiency and overall teacher satisfaction (Fuchs et al., 1988). Learners interacted with the computer while a program kept track of their progress in reading, spelling, or math. After saving their scores, data were graphed and analyzed in the teacher's data-management system program. The goal of more recent computerized curriculum-based measurement systems continues to focus on documenting learner progress "over time" and providing rich detail about subskill performance (Woodward & Carnine, 1993).

Precision Teaching

Precision teaching, introduced by Lindsley (1964), provides a set of systematic procedures to analyze rate-based behavior. The advantages of precision teaching are that assessment (a) emphasizes stage of learning, (b) matches the learning strategy, (c) matches instruction, and (d) provides a vehicle for error analysis. Standard procedures simplify monitoring and evaluation. However, precision teachers need training to learn how to use the procedures. Also, many teachers have difficulty isolating an appropriate response to measure behavior that will accurately reflect instruction, which is by nature complex. Furthermore, the need to change assessment probes to correlate with each pinpoint can be time consuming.

The first step in precision teaching is to precisely identify a movement cycle (i.e., *pinpoint*). A pinpoint must be observable, measurable, and repeatable. *Learning channels* (e.g., see to write), the *behavior* (e.g., spelling words), and the *aim* (e.g., at 75 letters per minute) are defined. The input learning channel describes the way in which a learner receives the stimulus (e.g., via seeing, hearing, thinking). The output learning channel refers to the response a learner makes (e.g., write, say, do). A myriad of academic, social, and life skill behaviors can be pinpointed. Each successive pinpoint builds on a previous skill (i.e., tool skill) and leads to the next skill. Aims are established based on peer performance or the fluency (i.e., automaticity) necessary to demonstrate proficiency.

Next, a *probe* is found or developed to assess the pinpoint. The *fair pair*, two incompatible behaviors that cannot occur simultaneously (e.g., correct letters and incorrect letters), is also identified. Setting up a standard behavior chart or standard celeration chart (see Figure 19.2 in Chapter 19 for an example of this chart) completes the preparatory steps. Information about the chart and charting conventions are given in Chapter 19.

The earlier example of measurement can also be assessed using precision teaching procedures. In this case the learner demonstrates proficiency by quickly identifying the capacity of various containers. Figure 5.8 provides an example of a probe sheet for assessing the pinpoint, "see to mark capacity of cup, pint, quart, and liter at 20 marks per minute." Learner performance data are collected daily. After timing the learner for a prespecified amount of time (e.g., 30 seconds, 2 minutes), rate-based data from the fair pair (e.g., correct marks and errors) are recorded and charted. For young learners the timing might be as short as 15 seconds. For low-rate behaviors or problem behaviors that occur throughout the day, the recording period could be as long as 24 hours. When at least 3 days of data have been charted, the teacher can make a decision about when and whether to modify the instructional program or change the pinpoint.

Time-Based Assessment

Time plays an important role in determining whether a learner has acquired a skill at a level that approximates normal performance. In many instances, it is not enough to know if a learner can perform a target skill accurately. It is also necessary to demonstrate proficiency over time, quickness, or endurance. Therefore, time-based assessment is frequently used concurrently with task analytic assessment or repeated measures assessment (i.e., discrete trial or opportunity).

Rate, also referred to as frequency, can be used to assess number of responses performed during a specified time (e.g., words read per minute, digits calculated per minute, silverware sorted per minute, items assembled per hour). The professional counts the number of events or items and times the length of the counting period with a stopwatch or wristwatch, or by noting start and stop times. Recording events without documenting time results in incomplete data and limits the comparison of potentially dissimilar information. Precision teaching and curriculum-based measurement are models for conducting time-based assessments associated with rate or frequency.

When proficiency is verified by how quickly a person begins to perform a task following the stimulus, then latency should be evaluated. For example, when greeted, it is important to respond immediately, or the greeter may leave. Or, when asked for a home telephone number, a quick answer indicates an automatic response. To determine latency, the

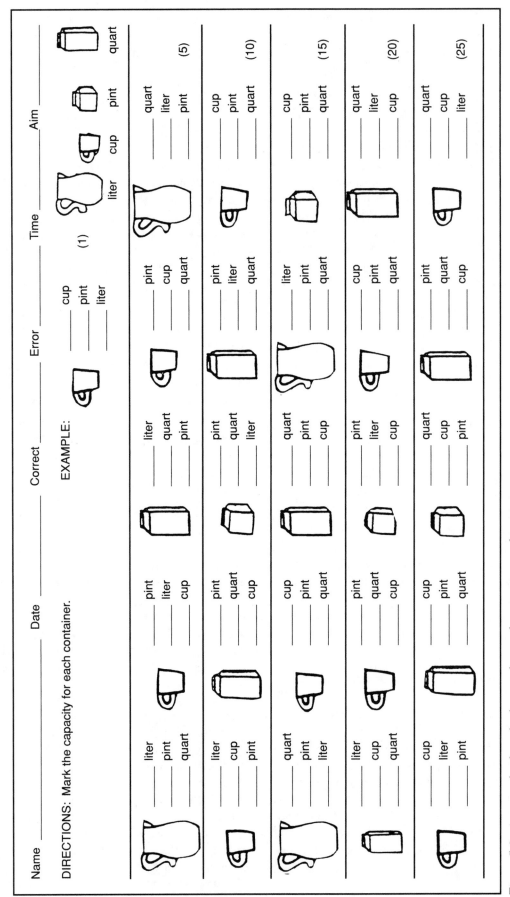

Figure 5.8. An example of a probe sheet used to conduct precision teaching timing.

professional times the interval between the stimulus and the response. A stopwatch or other timing device can be used for longer latencies. For shorter latencies, the professional may simply count mentally (e.g., "one thousand one, one thousand two, one thousand three").

In some instances the time needed to complete the skill demonstrates proficiency. In other instances the time spent engaged in a task demonstrates proficiency. In either case, the time-based method of assessment is duration. Dressing is a skill that under many circumstances must be done quickly (e.g., to get ready for school before the bus arrives, to change clothes after physical education before the next class). Even without time constraints, many tasks should be completed within a reasonable time limit. At the other end of the continuum are tasks that require endurance. The ability to work for periods of time without getting tired, needing a break, or requiring supervisor contacts (i.e., positive reinforcement or negative feedback) is often necessary in the workplace. Under those circumstances, it is important to measure and evaluate how long a person can maintain behavior. Again, stopwatches and other timing devices can be used. Timings can be continuous (i.e., learner responses are uninterrupted) or discontinuous (i.e., interrupted by teacher cues). In the latter, the timing starts when the learner begins to respond and is temporarily stopped for the next teacher cue, and then timing continues again while the learner responds.

Qualitative Assessment

Although the majority of assessment procedures address the gathering of quantitative information, qualitative information plays a vital role particularly in documenting social validity, especially when measuring skills in the generalization stage of learning. The following strategies can be used to collect qualitative data. Some skills, such as voice quality, public behavior, social skills, or culinary expertise, require judgment or ratings by others to determine appropriateness or satisfaction. If voice quality was the issue, an audiotape could be made and then played so that significant persons could judge the appropriateness of the person's voice. Likewise, the teacher could use a videotape or peer report to rate the appropriateness of a person's behavior at the bowling alley, school cafeteria, or football game. Along with ratings by others, self-report, role play, or behavioral interview can be used to assess social competence. Taste tests, ratings on key attributes, requests for more, or positive remarks and body language could document satisfaction with prepared food items. For young learners or nonreaders, pictures of facial expressions (e.g., smiling face, neutral face, frowning face) could be used to measure feelings or level of satisfaction. A representative sample or collection of permanent products (i.e., portfolio) can substantiate changes over time (e.g., writing skills) or document cumulative effects (e.g., art work). Portfolio items may be similar (e.g., spelling tests) or reflect different modalities (e.g., videotaped performance, worksheet, product). Examples may be added on a schedule to reflect ongoing performance or as reasonable to highlight various accomplishments.

In an effort to enhance current assessment methods of social skills in children with disabilities, Irvin and Walker (1993) developed a prototype microcomputer-based videodisc program. The purpose of the program is to assess social competence, knowledge, and perception. Their research suggests that the use of videodiscs rather than videotapes and a computerized scoring program improved the examiner's ability to gather accurate data about children's choices and behavior and integrate it with more traditional approaches. Further work remains to complete the project. However, the application of technology to qualitative assessment appears promising.

Assessment Guidelines

Effective practice indicates that, to gather the best and most accurate information, several general-purpose guidelines should be followed during instructional assessment. These guidelines apply whether measurement is formal or informal, commercial or teacher made. They can guide selection of the most appropriate tool or designing assessments. First, assessment should reflect the natural context or environment in which the learner with a disability will ultimately use the target skill. However, when assessment takes place in the community or generalization environment, the professional must realize that traditional clipboards and stopwatches may look out of place or call attention to the assessment process (Browder, 1991). The presence of such assessment tools can modify the environment to such an extent that it may "contaminate" the natural environment. When this happens, the information gathered is not as accurate and decisions are made with less certainty.

Second, the learner should be motivated to participate in the assessment process; otherwise, the results may not reflect a person's true capabilities or best performance. However, it must be remembered that under normal circumstances a person would only have access to natural reinforcers present in the environment. Therefore, any extrinsic form of motivation must address only participation in the assessment process and not be given based on correct or incorrect answers. Feedback in any form (i.e., reinforcement or error correction), unless necessary to continue testing, should be reserved for instruction. To do otherwise will confound the data.

When assessment encompasses multiple skills, the assessment format must be carefully thought out. If each component, step, or phase (i.e., scope and sequence) is independent or developmentally sequential, then test administration can be hierarchically sequenced from easy to hard, from first to last, or in some other logical order. It would be futile to assess the ability to write numbers or letters if the person could not hold a pencil or make marks; thus testing proceeds from easy to hard. Similarly, most children learn to sit, crawl, stand, and walk in that order. Testing would begin at the earliest developmental skill and move forward from there. However, knowledge of the color red is independent of knowledge of the colors green, blue, or yellow; therefore, any logical order will do. In all cases, assessment stops when the learner becomes frustrated, repeatedly answers incorrectly, or cannot perform the task.

If the skills in the scope and sequence are correlated or dependent on each other, however, then assessment must proceed from hard to easy, independent to prompted, or last to first; otherwise, there is a risk that assessment will turn into instruction. Instead of providing an accurate picture, performance could be inflated. For example, if a teacher wants to know if a person can identify a penny, assessment should begin with the hardest skill: identifying the penny with three distracters or nonexamples (e.g., nickel, dime, quarter) present. If the learner errs, then assessment moves to the next lower skill: identifying the penny with two distracters present. In this scenario, assessment stops when the learner answers correctly. Teaching or learning probably will not take place within the context of assessment. If, on the other hand, assessment begins with the easiest skill—identifying the penny with no distracters present—the learner would probably be successful. When tested on the next higher skill—identifying the penny with one distracter present—there is a chance that the learner could now give the correct answer based on previous performance.

The same principle applies when administering a task analytic assessment. Assessment begins by expecting an independent response. When an error occurs or the learner is unable to perform independently, two options exist. If using a single-opportunity probe format, testing would stop or the learner could continue without interference and independently complete as many additional steps as possible. With a multiple-opportunity probe, the teacher delivers an error correction procedure or provides a prompt or series of prompts until the learner responds (see Figure 5.5). Information about the level of prompt needed to respond is very helpful in establishing a starting point for instruction. Also, it is much more efficient to shift between independent behavior and the various prompt levels (e.g, verbal, model, physical assistance) on each step than to repeat the total task at each level. Later, information from a single-opportunity probe can confirm generalization and maintenance within the natural context.

In many instances, it will be necessary to shift formats when sequencing multiple skills. For example, when assessing coin identification, the most appropriate format is hard to easy, as described previously. However, when assessing coin values, (e.g., 1¢, 5¢, 10¢, 25¢), answers are independent. Overall, though, the assessment format would be sequential. It would be more appropriate to assess basic skills such as coin identification and value before advanced skills such as counting change.

Regardless of the format or type of assessment, professionals must ensure the accuracy of data collection. Without appropriate or accurate information, quality decisions cannot result.

Despite these guidelines, the need for individual considerations must always be anticipated during assessment. The professional's best judgment should guide on-the-spot decisions. On the basis of a learner's performance, the professional may stop testing sooner than planned or add more items. It is certainly not appropriate to drag out the assessment process, or to repeat similar items needlessly. Like Goldilock's assessment of the porridge: Professionals want it not "too hot" and not "too cold"; they want it "just right."

Conclusion

The process of assessment is time consuming, but without measurement and evaluation there is no accountability or assurance of learning. Effective professionals cannot allow themselves to be anything less than highly qualified, scientific practitioners and technicians with humanistic, value-driven qualities. If educators fail to assess learners in a timely and competent manner, problems may go undiagnosed, learners may be inappropriately placed in programs, curricular goals may be set too low or too high, and/or instructional decisions may not be made in a timely fashion. Depending on need and individual characteristics, assessment can be quantitative or qualitative; the paradigm can shift from behavioral to cognitive to constructivist; and evaluation can be formative or summative. Whether formal or informal, commercial or teacher made, a real-world need exists to measure and evaluate the performance of persons with developmental disabilities. Regardless of federal mandate, to do otherwise is to engage in less than best practice.

Acknowledgment

I wish to thank Emily A. Johnson for her generous support in helping to edit earlier versions of this manuscript; Alan Hilton for his support and direction as co-editor; and K. Richard Young for his support as friend, colleague, and mentor in learning, teaching, researching, and writing about assessment.

QUESTIONS

1. When would it be appropriate to use a norm-referenced test?

2. What are the key differences between initial assessment and ongoing assesment?

3. What are the advantages of teacher-made assessment protocols?

4. Why is time an important component of assessment?

5. How can parents and professionals use the results of assessment to determine learner priorities?

References

American Association on Mental Retardation. (1992). *Mental retardation: Definition, classification, and systems of support* (9th ed.). Washington, DC: Author.

Baer, R., Ferrara, J. M., Althouse, B., & Reavis, K. (1988). *CLASS.BD: An expert system for classifying behaviorally disordered students* [Computer program]. Logan: Utah State University, Developmental Center for Handicapped Persons.

Bayley, N. A. (1993). *Bayley Scales of Infant Development* (2nd ed.). San Antonio: Psychological Corp.

Blair, M., Macfarlane, C. A., & Young, K. R. (1991). *Reinforcer evaluation*. Unpublished manuscript, Department of Special Education, Utah State University, Logan.

Brigance, A. H. (1991). *Brigance Diagnostic Inventory of Early Development–Revised*. North Bilerica, MA: Curriculum Associates.

Browder, D. M. (1991). *Assessment of individuals with severe disabilities: An applied behavior approach to life skills assessment* (2nd ed.). Baltimore: Brookes.

Browder, D. M., & Snell, M. E. (1988). Assessment of individuals with severe handicaps. In E. S. Shapiro & T. R. Kratochwill (Eds.), *Behavioral assessment in schools: Conceptual foundations and practice applications* (pp. 121–160). New York: Guilford Press.

Brown, F., Evans, I. M., Week, K. A., & Owen, V. (1987). Delineating functional competencies: A component model. *Journal of the Association for Persons with Severe Handicaps, 12,* 117–124.

Brown, F., & Snell, M. (1993a). Meaningful assessment. In M. E. Snell (Ed.), *Instruction of students with severe disabilities* (4th ed., pp. 61–98). New York: Merrill.

Brown, F., & Snell, M. (1993b). Measurement, analysis, and evaluation. In M. E. Snell (Ed.), *Instruction of students with severe disabilities* (4th ed., pp. 152–183). New York: Merrill.

Brown, L., Branston, M. B., Hamre-Nietupski, S., Pumpian, I., Certo, N., & Gruenewald, L. (1979). A strategy for developing chronological-age-appropriate and functional curricular content for severely handicapped adolescents and young adults. *Journal of Special Education, 13,* 81–90.

Burgemeister, B. B., Blum, L. H., & Lorge, I. (1972). *Columbia Mental Maturity Scale* (3rd ed.). San Antonio: Psychological Corp.

Choate, J. S., Enright, B. E., Miller, L. J., Poteet, J. A., & Rakes, T. A. (1992). *Curriculum-based assessment and programming*. Needham Heights, MA: Allyn & Bacon.

Connolly, A. J. (1988). *KeyMath Revised: A diagnostic inventory of essential mathematics*. Circle Pines, MN: American Guidance Service.

Cronin, M. E., & Patton, J. R. (1993). *Life skills instruction for all students with special needs: A practical guide for integrating real-life content into the curriculum*. Austin, TX: PRO-ED.

Durand, V. M. (1990). *Severe behavior problems: A functional communication training approach*. New York: Guilford Press.

Education for All Handicapped Children Act of 1975, 20 U.S.C. § 1400 *et seq.*

Ferrara, J. M., & Hofmeister, A. M. (1986). *CLASS.LD2: An expert system for classifying learning disabled students* [Computer program]. Logan: Utah State University, Developmental Center for Handicapped Persons.

Ferrara, J. M., Williams, D., & Giere, S. (1987). *CLASS.IH: An expert system for classifying intellectually handicapped students* [Computer program]. Logan: Utah State University, Developmental Center for Handicapped Persons.

Fuchs, L. S., & Fuchs, D. (1986). Effects of systematic formative evaluation: A meta-analysis. *Exceptional Children, 53,* 199–208.

Fuchs, L. S., & Fuchs, D. (1990). Traditional academic assessment: An overview. In R. A. Gable & J. M. Hendrickson (Eds.), *Assessing students with special needs: A sourcebook for analyzing and correcting errors in academics* (pp. 1–13). New York: Longman.

Fuchs, L. S., Fuchs, D., Hamlett, C. L., & Hasselbring, T. S. (1987). Using computers with curriculum-based monitoring: Effects on teacher efficiency and satisfaction. *Journal of Special Education Technology, 8*(4), 14–27.

Fuchs, L. S., Hamlett, C. L., Fuchs, D., Stecker, P. M., & Ferguson, C. (1988). Conducting curriculum-based measurement with computerized data collection: Effects on efficiency and teacher satisfaction. *Journal of Special Education Technology, 9,* 73–86.

Giangreco, M. F., Cloninger, C. J., & Iverson, V. S. (1993). *Choosing options for accommodations for children: A guide to planning inclusive education*. Baltimore: Brookes.

Glover, M. E., Preminger, J. L., & Sanford, A. R. (1988). *Early Learning Accomplishment Profile*. Winston-Salem, NC: Kaplan.

Hasselbring, T. S., & Moore, P. (1990). Computer-based assessment and error analysis. In R. A. Gable & J. M. Hendrickson (Eds.), *Assessing students with special needs: A sourcebook for analyzing and correcting errors in academics* (pp. 102–116). New York: Longman.

Hiskey, M. (1966). *Hiskey–Nebraska Test of Learning Aptitude*. Lincoln, NE: Author.

Irvin, L. K., & Walker, H. M. (1993). Improving social skills assessment of children with disabilities: Construct development and applications of technology. *Journal of Special Education Technology, 12,* 63–70.

Kazdin, A. E. (1977). Assessing the clinical or applied importance of behavior change through social validation. *Behavior Modification, 1,* 427–452.

Kazdin, A. E. (1980). *Behavior modification in applied settings* (2nd ed.). Homewood, IL: Dorsey Press.

Lindsley, O. R. (1964). Direct measurement and prosthesis of retarded behavior. *Journal of Education, 147,* 62–81.

Markwardt, F. C. (1989). *Peabody Individual Achievement Test–Revised.* Circle Pines, MN: American Guidance Service.

Mercer, J. R., & Lewis, J. F. (1978). *System of Multicultural Pluralistic Assessment.* San Antonio: Psychological Corp.

Meyer, L. H., & Evans, I. M. (1989). *Non-aversive intervention for behavior problems: A manual for home and community.* Baltimore: Brookes.

Neel, R. S., & Billingsley, F. F. (1989). *IMPACT: A functional curriculum handbook for students with moderate to severe disabilities.* Baltimore: Brookes.

O'Neill, R. E., Horner, R. H., Albin, R. W., Storey, K., & Sprague, J. R. (1990). *Functional analysis of problem behavior: A practical assessment guide.* Sycamore, IL: Sycamore Publishing.

Polloway, E. A., Patton, J. R., Payne, J. S., & Payne, R. A. (1989). *Strategies for teaching learners with special needs* (4th ed.). New York: Merrill.

Sparrow, S. S., Balla, D. A., & Cicchetti, D. V. (1985). *Vineland Adaptive Behavior Scales.* Circle Pines, MN: American Guidance Service.

Thorndike, R. L., Hagen, E., & Sattler, J. (1986). *Stanford–Binet Intelligence Scale: Fourth Edition.* Chicago: Riverside.

Turnbull, H. R., III. (1990). *Free appropriate public education: The law and children with disabilities* (3rd ed.). Denver: Love.

Venn, J. (1994). *Assessment of students with special needs.* New York: Merrill.

Voeltz, L. M., & Evans, I. M. (1983). Educational validity: Procedures to evaluate outcomes in programs for severely handicapped learners. *Journal of the Association of the Severely Handicapped, 8*(1), 3–15.

Waterman, B. B. (1994). Assessing children for the presence of a disability. *National Information Center for Children and Youth with Disabilities (NICHCY) News Digest, 4*(1), 1–25.

Wechsler, D. (1991). *Wechsler Intelligence Scale for Children–Third Edition.* San Antonio: Psychological Corp.

Witt, J. C., Elliott, S. N., Kramer, J. J., & Gresham, F. M. (1994). *Assessment of children: Fundamental methods and practices.* Madison, WI: WCB Brown & Benchmark.

Wolf, M. M. (1978). Social validity: The case for subjective measurement, or how applied behavior analysis is finding its heart. *Journal of Applied Behavior Analysis, 11,* 203–214.

Woodcock, R. (1987). *Woodcock Reading Mastery Tests–Revised.* Circle Pines, MN: American Guidance Service.

Woodward, J., & Carnine, D. (1993). Uses of technology for mathematics assessment and instruction: Reflection on a decade of innovations. *Journal of Special Education Technology, 12,* 38–48.

Young, K. R., Kemblowski, E. J., Blair, M. E., & Macfarlane, C. A. (1992). *DECEL* [Computer program]. Logan, UT: Utah State University, Department of Special Education.

Young, K. R., West, R. P., & Macfarlane, C. A. (1994). Program development, evaluation, and data-based decision making. In E. C. Cipanie & F. Spooner (Eds.), *Curricular and instructional approaches for persons with severe disabilities.* Needham Heights, MA: Allyn & Bacon.

Ysseldyke, J. E., & Christenson, S. L. (1987). *The Instructional Environmental Scale.* Austin, TX: PRO-ED.

Assessment for Instruction of Students with Developmental Disabilities

CHAPTER 6

Andrea Rosenthal-Malek

Learning Outcomes

After reading this chapter, you should be able to

- Discuss the various types of assessment instruments that are used for teaching students.

- Discuss the four phases of the assessment-based instruction model of teaching.

- Discuss various informal techniques used for the assessment of academic and functional skills.

- Discuss various informal methods for assessing specific social skills, as well as social-cognitive and metacognitive skills.

TERMS

The following terms are important for the understanding of this chapter:

Assessment: A generic concept that includes any source of data that contributes to the understanding of a student's strengths and weaknesses.

Assessment-based instruction: Instruction based on a test–teach–test format, which incorporates four cyclical phases—assessment, planning, implementing, and evaluating.

Criterion-referenced tests: Tests that measure students' skills in terms of absolute levels of mastery.

Curriculum-based assessment: Informal assessment that is conducted within the framework of the curriculum. The purpose of the assessment is to decide whether specific instructional objectives have been accomplished and to directly monitor the progress being taught in the curriculum.

Informal assessment: Any assessment that involves collection of data by anything other than norm-referenced tests.

Introduction

Much too often, the assessment of students prematurely ends after diagnosis or classification. Teachers are often given little more than a label (e.g., developmental disabilities) and general information about a student's strengths and weaknesses. When this happens, Individualized Education Programs (IEPs) are often subjective and of little use because they do not share meaningful information. For assessment to be relevant, teachers need to know specifically what to do for and with students (Witt, Elliott, Kramer, & Gresham, 1994). Therefore, further assessment is necessary for educational instruction.

Before a teacher can make appropriate educational programming and teaching decisions regarding how and what to teach a student with developmental disabilities, he or she not only must be familiar with basic assessment issues but also must know how to link assessment with instruction (Hickson, Blackman, & Reis, 1995). Assessment and instruction should be considered interrelated, and approached using a test–teach–test format.

Many models based on a test–teach–test format are applicable to students with developmental disabilities. This chapter focuses on describing a model whose format is based on Stephens's (1976) four-phase (assess, plan, implement, and evaluate) behavioral model, with an additional cognitively based developmental component (Bronson, 1985, 1994; Sapir, 1985). This model is discussed as it applies to students with developmental disabilities. The model can be used for all levels of disability, although a separate section is included to discuss the assessment of the severely disabled with regard to life skills.

An Assessment-Based Instructional Model

Teachers of students with developmental disabilities are most effective when they use a systematic approach to teaching. By using a deliberate and planned approach to instruction, a teacher is better able to enhance performance. To develop an appropriate plan for a student, the teacher must first know both the student and the curriculum. Thus, it is presumed in this model that the appropriate person to assess a student is the teacher with appropriate training in assessment or someone else who works with the student on a regular basis who has that training. It is also presumed that assessment is an ongoing process and that teaching is directly related to assessment (Stephens, 1976). In other words, the assessment-based model stresses a cyclical, repeated process of assessment and teaching (Polloway & Patton, 1997).

This diagnostic model is a system of teaching consisting of assessing students' academic and social performance; planning instruction based on the assessment information; implementing the instructional strategies in the plan; and evaluating the effects of instruction based on the original assessment, while incorporating aspects of the whole student into the evaluation. The remainder of this chapter discusses each of these phases, but concentrates on the assessment phase.

The Assessment Phase

The goal of the assessment phase of teaching is to gather information about the strengths and weaknesses of a student in order to develop an IEP and provide information that will guide further assessment for instruction. Effective practices in the implementation of instruction dictate that teachers begin teaching exactly where the student is functioning. Thus, before any instruction begins, the teacher must gather descriptive information about the student that is instructionally relevant, that is, specific descriptions of current academic and social behavior. Descriptive information that is gathered should include examples of the student's functional and academic performance, social behavior, cognitive style (including metacognitive awareness), personality variables, and, if possible, reinforcement preferences. Descriptive information should be written in behavioral terms (e.g., "The student bites other students" rather than "The student is physi-

cally aggressive," or "The student orally counts to 5" rather than "The student knows numbers to 5").

Assessment of five types of information—functional and academic skills and concepts, social behavior, use of specific sensory modalities (learning or cognitive styles), affective and personality variables, and generalization of newly acquired skills—is important for teaching students with developmental disabilities. The following sections describe procedures for acquiring relevant information regarding these five areas.

Assessing Functional and Academic Skills and Concepts

Two types of assessment tools are commonly used in the assessment of functional and academic skills: (a) formal standardized tests, which are designed to measure school achievement, and (b) informal teacher-devised tests, which are usually given to students prior to and following a period of instruction. Because teachers need much more detailed information about students' academic skills than is yielded in most standardized tests, and because information regarding academic performance must be highly specific to be helpful for teaching, it is necessary to either adapt presently available tests or to develop tests of achievement that isolate skills and principles that students know and do not know. Although informal techniques lack the specific kinds of scores given by standardized tests, the major advantage of informal assessment techniques is their relevance to instruction. Specifically, informal techniques provide information about students' current levels of performance, aid in the selection of instructional goals and objectives, document student progress, and help pinpoint directions for further assessment (McLoughlin & Lewis, 1994).

Curriculum-Based Assessment. When the informal assessment is conducted within the framework of the curriculum, the assessment process is often referred to as curriculum-based assessment. Specifically, this type of assessment is the process teachers use to determine students' instructional needs within a curriculum by directly assessing specific curriculum skills (Choate, Enright, Miller, Poteet, & Rakes, 1995). The curriculum can be considered a structured set of learning tasks that teachers often refer to as objectives. These objectives are sequenced and organized to enhance learning (Howell, Fox, & Morehead, 1993).

Because curriculum-based assessment techniques are performed in conjunction with the instructional process, they serve not only as an evaluation of the student but also as a basis for evaluation and modification of the curriculum (McLoughlin & Lewis, 1994). Curriculum-based procedures often include curriculum-based measurement, criterion-referenced tests, portfolios, work sample analyses, task analyses, and informal inventories.

CURRICULUM-BASED MEASUREMENT. In curriculum-based measurement (McLoughlin & Lewis, 1994), short probes are used to collect samples of target skills, such as reading sentences aloud or writing words. For example, these probes might consist of having a student orally read a paragraph from a text for 2 minutes while the teacher tallies the words read correctly and incorrectly. This type of probe is administered a few times a week or more, the data are graphed, and the results are analyzed against established norms.

CRITERION-REFERENCED TESTS. Criterion-referenced testing is one of the most effective ways to initially measure a student's academic and functional performance in relation to curricula. Criterion measures are often teacher made; thus, they have excellent value for immediate instructional needs in that they reveal exactly what the teacher needs to teach to the specific student (Stephens, 1976).

Criterion-referenced tests can be used to assess any behavior for which an instructional objective is specified. They are simple to design but do require an investment of time. For the teacher to develop appropriate criterion-referenced tests, the teacher must know the sequence of skills that are to be taught. With this information the teacher can select items to be taught that not only are at the appropriate level but do not require prerequisites that the student has not yet learned. The following are suggested effective practices that teachers can take when developing criterion-referenced measures (Stephens, 1976, pp. 61–62):

1. Decide what content to teach, as well as the specified time period.

2. Sequence the content by analyzing and recording each skill in the order it appears in the text. For record keeping, record the page numbers of each skill.

3. Refer to another source that contains similar content but at an easier level and repeat Step 2.

4. Refer to another source that contains similar content but at a more difficult level and repeat Step 2.

5. Return to the pages that were recorded in Steps 2, 3, and 4 and develop items to measure each skill. Use a format similar to that shown in Figure 6.1.

6. Field-test the assessment measures with students. Revise if needed.

Criterion-referenced measures should consist of specific tasks, a minimum criterion for demonstrating that each task has been learned, directions for using the measure, and test items. According to Stephens (1976, p. 89) criterion measures should

1. Be used to assess students' knowledge and performance of a specific skill.

2. Always include a criterion for indicating to teachers and students the level of accuracy required to have mastered the skill.

3. Contain at least eight items in order that students' proficiencies on each skill can be adequately assessed.

4. Indicate the modality needed by students in responding.

5. Provide instruction to the teacher.

6. Indicate materials needed to conduct the assessment.

An example of a criterion-referenced test that measures the objective "When told to orally read short vowel words, the student will say each word with no pronunciation errors" is shown in Figure 6.1.

Teachers are often faced with the problem of where to begin assessing students once criterion-referenced measures are devised. One procedure for determining where to begin an assessment of students is to develop entry-level assessment measures. These measures are sample items from the previously constructed assessment measures and are used to survey students across a number of different curriculum areas. Entry-level measures are actually abbreviated items selected from each subcategory in the curriculum to be assessed. Instruction begins for those students who fail to meet the criterion on any of the items in that particular subcategory.

PORTFOLIO ASSESSMENT AND WORK SAMPLE ANALYSIS. Portfolio assessment has been defined as a sample of student's

---

Objective: When told to orally read short vowel words, the student will say each word with no pronunciation errors.

Task: To orally read 10 short vowel words. The words will be written on a 3 × 5 card. The student will be given 3 seconds to orally read each word.

Criterion: 100% (10/10)

Modality: Visual

Directions: Orally read these words in order:

1. bit	6. rug
2. cat	7. fog
3. fun	8. dad
4. pen	9. run
5. tip	10. bed

Scoring: Count correct if the student pronounces each word correctly.

Figure 6.1. Example of a criterion-referenced test in the academic domain.

work collected over time (Feuer & Fulton, 1993). Teachers use portfolios to study students' products. The teacher gathers a sample of the student's work, whether a test, a written assignment, oral reading, and so on, and analyzes the work to determine areas of strength and weakness. Portfolios may also contain different types of documents, including teacher observations, questionnaires, self-evaluations, and so forth.

In work sample analysis, the teacher routinely collects and analyzes assignments that the student completes. The teacher must calculate the number of errors as well as analyze the types of errors (e.g., the student writes "6" for "9" in four out of five problems on a math worksheet). This type of analysis is often called error analysis.

TASK ANALYSIS. Task analysis focuses on curricular tasks instead of student performance and presumes that students must learn the subcomponents, or prerequisites, of a task if the student is to learn the task. Task analysis is an instructional technique as much as it is an assessment strategy.

In instruction, task analysis follows specific steps. An instructional goal is selected, then analyzed and broken down into subskills, which are then arranged in a sequence for instruction. Subtasks are simply smaller or more elementary tasks that are required for the final performance of the task or objective (McLoughlin & Lewis, 1994). For example, if sound-symbol letter recognition is required to read sight words, then sound-symbol letter recognition is a subtask for reading vocabulary. However, if naming each letter in a word is not required for the final performance of reading the word, then naming individual letters is not a subtask even though the skill might be considered a simpler task. Subtasks must have all the same elements as tasks, or they are not complete.

There are two major types of task analysis: analysis of temporal order and analysis of developmental sequence. The type of analysis completed depends on the specific tasks. Temporal analysis is performed when a task naturally follows a temporal order. For example, when a student is expected to use a knife to cut food, the student must first pick up the knife before he or she can cut the food. Developmental sequence analysis is necessary when gradual progressive steps of learning are based on previously learned subskills. An example of a developmental hierarchy is the traditional curriculum. When using this type of task analysis, the evaluator must first identify the subskills of each skill to be taught, then assess the student's knowledge of each subskill. A number of strategies can be used when analyzing subskills. If the subskills are part of a standard curriculum, the teacher can simply use standard curriculum guides, or scope-and-sequence charts. If the skills do not fall within a standard curriculum, the teacher must develop the sequence using primarily logic. Although this method is somewhat subjective, it can be checked for flaws by observing how the stu-

dent performs the subskill and determining where the errors lie (McLoughlin & Lewis, 1994).

CHECKLISTS AND RATING SCALES. Checklists and rating scales are used to obtain additional information that is relevant to instruction. They are both structured assessment techniques in that specific questions are given, and the student selects a response. Although checklists and rating scales can be used to obtain similar information, their formats differ. Checklists ask the informant to check the responses that best describe him or her, whereas rating scales ask the respondent to rate a particular skill. Rating scales are often in the form of Likert-type scales (Likert, 1932) in which each response is tied to a numerical value (McLoughlin & Lewis, 1994).

One advantage of using these instruments is that they can be given to parents, former teachers, or any other significant person in the student's life. Checklists and rating scales serve the additional purpose of pinpointing areas of difficulty, which can be task-analyzed and then used to develop instructional objectives. See Figure 6.2 for an example of a checklist and Figure 6.3 for an example of a rating scale, each used to assess personality, temperament, and motor skills.

Strengths and Weaknesses of Informal Assessment Results. A major advantage of informal assessment is its relevance to instruction. Because informal assessment is designed specifically by teachers for specific students, the

---

Directions: Read through the following list carefully and check each phrase that describes the student.

Personality		Physical/Motor	
Strong self-esteem	☐	Coordinated gross motor	☐
Respectful control	☐	Coordinated fine motor	☐
Assertive	☐	Physically fit	☐
Enthusiastic	☐	Eye-tracking ability	☐
Autonomous	☐		

Temperament	
Attentive	☐
Even rhythm	☐
Reflective	☐
Focused	☐
Perseveres	☐
Flexible	☐

Figure 6.2. Example of a checklist for personality, temperament, and motor variables.

Directions: Rate the student on the following items using the following code.

5 = Totally like the student
4 = Moderately like the student
3 = Somewhat like the student
2 = Slightly like the student
1 = Not at all like the student

Personality

Strong self-esteem ☐
Respectful control ☐
Assertive ☐
Enthusiastic ☐
Autonomous ☐

Physical/Motor

Coordinated gross motor ☐
Coordinated fine motor ☐
Physically fit ☐
Eye-tracking ability ☐

Temperament

Attentive ☐
Even rhythm ☐
Reflective ☐
Focused ☐
Perseveres ☐
Flexible ☐

Figure 6.3. Example of a rating scale for measuring affective variables of personality, temperament, and motor control.

results are directly applicable to instruction. Specifically, the assessment results help the teacher to describe the student's present classroom performance, identify areas for further assessment, and plan and modify instructional strategies (McLoughlin & Lewis, 1994).

Despite its many advantages, informal assessment also has numerous disadvantages. Among the disadvantages are the difficulty in selecting the appropriate tools for the assessment, the inability to obtain an overall objectively based sample of behavior, and the subjectiveness of the chosen criterion level (McLoughlin & Lewis, 1994). An additional major limitation of informal assessment is the lack of information about reliability and validity. For example, in many cases the teacher does not know whether a specific informal procedure is technically adequate. Therefore, one must remember that, if technical data are not available for an instrument, caution must be used in interpreting the results.

Although it may be difficult to obtain technical information regarding a specific assessment instrument, at minimum, content validity should be evaluated. Content validity refers to how well the instrument achieves its purpose. The most important areas of concern are whether the assessment

instrument includes a representative sample of the content domain and whether the assessment tasks are appropriate. For example, if the student's problem is oral reading, the assessment task should be reading aloud, not matching words and pictures (McLoughlin & Lewis, 1994).

Assessing Social Behavior

School-related social behavior is easily observed by the average teacher; however, observing instructionally relevant social behavior is somewhat more problematic. Without carefully observing all aspects of the behavior, teachers may infer rather than describe in precise terms the behavior they observed.

When assessing social behavior, teachers can use the same techniques used for assessing functional and academic skills. One of the most practical ways to assess social behavior is to first informally evaluate the students, then use either a checklist or behavioral inventory to more formally assess it.

When an evaluator is assessing social behavior, the evaluator must be clear as to the purpose of the evaluation. There are three basic reasons for evaluating social behavior: (a) to analyze the amount of inappropriate social responding and thus curtail misbehavior, (b) to analyze specific social skills in order to train the particular skill that the student is lacking, and (c) to analyze the social cognitive and metacognitive levels in order to train the general cognitive skills that are lacking.

Assessment of Misbehavior. Effective teachers are constantly listening and watching their students. By observing what their students say and do, teachers are performing simple assessment. The teacher can begin more systematic observational procedures only after noting a problem while casually observing the student.

Systematic observations are used to study a particular student's behavior in the particular learning environment over a period of time. The purpose of these observations is to describe patterns of behavior, including classroom interactions with peers and teachers, in both academic and social settings. Systematic observation techniques aid the teacher in clarifying, recording, and analyzing the student's behaviors both academically and socially.

In its simplest form, continuous recording (Cooper, 1981) is an observational technique in which the teacher simply observes and records target behaviors that a student exhibits during a specified time period. This type of observation technique is best used to help the teacher decide if further testing is required. Figure 6.4 presents an example of a continuous observation in which the casual observation that Jason appeared to be "constantly" bothering the other students, especially during seatwork time, was confirmed.

```
┌─────────────────────────────────────────────────────────────────────┐
│                                                                       │
│  Student:      Jason          Date:  September 10, 1995               │
│                                                                       │
│  Observer:    Mr. Smith                                               │
│                                                                       │
│  Classroom Activity:   Independent Seatwork                           │
│                                                                       │
│  Reason for Observation: Jason appears to be bothering other          │
│  students during seatwork.                                            │
│                                                                       │
│  ─────────────────────────────────────────────────────────────────   │
│  Time                    Event                                        │
│  ─────────────────────────────────────────────────────────────────   │
│  1:00–1:02     While walking to his desk, Jason trips John.           │
│                                                                       │
│  1:02–1:04     Jason sits while teacher passes out assignments.       │
│                                                                       │
│  1:04–1:07     Jason reads assignment and gets out pencil.            │
│                                                                       │
│  1:07–1:10     Jason gets up, hits Kim in the back of her head,       │
│                and sits down.                                         │
│                                                                       │
│  1:10–1:14     Jason writes on worksheet.                             │
│                                                                       │
│  1:14–1:15     Jason pretends to have a coughing spell.               │
│                                                                       │
│  1:15–1:19     Jason writes on worksheet.                             │
│                                                                       │
│  1:19–1:21     Jason gets up, walks to Jill's desk, and knocks        │
│                books off desk.                                        │
│                                                                       │
│  1:21–1:26     Jason returns to seat and writes on worksheet.         │
│                                                                       │
│  1:26–1:30     Jason gets up, walks over to Jan's desk, and con-      │
│                tinues to talk to Jan.                                 │
│                                                                       │
└─────────────────────────────────────────────────────────────────────┘
```

Figure 6.4. Example of continuous observation.

Another modified version of this recording system consists of adding the teacher's response to each incidence.

To change students' behavior, the teacher must know conditions in which behavior takes place. It is not sufficient to describe responses, and when and how often they occur; the teacher must also be able to specify the stimuli that provoke reactions. For example, is the misbehavior a reaction to instruction, to others, or to assignments? When all these factors are combined, a teacher is ready to develop a behavior management plan for the student.

Assessing Specific Social Skills. Unlike the goal of behavioral assessment, in which the teacher is attempting to pinpoint misbehavior in order to develop an appropriate behavior management system, the goal of specific social skills assessment is to pinpoint the level of functioning for a specific social skill in order to increase the level of that particular skill. Many assessment techniques can be used to assess a student's ability in a specific social skill. For example, assessment techniques can be used to assess both the verbal and nonverbal components of a specific skill, such as conversational skills for dealing with criticism, or such skills as voice tone, eye contact, and body posture (Sherman, Sheldon, Harchik, Edwards, & Quinn, 1992).

A common effective practice procedure consists of the following steps (Polloway & Patton, 1997, pp. 465–467):

1. Task-analyze the specific social skill.

2. Devise definitions for each behavioral component of the skill.

3. Develop a rating scale to assess each behavioral component.

4. Check for reliability by using an outside observer.

5. Assess the student in a real-life situation where he or she must use the specific skill.

6. Individually assess the student.

7. Use ongoing assessment for continued evaluation of the specific skill.

Assessing Social Cognition. Unlike the assessment of specific social skills, in which the teacher is looking to pinpoint what the student knows or does not know, the assessment of social cognition involves the attempt to pinpoint how a student uses social skills during social interactions. Specifically, social cognition can be defined as the process of thinking about emotions, feelings, and the ways in which people interact with one another. It is a developmental process that is considered to play a major role in the acquisition of social skills, and in the ability to engage in interpersonal problem solving (Feinburg & Mindess, 1994).

Two major areas of social cognition are often assessed: (a) the ability to decode social information and (b) the ability to make decisions on that information. The skill of decoding involves the ability to read cues that indicate another's intention in a social interaction. An example of a typical assessment procedure for the decoding of nonverbal cues is to show students pictures of other students with various body postures and ask the student to explain the pictures. The tester then notes whether the explanations were accurate (Polloway & Patton, 1997). A student also must be able to make decisions and execute a plan of action in response to a particular social situation. This plan of action needs to follow specific steps, such as the following: (a) decode social cues so that a problem can be identified, (b) generate a number of possible solutions to the problems, (c) predict the effectiveness of each generated solution, (d) determine the most effective solution, (e) identify the skills necessary to implement the solution, (f) implement the solution, and (g) evaluate the outcome (Polloway & Patton, 1997, p. 486).

To assess each of these steps, a teacher should invent a hypothetical situation that addresses each step and have the student talk through the solution to each problem. The student is instructed to state all the possibilities for solving the problem and discuss why he or she made specific choices (Polloway & Patton, 1997).

Assessing Cognitive Styles

Two major types of cognitive assessment are relevant to students with developmental disabilities: the assessment of preferred use of learning modalities and the assessment of cognitive, metacognitive, and executive strategy use.

Assessing Learning Modalities. When assessing functional, academic, and social skills, a teacher is concerned with what is to be taught. When assessing a student's preferred use of sensory modalities, a teacher is concerned with how a student learns. Specifically, learning is dependent on a student's ability to assimilate sensations from his or her environment. In other words, in order to learn, a student is required to discriminate and select relevant stimuli from the environment and then be able to effectively relate the stimuli to previous experiences and respond appropriately (Piaget, 1951). In education, the use of a preferred sensory modality while learning is often referred to as learning style.

The study of sensory modalities is intertwined with recent brain research investigating the differences in left and right hemispheric dominance. In the last decade, new techniques have allowed scientists to research areas that previously had been restricted to speculation (Cherry, Godwin, & Staples, 1989; Williams, 1986).

According to a number of educational researchers (e.g., Carbo, Dunn, & Dunn, 1986; Cherry et al., 1989), students learn best when information is presented in their preferred sensory modality (auditory, visual, or kinesthetic). For example, a student who prefers auditory input will retain more information when the lesson is taught by the lecture technique. On the other hand, if a student prefers the kinesthetic modality, the teacher would do best by providing manipulatives, such as number lines when teaching math.

Effective practice would dictate that teachers consider the following suggestions when assessing students' sensory modalities or learning styles (Stephens, 1976, p. 118):

1. Assess in relation to the academic task. For example, assess the same skill using two different modalities to see if there is a difference in the student's performance.

2. To avoid time-consuming and inefficient approaches, assess only if teaching will be based on the assessment results.

3. If the student demonstrates adequate performance on a task, do not assess his or her modalities. Merely state the modality needed to complete the task.

4. Students with developmental disabilities do not necessarily have problems in sensory discrimination.

Assessing Executive Competence and Metacognitive Strategy Use.

A number of theorists in the field of developmental disabilities (e.g., Brown, 1987; Lezak, 1982) feel that the assessment of executive or metacognitive processes offers a viable alternative for the evaluation of students with developmental disabilities. The term *executive* is used in the information processing sense of executive routines or programs that organize and guide incoming and outgoing data. Executive skill implies ability to recognize or identify relevant cues and parameters of a situation, to predict and plan possible sequences of events and outcomes of a situation, and to organize and control both the self and the social or material "other" in order to effectively reach chosen goals (Bronson, 1985; Brown, 1987). Metacognition is defined as knowledge concerning one's own cognitive processes and products or anything related to them (Flavell, 1979). In practice, the concept of executive competence is embedded in the definition of metacognition, and the terms are often used interchangeably.

Unfortunately, researchers (e.g., Lezak, 1982) involved with the study of executive abilities and metacognitive strategy use have found the measurement of these processes to be somewhat problematic. First, few assessment methods are available for examining these skills for students with developmental disabilities. Second, few standardized methods exist for making objective or reliably replicable estimates of gradations of impairment of these functions. Further, there are no methods for making intra- and interindividual comparisons (Lezak, 1982). More recent research has corroborated Lezak's findings (Rosenthal, 1990).

In addition, executive skills or metacognitive strategy use is not revealed in simple right or wrong answers. It is instead demonstrated in a person's total approach to a situation or a problem. For example, executive skills are revealed in the manner in which the person construes the problem or situation, the nature of the plan generated to cope with the problem, the appropriateness of the strategies used, the adequacy of monitoring techniques, the flexibility for modifying plans when necessary, and the accuracy of the appraisal of the outcome (Bronson, 1985; Brown, 1987). For a detailed description of metacognitive and executive functions, see Chapter 12 in this text.

Because it is much easier to conceptualize and observe behavior when dealing with cognitive deficits than executive deficits, researchers have successfully used a number of methods to test executive and metacognitive functioning with students who have developmental disabilities (Paris & Meyers, 1981). The technique that is most applicable to the teacher is the systematic coding of students' in-class behaviors through the use of observational profiles. The use of these profiles allows the teacher to go beyond the identification of one type of executive or metacognitive activity and to examine where the activity occurs in the stream of cognition (Lawson, 1984). These instruments are best used in the natural classroom environment. Although numerous problems are associated with naturalistic observation, it is felt that the advantages outweigh the disadvantages, especially given the difficulty of reliably testing this population of students (Rosenthal, 1990).

No formal inventories for the assessment of cognitive and metacognitive strategy use have been devised specifically for students with developmental disabilities. *The Bronson Social and Task Skill Profile* (Bronson, 1985) assesses both academic and social executive skills at the preschool and kindergarten level and has been used successfully with students with developmental disabilities (Hauser-Cram, Bronson, & Upshur, 1993; Rosenthal, 1990; Rosenthal-Malek & Yoshida, 1994). The profile provides a way of evaluating students' academic and social behaviors and their use of time, all within a natural setting. This inventory is an observational measure that uses structured observation categories and trained observers to assess the behavior of individual students. The profile is designed to measure the level of executive competence in both academic and social situations for students who are functioning at the preschool and primary school level.

The skills assessed in the profile are divided into three categories. The first is *use of time,* in which both the social and the nonsocial focuses of the student are assessed. The social focus is measured during free play and assesses parallel, associative, and cooperative play levels, as well as noninvolvement. The nonsocial focus describes the student's sustained directed activities other than social activities (i.e., fantasy, gross motor, and mastery activities). This part of the instrument also measures the amount of watching of social and nonsocial activities in which the student engages.

The second category assessed is *social skills.* This section assesses such skills as the ability to control a situation, to converse, to accept rules, to lead versus follow, to assert rights, and to show sympathy/empathy, as well as the level of competition and the use of cooperative strategies such as the ability to take turns, to help, to trade, to share, and to use a joint effort in a social task. The highest level of cooperative strategies is called planning or executive strategies and includes the ability to state the rules of the game, to assign roles, and to make the play suggestions. The ability to achieve one's social goal without infringing on the rights of others (getting other students to play the game the student wants) is considered a higher level of social executive skill and is considered desirable (Bronson, 1985).

The third category assessed in the inventory is *nonsocial skills.* In this section, areas such as the use of coping strategies, distractibility, the ability to dual focus, the ability to notice novel discrepancies, persistence, the ability to correct oneself, and the ability to complete assignments are assessed. See Figure 6.5 for the protocol of the Bronson Profile.

Assessing Affective and Personality Variables

The final area of assessment discussed is the assessment of affective and personality variables. Sapir (1985) suggested

that, in addition to the previously mentioned areas of assessment, a teacher needs to assess affect and personality, temperament, and physical–motor characteristics. In other words, all aspects of the student that are relevant to teaching need to be assessed on an ongoing basis.

Personality and Affect. The nature of a student's responses and the way the student defends himself or herself against failure are the keys to the analysis of the personality of the student. Feelings of inadequacy may be expressed in many ways, such as hiding, clowning, denial, or aggression. A student may be enthusiastic or lack enthusiasm, may be autonomous or intrusive, may have respectful control or arbitrary control, or may be appropriately assertive or manipulative or submissive.

Temperament. The temperament characteristics assessed include activity level, distractibility, adaptability, attention span, persistence, intensity of reaction, and appropriate focus. These innate characteristics are seen as apparent almost from birth, remain relatively constant over time, and affect all learning experiences. For example, one student might be hyperactive, be impulsive, have poor attention, be distractible, and be unable to focus on a task, whereas another student might be passive, slow paced, and in need of much stimulation in order to complete a task.

Physical–Motor. Physical makeup, general body tone and coordination, eye-tracking ability, and gross and small motor coordination all play a role in the students' exploration of the environment and development of self-esteem. For example, one student might have excellent physical coordination and a sense of competence in this area, whereas another student might be clumsy, have difficulty making things with his or her hands, and lack confidence in his or her motor ability.

Assessment Techniques for the Affective Domain

The following is an example of an assessment technique that can be used for the various dimensions listed above (Sapir, 1985):

1. Begin by recording the observations of the student and state exactly what is happening.

2. Write a paragraph describing the student. Include a summary statement for each dimension.

3. Develop and use a form that will allow for a brief description of the student's strengths and weaknesses in each dimension.

Each teacher can devise a protocol that best suits his or her students' needs. An example of a checklist that addresses these dimensions is shown in Figure 6.2, and an example of a rating scale is in Figure 6.3.

Child's Name: _____
Age: _____
Sex: _____
Date: _____
Place: _____
Time: _____
Observer: _____
Observation Number: _____

ACTIVITIES / COMMENTS

USE OF TIME

Social Focus:
- Parallel
- Associative
- Cooperative, Conversing

Nonsocial Focus:
- Mastery
- Exploratory, Gross Motor, Fantasy
- Uninvolved

SOCIAL BEHAVIORS
- Social Control - S/N (V-P-D)
- Controlled
- Asks Social Help - S/N
- Negative Behavior
- Accommodating Strategies - H, S, T, TT, JE, TO, CR
- Planning Strategies - PS, AR, RS

NONSOCIAL BEHAVIORS
- Notices
- Dual Focus
- Distracted, Interrupted
- Gives Up, Asks Help S/N
- Corrects Self, Tries Again S/N
- Completes/No S/N
- Task Attack Strategy - GAM, CS, GM, AFC, CC, VR, CSDC, NF, CF, CD

Code:
H = Helps
S = Shares
T = Trades
TT = Takes Turns
TO = Trades Off
JE = Joint Effort
CR = Combine Resources
AS = Assigns Roles
RS = Rule States
PS = Play Suggestions
P = Physical
D = Demonstrates
V = Verbal
S = Successful
N = Not successful
GAM = GAthers Material
CS = Chooses Sites
GM = Groups Material
CC = Chooses Consistently
NF = Notices Features
VR = Verbalizes Rules
CD = Corrects Discrepancies
CSDC = Carefully Scans or Delay Choice
AFC = Arranges Feedback Contingencies
CF = Checks Feedback

Figure 6.5. Protocol for *The Bronson Social and Task Skill Profile*. From *Bronson Social and Task Skill Profile*, by M. B. Bronson, 1985, Chestnut Hill, MA: Boston College. Copyright 1985 by Boston College. Reprinted with permission.

Assessing Generalization of Skills

Although students' skill acquisition takes much of a teacher's instructional time, generalization of skills may be the most important aspect of the learning process. Behaviors are generalized if they occur outside the instructional situation, without the cues, prompts, and materials the teacher used; without the presence of the teacher who provided the instruction; and at places and times other than where and when the instruction took place (Matlock, Lynch, & Paeth, 1990).

Researchers such as Browder (1991) and Haring (1988) have suggested that, when assessing for generalization, teachers may observe performance in novel situations or collect information from significant others. More specifically, Browder (1991) suggested use of the following methods for making generalization probes a part of the assessment: (a) direct observation by the instructor, (b) direct observation by others, and (c) retrospective reports. Each of the formats is useful for different situations (Browder, 1991).

The best method for direct observation is to covertly observe the individual from a distance. If this is not possible, ask a person whom the student does not know or someone who would normally be in the natural environment to complete the observation. Directly observing a student's performance enables one to obtain firsthand information about the generalized performance. The problem with direct observation is that the presence of an adult may act as a signal for the student to perform the skill.

Generalization should be assessed on an ongoing basis. The evaluation of generalization might be scheduled at several phases: during acquisition, concurrently with instruction, and concurrently with maintenance probes (Browder, 1991; Haring, 1988).

Assessment of Individuals with Severe Developmental Disabilities

Since the 1980s many programs for individuals with severe developmental disabilities have extended outside the classroom into the communities. The importance of preparing these individuals for life outside the classroom has become an additional priority for their instructors. It has become increasingly important to incorporate an ecological model into the assessment of students with severe disabilities.

Although skills such as learning to maintain a home, hold a job, and use public facilities remain key components of any curricula for people with severe disabilities, professionals are becoming increasingly aware that social skills and maintenance and generalization of acquired skills are equally important. Therefore, it is important to not only specific functional and academic skills but also social skills and maintenance and generalization. The assessment needs to be ongoing and linked over many years.

Browder (1991) proposed an effective practice model based on a behavioral–ecological model for assessing life skills. Life skills are divided into two basic categories: skills related to the home and skills related to the community.

Assessment Related to the Home. Traditionally, assessment of home-related skills focused on basic self-help and housekeeping skills. Because of the current emphasis on inclusive education, the goal has been expanded to identify skills needed to function independently within domestic environments and to participate as a contributing member of the family, the household, and the immediate community (Eshilian, Haney, & Falvey, 1989). Assessment related to the home requires consideration of the caregivers' interests and resources and use of a collaborative model of assessment.

The first step in any ecological assessment is to get to know the family (i.e., people who live together and care for each other). Areas to be covered include family membership, cultures and values, interactive styles, and present life cycle stage (Benson & Turnbull, 1986). The second step in the assessment process is to select the skills to be assessed. The teacher must begin by reviewing records. The third step is to task-analyze the curriculum, looking for any discrepancies between the student's performance and the performance of normal developing peers. The teacher should look not only at specific skill discrepancy but also at processes of interactions. The final step is to prioritize the skills needed for daily functioning. The use of ongoing assessment and evaluation is essential throughout the process.

The investigator can use an interview, survey, or observation format. The important issue is that the assessor respect the many differences in family lifestyles when planning for instruction.

Assessment Related to the Community. The overall goal for people with severe developmental disabilities is to function in a community setting. Because maintaining a job is an integral aspect of successful integration into the community, one purpose of assessment in community settings is to assess the person's ability to maintain a job. This entails looking at both job-specific tasks and job-related social skills. Thus, the assessor must go into the community to assess the actual use of the skills on the job using ecologically oriented inventories.

Because living in a community requires frequent use of public facilities to shop, participate in recreation, and so forth, the second area of assessment is the ability of the person with severe developmental disabilities to use the community facilities. This assessment should begin with analyzing the community and developing a plan for the individual. The skills needed to participate in the activities should be task-analyzed and a determination made of the person's deficits in performing these skills. Again, the use of ongoing assessment throughout the process is essential.

The Planning Phase

Assessment information regarding academic and social behavior is useful only if it is used for planning instruction. Only after teachers have accumulated instructionally relevant information do they have a basis for planning and developing learning tasks and teaching strategies that are appropriate for the student. Specifically, in the planning phase of the program, specific goals and objectives are developed for the student's IEP, materials are gathered, and behavior management techniques are developed.

The Implementation Phase

Once the skills to be taught and the method of instruction are known, and the goals and objectives have been established, the teacher is ready to begin instruction. Specifically, teaching is the implementation of the instructional strategies, which consist of tasks, terminal criteria, presentation modes, instructional materials, and evaluation techniques. Tasks should be chosen on the basis of improving student functioning, assisting students in becoming more responsible and independent, and enhancing their quality of life (making living more pleasurable).

It is the teacher's responsibility to properly design and present tasks. When students fail at tasks, the teacher must redesign the tasks and instructional activities. Only tasks that are within the students' instructional range should be chosen. In other words, students must have the prerequisite skills before they can accomplish a task with reasonable effort.

The Evaluation Phase

Evaluation involves comparing terminal criteria with actual performance. When performance equals or exceeds original criteria, the tasks have been learned and mastered. When mastery has occurred, other tasks should be chosen for instruction.

Evaluation should occur minimally at the end of each area of instruction or it can occur daily and be part of the instruction. Evaluation will provide the teacher with information as to what instruction needs to be continued, what instruction needs to be reviewed, and what prerequisite skills need to be addressed. In other words, when evaluation is administered prior to and following instruction, the results can be used as both measures of learning and indicators of what should be retaught. The process continues and reenters the assessment cycle.

Summary

This chapter has discussed the concept of assessment within the framework of decision making. The two major decision areas include (a) assessment for screening, classification, and placement and (b) assessment for teaching.

Decisions involving screening, classification, or placements of students with developmental disabilities require the evaluator to make global comparisons between a student and his or her peers in order to decide if the student qualifies for special education services. This objective requires more formalized norm-referenced and criterion-referenced tests.

Assessment for teaching, on the other hand, entails the specific evaluation of strengths and weaknesses in many areas of development, including academic and functional skills, social skills, cognitive strategy use and metacognitive awareness, learning styles, personality variables, and generalization of newly learned skills. Assessment procedures include curriculum-based assessment, curriculum-based measurement, criterion-referenced tests, portfolio assessment, checklists, and so forth. The overall goal is to develop a profile of the student that can be used to help the teacher make decisions on what and how to teach the student. Teaching is seen as a four-stage cycle of assessing, planning, implementing, and evaluating.

 QUESTIONS

1. What type of assessment instruments would you use when assessing students for placement? What type of assessment instruments would you use when assessing students for teaching?

2. Name the four phases of the assessment-based instructional model and describe each phase.

3. Describe five informal assessment techniques that could be used for assessing functional and academic skills.

4. Describe two assessment techniques for evaluating students with more severe developmental disabilities.

5. Name the three purposes of assessing social behavior and discuss which assessment techniques you would use for each.

References

Benson, H. A., & Turnbull, A. P. (1986). Approach families from an individualized perspective. In R. H. Horner, L. H. Meyer, & H. D. Fredericks (Eds.), *Education of learners with severe handicaps: Exemplary service strategies* (pp. 127–157). Baltimore: Brookes.

Bronson, M. B. (1985). *Manual for the Bronson Social and Task Skills Profile.* Chestnut Hill, MA: Boston College.

Bronson, M. B. (1994). The usefulness of an observational measure of children's social and mastery behaviors in early childhood programs. *Early Childhood Research Quarterly, 9,* 19–43.

Browder, D. M. (1991). *Assessment of individuals with severe disabilities: An applied behavior approach to life skills assessment.* Baltimore: Brookes.

Brown, A. L. (1987). Metacognition, executive control, self-regulation and other mysterious mechanisms. In F. E. Weinert & R. H. Klewe (Eds.), *Metacognition, motivation and understanding* (pp. 65–116). Hillsdale, NJ: Erlbaum.

Butterfield, E. C., & Belmont, J. M. (1977). Assessing and improving the executive cognitive functions of mentally retarded people. In I. Bigler & M. Sternlicht (Eds.), *The psychology of mental retardation: Issues and approaches (pp. 277–318).* New York: Psychological Dimensions.

Carbo, M., Dunn, R., & Dunn, K. (1986). *Teaching students to read through their individual learning styles.* Englewood Cliffs, NJ: Prentice-Hall.

Cherry, C., Godwin, D., & Staples, J. (1989). *Is the left brain always right? A guide to whole child development.* Belmont, CA: Fearon Teacher Aids.

Choate, J. S., Enright, B. E., Miller, L. J., Poteet, J. A., & Rakes, T. A. (1995). *Curriculum-based assessment and programming* (3rd ed.). Needham Heights, MA: Allyn & Bacon.

Cooper, J. O. (1981). *Measuring behavior* (2nd ed.). New York: Merrill/Macmillan.

Eshilian, L., Haney, M., & Falvey, M. A. (1989). Domestic skills. In M. A. Falvey (Ed.), *Community-based curriculum: Instructional strategies for students with severe handicaps* (2nd ed., pp. 115–140). Baltimore: Brookes.

Feinburg, S., & Mindess, M. (1994). *Eliciting children's full potential.* Pacific Grove, CA: Brooks/Cole.

Feuer, M. J., & Fulton, K. (1993). The many faces of performance assessment. *Phi Delta Kappan, 74,* 478.

Flavell, J. H. (1979). Metacognitive and cognitive monitoring: A new area of cognitive-developmental inquiry. *American Psychologist, 34,* 906–911.

Haring, N. G. (1988). *Generalization for children with severe handicaps: Strategies and solutions.* Seattle: University of Washington Press.

Hauser-Cram, P., Bronson, M. B., & Upshur, C. C. (1993). The effects of the classroom environment on the social and mastery behavior of preschool children with disabilities. *Early Childhood Research Quarterly, 8,* 479–497.

Hickson, L., Blackman, L. S., & Reis, E. M. (1995). *Mental retardation: Foundations of educational programming.* Needham Heights, MA: Allyn & Bacon.

Howell, K. W., Fox, S. L., & Morehead, M. K. (1993). *Curriculum-based evaluation: Teaching and decision making* (2nd ed.). Pacific Grove, CA: Brooks/Cole.

Lawson, M. J. (1984). Being executive about metacognition. In J. Kirby (Ed.), *Cognition, development and instruction* (pp. 89–109). New York: Academic Press.

Lezak, M. D. (1982). The problem of assessing executive functions. *International Journal of Psychology, 17,* 281–297.

Likert, R. (1932). A technique for the measurement of attitudes. *Archives of Psychology,* No. 140.

Matlock, B., Lynch, V., & Paeth, M. A. (1990). *Decision rules and strategies for skill generalization trainers' kit.* Seattle: University of Washington Press.

McLoughlin, J. A., & Lewis, R. B. (1994). *Assessing special students* (4th ed.). New York: Macmillan.

Paris, S., & Meyers, M. (1981). Comprehension monitoring memory and study strategies of good and poor readers. *Journal of Reading Behavior, 13,* 5–22.

Piaget, J. (1951). *The child's conception of the world.* London: Routledge & Kegan Paul.

Polloway, E. A., & Patton, J. R. (1997). *Strategies for teaching learners with special needs* (6th ed.). Columbus, OH: Merrill.

Rosenthal, A. L. (1990). The effects of metacognitive strategy training on the social executive competence of moderately retarded children (doctoral dissertation, Fordham University, 1990). *Dissertation Abstracts International, 51,* 1961A.

Rosenthal-Malek, A. L., & Yoshida, R. K. (1994). The effects of metacognitive strategy training on the acquisition and generalization of social skills. *Education and Training in Mental Retardation and Developmental Disabilities, 29*(3), 213–321.

Sapir, S. G. (1985). *The clinical teaching model: Clinical insights and strategies for the learning disabled.* New York: Brunner/Mazel.

Sherman, J. A., Sheldon, J. B., Harchik, A. E., Edwards, K., & Quinn, J. M. (1992). Social evaluation of behaviors comprising three social skills and a comparison of the performance of people with and without mental retardation. *American Journal of Mental Retardation, 94,* 419–431.

Stephens, T. M. (1976). *Directive teaching of children with learning and behavioral handicaps* (2nd ed.). Columbus, OH: Merrill.

Williams, L. V. (1986). *Teaching for the two-sided mind: A guide to right brain/left brain education.* New York: Simon & Schuster.

Witt, L. C., Elliott, S. N., Kramer, J. J., & Gresham, F. M. (1994). *Assessment of children: Fundamental methods and practices.* Madison: Brown & Benchmark.

Appropriate Curriculum for Students with Developmental Disabilities

CHAPTER 7

Earle Knowlton

Learning Outcomes

After reading this chapter, you should be able to

■ Describe assessment practices and procedures that lend themselves to the development and implementation of appropriate curriculum for students with developmental disabilities.

■ Explain the concepts of independence and lifestyle quality as they pertain to curricular planning.

■ Define curriculum augmentation, adaptation, and alteration.

■ Discuss three practices that can enhance the delivery of appropriate curriculum in inclusive settings.

TERMS

The following terms are important for the understanding of this chapter:

Authentic demonstration: Direct assessment of responses to actual environmental demands.

Collaborative person-centered planning: A program planning model in which the person with developmental disabilities and an array of significant others engage in longitudinal planning and procurement of resources in natural settings.

Community-based instructional integration: An instructional delivery model that facilitates inclusion by engaging students without disabilities in relevant community-based instruction with their peers with developmental disabilities.

Cooperative teaching: An instructional delivery model that facilitates inclusion through the use of a general educator and a special educator teaching together in a heterogeneous classroom.

Curricular personalization: Molding the standard general education curriculum through augmentation, adaptation, and/or alteration in order to achieve maximum independence and the highest possible quality of life in a manner that is as inclusive as possible.

Ecological analysis: Procedures leading to the identification of environmental demands to which people respond to obtain what they need or want.

Independence: Exhibiting behavior appropriate to settings frequented by peers in a manner requiring as little assistance as possible.

Quality of life: A personally satisfying lifestyle that, within social norms, is characterized by competence, choice, community presence, and social networking.

Standard general education curriculum: The locally determined, state-approved outcomes and content taught to students without disabilities.

Introduction

Curriculum has been defined as everything from a course of study in school to the totality of schooling itself (Seguel, 1966). Although many theorists confine the defini-

tion of curriculum to subject matter, others define it in broader terms, typically inclusive of learning outcomes or instructional methods associated with the subject matter (M. Johnson, 1967; Renzulli, 1988). Perusal of the literature addressing curriculum for students with developmental disabilities similarly reveals widely ranging perspectives on what should be learned in school (cf. Cronin & Patton, 1993; Cronis, Smith, & Forgnone, 1986; Dever, 1989; Polloway, Patton, Epstein, & Smith, 1989; York, Doyle, & Kronberg, 1992).

Most salient among the factors influencing curricular perspectives in developmental disabilities is the evolution of prevailing issues and related trends about what and where students should be taught. Chief among the current issues facing the field are the questions of what constitutes an appropriate curriculum (Beck, Broers, Hogue, Shipstead, & Knowlton, 1994; Cronis et al., 1986; Knowlton, 1994) and where such a curriculum should be delivered (cf. D. Fuchs & Fuchs, 1994; Kauffman, Gerber, & Semmel, 1988; Reynolds, Wang, & Walberg, 1987; Stainback & Stainback, 1992). Related trends involve the development of strategies and tactics for achieving what has come to be known as inclusion, and balancing the need to comply with inclusion policies with the need to provide curricula appropriate to the needs of students with developmental disabilities (Knowlton, 1994).

A curriculum appropriate to the needs of these students is one from which programs are personalized continuously for any one student toward the ends of maximum independence and the highest possible lifestyle quality (Dever, 1989; Halpern, 1993; Schalock, 1990). The what (curricula and programs), where (settings), and how (methods and instructional resources) of special education for students with developmental disabilities serve as means to these ends, not ends unto themselves.

Essentially, the development of an appropriate curriculum hinges first on consensual determination, among professionals, family members, and the student with developmental disabilities, of the degree of independence and style of life desired, and then on creative planning through which instructional programs, and their goals and objectives, are identified and sequenced. This chapter discusses this process of building an appropriate curriculum for students with developmental disabilities. The bulk of the chapter is devoted to this curriculum planning process. A brief overview of the assessment procedures necessary to achieve an appropriate curriculum is provided first.

Assessment Practices

This section describes first the roles of curriculum-based assessment and ecological analysis in the process of determining curriculum. It concludes with a look at the roles of newer assessment trends: portfolio assessment, authentic demonstration, and the emergence of technology-based assessment procedures.

Curriculum-Based Assessment

Curriculum-based assessment is characterized by regular (usually daily or weekly) sampling of student performance with material from that student's own curriculum. Designed initially as a tool to provide teachers with procedures for evaluating their instructional interventions, curriculum-based assessment has become widespread in both general and special education. Curriculum-based assessment serves as an alternative measurement system that incorporates sound, accurate measurement procedures for indexing overall student proficiency in the basic skills (L. Fuchs & Fuchs, 1991; Shinn & Habedank, 1992; Vergason & Anderegg, 1991).

Graham, Harris, and Reid (1990) listed five essential elements of curriculum-based assessment:

1. Specification of objectives with performance criteria

2. Collection of baseline data

3. Initiation of instruction

4. Collection of progress data

5. Appropriate modification of the Individualized Education Program

Use of these procedures involves the following steps: First, teachers identify the curriculum and the level within that curriculum that they expect the student to master by the end of some predetermined time frame. Second, teachers administer curriculum-based tests (sometimes called skill probes) to obtain a baseline assessment of student ability. Third, teachers measure and graph student performance on a regular basis and compare these repeated measures with the baseline (L. Fuchs & Fuchs, 1991; Perkins, 1989).

For its content, curriculum-based assessment relies on the curriculum that is actually presented in the classroom. Students are assessed with direct reference to the curricula that they are expected to learn. Their performance can be compared with their own previous performance, and with the performance of other children in the same instructional environment who are considered to be benefiting from the curriculum and current instructional practices. The teacher can appraise each student's performance and determine which specific skills need to be taught, reviewed, or passed over due to mastery performance (Shinn & Habedank, 1992).

The criteria for mastery of each skill area's stated objectives are based either on the previously demonstrated performance level of peers who have mastered the specific skill or on the student's own previously measured learning. Mastery criteria should be appropriately ambitious for the individual student. Long-range goals can be based on the difference between the student's baseline score and the mean or median score of an available comparison group (L. Fuchs & Fuchs, 1991; Perkins, 1989).

Curriculum-based assessment can be an effective tool for general and special educators of students with developmental disabilities for several reasons. Systematic, ongoing monitoring of student progress is frequently cited as a critical feature of effective practices. L. Fuchs (1992) found that special education teachers who used curriculum-based assessment adapted their students' programs more frequently and relied more on objective data than those who did not. Moreover, curriculum-based assessment places assessment in a more proper and efficient role in the instructional process. Teachers can work within a teach–test–teach rather than test–teach–test framework, the former wasting far less time and producing far more valid instructional data (L. Fuchs & Fuchs, 1991). Finally, curriculum-based assessment often compares the performance of students with that of their peers in the same educational setting. Comparison with this type of local reference group is seen as more relevant than comparisons with nationally normed groups, the latter a general practice in commercially developed standardized tests (Hallahan & Kauffman, 1994).

Ecological Analysis

Ecology refers to the relationships among organisms and their environments. Effective practitioners conduct ecological analyses to determine the "fit" between environmentally imposed demands on persons with developmental disabilities and their adaptive skills in relation to such demands. Personalizing curricula for specific instructional programs is predicated on this determination of the relationship between demands and skills required in a particular setting.

To perform an ecological analysis, a useful starting point is to identify and count, in reference to the person with developmental disabilities, the number of current environments in which he or she participates, and the number of environments in which nondisabled peers participate (Brown et al., 1979; Cronis et al., 1986; Falvey, 1989). Next, specific subenvironments within each set are identified. If one of the community environments identified is the bank, subenvironments might include entry–exit areas, teller counters, safe deposit repositories, and automatic teller machines (ATMs).

Once current and future environments have been delineated, the demands of those environments and subenvironments can be identified by observing and categorizing the activities people perform in order to obtain what they need and/or want (Falvey, 1989). Discrete chains of behavior are performed, for example, at an ATM toward fulfillment of at least three outcomes: to obtain cash, to make a deposit, and to obtain account information. Thus, an ATM machine presents a set of demands to which people must respond if they wish to engage in activities that provide them with what they want and/or need. The ATM demands of users chains of behavior that constitute proper operation. They must insert a card, push buttons in response to various printed prompts, obtain cash and a receipt, and retrieve the card. They must also respond appropriately when the machine does not function.

In essence, ecological analysis provides a useful and relevant context for curriculum and instructional programming. It enables the specification of relevant environments and of the explicit demands of those environments. When these demands have been identified, pertinent program objectives can be specified. For example, two specific ATMs might be selected as training subenvironments, and a task analysis of a sequence of behaviors that are chained serially or concurrently can be performed (Ferguson & McDonnell, 1991).

Alternative Performance Assessment

In recent years, alternatives to traditional assessment procedures have evolved in response for the most part to the numerous calls for more stringent accountability by schools for students' achievement of desired outcomes (Ysseldyke, Thurlow, & Bruininks, 1992). During the 1980s, several federal and independent commissions recommended direct accountability measures to assure consumers that public schooling was not without efficacy; states responded with various configurations of accreditation policies that focus on schools' "quality performance" (e.g., Kansas State Board of Education, 1992). These policies spurred the development of alternative performance assessment procedures, directly reflective of student outcomes, with which state oversight agencies could determine the accreditation status of local schools.

Despite the accountability character and motives of alternative performance assessment, specific alternative procedures provide useful data for curricular and programmatic decisions affecting students with developmental disabilities. Rudner and Boston (1994) explicated a variety of specific techniques that comprise alternative performance assessment. Of these procedures, portfolios and authentic demonstrations aptly facilitate the development of appropriate curricula for students with developmental disabilities.

Portfolio Assessment

Portfolio procedures stress the cumulative appraisal of skills. As such, they can provide a longitudinal rather than snapshot perspective on student performance (Feuer & Fulton, 1993). Grady (1992) suggested that the portfolio consist of records of teacher observations and collections of student work, among other contents. For students with developmental disabilities, observations might consist of comparative data across time and settings reflective of the degree of independent functioning within relevant environments and subenvironments. Evidence of student performance might take the form of photographs, audiotapes, and/or videotapes.

Authentic Demonstration

The term *authentic*, applied to developmental disabilities, implies that assessment is directly pertinent to maximum independence and lifestyle quality in relevant environments. In short, authenticity is real rather than contrived. Attempts to assess whether a student can board the correct bus, pay the fare, emit acceptable social behavior, and debark at the proper location can proceed in two ways. In a special education classroom, assuming a connect-the-dots-to-draw-the-bus worksheet is eschewed, a cardboard facsimile of a bus could be used to train pertinent bus-riding behaviors. However, when the demand to ride the actual bus emerges, one need not wonder why students, desiring to take in a ball game at the Vet in South Philadelphia, end up in Palmyra, New Jersey (Knowlton & Clark, 1990). On the other hand, an authentic demonstration of skills in response to bus-riding demands could simply entail independent entry onto, use of, and exit from the bus—unobtrusively, or even covertly, observed by the teacher (J. D. Chaffin, personal communication, March 10, 1992). Further, permanent records of authentic demonstrations, such as videotapes, should be part of the student's portfolio.

Technological Tools for Assessment

Recent advances in microcircuitry and software, as well as federal legislative requirements and incentives, have paved the way for technological applications to numerous educational functions, including those devoted to assessment. For example, it is now possible to employ electronic systems to assess (a) social interaction, (b) retrieve intervention studies directly related to problem behaviors, and (c) observe and tabulate numerous behaviors of an entire class simultaneously.

It has long been recognized that active participation in the pragmatics of interpersonal interactions can facilitate social learning on the part of persons with developmental disabilities (Lavalli & Levine, 1954). Before microcircuitry, social skills were assessed and taught primarily through the use of simulations and role playing (e.g., Blackhurst, 1966; Nietupski, Hamre-Nietupski, Clancy, & Veerhusen, 1986). With the advent of interactive videodisc technology, the active engagement properties of social learning are greatly enhanced (Browning & White, 1986; Irvin & Walker, 1994). Reflective of current effective practices in this regard is the computer–videodisc interface system used by Irvin and Walker (1994) to assess how well students can (a) recognize

social cues, (b) select social response alternatives, and (c) anticipate the consequences of their actions.

Severe behavioral problems accompany cognitive deficits in a large number of students with developmental disabilities (Cipani, 1989). Ethical as well as pragmatic considerations often obviate extensive assessment of behaviors that are dangerous to self and/or others. Computer-based expert system technology enables the quick retrieval of intervention programs so that implementation can commence immediately. Expert systems provide the practitioner with electronic databases and retrieval rules, which collectively serve as a computerized version of the expertise offered by a human consultant (Hayes-Roth, Waterman, & Lenat, 1983). For example, The Center for Persons with Disabilities at Utah State University has developed 16 expert systems for a variety of problem-solving domains, including the retrieval of interventions appropriate to specific characteristics of problem behavior (Hoffmeister et al., 1994). Practitioners enter data descriptive of the behavior(s), student, environment, teacher, and available resources. The system then provides a ranked list of citations of research-based intervention procedures matched to these input characteristics.

Direct observation long has been a foundation of special education practices (Cartwright & Cartwright, 1984). Recent advances in portability and power allow practitioners to observe more students and more behaviors in less time, free of pencils, counters, and stopwatches. Greenwood, Carta, Kamps, Terry, and Delquadri (1994) described software used with laptop computers that facilitates collection, analysis, and storage of numerous setting, teacher, and student observational variables. In addition, Knowlton and Sanders (1995) implemented a schoolwide observation system in which students with developmental disabilities and their nondisabled peers, in classroom and community settings, can be observed simultaneously along a variety of behavioral and performance dimensions using a credit card–sized bar-code scanner and a computer-interfaced data uploader.

Effective Practices in Curricular Planning

Educators waste years of valuable opportunities for meaningful learning when they reference curriculum for students with developmental disabilities to outcomes devoid of direct relevance to ultimate independence and lifestyle quality. Although current employment and adjustment data for persons with developmental disabilities appear less grim than they did in the 1980s (cf. Hasazi et al., 1985; Hasazi, Johnson, Hasazi, Gordon, & Hull, 1989; Levine & Edgar, 1994; U.S. Department of Education, 1994), these data nevertheless continue to suggest the necessity of an adult-outcomes orientation to curricula and instructional programs (Cronin & Patton, 1993). Furthermore, curriculum consistent with this orientation often requires delivery in community rather than classroom environments. Thus, for many students with developmental disabilities, a significant dilemma emerges with respect to curricular planning: how to facilitate the goals of maximum independence and the highest possible quality of life while maximizing inclusive educational experiences for these students (Beck et al., 1994; Knowlton, 1994).

This dilemma's sensible resolution is suggested in the following curricular planning process. First, curriculum goals for students with developmental disabilities in relation to the standard general education curriculum are addressed. Next, strategies for delivering appropriate curriculum and instructional programs in inclusive educational settings are presented. Finally, principles for collaborative, person-centered instructional planning that can facilitate curriculum development and implementation are described.

Goals of Curricular Planning

Curriculum decisions for students with developmental disabilities, as stated previously, are predicated on the goals of maximum independence and the highest possible quality of life. These interdependent goals must be clarified for any one individual as a function of collaborative longitudinal planning on the part of professionals, the student, and members of his or her family.

Independence

Dever (1989) defined independence as "exhibiting behavior patterns appropriate to the behavior settings that are frequented by others of the person's age . . . in such a manner that the individual is not perceived as requiring assistance" (p. 396). The curriculum should provide the skills necessary to achieve as close an approximation to independence as possible, that is, maximum independence within community environments related to work, residential living, and leisure.

Dever's (1989) definition could be amended by suggesting that the emphasis should shift from the *perception* of the need for assistance to the *actual degree of assistance necessary* for an individual to participate in a particular environment. Viable functioning by the person with developmental disabilities would appear to be a more useful curricular concern than would assurances that others' perceptions of the person are positive. Wolfensberger (1983) argued that public perceptions, be they positive, paternalistic, or pejorative, are entrenched in the cultural value that the social role "developmental disabilities" connotes rather than in any bona fide

judgments about the abilities that individuals with such disabilities actually or apparently demonstrate. Like it or not, the individual is "seen" by others as "retarded" regardless of how much or how little assistance he or she actually needs. Of higher priority than others' perceptions are the person's own competence and volition while engaging in maximum participation within a given environment (D. Ferguson & Baumgart, 1991).

Quality of Life

The notions of competence and volition also are involved in the second goal of curricular planning: quality of life. When the issue of lifestyle quality is raised, immediate difficulty emerges in regard to its definition. Attempts to conceptualize or measure lifestyle quality (cf. Halpern, 1993; Hughes, Hwang, Kim, Eisenman, & Killian, 1995; Schalock, 1990) present problems since one's quality of life is obviously and decidedly phenomenological (Ward, 1990). Worse, objective means for determining one's quality of life open the door for the imposition of "idiosyncratic definitions . . . [and determinations by] . . . individuals outside the disability community" (Luckasson, 1990, p. 211). Halpern (1993) observed that the conceptualization of lifestyle quality requires the careful reconciliation of several dichotomies that pit personal choices and needs against societal norms and expectations.

Notwithstanding the conceptual issues confronting attempts to define quality of life, guidelines presented by Luckasson et al. (1992) are helpful in formulating lifestyle goals in a practical manner for students with developmental disabilities. Reported by Schalock and Spitalnik (1991), these guidelines offer a framework for collaborative curricular planning toward the enhancement of lifestyle quality that veers away from a focus on the person per se and, instead, centers on optimal interactions of the person and the environment. The first, *competence*, refers to the person's ability over time to learn and perform functional activities in relation to environmental demands. An activity is functional for an individual with developmental disabilities if it is integral to participation in a given environment, and a nondisabled person would need to perform all or part of the activity for the person if he or she cannot perform it independently (Brown et al., 1984).

Competence within a particular environment is not an all-or-none proposition. Absolute competence, although a worthy aim, should take a back seat to the opportunity to participate as long as such participation is desired and not harmful. Independent use of a restaurant requires, for example, competence related to payment of the check. If the student with developmental disabilities, however, has not been able to recognize that he or she is receiving the correct change, an important instructional decision regarding the degree of competence emerges. Should teachers continue to engage in instruction concerning change recognition? Or do they circumvent that particular demand in some way so that continued participation is assured? The decision to continue instruction should be based on program data, the student's age, and the student's and family's preferences. On the other hand, circumvention options might include instruction in the estimation of the nearest dollar amount, calculation before the fact of the exact cost of the meal, or assistance from a nondisabled companion.

The second characteristic of optimal environmental interactions is *choice*. Personal choice is characterized by autonomy and volition; that is, within social laws and norms, people exercise control and make decisions that concern their manner of living. The autonomy to make choices, even within law and reason, is a matter of sensible balance. Schools and adult service agencies often justify what, in some cases, are unnecessary intrusions in personal autonomy for the sake of educational and habilitative aims (Bannerman, Sheldon, Sherman, & Harchik, 1990). The quality of one's life within the constraints of state-funded adult service bureaucracies might still be seen as acceptable by that person despite bureaucratic regulations concerning, for example, heterosexual relationships. However, relevant curriculum and effective instruction attendant to such relationships ultimately would enable the individual to engage with others in important decisions regarding the trade-off between the benefits (and costs in autonomy) of participation in the adult service system, and the freedom to participate fully in a safe heterosexual relationship (Knowlton, Turnbull, Backus, & Turnbull, 1988).

The third and fourth characteristics, *community presence* and *social networking*, are related. Community presence refers to the civil right of a person with developmental disabilities to share in the ordinary places that define community life. As the movement to segregate and institutionalize persons with developmental disabilities accelerated during the early and mid-20th century (Lazerson, 1983; Scheerenberger, 1983), this right of sharing was dampened and finally snuffed. The latter part of the century saw the rekindling of this right of community presence and a companion emphasis: social networking. Networking is the normalized experience of steadily enhancing one's social framework of friends and family. A network requires the support and participation of all its members, and the acquisition of networking skills requires a curriculum in which an emphasis on social pragmatics is pervasive. Snell and Drake (1994), among others, suggested caution in curriculum design so that obviously pervasive skill domains such as communication and social skills are not artificially partitioned for instruction. Because community presence and networking involve such a variety of environments and are so fundamental to lifestyle quality,

social and communication skills curricula focusing on conversational pragmatics, friend keeping, phone skills, recreation, resource usage, and the like, need to be distributed across a variety of environments.

Planning in Relation to the Standard Curriculum

Curriculum planning toward the goals of maximum independence and the highest possible lifestyle quality for students with developmental disabilities begins with reference to the standard curriculum. For the purposes of this discussion, the standard curriculum refers to the locally determined, state-approved general education curriculum from which nondisabled students are instructed. Unlike yesteryear's "watered down" versions of the standard curriculum, where improper emphasis was placed on developmental prerequisites to academic skills, today's effective curricular practices center on adult- and community-oriented modifications that can enhance the individual's ultimate functioning as an adult (Beck et al., 1994; Cronin & Patton, 1993). Given the momentum of the inclusion movement, use of the standard curriculum as a benchmark for modifications is for the purpose not of thinning it, but rather of personalizing it so that the student with a developmental disability is taught with a curriculum keyed to ultimate independence and lifestyle quality in a manner that is as inclusive as possible. Curriculum outcomes and resultant instructional programs are personalized in one or a combination of the following three ways with reference to the standard curriculum: augmentation, adaptation, and alteration (Knowlton & Friedman, 1993).

Augmenting the Curriculum

When the standard curriculum is augmented, it is fortified with content relating to the use of metacognitive or executive processing strategies for acquiring and generalizing standard curriculum skills—a "meta" curriculum, superimposed over the standard general education curriculum. In the field of special education, the learning strategies model (Ellis, Deshler, Lenz, Schumaker, & Clark, 1991) has reaped considerable notoriety, assisting in the mastery of standard academic content by students with learning disabilities. In developmental disabilities, two of the more notable augmentations concern cognition (Belmont & Mitchell, 1987; Borkowski, Weyhing, & Turner, 1986) and self-regulation (Mithaug, 1993; Paris & Oka, 1986). Each augmentation enables students, through training in selected strategies, to perform more effectively with reference to standard curricular objectives. Neither option modifies or alters the standard curriculum; rather, the curriculum is enhanced with overlaying content geared to facilitate mastery, generalization, and problem solving in relation to standard content.

Adapting the Curriculum

An adapted curriculum is one that is adjusted to accommodate and support diverse learning characteristics and styles. Many adaptations of standard content are simple, cost free, and instructional rather than curricular or programmatic in nature (e.g., font size of instructional materials is enlarged, printed or figural stimuli are enhanced with visual cues, 10 rather than 20 repetitions are accepted as performance evidence). However, there are instances when necessary adaptations can become cost and time intensive. Some students require customized computer-assisted language boards with speech synthesis to facilitate the communication necessary to master standard content. Others, while not requiring assistive devices or other intensive accommodations, need remedial programs that can provide additional instruction on standard content. Still others need extensive adaptations of stimulus materials for learning. Curricular materials related to word recognition and reading comprehension, for example, are adapted to include photos and pictorial icons which, during instruction, can be faded systematically (e.g., Knowlton, 1982) or otherwise shifted into stimuli that begin to approximate orthography (e.g., T. Johnson, Knowlton, Adams, & Swall, 1992). In such cases, curriculum and instruction are adapted in terms of the time and intensity necessary for eventual mastery.

Altering the Curriculum

Whereas augmentation and adaptation involve enhancing and modifying the curriculum, respectively, curriculum alteration substantively changes the standard content to achieve a match between the content and the student's functional needs. Polloway et al., (1989) identified two distinct orientations of altered curriculum: vocational and life skills. The former orientation typically focuses on career–vocational education and work–study experiences as the student progresses through his or her schooling. The latter stresses basic daily living needs, such as eating, dressing, social interactions, and safety. Although it is tempting to view an altered curriculum as a "functional curriculum," it should be noted that any curricular plan for any student with developmental disabilities must *function* ultimately as the delineation of knowledge and skills necessary for maximum independence and lifestyle quality. In addition, there is a tendency to equate an altered curriculum with a physically separate, segregated setting for its delivery. Any of these three ways of curricular personalization, including altering the curriculum, can be implemented in settings where students with developmental disabilities and their peers are served.

Delivering Appropriate Curriculum in Inclusive Settings

Educational experiences for students with developmental disabilities occur in classrooms and community settings. In either setting, students with and without developmental disabilities increasingly are being educated together (Beck et al., 1994; U.S. Department of Education, 1994). Despite the meta-analytic findings of Carlberg and Kavale (1980) with respect to the possible academic benefits of general education instruction for students with developmental disabilities, the equivocal nature of inclusion's cost–benefits (Kauffman, 1989) and the avoidance of crucial efficacy issues through rhetorical skirmishes (Edgar, 1994) lead rational persons to the conclusion drawn by the Board of Directors of the Mental Retardation and Developmental Disabilities Division of the Council for Exceptional Children with respect to the role of inclusion in program design for students with developmental disabilities. The board recommended, in essence, that students' individual curricular and instructional needs override blanket policies to include or not include them in general education settings (Smith & Hilton, 1994).

Nevertheless, most states have initiated policies consistent with the federal government's call for inclusion that began with Will's (1986) Regular Education Initiative charge, which in turn emanated in part from Reynolds's (1976) persuasive critique of the role of the placement continuum promulgated on the heels of passage of the Education for All Handicapped Children Act of 1975 (P.L. 94-142). Public criticism of special education (e.g., Shapiro et al., 1993), coupled with continuing political sentiments of fiscal conservatism (Kauffman, 1989) and the potential for low-cost staffing patterns that inclusion promises administrators (see McLaughlin & Warren, 1994), has encouraged a host of professional and consumer organizations to endorse inclusion policies (Kauffman & Hallahan, 1995). These events in cumulative fashion have buttressed philosophic appeals to the heart for one unified educational system for all (e.g., Gartner & Lipsky, 1987) and, as a result, have rendered inclusion as a movement of momentum.

Within the context of this reality, professionals thus are asked to implement appropriate curriculum for students with developmental disabilities in ways that maximize independence and quality of life and, at the same time, facilitate the inclusion of these students in general education settings, whether they be classroom (Becker-Staab, 1994) or community environments (Beck et al., 1994). Unlike the earlier mainstreaming era, the inclusion era brings with it a few somewhat promising models for attenuating the dilemma between the delivery of appropriate curriculum and the implementation of inclusion policies (Knowlton, 1994). Two such models—the Cooperative Teaching Model for classroom settings, and the Community-Based Instructional Integration Model for community settings—are described in the following text.

Cooperative Teaching Model

Grounded in the collaborative consultation process (Idol, 1989; Morsink, Thomas, & Correa, 1991), cooperative teaching is a set of teaching configurations designed to address diverse curricular and instructional needs in the general education classroom (Bauwens & Hourcade, 1995; Bauwens, Hourcade, & Friend, 1989; Friend, Reising, & Cook, 1993; Hudson, 1991). The model requires general and special education teachers to maintain joint responsibility for planning and teaching. Despite the workable, flexible nature of the specific configurations described below, critics caution that the presence of a special educator in a general education classroom removes that teacher from students who need more intensive instruction and that a predictable administrative solution—the special education co-teacher supplanted by a paraprofessional or volunteer (McLaughlin & Warren, 1994)—dilutes the effectiveness of the model and of special education.

Nevertheless, adequate planning time and a good working relationship between general and special educators can yield the delivery of personalized curricula in the general education setting through the use of at least five specific co-teaching configurations (Becker-Staab, 1994). The first configuration, teach–assist, focuses on whole-group instruction and is common in a two-teacher classroom. One teacher leads the lesson while the other provides (a) complementary teaching or (b) supportive learning activities as necessary for individuals or small groups of students (Bauwens et al., 1989). In the former, one teacher maintains responsibility for the curricular subject matter and the other takes responsibility for employing methods to assure skill mastery. If the teachers were presenting a reading lesson to third graders, for example, one teacher would instruct the whole group on vowel–consonant patterns while the other would employ a direct instruction approach with practice materials. For the latter, one teacher would present a lesson on subtraction with regrouping while the other would demonstrate regrouping using multipurpose blocks or other supplementary materials to enhance students' comprehension of place value.

Three other related configurations are station teaching, parallel teaching, and alternative teaching (Becker-Staab, 1994; Friend et al., 1993). In station teaching, the class is divided into as many stations or centers as there are co-teachers. Curriculum is segmented so that each teacher is responsible for a part of the whole. In tandem, these parts are presented followed by practice and application at the appropriate center. An eighth-grade civics class presentation on local government might include a station on governmental bodies and access to those bodies (whom to call about a problem), with each teacher assuming responsibility for one

of these segments. Parallel teaching involves a unified, rather than segmented, lesson delivered simultaneously by each teacher to a portion of the class. Essentially, this configuration forms a class-within-a-class (Hudson, 1991) where students with developmental disabilities are grouped together and taught curriculum that parallels that presented to nondisabled students in the same classroom (Becker-Staab, 1994). Alternative teaching involves the simultaneous delivery of substantively different curricula. The configuration is similar to parallel teaching but the content delivered to each group is distinct. In a language arts class, students with developmental disabilities may be taught with an altered curriculum, focusing on conversational skills, by the special educator, while their nondisabled peers are being taught sentence structure.

Finally, team teaching is a cooperative configuration in which teachers literally teach together rather than in tandem or segments. Two or more teachers instruct the whole class via dialogue between themselves and among themselves and the students. Ideally, there is a merger rather than a division of responsibilities and interactions. For example, a high school class covering current events might be taught in debate format with each of two teachers taking opposing positions on an issue. Students with developmental disabilities and nondisabled students might have different curricular outcomes, but the presentation directed toward those outcomes is delivered by a team of two or more teachers.

Community-Based Instructional Integration Model

Based on early work, Beck et al. (1994) developed the Community-Based Instructional Integration Model, designed to integrate students with developmental disabilities and their peers without disabilities with a focus on functional, community-based curriculum consisting of age-appropriate content and sequences that can enhance the student's likelihood of ultimately functioning with maximum independence in home, work, and community environments (Cronis et al., 1986; Falvey, 1989; Knowlton, 1994). For students without disabilities, instruction focuses on selected elements of the standard curriculum that can be taught in community environments. For students with developmental disabilities, an altered curriculum is planned and implemented with direct reference to current and/or future independent functioning within the home, work, and community environments, as well as any other environments that might be relevant to a given student. Curricular objectives and learning activities are embedded within rather than separated from actual daily living and community experiences, and are related to the ultimate demands of adult life and work (Beck et al., 1994).

The key elements of community-based instructional integration are (a) the use of curriculum that is functional for students with developmental disabilities (Cronis et al., 1986) and their nondisabled peers (Thousand & Villa, 1991) and (b) the inclusion of nondisabled peers in instruction at community-based sites (Beck et al., 1994). Growing out of the educational reform movement has been the concern that students exiting high school lacked the skills necessary for making wise purchases, maintaining a bank account, presenting themselves well at a job interview, and so forth. There are those who advocate that these functional skills, normally thought to be appropriate exclusively for students with disabilities, particularly developmental disabilities, be taught to general education students as well (Goodlad, 1980, 1984; Thousand & Villa, 1991). Functional curriculum content for independent living in the home includes personal care, emergency management, food storage and preparation, and household upkeep and management. Content for work environments includes career awareness, social interactions, and work-related values and habits. For community environments, curricular content includes oral and written communication, safety skills, access to community and governmental resources, money management, judicious purchase of goods and services, access to transportation services, and the satisfying use of leisure time.

Thus, community-based instructional integration might include the following instructional scenarios involving general and special educators. Whereas a general educator using a standard curriculum might teach the calculation of decimals, a special educator might assist all students in calculating the sales tax for items they would actually purchase at a clothing store. Whereas a general educator might address critical thinking processes, a special educator might assist students in evaluating the advantages and drawbacks of two or three options for apartment living. Whereas a general educator provides a bank of sight words for students to master, a special educator and the teacher might assist students in the mastery of words directly related to independent functioning in the community.

Whereas many students without disabilities typically generalize the application of general curriculum subjects to various environmental demands without formal assistance, some do not. These students, as well as students with developmental disabilities, can benefit from community-based instruction (Beck et al., 1994; Knowlton, 1994; Thousand & Villa, 1991).

Collaborative Person-Centered Planning

Person-centered instructional planning is a relatively new approach to planning, emphasizing a longitudinal perspective and consensus building relative to the best interests of the person with developmental disabilities. It is perhaps best exemplified by the McGill Action Planning System (referred to as MAPS), originally developed at the Centre for Integrated Education in Canada (Vandercook, York, & Forest, 1989). When a person-centered model is used to plan for the future of an individual with developmental disabilities, the process of and the setting for the actual planning session are natural ones where all concerned can focus on the strengths and abilities of the individual and his or her inclusion within community life.

The goals of person-centered curriculum planning are to recognize the person's abilities and future aspirations, and to reach consensus concerning the necessary supports and services. The focus of control in this process shifts from the interdisciplinary team to the person with developmental disabilities and members of his or her family. The person is the center of the future planning process, and every effort is made to customize supports so that the person can achieve maximum independence and experience as high a quality of life as possible. The objective for all concerned is that the person involved be allowed to make as many of the normal choices that a person without disabilities makes relative to lifestyle, support networks, and access to school and community services.

Person-centered planning sessions are held in a home, restaurant, or other setting free of the formal bureaucratic trappings (e.g., voluminous folders, cramped conference quarters) of a school or service agency. A relatively large variety and number of people form what is termed the Action Planning Group: the person, family members (parents, siblings, grandparents, and others interested in the person's progress), classroom teachers, the principal or agency director, special education and human services personnel, the person's classmates, and anyone else who has an interest in the person's well-being. One person facilitates the meeting where, ideally, everyone is seated in a large circle and not separated from one another by a table. The person rather than the cumulative file is at the center of concern. The facilitator makes notes of relevant points of discussion on a flip chart so that everyone present can follow the course of the discussion.

Everyone is invited to contribute input concerning the following questions:

1. What are the significant facts and circumstances pertinent to the individual?

2. What is your dream (for the person)?

3. What is your nightmare?

4. Who is the individual? (Short descriptions are given by participants.)

5. What are this individual's strengths, gifts, abilities, and needs?

6. What would the person's ideal day at school or other setting be like?

As responses to these questions emerge and significant themes become apparent, goals and objectives are derived. Then, natural and created support resources are identified and assembled. Initially, this process is very time intensive, yet the carrying out of suggested outcomes usually takes less time

Table 7.1

Contrasting Traditional and Person-Centered Planning

Traditional Planning	Person-Centered Planning
Directed by professionals. In attendance: 3 or 4 professionals, 1 parent.	Person-focused. In attendance: the student, parents, professionals, family, classmates, any other interested parties.
Structured and regimented; routinized.	Open, reflective, creative; encourages brainstorming.
Regulated; requires compliance paperwork.	Nonregulated; content driven by person-based goals, objectives, and actions.
Held in schools; professionals often seen as intimidating to parents.	Informal settings; no tables or folders; conversational tone.
Directive, serious, business-like; no food and fun.	Relational and fun; plenty of pizza.
Meets annually.	Regular and ongoing.
Annual goals; no long-term vision.	Longitudinal perspective; small steps and ongoing adjustments.
Teacher monitors student progress.	Everyone monitors.
Membership shrinks as years go by.	Membership grows.
Takes less time, but more time to implement.	Takes more time, but less time to implement.
Professionals have power and answers.	Power is equally distributed among the group.

Note. Adapted from *Exceptional Lives*, by A. Turnbull, H. R. Turnbull, M. Shank, and D. Leal, 1995, Englewood Cliffs, NJ: Merrill/Prentice-Hall.

than with traditional programming models because many more people are involved in the provision of support. Person-centered planning can contrast starkly to some traditional planning models that tend to look at available options first, and try to fit the person into one of those options. Table 7.1 summarizes the differences between a traditional planning model and a person-centered model, as adapted from Turnbull, Turnbull, Shank, and Leal (1995).

Skeptics encounter little difficulty finding reasons not to implement person-centered planning. Nearly all criticisms of this approach can be valid: too much time, relinquishment of control, recalcitrant parents, submissive parents, apathetic parents, lack of fairness to students without disabilities, difficulty in documentation for accountability purposes, difficulty in reaching consensus, and so on. If educators can tolerate these realities, commitment can overcome them. Consequently, person-centered planning will result in a truly personalized curriculum that is characterized by continuity and consensus.

Summary

Outcome data for persons with developmental disabilities, while improving, continue to suggest that these individuals are not receiving educations appropriate to their needs. In this chapter, considerations have been presented for practitioners who engage in curriculum planning for students with developmental disabilities. A premise for planning an appropriate curriculum has been offered: that the goals of maximum independence and the highest possible quality of life should guide all other decisions regarding what should be taught. Moreover, curricular planning in the context of these goals needs to be collaborative, free of prevailing one-size-fits-all policies and philosophies, and personalized on a longitudinal basis. In this way, curriculum, along with placement, has been placed in its proper perspective—as means toward the ends of independent functioning and a high quality of life.

 QUESTIONS

1. Once you have identified selected environments and subenvironments that a person with developmental disabilities should be able to access, how would you proceed to identify the specific demands those settings would place on the person?

2. Why is quality of life a difficult concept to define and apply? As a practitioner, what does quality of life mean to you?

3. What advantages and disadvantages might a general educator see in cooperative teaching?

4. What advantages and disadvantages might a general educator see in community-based instructional integration?

5. As a practitioner, what features of collaborative person-centered planning could immediately be incorporated within the current planning model used in your school district or agency? What features would require considerable change in current practices?

References

Bannerman, D., Sheldon, J., Sherman, J., & Harchik, A. (1990). Balancing the right to habilitation with the right to personal liberties: The rights of people with developmental disabilities to eat too many doughnuts and take a nap. *Journal of Applied Behavior Analysis, 23,* 79–89.

Bauwens, J., & Hourcade, J. (1995). *Cooperative teaching.* Austin, TX: PRO-ED.

Bauwens, J., Hourcade, J., & Friend, M. (1989). Cooperative teaching: A model for general and special education integration. *Remedial and Special Education, 10*(2), 17–22.

Beck, J., Broers, J., Hogue, E., Shipstead, J., & Knowlton, H. E. (1994). Strategies for functional community-based instruction and inclusion of children with mental retardation. *Teaching Exceptional Children, 26*(2), 44–48.

Becker-Staab, M. (1994). *Classroom strategies.* Unpublished manuscript, Department of Special Education, University of Kansas, Lawrence.

Belmont, J., & Mitchell, D. (1987). The general strategies hypothesis as applied to cognitive theory in mental retardation. *Intelligence, 11,* 91–105.

Blackhurst, A. E. (1966). Sociodrama for the adolescent mentally retarded. *Training School Bulletin, 63,* 136–142.

Borkowski, J., Weyhing, R., & Turner, L. (1986). Attributional retraining and the teaching of strategies. *Exceptional Children, 53,* 130–137.

Brown, L., Branston, M., Hamre-Nietupski, S., Pumpian, I., Certo, N., & Gruenewald, L. (1979). A strategy for developing chronological age appropriate and functional curricular content for severely handicapped adolescents and young adults. *Journal of Special Education, 13,* 81–90.

Brown, L., Sweet, M., Shiraga, B., York, J., Zanella, K., & Rogan, P. (1984). Functional skills in programs for students with severe handicaps. In L. Brown, M. Sweet, B. Shiraga, J. York, K. Zanella, P. Rogan, & R. Loomis (Eds.), *Educational programs for students with severe handicaps* (Vol. 14, pp. 55–60). Madison, WI: Madison Metropolitan School District.

Browning, P., & White, W. (1986). Teaching life enhancement skills with interactive video-based curricula. *Education and Training of the Mentally Retarded, 21,* 236–244.

Carlberg, C., & Kavale, K. (1980). The efficacy of special versus regular class placement for exceptional children: A meta-analysis. *Journal of Special Education, 14,* 295–309.

Cartwright, C., & Cartwright, G. P. (1984). *Developing observation skills* (2nd ed.). New York: McGraw-Hill.

Cipani, E. (1989). *The treatment of severe behavior disorders.* Washington, DC: American Association on Mental Retardation.

Cronin, M., & Patton, J. (1993). *Life skills instruction for all students with special needs: A practical guide for integrating real life content into the curriculum.* Austin, TX: PRO-ED.

Cronis, T., Smith, G., & Forgnone, C. (1986). Mild mental retardation: Implications for an ecological curriculum. *Journal of Research and Development in Education, 19*(3), 72–76.

Dever, R. (1989). A taxonomy of community living skills. *Exceptional Children, 55,* 395–404.

Edgar, E. (1994, September–October). A profession in denial: The consequences of ignoring the condition of mild mental retardation. Keynote Address to the Fourth International Conference of the Council for Exceptional Children, Division on Mental Retardation/Developmental Disabilities, Arlington Heights, IL.

Education for All Handicapped Children Act of 1975, 20 U.S.C. § 1400 *et seq.*

Ellis, E., Deshler, D., Lenz, B., Schumaker, J., & Clark, F. (1991). An instructional model for teaching learning strategies. *Focus on Exceptional Children, 23*(6), 1–23.

Falvey, M. (1989). *Community-based curriculum* (2nd ed.). Baltimore: Brookes.

Ferguson, B., & McDonnell, J. (1991). A comparison of serial and concurrent sequencing strategies in teaching generalized grocery item location to students with moderate handicaps. *Education and Training in Mental Retardation, 26,* 292–304.

Ferguson, D., & Baumgart, D. (1991). Partial participation revisited. *Journal of the Association of Persons with Severe Handicaps, 16,* 218–227.

Feuer, M., & Fulton, K. (1993). The many faces of performance assessment. *Phi Delta Kappan, 74,* 478.

Friend, M., Reising, M., & Cook, L. (1993). Co-teaching: An overview of the past, a glimpse at the present, and considerations for the future. *Preventing School Failure, 37,* 6–10.

Fuchs, D., & Fuchs, L. (1994). Inclusive schools movement and the radicalization of special education reform. *Exceptional Children, 60,* 294–309.

Fuchs, L. (1992). Teacher planning for students with learning disabilities: Differences between general and special educators. *Learning Disabilities Research and Practice, 7*(3), 120–128.

Fuchs, L., & Fuchs, D. (1991). Curriculum-based measurement: Current applications and future directions. *Preventing School Failure, 35*(3), 6–11.

Gartner, A., & Lipsky, D. (1987). Beyond special education: Toward a quality system for all students. *Harvard Educational Review, 57,* 367–395.

Goodlad, J. (1980). How fares the common school? *Today's Education, 69*(2), 37–40.

Goodlad, J. (1984). *A place called school: Prospects for the future.* New York: McGraw-Hill.

Grady, E. (1992). *The portfolio approach to assessment.* Bloomington, IN: Phi Delta Kappa Foundation.

Graham, S., Harris, K. R., & Reid, R. (1990). Learning disabilities. In E. Meyen (Ed.), *Exceptional children in today's schools* (2nd ed., pp. 193–222). Denver: Love.

Greenwood, C., Carta, J., Kamps, D., Terry, B., & Delquadri, J. (1994). Development and validation of standard classroom observation systems for school practitioners: Ecobehavioral assessment system software. *Exceptional Children, 61,* 197–210.

Hallahan, D. P., & Kauffman, J. M. (1994). *Exceptional children* (6th ed.). Englewood Cliffs, NJ: Prentice-Hall.

Halpern, A. (1993). Quality of life as a conceptual framework for evaluating transition outcomes. *Exceptional Children, 59,* 486–498.

Hasazi, S., Gordon, L., Roe, C., Hull, M., Finck, K., & Salembier, G. (1985). A statewide follow-up on the post high school employment and residential status of students labeled mentally retarded. *Education and Training of the Mentally Retarded, 20,* 222–234.

Hasazi, S., Johnson, A., Hasazi, J., Gordon, L., & Hull, M. (1989). Employment of youth with and without handicaps following high school: Outcomes and correlates. *Journal of Special Education, 23,* 243–255.

Hayes-Roth, F., Waterman, D., & Lenat, D. (1983). *Building expert systems.* London: Addison-Wesley.

Hoffmeister, A., Althouse, R. B., Likins, M., Morgan, D., Ferrara, J., Jenson, W., & Rollins, E. (1994). SMH.PAL: An expert system for identifying treatment procedures for students with severe disabilities. *Exceptional Children, 61*, 174–181.

Hudson, F. (1991). *Class within a class: A shared responsibility of regular and special education*. Kansas City: Department of Special Education, University of Kansas Medical Center.

Hughes, C., Hwang, B., Kim, J., Eisenman, L., & Killian, D. (1995). Quality of life in applied research: A review and analysis of empirical measures. *American Journal on Mental Retardation, 99*, 623–641.

Idol, L. (1989). The resource/consulting teacher: An integrated model of service delivery. *Remedial and Special Education, 10*(6), 38–48.

Irvin, L., & Walker, H. (1994). Assessing children's social skills using video-based microcomputer technology. *Exceptional Children, 61*, 182–196.

Johnson, T., Knowlton, H. E., Adams, S., & Swall, R. (1992). Effects of personal photographs on verbal responses to figural stimuli by students with moderate mental retardation: A Brunerian approach. *Education and Training in Mental Retardation, 27*, 367–378.

Johnson, M. (1967). Definitions and models in curriculum theory. *Educational Theory, 17*, 127–140.

Kansas State Board of Education. (1992). *Kansas Quality Performance Accreditation*. Topeka, KS: Author.

Kauffman, J. (1989). The Regular Education Initiative as Reagan–Bush education policy: A trickle-down theory of education of the hard-to-teach. *Journal of Special Education, 23*, 256–289.

Kauffman, J., Gerber, M., & Semmel, M. (1988). Arguable assumptions underlying the Regular Education Initiative. *Journal of Learning Disabilities, 21*, 6–11.

Kauffman, J., & Hallahan, D. (Eds.). (1995). *The illusion of full inclusion*. Austin, TX: PRO-ED.

Knowlton, H. E. (1982). The QC approach to teaching basic skills. *Directive Teacher, 4*(2), 20–24.

Knowlton, H. E. (1994, September–October). *Resolving the inclusion-curriculum dilemma: Strategies for delivering functional curriculum in integrated settings*. Paper presented at the Fourth International Conference of the Council for Exceptional Children, Division on Mental Retardation/Developmental Disabilities, Arlington Heights, IL.

Knowlton, H. E., & Clark, G. (1990). *National study of high school programs for handicapped youth in transition: Volume I. Qualitative component*. Lawrence: University of Kansas, Department of Special Education. (ERIC Document Reproduction Center No. Ed 314 918)

Knowlton, H. E., & Friedman, R. (1993). *Preparation of personnel for careers in special education: Cross-categorical curriculum specialists*. Lawrence: University of Kansas, Department of Special Education.

Knowlton, S., & Sanders, S. (1995, February). *Use of the Learner Profile Observational System*. Paper presented at the Second Annual Kaw Valley Regional Quality Performance Accreditation Conference, Lawrence, KS.

Knowlton, H. E., Turnbull, A., Backus, L., & Turnbull, H. R. (1988). Letting go: Consent and the "yes, but . . ." problem in transition. In B. Ludlow, A. Turnbull, & R. Luckasson (Eds.), *Transitions to adult life for people with mental retardation* (pp. 45–66). Baltimore: Brookes.

Kavalli, A., & Levine, M. (1954). Social and guidance needs of mentally handicapped adolescents as revealed through sociodrama. *American Journal of Mental Deficiency, 60*, 93–99.

Kerzerson, M. (1983). The origins of special education. In J. Chambers & W. Hartman (Eds.), *Special education policies: Their history, implementation, and finance* (pp. 15–47). Philadelphia: Temple University Press.

Levine, P., & Edgar, E. (1994). An analysis by gender of long-term postschool outcomes for youth with and without disabilities. *Exceptional Children, 61*, 282–300.

Luckasson, R. (1990). A lawyer's perspective on quality of life. In R. Schalock (Ed.), *Quality of life* (pp. 211–214). Washington, DC: American Association on Mental Retardation.

Luckasson, R., Coulter, D., Polloway, E., Reiss, S., Schalock, R., Snell, M., Spitalnik, D., & Stark, J. (1992). *Mental retardation: Definition, classification, and systems of supports* (9th ed.). Washington, DC: American Association on Mental Retardation.

McLaughlin, M., & Warren, S. (1994). The costs of inclusion. *The School Administrator, 51*(10), 8–19.

Mithaug, D. (1993). *Self-regulation theory: How optimal adjustment maximizes gain*. Westport, CT: Praeger.

Morsink, C., Thomas, C., & Correa, V. (1991). *Interactive teaming: Consultation and collaboration in special programs*. Columbus, OH: Merrill.

Nietupski, J., Hamre-Nietupski, S., Clancy, P., & Veerhusen, K. (1986). Guidelines for making simulation an effective adjunct to in vivo community instruction. *Journal of the Association for Persons with Severe Handicaps, 11*, 12–18.

Paris, S., & Oka, E. (1986). Self-regulated learning among exceptional children. *Exceptional Children, 53*, 103–108.

Perkins, C. B. (1989). Curriculum based assessment: A new approach. *Principal, 69*(2), 44–45.

Polloway, E., Patton, J., Epstein, M., & Smith, T. E. C. (1989). Comprehensive curriculum for students with mild handicaps. *Focus on Exceptional Children, 21*(8), 1–12.

Renzulli, J. (1988). The multiple menu model for developing differential curriculum for the gifted and talented. *Gifted Child Quarterly, 32*, 298–309.

Reynolds, M. (1976, November). *New perspectives on the instructional cascade*. Paper presented at the conference Least Restrictive Alternatives: A Partnership of General and Special Education, sponsored by the Special Education Division, Minneapolis Public Schools, Minneapolis.

Reynolds, M., Wang, M., & Walberg, H. (1987). The necessary restructuring of special and regular education. *Exceptional Children, 53*, 391–398.

Rudner, L., & Boston, C. (1994). Performance assessment. *ERIC Review, 3*(1), 2–12.

Schalock, R. (1990). *Quality of life*. Washington, DC: American Association on Mental Retardation.

Schalock, R., & Spitalnik, D. (1991). Environmental considerations. In R. Luckasson, D. Coulter, E. Polloway, S. Reiss, R. Schalock, M. Snell, D. Spitalnik, & J. Stark, *Classification in mental retardation* (9th ed., Draft). Washington, DC: American Association on Mental Retardation.

Scheerenberger, R. C. (1983). *A history of mental retardation*. Baltimore: Brookes.

Seguel, M. (1966). *The curriculum field: Its formative years*. New York: Teachers College Press.

Shapiro, J., Loeb, P., Bowermaster, D., Wright, A., Headden, S., & Toch, T. (1993, December 13). Separate and unequal: Examining special education. *U.S. News and World Report, 115*, pp. 46–50, 54–56, 60.

Shinn, M. R., & Habedank, L. (1992). Curriculum-based measurement in special education problem identification and certification decisions. *Preventing School Failure, 36*(2), 11–15.

Smith, T. E. C., & Hilton, A. (1994). Program design for students with mental retardation. *Education and Training in Mental Retardation and Developmental Disabilities, 29*, 3–8.

Snell, M., & Drake, G. (1994). Replacing cascades with supported education. *Journal of Special Education, 27,* 393–409.

Stainback, S., & Stainback, W. (1992). *Curricular considerations in inclusive classrooms: Facilitating learning for all students.* Baltimore: Brookes.

Thousand, J., & Villa, R. (1991). A futuristic view of the REI: A response to Jenkins, Pious, and Jewell. *Exceptional Children, 57,* 556–562.

Turnbull, A., Turnbull, H. R., Shank, M., & Leal, D. (1995). *Exceptional lives.* Englewood Cliffs, NJ: Merrill/Prentice-Hall.

U.S. Department of Education. (1994). *To assure the free, appropriate public education of all children with disabilities: Sixteenth annual report to Congress on the implementation of IDEA.* Washington, DC: Author.

Vandercook, T., York, J., & Forest, M. (1989). The McGill Action Planning System (MAPS): A strategy for building the vision. *Journal of the Association for Persons with Severe Handicaps, 14,* 205–215.

Vergason, G., & Anderegg, M. (1991). Beyond the Regular Education Initiative and the resource room controversy. *Focus on Exceptional Children, 23*(7), 1–7.

Ward, N. (1990). Reflections on my quality of life: Then and now. In R. Schalock (Ed.), *Quality of life* (pp. 9–16). Washington, DC: American Association on Mental Retardation.

Will, M. (1986). Educating children with learning problems: A shared responsibility. *Exceptional Children, 52,* 411–415.

Wolfensberger, W. (1983). Social role valorization: A proposed new term for the principle of normalization. *Mental Retardation, 21,* 234–239.

York, J., Doyle, M. B., & Kronberg, R. (1992). A curriculum development process for inclusive classrooms. *Focus on Exceptional Children, 25*(4), 1–16.

Ysseldyke, J., Thurlow, M., & Bruininks, R. (1992). Expected educational outcomes for students with disabilities. *Remedial and Special Education, 13*(6), 19–30.

Meeting the Life Skill Needs of Students with Developmental Disabilities in Integrated Settings

CHAPTER 8

H. Roberta Weaver, Shauna M. Adams, Mary F. Landers, and Yvonne Bullock Fryberger

Learning Outcomes

After reading this chapter, you should be able to

- Understand the authentic activity thinking process and its importance for making curricular decisions in integrated settings.

- State how effective practice relates to instructional environment, authentic adaptations, and employability skill building.

- Use the *Employability/Life Skills Assessment* (Weaver & DeLuca, 1989) as a tool for understanding how the life skills needs of students with mild developmental disabilities can be met through the general education curriculum.

- Begin making curricular decisions that are centered in student interests, motivations, and skills.

TERMS

The following terms are important for the understanding of this chapter:

Authentic activities: Real-life experiences that are naturally occurring within age-appropriate environments.

Authentic teaching: Using the child's interests, motivation, and skill levels to design and implement meaningful learning activities in various environments.

Community-based instruction: Using the local community (school, shopping mall, bus transportation system, etc.) to teach students the skills needed to function in that environment.

Employability skills instruction: The practice of making curricular decisions based on teaching students the skills that adults use in gaining and maintaining employment.

Life skills approach: The practice of making curricular decisions based on teaching students the skills that adults use in daily living (communication, transportation, food preparation, home maintenance, etc.).

Introduction

The movement toward greater integration of individuals with mental retardation into general education has presented special educators the problem of how to incorporate into the integrated setting the life skills and vocational training that have been considered effective practices in the past. The purpose of this chapter is to address this problem by demonstrating how the life skills approach, which has traditionally been implemented in special education classrooms, can be addressed in the general education classroom using the authentic activities thinking process (Weaver, Landers, & Adams, 1991) and the *Employability/Life Skills Assessment* (Weaver & DeLuca, 1989).

This chapter discusses the purpose of special education and provides evidence that traditional programming has failed to address that purpose. Approaches to special education curriculum, including functional skills, life skills, employability skills, and an authentic thinking process are presented. A historical perspective of special education approaches compares and contrasts typical learning, project-oriented and community-based learning, and authentic learning. A discussion of the authentic thinking process and employability/life skills leads the reader to an understanding of integrated education.

Examples of effective practice related to instructional environment, authentic adaptations, and employability applications are given. Finally, the case is made for merging authentic thinking and employability/life skills with general education to create an integrated experience for the student with developmental disabilities.

The Purpose of Special Education

The philosophy and/or mission statement of just about any school district in this country states that the purpose of education is to "produce skilled and knowledgeable adults who can function successfully within and contribute to their communities" (Patton, Cronin, Polloway, Hutchison, & Robinson, 1989, p. 23). This philosophy is held by professionals in both general education and special education. Thus, the philosophical purpose of special education is not different from that of education in general. They do differ, however, in the manner in which this philosophy is implemented, on a daily basis, in the classrooms.

Halpern (1985) equated the purpose of special education to the ability to establish a social and interpersonal network so that individuals with disabilities might successfully live "in one's community" (p. 480). Will (1984) suggested that the goal of special education is "an outcome-oriented process encompassing a broad array of services and experiences that lead to employment" (p. 1). Adult independence is a frequent theme in the literature and exists as a major goal of special education instruction whether services are provided in the special education classroom or in the mainstream. However, research (Edgar, 1987) demonstrates that past practices in special education have not been successful in preparing students for independence as adults.

High school dropout rates among students with mild disabilities have been increasing at an alarming rate. Over 30% of the students in secondary special education programs drop out of school. Of those students who manage to earn their diplomas, less than 15% obtain employment with a salary above minimum wage (Edgar, 1987). Unemployment and underemployment, as well as high dropout rates, suggest that goals for adult independence for students in special education are not being met. "Few mildly handicapped students (and virtually no severely involved students) move from school to community jobs that allow for independent living" (Edgar, 1987, p. 560).

Many students with mild disabilities leave school without the necessary skills to gain and maintain employment and are not prepared for the demands of adulthood (Burnham & Housley, 1992; Hasazi, Gordon, & Roe, 1985; Polloway, Patton, Epstein, & Smith, 1989). Further, Harris and Evans (1994) estimated that "as many as one third of the nation's school age children in their current circumstances, are at risk of either failing in school, dropping out or becoming a victim of crime, alcohol . . ." (p. 8). These data have

brought to focus the need for change. Some would suggest that a change to a reality-based curriculum (real-world functioning) is the primary way to improve the graduation rate, employability, and quality of life of students with mild disabilities (Polloway et al., 1989; Weaver et al., 1991). The key, however, is to be congruent in conceptualization of needed change and implementation of that change, a practice that Krom and Prater (1993) found was difficult for practitioners. In examining the relationship between Individualized Education Program (IEP) goals of intermediate-aged students with mild mental retardation and teacher self-reports of what was being taught, Krom and Prater (1993) found wide discrepancies between the number of goals written in the nonacademic areas and teachers' self-reports of the content the students were taught. The teachers reported that the majority of students were receiving vocational and/or prevocational skills instruction when, in fact, only 33% of the students had IEP goals written for these areas. Classroom observation to determine exactly what was being taught was not done.

Approaches to Special Education

Special education instruction has traditionally been based on one of three curricular orientations: remedial, maintenance, or functionality (Polloway & Patton, 1993). The remedial and maintenance orientations typically focus on basic skills instruction, whereas the functional approach centers on vocational and life skills. It is rare for a special education program to be based on only one of these curricular orientations. A more common practice is to employ a combination of these approaches (Patton et al., 1989).

Functional skills curriculum is based on traditional academics or basic skills, with subject content being taught within the context of practical application. Most commonly, this approach is implemented in separate self-contained classes taught by special teachers. There is often a focus on survival skills that students need for functioning in society (Gloeckler & Simpson, 1988). For example, it might be determined that a student needs to develop sentence writing skills. In a functional curriculum, the student would work toward this traditional goal within the context of real life. Survival for that student might suggest that learning to write notes to a parent or take phone messages is necessary; sentence writing would then be taught in the context of note writing or message taking.

The life skills approach begins by determining those skills required for adult independence. The specific skills, academic as well as survival, are identified and become the basis for the curriculum. If the development of physical health through a knowledge of nutrition is a skill required for adult independence, then learning to evaluate food choices based on the student's personal and family medical history becomes part of the student's curriculum. One attractive feature of this approach is that it "emphasizes topics which are meaningful to students, thus increasing the chances that they will become actively involved in its instructional components" (Patton et al., 1989, p. 25).

The Philosophy of Employability Skills Instruction

Some authors suggest that a functional or life skills program is more appropriate for secondary students who have academic skills that are below the fourth-grade level (Mercer & Mercer, 1989). Others advocate that functional living skills must be taught directly and systematically beginning early in a student's educational career (Kokaska & Brolin, 1985). If students with mild developmental disabilities do not receive this direct and systematic instruction at an early age, they may never learn these skills (Kokaska & Brolin, 1985).

Employers expect workers to be responsible, show initiative, and work cooperatively with their colleagues and supervisors. These skills and attitudes develop over time, and unfortunately many special educators do not address these employability skills until the secondary level, missing the formative years for providing systematic employability skills training.

Providing systematic employability skills training is the driving force behind Ohio's Employability Skills Project (Beck, n.d.) and the *Employability/Life Skills Assessment* (ELSA). This project is designed to "assist educators in meeting the changing needs of business and industry by preparing students for independence as successful adults" (Beck, n.d., p. 9). The project emphasizes that employability skills must begin early in the child's educational experience and be monitored through the use of the ELSA, which is an ongoing observational assessment of the student's employability skills acquisition.

Figure 8.1 shows the checksheet of the *Employability/Life Skills Assessment*. The checksheet is applicable to children ages 6 to 21 and relies on the teacher's understanding that the work habits of a 6-year-old are clearly different from those of a 17-year-old. It is useful for charting student skills observed in the classroom, the community, or any other instructional environment. It could be used as a checklist in the grading process and in the development of IEP objectives. The ELSA structures the teacher's observations of students in eight personal and/or interpersonal areas that are believed to demonstrate a set of attitudes, abilities, and behaviors associated with a sense of responsibility, self-discipline, pride, teamwork, and enthusiasm. These are skills that employers think schools are not developing (Congressional Committee for Economic Development, 1985).

The effectiveness of teaching students to work and problem solve collaboratively has been understood since the mid-1970s (Johnson & Johnson, 1975). The current cooperative learning movement emphasizes some of the skills found on the ELSA, such as quality of work, relationship to peers, and work attitudes. Thus, employability skills training and cooperative learning are two key elements to a functional skills, reality-based curriculum.

The Authentic Teaching Philosophy

The authentic teaching philosophy is grounded in the way one thinks about knowledge. The emphasis is not on what knowledge is being taught, but rather on how that knowledge is being presented. Brown, Collins, and Duguid (1989) used the term "situated" to describe knowledge, since they explained knowledge as, in part, a product of the activity, context, and culture in which it is developed and used. They defined authentic activities as the "ordinary practices of the culture" (p. 34). They also promoted the use of authentic activities as a means of acquiring knowledge in the same manner that "just plain folks" (p. 33) learn.

To exemplify how just plain folks might learn, Weaver et al. (1991) described why the average person would need to compute the areas of circles, squares, and rectangles when faced with the tasks of buying carpets, grass seed, insulation, and so forth. The just plain folks theory suggests selecting applications of learning by examining the tasks with which folks are confronted in daily life.

Clinchy (1995) wrote of "recontextualizing" the schools to enable students to make the connection between what is being taught and how that relates to what takes place in the real world. He argued that public schools are rote, mechanical, relentlessly academic, out-of-context institutions that do not provide genuine meaning and relevant learning for students. The approach he recommended is the creation in school of simulations of the "real," or nonschool, world. Thus, according to Clinchy, the goal is to make the learning activities important to the student by building an environment in which the student will invest. In special education, this has traditionally been called life skill development or reality-based education.

According to Woolfolk (1995, p. 268), "Perhaps the best single method for helping students remember what they learn is to make each lesson as meaningful as possible." In discussing how all teachers, special educators, and general educators alike might better motivate their students to learn, Brophy (1988) suggested that teachers base classroom activities on their students' interests, such as sports, music, common problems with families, fads, or other important aspects of their lives. Dewey (1937) supported the concept of "learning by doing," and Glasser (1990) expounded on the value of the power of motivation, which is evident when students are aware of the application of their learning.

Neither the concept of authentic teaching nor its benefits for students with developmental disabilities are new. All learners can benefit from the constructs of authentic

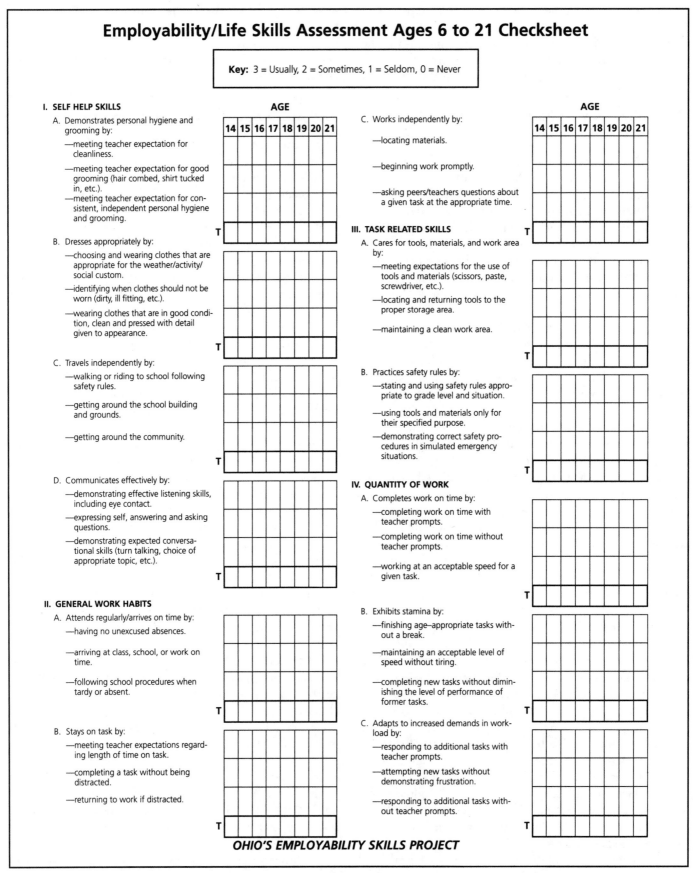

Figure 8.1. Employability Life Skills Assessment Checksheet. Developed by H. R. Weaver and J. R. DeLuca and funded through the Ohio Department of Education, Division of Special Education. Title VI-B, P.L. 94-142, 1989, Columbus: Ohio

Employability/Life Skills Assessment Ages 6 to 21 Checksheet

Key: 3 = Usually, 2 = Sometimes, 1 = Seldom, 0 = Never

V. QUALITY OF WORK

AGE

	14	15	16	17	18	19	20	21

A. Makes appropriate choices and decisions by:
—choosing an appropriate solution when given options.

—making age–appropriate decisions with teacher intervention.

—responding to a problem situation with reasonable alternative solutions.

T

B. Recognizes and corrects mistakes by:
—examining work for errors before submitting it.

—using self check methods to evaluate work.

—making corrections once an error has been identified.

T

VI. RELATIONSHIP TO SUPERVISOR/ TEACHER

A. Accepts constructive criticism from supervisor/teacher by:
—listening to constructive criticism without making inappropriate gestures or comments.

—making specified changes based on constructive criticism.

—identifying that changes have been made and that performance has improved.

T

B. Follows directions from supervisor/ teacher by:
—correctly completing tasks following verbal directions.

—correctly completing tasks following written directions.

—communicating and accepting consequences for not following directions.

T

C. Seeks help when needed by:
—identifying when help is needed.

—asking for assistance when help is needed.

—using requested information to remedy the problem.

T

VII. RELATIONSHIP TO PEERS

A. Works cooperatively with peers by:
—working well with others.

—seeking help from co-workers.

—directing co-workers without being overbearing.

T

AGE

	14	15	16	17	18	19	20	21

B. Shows respect for the rights and property of others by:
—taking turns.

—asking permission to use another's property.

—treating borrowed property with respect.

T

C. Uses appropriate language and manners with peers by:
—using everyday manners (please, thank you).

—avoiding teasing/ridiculing others.

—using language appropriate for a given situation.

T

VIII. WORK ATTITUDES

A. Develops and seeks personal goals by:
—demonstrating short term personal goals such as completing daily work.

—explaining planned activities for after school, weekend, or vacation.

—seeking and developing personal goals that are viable and consistent with abilities and limitations.

T

B. Shows initiative by:
—beginning a task as soon as requested to do so.

—beginning a task without prompting.

—asking for additional work or directions once a task is completed.

T

C. Accepts societal values and rewards by:
—acknowledging various types of rewards for work well done (stickers, free time, etc.).

—recognizing when good work has been done.

—responding appropriately when praised for doing a good job.

T

D. Takes pride in working by:
—sharing accomplishments with others (takes papers home, collects stickers, responds to point systems/grades).

—working for positions requiring improvement in skills.

—contributing to the common good of the group.

T

OHIO'S EMPLOYABILITY SKILLS PROJECT

Figure 8.1. Continued.

teaching—teaching that utilizes the child's interests, motivation, and skill levels to design and implement meaningful learning activities in various environments.

The Curriculum Perspective

Curriculum, as defined by Bigge (1988), is the total content of instruction that meets the needs of both students and society. Special education was born out of the belief that the content of instruction provided to the general school population did not meet the needs of students with disabilities. This belief about the mismatch between the individual with special needs and the adopted curriculum resulted in the creation of separate curricula—that for the general population and that for students with special needs. This resulted in groups of children (e.g., typically developing, mildly/moderately delayed, moderately/severely delayed) receiving specialized instruction from differently trained teachers (general educators and special educators). These curricular decisions led to the segregation of same-aged peers. Even though reading, math, social studies, and so forth, remained the topics of curriculum, the mode of instruction and the pace of presentation were varied. Thus, students were clustered by labels and taught similar content in differing ways.

Figure 8.2 (which contrasts the use of three types of activities to teach students) exemplifies in Column 1 how various student groupings with the same educational goal, "to demonstrate knowledge of basic math facts," might have been taught differently under the segregated system. Examples in Column 2 illustrate the belief that typically developing students learned using memory and timed practice; that students with mild/moderate delays needed more hands-on, purposeful activities related to their everyday functioning; and that students with moderate/severe delays had difficulty learning math facts but were capable of understanding numbers as related to essential elements within their daily functioning. These examples further show how each student's age and skill level determined the complexity and the appropriateness of the learning activity. Because these activities appeared so different, most educators and the general public initially accepted the practicality of separate instruction.

Teachers, over time, discovered that, even with groupings of similarly functioning students, there remained a diversity of abilities among the students. They neither performed the same task equally well nor learned at the same pace. This discovery caused educators to, once again, explore curriculum and look for instructional options to meet the needs of a greater diversity of students. Project-oriented and community-based instruction emerged as two approaches that allowed educators to teach across curricular areas and meet the needs of these diverse learners. Projects such as "On Your Own" (Miller, 1994) provide opportunities for students with mild disabilities to work in small groups on pro-

jects relevant to their interests while utilizing the diversity of individual talents within the group. For example, Miller (1994) described how using themes such as "Choosing a Career" and "Finding an Apartment" increases student motivation and helps teach academics (reading, math, writing, geography, etc.) as well as life skills (budgeting, using the newspaper, traveling, etc.) to adolescents.

Community-based instruction also accommodated a diverse group of learners. According to proponents of this type of instruction, community, defined as that social reality in which the students function on a daily basis, provides students the opportunity to recognize the need, in context, for academic skills, social skills, and life skills. "Students with disabilities should receive instruction in environments that increase and expand from the home, to the general classroom, to the school at large, to the community and integrated work environments" (Snell, 1993, p. 19). The time spent in the community is directly related to the age of the student. Older students spend a greater amount of their time in the community and younger students spend small portions of their time there. Thus, for an elementary-aged student, the total school would be the environment of choice for instruction. For example, eating in the cafeteria presents opportunities for learning health and safety skills, social skills, money skills, conversational skills, science applications, and so forth. By approaching the learning of content within a meaningful, student-oriented context, more diverse students are able to gain from the learning experience. The curricular goals do not necessarily change, but the project-oriented or community-based activities tend to differ and the practice of keeping students separate remain. As seen in Column 3 of Figure 8.2, despite having the same educational goal, the students in various groupings engage in different project-oriented or community-based activities.

According to this type of instruction, even though the same project-oriented or community-based activities might be valuable experiences for each of the student groupings, different priorities are given such instructional activities for the different groups. Most typically developing students can learn the skills in the classroom and generalize them to projects done in postschool environments; therefore, no good argument exists for routinely spending the time away from the classroom or spending the money required to support off–school site instruction for typically developing students. The students with disabilities, however, are not as able to generalize their knowledge from in-class to out-of-class school activities; thus, learning across environmental situations have become practice for students with disabilities, especially those with more limited academic abilities.

Providing different curricular foci in different instructional settings for students with different labels, as in the types of instruction described, appeared to be sound practice, but, as stated earlier, students in the special education programs dropped out of school at a high rate and those who

Student Groupings	Typical Learning Activities	Project/Community-Based Learning Activities	Authentic Learning Activities
Typically Developing ELEMENTARY General Education	Flashcard races and/or timed tests of facts from memory	Take a field trip and calculate total miles traveled, total amount spent for lunches, total time spent, etc.	Keep track of points earned by cooperative learning team members
Mildly/Moderately Delayed ELEMENTARY (Self-Contained)	Construct basic facts from dice used in a learning game	Purchase raw materials to make an item to sell or give as a gift	Run the school store 2 days a week
Mildly/Moderately Delayed SECONDARY (Self-Contained)	Calculate, on worksheets, the minimum amount of money needed to get through one typical school week	Keep personal record of money earned through High School Junior Achievement Company	Calculate from paystub the accuracy of wages earned at part-time florist job
Moderately/Severely Delayed ELEMENTARY (Self-Contained)	Verbalize one with a single clothing item and two with pairs as they put them on to go outside	Match coins needed to make a purchase in replicated grocery store in classroom; make the purchase	Go to school store or cafeteria and make a purchase
Moderately/Severely Delayed SECONDARY (Self-Contained)	Select cardboard coins needed to purchase soda from a machine	Buy soda from classroom refrigerator using real coins	Locate a soda machine in environments typically frequented (i.e., student lounge/cafeteria) and purchase a soda

Figure 8.2. A Contrast of Learning Activities for Different Student Groupings with the Same Educational Goal: To Demonstrate Knowledge of Basic Math Facts.

graduated tended not to be successful as adults (Edgar, 1988). Educators had failed to prepare the students for their future, or as Polloway, Patton, Smith, and Roderique (1991) stated, the students were not prepared for the "subsequent environments" (p. 143) in which they would need to adapt and function.

All students must be prepared to function in a world that embraces a diverse population, rather than limited groups with labels similar to those under which the school experience had been organized. Thus, once again, the purpose of schooling came under scrutiny (Harris & Evans, 1994). It became increasingly apparent that a glaring omission within the segregated system was the opportunity to learn cultural values, norms, attitudes, and skills from peers. If becoming independent adults and functioning citizens is the goal of education, then school must be defined beyond academic skills. The focus must change from a curriculum-centered approach to a child-centered approach, and this must be a pervasive attitude (Polloway et al., 1991). Child centered does not mean negating curriculum. It simply means making the academic content meaningful for the individual student and relevant to that student's life span development. This is a thinking process for the teacher. There cannot be a static curriculum. "Figuring out what is

most important for students to learn and how to most effectively teach it is an ongoing process" (York, Doyle, & Kronberg, 1992, p. 4).

Implementation Strategies

What are the tools teachers need to effectively teach a diverse student population in a meaningful manner today for tomorrow's future? Educators have the essential tools: written curriculum, knowledge of growth and development, theories of learning, and a myriad of teaching strategies. What is needed is a structure for making decisions about curriculum implementation. Teachers need to implement the authentic thinking process and to use the *Employability/Life Skills Assessment* (Weaver & DeLuca, 1989). The authentic thinking process and the ELSA provide a framework for making instructional decisions.

Authentic Thinking Process

Authentic thinking requires teachers to walk in the shoes of the students, to see through the students' eyes, to identify the students' interests, and to discover the elements of curriculum that naturally occur in the students' daily lives. A teacher or a team of teachers, using this knowledge of students, creates meaningful contexts for implementing the school's adopted curriculum that will meet the needs of all the learners in the group.

Authentic thinking is a three-step process: First, assess student need; second, determine the functional value of each student need; and third, teach through an authentic activity. First the teacher asks, "What does the student need to learn?" If the answer is, for example, "To demonstrate knowledge of basic math facts," then the teacher moves to Step 2. The following questions might be asked to determine the functionality of that knowledge: Is there a meaningfulness, an authenticity, a reality, about that knowledge for the student? Is this a part of the student's reality now and in the future? What are the natural consequences if the knowledge is not learned? If the responses to the functionality questions are positive and the failure to learn is a negative, Step 3 requires the teacher to identify potential authentic activities to serve as the vehicle for learning. Authentic activities are real-life experiences that are naturally occurring within age-appropriate environments. For example, in the case of the goal, "To demonstrate knowledge of basic math facts," the teachers of various groups of students might identify activities as shown in Column 4 of Figure 8.2.

The typical learning activities are contrasted in Figure 8.2, not only with project/community-based activities, but also with the authentic activities to show how the authentic exists within meaningful contexts (e.g., cooperative learning, operating a school store, making purchases at school, functioning as a member of the community workforce). Teaching within meaningful contexts provides not only more options for meeting individual needs but also more opportunities for developing the personal and interpersonal skills needed for employment and community participation. This three-step authentic thinking process is the tool teachers can use to establish the authenticity (student value) of a lesson for a variety of learners.

Employability Skills

Classified advertisements for job openings generally list wages, skill requirements, educational requirements, time requirements, and so on; however, jobs are lost because of employee absence, inability to get along with others, and poor work habits, to mention a few reasons. Employment requires the individual to have a salable skill, plus the ability to function as a member of a community. Teachers, just as they sequence academic skill development, need to systematically develop the personal and interpersonal skills needed by successful employees. The ELSA provides teachers with a listing of "those personal social behaviors and daily living habits . . . essential for obtaining employment and for success in the work place" (Weaver & DeLuca, 1989, p. 1).

The ELSA (see Figure 8.1) assesses the following eight areas of employability: Self Help Skills (i.e., dress, travel, communication), General Work Habits (i.e., attendance, distractibility, independence), Task Related Skills (i.e., care of tools, safety habits), Quantity of Work (i.e., speed, stamina, adaptation to workload), Quality of Work (i.e., problem solving, self-checking), Relationship to Supervisor/Teacher (accepts criticism, follows directions, seeks help), Relationship to Peers (i.e., cooperation, respect, mannerliness), and Work Attitudes (i.e., goal setting, initiative, pride in work, values). Figure 8.3 shows examples of how typical activities provide the opportunity for teaching and/or reinforcing employability skills.

Figure 8.3 shows one category of each of the eight ELSA areas of employability/life skills (i.e., I.D. Communicates Effectively, II.B. Exhibits Stamina, etc.). The subskills within each category that can be taught through the typical learning activities are listed under that category and across from the typical learning activity. The subskills referenced to each of the typical activities are written as they appear on the ELSA Checksheet. Thus, in Figure 8.3, the elementary, general education, "flashcard races and/or timed tests of facts from memory" activity is referenced to the subskill, "meeting expectations for the use of tools and materials (scissors, paste, screwdriver, etc.)" for Category III.A. In this particular situation, the tools and materials refer to flashcards, pencil, and paper. The tools and materials also could refer to a computer, a bus schedule, a cafeteria tray, and so on.

Subskills in categories such as Communicates Effectively, Exhibits Stamina, Recognizes and Corrects Mistakes, and Accepts Societal Values and Rewards are not necessarily implicit in each activity, but affect the quality of the final product. These subskills are the ones required for the student to demonstrate the knowledge implicit within the activity. Often these skills are expected to be present or are taught incidentally, rather than in an explicit, sequential manner.

Area I, Self Help Skills, and Area VII, Relationship to Peers, both imply that the teacher's structuring of the learning activity can influence the opportunity for students to engage in employability skill development. For example, if the task of "constructing basic facts from dice used in a learning game" is done by small groups or in pairs, then many of the "Relationship to Peer" skills may be developed. This is the contextual issue that teachers must address persistently.

Figure 8.4 is designed in the same manner as Figure 8.3. They differ in that Figure 8.4 addresses the authentic activities, which occur within contexts. It shows, when contrasted with the typical activities chart (Figure 8.3), how the authentic activities provide a greater opportunity for directly teaching and/or reinforcing employability skills.

These activities, as critiqued, show that most of the subskills can be directly taught as a part of the functioning within the activity. For example, the subskills in Category III.A, Cares for Tools, Materials, and Work Area (Figure 8. 4), are implicit to a storekeeper's image. Teachers have a natural opportunity to raise student awareness of this issue by having students observe shopkeepers and apply the neatness and maintainence standards to the operation of the school store (Elementary: Mildly/Moderately Delayed Activity).

Figure 8.4 also indicates that the context allows for acquisition of skills over time as the student performs a variety of tasks within that context. For example, calculating accuracy of wages earned at a part-time florist job (High School: Mildly/Moderately Delayed Activity) is only one task related to the student's functioning as a worker. The job situation opens the door to discussing communication with supervisors, other workers, and customers; working independently; proper hygiene; transportation to and from work; and so on.

Figures 8.3 and 8.4 show the instructional environments as categorical (e.g., General Education, Mildly/Moderately Delayed Elementary and Secondary) to allow the reader to relate to specific populations and to see how similar skills are being taught across various student groupings and grade levels. The charts also provide the basis for entertaining the challenge of merging, and thus integrating, populations within meaningful, authentic projects and activities for the purpose of acquiring skills needed for functioning in a diverse society.

Integrated Education

Using both the ELSA and the authentic thinking process permits teachers to develop meaningful lessons that reflect the adopted curriculum. Additionally, they provide individual teachers and interested teaching teams a framework within which to examine changes needed in their respective school's curriculum that will facilitate the integration of all students. Change can become evolutionary. Curriculum (written by content area, and learning environments, organized by categories of students or subject areas) needs to be reconceptualized so that teaching through authentic activities and across content areas is the standard. Teachers, parents, and administrators will have to make a concerted effort to "think through" the changes needed. The first step of this think-through, evolutionary process is to examine the curriculum that is currently being provided students with and without special needs. To what degree are the authentic activities and employability skills now being provided in an integrated setting? An analysis of Jody's day at school provides some answers to this question (see Figure 8.5).

Jody's Day at School description is a composite of many students. Jody is included in the same class as her peers and is expected to gain knowledge from the learning activities provided. She is expected to participate in the lessons just as her peers unless an adaptation is noted. Some of the instruction provided is done within authentic, real-life, everyday occurrences, meaningful to the student, and others are more academically oriented. Even though Jody might be able to perform some of the academically oriented activities successfully because of the amount of assistance she is given, these activities may not meet the test of being authentic for her.

For example, is the language arts writing and editing task one that Jody will use functionally now or in the future? With her limited reading and writing skills, she will probably not, in the future, be writing paragraphs on "How To . . . ." She will probably use writing for messages and/or personal letters. Thus, an on-the-job situation where she needs to use writing skills or an ongoing pen pal situation would make learning editing skills more meaningful. Does that mean that Jody should not be in language arts? The answer to that question is child specific. Seven of the eight employability skills can be directly taught or reinforced through the language arts activities, as designed. Are the socialization opportunities and employability skills provided sufficient reason for Jody to be a part of the language arts class? If Jody, her parents, and teachers agree that socialization and employability skills are sufficient reasons for her to be in the language arts class, then it is an appropriate placement. If these are not agreed to as sufficient reasons to be in language arts, then teachers need to look at how activities can be more individualized, as in the science class. If no authentic situation or individualization can be created to meet the needs of all the students, including Jody, then Jody should be provided some alternate opportunity during the teaching of this particular unit.

By doing an analysis of the way in which students are scheduled and the activities in which they are expected to engage, teachers can identify current programming that is appropriate for all students. Such an analysis raises questions about the appropriateness of a student's presence in an integrated setting just because the student can be made to function if enough help is given.

Jody exemplifies inclusion within a traditional setting, following the traditional schedule for an in-school program. As students get older and/or are more limited, integration options are found primarily in the community. Jerry, a 19-year-old with limited academic skills but good interpersonal skills and an adventuresome spirit, exemplifies the latter situation (see Figure 8.6). Jerry's day is not oriented to the typical school class period schedule. Segments of his day are dictated by daily events in the community, such as bus schedules, office operations, lunch time, and peer-partner availability. Jerry must adapt to the various environments with which he interacts. His use of academics (e.g., reading, math, geography, science, physical education) is directly related to those necessary to get him through the day. Even when he receives instruction during class time, 2 days a

(text continues on page 102)

Instructional Groupings	Typical Learning Activities	I. Self Help Skills — D. Communicates Effectively	II. General Work Habits — C. Works Independently	III. Task Related Skills — A. Cares for Tools, Materials, and Work Area	IV. Quantity of Work — B. Exhibits Stamina
Typically Developing ELEMENTARY General Education	Flashcard races and/or timed tests of facts from memory	• Demonstrating effective listening skills, including eye contact • Expressing self, answering and asking questions	• Locating materials • Beginning work promptly • Asking peer/teacher questions about a given task at the appropriate time	• Meeting expectations for the use of tools and materials (scissors, paste, screwdriver, etc.)	• Finishing age-appropriate tasks without a break • Maintaining acceptable level of speed without tiring
Mildly/Moderately Delayed ELEMENTARY (Self-Contained)	Construct basic facts from dice used in a learning game	Same as above, depending on how task is structured	All three above	Same as above plus • Locating and returning tools to proper storage area • Maintaining a clean work area	Same as above
Mildly/Moderately Delayed SECONDARY (Self-Contained)	Calculate, on worksheets, the minimum amount of money needed to get through one typical school week	Same as above, depending on how task is structured	All three above	All three above	Same as above

Figure 8.3. Examples of Employability Skill Development Through Typical Learning Activities.

Instructional Groupings	Typical Learning Activities	V. Quality of Work B. Recognizes and Corrects Mistakes	VI. Relationship to Supervisor/Teacher A. Accepts Constructive Criticism from Supervisor/Teacher	VII. Relationship to Peers B. Shows Respect for the Rights and Privacy of Others	VIII. Work Attitudes C. Accepts Societal Values and Rewards
Typically Developing ELEMENTARY General Education	Flashcard races and/or timed tests of facts from memory	• Making corrections once an error has been identified	• Listening to constructive criticism without making inappropriate gestures or comments	If structured as small group or pair work, then these sub-skills will apply	• Acknowledging various types of rewards for work well done (stickers, free time, etc.) • Recognizing when good work has been done • Responding appropriately when praised for doing a good job
Mildly/Moderately Delayed ELEMENTARY (Self-Contained)	Construct basic facts from dice used in a learning game	Same as above plus • Examining work for errors before submitting it • Using self-check methods to evaluate work	Same as above plus • Making specified changes based on constructive criticism • Identifying that changes have been made and that performance has improved	If structured as small group or pair work, then these sub-skills will apply	All three above
Mildly/Moderately Delayed SECONDARY (Self-Contained)	Calculate, on worksheets, the minimum amount of money needed to get through one typical school week	All three above	All three above	If structured as small group or pair work, then these sub-skills will apply	All three above

Figure 8.3. Continued.

Instructional Groupings	Authentic Learning Activities	I. Self Help Skills D. Communicates Effectively	II. General Work Habits C. Works Independently	III. Task Related Skills A. Cares for Tools, Materials, and Work Area	IV. Quantity of Work B. Exhibits Stamina
Typically Developing ELEMENTARY General Education	Keep track of points earned by cooperative learning team members	• Demonstrating effective listening skills, including eye contact • Expressing self, answering and asking questions • Demonstrating expected conversational skills (turn taking, choice of appropriate topics, etc.)	• Locating materials • Beginning work promptly • Asking peer/teacher questions about a given task at the appropriate time	• Meeting expectations for the use of tools and materials (scissors, paste, screwdriver, etc.)	• Finishing age-appropriate tasks without a break • Maintaining acceptable level of speed without tiring
Mildly/Moderately Delayed ELEMENTARY (Self-Contained)	Run the school store 2 days a week	All three above	All three above	Same as above plus • Locating and returning tools to proper storage area • Maintaining a clean work area	Same as above plus • Completing new tasks without diminishing the level of performance of former tasks
Mildly/Moderately Delayed HIGH SCHOOL (Self-Contained)	Calculate from paystub accuracy of wages earned at part-time florist job	All three above	All three above	All three above	All three above

Figure 8.4. Examples of Employability Skill Development Through Authentic Learning Activities.

Instructional Groupings	Authentic Learning Activities	V. Quality of Work B. Recognizes and Corrects Mistakes	VI. Relationship to Supervisor/Teacher A. Accepts Constructive Criticism from Supervisor/Teacher	VII. Relationship to Peers B. Shows Respect for the Rights and Property of Others	VIII. Work Attitudes C. Accepts Societal Values and Rewards
Typically Developing ELEMENTARY General Education	Keep track of points earned by cooperative learning team members	• Examining work for errors before submitting it • Using self-check methods to evaluate work • Making corrections once an error has been identified	• Listening to constructive criticism without making inappropriate gestures or comments • Making specified changes based on constructive criticism • Identifying that changes have been made and that performance has improved	• Taking turns • Asking permission to use another's property • Treating borrowed property with respect	• Acknowledging various types of rewards for work well done (stickers, free time, etc.) • Recognizing when good work has been done • Responding appropriately when praised for doing a good job.
Mildly/Moderately Delayed ELEMENTARY (Self-Contained)	Run the school store 2 days a week	All three above	All three above	All three above	All three above
Mildly/Moderately Delayed HIGH SCHOOL (Self-Contained)	Calculate from paystub accuracy of wages earned at part-time florist job	All three above	All three above	All three above	All three above

Figure 8.4. Continued.

Jody: A 15-year-old ninth grader. She reads at a third- to fourth-grade level; spells creatively; and can do basic computations (addition, subtraction, multiplication, and division) with and without the use of a calculator. She can tell time and is fairly accurate in exchanging money up to $10. She tends to process information auditorily and communicates orally with meaning. Sometimes the listener needs to question her to be sure she has comprehended the information discussed. She has reasonable social skills and has a sense of right and wrong.

Vision: Jody will acquire independent living skills, will hold a paying job, will be productive in her community, will enjoy leisure time activities, will be "street smart," and will be socially acceptable in the community.

Class Period: Arrival

A. Learning Activities

1. *Peers*—Get off bus; go to locker; go to homeroom.

2. *Jody Adaptation*—Uses a "locker combination reference card" to help with sequencing of numbers to open locker.

B. Employability Skills Addressed[a]

1. Self Help Skills: Travels to school and around building

2. General Work Habits: Stays on task with time and completion

3. Relationship To Supervisor/Teacher: Follows directions; correctly completes task following written directions

C. Is the Learning Activity Authentic? Yes

Class Period: Homeroom

A. Learning Activities

1. *Peers*—Listen for announcements; counted as present.

2. *Jody Adaptation*
   Teacher: Ask Jody if she heard pep rally announcement and if she knows which schedule to follow.
   Jody: Replies, "Yes, I follow the blue schedule today."

B. Employability Skills Addressed

1. Self Help Skills: Communicates using listening and answering

2. General Work Habits: Arrives at class on time

C. Is the Learning Activity Authentic? Yes

Class Period: Language Arts

A. Learning Activities

1. *Peers*—Exchange "How to . . ." papers, follow directions, and edit first draft. Use following steps:
   a. Read each sentence aloud to partner.
   b. Partner carries out each step.
   c. Use thesaurus, dictionary, and English books to check spelling, vocabulary, and grammar.
   d. Revise per editing and hand in by Friday.

2. *Jody Adaptation*—Uses following steps:
   a. Partner reads each sentence of each paper aloud.
   b. Jody carries out each step (i.e., follows directions).
   c. Jody and partner take hard copy, computer disk, and go to media center.
   d. Jody and partner use computer to check spelling, vocabulary, and grammar.
   e. Print out edited version and hand in by Friday.
      Teacher: Checks that Jody recorded on her weekly schedule the due date of revision.

B. Employability Skills Addressed

1. Self Help Skills: Communicates by listening and answering

[a]Listed by areas found on Figure 8.1, *Employability/Life Skills Assessment.*

Figure 8.5. Jody's day at school.

2. General Work Habits: Stays on task

3. Task Related Skills: Cares for tools and uses for specified purpose

4. Quantity of Work: Completes work on time with teacher prompt

5. Quality of Work: Recognizes and corrects mistakes with partner help

6. Relationship to Peers: Works cooperatively, shows respect, and uses appropriate language/manners

7. Work Attitudes: Demonstrates personal goal, shows initiative, accepts societal value of recognizing good work, and contributes to the common good of the group

C. Is the Learning Activity Authentic? No

Class Period: Basic Math

A. Learning Activity

1. *Peers*—Students work in pairs at seats using hands-on manipulatives to illustrate math problems being taught. Pairs go to chalkboard to illustrate computation for whole class. Everyone takes one of two quizzes over concept presented today.

2. *Jody Adaptation*—None. Takes the quiz that requires student to show problem with manipulatives before doing computation.

B. Employability Skills Addressed

All eight areas are addressed.

C. Is the Learning Activity Authentic? No

Class Period: General Science

(Team-taught by General Education Science Teacher and Special Education Teacher)

A. Learning Activities

1. *Peers*—Three groups to investigate "electricity" and report to whole class their findings.

Group 1 (one fourth of class)   Brainstorm: "What would life in local city or town be like without electricity for 24 hours? For 1 week?"

Group 2 (one half of class)   With Special Education Teacher: Design a radio or TV report on "What a day in the life of a typical teenager would be like without electricity."

Group 3 (one fourth of class)   With Science Teacher: Tour school with custodian and identify what would not operate in various parts of school if there were no electricity.

2. *Jody Adaptation*—None. She is a member of Group 3.

B. Employability Skills Addressed
I, IV, V, VI, VII, VIII

C. Is the Learning Activity Authentic? Yes

Class Period: Elective and Lunch

A. Learning Activities

1. *Peers*—Class or Study Hall and Lunch.

2. *Jody Adaptation*—None.
Works first half of period: Goes to media center to serve as aide. (This job was assigned per Jody's skills, IEP objectives, and interests.) Eats second half of period: Goes to lunch with a friend when other students go.

Lunchroom worker: Checks that Jody uses "reasonable" bills and coins to pay for purchases. Observations are reported to Special Education Teacher.

B. Employability Skills Addressed (Listed by areas found on Employability/Life Skills Assessment)—All eight areas are addressed, including grooming and appropriate dress for work.

C. Is the Learning Activity Authentic? Yes

Figure 8.5. Continued.

Class Period: History

A. Learning Activities

1. *Peers*—Teacher introduces chapter on Europe by using a map and associating pictures of products exported with specific countries. Students are given a homework reading assignment from the text and from the chapter work packet. They use end of period to begin homework.

2. *Jody Adaptation*—Takes "adapted worksheet," and goes to work with tutor/peer/volunteer who helps Jody design "a plan of action" for how to get work done; begins to work until period is over.

B. Employability Skills Addressed
   All areas except Area III are addressed.

C. Is the Learning Activity Authentic? No

Class Period: Chorus

A. Learning Activities

1. *Peers*—Learning music for spring concert.

2. *Jody Adaptation*—Stands next to peer who can read music and lyrics. Listens to and hums tune. Repeats words to music as read by class.
   Music Teacher: Checks to see that Jody recorded on weekly calendar time in resource room to review and reinforce memorization of lyrics.

B. Employability Skills Addressed
   All areas except Area III are addressed.

C. Is the Learning Activity Authentic? Yes—If Jody has a good voice and can learn lyrics independently. No—If she needs a lot of help to perform or can't carry a tune.

Figure 8.5. Continued.

week, that instruction is based on Jerry's needs as observed in the various environments in which he functions throughout the school day. Jerry also receives instruction in context. For example, if he is not counting out enough place settings, the teacher or supervisor immediately points out his error and has him correct it. Figure 8.6 shows how Jerry uses the knowledge of basic math during his day.

Jerry's entire school day is about building employability skills. The description indicates where, during the day, various employability skills are emphasized. Chances are that Jerry will always need supported living and supported employment, but he can be integrated with his same-age peers. His inclusion fits the "just plain folks" theory in that he functions in environments with other folks as both he and they go about their daily lives. Jerry is another member of the community who goes to and from home, does his job, and uses recreational resources.

Summary

The school day examples presented are based on the premise that teachers have the essential tools related to student development, curriculum, and learning strategies to teach a variety of students. The authentic thinking process and the employability skills development focus provide a framework for creating the activities and the learning environments that support integration while meeting the needs of all students, general and special. The examples are also intended to show that integration is reality based and that reality is child specific.

The intent of this chapter has been to provide educators with examples of how to think about integrating students into a number of learning environments (e.g., general education classrooms, community settings). Topics such as parental involvement, team teaching, and administrative support were not addressed. The importance of these issues is recognized; however, the key to making curriculum student centered and authentic is the teacher or teachers who implement instruction on a daily basis. These are the educators to whom this chapter is directed. With the appropriate mindset, teachers can make a difference for students immediately and gradually have an impact on the other significant players (i.e., parents and administrators).

Jerry: A 19-year-old "senior." His reading skills are limited to emergency sight words, his name, the names of his immediate family members, his address, and a few common signs (e.g., McDonald's). His math skills are at kindergarten to first-grade level. He does know that paper money is worth more than coins. He understands the passage of time and can tell time to the half hour. He is travel trained to go back and forth from home to his class, which is located on the campus of a local university. He is verbal, personable, and ambulatory.

Vision: Jerry will graduate from the high school special education program and become an active participant in the community. He will live in a supported living setting and will work in a supported employment setting.

Instructional Environment—Community Based: Jerry attends a special education class that is situated on the campus of a local university.

Time	Learning Activities	Employability Skills[a]
(Daily) 6:45 A.M. to 7:25 A.M.	Getting Ready for School • Check temperature to ascertain what to wear. • Use bus schedule and clock to know when to catch bus.	I. Self Help Skills would be emphasized here—A parent checks his functioning or he completes a checklist when he arrives at class
(Daily) 7:25 A.M. to 7:30 A.M.	Catching Bus • Leave house and walk to bus stop (3-minute walk). • Recognize correct bus number. • Check watch for timeliness of bus. • Pay bus fare. • Carry emergency telephone numbers for use in case bus is late or some other emergency arises.	I. Self Help Skills in the area of travel V. Quality of Work in the area of making choices (again a self-report method would be appropriate)
(Daily) 8:15 A.M. to 8:30 A.M.	Arrive on Campus • Check arrival time; must be in class by 8:30 A.M. (5-minute walk). • Locate class room number. • Sign into class using correct time and date (digital clock and calendar are available in the classroom).	II. General Work Habits in the area of attendance
(Daily) 8:30 A.M. to 8:50 A.M.	Organize for the Day • With teacher review of day's schedule, assess performance of previous day's activities.	II. General Work Habits
(Mon–Wed–Fri) 8:50 A.M. to 10:30 A.M.	Volunteer Job Exploration Site • Locate curriculum materials center by room number (10 minutes). During this experience, Jerry needs to read numbers on elevator, find rooms to which he must make deliveries, count out materials to fill orders, and file by number and by initial alphabet. (90 minutes).	II. General Work Habits III. Task Related Skills V. Quality of Work VI. Relationship to Supervisor VIII. Work Attitudes
(Tues–Thurs) 8:50 A.M. to 10:30 A.M.	In-Class Instruction This time is used to give Jerry instruction on skills that will help him function better (telling time, moving more quickly from one location to another, etc.).	Varies, but primarily: VI. Relationship to Supervisor

[a]Listed by areas found on Figure 8.1 *Employability/Life Skills Assessment.*

(continues)

Figure 8.6. Jerry's school day.

Time	Learning Activities	Employability Skills
(Daily) 10:30 A.M. to 11:10 A.M.	Lunch • Go to food court in another building (2-minute walk). • Pay for food selected, staying within a budget.	I. Self Help Skills—Communicates effectively by demonstrating expected conversation skills
(Daily) 11:10 A.M. to 11:25 A.M.	Prepare to Work • Go to kitchen area and locate employee locker by number. • Open locker using correct number combination. • Put on smock and prepare to "bus" tables.	I. Self Help Skills III. Task Related Skills
(Daily) 11:25 A.M. to 1:30 P.M.	Job • Clear and wipe tables. • Count out number of place settings for each table (set in groups of 2 to 10) and reset tables as needed .	Every employability skill could be observed; most important would be II. General Work Habits III. Task Related Skills IV. Quantity of Work V. Quality of Work VI. Relationship toSupervisor VIII. Work Attitudes
(Daily) 1:30 P.M. to 1:45 P.M.	Transition • Return to locker; open using combination lock. • Put dirty smock in laundry basket. • Walk to recreation area (2 minutes).	Will not be observed. If difficulty getting material from locker or being late for next activity, then observation will be done.
(Daily) 1:45 P.M. to 2:30 P.M.	Peer Recreation Activity • Meet university peer for billiards or bowling. • Pay deposit on billiard table or on bowling shoes. • Recognize 8 ball in billiards; shoe size in bowling. • Count pins knocked down in bowling. • Pay for number of games played. • Pay for a drink or snack.	I. Self Help Skills—Communicates effectively by demonstrating expected conversation skills VII. Relationship to Peers
(Daily) 2:30 P.M. to 2:45 P.M.	Check Out For Day • Return to classroom (3-minute walk). • Check for any personal messages from teacher, employer, or peers. • Sign out for the day using same procedure as in morning.	II. General Work Habits
(Daily) 2:45 P.M. to 3:00 P.M.	Travel Home • Use bus schedule and clock to know when to catch bus. • Get to bus stop on time (5-minute walk). • Recognize correct bus number. • Check watch for timeliness of bus. • Pay bus fare. • Carry emergency telephone numbers for use in case bus is late or some other emergency arises.	I. Self Help Skills—Travel

Figure 8.6. Continued.

QUESTIONS

1. What is the difference between functional curriculum, the life skills approach, employability skill building, community based instruction, and the authentic activity thinking process?

2. What are the benefits of using the structure for making decisions about curriculum as described in this chapter over the notion of a traditional curriculum?

3. The dynamic nature of the authentic activity thinking process dictates that instructional decisions are based on the information gleaned from a series of questions. What are the questions and what is the significance of the information gathered from each?

4. What impact can the use of the *Employability/Life Skills Assessment* and the authentic thinking process have on examining curriculum for inclusive educational settings?

5. In examining the descriptions of Jody's and Jerry's school days, how does age play a factor in the types of learning activities developed for each student?

References

Beck, S. L. (n.d.). *Ohio's Employability Skills Project* (Project No. 684A-6B-87-X). Columbus: Ohio Department of Education, Division of Special Education.

Bigge, J. (1988). *Curriculum based instruction for special education students.* Mountain View, CA: Mayfield.

Brophy, J. E. (1988). On motivating students. In D. Berliner & B. Rosenshine (Eds.), *Talks to teachers* (pp. 201–245). New York: Random House.

Brown, J. B., Collins, A., & Duguid, P. (1989, January/February). Situated cognition and the culture of learning. *Educational Researcher,* pp. 32–42.

Burnham, S. C., & Housley, W. F. (1992). Pride in work: Perceptions of employers, service providers and students who are mentally retarded and learning disabled. *Career Development for Exceptional Individuals, 15*(1), 101–108.

Clinchy, E. (1995). Learning in and about the real world. *Phi Delta Kappan, 76*(5), 400–404.

Congressional Committee for Economic Development. (1985). *Investing in our children: Business and the public school. A statement of the Research and Policy Committee of the Committee for Economic Development.* Washington, DC: U.S. Government Printing Office.

Dewey, J. (1937). *Democracy and education: An introduction to the philosophy of education.* New York: Macmillan.

Edgar, E. (1987). Secondary programs in special education: Are many of them justifiable? *Exceptional Children, 53,* 555–561.

Edgar, E. (1988). Employment as an outcome for mildly handicapped students: Current status and future directions. *Focus on Exceptional Children, 21*(1), 1–8.

Glasser, W. (1990). *The quality school.* New York: Harper & Row.

Gloeckler, T., & Simpson, C. (1988). *Exceptional students in regular classrooms: challenges, services and methods.* Mountain View, CA: Mayfield.

Halpern, A. S. (1985). Transition: A look at the foundations. *Exceptional Children, 51,* 479–486.

Harris, D. M., & Evans, D. W. (1994). Integrating school restructuring and special education reform. *Case In Point, 8*(2), 7–9.

Hasazi, S. B., Gordon, L. R., & Roe, C. A. (1985). Factors associated with the employment status of handicapped youth exiting high school from 1979 to 1983. *Exceptional Children, 51,* 455–469.

Johnson, D., & Johnson, R. (1975). *Learning together and alone: Cooperation, competition, and individualization.* Englewood Cliffs, NJ: Prentice-Hall.

Kokaska, C. J., & Brolin, D. E. (1985). *Career education for handicapped individuals* (2nd ed.). Columbus, OH: Merrill.

Krom, D. M., & Prater, M. A. (1993). IEP goals for intermediate-aged students with mild mental retardation. *Career Development for Exceptional Individuals, 16*(1), 87–95.

Mercer, C. D., & Mercer, A. R. (1989). *Teaching students with learning problems* (3rd ed.). Columbus, OH: Merrill.

Miller, D. E. (1994). "On your own": A functional skills activity for adolescents with mild disabilities. *Teaching Exceptional Children, 26*(3), 29–32.

Patton, J. R., Cronin, M. E., Polloway, E. A., Hutchison, D., & Robinson, G. A. (1989). Curricular considerations: A life skills orientation. In G. A. Robinson, J. R. Patton, E. A. Polloway, & L. R. Sargent (Eds.), *Best practices in mild mental disabilities* (pp. 21–37). Reston, VA: The Division on Mental Retardation of the Council for Exceptional Children.

Polloway, E. A., & Patton, J. R. (1993). *Strategies for teaching special needs learners* (4th ed.). Columbus, OH: Merrill.

Polloway, E. A., Patton, J. R., Epstein, M. H., & Smith, T. E. C. (1989). Comprehensive curriculum for students with mild handicaps. *Focus on Exceptional Children, 21*(8), 1–12.

Polloway, E. A., Patton, J. R., Smith, J. D., & Roderique, T. W. (1991). Issues in program design for elementary students with mild retardation: Emphasis on curriculum development. *Education and Training in Mental Retardation, 26*(2) 142–150.

Snell, M. E. (Ed.). (1993). *Instruction of students with severe disabilities* (4th ed.). New York: Macmillan.

Weaver, H. R., & DeLuca, J. R. (Developers). (1989). *Employability/Life Skills Assessment* (Project No. 674A-6B-87-X). Columbus: Ohio Department of Education, Division of Special Education.

Weaver, H. R., Landers, M. F., & Adams, S. M. (1991). Making curriculum functional: Special education and beyond. *Intervention in School and Clinic, 26*(5), 284–287.

Will, M. C. (1984). *OSERS programming for the transition of youth with disabilities: Bridges from school to working life.* Washington DC: Office of Special Education and Rehabilitation Services (OSERS), U.S. Department of Education.

Woolfolk, A. E. (1995). *Educational psychology* (6th ed.). Needham Heights, MA: Allyn & Bacon.

York, J., Doyle, M. B., & Kronberg, R. (1992). A curriculum development process for inclusive classrooms. *Focus on Exceptional Children, 25*(4), 1–16.

Development of Friendships and Social Competence

CHAPTER 9

Andrea Rosenthal-Malek

Learning Outcomes

After reading this chapter, you should be able to

■ Understand the interrelationship between social competence and the development of friendships.

■ Understand the interrelationship between play and social competence.

■ Differentiate between behavioral, cognitive, and metacognitive techniques for training social skills and social strategy use.

■ Describe various methods of training for generalization of social skills.

TERMS

The following terms are important for the understanding of this chapter:

Self-interrogation strategies: A series of questions that students ask themselves while solving problems.

Social cognition: The process of thinking about emotions, feelings, and how people interact with one another.

Social competence: The ability to move from one environment to another, while recognizing the social rules of each environment and acting in accordance with the rules.

Social executive skills: An individual's effectiveness in receiving, sorting, and processing information and in generating effective strategies for coping with social situations in order to constructively influence others.

Social perspective taking: A process whereby students are able to assume the point of view of the other students and relate it to their own.

Social skills (behavioral view): Specific learned social responses that are rule governed, goal oriented, and directly observable. These skills are situation specific, and vary depending on social context. These skills could include, among others, friendship-making skills, classroom survival skills, skill alternatives to aggression, and skills for dealing with stress.

Social skills (cognitive view): Students' ability to think and be in control of their own social behavior.

Introduction

Much of the movement to include students with developmental disabilities in the mainstream is based on the rationale of the social benefits for the students (Altman & Lewis, 1990; Hamre-Nietupski, Hendrickson, Nietupski, & Shokooi-Yektka, 1994). Advocates for inclusion believe that when students with developmental disabilities are placed with their nondisabled peers, the students with disabilities will model the more appropriate behavior exhibited by the stu-

dents without disabilities, and this in turn will automatically increase their own interpersonal social competence and help them to develop friends (Amado, 1993).

Unfortunately, research data have shown that the mere placement of students with developmental disabilities into the mainstream or into the community setting has not automatically produced spontaneous improvement of social skills or friendships between the two groups (Hilton & Liberty, 1992; Jenkins, Odom, & Seltz, 1989; Sabornie, Kauffman, & Cullinan, 1990). In fact, students with disabilities often have been socially rejected by peers, display more social isolation, and demand more teacher time (Polloway, Epstein, Patton, Cullinan, & Luebke, 1986). Further, it has been found that, when students without disabilities were asked whom they would like to have as a playmate, these students were less likely to choose students with developmental disabilities than their nondisabled peers (Sabornie et al., 1990).

Because the integration experiences of students with developmental disabilities have not been totally successful (Polloway & Patton, 1997), research has begun to look at the possible causes for some of these unsuccessful integration experiences. One primary explanation has emerged: Students with developmental disabilities lack the social competencies necessary to develop meaningful friendships (Chadsey-Rusch, 1992; Guralnick & Groom, 1988). The following section discusses social competency in relation to the development of friendships.

Development of Friendships

To understand what factors contribute to the development of the social interpersonal competencies that lead to the ability to acquire friends, researchers have looked at the development of these skills in both students with disabilities and students without disabilities. Research has shown that most students derive an enormous amount of information regarding appropriate social interactions from actual interactions with other students (Levine, 1993). The question then becomes which type of social interactions would best contribute to the development of friendships.

One group of researchers (Guralnick, 1986; Guralnick & Groom, 1988) have specifically analyzed the various types of social interactions in which students engage. They found two major types of interactions: adult–child type interactions where one person is always taking a lead role and child–child type interactions where the lead role is reciprocal. These researchers found that child–child type interactions had a more positive impact on the development of social interactive skills among the students with developmental disabilities than did adult–child type interactions. One explanation for these results is that the student who takes on the adult-type role provides a highly anticipatory social environment for the other student who merely responds. In contrast to adult–child type interactions, child–child type interactions rely on the effective participation and balanced contributions of both participants. It may be the balanced contribution and the ability to take the lead that allow the student to practice and eventually internalize the skills he or she is observing.

In line with this reasoning, it is felt that one possible explanation for the unsuccessful mainstreaming attempts, especially for students with moderate and severe developmental disabilities, may be that their relationships that have developed in the mainstream are not child–child type relationships, but rather older sibling–child or parent–child type relationships (Guralnick, 1986). In other words, what is actually happening in the mainstream is that the students without disabilities are taking a parental or older sibling type role with the students with disabilities, and thus a co-equal relationship never develops. Because the students with developmental disabilities are not considered equal, they rarely take the initiative, and thus social skills do not become internalized. This would also explain why students with developmental disabilities do not generalize newly learned social skills. Even when they imitate positive behavior, they have not assimilated the essential social skills.

Following this line of reasoning, older students with developmental disabilities should have a more difficult time with integration than younger students, because the older student without disabilities would be even more likely to take on an older sibling or parental type role. In fact, research does bear this out, as most of the successful integration attempts have been in preschool or early primary grades (Odom, McConnell, & Chandler, 1994), whereas the mainstreaming of adolescents has been more problematic (Sabornie, 1985; Sabornie & Kauffman, 1987).

Besides the possibility that the older students without disabilities are taking a parental type role, one other explanation for these results may rest in findings in the area of social cognitive research, particularly in the area of the changing aspects of friendships during the school years. Social cognition is the developmental process of thinking about emotions, feelings, and ways that people interact with each other. Social cognition links cognition and social-emotional behavior in that the stage of cognitive development influences social-emotional behavior. Further, social cognition plays a critical role in the acquisition of social skills, the ability to engage in interpersonal problem solving, and the ability to make friends (Feinburg & Mindess, 1994). Although social cognition encompasses many areas of investigation, the area most relevant to this chapter is friendship patterns, which is discussed in the next subsection.

Friendship Patterns

Young students construct an understanding of friendship through repeated encounters with others. This understanding is influenced by students' unique qualities, growth patterns, and daily experiences (Feinburg & Mindess, 1994). Thus, age greatly affects students' understanding of friendships. For example, researchers have found that students' perception of the word *friendship* changes with age (Feinburg & Mindess, 1994). Youniss and Volpe (1978) compared students' feelings regarding friendships. They asked students of different ages what a person would need to do to maintain a positive social relationship with them. These researchers, like others (e.g., Edwards, 1986), found that younger students associated the sharing of material goods or enjoyable activities with friendship, whereas older students described the sharing of private thoughts and feelings as essential ingredients (Levine, 1993). For example, when a 4-year-old says, "I don't want to be your friend," the child actually means, "I don't want to play with you right now." The same statement made by a 7-year-old has a much more enduring quality and means, "I will not share my inner feelings with you for a long time."

Another important issue in the development of friendships is social perspective taking (Levine, 1993). Social perspective taking is a process through which students are able to assume the point of view of the other student and relate it to their own. This represents a major departure from the egocentricity of preschool. Selman (1981) proposed three stages of friendship through which students progress: (a) the student is unable to distinguish his or her own perspective from that of others (ages 3 to 7), (b) the student first begins to understand that another student may have a different perspective (ages 4 to 9), and (c) the student can distinguish his or her perspective from all others involved (ages 9 to 15). Thus, according to Selman (1981), as students grow, the meaning of friendship becomes increasingly diverse and complicated. To the preschool and primary school student, friendship simply means a facilitator of play, whereas for the high school student, friendship represents a mixing of personalities at multiple levels (Levine, 1993). The research on the changing roles of friendship, as well as what is known about students with developmental disabilities, can be used to consider which grade levels would be most conducive to mainstreaming.

Social Play

Because social play can be seen as intertwined with friendships and social competence, play is discussed in this section in relation to the development of both social competence and friendships. The discussion centers around the development of play in young students without disabilities, with the idea that if we want students with developmental disabilities to derive the same benefits from play, we must allow them the same opportunity to participate as their peers without disabilities.

Researchers in the field of early childhood education are beginning to change their views on the benefits of play (Krogh, 1994). Researchers once felt that students' play was merely an outlet for physical energy, and thus unimportant for study (Frost & Sunderlin, 1985). However, play is now seen as a natural way for students to learn. It is felt that good play experiences unite all aspects of development, including social, emotional, physical, and cognitive (Eliason & Jenkins, 1994).

Thus, a major goal of preschool is to become competent at play (Riddick, 1982). Competent players are skilled at

symbolically representing their experiences in self-initiated improvisational drama. This improvisation can take place alone or in collaboration with others. Students play out their fantasies and the events in their daily lives. Through pretend play young students consolidate their understanding of the world, their language, and their social skills. Therefore, the effective teacher of young students is one who makes such play possible and helps students to continually improve their play skills (Jones & Reynolds, 1992). The following is a discussion on one particular view of play, the cognitive-developmental view.

Cognitive-Developmental View of Play

Cognitive-developmental theorists have linked play with cognitive stages of development (Feinburg & Mindess, 1994; Wortham, 1985). Like other areas of development, play progresses through stages, with one stage preparing a student for the next (Dolinar, Boser, & Holm, 1994). If a student skips a stage, he or she will enter into the next stage unprepared and this will affect all future stages (Eliason & Jenkins, 1994). In other words, play experiences provide an opportunity to try out social behaviors, and thus put development and thought into action. Each level builds the social skills necessary to move to the next higher level.

Specifically, Piaget (1951) described the play of students as dependent upon cognitive structures. In other words, play is dependent upon the thinking processes available to the student at each stage of development. As the student develops, the student's cognitive style influences the complexity of play. At the same time, the student uses play to influence cognitive development. For example, when a new behavior is learned, the student repeats it as a playful or pleasurable experience (Ellis, 1973).

One classical developmental view of play, first proposed by Parten (1932), is still considered the state of the art in the area of play. The four stages of play according to this model are as follows:

1. *Solitary play* is when the student plays alone and independently without reference to others. The student may use this stage to watch others.

2. *Parallel play* is when the student plays independently but alongside others. Its purpose may be to allow students to become acquainted with one another or to gain social acceptance.

3. *Associative play* is when the student plays with others in a similar activity but with no negotiation, cooperation, or interest in subordinating the interests of self to the interests of the group. During this stage, the teacher takes an active role in problem solving with the students.

4. *Cooperative play* is when the student plays with others in a complementary way. The negotiation,

cooperation, and subordination that were absent in associative play become more the norm. The students are able to work out compromises without any assistance from the teacher.

One must remember that individuals, including those with developmental disabilities, develop according to their own schedules but for the most part progress through the same sequence (Eliason & Jenkins, 1994). Therefore, it would be inappropriate to push a student into a cooperative situation if the student is functioning at the solitary play level. In other words, it is important to have all students participate in play situations that are at an appropriate level for their development.

Students without disabilities, given normal circumstances, seem to progress through the stages of play with little help from adults. However, students with disabilities often have difficulty in playing and, therefore, need to be given more structured help from an early age (Riddick, 1982).

Fostering Meaningful Play Experiences

For all students, including students with developmental disabilities, the most important aspect of fostering meaningful play experiences is the contact with adults and students. Students develop understanding, empathy, and sensitivity to each other by relating to, not by merely watching, others (Eliason & Jenkins, 1994). In short, play is one avenue in developing social competence in which students take an active role. Teachers can provide the model, merely set the stage, or act as a mediator when problems arise, but the students must be active participants if real friendships are to develop (Jones & Reynolds, 1992).

Although students take an active role in play, teachers can enhance the social competence of students by either directly training social skills or by training the underlying cognitive functions that mediate competence. Both of these types of training are discussed in the next section.

Social Competence

Social competence has been broadly defined as a person's overall ability to achieve his or her goals and desires in the personal and social aspects of life (Ford, 1985). For example, a socially competent person is able to move from one environment to another while recognizing the social rules of each setting and acting accordingly. Social ability, like other abilities, is developed during childhood. The following topics are discussed in the remainder of this section: the development of specific social skills, the development of social–cognitive strategies, and the generalization of these skills and strategies.

Approaches to Teaching Social Competence

Two major approaches for improving social competence are identified in the professional literature: specific social skills training and interpersonal cognitive and metacognitive strategy training (Hollinger, 1987). The former is skills based and the latter is strategy based. Social skills training assumes that key skills underlie social competence and that these skills can be systematically identified and taught. Social-cognitive strategy training, on the other hand, focuses on teaching generic strategies that students can use when responding to social situations. These strategies are adaptive and, when used, are considered social competence. Skills-based approaches rely on directly training specific skills, whereas strategy-based approaches focus on developing improved social awareness (Walker, Colvin & Ramsey, 1995).

The purposes of the following discussions are to describe effective practice procedures and recommended guidelines for implementation of social skills training programs from both a behavioral perspective and a cognitive strategy perspective. Topics covered include examples of best practices in both specific skills and social strategy training programs, issues in the use of each program type, and recommendations and guidelines governing best practices in social skills intervention in the schools.

Specific Social Skills Training

Behavioral researchers involved in social skills training of students with developmental disabilities have focused on developing specific social skills, whether physical behaviors, overt social behaviors, or social-cognitive behaviors (Davies & Rogers, 1985). This approach targets a specific behavior, then uses behavioral and social learning techniques to promote the behavior. Finally, this approach uses behavioral techniques to directly train for the generalization of the learned skill. Targeted social skills have ranged from assertiveness (Bregman, 1984) to cooperative play responses (Springler & Marshall, 1983). Intervention procedures have included homework, contingent reinforcement, modeling, behavior rehearsal, instruction feedback, and other social learning procedures (e.g., Foxx, McMorrow, & Mennemeier, 1984; Schloss & Schloss, 1984). Researchers have demonstrated that, with the use of behavioral techniques, students at all levels can be taught to display a number of positive social behaviors (Stephens, 1992).

Effective Practice: A Behavioral Approach to Training Social Skills

One example of a social skills training program that utilizes a behavioral model is that developed by Stephens (1992). This model can be modified for all levels of developmental disabilities. In this model, specific social skills are taught directly, just like all other skills. The teacher begins by defining and stating in behavioral terms the behavior to be trained, as well as the conditions under which the behavior occurs. The teacher then assesses the present level of performance of the specific skill. Finally, the teacher prescribes strategies to fit the student's needs as determined by the assessment. Specifically, the teaching process employs the following steps:

1. Define, in behavioral terms, the behavior to be taught.
2. Assess the target behavior.
3. Develop an instructional strategy.
4. Evaluate the effectiveness of the strategy.

In this model, the teaching strategies include three types: social modeling, social reinforcement, and contingency management. The particular strategy is chosen depending on the results of the assessment. Progress is routinely evaluated, and strategies are changed to fit the student's level of performance.

Generalization of Trained Social Skills

It appears that individuals with developmental disabilities do not automatically transfer learning and that skills or strategies that will promote generalization of social skills must be employed if transfer of learning is to take place (Haring, 1988; Haring et al., 1985). Generalization in the social domain has been defined as the use of acquired social skills with people other than the instructor, across environments other than the instructional setting, and applied to situations other than those experienced during instruction of the social skill (Haring & Liberty, 1990). Generalization is important in that the true purpose of learning a new skill is to be able to use the skill in other settings, at other times, and with other people.

Social skills training programs based on a behavioral model have relied on directly training for generalization either after a new skill has been learned or throughout the entire learning process including during the acquisition phase (Haring, 1988; Meese, 1994). For a more detailed explanation of generalization of trained skills, see Chapter 12 in this text.

Recommendations for Effective Practices in Behavioral Social Skills Interventions

The following is a list of effective practice suggestions for conducting generic social skills training programs:

1. Social skills or social strategies should be directly taught like any other academic subject.

2. To be effective, social skills instruction must be accompanied by the opportunity to use the newly learned skills, appropriate feedback, and incentive systems in natural settings.

3. Generalization probes should be systematically administered into the natural environment.

4. Opportunities for feedback from the targeted generalization setting must be incorporated into the training.

5. Social skills training can be used in conjunction with behavioral reduction techniques for acting-out students.

Issues Regarding Behavioral Social Skills Training and Generalization

Although researchers have successfully trained all levels of students with developmental disabilities to use specific social skills, there are contradictory research results regarding the generalization of these trained social skills, even in studies that attempted to directly train for generalization (Misra, 1992; Whitman, 1990). The emerging theoretical issue from both successful and unsuccessful attempts to promote generalization of trained social skills is the identification of the underlying mechanisms that produce the generalization (Burger, Blackman, & Clark, 1981). A number of cognitive theorists have directly addressed the issue of generalization and claim that social skills generalization will occur only through the use of social metacognitive strategies (e.g., Brown, 1987) or the use of social executive skills (e.g., Butterfield & Belmont, 1977). These authors feel that both social metacognitive strategy use and social executive functioning are transsituational, and thus this type of training lends itself to automatic generalization (Brown, 1987).

Both these skills address the process of thinking rather than the mastering of specific social skills or strategies. The following section discusses the cognitive view of social skill acquisition and generalization. See Chapter 12 for a complete analysis on cognitive, metacognitive, and executive skill strategy training.

Cognitive and Metacognitive Social Skills Training

When cognitive theorists talk about social skills training, they are not referring to skills that adults teach students or skills that students learn through imitation and modeling. The term in the cognitive-developmental framework refers to students' ability to think about and be in control of their own social behavior. The cognitive-developmental teacher's goal is to increase students' understanding and to enhance their natural development. It is assumed that all students, including students with developmental disabilities, will develop socially. One could say that the teacher's role includes being an observer and evaluator, a planner and stimulator, and a mentor and collaborator (Feinburg & Mindess, 1994).

The following subsections discuss both the theory and application of executive and metacognitive social skills training for students with developmental disabilities. Although these areas are dealt with separately for understanding, they should be thought of as being used concurrently.

Social Executive and Metacognitive Functioning

Investigators involved in executive and metacognitive functioning (Brown, 1987; Butterfield & Belmont, 1977) believe that students with developmental disabilities possess the ability required for competent performance but lack the spontaneous access to the process needed to coordinate specific abilities. In other words, they are lacking executive or metacognitive ability. The term *executive* is used in the information processing sense of executive routines or programs that organize and guide incoming and outgoing data. Executive skill in the social domain implies skill in recognizing or identifying relevant cues and parameters of a social situation, skill in predicting and planning possible sequences of events and outcomes of a situation, and skill in organizing and controlling both the self and the social "other" in order to effectively reach a chosen social goal (Bronson, 1985). On the other hand, metacognition is defined as knowledge concerning one's own cognitive processes and products or anything related to them (Flavell, 1979). Both metacognition and executive functioning address the process of thinking, rather than the mastering of specific social skills or strategies.

The following is a discussion of a social skills training program based on the use of a metacognitive and executive skills training approach. This approach has been successfully used with students with moderate developmental disabilities between the chronological ages of 9 and 14 years and with the mental ages of 3 to 7 years (Rosenthal, 1990; Rosenthal-Malek & Yoshida, 1994).

Effective Practice: A Social Metacognitive Strategy Training Program

This social skills training program is designed to be used with the whole class. The students participate in three phases of the program: the formal self-interrogation strategy training phase, the informal phase, and the generalization phase.

This program focuses on two specific skill areas: use of time and social skills. The use of time portion of the program focuses on developing the student's social interaction skills to a cooperative level without teacher assistance. The social skills portion of the program targets the development of cooperative strategies, such as helps, shares, trades, takes

turns, makes play suggestions, and states rules. This portion of the program also targets for the elimination of hostile, aggressive behavior. This program is designed to be used for 1 hour every day as part of the general curriculum. The premise is that all students, including students with developmental disabilities, need to proceed through a "kindergarten" type experience where they gain social interaction skills before they are ready to participate in a functional or academically oriented program (Rosenthal-Malek, 1997; Rosenthal-Malek & Yoshida, 1994). Thus, the development of leadership or executive skills, prosocial behavior, and cooperative social skills is emphasized.

Although this program was developed for students with moderate mental retardation between the ages of 9 and 14 with mental ages of 3 to 7 (Rosenthal, 1990; Rosenthal-Malek, 1997; Rosenthal-Malek & Yoshida, 1994), the self-interrogation questions can be modified for the individual levels of various students. However, it is suggested that students should be functioning at a developmental level of at least 3 years to use this program.

Three stages are essential for effective implementation of this training program. First, students participate in a 10-minute formal, teacher-directed lesson in which they are taught self-interrogation strategies that are chosen by the teacher. Self-interrogation strategies refer to a series of statements and questions that the students ask themselves while solving problems, in this case social problems (Brown, 1987). The same questions are repeated daily, beginning with the first statement and adding a question each day until all questions are internalized. The meanings of the statement and questions are discussed at the time they are introduced. The self-interrogation questions are taught by having the students orally repeat the questions, writing the questions on the blackboard, and applying the questions in a gamelike manner.

The following is an example of the self-interrogation statements and questions:

1. Stop and Think!
2. What (or whom) do I want to play with?
3. What will happen if I do?
4. How do I feel (happy, sad, angry, etc.)?
5. How does my friend feel (happy, sad, angry, etc.)?
6. What (or whom) else could I play with? (Rosenthal-Malek, 1997, p. 30)

During the second phase of the program, the students participate in a 50-minute student-directed free-play situation in the classroom. During this time, the students are encouraged to use the newly learned strategies in a more naturalistic play setting. During the free-play situation, the students are instructed to choose with what and whom they want to play. The teacher observes the students closely, and acts as mediator only when a student requests or needs help. The teacher attempts to promote more positive play by reminding and praising the students for successful use of the learned questions. Reinforcement of the learned strategies is given at the moment a student elicits the targeted social strategy. The following are examples of the types of free-play situations in which specific strategy intervention might take place: (a) the student cannot decide what to play, (b) the student wants to play with a group that does not want to play with the student, (c) the student was physically abused by another student, or (d) someone upset the student.

There are three important points to remember during the informal training: (a) training should take place during regularly scheduled play periods; (b) activity materials should be arranged to promote interaction and cooperative play; and (c) the teacher should intervene only when a student does not exhibit the particular social skill.

Because a major goal of this program is to have the students generalize the newly learned social skills to other settings and to use self-interrogation strategies without teacher assistance, the students are taken someplace other than the classroom (e.g., the school playground), where they practice the learned strategies with as little teacher intervention as possible. Also, the teacher must promote interaction between classmates throughout the day, and continually make statements that will promote generalization.

Recommendations for Best Practices in Cognitive Social Skills Interventions: A Cognitive Approach

The following is a list of best practice suggestions for conducting generic cognitive social skills training programs:

1. Train within the natural setting.

2. Reduce the use of adult authority and encourage students to regulate the play.

3. When conflicts arise, support and help students discuss rules and reach mutual agreement about how to play the game or what is fair.

4. When students ask for advice on what to do in specific situations, turn the decision making back to the students. If a student has no ideas about what to do, make suggestions, but always make sure the suggestions are acceptable to the student.

5. Encourage students to invent games. Discuss techniques for establishing rules of the game.

6. Keep the games at a developmentally appropriate level.

Issues Regarding Social-Cognitive Strategy Training

Professionals involved in the training of skills for students with developmental disabilities have debated the relative effectiveness of directly training specific social skills versus teaching those cognitive strategies that are ostensibly foundations to a broader range of skill development (Blackman & Lin, 1984). Cognitive strategy training appears to be favored for younger students and students with mild developmental disabilities. On the other hand, direct training of specific skills is advocated primarily for students with more profound and severe disabilities (Hickson, Blackman, & Reis, 1995).

Although some professionals (e.g., Hickson et al., 1995) are questioning the potential use of cognitive training for persons with moderate developmental disabilities, there has been recent research (Rosenthal, 1990; Rosenthal-Malek & Yoshida, 1994) that has successfully used a cognitive strategy approach with students with moderate developmental disabilities, increasing their social executive competence in both a free-play situation in the classroom and a generalized situation. Although these results are encouraging, more research is needed to verify the use of metacognitive strategy training with persons with moderate developmental disabilities.

Summary

This chapter has discussed a number of issues involved in the lack of development of friendships in the mainstream and the lack of social competence of students with developmental disabilities. Social play is seen as one avenue for the development of friendships in the mainstream and the enhancement of social competence. Unfortunately, research has shown that students with developmental disabilities are not able to gain the abilities they need to develop friendships through play in the mainstream. One explanation is that the students without disabilities are taking on a parent or older sibling role and not allowing the students with developmental disabilities to be an equal contributor to the play situation. These students with disabilities may not be internalizing the skills needed to acquire friendships because they do not get a chance to practice the social skills that they have observed.

Another possible explanation for their unsuccessful attempts at friendships is the effects of age on the changing patterns of friendships. As students without disabilities mature, they change their perceptions of friendships from merely viewing a friend as someone with whom to play to viewing a friend as someone with whom to share their innermost secrets. This change may be affecting their ability to accept the students with developmental disabilities as true friends.

Thus, students with developmental disabilities need to be trained in social skills and social strategies in order to raise their level of social competence and thus enhance their ability to make friends. One way to increase social competence is to directly train social skills or strategies or train the underlying mechanisms that enhance competence. Two major training programs were discussed: a behavioral training model that trains discrete social skills and a meta- cognitive training model that addresses the process of thinking during social situations. Strengths and weaknesses and effective practices for both were discussed.

QUESTIONS

1. What factors contribute to the development of friendships?

2. What are the advantages of social play in relation to the development of social competencies and friendships.

3. Compare and contrast the behavioral, cognitive, and metacognitive approaches to teaching social skills and social strategy use.

4. Discuss various techniques for training for generalization of social skills.

5. Do students' views regarding friendships change with age? If so, how do they change and how will this change affect students with disabilities?

References

Altman, R., & Lewis, T. J. (1990). Social judgments of integrated and segregated children with mental retardation toward their same-age peers. *Education and Training in Mental Retardation, 25,* 107–112.

Amado, A. N. (1993). *Friendships and community connections between people with and without developmental disabilities.* Baltimore: Brookes.

Blackman, L. S., & Lin, A. (1984). Generalization training in the educable mentally retarded: Intelligence and its educability revisited. In P. H. Brooks, R. Sperber, & C. McCauly (Eds.), *Learning and cognition in the mentally retarded.* Hillsdale, NJ: Erlbaum.

Bregman, S. (1984). Assertiveness training for mentally retarded adults. *Mental Retardation, 22,* 12–16.

Bronson, M. B. (1985). *Manual for the Bronson Social and Task Skill Profile.* Westport, CT: Mediax Interactive Technologies.

Brown, A. L. (1987). Metacognition, executive control, self-regulation and other more mysterious mechanisms. In F. E. Weinert & R. H. Klewe (Eds.), *Metacognition, motivation and understanding* (pp. 65–116). Hillsdale, NJ: Erlbaum.

Burger, A. L., Blackman, L. S., & Clark, H. T. (1981). Generalization of verbal abstraction strategies by EMR children and adolescents. *American Journal of Mental Deficiency, 86,* 405–413.

Butterfield, E. C., & Belmont, J. M. (1977). Assessing and improving the executive cognitive functions of mentally retarded people. In I. Bigler & M. Sternlicht (Eds.), *The psychology of mental retardation: Issues and approaches* (pp. 277–318). New York: Psychological Dimension.

Chadsey-Rusch, J. (1992). Toward defining and measuring social skills in employment settings. *American Journal on Mental Retardation, 98,* 405–418.

Davies, R. R., & Rogers, E. S. (1985). Social skills training with persons who are mentally retarded. *Mental Retardation, 23,* 186–196.

Dolinar, K., Boser, C., & Holm, E. (1994). *Learning through play: Curriculum and activities for the inclusive classroom.* Albany, NY: Delmar.

Edwards, C. P. (1986). *Promoting social and moral development in young children: Creative approaches for the classroom.* New York: Columbia University, Teachers College Press.

Eliason, C., & Jenkins, L. (1994). *A practical guide to early childhood curriculum* (5th ed.). New York: Merrill.

Ellis, J. J. (1973). *Why people play.* Englewood Cliffs, NJ: Prentice-Hall.

Feinburg, S., & Mindess, M. (1994). *Eliciting children's full potential.* Pacific Grove, CA: Brooks/Cole.

Flavell, J. H. (1979). Metacognitive and cognitive monitoring: A new area of cognitive-developmental inquiry. *American Psychologist, 34,* 906–911.

Ford, M. E. (1985). The concept of competence: Themes and variations. In H. A. Marlow & R. B. Weinberg (Eds.), *Competence development: Theory and practice in special populations* (pp. 3–38). Springfield, IL: Charles C Thomas.

Foxx, R. M., McMorrow, M. J., & Mennemeier, M. (1984). Teaching social/vocational skills to retarded adults with a modified table game: An analysis of generalization. *Journal of Applied Behavior Analysis, 17,* 343–352.

Frost, J. L., & Sunderlin, S. (1985). *When children play: Proceedings of the International Conference of Play and Play Environments.* Wheaton, MD: Association for Childhood Education International.

Guralnick, M. J. (1986). The peer relations of young handicapped and nonhandicapped children. In P. Strain, M. J. Guralnick, & H. M. Walker (Eds.), *Children's social behavior: Development, assessment and modification* (pp. 93–131). New York: Academic Press.

Guralnick, M. J., & Groom, J. M. (1988). Peer interactions in mainstreamed and specialized classrooms: A comparative analysis. *Exceptional Children, 54,* 415–425.

Hamre-Nietupski, S., Hendrickson, J., Nietupski, J., & Shokoohi- Yektka, M. (1994). Regular educators' perceptions of facilitating friendships of students with moderate, severe, or profound disabilities with nondisabled peers. *Education and Training in Mental Retardation and Developmental Disabilities, 29,* 102–117.

Haring, N. G. (1988). *Generalization for students with severe handicaps: Strategies and solutions*. Seattle: University of Washington Press.

Haring, N., & Liberty, K. (1990). Matching strategies with performance in facilitating generalization. *Focus on Exceptional Children, 22*(8), 1–16.

Haring, N., Liberty, K., Billingsley, F., White, O., Lynch, V., Kayser, J., & McCarty, F. (1985). *Investigating the problem of skill generalization*. Seattle: Washington Research Organization, University of Washington. (ERIC Document Reproduction Service No. ED 181 385)

Hickson, L., Blackman, L. S., & Reis, E. M. (1995). *Mental retardation: Foundations of educational programming*. Boston: Allyn & Bacon.

Hilton, A., & Liberty, K. (1992). The challenge of ensuring educational gains for students with severe disabilities who are placed in more integrated settings. *Education and Training in Mental Retardation, 27*, 167–175.

Hollinger, J. (1987). Social skills for behaviorally disordered children as preparation for mainstreaming: Theory, practice and new directions. *Remedial and Special Education, 8*(4), 17–27.

Jenkins, J. R., Odom, S. L., & Seltz, M. L. (1989). Effects of social integration on preschool children with handicaps. *Exceptional Children, 55*, 420–428.

Jones, E., & Reynolds, G. (1992). *The play's the thing: Teachers' roles in children's play*. New York: Teachers College Press.

Krogh, S. L. (1994). *Educating young children: Infancy to grade three*. New York: McGraw-Hill.

Levine, M. D. (1993). *Developmental variation and learning disorders*. Cambridge, MA: Educators Publishers.

Meese, R. L. (1994). *Teaching learners with mild disabilities: Integrating research and practice*. Pacific Grove, CA: Brooks/Cole.

Misra, A. (1992). Generalization of social skills through self-monitoring by adults with mild mental retardation. *Exceptional Children, 58*, 495–507.

Odom, S. L., McConnell, S. R., & Chandler, L. K. (1994). Acceptability and feasibility of classroom-based social interaction interventions for young children with disabilities. *Exceptional Children, 60*, 226–236.

Parten, M. B. (1932). Social participation among preschool children. *Journal of Abnormal and Social Psychology, 27*, 243–269.

Piaget, J. (1951). *The child's conception of the world*. London: Routledge & Kegan Paul.

Polloway, E. A., Epstein, M. H., Patton, J. R., Cullinan, D., & Luebke, J. (1986). Demographic, social and behavioral characteristics of students with educable mental retardation. *Education and Training in Mental Retardation, 21*, 27–34.

Polloway, E. A., & Patton, J. R. (1997). *Strategies for teaching learners with special needs* (6th ed.). Columbus, OH: Merrill.

Riddick, B. (1982). *Toys and play for the handicapped child*. New York: Rutledge, Chapman & Hale.

Rosenthal, A. L. (1990). The effects of metacognitive strategy training on the social executive competence of moderately retarded children (Doctoral Dissertation, Fordham University, 1990). *Dissertation Abstracts International, 51*, 1961A.

Rosenthal-Malek, A. L. (1997). Stop and Think! Using metacognitive strategies to teach social skills. *Teaching Exceptional Children, 29*(3), 29–31.

Rosenthal-Malek, A. L., & Yoshida, R. K. (1994). The effects of metacognitive strategy training on the acquisition and generalization of social skills. *Education and Training in Mental Retardation and Developmental Disabilities, 29*, 213–321.

Sabornie, E. J. (1985). Social mainstreaming of handicapped students: Facing an unpleasant reality. *Remedial and Special Education, 6*(2), 12–16.

Sabornie, E. J., & Kauffman, J. (1987). Assigned, received, and reciprocal social status of adolescents with and without mild mental retardation. *Education and Training in Mental Retardation, 24*, 139–149.

Sabornie, E., Kauffman, J., & Cullinan, D. (1990). Extended sociometric status of adolescents with mild handicaps: A cross-categorical perspective. *Exceptionality, 1*, 197–207.

Schloss, P. J., & Schloss, C. N. (1984). Evaluation of a table game designed to promote the acquisition of vocationally oriented social skills with mildly and moderately retarded adults. *Journal of Industrial Teacher Education, 21*, 12–25.

Selman, R. L. (1981). The child as a friendship philosopher. In S. R. Asher & J. M. Gottman (Eds.), *The development of children's friendships*. Cambridge, England: Cambridge University Press.

Springler, P., & Marshall, A. (1983). The unit play manager as facilitator of purposeful activities among institutionalized profoundly and severely retarded boys. *Journal of Applied Behavior Analysis, 16*, 345–349.

Stephens, T. M. (1992). *Social skills in the classroom*. Odessa, FL: Psychological Associates Resources.

Walker, H. M., Colvin, G., & Ramsey, E. (1995). *Antisocial behavior in school: Strategies and best practices*. Pacific Grove, CA: Brooks/Cole.

Whitman, T. L. (1990). Self-regulation and mental retardation. *American Journal of Mental Retardation, 94*, 347–362.

Wortham, S. C. (1985). A history of outdoor play 1900–1985: Theories of play and play environments. In J. L. Frost & S. Sunderlin (Eds.), *When children play: Proceedings of the International Conference on Play and Play Environments*. Wheaton, MD: Association for Childhood Education International.

Youniss, J., & Volpe, J. A. (1978). A relational analysis of children's friendships. In W. Damon (Ed.), *New directions for child development*. San Francisco: Jossey-Bass.

Specific Instructional Strategies

SECTION III

Best Practices

The use of instructional strategies that meet the needs of the individual are considered a best practice. This means that instructional strategies are determined from analysis of individualized assessment and objectives found in the individual program developed for the student. In most cases such strategies are effective practices that have been shown to work with students who have developmental disabilities, but often can also be effective instructional practices for all students. A set of promising practices for individuals with developmental disabilities is emerging within the context of the inclusion of students with developmental disabilities into general education classrooms.

The standard practices that many have said define special education are critical to the appropriate instruction of students with disabilities and should be used no matter in what setting the student is placed. These include such practices as the development of instructional plans that reflect the identified goals and objectives; instructional plans developed from a task analytic approach; use of a consistent cue hierarchy, especially during acquisition; high levels of instructional time; varied reinforcement strategies; and appropriate grouping. All of these have been proven to be effective for special education students when properly used. Other promising and effective practices include instruction in a variety of settings; promotion of generalization of skills for use in other settings; integrating instruction into natural routines; individual and small group instruction; constant cue hierarchy; extended practice of new skills; and the partial or full participation of students with developmental disabilities in all activities.

This Section of the Book

The chapters in Section III focus on instruction. Chapter 10 provides a general discussion of instructional interventions for students with developmental disabilities. From that discussion follow three chapters that present effective specific instructional approaches: Chapter 11 on small group instruction, Chapter 12 on teaching that has outcomes in generalized functioning, and Chapter 13 on methods of fading instructor assistance. All three approaches have been shown to be effective for teaching students with developmental disabilities, and the chapters contain a number of promising practices for the implementation of these approaches. Chapter 14 concludes the section with a general discussion of multicultural teaching practices. This last chapter underscores the message presented in the preceding four chapters—that is, the need for specific instruction approaches if the needs of the students are to be provided for.

Effective Instructional Interventions for Students with Developmental Disabilities

CHAPTER 10

Deborah Huntington

Learning Outcomes

After reading this chapter, you should be able to

- Identify three types of indirect ways to assist students through systematic instruction.

- Select a target behavior and apply a direct method of student assistance.

- Differentiate color redundancy cuing from form cuing.

- Describe how self-modeling could be used to teach a social or academic skill to an adolescent.

- Compare and contrast the decreasing prompt hierarchy with time delay.

TERMS

The following terms are important for the understanding of this chapter:

Gesture: Instructor draws the student's attention to the teaching material without any physical contact with the student.

Model: Instructor demonstrates desired behavior so it can be imitated.

Physical prompt: Instructor bodily assists the student through the desired action.

Response shaping: Successive approximations of the target behavior are reinforced.

Stimulus fading: The irrelevant characteristics of the stimulus are gradually changed from maximum cues to minimal cues.

Stimulus shaping: The critical characteristics of the stimulus being presented to the student are changed as instruction progresses from a maximum contrast to a minimum contrast.

Verbal prompts: Instructor verbalizes directions prior to and or during the performance of the requested behavior.

Introduction

Students with developmental disabilities are increasingly being served in inclusive settings (Chira, 1993). Although little research has been conducted as to the most effective ways to instruct students with developmental disabilities in inclusive settings, preliminary research indicates that program planning should focus on the characteristics and needs of individual students being served in relation to the corresponding salient social and academic features of a particular instructional setting (Altman & Kanagawa, 1994). Individuals with developmental disabilities are often characterized as inefficient learners who acquire skills at a slower rate and may make more errors initially than their normally achieving peers. When an instructor provides systematic instruction, these students have the opportunity to attain new skills and activities.

Successful teachers modify the learning environment through the provision of direct and indirect assistance to students with developmental disabilities, providing these learners the opportunity to acquire skills more quickly while reducing the error rate of their learning. The successful teacher demonstrates use of the knowledge and skills of assessing the characteristics and needs of the individual learner, determining the salient social and academic features of various instructional settings, selecting appropriate instructional methods and teaching activities, and developing systematic instruction to support these individuals in their learning.

Errorless Procedures of Systematic Instruction

Successful teachers correct student errors immediately and continue instruction until students achieve a success rate of at least 85% (Browder, Morris, & Snell, 1981; Koury & Browder, 1986). Some researchers have investigated obtaining a higher level of achievement, and this research has come to be known as errorless learning. Originally used with students with moderate and severe disabilities (LeBlanc & Ruggles, 1982; Snell & Brown, 1993), errorless procedures also have been applied to students with mild disabilities (Kinney, Stevens, & Schuster, 1988; Stevens & Schuster, 1987; Wolery, Cybrisky, Gast, & Boyle-Gast, 1991). These procedures are based on the assumption that learning will be more rapid and efficient if it is arranged to prevent errors. Even when teaching includes all elements of effective instructional design and effective teaching practices are used, some students will continue to make errors and have a slow rate of acquisition. However, when stimulus control is established, the result is a reduction in the occurrence of errors.

Errorless stimulus control can be established both indirectly and directly. The less intrusive approach would be to establish stimulus control indirectly, as when a teacher systematically fades a picture cue next to a reading word. A more intrusive approach would be to use direct assistance, such as providing response prompts, as when a teacher puts his or her hands over the student's hands and guides the student through the steps of tying a shoe.

Stimulus control established through use of indirect assistance, such as stimulus shaping, stimulus fading, and response shaping, is presented next. This discussion is followed by the presentation of more direct means of establishing stimulus control—response prompts such as verbal directions, gestures, models, cues, and physical prompts. Finally, response prompting and fading strategies, such as increasing prompt hierarchy, decreasing prompt hierarchy, and time delay, are presented.

Indirect Assistance

Stimulus control can be established by indirect assistance, such as stimulus shaping, stimulus fading, and response fad-

ing. In stimulus shaping, changes are made in the stimuli being presented to the student and, as a result, there is a change in stimulus control. The critical characteristics of the stimulus (those characteristics being taught) are changed as training progresses. More specifically, the exemplars and/or nonexemplars in an array of symbols are changed from a maximum contrast to a minimum contrast (Snell & Zirpoli, 1987). For example, the Edmark Reading Program (Edmark, 1994) makes use of stimulus shaping. The target word is presented in an array of cards with distractor symbols. Initially the distractors, horizontal lines, are very different in appearance from the target word. Later, distractors acquire more characteristics of the target word, such as the use of letters and word length. By the last trials, the distractors and the target word are very similar. This approach has the advantage of teaching students to attend to every stimulus feature in order to make the discrimination. Stimulus shaping can be easily implemented by the instructor. For example, if stimulus shaping were used to teach Joe to read the word *stop*, instruction would begin with a small drawing of a stop sign, proceed to the letters s-t-o-p above an octagonal shape, and end with the word "stop" (Bailey & Wolery, 1984).

In contrast to stimulus shaping, in stimulus fading the irrelevant characteristics are gradually changed (Dorry, 1976; Dorry & Zeaman, 1973, 1975). Stimulus fading takes many forms and may include variation of many different dimensions of the stimulus. For example, Dorry (1976) compared four conditions in which graphic fading was used in teaching 48 students with mild intellectual disabilities to read pre-primer words. Students were randomly assigned to four experimental groups. The first group received instruction in which the picture was faded out. For the second group, the word was gradually faded in. The third group received a double fade: The picture was faded out and the word was faded in. The fourth group, which served as the control group, received instruction without use of a fading technique. Two lists of words were used for instruction. A third list of words was used to assess transfer generalization. An analysis of group means on tests of acquisition, retention, and transfer demonstrated that the fading picture out and double-fade conditions were significantly superior to the other conditions. Dorry concluded that it was not the stimulus change that produced the better performance, but rather the technique of fading the picture.

The successful practitioner makes use of stimulus fading during instruction. For example, to enhance Sue's discrimination of the word *when* from the word *where*, the word card for *when* could be placed closer to Sue's arm, or the word *where* could be written in Sue's favorite color. To ensure that the student is responding to the correct characteristic of the stimulus, the incorporated cue (e.g., distance and color) is gradually removed (Bailey & Wolery, 1984). The card for the word *when* could be gradually moved closer to the card for *where* until they are equal distance from Sue. The color could be removed gradually, shade by shade, until both words are presented on white cards. If Sue continues to respond correctly, then there has been a shift in stimulus control. She has shifted from responding to irrelevant characteristics (distance and color) to relevant characteristics of the stimulus target (sight word recognition).

In response shaping, successive approximations of the target behavior are reinforced (Bailey & Wolery, 1984). During the initial phases of instruction, the teacher might reinforce a response that is considerably inferior to the target behavior. Thereafter, closer approximations of the target behavior are gradually required before reinforcement is given. For example, in teaching Bill the meaning of *poison*, the teacher may initially accept "sick." Approximations may include different levels of complexity and accuracy such as "bad," to "hurts," to "chemicals that harm living things," and ultimately getting to the term "poison" as the response.

Direct Assistance

One of the most powerful ways a student can be supported in instruction is the provision of response prompts. The prompt sufficient to produce the desired behavior for a particular student in a particular situation is called the controlling prompt. The prompt guarantees that the student will complete the correct response. Types of response prompts include verbal directions, gestures, models, cues, and physical guidance.

Verbal directions serve as guides for responding (Snell & Zirpoli, 1987). Verbal prompts can be one word, several words, or even a paragraph in length. Verbal directions are used routinely in instruction and may be presented prior to, as well as during, the performance of the behavior.

The language demands of a verbal prompt should be carefully considered. It is recommended that instructors assess the ability of students with developmental disabilities to follow verbal directions and to adjust instruction accordingly. Cuvo and Davis (1980) recommended three methods of verbal instruction for students with moderate to severe developmental disabilities. The instructor can state or restate the response requested. The instructor may say, "Mike, write your name." A second method of verbal instruction is to ask questions. After waiting several seconds, the instructor may say, "Mike, what letter do you write next?" A third method of verbal instruction is to provide a procedural description. The instructor states the first step in the procedure. If the student has been asked to write his name, the instructor may say, "Mike, pick up your pencil." The teacher's instructions must match aspects of the student's language abilities. Specific considerations include the number of instructions given simultaneously, their length, their complexity, and the presence or absence of accompanying gestures and demonstrations.

In addition to considering the language demands of the verbal prompt, successful teachers employ the systematic use of both direct and indirect forms of a verbal prompt. An indirect verbal prompt provides minimal assistance to the student. An example of an indirect verbal prompt is for the instructor to say, "What do you do next?" A direct verbal prompt provides greater assistance to the student, by providing complete information about the expected response. An example of a direct verbal prompt is "Write your name at the top of this page."

A second type of response prompt is the use of *gestures*. Gestures are movements that draw a student's attention to the teaching materials. Gestures differ from physical prompts in that, with gestures, no physical contact is involved. Using the previous illustration, when Mike fails to pick up his pencil after being directed to write his name, the teacher may use a gestural prompt by merely pointing to the pencil. Simple pointing can be effective for some students. Gestural prompts can also be combined with verbal prompts (words or signs with words) if the verbal prompts are meaningful to the student.

Modeling involves demonstrating the desired behavior so that it can be imitated (Baer, Peterson, & Sherman, 1967; Cooper, Heron, & Heward, 1987; Martin, 1975). Modeling prompts are slightly more intrusive than verbal and gestural prompts in that the teacher must demonstrate the correct response. Models can be actual demonstrations or they can be done symbolically. The teacher of a student with severe developmental disabilities may provide an actual demonstration of a task. Using the previous illustration, Mike may observe as the teacher writes his name at the top of the paper, using self-talk to verbalize actions as they are being monitored (i.e. "I can't remember which way to make the letter e. Oh, that's right—start in the middle and go to the right"). Symbolic modeling can be presented in media such as books, movies, and television. For example, a symbolic model of dressing appropriately is provided when students view a film illustrating individuals dressed for different occasions.

Self-models can be used to improve behaviors. A self-model is the repeated observation of oneself on videotapes that show only the desired target behavior. Dowrick and Dove (1980) used self-models to improve the swimming ability of children with spina bifida. The use of self-models is undeniably an effective practice. Instruction that includes photographs and videos of students is intrinsically meaningful and interesting to students. This is an appropriate and suitable approach for use with all age groups in a variety of situations.

Martin (1975) used imitative modeling and imitative behaviors to increase the use of descriptive adjectives by two children with mild to moderate intellectual disabilities. Both students who participated in the study had previously developed an imitative repertoire. Teachers indicated that neither child used color or size adjectives. Direct observation and administration of a pretest were used for baseline assessment. Data indicated that students had previously acquired receptive use of color and size adjectives. Imitative training was provided in which students were asked to imitate 12 sentences modeled verbally for them. During baseline, no color or size adjectives were used. During Phase II, both color and size adjectives were used. Each child was praised for correct imitation of sentences, and both were prompted or corrected until all 12 sentences were imitated without errors. Generalization was assessed by showing the children animal pictures and asking, "What is this?" No feedback was given by the instructor following students' verbal responses. Results indicated that the intervention was effective in increasing the amount of descriptive adjective use in the children's verbal behavior. Transfer of effects occurred across different tasks, instructors, and settings. The children's responses transferred to a different instructor without additional instruction, as well as in different settings and at different times of day.

Systematic instruction can also incorporate color redundancy cuing and form cuing (Fisher & Zeaman, 1973; Gold, 1972; Zeaman & House, 1963). Using *cuing*, one or more dimensions of the color, shape, size, or position can be matched with the correct choice. For example, the correct choice can always be placed on a white piece of paper while other choices are placed on colored paper, or the correct choice can be physically larger than the other choices.

Gold (1972) compared the effectiveness of color-redundancy cuing and form cuing in teaching adults with severe intellectual disabilities to construct bicycle brakes in a sheltered workshop setting. Color cues were placed on parts so that, when assembled correctly, the color cues of each of the parts faced the worker. The subjects who used color-redundancy cuing acquired skills faster and retained skills longer than those who learned using form cuing. A successful practitioner can easily implement the use of cuing in instructional materials. For example, a vocational teacher could provide a standard screwdriver with a large silver handle, and a Phillips-head screwdriver with a small black handle.

The fifth type of response prompt, *physical guidance*, involves bodily assisting a student through an action (Snell & Brown, 1993). Physical guidance is the most intrusive of the response prompts presented in that it requires the teacher to be directly involved with the student. In some situations, verbal directions, gesturing, modeling, and cuing may not provide enough support for a student to perform a task successfully. It may be necessary to provide partial or full physical guidance. For example, Beth is learning to boot the computer. Although she has already received verbal directions and the teacher has modeled the behavior, Beth is still having difficulty sequencing the actions. Using physical guidance, the teacher may place her hands on top of Beth's and move Beth's hands through the steps of booting the computer.

In some cases it is more efficient to combine prompts. For example, some students may need both auditory and visual prompting to elicit the correct response. Beth may need to hear one word prompt as well as read the directions and observe the example on the card before she can proceed. Therefore, whatever prompt is sufficient to elicit a correct response for a particular student in a particular situation is utilized. There is mounting evidence that providing prompts prior to students' responses decreases the probability of errors and increases the probability of error-free learning. Direct assistance in the form of a response prompt ensures that learning will be errorless (Ault, Wolery, Doyle, & Gast, 1989).

For the student to learn to complete a task independently, prompts must be faded. This can be accomplished through eliminating prompts for some of the trials. Another method of fading is to decrease the force of the prompt. In the example given, Beth will eventually remember the steps to boot a computer when she has been given a gestural prompt. The teacher can fade the prompt by holding fingers in position above, but not completely touching, the appropriate keys of the keyboard. Eventually, it will be necessary only for the teacher to begin to raise her fingers to elicit the desired behavior, and ultimately the student will perform the task independently.

Response Prompting and Fading Strategies

Three response prompting and fading strategies have often been used to teach new skills and activities to students with developmental disabilities. These include the increasing prompt hierarchy, the decreasing prompt hierarchy, and time delay (Billingsley & Romer, 1983; Snell & Browder, 1986; Wolery & Gast, 1984). The *increasing prompt hierarchy* is designed to provide increasing levels of support to students following an error (Snell & Brown, 1993). During each instructional trial and/or session, the student is provided the opportunity to perform the skill without assistance. In the event that an error does occur, the teacher provides increasing levels of assistance until the student completes the target response. For example, immediately upon reaching the job site, Sue is expected to go to her locker and store personal belongings. If Sue does not initiate the target response within an acceptable period of time, the instructor may make an indirect verbal cue, such as "What do you do now?" If this prompt is not sufficient, a direct verbal prompt may be provided, such as "Go put your things in your locker." If Sue completes the response, she is praised. If the prompt is not sufficient, the teacher provides an increased level of assistance by providing a verbal prompt with a gestural prompt, such as pointing to the locker room and saying "Put your things away now."

In the *decreasing prompt hierarchy*, students are provided with assistance before they make a response (Snell & Brown, 1993). The level of assistance provided is systematically reduced across instructional trials and/or sessions. Using the illustration above, upon entering the job site, the teacher initially gives Sue both a direct verbal and a gestural prompt, such as pointing to the locker room and saying "Sue, go to your locker." Once Sue consistently goes to her locker with this level of assistance, the teacher reduces the amount of assistance by providing an indirect verbal prompt, such as "Sue, what do you do now?" Finally, the indirect verbal prompt is eliminated and Sue is expected to complete the task without assistance.

A third response prompting and fading strategy is *time delay* (Ault, Gast, Wolery, & Doyle, 1992). Similar to the decreasing prompt hierarchy, time delay is also designed to prevent students from making errors during instruction. This approach differs from a decreasing prompt hierarchy in that, when using time delay, no attempt is made to reduce the amount of assistance provided to the student across instructional trials and/or sessions. Prompts are faded by systematically increasing the time period between the presentation of the natural environmental cue and the teacher prompt.

There are two different types of time delay: progressive time delay and constant time delay. In *progressive time delay*, instruction begins by pairing the teacher's prompt with the environmental cue. Systematically, the period of time is increased between the presentation of the environmental cue and the teacher prompt. This procedure continues until the teacher is delaying the prompt beyond the maximum expected time limit for response performance.

Constant time delay differs from progressive time delay in terms of the periods of time the prompt is delayed. In progressive time delay the length of time between the presentation of the environmental cue and the teacher prompt is systematically increased, whereas in constant time delay the period of time the prompt is delayed remains stable throughout all instructional trials and/or sessions.

Schuster, Gast, Wolery, and Guiltinan (1988) used constant time delay to teach five elementary-aged students with moderate intellectual disabilities to prepare food by following recipes. Students received one-on-one instruction using a 9 12 recipe card and multiple exemplars. A multiple-probe design across subjects was used to assess the effectiveness of the intervention. Students reached a criterion of 100% correct anticipations on a fixed-ratio 16 reinforcement schedule and maintained skills over a period of 60 days.

In general, research supports the use of the decreasing prompt hierarchy and time delay to prevent student errors during instructional periods (Bennett, Gast, Wolery, & Schuster, 1986; Day, 1987). Successful teachers choose to use decreasing prompt hierarchy or time delay when teaching new skills and activities to students with developmental disabilities. Although little comparative research has been conducted at this time, it appears that the decreasing prompt hierarchy and time delay are equally effective (Billingsley & Romer, 1983; Snell & Browder, 1986). The decreasing prompt hierarchy is usually preferable for teaching most students and most activities in that it is easier to implement. Time delay is often difficult to implement in behavior chains (Billingsley & Romer, 1983; Snell, 1982; Wolery & Gast, 1984); however, time delay is more appropriate for use with students who are prompt dependent. Research suggests that prompt-dependent students learn more efficiently with time delay because it provides sufficient structure to encourage self-motivation of response by these students (Snell & Brown, 1993).

Summary

Successful teachers modify the learning environment through the provision of direct and indirect assistance to students with developmental disabilities, providing these learners the opportunity to acquire skills more quickly while reducing the error rate of their learning. The successful teacher demonstrates use of the knowledge and skills of assessing the characteristics and needs of the individual learner, determining the salient social and academic features of various instructional settings, selecting appropriate instructional methods and teaching activities, and developing systematic instruction to support these individuals in their learning. Ways in which stimulus control could be established through use of indirect assistance, such as stimulus shaping, stimulus fading, and response shaping, were described. Response prompts, more direct means of establishing stimulus control, were described, including verbal directions, gestures, models, cues, and physical prompts. Finally, response prompting and fading strategies—the increasing prompt hierarchy, the decreasing prompt hierarchy, and time delay—were presented.

These approaches are used by an effective teacher to provide sufficient support to enable students to learn new skills and activities more successfully. Through systematic instruction, teachers can ensure progress for many students with developmental disabilities.

QUESTIONS

1. Identify three types of indirect ways to assist students through systematic instruction.

2. Select a target behavior and apply a direct method of student assistance.

3. Differentiate color redundancy cuing from form cuing.

4. Describe how self modeling could be used to teach a social or academic skill to an adolescent.

5. Compare and contrast the decreasing prompt hierarchy with time delay.

References

Altman, R., & Kanagawa, L. (1994). Academic and social engagement of young children with developmental disabilities in integrated and nonintegrated settings. *Education and Training in Mental Retardation and Developmental Disabilities, 29*, 184–193.

Ault, M. J., Gast, D. L., Wolery, M., & Doyle, P. M. (1992). Data collection and graphing method for teaching chained tasks with the constant time delay procedure. *Teaching Exceptional Children, 24*(2), 28–33.

Ault, M. J., Wolery, M., Doyle, P. M., & Gast, D. L. (1989). Review of comparative studies in the instruction of students with moderate and severe handicaps. *Exceptional Children, 55*, 346–356.

Baer, D. M., Peterson, R. F., & Sherman, J. A. (1967). The development of imitation by reinforcing behavioral similarity of a model. *Journal of Experimental Analysis of Behavior, 10*, 405–416.

Bailey, D. M., & Wolery, M. (1984). *Teaching infants and preschoolers with handicaps.* Columbus, OH: Merrill.

Bennett, D. L., Gast, D. L., Wolery, M., & Schuster, J. (1986). Time delay and system of least prompts: A comparison in teaching manual sign production. *Education and Training of the Mentally Retarded, 21*, 117–129.

Billingsley, F. F., & Romer, L. T. (1983). Response prompting and the transfer of stimulus control: Methods, research, and a conceptual framework. *The Journal of the Association for the Severely Handicapped, 8*(2), 3–12.

Browder, D. M., Morris, W. W., & Snell, M. E. (1981). Using time delay to teach manual signs to a severely retarded student. *Education and Training of the Mentally Retarded, 16*, 252–258.

Chira, J. J. (1993, May 19). When disabled students enter regular classrooms. *The New York Times*, pp. A1, A17.

Cooper, J. O., Heron, T. E., & Heward, W. L. (1987). *Applied behavioral analysis.* Columbus, OH: Merrill.

Cuvo, A. J., & Davis, P. K. (1980). Teaching community living skills to mentally retarded persons: An examination of discriminative stimuli. *Gedrag, 8*, 14–33.

Day, H. M. (1987). Comparison of two prompting procedures to facilitate skill acquisition among severely mentally retarded adolescents. *American Journal of Mental Deficiency, 91*, 366–372.

Dorry, G. W. (1976). Attentional mode for the effectiveness of fading in training reading-vocabulary with retarded persons. *American Journal of Mental Deficiency, 81*, 271–279.

Dorry, G. W., & Zeaman, D. (1973). The use of a fading technique in paired-associate teaching of a reading vocabulary with retardates. *Mental Retardation, 11*(6), 3–6.

Dorry, G. W., & Zeaman, D. (1975). Teaching a simple reading vocabulary to retarded children: Effectiveness of fading and nonfading procedures. *American Journal of Mental Deficiency, 79*, 711–716.

Dowrick, P. W., & Dove, C. (1980). The use of self-modeling to improve the swimming performance of spina bifida children. *Journal of Applied Behavior Analysis, 13*, 51–56.

Edmark Associates. (1994). *Edmark Reading Program Software Levels 1 and 2* [Computer Program]. Richmond, WA: Author.

Fisher, M. A., & Zeaman, D. (1973). An attention–retention theory of retardate discrimination learning. In N. R. Ellis (Ed.), *The international review of research in mental retardation* (Vol. 6, pp. 169–256). New York: Academic Press.

Gold, M. (1972). Task analysis of a complex assembly task by the retarded blind. *Exceptional Children, 43*(2), 78–84.

Kinney, P. G., Stevens, K. B., & Schuster, J. W. (1988). The effects of CAI and time delay: A systematic program for teaching spelling. *Journal of Special Education Technology, 9*, 61–72.

Koury, M., & Browder, D. M. (1986). The use of time delay to teach sight words by peer tutors classified as moderately mentally retarded. *Education and Training of the Mentally Retarded, 21*, 252–258.

LeBlanc, J. M., & Ruggles, R. C. (1982). Instructional strategies for individual and group teaching. *Analysis and Intervention in Developmental Disabilities, 2*, 129–137.

Martin, J. A. (1975). Generalizing the use of descriptive adjectives through modeling. *Journal of Applied Behavioral Analysis, 8*, 203–209.

Schuster, J. W., Gast, D. L., Wolery, M., & Guiltinan, S. (1988). The effectiveness of a constant time-delay procedure to teach chained responses to adolescents with mental retardation. *Journal of Applied Behavior Analysis, 21*, 169–178.

Snell, M. E. (1982). Teaching bedmaking to severely retarded adults through time delay. *Analysis and Intervention in Developmental Disorders, 2*, 139–155.

Snell, M. E., & Browder, D. M. (1986). Community-referenced instruction: Research and issues. *The Journal of the Association for Persons with Severe Handicaps, 11*, 1–11.

Snell, M. E., & Brown, F. (1993). Instructional planning and implementation. In M. E. Snell (Ed.), *Instruction of students with severe disabilities* (4th ed., pp. 99–151). New York: Macmillan.

Snell, M. E., & Zirpoli, T. J. (1987). Functional academics. In M. E. Snell (Ed.), *Systematic instruction for persons with severe handicaps* (3rd ed., pp. 110–150). New York: Macmillan.

Stevens, K. B., & Schuster, J. W. (1987). Time delay: Systematic instruction for academic tasks. *Remedial and Special Education, 9*(5), 16–21.

Wolery, M., Cybrisky, C. A., Gast, D. L., & Boyle-Gast, K. (1991). Use of constant time delay and attentional responses with adolescents. *Exceptional Children, 57,* 462–473.

Wolery, M., & Gast, D. L. (1984). Effective and efficient procedures for the transfer of stimulus control. *Topics in Early Childhood Special Education, 4*(3), 52–77.

Zeaman, D., & House, B. J. (1963). The role of attention in retardate discrimination learning. In N. F. Ellis (Ed.), *Handbook of mental deficiency* (pp. 159–223). New York: McGraw-Hill.

Small-Group Direct Instruction for Students with Moderate to Severe Disabilities

CHAPTER 11

Dennis D. Munk, Toni Van Laarhoven, Steven Goodman, and Alan C. Repp

Learning Outcomes

After reading this chapter, you should be able to

■ Define small-group direct instruction and identify the different small-group models.

■ List important variables to consider when planning a small-group lesson.

■ Determine the types of skills that can be taught successfully within a small-group format.

■ Plan a small-group lesson to teach skills to students with moderate or severe disabilities.

TERMS

The following terms are important for the understanding of this chapter:

Incidental learning: A process whereby students learn skills that are being taught without engaging in direct instruction. The students may incidentally learn skills by observing another student who is engaged in direct instruction.

Novel tasks or stimuli: Instructional materials or tasks that have not been presented during instruction. The materials or tasks are novel in that the student has not had prior exposure to them. Novel tasks are used to test generalization of skills.

Stimuli: Materials that are presented to the students during instruction.

Introduction

Many, if not most, special education professionals deliver a portion of their instructional curriculum in small-group format. Educators of students with mild disabilities undoubtedly consider group instruction, involving small and large groups, to be the principal format for delivering instruction. However, educators of students with moderate to severe disabilities may perceive group instruction to be less efficacious than individual instruction due to the need for intense and systematic instructional procedures known to be effective for these learners. For some educators, group instruction may present a trade-off; more students receive instruction requiring less staff time, but the perceived efficacy of the instruction may be less than desired or of that achieved with individual instruction. Researchers have provided a substantial body of work comparing the effects of small-group and individual instruction.

This chapter describes research outcomes for small-group direct instruction, an instructional format previously discussed by several authors (e.g., Brown, Holvoet, Guess, & Mulligan, 1980; Collins, Gast, Ault, & Wolery, 1991; Johnson, Flanagan, Burge, Kauffman-Debriere, & Spellman, 1980; Reid & Favell, 1984). Small-group direct instruction is a teacher-directed, data-based activity in which two or more students receive instruction from an educator who provides modeling, response prompting, and feedback. Thus, this format shares many features of effective individual instruction for learners with disabilities. Small-group direct instruction differs from less structured group formats, in which an educator presents information to the group as a whole but provides no individual instruction or evaluation of individual performance. Small-group direct instruction also differs from activity-based group instruction, in which an educator generally guides learners through an activity that requires performance of subskills that are taught through modeling and verbal instruction but without emphasis on mastery of the subskill by each group member.

Reid and Favell (1984) summarized research on small-group direct instruction into three models, defined by the manner in which each group member is instructed. In the *sequential model*, learners are taught consecutively (one at a time), with those not receiving instruction at a given moment remaining in the group and observing others or working on other tasks. The combination *concurrent–sequential model* involves concurrent (simultaneous) instruction for some tasks and sequential instruction for other tasks. For multiple-step tasks, learners may receive some instruction simultaneously but receive more difficult instruction on an individual basis in a sequential fashion. In the tandem *individual-to-group model*, group members receive individual instruction until a criterion for inclusion in a group is met. This model allows training of prerequisite skills (e.g., remaining seated, watching the teacher) needed to benefit from small-group direct instruction. Pretraining in an individual instruction model also prepares learners to participate effectively in groups containing learners with more advanced skills or focusing on a more complex curriculum. The existence of distinct models suggests that small-group direct instruction can be matched to the characteristics of the learners and curriculum, and that educators should consider these issues when implementing group instruction.

The three models are differentiated based on how group instruction may be structured to provide various types of instruction and curriculum. Within each model, students may engage in varying levels of interaction with fellow group members. When each student receives individual instruction within the group, with no structured interaction with other members, an intrasequential format exists. An alternative, intersequential format may be implemented when student–student interactions may facilitate acquisition and generalization. Under this structure, interactions between group members are facilitated when group members perform a series of subskills needed to complete a complex skill, or when members prompt or question each other or share materials.

Proponents have asserted that small-group direct instruction is an effective instructional format for learners with disabilities because it (a) facilitates motivation of a learner by allowing the educator to interact and reinforce the learner's peers; (b) facilitates incidental learning; and (c) promotes generalization across persons, settings, and materials (Brown et al., 1980). In a review of published studies on group instruction with learners with moderate to severe disabilities, Reid and Favell (1984) concluded that evidence existed to support use of small-group direct instruction. Less clear, however, were the advantages of small-group direct instruction over individual instruction (comparisons were equivocal) and the type of activities for which small-group direct instruction would, or would not, be appropriate. Despite limitations in the number and methodologies of published studies, Reid and Favell (1984) concluded that small-group direct instruction is a potentially effective format for instructing learners with disabilities and that future research could clarify issues of when and how to make effective use of small-group direct instruction in the classroom.

The purpose of this chapter is to inform special education professionals of best practices in small-group direct instruction for students with moderate to severe disabilities. Specifically, we describe (a) outcomes for small-group direct instruction when used to teach content drawn from different skill domains and (b) effective practices for determining group composition, delivering instruction, and supervising and evaluating group instruction.

Research on Small-Group Direct Instruction

In this section, we describe research on applications of small-group direct instruction with learners with moderate to severe disabilities. So as to include several informative studies, we present research conducted since 1980. Thus, we describe some studies previously reviewed by Reid and Favell (1984). To facilitate use by educators, we have categorized studies by the skill domain from which tasks or activities were selected. To date, skill domains addressed with small-group direct instruction include functional academics, daily living skills, social skills, and language skills.

Functional Academics

Several investigators compared the effects of small-group direct instruction and individual instruction on performance of functional academic skills, which typically involved discrimination of positive examples of words, objects, or concepts that were presented with negative examples (distractors). Oliver and Scott (1981) found small-group direct instruction with intrasequential responding to be more effective than individual instruction for teaching eight students to discriminate examples of "hard" and "heavy." Although students mastered the discrimination under both individual instruction and small-group direct instruction, students receiving group instruction also generalized their skills to novel stimuli, a positive effect not observed for those receiving individual instruction. Advantages of small-group direct instruction were also reported by Westling, Ferrell, and Swenson (1982), who taught a series of skills from an early intervention curriculum to nine young children with multiple disabilities. Students were taught skills by either individual instruction or small-group direct instruction with sequential responding. Results indicated that, although the individual instruction condition resulted in relatively more instructional time, resulting mean percentages of correct responding and mean number of objectives passed were similar for individual instruction and small-group direct instruction. Thus, the additional time required for individual instruction did not appreciably improve student performance. The authors interpreted these results as favorable for small-group direct instruction because of the reduced instructional time needed to teach an equivalent number of skills. Fink and Sandall (1980) compared the effects of small-group direct instruction (type of responding not specified) and individual instruction on recognition of six common words by four children, ages 4 to 5. Results indicated that, although percentages of correct responding were slightly higher during individual instruction, overall performance was superior during small-group direct instruction. That is, the students mastered more words in less time and maintained their skills longer during and following small-group direct instruction.

Several researchers have compared the effects of small-group direct instruction and individual instruction on acquisition of skills from two or more instructional domains, including functional academics. Alberto, Jobes, Sizemore, and Duran (1980) compared the performances of 12 students under three instructional conditions: (a) control, in which students were individually presented with stimuli but no feedback; (b) individual instruction with feedback; and (c) small-group direct instruction with sequential responding and feedback. Two tasks, discriminating prepositions or colors, were selected from the functional academics domain. Performance on the discrimination tasks was contrasted with performance on a dressing skill selected from the daily living skills domain. Results indicated that both instructional conditions were superior to the control condition, with individual instruction producing slightly higher levels of correct responding for the functional academic tasks but significantly higher levels for the dressing task. The authors concluded that small-group direct instruction and individual instruction may be similarly effective for some types of tasks (e.g., discriminations) but less equivalent for multiple-step, motor tasks such as dressing. For this type of task, individual instruction may be indicated.

Bourland, Jablonski, and Lockhart (1988) assessed the performances of eight learners on sets of tasks selected from the functional academic (e.g., word recognition, name recognition, object recognition, discrimination of wet–dry) and prevocational domains. Learners were taught skills under three conditions: (a) individual instruction (1:1); (b) small-group direct instruction with a 2:1 student–teacher ratio; or (c) small-group direct instruction with a 4:1 ratio. Both small-group direct instruction conditions included sequential responding. Dependent measures included proportion of instructional interactions, frequency of disruptive behavior, percentages of correct responding, and proportion of on-task responding. Results indicated no significant differences in

levels of instructional interaction or percentage of correct responding across the three conditions. On-task responding was also similar across the three conditions, with four students engaging in more on-task responding during the 4:1 condition. Mixed results were observed for problem behaviors; however, the 4:1 conditions consistently produced lower levels than conditions with reduced staff-to-student ratios. The authors reported no differences in performance for functional academic versus prevocational tasks.

Kamps, Walker, Maher, and Rotholz (1992) conducted a pair of studies to assess the effects of two instructional conditions, individual and small-group direct instruction, with 41 (Study 1) and 25 (Study 2) individuals with mental retardation and autism, ages 5 to 21, divided into small groups of 3 to 5 students. Small-group direct instruction involved combination concurrent–sequential responding. Dependent variables for both studies were differences between pre- and posttest scores on criterion-referenced tests, percentages of correct responding, duration of on-task responding, and duration of stereotypical responding. Skills assessed by the tests and taught during individual or small-group direct instruction included functional academic skills, such as responses to interrogative (wh–) questions, and identification and demonstration of uses for commonly used objects. Language skills, shopping skills, and money skills (e.g., coin identification) were selected from the community living skill domain. Results of the two studies were similar, with small-group direct instruction producing significantly greater improvement in pre- to posttest scores for combined responding to all tasks. Percentages of correct responding for the instructional conditions were nearly equal (62% for small-group direct instruction and 60% for individual instruction). Mean durations for on-task responding and stereotypical responding were also nearly equivalent for small-group direct instruction and individual instruction. Like previous authors (e.g., Oliver & Scott, 1981), Kamps and colleagues (1992) interpreted the results of their study as favorable for small-group direct instruction due to comparable performances of learners under individual and small-group direct instruction, during which reduced overall instructional time was needed.

Finally, Oliver (1983) compared three learners' performances on symbol recognition tasks taught by (a) individual instruction, (b) small-group direct instruction in which all members responded to identical stimuli, and (c) small-group direct instruction in which members were presented with different stimuli. Both small-group direct instruction conditions involved sequential responding. Dependent measures were the number of instructed Bliss symbols and object–action–adjective sequences correctly identified, and the number of symbols presented to other students but correctly identified during probes. The latter variable represented the extent to which incidental learning occurred during group instruction. Results indicated that small-group direct instruction with the same symbol produced more rapid acquisition by two students, with the remaining student performing slightly better during individual instruction. All students learned at least one symbol taught to another student, with close physical proximity increasing the probability of incidental learning.

In addition to the comparative studies described above, two studies have assessed the utility of small-group direct instruction alone for improving student performance on functional academic tasks. These studies included applications of specific instructional procedures combined into a small-group direct instruction model. Karsh and Repp (1992) assessed the effects of a systematic instructional program, the Task Demonstration Model, on independent and prompted correct responding, and engagement of 11 students divided into three groups. The Task Demonstration Model incorporates concurrent responding, stimulus fading, rapid pace, mastery criterion, error correction, and differential reinforcement into an instructional package, which these authors compared to a standard prompting hierarchy, a least-to-most prompting sequence. Students were taught word recognition and clock minute-hand positions under each of the two instructional conditions. Results indicated that small-group direct instruction with the Task Demonstration Model was more effective than small-group direct instruction with the standard prompting hierarchy. Both methods significantly improved correct responding over baseline levels; however, small-group direct instruction with the Task Demonstration Model produced 10% more correct responding and, more important, a twofold increase in the rate of correct responding. Interestingly, engagement was roughly equivalent across baseline, small-group direct instruction with standard prompting hierarchy, and small-group direct instruction with Task Demonstration Model, suggesting that engagement may not be a sensitive measure for effectiveness of small-group direct instruction.

Finally, Gast, Wolery, Morris, Doyle, and Meyer (1990) taught five learners, in groups of two to five, to discriminate 40 environmental sight words. The purpose of the study was to assess the effectiveness of a constant time-delay prompting procedure when applied in a small-group direct instruction format with sequential responding. Results indicated that all students mastered words they were taught and responded correctly to 48% of words taught to other students—evidence of incidental learning. Results also indicated a reduction in trials, errors, and minutes of instruction with repeated exposure to the constant time-delay procedure.

Daily Living Skills

Several studies have investigated the effectiveness of small-group direct instruction for tasks from the daily living skills domain. Repp and Karsh (1992) assessed the efficacy of small-group direct instruction with the Task Demonstration Model (described in the previous section) for teaching

14 students, ages 16 to 21, to identify cooking utensils, food items, coins, and cleaning products. The students were divided into three groups. The authors measured correct responding, engagement, and maladaptive behavior (e.g., stereotypical responding, self-injury) during baseline, group instruction, and small-group direct instruction with the Task Demonstration Model. Results indicated significant increases in correct responding and engagement time for small-group direct instruction with the Task Demonstration Model. Maladaptive behaviors decreased for 8 of the 14 subjects despite the absence of specific procedures targeting these behaviors.

Kamps, Dugan, Leonard, and Daoust (1994) assessed the effects of small-group direct instruction incorporated into a package of effective procedures, termed enhanced group instruction, on the performance of 24 students, ages 5 to 12, with mental retardation and autism. Students were divided into small groups and exposed to enhanced group instruction that included (a) choral (concurrent) responding; (b) frequent opportunities to respond; (c) frequent student–student interactions; (d) task variation; and (e) interspersed, random, prompted responding. Skills taught included identifying and categorizing household items. Results indicated significant improvements in student performance during small-group direct instruction when compared with baseline levels. Although no significant increase was observed for individual opportunities to respond, opportunities for group and student–student interactions showed large increases. Benefits of small-group direct instruction for improving acquisition were evident, with students mastering twice as many skills in the enhanced group instruction as in baseline instruction.

Orelove (1982) investigated the extent of incidental learning by 12 learners taught to identify sight words related to cooking (e.g., *pour, cheese*). Learners were randomly assigned to pairs, with members of a pair instructed sequentially on a different set of words. Daily probes assessed the percentage of directly taught and incidentally presented words learned. Results indicated that learners acquired a significant percentage of directly taught words. Additionally, learners acquired a significant number of words taught to their partners, evidencing incidental learning.

Effectiveness of small-group direct instruction versus individual instruction for a multistep motor task has also been investigated. Ranieri, Ford, Vincent, and Brown (1984) taught 23 individuals with multiple disabilities to perform a task analysis for making a snack drink. The authors employed sequential responding within 3-person groups. The purpose of the study was to compare the mean task-related and counterproductive responses under the small-group direct instruction condition (total of 45 minutes) and the 1:1 (total of 15 minutes) plus free time condition (total of 30 minutes). Results indicated that individual instruction alone produced higher levels of task-related responding and lower levels of counterproductive responses than the small-group direct instruction condition. However, when responding during free time was averaged with individual instruction, the means for task responding were lower than those observed during the same duration of small-group direct instruction. A similar comparison indicated that counterproductive responses were higher during the individual instruction plus free time condition for two of the three groups.

Social Skills

One group of researchers has investigated the efficacy of small-group direct instruction with sequential responding for teaching social skills. Wildman, Wildman, and Kelly (1986) provided instruction on three conversational skills—questioning, complimenting, and self-disclosure—to seven individuals with moderate to severe disabilities. Small-group direct instruction was conducted twice weekly with members forming dyads when practicing skills. The authors reported significant increases in the two desirable responses of questioning (71% increase) and complimenting (29% increase) and a modest (6%) decrease in the discouraged response of self-disclosure. The study is unique in that vocal rather than motoric responses were taught.

Language Skills

In the lone study involving language skills, Faw, Reid, Schepis, Fitzgerald, and Welty (1981) implemented small-group direct instruction of manual signs depicting food or drink items. Learners were pretested, then divided into three-person teams for instruction, which consisted of the presentation of a picture and of the target sign followed by a prompt to name the sign. Group members responded concurrently, with individual trials conducted following incorrect responses. A second staff person stood behind the learners, prompted correct responses, and provided verbal praise and edible reinforcers. Results indicated a mean 67% increase in correct target signs for all learners. All subjects correctly identified a minimum of 90% of signs from at least one of the three sets.

Summary

Research outcomes suggest that educators should consider small-group direct instruction a viable and efficacious format for delivering instruction across several skill domains. Outcomes of comparison studies indicate that small-group direct instruction is equally or more effective than individual instruction for teaching word recognition, matching-to-sample, object identification, or verbal social responses. An exception appears to be multistep motor tasks, such as dressing, for which individual instruction may be more effective

(Alberto et al., 1980). However, when on-task responding rather than mastery is the dependent variable, small-group direct instruction may prove effective over an extended period including individual instruction plus free time (Ranieri et al., 1984). As reported previously by Reid and Favell (1984), sequential responding remains the most common form of small-group direct instruction. Exceptions include studies in which concurrent (Karsh & Repp, 1992; Repp & Karsh, 1992) and combined concurrent–sequential (Kamps et al., 1994) responding were implemented in instructional packages designed to promote increased rates of correct responding.

In the following sections, we describe effective practices educators may use to successfully implement small-group direct instruction. Specifically, we address the areas of group composition, delivery of instruction, and supervision and evaluation.

Group Composition

Prerequisite Skills

Although precise guidelines for selecting students and forming groups for small-group direct instruction have not been established, educators should consider determining prerequisite skills for participation. Researchers have identified prerequisite skills needed to benefit from small-group direct instruction. Examples of such skills include sitting quietly for extended periods of time (Gast et al., 1990; Oliver & Scott, 1981), following simple instructions or imitating simple responses (Alberto et al., 1980; Gast et al., 1990; Karsh & Repp, 1992; Oliver, 1983; Oliver & Scott, 1981; Orelove, 1982), and maintaining eye contact (Alberto et al., 1980; Oliver & Scott, 1981). As the above examples suggest, students should, at minimum, exhibit attending skills and be able to follow instructions similar in complexity to those used during small-group direct instruction. Prior to implementing small-group direct instruction, an educator (or paraeducator) may provide individual or small-group training on basic attending, imitating, and instruction-following responses (Storm & Willis, 1978).

Group Size

In general, small-group sizes in published studies have ranged from two to five students per educator. In the lone study to compare effects of different group sizes, Bourland and colleagues (1988) found no significant differences in on-task or correct responding for small-group direct instruction with 4:1 or 2:1 student-to-educator ratios. In the absence of more studies comparing effects of group size, educators may consider the following factors when determining group size: (a) similarity in skill levels of intended participants, (b) type of responding (e.g., sequential or concurrent) to be required, and (c) presence of a paraeducator to provide support during instruction.

Both smaller (e.g., two students) and larger (e.g., five students) groups possess potential advantages and disadvantages. A smaller group may allow more trials per student, and consequently reduce intertrial waiting. However, smaller groups may result in increased overall instructional time per student, and may therefore be less efficient. Smaller groups also provide fewer models for incidental learning, but may produce such learning if students are seated in close proximity (Faw et al., 1981). Relatively larger groups may decrease the instructional time required for each student in a classroom. Other benefits may include increased opportunities for incidental learning, particularly if the group possesses members who model correct responses and adaptive behavior. A potential problem may arise when members of a larger group possess significantly different skill levels, requiring different materials and instructions, or when they exhibit maladaptive behavior when intertrial periods (i.e., waiting times) become longer. In general, participants in studies have appeared to be quite similar in skill level and instructional needs. Given the considerable national interest in educating students with moderate to severe disabilities in regular education settings, research on efficacious procedures for cross-categorical grouping for small-group direct instruction is much needed.

Delivery of Instruction

In addition to determining group composition and type of responding to be required, the educator must identify procedures and materials to be used during instruction. We briefly describe four instructional variables relevant to small-group direct instruction: (a) type of task to be taught, (b) type of student response, (c) instructional materials to be used, and (d) effective instructional procedures embedded in group instruction.

Type of Task

As previously stated, research has for the most part involved functional tasks from the skill domains of functional academics, daily living, community living, social interaction, and functional language. Functional word recognition, money skills, shopping skills, and time telling have been the most popular tasks for small-group direct instruction. Such tasks are appropriate in that they are functional for learners with moderate to severe mental retardation and require an overt, usually motoric, response. When considering tasks for small-group direct instruction, educators should select those that are functional for the learner. When group members have different educational objectives, or are working at different

levels of complexity, the educator must identify tasks that are relevant to the domain and topic being taught, as well as to the skill level of each learner (Brown et al., 1980).

Type of Student Response

Prior to initiating instruction, the educator must determine the expected response mode for each learner. As would be expected, research with students with moderate to severe disabilities has involved primarily motoric responses, such as pointing to or touching a stimulus, or grasping and handing a stimulus to a peer or instructor. For learners with cognitive and language deficits that significantly limit vocal responding, motoric responses are appropriate because they (a) can be consistently produced by the learner, (b) can be taught with a prompting sequence, and (c) can be easily observed and evaluated. When learners possess the prerequisite language skills (e.g., comprehension, vocal production), vocal responses may be required. For nonverbal students, augmentative communication systems may be implemented. Examples of such systems include manual sign, picture books, or electronic devices, all of which allow the learner to respond verbally to educator-initiated questions, as well as to peer-initiated comments or questions.

Instructional Materials

In general, research has provided little guidance on material preparation and design for small-group direct instruction. Therefore, the educator is advised to follow general guidelines for developing instructional materials. Factors influencing material selection include (a) skill level of student (e.g., ability to match-to-sample vs. identify from verbal description), (b) type and number of positive and negative exemplars to be used in teaching discriminations or concepts, and (c) type of response (e.g., pointing, vocal response) required of student.

Type and number of positive and negative exemplars is an important consideration for any instructional format. Researchers recommend using multiple positive and negative examples of the concept (e.g., chair, complimenting others) being taught (Englemann & Carnine, 1982; Repp, Karsh, & Lenz, 1990). Studies on small-group direct instruction by Karsh and Repp (1992; Repp & Karsh, 1992) involved use of multiple examples of survival words or minute-hand positions. Positive examples included a range of words or clock faces that varied on all noncritical features (e.g., color, size) but never on the critical feature of spelling or minute-hand position. In these studies, students were seated at a U-shaped table, an arrangement that allowed stimuli to be passed from student to student so that each responded (concurrently) to a different positive example on each trial. Obviously, use of positive examples requires advanced preparation of stimuli and a group arrangement that allows sharing of materials by all members. Whenever possible, real rather than representational or analogue stimuli should be used during instruction. For example, real coins rather than cardboard representations should be used to teach money skills. Use of real stimuli facilitates generalization of skills from small-group direct instruction to each student's natural environment.

Sequencing of examples has been incorporated into an instructional package delivered via small-group direct instruction (Repp & Karsh, 1992). Sequencing materials may involve presenting easier tasks early, followed by more difficult tasks, or by employing stimulus fading during discrimination training. In the latter, negative examples gradually become more similar to positive examples, requiring the learner to identify the critical features of the concept or skills under instruction (Repp & Karsh, 1992).

Instructional Procedures Embedded Within Small-Group Direct Instruction

Other instructional variables included in research on small-group direct instruction include brisk pacing, feedback and reinforcement for correct responding, error correction, and signaling or unison responding. Two studies (Karsh & Repp, 1992; Repp & Karsh, 1992) incorporated brisk pacing during small-group direct instruction. These same authors, as well as Kamps and colleagues (1994), used teacher signaling for concurrent (also called unison or choral) responding. Both brisk pacing and concurrent responding produced increased opportunities for student responding and reduced waiting between turns.

Most studies on small-group direct instruction reported the use of positive feedback to students making a correct response, and error correction following an incorrect response. Verbal praise was the most commonly used form of positive feedback, a finding that is not surprising given the ease with which attention, praise, and touch can be delivered during group instruction. The most common form of error correction involved the educator's (a) saying "No" following the incorrect response, (b) modeling the correct response, then (c) retesting the student by repeating the instruction. When selecting an error correction procedure for small-group direct instruction, the educator should identify a procedure that can be easily and consistently implemented without requiring excessive attention to an individual student and thereby slowing the pace of instruction.

Supervision and Evaluation

Supervision and evaluation of student performance are well-recognized components of systematic, effective instruction (Kameenui & Simmons, 1990). Supervisory activities include

preparing and scheduling instructional formats and monitoring student performance during instruction. Evaluation activities may include collecting data on student responding and identifying and implementing strategies for improving performance. We briefly describe research-based and practical strategies for effectively supervising and evaluating student performance during small-group direct instruction.

Preparation and Scheduling

Preparation is a key factor in the delivery of systematic instruction. The general requirements for preparing instructional formats and materials are equivalent for individual or small-group direct instruction (Kameenui & Simmons, 1990). Prior to implementing a session of small-group direct instruction, an educator should (a) identify the antecedent instructions to be delivered by the educator or paraeducator; (b) identify the type of responding (e.g., sequential) to be used; (c) determine if and how student–student interactions will be facilitated during instruction; (d) select materials for the group or for individual students and place materials in convenient locations; and (e) determine the possible role of the paraeducator to prompt student responses, provide reinforcement, or record data. Published literature has not addressed practices for scheduling small-group direct instruction. In general, decisions regarding scheduling should be based on the learners' needs. For example, complex skills requiring many trials over several sessions would necessitate frequent sessions of small-group direct instruction. Frequent sessions would be particularly valuable if the opportunities to respond were reduced during small-group direct instruction, or if incidental learning was unlikely due to the extent of the students' disabilities or the complexity of the task. An additional advantage of frequent participation in small-group direct instruction may be that students learn the rules or expectations for group behavior. For example, students may learn to transition from individual instruction, independent seatwork, or free time to small-group direct instruction more rapidly and with less disruption if they are required to practice transitioning several times per day.

Roles for Classroom Staff

Although a single staff person, usually the classroom teacher, assumes responsibility for delivering small-group direct instruction, paraeducators or related services professionals (e.g., speech therapists) may support students during portions of the day. Presence of a second professional to support the educator delivering instruction is a critical element in effective small-group direct instruction, and supporting professionals should be prepared to perform the following functions: (a) remain behind students and contact all students during instructions, (b) provide prompts and feedback to individual group members, (c) reinforce students for waiting quietly between individual trials, and (d) record student responses. Educators and paraeducators may alternate between the leader and support person roles; however, we recommend that the support person avoid providing individual instruction to students who do not attend to instructions from the group leader.

Data Collection

Researchers have collected data on several student behaviors, including percentages of correct responses (Oliver & Scott, 1981), trials to criterion (Wolery, Ault, Gast, Doyle, & Mills, 1990), minutes of instruction needed to master a skill (Favell, Favell, & McGimsey, 1978), percentage or duration of on-task responding (Ranieri et al., 1984), frequency of student–student interactions (Kamps et al., 1994), percentage of session engaged in task responding (Karsh & Repp, 1992), and frequency of maladaptive behavior (Repp & Karsh, 1992). Obviously, recording data becomes more difficult as group size increases; therefore, goals and methods for recording should be defined prior to initiating instruction. Data should reflect the educators' goals for students in the group and should be useful for determining each student's progress on IEP goals. We recommend that educators follow these steps in designing data-collection methods for small-group direct instruction:

1. Identify the domain and skill to be taught.

2. Identify the type of student response of interest (e.g., correct responses, on-task responding).

3. Determine whether data will be recorded for each student per session, or for selected students during an individual session (probes).

4. Determine the desired student response mode (e.g., pointing, vocal response).

5. Create data-collection forms that allow rapid recording (e.g., a form with categories that the observer can check).

6. Determine if the observer will collect data on students during discrete trial responding, waiting, or a combination of both conditions.

7. Establish reliability by having a second observer record data on a percentage (e.g., 20%) of live or videotaped sessions.

Educators seeking more information on methods for collecting and summarizing data on a student performance are encouraged to review Brown and colleagues (1980) or Alberto and Troutman (1990).

Tactics for Improving Student Performance

Several researchers have implemented contingent reinforcement to maintain or improve student performance, particularly adaptive behavior during the intertrial interval. Bourland and colleagues (1988) delivered verbal praise every 30 seconds to students who waited quietly between turns. Oliver (1983) provided edible reinforcers on an intermittent schedule for correct responding on individual trials. Gast and colleagues (1990) implemented reinforcement procedures after several subjects failed to remain seated or observe peers while waiting for a turn. Although a discussion of reinforcement procedures plausible for use during small-group direct instruction is beyond the scope of this chapter, educators should consider such procedures when students fail to exhibit prerequisite skills or demonstrate slow progress.

When data indicate slow student progress or high levels of maladaptive behavior, an educator may be required to implement additional strategies. For example, a concurrent or combination concurrent–sequential model has been shown to increase opportunities to respond and receive reinforcement, and to reduce waiting time (Kamps et al., 1994; Karsh & Repp, 1992; Repp & Karsh, 1992). An additional strategy may be to provide supplemental individual instruction on difficult or novel tasks or activities. Supplemental instruction may be indicated when a student demonstrates prerequisite skills but exhibits low rates of correct responding, which subsequently reduces positive feedback from educators or peers.

 ## Case Study

Ms. Brown teaches 12 students with severe disabilities in a self-contained classroom in a public school. She is assisted by two paraeducators, who share responsibility for individual instruction. Over time, Ms. Brown has become increasingly frustrated over the time required to individually instruct each student in her class. Furthermore, students not receiving

instruction tend to wander around the room or engage in unproductive activities.

To increase her efficient use of instructional time, Ms. Brown has decided to implement group instruction. After reading several studies, she has concluded that small-group direct instruction is recommended for learners with moderate to severe disabilities. From her reading, Ms. Brown has created the following checklist of effective practices.

Checklist for Implementing Small-Group Direct Instruction

Group Composition

- [ ] Group comprises 2 to 5 students.
- [ ] Group members possess necessary prerequisite skills.
- [ ] Group members demonstrate similar levels of ability.

Curriculum

- [ ] Curriculum is functional for all members.
- [ ] Materials are prepared and conveniently located.
- [ ] Multiple positive and negative examples are prepared.
- [ ] Stimuli are sequenced so that less difficult tasks precede more difficult tasks.

Instructional Delivery

- [ ] Student response mode has been identified.
- [ ] Instructions or prompting sequence has been identified.
- [ ] Definitions of a correct and incorrect response are clear to all staff involved with instruction.
- [ ] Procedures for error correction, feedback, and reinforcement have been identified.
- [ ] Type of responding (e.g., sequential, concurrent, combined sequential–concurrent) has been identified.
- [ ] Decision whether to prompt student–student interactions via intersequential responding or provide only teacher–student interaction via intrasequential responding has been made.
- [ ] Students are seated in close proximity to promote incidental learning.

Supervision and Evaluation

- [ ] Paraeducators have been trained to support teacher during instruction.
- [ ] A precoded form and schedule for recording student responses have been created.
- [ ] Criteria for evaluating progress or need for additional motivational or instructional procedures has been established.

Having completed each task in the checklist, Ms. Brown is prepared to begin instruction. She identifies three students who are working on similar IEP goals and who demonstrate the ability to remain seated, observe while peers receive instruction, and follow two-step instructions. Because each of the group members is working on household cleaning and meal preparation, Ms. Brown will teach the concept "bowl" during small-group direct instruction. She gathers several examples of bowls, varying on noncritical features of size, color, or material. Ms. Brown selects negative examples of plates, cups, and spoons. All instructional stimuli are conveniently placed in a box near the area in which the group will meet.

Ms. Brown knows that she will not have time to record lengthy notes during instruction; therefore, she has created a form that includes spaces to record the student's name, instructional stimuli, and instructional objective (Figure 11.1). For each trial, the observer simply records a plus (+) for a correct response or a minus (−) for an incorrect response.

Prior to beginning instruction, Ms. Brown determines how she will deliver instruction. Students will be required to discriminate a bowl from a distractor (e.g., spoon); therefore, the response mode will be pointing or touching the correct object. Positive examples of bowls and negative examples (e.g., plates) will be placed in front of each student as he or she is seated at a kidney-shaped table. Providing instructional stimuli to each student will allow Ms. Brown to implement concurrent responding, which provides more trials per student.

Ms. Brown intends to implement small-group direct instruction in 20-minute sessions, one session each in the morning and in the afternoon. She begins the morning session by seating the three students at a kidney-shaped table, with her chair placed in the hollow. One paraeducator has been trained to assist during small-group direct instruction, while the other paraeducator supervises the remaining five students in a separate activity. The assisting paraeducator stands behind and near the students, in a position that allows him to quickly prompt and reinforce each student.

To begin the session, Ms. Brown instructs the students to place their hands down on the table and watch the teacher. This "ready" position was trained in previous sessions and is an important prerequisite skill for participating in small-group direct instruction. Next, she places a bowl in front of each student and says, "Everyone, touch the bowl." Students responding correctly are praised by the teacher and by the paraeducator. For students failing to respond, the teacher or paraeducator prompts the correct response, then the teacher repeats the trial.

Once all group members reach criterion (e.g., 90% independent correct responding), Ms. Brown presents examples of bowls with other objects serving as distractors. Delivery remains the same, with a prompt to touch the bowl, followed by praise for correct responses and error correction following incorrect responses. Ms. Brown sequences the negative examples so that early discriminations are easy (e.g., discriminate the bowl from a spoon), with later trials becoming increasingly difficult as negative examples become more similar to a bowl (e.g., plates, cups). When all students reach criterion on the most difficult discrimination, Ms. Brown plans to begin instruction on additional functional items for meal preparation.

Date: _____ Student: _____

Concept: Bowl

Instructional Stimuli

Positive Examples: **Negative Examples:**

  1. large wooden bowl   Easy—spoon
  2. medium plastic bowl   Moderately difficult—drinking cup
  3. small ceramic bowl   Very difficult—plate

Instructional Objective

Discriminate three examples of bowl when presented with easy negative example of spoon.

Trial	Pos. Ex.	Neg. Ex.	Initial Trial	Error Correction	Repeat Trial
1	1	spoon			
2	2	spoon			
3	3	spoon			
4	2	spoon			
5	3	spoon			
6	1	spoon			
7	3	spoon			
8	2	spoon			
9	1	spoon			
10	3	spoon			
Total					
Percentage Correct					

Figure 11.1. Form created to facilitate group instruction of "bowl" concept.

In addition to prompting and reinforcing student responses, the paraeducator assists Ms. Brown in recording student responses on the form. Because of the relatively small number of students in the group, all student responses are recorded. To assess students' performance, Ms. Brown sums the total number of correct responses and divides by the total number of responses to obtain the percentage of correct responses. In future sessions, Ms. Brown will compare her students' performances against her preestablished criterion. If performance lags, she will be prepared to implement additional strategies, such as (a) identifying more potent reinforcers (e.g., edibles, tokens exchangeable for privileges) or (b) providing additional individual instruction on particularly difficult tasks.

Conclusion

The purpose of this chapter has been to present special education professionals with an overview of small-group direct instruction for learners with moderate to severe disabili- ties. Toward this purpose we have presented a descriptive review of studies published since 1980. From these and ear- lier studies, we have highlighted effective practices to be implemented during group instruction. Although we have restricted our review and discussion to learners with moderate to severe disabilities, we believe that most of the specific practices or procedures discussed are appropriate for instructing students with milder disabilities.

In summarizing our review, we were struck by the relative decline in the number and changing characteristics of research studies conducted since 1990. It would appear that researchers, and perhaps practitioners, were convinced by earlier research that small-group direct instruction is an effective practice. Thus, the volume of studies has decreased. Also noticeable is a trend toward studies involving multi-component instructional packages that incorporate several effective practices (e.g., Collins et al., 1991; Kamps et al., 1992; Karsh & Repp, 1992; Repp & Karsh, 1992). We might conclude from this group of studies that more basic questions regarding the general efficacy of small-group direct instruction have been answered affirmatively. Following their review, Reid and Favell (1984) suggested that future research should focus on expanding knowledge of when and how small-group direct instruction can be best used in the classroom. Research since their review has helped clarify those issues. For example, small-group direct instruction has been used to teach skills across multiple domains. Comparative studies have also demonstrated the relative efficiency of group instruction versus individual instruction, even when group instruction requires more instructional time per student. Limitations of small-group direct instruction have been revealed during comparative studies. For example, multiple-step motor tasks that are typically taught in a task-analyzed sequence of steps are less appropriate for group instruction.

Perhaps the most exciting finding has been the potential for incidental learning during small-group direct instruction. Incidental learning, which has been shown to be facilitated by close proximity, increases the relative efficiency of group instruction in that learners may acquire skills for which they do not receive direct instruction. Evidence of incidental learning should affect educators' decisions regarding group composition. Heterogeneous groupings of students with varying levels of abilities may facilitate incidental learning because higher performing members serve as models for lower performing members. The extent to which heterogeneous grouping facilitates incidental learning warrants future research attention.

Future research should also address the increasing movement to include students with disabilities in regular education settings. For example, research investigating effective practices for instructing heterogeneous groups containing students with and without disabilities is needed. Such research should focus on selecting instructional objectives, materials, and response requirements for students with disabilities, and should provide guidelines for implementing small-group direct instruction in the regular education classroom.

QUESTIONS

1. Describe a small-group lesson using a concurrent format for teaching sight word vocabulary to students with moderate to severe disabilities. Be sure to include details such as group size, error correction procedures, data collection, and so on.

2. Describe how an educator could use small-group direct instruction to promote incidental learning of skills and concepts.

3. What types of skills are more conducive to being taught in a small-group format? What types of skills are more conducive to individual instruction?

4. Define and describe the differences between sequential, concurrent, and tandem models of small-group direct instruction.

5. List the variables that need to be considered when designing lessons within a small-group direct instruction format.

References

Alberto, P., Jobes, N., Sizemore, A., & Duran, D. (1980). A comparison of individual and group instruction across response tasks. *Journal of the Association for Persons with Severe Handicaps, 5,* 285–293.

Alberto, P. A., & Troutman, A. C. (1990). *Applied behavior analysis for teachers* (3rd ed.). New York: Merrill.

Bourland, G., Jablonski, E. M., & Lockhart, D. L. (1988). Multiple-behavior comparison of group and individual instruction of persons with mental retardation. *Mental Retardation, 26,* 39–46.

Brown, F., Holvoet, J., Guess, D., & Mulligan, M. (1980). The Individualized Curriculum Sequencing Model (III): Small group instruction. *Journal of the Association for Persons with Severe Handicaps, 5,* 352–367.

Collins, B. C., Gast, D. L., Ault, M. J., & Wolery, M. (1991). Small-group instruction: Guidelines for teachers of students with moderate to severe handicaps. *Education and Training in Mental Retardation, 26,* 18–32.

Englemann, S., & Carnine, D. (1982). *Theory of instruction: Principles and applications.* New York: Irvington.

Favell, J. E., Favell, J. E., & McGimsey, J. F. (1978). Relative effectiveness and efficiency of group vs. individual training of severely retarded persons. *American Journal of Mental Deficiency, 83,* 104–109.

Faw, G. D., Reid, D. H., Schepis, M. M., Fitzgerald, J. R., & Welty, P. A. (1981). Involving institutional staff in the development and maintenance of sign language skills with profoundly retarded persons. *Journal of Applied Behavior Analysis, 14,* 411–423.

Fink, W. T., & Sandall, J. R. (1980). A comparison of one-to-one and small group instructional strategies with developmentally disabled preschoolers. *Mental Retardation, 18*, 34–35.

Gast, D. L., Wolery, M., Morris, L. L., Doyle, P. M., & Meyer, L. L. (1990). Teaching sight word reading in a group instructional arrangement using constant time delay. *Exceptionality, 1*, 81–96.

Johnson, J. L., Flanagan, K., Burge, M. E., Kauffman-Debriere, S., & Spellman, C. R. (1980). Interactive individualized instruction with small groups of severely handicapped students. *Educational and Training of the Mentally Retarded, 4*, 230–236.

Kameenui, E. J., & Simmons, D. A. (1990). *Designing instructional strategies: The prevention of academic learning problems.* New York: Merrill.

Kamps, D. M., Dugan, E. P., Leonard, B. R., & Daoust, P. M. (1994). Enhanced small group instruction using choral responding and student interactions for children with autism and developmental disabilities. *American Journal on Mental Retardation, 99*(1), 60–73.

Kamps, D., Walker, D., Maher, J., & Rotholz, D. (1992). Academic and environmental effects of small group arrangements in classrooms for students with autism and other developmental disabilities. *Journal of Autism and Developmental Disorders, 22*(2), 277–293.

Karsh, K. G., & Repp, A. C. (1992). The Task Demonstration Model: A concurrent model for teaching groups of students with severe disabilities. *Exceptional Children, 59*, 54–67.

Oliver, P. (1983). Effect of teaching different tasks in group vs. individual training formats with severely handicapped individuals. *Journal of the Association for Persons with Severe Handicaps, 8*, 79–91.

Oliver, P. R., & Scott, T. L. (1981). Group versus individual training in establishing generalization of language skills with severely handicapped individuals. *Mental Retardation, 19*, 285–289.

Orelove, F. P. (1982). Acquisition of incidental learning in moderately and severely handicapped adults. *Education and Training of the Mentally Retarded, 17*, 131–136.

Ranieri, L., Ford, A., Vincent, L., & Brown, L. (1984). 1:1 vs. 1:3 instruction of severely multihandicapped students. *Remedial and Special Education, 5*, 23–28.

Reid, D. H., & Favell, J. E. (1984). Group instruction with persons who have severe disabilities: A critical review. *Journal of the Association for Persons with Severe Handicaps, 9*, 167–177.

Repp, A. C., & Karsh, K. G. (1992). An analysis of a group teaching procedure for persons with developmental disabilities. *Journal of Applied Behavior Analysis, 25*, 701–712.

Repp, A. C., Karsh, K. G., & Lenz, M. W. (1990). Discrimination training for persons with developmental disabilities: A comparison of the Task Demonstration Model and the Standard Prompting Hierarchy. *Journal of Applied Behavior Analysis, 23*, 43–52.

Storm, R. H., & Willis, J. H. (1978). Small-group training as an alternative to individual programs for profoundly retarded persons. *American Journal of Mental Deficiency, 83*, 283–288.

Westling, D. L., Ferrell, K., & Swenson, K. (1982). Intraclassroom comparison of two arrangements for teaching profoundly mentally retarded children. *American Journal of Mental Deficiency, 86*, 601–608.

Wildman, B. G., Wildman, H. E., & Kelly, W. J. (1986). Group conversational skills training and social validation with mentally retarded adults. *Applied Research in Mental Retardation, 1*, 443–458.

Wolery, M., Ault, M. J., Gast, D. L., Doyle, P. M., & Mills, B. M. (1990). The use of choral and individual spelling attentional responses in teaching sight word reading during small group instruction. *Remedial and Special Education, 11*, 47–58.

Beyond Acquisition: Teaching Generalization for Students with Developmental Disabilities

CHAPTER 12

Andrea Rosenthal-Malek and Arlene Bloom

Learning Outcomes

After reading this chapter, you should be able to

- Compare and contrast the cognitive and behavioral views on learning and generalization.

- Describe the four stages of learning, emphasizing the generalization phase.

- Describe a variety of behavioral probes that could be used to identify problems students have with generalization of newly learned skills and identify various behavioral strategies that would alleviate these problems.

- Identify the characteristics of the sensory registers, short-term memory, and long-term memory.

- Describe the three cognitive processes that help transfer information from the short-term memory store to the long-term memory store.

- Explain various best and effective practice approaches for generalization from both a behavioral and a cognitive perspective.

- Devise your own eclectic model of training for generalization.

TERMS

The following terms are important for the understanding of this chapter:

Cognitive processes: Internal actions that transform information, then transfer the information from one memory store to another.

Cognitive strategies: Cognitive operations, over and above the processes directly involved in carrying out a task, that help the student to attack a problem more effectively.

Encoding: The process of forming mental representations that are based on the critical features of a learning task.

Executive competence: A student's effectiveness in receiving, sorting, and processing information and in generating effective strategies. Specific competencies include planning, analyzing, monitoring, modifying, and evaluating.

Generalization (behavioral view): Responses given to similar but not identical stimuli that occur as a result of reinforcement. These responses can take place in different settings, or with different people or materials, or at a different time.

Generalization (cognitive view): The spontaneous use of a cognitive strategy in a unique situation.

Learning (behavioral view): An enduring change in observable behavior that occurs when the environment acts on learners.

Learning (cognitive view): A change in a student's mental structures that gives them the capacity to demonstrate changes in behavior.

Long-term memory: The permanent memory store from which information is able to be retrieved for reference use.

Metacognition: The awareness and monitoring of one's own thinking processes.

Rehearsal: The process of repeating information over and over, without altering its form, either aloud or mentally.

Self-regulation: The conscious use of cognitive strategies for encoding without directions from the teacher.

(continues)

Sensory registers: A memory store that holds an exact copy of stimuli for a very brief period of time and selects information that needs further processing.

Short-term memory: A memory store (commonly called working memory) where memory is held briefly until

forgotten or processed further and transferred to long-term memory.

Introduction

Many students with mild developmental disabilities and most students with moderate or severe developmental disabilities have difficulty transferring or generalizing newly learned skills from one context to another (Hunt & Marshall, 1994). In fact, although educators have successfully demonstrated the ability to teach social, functional, and academic skills to students with developmental disabilities, many of these newly learned skills are not generalized beyond the training situation (Blackhurst & Berline, 1993).

Generalization is considered important because the true purpose of teaching a new skill is to offer a person the means of adapting the skill to new situations, solving novel problems, and using the skill in different settings (Stainback, Stainback, & Strathe, 1983). Further, it is commonly accepted that the ability to generalize learned skills and strategies is an essential component to intellectual normalcy (Blackman & Lin, 1984). Therefore, researchers are now realizing that the teaching of generalization should not be left to chance and that, if generalization is to be achieved, strategies that promote generalization must be incorporated into a continuum of learning opportunities (Haring, 1988; Schloss & Schloss, 1985).

Although most professionals in the field of developmental disabilities agree that generalization should be directly trained, the specific approaches to the training are still a matter of discussion (Stokes & Osnes, 1988). Both behavioral and cognitive theorists believe that generalization of learned skills is embedded into the concept of learning and that, to understand the generalization process, it is important to understand how the learning process works (Eggen & Kauchak, 1994). However, each group of theorists views learning from a different perspective. Therefore, each group has a different view of generalization (Seifert, 1991). Various aspects of generalization from the behavioral, cognitive, and eclectic traditions are discussed in the remainder of this chapter.

Behavioral View of Learning and Generalization

Behavioral theorists emphasize what learners do. They examine observable signs of change and minimize the importance of the internal processes that might underlie behavior or

skills. They emphasize conditioning, stimulus–response, and reinforcement. More specifically, proponents of behaviorally oriented instruction view knowledge as being separated into components and taught by practice and reinforcement. Generally, learners are viewed as the recipients of knowledge given to them by the teacher.

Generalization from a behavioral perspective has been defined as responses given to similar but not identical stimuli that occur as a result of reinforcement (Eggen & Kauchak, 1994). In other words, generalization often refers to the application of a learned skill or strategy to a task structure that has been significantly altered, where the task and/or the demands and/or the materials have been changed (Blackman & Lin, 1984). It is felt that the closer the generalization is to the learning situation, the more chance for transfer. Generalization can take place in both the academic and the social domains. An example of generalization across persons in the academic or functional skill domain would be the ability to orally count to 10 when asked by a teacher who did not train the student. An example of generalization across settings in the social skills domain would be when the student who has learned to make successful overtures to another student in the classroom uses the same overtures in the gym.

More specifically, a number of theorists (e.g., Meese, 1994) conceptualize generalization as part of the stages of the learning process. According to Meese (1994), as students progress from a total lack of knowledge or limited knowledge of a skill, to knowing how to use the skill proficiently in differing contexts, they typically pass through four basic stages of learning; acquisition, proficiency, maintenance, and finally generalization. The following is a discussion of the four stages of learning and how these stages relate to the teaching of new skills.

Stages of the Learning Process

Acquisition is the initial stage of learning. At this stage, the student has either little or no knowledge of the skill and is not able to perform the skill without teacher assistance. During this stage, instruction is interactive and teacher directed. The teacher poses questions and gives the students many opportunities to correctly answer the questions. For example, if a student's long-term goal on his Individualized Education Program (IEP) was to count to 10 and at this point he could count only to 3 consistently, he would be considered at the acquisition stage of learning to count to 10. To teach the student to count to 10, the teacher would first ascertain exactly how far the student could count consistently, and then plan sequential direct instructional lessons focused on the short-term goal of counting to 10.

The *proficiency* stage of learning is the stage at which the students develop the ability to consistently use the newly learned skill automatically and fluently. At the onset of the proficiency stage, students perform the new skill but still make numerous errors and respond hesitantly. They often require much independent drill and practice until they become proficient in the newly learned skill. Instruction at this stage is still interactive. However, at this point, students may work with the paraprofessional or peer tutors for rehearsal of the newly learned skill.

The *maintenance* stage of learning is the stage at which the student is able to successfully complete the skill over time. This stage is essential because, once a student becomes proficient with a new skill, he or she must be able to maintain the information over time with little or no teacher assistance. At this stage the teacher offers periodic review or practice of the skill in order that the student maintain accuracy and speed. The review is often in the form of independent seatwork, homework, or group projects.

Generalization, the final stage of learning, has been defined as responses given to similar but not identical stimuli that occur as a result of reinforcement. During the generalization phase, the student appropriately uses the newly learned skill in novel situations, with different materials, or with new people. For example, in the previously mentioned skill of counting to 10, the student would be able to count to 10 no matter what adult requested him to do so, or in whatever room he was requested to do so. Unfortunately, students with developmental disabilities do not pass through these stages automatically (Meese, 1994). To enhance generalization, the behavioral teacher needs to specifically plan for each learning stage, changing instructional objectives and methods as students progress through the stages, while continuing to use behavioral techniques that promote generalization throughout the process (Haring, 1988; Meese, 1994; Wolery, Bailey, & Sugai, 1988). Behavioral theorists believe that generalization objectives should be written into all stages of learning, including the acquisition stage. They feel that an objective cannot be considered mastered unless the behavior is performed fluently with someone other than the person doing the training, in different settings, and in naturally occurring situations (Haring, 1988). Thus, behaviorists feel that teachers have a direct role in the training of generalization.

The Teacher's Role in Generalization Training: A Behavioral View

Traditionally, both academic and social skills generalization training for students with developmental disabilities has relied on developing discrete skills by using specific behavioral techniques, then either hoping or directly training for generalization by using various behavioral techniques (Haring, 1988). Because of the lack of success with this approach, some researchers from the behavioral tradition (Haring, 1988; Meese, 1994) have advocated the direct training of generalization throughout the entire learning process.

Effective Practice: A Behavioral Approach for Teaching Generalization

An effective behavioral approach that directly trains for generalization of newly learned skills from the onset of instruction was developed by Matlock, Lynch, and Paeth (1990a, 1990b), based on the research of Haring (1988). The program was developed for students with severe disabilities, but could be modified for students with higher skill levels. This program is based on the premise that generalization is the most critical phase of learning and, therefore, should be incorporated into all stages of the training.

In this model, there are five basic stages of generalization training: IEP development, assessment for generalization, assessment of the environment, strategy implementation to promote generalization, and ongoing evaluation of progress. In the first stage, formulation of the IEP objectives, the teacher (in conjunction with the IEP team) develops and incorporates the generalization objective during the acquisition stage of the training. This entails choosing the generalization objective from the onset of instruction and writing the generalization objective concurrently with the acquisition objective. One suggestion made by Matlock et al. (1990b) is to write the word "instruction" in parentheses after the phrase that discusses the instructional conditions, and to write the word "generalization" in parentheses after the generalization condition. For example, using the objective of orally counting to 10, the generalization objective would read, "The student will orally count to 10 when requested by the teacher (instruction) as well as when requested by a teacher who was not involved in the original training (generalization) with 80% accuracy." During the proficiency phase, the words "without hesitation" and "100% accuracy" would be added to the IEP. Proficiency (fluency) objectives are usually written prior to a terminal (acceptable level of competence to function under varied demand situations) generalization objective.

Once the behavioral objective is written, the next step is to conduct generalization probes. These probes assess whether the student is performing, as well as generalizing, the desired skill. A generalization probe is an assessment procedure that determines the use of a skill outside the instructional situation. The purpose of a probe is to use the information to make any necessary changes in the instructional procedures. Although the purpose of probes is identical to the purpose of assessments, there is a slight difference between assessment and probes. In probes, the teacher is assessing in some situation where he or she did not teach, with a person who did not teach the skill, using materials the original lesson did not use or testing at a different time, and so on. In other words, a probe assesses something, somewhere, or somehow that the teacher did not teach. To be considered a probe, at least one of the above-mentioned situations must be different from the original instruction.

To probe students with more severe developmental disabilities for generalization, the teacher would change only one condition at a time, whereas for students with mild developmental disabilities, the teacher may want to probe all three areas at once. For example, a student with profound disabilities who is being taught to sip liquid through a straw by the occupational therapist would be requested to sip liquid through a straw by the special education teacher, but all other conditions would remain the same.

On the other hand, a student with mild developmental disabilities may be taught by the special education teacher to kick a ball while playing with other students with disabilities in the gym. A generalization probe may take place in the school yard with a regular education teacher while the student is mainstreamed with students who are not disabled. To conduct a probe, the teacher can either ask the student, observe the student, or have someone else observe the student to obtain the desired information.

If the student is not successful at performing the generalization objective, the teacher must assess where the deficiency lies. In this model, three major areas are assessed: the time when the deficiency arises (either before, during, or after the response), the stimuli that may be affecting the response (positive, negative, or neutral), and the natural environmental variables (in either the generalized condition or the instruction condition) that may be affecting the response. Examples of specific problems that might occur during the generalization phase, as well as strategies that could be used to alleviate these problems, are listed in Table 12.1.

If the problem is not identified in the generalization phase, then the teacher should examine steps in the instructional phase. For example, the student may not have fully acquired the skill well enough to generalize it, or the reinforcers or schedule of reinforcement the teacher uses may not be available in the generalization situation. In short, by analyzing specific instructional stages, the teacher is better able to use strategies that will enhance generalization.

The final stage of the program, which actually is ongoing, is the evaluation of the effectiveness of strategies and the altering of any strategy that is ineffective. In other words, strategies can be added or dropped depending on their success.

Generalization Issues

Although professionals from the behavioral tradition have successfully trained specific skills to students with develop-

Table 12.1

Examples of Generalization Problems and Strategies that Would Be Used to Alleviate the Problems

General Problems	Strategies to Solve Problems
Limited generalization situation	Train in the target situation
Discrimination	Use frequent stimuli (examine generalization situation and select stimuli that occurs most frequently in the generalization condition)
	Use multiple exemplars (examine generalization situation, then select those stimuli that occur most frequently)
Competing behavior	Increase performance criterion for target skill (consider using adaptive equipment or add to or change the behavior in the training setting)
	Alter generalization contingencies (train people in the generalization situation to allow only new behavior to access reinforcer)
Competing or noncontingent reinforcer	Alter generalization contingencies
Reinforcing function	Introduce reinforcer that naturally occurs in generalization situation into training situation
	Use natural schedules (examine generalization situation and identify natural schedules of reinforcers, then provide the same natural schedule during training)
	Use natural consequences (in the training situation, introduce consequences that occur naturally in generalization situation)
	Teach self-reinforcement

mental disabilities, contradictory research results exist regarding the generalization of the trained skills, even when direct instruction for generalization was employed (Misra, 1992; Whitman, 1990). Despite the contradictory research results regarding generalization, many professionals from the cognitive tradition state that students with developmental disabilities can be taught to successfully generalize newly learned academic skills (Blackman & Lin, 1984; Lin, Blackman, Clark, & Gordon, 1983) and newly learned social skills (Rosenthal-Malek, 1997; Rosenthal-Malek & Yoshida, 1994).

In order to enhance generalization, cognitive theorists (e.g., Pressley, Burkell, et al., 1990; Sheid, 1993) have attempted to expand the concept of learning and generalization from focusing on observable behavior and manipulation of environmental variables to identifying the underlying mechanisms that produce the learning and generalization (Burger, Blackman, & Clark, 1981). These theorists focus their investigations on the processes students use to obtain, organize, and store information. Cognitive theories of learning and generalization are discussed in the following section.

Cognitive View of Learning and Generalization

In contrast to behavioral theorists, cognitive theorists focus on the relationships between a student's actions and his or her thoughts. The cognitive theories differ from behavioral theories of learning in that they do not emphasize observable behavior, conditioning, stimulus–response, or reinforcement, but rather emphasize attention, memory, recognition, meaning, organization of ideas, and information processing (Seifert, 1991).

Cognitive learning theories have been defined as "explanations for learning that focus on the internal mental processes people use in their effort to make sense out of the world" (Eggen & Kauchak, 1994, p. 305). Further, proponents of cognitively oriented instruction view learning as a process in which the students are responsible for constructing meaning from information and for controlling their own learning processes through application of learning strategies (Sheid, 1993). These processes can be used for complex problem solving or simple decisions, such as "Do I need a fork or spoon to eat this piece of cake?"

Generalization from a cognitive perspective has been defined as the spontaneous use of a cognitive strategy in a unique situation (Eggen & Kauchak, 1994). Transfer or generalization ranges on a continuum from closely related (specific transfer) to basically unrelated (general transfer). For example, specific transfer takes place when a student answers questions on a test that are similar to questions previously discussed in class, or when students use an appropriate social skill in the lunchroom that had been taught in the classroom. General transfer, on the other hand, takes place when a student applies previously learned knowledge to a unique situation (e.g., when the student says, "Hmmm, isn't this problem similar to the one we did the other day?"). As is probably obvious, specific transfer is much more likely to occur than general transfer and is also much easier to teach.

The goal of teachers using the cognitive approach is to make generalization or transfer as general and meaningful as possible (Brown & Kane, 1988). The more associations between the items to be stored in long-term memory, the more likely the newly learned skills will generalize. Thus, generalization depends on the students' ability to access and connect information in the long-term memory store (Prawat, 1989).

This section discusses cognitively oriented learning theories, their relation to generalization, and their application to teaching. The section is divided into three major areas. The first subsection focuses on theoretical concepts of the information processing theories (because of their relevance to generalization). This subsection focuses specifically on the information stores of memory, the cognitive processing, and the metacognitive processes. Included in this subsection is a discussion on the developmental aspects of cognitive and metacognitive ability and their relationship to students with developmental disabilities. The second subsection looks at use of both cognitive and metacognitive strategies and their relationship to generalization. The third subsection focuses on the teacher's role in the facilitation of generalization through strategy training. This subsection includes general guidelines for strategy instruction, examples of cognitive strategies that would help promote generalization, and an example of an effective metacognitive strategy training program.

Information Processing Theory

The most widely accepted of the cognitive theories is the information processing theories, which range from relatively general descriptions of processing strategies (Miller, Galanter, & Pribram, 1960) to fine-grained analyses of processing programs that simulate behavior in a task (Klahr & Wallace, 1972; Simon & Newell, 1971). The theories conceive of the human mind as a system, like a computer, and draw a parallel between computer processing and human cognition. Researchers in the area have been concerned with tracing the flow of information through the system. They describe cognition in terms such as input, processing, subroutine, and feedback. Their emphasis is on process rather than information, and they look at cognition as knowing how to perform a task. They assume that people control their internal behavior of thinking by programs and subroutines or strategies that are stored in long-term memory and are modifiable (Simon, 1972).

The information processing model described here represents one current view of the manner in which the mind processes and remembers information (Eggen & Kauchak, 1994). This model contains three component parts: the information stores, the cognitive processes, and the metacognitive and executive processes. The model is derived from the work of several theorists, including Atkinson and Shiffrin (1968) and Simon (1972). A graphic representation of the manner in which students process information is shown in Figure 12.1. Although all the components act in coordination with each other, each component part of this model is discussed separately for better understanding.

Information Stores

The three information areas—the sensory registers, the working or short-term memory, and the long-term memory—are

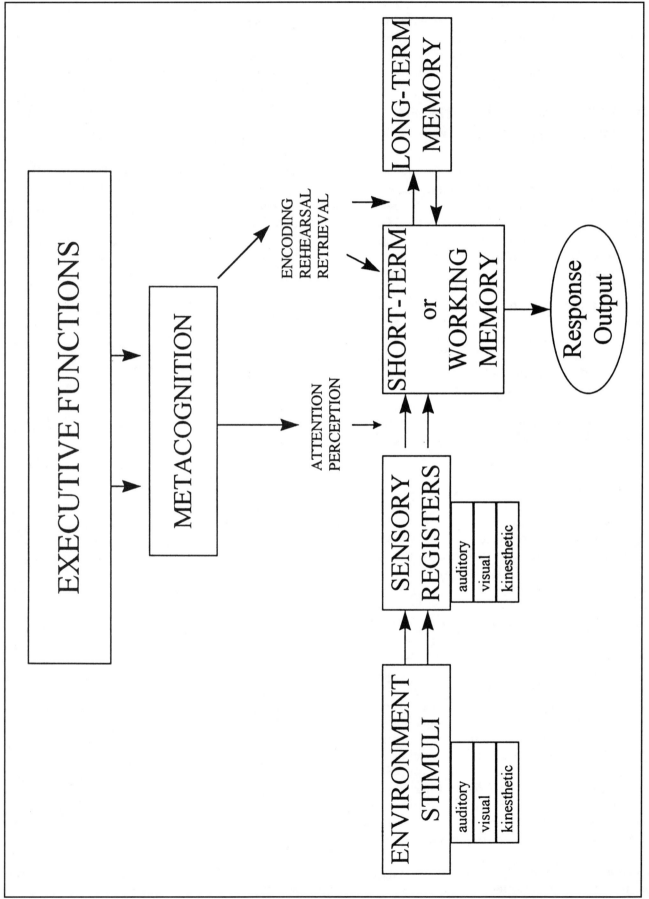

Figure 12.1. An example of an information processing model.

used to hold or store information. These stores have been compared to the storage units (the central processing unit and the hard drive) in a computer. The sensory registers are the information stores that receive stimuli from the environment and hold an exact copy of the stimuli for a brief period of time (about 1 second for visual information and about 4 seconds for auditory information) (Moates & Schumacher, 1980). In general, either the information is lost or the sensory registers hold the information, through the use of the cognitive processes of attention and perception, just long enough for the student to recognize and transfer it into the second information store, short-term or working memory.

In short-term or working memory, conscious thinking and processing of information take place. Because short-term memory is very sensitive to interference or interruptions, information is held for only about 20 seconds. Either a response is elicited immediately, or the information is lost, or the information is transferred by the cognitive processes of rehearsal, encoding, and retrieval into the long-term memory store. However, information is transferred only if the information is important and meaningful, or has been actively rehearsed.

Long-term memory is the permanent information store in which memory capacity is unlimited (Ashcraft, 1989). Long-term memory has been compared with a library of millions of entries and a network (learning strategies) that allows the entries to be retrieved for use. Most learning strategies are stored in long-term memory but operate in short-term memory. In other words, students, including those with developmental disabilities, transfer memories that are needed at the moment out of long-term memory, through the process of retrieval, back into short-term memory where it elicits a response. Thus, for all students, the effectiveness or limitations of information processing depend on the contents, limitations, and capabilities of both short-term and long-term memory (Rafoth, Leal, & DeFabo, 1993).

Cognitive Processes

The cognitive processes are the processes that transfer information from one information store to another. Five processes—attention, perception, rehearsal, encoding, and retrieval—make up these cognitive processes (Eggen & Kauchak, 1994). Although attention and perception are important aspects of the information processing system, and students with developmental disabilities have been shown to be deficient in these processes (Morrison & Polloway, 1995), this chapter focuses on the latter three processes because of their relevance to generalization. The three cognitive processes of rehearsal, encoding, and retrieval all aid in the transfer of information from the short-term store to the long-term store and, through retrieval, back again to the short-term or working memory store.

The cognitive process of *rehearsal* involves the repeating of information over and over, either mentally or out loud, without altering the form (Eggen & Kauchak, 1994). Rehearsal has two functions, retention of short-term memory and transfer into long-term memory. When a student repeats a telephone number over and over immediately before dialing, the student is retaining information in the short-term memory for immediate use. On the other hand, when a student repeats the multiplication tables over and over again, the student is transferring information into the long-term store for future recall.

The process of *encoding* addresses the issue of meaningfulness and organization. Specifically, encoding is the process of forming mental pictures based on the critical features of the learning task, organizing the information, and putting the information into a meaningful context (Seifert, 1991). Encoding is accomplished by using information that already exists in long-term memory and attaching new information to the old. Meaningful encoding is the opposite of rote learning by repetition, in which no meaning is attached to the newly learned material. A number of strategies that put together meaning where there is none include organizational strategies, such as graphic organizers, and mnemonic devices, such as the key word method. These strategies, as well as others, are discussed in detail in the effective cognitive strategies section of this chapter.

The cognitive process of *retrieval* involves the accessing of information from either the short-term or the long-term memory store and transferring to the other memory store. Lack of retrieval has been compared with placing files in a folder but not remembering where the folder has been placed. Once the folder is found, all the information is retrieved. Many researchers believe that students, including those with developmental disabilities, have not forgotten the information but do not know from where to retrieve it (Ashcraft, 1989).

Metacognitive and Executive Processes

The discussion up to this point has given general explanations of how students store, rehearse, encode, and retrieve information—in other words, how a student thinks. The metacognitive and executive processes, which comprise the third component of the information processing system, regulate and control the other cognitive processes and are essential for generalization. In actuality, these two processes are used in conjunction with each other, but are discussed separately for better understanding.

The concept of metacognition was originally proposed by Flavell (1976) to explain why students of different ages approach learning tasks in different ways. In contrast to cognition, which essentially refers to the ways in which information is processed (Seifert, 1991), metacognition refers to the students' knowledge about those operations and about how they might best be used to achieve a learning goal (Flavell, 1976). In other words, the cognitive processes are not simple mechanisms that automatically turn on or off. As students develop, they learn to understand and control these mechanisms through the use of metacognitive strategies.

Specifically, metacognition refers to one's knowledge concerning one's own cognitive processes and products or anything related to them (Flavell, 1976). In other words, a student with intact metacognitive awareness is one who is aware of the capacity of his or her own cognitive system in relation to the complexity of problems with which he or she is faced. An example in the social domain is when a lesson has started and the student realizes that she must stop daydreaming and pay attention to what is being said. An example of metacognition in the academic or functional domain is when a student perceives that he has learned A better than B, or realizes that he needs to double-check his answer on a task before he accepts the answer as correct (Flavell, 1976).

Metacognition, as Flavell (1976) proposed, involves knowledge of person variables, task variables, and strategy variables. Knowing that one learns mathematics material better than verbal material is an example of a person variable. Being aware that reading a selection comprised only of words is more difficult to comprehend than a selection containing few words and more pictures is an example of a task variable. An example of a strategy variable is knowing that rereading, reading, or slowing down one's pace will enhance one's ability to comprehend unfamiliar concepts. In short, metacognition is a very broad concept that covers everything a student can know that relates to how he or she processes information.

Executive competence has much in common with the concept of metacognition. In practice, many educators incorporate the concept of executive competence into the definition of metacognition, as the two are hard to separate (Bronson, 1984).

Specifically, executive competence is seen as the processes that are responsible for the regulation and marshalling of the other cognitive processes (Butterfield & Belmont, 1977; Lezak, 1982). These executive processes keep track of what the mind has learned, know where to look for the best solutions, and recognize when a problem has been solved. In other words, the executive functions comprise those mental capacities that are essential for formulating goals, planning the achievement of these goals, and carrying out the plans effectively (Bronson, 1985).

Authors (e.g., Butterfield & Belmont, 1977; Lawson, 1984) involved in the study of executive functioning have focused on five major types of executive activities: planning, analysis, monitoring, modification, and evaluation. Each of these is considered to be directly involved in the control of other cognitive processes during performance of a task or

during interpersonal socialization (Lawson, 1984). These skills are considered transituational and thus lend themselves to automatic generalization. In fact, a number of theorists (e.g., Brown, 1987) believe that problems with generalization are due to problems with metacognition and executive functioning.

Cognitive and Metacognitive Learning Strategies: The Link Between Theory and Practice

Although the cognitive processes play a major role in generalization, these processes do not become activated automatically, especially with students who are developmentally disabled (Pressley & McCormick, 1995). Learning strategies are often needed to activate the cognitive processes in order to help students move information from one memory store to another, as well as aid students in attacking a problem more effectively (Eggen & Kauchak, 1994).

Cognitive learning strategies have been defined as cognitive operations over and above the processes directly involved in carrying out a task (Pressley, Burkell, et al., 1990). Strategies apply cognitive theories to concrete learning tasks. They are potentially conscious and controllable activities and achieve cognitive purposes such as memorizing. In other words, cognitive learning strategies are general methods of thinking that promote learning in a variety of situations (Pressley & McCormick, 1995).

For example, decoding the words in a reading passage and reading from front to back would not be considered learning strategies because these activities are considered essential activities for the successful completion of the task. There are, however, many reading-related activities that would be considered learning strategies. For example, students might skim a story before actually reading it, ask questions to themselves regarding specific outcomes, or self-test themselves for recall. In short, all the processes that a student executes that are over and above simply decoding words and reading from front to back are considered learning strategies (Pressley & McCormick, 1995).

These learning strategies are important to generalization because they are ways of increasing students' chances of transferring information between short- and long-term memory stores and, thus, increasing the chances for generalization (Seifert, 1991). In fact, according to Wong (1985), the primary reason for the current interest in teaching cognitive learning strategies is the assertion that strategy training may constitute one of the key ingredients in achieving generalization.

It is important to remember, however, that teaching a student how to carry out a strategy does not ensure that the student understands how the strategy benefits performance. It is this understanding of strategy benefits (metacognitive and executive awareness) that ensures that students will continue to use a strategy-following instruction and will, thus, generalize the strategy to unique situations. In other words, cognitive strategy training without metacognitive and executive skill training may not ensure generalization (Pressley & McCormick, 1995).

Developmental Aspects of Cognitive and Metacognitive Strategy Use

Because cognitive and metacognitive strategy training has been shown to be related to developmental age (Pressley & McCormick, 1995), this section discusses the developmental aspects of cognitive and metacognitive strategy use. The understanding that children move through stages of development at different rates derives from Piaget's (1951) work. In that sufficient short-term memory capacity is needed to carry out strategies, the ability to use cognitive and metacognitive learning strategies develops through stages as do other skills. The student's developmental progress depends on genetic potential, maturation, and the opportunities that the student has to experience the world. In short, cognitive development affects the student's ability to use both cognitive and metacognitive strategies (Pressley & McCormick, 1995).

In fact, reviews of the literature on cognitive and metacognitive strategy use indicate that the use of these strategies follows a developmental sequence. Specifically, the use of memory strategies has been shown to follow a developmental pattern by age for children without disabilities (Rafoth et al., 1993). For example, by the age of 2, children independently display preliminary memory strategy use. They use simple, direct strategies that require little processing time. They use either pointing, looking, or naming when asked to remember objects, their locations, or events (Baker-Ward, Ornstein, & Holden, 1984; DeLoache, Cassidy, & Brown, 1985). Rehearsal strategies undergo developmental changes as well. For example, younger children rehearse one item at a time, whereas older children tend to use more sophisticated rehearsal strategies such as combining the items into sets (Ornstein, Naus, & Liberty, 1975).

Researchers (e.g., Kail, 1984) have also shown that metacognitive and executive strategy use develop with age. For example, studies of younger and older students without disabilities (Duell, 1986) indicated differences in metacognitive awareness and the use of executive strategies. Specifically, the older students were able to use more sophisticated strategies than the younger students.

The obvious implication of this research for students with developmental disabilities is the question of whether or not individual students will gain any benefits from cognitive or metacognitive strategy instruction at specific chronological or mental age levels. Some professionals believe that cog-

nitive and metacognitive strategies should be beneficial for students with mild developmental disabilities but that students with moderate or severe disabilities may never reach the cognitive level at which strategy training would become widely beneficial (Hickson, Blackman, & Reis, 1995). However, other professionals (Rosenthal-Malek & Yoshida, 1994) disagree and feel that limited cognitive and metacognitive strategy training is appropriate for students with moderate developmental disabilities who are functioning at least at a mental age of 3 years (this is the same chronological age that children without developmental disabilities begin to use simple strategies). In other words, the barometer of the ability to use a specific strategy lies in the student's mental age rather than the classification of mild or moderate developmental disabilities (Rosenthal-Malek & Yoshida, 1994).

Although students with developmental disabilities have trouble at all levels of the cognitive process, this section of the chapter focuses primarily on the area of memory and use of strategies because of their relevance to generalization. Research has shown that most students with developmental disabilities have difficulty with memory, particularly with attention, short-term memory, and the strategies necessary to enhance short-term memory (Hunt & Marshall, 1994; Morrison & Polloway, 1995). Although controversy surrounds the issue of exactly where students with developmental disabilities have most of their problems, most cognitive researchers and theorists agree that the major deficiency lies in transferring information between the memory stores and in metacognitive and executive ability (Morrison & Polloway, 1995).

Researchers have studied the use of strategies by children with developmental disabilities compared with that of children without disabilities. Specifically, researchers have found that, whereas many children without disabilities successfully use cognitive or metacognitive strategies with or without training, children with developmental disabilities appear to not use appropriate cognitive or metacognitive strategies unless specifically trained to do so (Brown, 1987).

In addition, children with mild developmental disabilities use memory strategies similar to those of younger children without disabilities (Brown & Barclay, 1976; Wong & Wilson, 1984). Younger children without disabilities and children with developmental disabilities generally know fewer strategies and have little awareness of when and how to use the strategies that they know (Rafoth et al., 1993). Further, it has been found that children with disabilities use strategies only when asked to remember or when the object is familiar (Schneider & Sodian, 1988).

Researchers also have looked at the ability of students with developmental disabilities to monitor their own cognitive processes, that is, to use metacognitive and executive processes. In fact, investigators involved in metacognitive and executive functioning (e.g., Brown, 1987; Butterfield &

Belmont, 1977) believe that students with developmental disabilities possess the ability required for competent performance, but lack the spontaneous access to the processes needed to coordinate specific abilities. In other words, they are lacking metacognitive and executive ability. Further, some researchers (e.g., Brown, 1987) feel that most academic and some of the life skills difficulties of individuals with developmental disabilities are related to dysfunctions in metacognitive and executive skill capabilities. However, although students with developmental disabilities do not use metacognitive and executive skills automatically, it is felt that these students are capable of being trained in these skills (Brown, 1987; Butterfield & Belmont, 1977; Rosenthal-Malek & Yoshida, 1994) and that it is the teacher's responsibility to train these skills.

The Teacher's Role in Facilitating Generalization: Teaching Cognitive Strategies

Unlike behavioral strategy training, in which the teacher promotes learning and the students are the recipients, cognitive strategy training assumes that learners are mentally active and construct their own understanding. It has as its ultimate goal the self-regulation of learning by students. Students need to be self-confident that they are able to control their own cognitive performance and learn effectively. Although it is the teacher's role to facilitate these feelings of confidence and the ability to self-regulate, in the end the student must take responsibility for his or her own learning. In short, the goal of cognitive strategy instruction is for self-regulated learners to be able to select, apply, monitor, and assess the effectiveness of strategies so that they can use appropriate strategies for a specific task as well as generalize them to other learning tasks (Pressley, Burkell, et al., 1990; Sheid, 1993).

Teachers using cognitive strategies should consider a number of issues when applying strategy training. The appropriate location of the strategy training is one consideration. Research has shown that when cognitive strategy training takes place outside of the classroom or is not integrated with the subject matter, generalization does not take place (Blackman, Burger, Tan, & Weiner, 1982; Blackman & Lin, 1984). In other words, effective cognitively oriented instruction should take place in the student's classroom and be integrated into the curriculum (embedded strategies approach), rather than being taught in isolation (detached strategy training approach).

Another consideration for the teacher is the specific techniques to be used for effective strategy training. Rafoth et al., (1993, p. 71) presented a helpful mnemonic method for teaching strategies effectively:

M - Model the strategy; explain how to carry it out
I - Inform the students about when and how to use it
R - Remind the students to use the strategy

R - Repeat the strategy; practice, practice, practice
O - Outline the strategy's usefulness via constant feedback
R - Reassess the student's performance as a result of using the strategy
S - Stress strategy generalization

From a pragmatic point of view, models of how to teach strategies differ somewhat but generally include the steps delineated in MIRRORS, as well as the following components (Pressley, Burkell, et al., 1990; Rafoth et al., 1993; Sheid, 1993).

1. Teach a few strategies at a time thoroughly as part of the academic curriculum.

2. Model monitoring performance of strategy use.

3. Incorporate assessment throughout instruction and modify students' application through appropriate feedback based on this ongoing assessment.

4. Teach students to monitor how they are doing when they use strategies.

5. If necessary, repeat above steps if students do not appear to understand the strategy use.

6. Motivate students to use strategies by providing explicit information about the usefulness of the strategies and its promise for improving their functioning.

7. Provide consistent feedback about students' improved performance due to strategy use.

In addition to the previously mentioned techniques, the strategy of scaffolding is useful for cognitively oriented teachers. Specifically, scaffolding is defined as the framework or the support that adults provide for students' learning (Feinburg & Mindess, 1994). To better understand scaffolding, it is helpful to visualize a physical scaffold used when a building is being constructed. As the building becomes self-supporting, the scaffold is gradually removed. In a similar manner, teachers scaffold instruction through adult–child interactions in which, as the student progresses, teacher support is gradually removed. Through careful monitoring, the teacher provides only enough supports and assistance that the student does not fail. The teacher who is using scaffolding techniques attempts to lead the student to important understandings about accomplishing a particular task. Thus, the ultimate goal in scaffolding instruction is that the student will eventually not need any supports and that the control of strategies will gradually be transferred from the teacher to the student (Pressley & McCormick, 1995).

Finally, all strategy programs should be individually developmentally appropriate, that is, used only with students who are functioning at an appropriate mental age for each strategy taught.

Effective Practices: Developing Strategic Learning Capabilities

This section focuses on best and effective practices in the area of cognitive strategy training. Although various strategies are discussed separately for understanding, it is important to keep in mind that they operate interactively. Strategies generally are not used in isolation but are integrated into sequences that accomplish complex cognitive goals (Pressley, Burkell, et al., 1990). For example, a reader may combine strategies such as those for activating prior knowledge, self-questioning, careful reading, and rereading.

Specifically, although cognitive strategies can be used in many subject areas, this effective practice section includes only examples of cognitive strategies designed to develop strategic listening, reading capabilities, and writing capabilities. In addition, the students' level of cognitive development needed to complete a particular task is discussed. In general, those strategies requiring reading or writing ability are best used with students who are functioning at the mild or moderate level and have a minimum mental age of 6 years. Strategies using visual or oral input of information can be used with students who have a minimum mental age of 2 years.

Specifically, integrated multimedia computer programs, videos, oral storytelling, and pictures can be used to facilitate cognitive strategy instruction for students functioning at lower cognitive levels. Color is a salient cue for lower functioning students. It is one of the first taxonomic categories that young students use to organize materials (Rafoth et al., 1993). In presenting cognitive strategy instruction to students with lower mental ages, decreasing the amount of material presented and color-coding information increases students' selective attention to relevant stimuli, thereby promoting successful strategy use even in students with mental ages of 2 years.

The following sections focus specifically on how various learning strategies help teachers and students with developmental disabilities in classroom situations. Examples of strategies that are applicable to students with developmental disabilities are included. In the following effective practice section, the term *higher functioning student* is used to refer to students with developmental disabilities with mental ages above 6 years, whereas *lower functioning students* refers to students with mental ages between 2 and 6 years.

Rehearsal Strategies

Rehearsal strategies attempt to facilitate retention through the use of repeated practice (Seifert, 1991). Rehearsal strategies have obvious benefits for improving recall of both simple information, such as telephone numbers, and more complex information, such as a list of grocery store items. At a very simple level, rehearsal strategies are appropriate for lower functioning students with mild and moderate developmental disabilities. Students under the mental age of 7 years do not spontaneously use rehearsal strategies; however, when instructed, these students are able to use the strategies and memory improves (Glover, Ronning, & Brunning, 1990). Shadowing and verbatim notes are specific examples of rehearsal strategies used in literacy instruction.

Shadowing. Shadowing is a verbal strategy that involves repeatedly reading a selection aloud verbatim. Vocalized thinking, or thinking aloud, is a broader strategy in which the student orally paraphrases or reorganizes ideas from the text (Seifert, 1991). At a lower level, the student would repeat material presented orally verbatim. For example, the student would repeat his or her name and address aloud verbatim.

Verbatim Notes. Verbatim notes is a written strategy that involves copying sections of text. Teachers should monitor students' verbal or written rehearsal to make sure that they do not use rehearsal ineffectively. An example of this might be a student who writes in a column the first letter of a spelling word five times, then the second letter, and so on. Rehearsal must be accurate to be effective.

Encoding and Retrieval

Encoding and retrieval strategies are closely linked because efficient retrieval cannot take place unless the information has been efficiently encoded. In other words, efficient storage facilitates retrieval (Seifert, 1991). Therefore, in the effective practices discussed in this chapter, retrieval strategies are embedded in the encoding strategies. In other words, it is presumed that encoding strategies are necessary for retrieval.

Encoding is possibly the most critical cognitive process. If students did not use the process of encoding, all information would be stored for only a short period of time and would therefore need to be continually relearned (Seigler, 1991).

The encoding strategies are divided into two major categories (a) organization and elaboration and (b) mnemonics. These strategies are best used with higher functioning students with mild developmental disabilities.

Organization and Elaboration. Organization and elaboration are two important encoding strategies. The process of organization involves clustering information into categories or patterns (Eggen & Kauchak, 1994). An example of this is the use of outlining. Elaboration is the process of increasing the number of associations in information either by forming additional links in existing knowledge or by adding new knowledge. Analogies are examples of elaboration. Strategies promoting elaboration and organization are described in the same section because students generally engage in these processes simultaneously.

GRAPHIC ORGANIZERS. A graphic organizer is a visual representation of important aspects of a concept, topic, or unit of study which are identified and arranged in a nonverbal framework with appropriate verbal labels (Bloom, 1991). Graphic organizers can be used for reading or writing and may take various forms, such as story maps or webs and Venn diagrams, that help students understand and recognize patterns and organizations of writing. Organizational strategies may be promoted by having students verbalize how different items and events are similar, different, and the same. An example of a Venn diagram is shown in Figure 12.2. This diagram (Bloom, 1991) depicts an actual dictation to a teacher by a student with developmental disabilities with a mental age of 5 years. The student compared two characters in a story that was read aloud by the teacher. The student then went on to retell the story. Subsequently, pictures were used and, by placing them on a story map, the student again retold the story in sequential order.

Graphic organizers can be used with higher functioning students with both mild and moderate developmental disabilities. Graphic organizers using pictures can be used by lower functioning students. Figure 12.3 is an example of a graphic organizer that can facilitate children's performance in the academic curriculum area of reading. The comprehension of narrative (or storylike) text increases the student's knowledge of story structure. This graphic organizer is designed to promote knowledge of story structure by analyzing narrative text read by the students or to the students with developmental delays. Students analyze text and retell the plot of the story by listing under the appropriate headings information that addresses elements of story structure. Most narratives contain the elements of *characters* (Someone), *plot* (Tried—problem that a character must solve), and different *events* (But) that take place in the story. At the end of the story, there is a *solution* or resolution (So).

The teacher models the use of this strategy and teaches the strategy using appropriate procedures. The more experience students have with comprehending story structure, the more effectively they will generalize this strategy to other narratives.

SEMANTIC MAPPING. Semantic mapping, which is used to enhance vocabulary learning, involves presenting a new vocabulary word to students and having them brainstorm about related vocabulary. See Figure 12.4 for an example of a semantic map that would be appropriate for higher functioning students. With lower functioning students, pictures and integrated multimedia computer programs may be used instead of words to brainstorm about vocabulary or to activate prior knowledge about concepts.

QUESTION–ANSWER RELATIONSHIPS. Question–answer relationships are designed to assist higher functioning students with mild or moderate developmental disabilities who do not know where to find answers to questions about the text. Students are taught to analyze questions to determine whether the answer is stated literally in the text ("right there"), or could be inferred by two or more sentences ("think and search") or by information in the student's knowledge base ("on my own") (Rapheal & McKinney, 1993; Raphael & Pearson, 1985). Students who have a mental age of at least 3 years may use these strategies in response to videos, stories read to them, and pictures or integrated multimedia computer programs.

Mnemonics. Mnemonics are strategies that form associations that do not exist naturally in the content (Eggen & Kauchak, 1994). The following is an example of a mnemonic strategy that could be used with higher functioning students.

THE KEY WORD METHOD. The key word method is a mnemonic strategy based on mental imagery. Research has shown that students with moderate and mild developmental disabilities have benefitted by instruction in this method when pictorial supports are provided (Scruggs, Mastropieri, & Levin, 1985).

The key word method facilitates associative aspects of learning, such as learning associations between new vocabulary words and their meaning. This strategy uses a key word mediator to facilitate remembering. It consists of two stages, an "acoustic-link" stage and an "imagery-link" stage (Pressley, Levin, & McDaniel, 1987). A key word can be a word that sounds similar (e.g., *pencil* for *Pennsylvania*), is spelled in a similar manner (e.g., *cat* for *cart*), or is part of the actual word to be learned (e.g., *car* for *carpet*). During the imagery-link stage, the student forms a visual image in which the key word and the definition interact.

RHYMES. Mnemonic poems are commonly used to remember information that is essentially arbitrary. For example, many children are taught the following poem about the duration of the months: "Thirty days hath September, April, June and November . . ." Using rhymes and rhythmic activities will improve memory as students recite their spelling words, number facts, or other information. Less mature students could be taught to identify their fingers with a rhythmic activity such as "Where is Thumbkin." Commercially prepared audiotapes and videotapes that present information about the alphabet, numerals, and other content may be used in presenting cognitive strategy instruction appropriate for lower functioning students. Using rhymes and rhythmic activities will improve memory as students recite their spelling words, number facts, or other information.

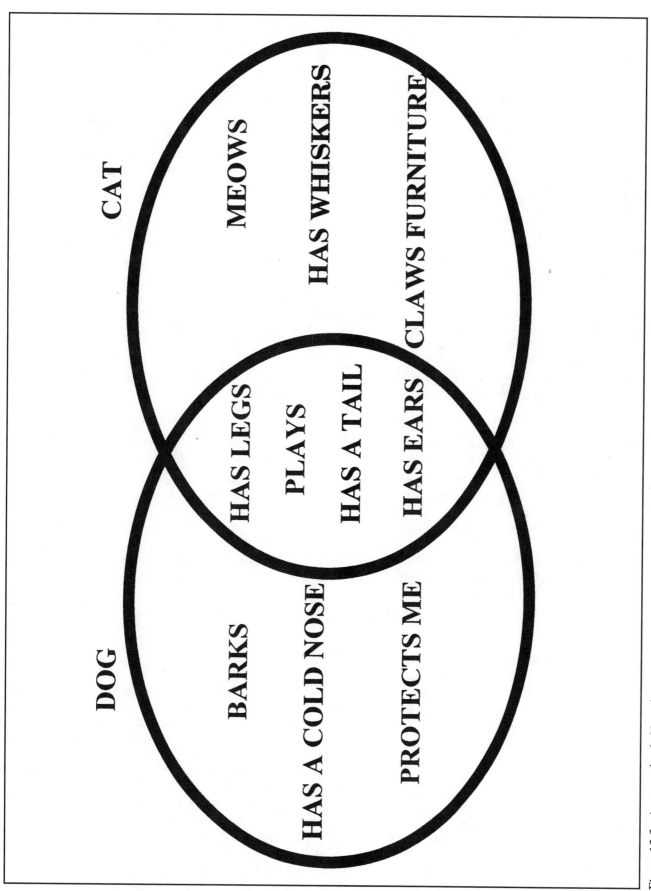

Figure 12.2. An example of a Venn diagram.

In addition to cognitive strategy training, metacognitive and executive skill training is also necessary for generalization. The following section describes an approach that has been used successfully with students with mild and moderate developmental disabilities functioning at least at a 3-year mental age, in both the academic and social domains (Rosenthal-Malek & Yoshida, 1994; Rosenthal-Malek, 1997).

Promising and Effective Practice: An Example of a Metacognitive Strategy Training Program

Researchers have attempted to translate what has been learned regarding metacognitive and executive ability into training programs for students with developmental disabilities.

Brown (1978, 1987) developed an approach called general metacognitive strategy training, which covers areas including functional, academic, memory, and social skills training. In this training, students learn to (a) become aware of what they know or do not know concerning a particular problem, (b) predict outcomes (be able to imagine acts before doing them), (c) plan appropriately for future recall, and (d) check and monitor performance. During the final stage, checking and monitoring, the student must be able to notice contradictory and/or incompatible responses; see that the response makes sense; understand procedures used; and have insight into the flexible, efficient, and intelligent use of rules and strategies in the solution of problems.

To make these four areas of metacognition operational, Brown (1978) recommended the use of a self-interrogation questioning procedure. This procedure consists of questions that the students ask themselves. These questions, according to Brown (1978), stimulate the thinking process, which in turn automatically promotes generalization. Examples of these questions are (a) What do I need to do? (b) What will happen if . . .? (c) How am I doing? and (d) Did that work achieve my goal? The teacher formally teaches the questions, after which the student models the questioning procedure, and then practices the questioning procedure in real situations with as little teacher intervention as possible. The teacher acts as a mediator, helping the student to achieve the goal.

Someone	Tried	But	So
The three billy goats gruff	to get to the green grass	a troll stopped the goats	the big goat butted the troll off the bridge

Figure 12.3. An example of a graphic organizer.

A Cognitive–Behavioral Model for Generalization

Meichenbaum (1985) proposed that both the behavioral and the cognitive views have something to offer to teachers regarding techniques that enhance generalization and are not mutually exclusive. Therefore, it is proposed that the following examples of instructional techniques, which are taken from both the behavioral and cognitive viewpoints, be implemented.

1. Training generalization as a skill in and of itself
2. Use of detailed extensive training
3. Use of self-instructional procedures
4. Use of explicit feedback regarding the use of the strategy
5. Use of reinforcement techniques at the moment when the behavior occurs
6. Use of a gamelike situation
7. Training of skills that are general enough to fit different situations
8. Use of different people, settings, and/or materials
9. Training of several tasks at once
10. Direct training of self-regulating or executive skills such as checking and monitoring

These techniques have all been used successfully with students with developmental disabilities (Rosenthal, 1990; Rosenthal-Malek & Yoshida, 1994).

Summary

This chapter has reviewed current issues and trends involved in the training of generalization. Researchers have found that students with developmental disabilities often have trouble generalizing newly learned skills and strategies to untrained situations and do not actively employ cognitive strategies that might promote generalization. This chapter has reviewed both theory and techniques that students with developmental disabilities could use to promote generalization of skills and strategies.

Although both behaviorally and cognitively oriented theorists have addressed the issue of generalization and both traditions believe that generalization is an important aspect of learning, there is still much discussion on exactly what causes generalization and how to train for generalization. Behaviorists focus generalization training on manipulation of the environment, assuming that the closer the training

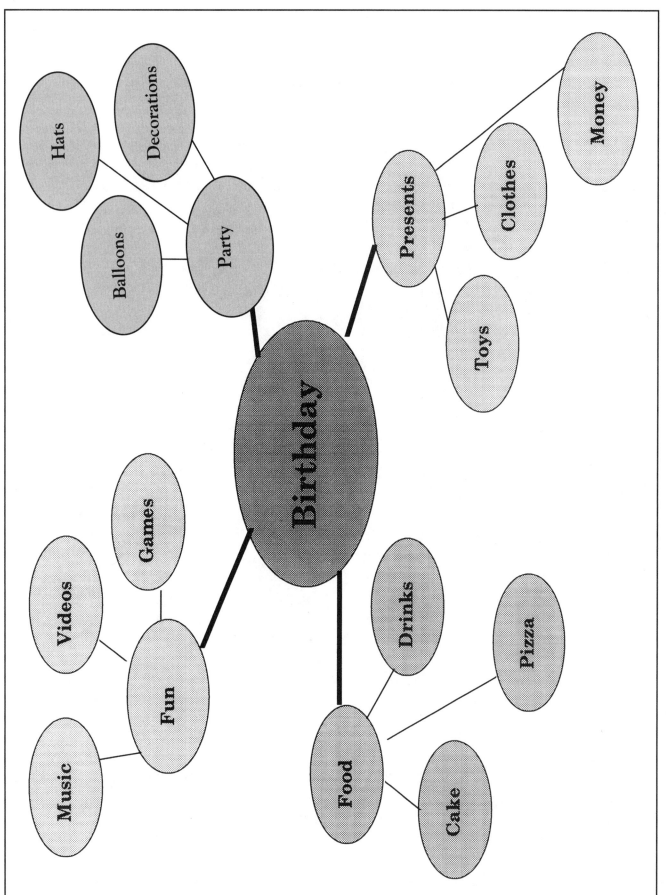

Figure 12.4. An example of a semantic map.

environment is to the generalization situation, the more likely generalization will occur. Behavioral teachers see their role in training for generalization as active manipulators of the environment. On the other hand, cognitive theorists focus on the thinking processes as well as on cognitive and metacognitive strategy training. Cognitive professionals attempt to empower students by facilitating the students until they become self-regulators of their own learning. Examples of best and effective practices from each tradition were discussed and an eclectic model was proposed.

 ## QUESTIONS

1. What are the major differences between the behavioral and cognitive views on techniques to promote generalization of newly learned skills and strategies?

2. What are the four stages of learning? Describe each.

3. What are generalization probes and how do they differ from assessment?

4. What are the three component parts of the information processing system? Describe each in detail.

5. What types of cognitive and metacognitive strategies must a student perform in order to promote generalization? Give examples of each and describe.

References

Ashcraft, M. (1989). *Human memory and cognition.* Glenview, IL: Scott, Foresman.

Atkinson, R. C., & Shiffrin, R. M. (1968). Human memory: A proposed system and its control processes. In K. W. Spence & J. T. Spence (Eds.), *The psychology of learning and motivation: Advances in research and theory* (Vol. 2). New York: Academic Press.

Baker-Ward, L., Ornstein, P. A., & Holden, D. J. (1984). The expression of memorization in early childhood. *Journal of Experimental Child Psychology, 37,* 555–575.

Blackhurst, A. E., & Berline, W. H. (1993). *An introduction to special education* (3rd ed.). New York: Harper Collins.

Blackman, L. S., Burger, A. L., Tan, N., & Weiner, S. (1982). Strategy training and the acquisition of decoding skills in EMR students. *Education and Training of the Mentally Retarded, 17,* 83–87.

Blackman, L. S., & Lin, A. (1984). Generalization training in the educable mentally retarded: Intelligence and its educability revisited. In P. H. Brooks, R. Sperber, & C. McCauley (Eds.), *Learning and cognition in the mentally retarded.* Hillsdale, NJ: Erlbaum.

Bloom, A. (1991, November). *Language arts strategies for handicapped and integrated classes.* Paper presented at the annual Conference of the College Reading Association, Washington, DC.

Bronson, M. B. (1984). *The concept of executive skills: Definition and measurement.* Paper presented at the Conference on Human Competence, Washington, DC.

Bronson, M. B. (1985). *Manual for the Bronson Social and Task Skill Profile.* Westport, CT: Mediax Interactive Technologies.

Brown, A. L. (1978). Knowing when, where, and how to remember: A problem with metacognition. In R. Glaser (Ed.), *Advances in instructional psychology* (pp. 77–165). Hillsdale, NJ: Erlbaum.

Brown, A. L. (1987). Metacognition, executive control, self-regulation and other more mysterious mechanisms. In F. E. Weinert & R. H. Klewe (Eds.), *Metacognition, motivation, and understanding* (pp. 65–116). Hillsdale, NJ: Erlbaum.

Brown, A. L., & Barclay, C. R. (1976). The effects of training specific mnemonics on the metamnemonic efficiency of retarded students. *Child Development, 47,* 71–80.

Brown, A., & Kane, M. (1988). Preschool children can learn to transfer: Learning to learn and learning from example. *Cognitive Psychology, 20,* 493–523.

Burger, A. L., Blackman, L. S., & Clark, H. T. (1981). Generalization of verbal abstraction strategies by EMR students and adolescents. *American Journal of Mental Deficiency, 86,* 405–413.

Butterfield, E. C., & Belmont, J. M. (1977). Assessing and improving the executive cognitive functions of mentally retarded people. In I. Bigler & M. Sternlicht (Eds.), *The psychology of mental retardation: Issues and approaches* (pp. 277–318). New York: Psychological Dimensions.

DeLoache, J. S., Cassidy, D. J., & Brown, A. (1985). Precursors of mnemonic strategies in very young students' memory. *Child Development, 56,* 125–137.

Duell, O. K. (1986). Metacognitive skills. In G. D. Phye & T. Andre (Eds.), *Cognitive classroom learning.* Orlando, FL: Academic Press.

Eggen, P., & Kauchak, D. (1994). *Educational psychology: Classroom connections* (2nd ed.). New York: Macmillan.

Feinburg, S., & Mindess, M. (1994). *Eliciting children's full potential: Designing and evaluating developmentally based programs for young children.* Pacific Grove, CA: Brooks/Cole.

Flavell, J. H. (1976). Metacognitive aspects of problem solving. In L. B. Resnick (Ed.), *The nature of intelligence.* Boston: University Park Press.

Glover, J. A., Ronning, R. H., & Brunning, R. H. (1990). *Cognitive psychology for teachers.* New York: Macmillan.

Haring, N. G. (1988). *Generalization for children with severe handicaps: Strategies and solutions.* Seattle: University of Washington Press.

Hickson, L., Blackman, L. S., & Reis, E. M. (1995). *Mental retardation: Foundations of educational programming.* Needham Heights, MA: Allyn & Bacon.

Hunt, N., & Marshall, K. (1994). *Exceptional children and youth: An introduction to special education*. Boston: Houghton Mifflin.

Kail, R. (1984). *The development of memory in students* (2nd ed.). San Francisco: Freeman.

Klahr, D., & Wallace, K. G. (1972). Class inclusion processes. In S. Farnham-Diggory (Ed.), *Information processing in children* (pp. 144–170). New York: Academic Press.

Lawson, M. J. (1984). Being executive about metacognition. In J. Kirby (Ed.), *Cognitive strategies and educational practices* (pp. 89–109). New York: Academic Press.

Lezak, M. D. (1982). The problem of assessing executive functions. *International Journal of Psychology, 17*, 281–297.

Lin, A., Blackman, L. S., Clark, H. T., & Gordon, R. (1983). Far generalization of visual analogies strategies by impulsive and reflective EMR students. *American Journal of Mental Deficiency, 88*, 297–306.

Matlock, B., Lynch, V., & Paeth, M. A. (1990a). *Decision rules and strategies for skill generalization trainers' kit*. Seattle: University of Washington Press.

Matlock, B., Lynch, V., & Paeth, M. A. (1990b). *Probing for generalization trainer's kit*. Seattle: University of Washington Press.

Meese, R. L. (1994). *Teaching learners with mild disabilities: Integrating research and practice*. Pacific Grove, CA: Brooks/Cole.

Meichenbaum, D. (1985). Teaching thinking: A cognitive–behavioral perspective. In J. Segal, S. Chipman, & R. Glaser (Eds.), *Thinking and learning skills: Vol. 2. Research and open questions*. Hillsdale, NJ: Erlbaum.

Miller, G. A., Galanter, E., & Pribram, K. (1960). *Plans and the structure of behavior*. New York: Holt, Rinehart and Winston.

Misra, A. (1992). Generalization of social skills through self-monitoring by adults with mental retardation. *Exceptional Students, 58*(6), 495–507.

Moates, D., & Schumacher, G. (1980). *An introduction to cognitive psychology*. Belmont, CA: Wadsworth.

Morrison, G. M., & Polloway, E. A. (1995). Mental retardation. In E. L. Meyan & T. M. Skrtic (Eds.), *Special education and student disability: An introduction* (pp. 215–269). Denver: Love.

Ornstein, P. A., Naus, M. J., & Liberty, C. (1975). Rehearsal and organizational processes in students' memory. *Child Development, 46*, 818–830.

Piaget, J. (1951). *The child's conception of the world*. London: Routledge & Kegan Paul.

Prawat, R. (1989). Promoting access to knowledge, strategy, and disposition in students: A research synthesis. *Review of Educational Research, 59*, 1–41.

Pressley, M., Burkell, J., Cariglia-Bull, T., Lysynchuk, L., McGoldrick, J. A., Schneider, B., Symons, S., & Woloshyn, V. E. (1990). *Cognitive strategy instruction that really improves students' academic performance*. Cambridge, MA: Brookline Books.

Pressley, M., Levin, J. R., & McDaniel, M. A. (1987). Remembering versus inferring what a word means: Mnemonic and contextual approaches. In M. McKeown & M. E. Curtis (Eds.), *The nature of vocabulary acquisition* (pp. 107–127). Hillsdale, NJ: Erlbaum.

Pressley, M., & McCormick, C. (1995). *Cognition, teaching, and assessment*. New York: Harper Collins College.

Pressley, M., Woloshyn, V., Lysynchuk, L., Martin, V., Wood, E., & Wiloughby, T. (1990). A primer of research on cognitive strategy instruction: The important issues and how to address them. *Educational Psychology, 2*, 1–58.

Rafoth, M., Leal, L., & DeFabo, L. (1993). *Strategies for learning and remembering*. National Education Association of the United States.

Raphael, T. E., & McKinney, J. (1993). An examination of fifth and eighth grade students' question answering behavior: An instructional study in metacognition. *Journal of Reading Behavior, 15*, 67–86.

Raphael, T. E., & Pearson, P. D. (1985). Increasing students' awareness of sources of information for answering questions. *American Educational Research Journal, 22*, 217–236.

Rosenthal, A. L. (1990). The effects of metacognitive strategy training on the social executive competence of moderately retarded students. (Doctoral dissertation, Fordham University, 1990). *Dissertation Abstracts International, 51*, 1961A.

Rosenthal-Malek, A. (1997). Stop and Think! Using metacognitive strategies to teach students social skills. *Teaching Exceptional Children, 29*(3), 29–31.

Rosenthal-Malek, A. L., & Yoshida, R. K. (1994). The effects of metacognitive strategy training on the acquisition and generalization of social skills. *Education and Training in Mental Retardation and Developmental Disabilities, 3*, 213–321.

Schloss, P. J., & Schloss, C. N. (1985). Contemporary issues in social skills research with mentally retarded persons. *Journal of Special Education, 19*, 269–282.

Schneider, W., & Sodian, B. (1988). Metamemory–memory relationships in preschool students: Evidence from memory for location task. *Developmental Psychology, 37*, 209–233.

Scruggs, T. E., Mastropieri, M. A., & Levin, J. R. (1985). Vocabulary acquisition by mentally retarded students under direct mnemonic instruction. *American Journal of Mental Deficiency, 89*, 546–551.

Seifert, K. L. (1991). *Educational psychology* (2nd ed.). Boston: Houghton Mifflin.

Seigler, R. S. (1991). *Children's thinking* (2nd ed.). Englewood Cliffs, NJ: Prentice-Hall.

Sheid, K. (1993). *Helping students become strategic learners*. Cambridge, MA: Brookline Books.

Simon, H. A. (1972). On the development of the processor. In S. Farnham-Diggory (Ed.), *Information processing in students* (pp. 5–22). New York: Academic Press.

Simon, H. A., & Newell, A. (1971). Human problem-solving: The state of the theory in 1970. *American Psychologist, 26*, 145–159.

Stainback, W., Stainback, S., & Strathe, M. (1983). Generalization of positive social behavior by severely handicapped students: A review and analysis of research. *Education and Training of the Mentally Retarded, 18*, 283–290.

Stokes, T. F., & Osnes, P. G. (1988). Programming the generalization of students' social behavior. In P. S. Strain, M. Guralnick, & H. Walker (Eds.), *Children's social behavior, development, assessment, and modification* (pp. 407–443). Orlando, FL: Academic Press.

Whitman, T. L. (1990). Self-regulation and mental retardation. *American Journal on Mental Retardation, 94*, 347–362.

Wolery, M., Bailey, D. B., & Sugai, G. M. (1988). *Effective teaching: Principles and procedures of applied behavior analysis with exceptional students*. Boston: Allyn & Bacon.

Wong, B. Y. L. (1985). Self-questioning instructional research: A review. *Review of Educational Research, 55*, 227–268.

Wong, B. Y. L., & Wilson, M. (1984). Investigating awareness of and teaching passage organization in learning disabled children. *Journal of Learning Disabilities, 17*, 477–482.

Behaving Independently: Considerations in Fading Instructor Assistance

CHAPTER 13

Felix F. Billingsley

Learning Outcomes

After reading this chapter, you should be able to

- Describe the nature and purpose of response prompts.

- Identify critical characteristics, as well as advantages and disadvantages, of systems designed to fade response prompts.

- Discuss factors that an educator should consider in selecting a particular prompt fading system.

- Describe considerations for the use of prompt fading systems in general education settings.

TERMS

The following terms are important for the understanding of this chapter:

Discriminative stimulus: A person, object, or event in the presence of which it is more (or less) likely that a behavior will occur than in its absence. Such a stimulus is able to influence the likelihood that a behavior will occur because the behavior has previously been reinforced or punished when the stimulus was present.

Fading: In this chapter, the systematic removal of instructor assistance so that students learn to respond independently to appropriate natural cues.

Full physical assistance: Instructor-provided assistance in which the student is physically guided through the movements necessary to complete a task or task step.

Gesture: A movement by the instructor that does not involve physical contact, but that is intended to evoke correct behavior on the part of the student. Gestures may involve, for example, pointing (as to a correct choice or an item required for task completion), facial expressions, or body language.

Modeling: A demonstration of correct task performance.

Natural cues: Persons, objects, or events that should act as "signals" for learned behaviors to occur outside of instructional situations; natural discriminative stimuli.

Partial physical assistance: Instructor assistance that involves physical contact with the student, but to a lesser degree than full physical assistance. Partial physical assistance might vary from a light touch or tap to providing guidance part of the way through some movement.

Performance criterion: A standard of learner behavior that the instructor will use in order to determine whether a change should be made, or whether mastery has been achieved, in an educational program.

Self-fading: The elimination of prompts without procedural modifications on the part of the instructor as learning progresses.

Shadowing: A step that has been used in fading physical assistance in which the instructor follows the movements of the student with his or her hands, but does not make physical contact.

Trial: Opportunity for a student to perform for instructional and/or evaluation purposes. Performance requirements may be very narrow (e.g., a single, discrete communication response) or quite broad (e.g., all of the steps in a community shopping routine).

Verbal prompt: A verbal statement by the instructor that tells a student how to respond appropriately. Such statements may be direct (e.g., "Take the top one off") or indirect (e.g., "What's next?").

Introduction

Carleen, who has multiple disabilities including profound mental retardation, is learning to drink liquids from a can. After she brings the can to her mouth, she simply holds the can upright against her lower lip and attempts to lick the drink out with her tongue. As part of the instructional plan, her teacher physically assists her to tilt the can up to an appropriate angle so that the liquid pours into her mouth.

Jeremy, a youth with significant intellectual disabilities, is learning to read aisle labels relevant to several community shopping environments (e.g., drug stores, grocery stores, hardware stores). One element of his program requires that he read the labels aloud when shown pictures of the labels as displayed in a number of the stores. To get him started, an instructional assistant states the correct response as each word is presented and Jeremy imitates her.

Lorraine, a preschooler with autism and moderate mental retardation, is learning to put away her toys after a free-play period. Her typically developing classmate and friend, Mariana, points out the bins appropriate for the storage of each type of toy.

The above examples illustrate the use of response prompts, that is, extra assistance provided by one person to promote the acquisition of some skill by another. Few strategies share the versatility of such prompts as an instructional tool. Among their desirable characteristics are the following:

1. They do not require the preparation of special materials and are free.

2. They are transportable and can be made available in almost any instructional context (school, home, community, vocational setting, etc.).

3. They are a common part of the educational experience for learners with diverse abilities, including typically developing students.

4. They can be used in conjunction with a variety of other instructional practices, such as stimulus manipulations (e.g., Mosk & Bucher, 1984) and shaping.

5. They can be easily and efficiently modified to meet the needs of individual learners.

6. They can be changed (once again, easily and efficiently) across time in response to student progress.

7. They are useful in the instruction of many types of skills.

Given such advantages, it is not surprising that the use of response prompts has acquired best practice status in the instruction of students with moderate to profound disabilities.

The specific nature of response prompts can vary widely. In general, however, learners receive assistance in auditory, visual, or tactile–kinesthetic modes. Prompts in the auditory mode are usually verbal cues in which the teacher makes requests or gives instructions that are more specific than those evident in the task itself (Hourcade, 1988). Wolery, Ault, and Doyle (1992) identified five types of verbal prompts that may be used, depending on the ability of the learner, to "understand the meaning of the statement" (p. 39): (a) explaining how to perform the behavior, (b) explaining how to do a portion of the behavior, (c) providing a rule, (d) offering indirect verbal information, and (e) giving verbal options.

Visual prompts offered by instructors can include both gestures and modeling (or demonstration). Teachers using gestures might touch, tap, or point to items, events, or other stimuli to which students should respond (Hourcade, 1988; Snell & Zirpoli, 1987) or motion in a manner that suggests the appropriate movement (Billingsley & Romer, 1983). When modeling is employed, the teacher provides a demonstration of the target behavior for the student.

Tactile–kinesthetic prompts range from touches to partial physical assistance to full physical guidance. The intent of such prompts is to direct the movement of the student and/or to mold the appropriate topography.

It is critical to note that, for assistance to serve a prompting function, the type of assistance offered must control the target behavior. Modeling, for instance, should not be selected simply because it has frequently proven to be a powerful instructional tool. Rather, it should be selected because the learner possesses imitative skills and will perform desired behaviors when presented with a demonstration. If the learner does not imitate, it is necessary to teach him or her to profit from demonstrations (see Charlop & Walsh, 1986; Schoen, 1989; Sternberg, McNerney & Pegnatore, 1985; Venn et al., 1993) or to use some other type of prompt. Similarly, learners who react negatively to physical guidance are not likely to attend to the input provided by that form of prompt. In those cases, it may be necessary that steps be taken to establish contact as a conditioned reinforcer prior to the successful use of tactile prompts for instructional purposes (Wolery, Bailey, & Sugai, 1988).

To ensure that appropriate assistance procedures are selected for instructional purposes, it is important that various forms and degrees of assistance be tried, and that the type chosen for use be one that will reliably and efficiently evoke the desired response (Bijou, 1981; Neel & Billingsley, 1989). Such an assessment process is also important to guard against the routine use of those prompts that are most intrusive (e.g., full physical assistance) and that may draw negative attention to students with disabilities in community and general education settings (see Billingsley & Kelley, 1994).

Although response prompts have long been considered a component of educational best practice for students with significant intellectual disabilities, they cannot be considered effective in promoting independent, adaptive performance unless they are included as part of a broader instructional plan. When teacher assistance is scheduled, a method to transfer control of pupil behavior to appropriate natural cues should, in most instances, be identified. By the end of instruction, a peer's greeting, rather than a teacher's partial physical assistance, ought to evoke an appropriate response from a student on a communication board. In a similar manner, the student should kick when the ball approaches in an adapted soccer game instead of requiring the verbal directive to "Kick the ball"; completion of the second step needed to activate a computer game should supplant a gestural prompt as the stimulus for initiation of the third step; and so forth. The purpose of this chapter, then, is to describe and examine several techniques that can be used to reduce the dependence of students on teacher-provided prompts. Important limitations of these techniques are identified, recommendations for choosing among them are presented, and their potential for application in inclusive school settings is explored.

Transfer of Stimulus Control from Instructor Assistance to Natural Cues

Four general systems designed to achieve transfer of stimulus control (i.e., to fade response prompts) have frequently been employed with success in programs for students with significant disabilities. These systems include increasing assistance, decreasing assistance, graduated guidance, and time delay.

Increasing Assistance

Increasing assistance (also known as system of least prompts, least-to-most prompting, and least intrusive prompts) requires that prompts be arranged in a presumed order, or hierarchy, of lesser to greater assistance and applied sequentially as a consequence for errors or failures to respond. The types and number of prompts that educators have employed in this method have varied widely. Typically, however, sequences have involved progressing from auditory prompts (direct and/or indirect verbal assistance), to visual prompts (gestures and/or modeling), to tactile prompts (partial or full physical assistance).

An instructional procedure described by Giangreco (1983), in which a young adult with severe disabilities was taught basic photography skills, provides a good illustration of the use of the increasing assistance method. In Phase I of the program, task steps included looking at the number indicator on the back of the camera, opening the film compartment of the camera if no number appeared in the indicator,

removing the old film, opening the new film pack, loading new film, and closing the film compartment. Taking the third step as an example, if the student did not remove the used film within 3 seconds after the camera was opened, the instructor provided a verbal direction to remove the film. If the learner did not take the film out within 3 seconds following the direction, or responded incorrectly, a gestural prompt was provided. If the correct response was not performed after 3 more seconds, the instructor demonstrated the behavior. Finally, if the film was not removed by the student after 3 additional seconds, physical guidance was offered. Each prompt was also accompanied by a verbal direction. When the student removed the film, he had the opportunity to perform the next step independently, followed by increasing levels of assistance if necessary. This approach continued until all steps of the task were completed.

In Giangreco's (1983) and other examples of the increasing assistance procedure, the same sequence of events has generally been followed on each trial, with prompts dropping out as students make increasing numbers of correct responses earlier in the sequence. Steege, Wacker, and McMahon (1987), however, found that instructional efficiency could be improved by employing a "prescriptive procedure" in which the beginning prompt in the sequence could vary across instructional trials depending upon prior student performance.

The increasing assistance method can be conceptualized as a self-fading system (Lent, 1974) because prompts considered to be more intrusive ideally will be eliminated without procedural modification as learning progresses. Further, it has been employed successfully to teach a wide variety of skills to students with mild to severe disabilities (Billingsley & Romer, 1983; Wolery et al., 1992). For such reasons, this approach is a frequently used and recommended instructional technique. Several potential disadvantages exist, however. Falvey, Brown, Lyon, Baumgart, and Schroeder (1980) and Schoen (1986) have suggested that the sequential presentation of prompts is not consistent with events in natural environments and that students could learn to delay through a series of prompted steps in order to gain teacher guidance and reinforcement. In addition, because the initial prompts in a sequence do not control responding, relatively high error rates are likely during the early stages of training. Such an outcome is of concern for several reasons:

1. Frequent errors and corrections may be associated with the appearance of undesirable behaviors (Bellamy, Horner, & Inman, 1979; Carr & Durand, 1985; Horner, 1988; Weeks & Gaylord-Ross, 1981).

2. When errors begin to be made, they may tend to persist (Bereiter & Engelmann, 1966; Terrace, 1963).

3. Motivation to perform may be adversely affected by excessive errors (Koegel & Egel, 1979).

4. When natural cues reliably evoke desired behaviors, they are said to have become discriminative stimuli. Discriminative stimuli gain their controlling power as a result of the frequent reinforcement of behaviors that occur in their presence. High proportions of errors could reduce opportunities for the appropriate behavior to be reinforced in the presence of the natural cue and, thereby, delay the establishment of that cue as an effective discriminative stimulus. In other words, using an instructional strategy that results in large numbers of errors could delay the student's learning to respond to cues that should influence the appearance of behaviors in natural environments.

Where increasing assistance is selected as a prompt fading system, educators should attempt to reduce error opportunities. Error reduction might be achieved, for example, by employing a variation such as that described by Steege and colleagues (1987). In applying that procedure, the instructor first presented the natural cue for the target behavior. If the student did not respond correctly, the instructor then presented the prompt that was considered to be just above (in terms of less assistance) the prompt that had successfully occasioned responding on the previous trial. If, for example, a student responded correctly when provided with partial assistance, an incorrect response to the natural cue on the next trial would result in the provision of, say, a demonstration on the part of the instructor rather than the provision of the initial prompt in the sequence originally devised (e.g., direct verbal assistance). Another option for reducing errors might be to modify materials so that learners would be more likely to achieve success (Mosk & Bucher, 1984).

Decreasing Assistance

As in increasing assistance systems, educators using decreasing assistance (also known as most-to-least prompting) typically select several types of prompts to apply sequentially. Rather than beginning with the prompt that provides the presumed least amount of assistance, however, instruction starts with a prompt that has a high probability of evoking the correct response. After the student achieves a performance criterion with the initial prompt, the level of assistance is decreased by presenting the next prompt in the sequence. Prompts continue to be removed successively, contingent on correct responding by the student. If errors are made when a specific type of prompt is employed, the teacher usually returns to a prompt used earlier in the sequence, or to some intermediate point, in order to provide more assistance. Neel and Billingsley (1989), discussed below, and Wolery and colleagues (1992) discuss criteria for changes in amounts or types of assistance.

Decreasing assistance approaches can be used within an error correction format (e.g., Miller & Test, 1989), and the prompt used initially is often full physical assistance (e.g.,

Csapo, 1981; Luyben, Funk, Morgan, Clark, & Delulio, 1986). It is preferable, however, to provide the controlling prompt prior to the initial response in order to maximize correct responding and to base selection of the controlling prompt on assessment data (e.g., McDonnell & Ferguson, 1989; see also Neel & Billingsley, 1989; Wolery et al., 1992; Wuerch & Voeltz, 1982), thus ensuring that more assistance is not being given than is necessary.

Educators should also refer to some set of rules to determine when changes in assistance should be implemented. One possible set of decision rules is that presented in the IMPACT curriculum (Neel & Billingsley, 1989). Those rules presume that the initial controlling prompt has been selected on the basis of the outcomes of three assessment trials. Performance data from blocks of three instructional trials are then employed to make decisions regarding decreases or increases in assistance. If student responses are correct on each of the three trials for any step of a task, it is recommended that the instructor reduce assistance on that step; however, if correct responses occur on only one, or none, of the trials, it is recommended that the program be changed to provide more assistance or to increase student motivation. If responses are correct on two of the three trials, the decision rules specify that another block of three trials be administered and, if fewer than three correct responses are observed, the program be changed in ways that are likely to improve learner performance. If all three responses are correct, instructor assistance is reduced.

Following recommendations outlined above, instruction in removing film from an opened camera using a prompting sequence similar to that employed by Giangreco (1983) might proceed as follows:

1. Three assessment trials are conducted to determine the type of assistance sufficient to evoke film removal. A demonstration by the instructor seems to do it.

2. As soon as the student finishes opening the camera, the selected prompt (demonstration) is applied. If three trials are completed successfully, the next, presumably less intrusive, prompt in the sequence (a gesture) is used. Prompts continue to be changed from gestural to verbal as the student continues to demonstrate successful performance across three trial blocks. Finally, the verbal direction is eliminated.

3. If errors are made when a new prompt is introduced, a different prompt is provided (in accordance with decision rules) that is more likely to control the behavior. Note that it is not necessary to revert to the last prompt in the sequence that controlled the behavior, but to any intermediate prompt that will evoke the desired response. For example, rather than moving from gestures back to demonstration if errors occurred, the gesture might be modified in ways intended to provide the student with an increased amount of information.

Usually, transfer of stimulus control is achieved in both decreasing and increasing assistance systems by moving through a presumed hierarchy of prompts that vary across sensory input channels (i.e., auditory, visual, tactile) as in the above example. It is also frequently the case that verbal cues are paired with other prompts throughout the fading process. Variations of these typical methods, however, may be effectively employed. Assistance could be reduced within a selected sensory modality, for example, by systematically reducing the intensity or location of physical assistance (Hunt, Staub, Alwell, & Goetz, 1994) or by moving from direct to indirect verbal cues. Tentative support for such an approach was recently provided by Moran (1994), who investigated the comparative effects of across-modality (multimodal) and within-modality (unimodal) prompting on the performance of juice and snack preparation tasks by learners with severe disabilities. Moran found that, generally, learners tended to make fewer response errors when the instructor remained in a single sensory modality as prompts were faded than when the instructor moved across modalities. The unimodal approach also tended to be the more efficient of the two procedures during the prompt fading process. In another possible variation, only one prompt at a time might be used to avoid establishing the controlling power of a previously ineffective stimulus, such as a verbal direction (e.g., "More! Sign 'more'"), that is unlikely to be provided in nontraining situations (Neel & Billingsley, 1989).[1]

A possible disadvantage of decreasing assistance systems in which antecedent prompts are employed may be their potential to conceal pupil progress. Billingsley, Liberty, and White (1994) noted that, "Because the controlling prompts are provided before the student has a chance to respond to the natural cue without assistance (or with less assistance) . . . the student may be capable of performing with greater independence than can be observed" (p. 93). When decreasing assistance procedures are used, periodic assessments (independence probes) should be conducted to determine whether assistance may be reduced more rapidly or omitted altogether. The timing of those assessments should be based on the frequency with which instructional trials are provided. Neel and Billingsley (1989), for example, suggested that independence probes be administered approximately once every 2 weeks when only one or two trials are provided each day.

Graduated Guidance

Graduated guidance begins by providing the learner with the amount of physical assistance that is required for correct task performance. The amount of assistance is then changed within rather than across trials. Moment-by-moment judgments regarding changes in degree of assistance are then made by the instructor on the basis of student performance (Schoen, 1986; Wolery et al., 1992); that is, correct responses are followed by reductions in assistance, and errors, or failures to respond, are followed by increases. Typically, prompts are faded by reducing their intensity or by changing their location. Prompt intensity could be reduced by providing guidance with the entire hand, then with a two-finger touch, and then by simply shadowing the student's movements by following the response, but not actually touching the student. If the student begins to err or ceases to respond during a trial, assistance could be increased to the amount required to once again secure correct performance. Changing the location of a prompt could be accomplished, for instance, by moving the site of teacher assistance from the student's wrist to forearm and then to shoulder.

Graduated guidance trials continue uninterrupted until the response or the response sequence is completed. Reinforcement is provided immediately after a trial following withdrawal of teacher contact. In addition, verbal praise is given during trials for active student participation. Extensive guidelines for the use of graduated guidance have been provided by Foxx and Azrin (1973) and Foxx (1982).

Graduated guidance procedures allow teachers to quickly modify the amount of assistance provided in order to meet the changing needs of students throughout task performance and across instructional trials. Because these procedures rely so heavily on subjective judgments of the teacher, however, and because judgments must be made very rapidly, students may receive either too little or too much help in task completion. Where help is insufficient, undesirable levels of error responding may occur. Where more help is given than is required, the danger exists that students will respond to the extensive physical guidance by attempting to exert countercontrol (Schoen, 1986; Schoen, Lentz, & Suppa, 1988) or will become dependent on such guidance (Wolery & Gast, 1984). Although descriptions of graduated guidance consistently include the use of physical assistance (e.g., Cipani, Augustine, & Blomgren, 1982; Foxx & Azrin, 1973), Schoen (1986) indicated that other prompts could potentially be used within a graduated guidance format: "For example, a teacher may watch a student's use of a vending machine and provide prompts such as "put in the money, push the button," and so forth. If the student moves in the correct direction, the teacher would discontinue prompting. This description meets the criteria for graduated guidance, with the exception of the physical prompt component" (Shoen, 1986, p. 66).

---

[1]Teachers could, of course, pair ineffective with controlling prompts as a systematic strategy to teach pupils to respond to cues that are not currently effective. As an example, Wolery and colleagues (1992) suggested that demonstrations might be paired with physical assistance to teach imitation skills to pupils who have not previously exhibited imitation.

Time Delay

The prompt fading methods described previously are designed to achieve transfer of stimulus control through systematic variations in the type of prompt, or amount of assistance, provided. Time delay procedures, on the other hand, employ systematic temporal variation to achieve desired outcomes (Billingsley & Romer, 1983; Wolery et al., 1992). Two major types of time delay have been successfully employed in programs for students with severe disabilities: progressive time delay (e.g., Godby, Gast, & Wolery, 1987; Snell, 1982) and constant time delay (e.g., Kleinert & Gast, 1982; McDonnell, 1987).

Progressive time delay involves the presentation of a controlling prompt concurrent with the presentation of the natural cue for some number of trials. Following those concurrent presentations, trials are provided during which a brief time interval (e.g., 1 second) is inserted between the natural cue and the prompt delivery. During that time, the student has the opportunity to respond independently. If an independent response is obtained (an anticipation), reinforcement is provided as appropriate and the next trial or next skill step is presented. If the correct response does not occur during the interval, it is prompted and, as in the case of an independent response, any scheduled reinforcers are delivered and the learner moves to the next trial or step in the skill sequence. If transfer appears to be delayed by the continued reinforcement of prompted responses as instruction progresses, Gast, Wolery, Ault, Doyle, and Alig (1988) recommended that reinforcers be provided only for unprompted correct responses.

In trials that follow, the delay is incrementally increased to a teacher-determined maximum length. Increases occur contingent upon some preselected number of independent or prompted correct responses. Although increments of various sizes have been employed, findings of Walls, Haught, and Dowler (1982) suggest that short increments of 1 second may result in more desirable outcomes than longer increments of 3 or 5 seconds. If a maximum interval of 5 seconds is selected, a 1-second delay might be extended by 1 additional second whenever the student makes two prompted or unprompted correct responses in a row. Additional seconds are added until the maximum interval of 5 seconds is achieved. Billingsley et al. (1994) noted, "The effect of the increasing interval is to gradually delay reinforcement; if the reinforcer is powerful enough and the student can perform the behavior, the learner should respond before the prompt in order to avoid the delay" (p. 95). When an error is made, the delay is decreased and/or a brief period of time-out or a response correction procedure is applied.

As in the case of progressive time delay, constant time delay begins with a set or sets of trials during which the prompt and natural cue are presented simultaneously. In contrast to the progressive delay method, however, simulta-neous presentation sets are followed by trials that include a constant, rather than changing, delay interval between the natural cue and the prompt. The teacher, therefore, might devise a program in which one session of no-delay trials is followed by sets of trials in which the delay begins and remains at 5 seconds.

Although the constant time delay procedure has been used extensively for teaching discrete skills, such as manual sign production (Kleinert & Gast, 1982) and sight word reading (Koury & Browder, 1986), to learners with moderate to severe disabilities, it has also been effectively employed in the instruction of chained skills. Hall, Schuster, Wolery, Gast, and Doyle (1992) provided the following description of the application of constant time delay within a dyadic instructional format for teaching food preparation to students with moderate mental retardation:

> A 0–4-s constant time delay procedure was used to teach each dyad the three cooking skills. The dyads were given one trial on each step of the task analysis in each instructional session. A 0-s delay interval was used during the first two instructional sessions for each dyad and each skill. This gave both students in the dyad an opportunity to complete the chain at the 0-s delay. A 0-s session began by the instructor ensuring an attending response from each student in the dyad, delivering the task direction (e.g., "Make a microwave cake") to the target student, and immediately providing the controlling prompt (a verbal description and model of the correct response on a second set of materials). Following delivery of the prompt, students were given 4 s to initiate the response and on the majority of steps, 20 s to complete the response. This continued until each step in the task analysis was completed. During all subsequent sessions, a 4-s delay interval was inserted between presentation of the task direction and delivery of the controlling prompt. Once a response occurred within the 4-s response interval, either before or after the prompt, the student was given 20 s to complete the response. (pp. 264–265)

Perhaps the greatest disadvantage of time delay systems is that they can be relatively complicated to apply, particularly in the case of skill sequences (McDonnell & Ferguson, 1989; Snell, 1982), and other prompt fading methods (i.e., decreasing assistance) may be preferred by some educators (McDonnell & Ferguson, 1989). Constant delay methods, however, are usually easier to manage than progressive delay techniques because they require fewer procedural changes (Ault, Gast, & Wolery, 1988).

Regardless of the potential for complication, many variations of the two basic time delay procedures have been described and successfully applied in instructional programs for students experiencing significant disabilities (see Handen & Zane, 1987). In fact, a number of investigations have demonstrated the use of time delay methods within group instructional formats (e.g., Farmer, Gast, Wolery, & Winterling, 1991). Browder and Snell (1993) provided the following guidelines for applying time delay for the group instruction of sight word reading:

1. Because observational learning is an advantage of the group format, students should be prompted to attend to the word or symbol (e.g., "Everybody, look"). Praise should then be provided to the students for their attention at the conclusion of the trial.

2. One student should be provided with the opportunity to respond per trial as the other students in the group attend. It is important to name the student who is to respond prior to presenting the word to be read in order to discourage responses from other students in the group. The appropriate delay interval is provided before delivery of the prompt and praise or prior to delivering a correction procedure.

3. At least one round of trials should be implemented with no delay between the target word(s) and the prompt. Follow no-delay trials with multiple sets of trials in which the appropriate delay interval is introduced. Because observational learning is anticipated, it is not critical that all students read all words during every round. At least one opportunity for each student to read each word should be provided, however, so that adequate amounts of individual student data may be collected to effectively monitor progress.

Gast and colleagues (1988) and Schuster and Griffen (1990) provided a number of sound, practical suggestions for developing, implementing, and evaluating time delay. An examination of those sources, and a consideration of the contexts in which time delay variations have been found effective, should enable educators to customize systems that will fit the requirements of many instructional situations.

Other Methods

Although the four methods discussed above have had most frequent application in the education of learners with moderate to profound intellectual disabilities, Ault, Wolery, Doyle, and Gast (1989) and others (e.g., Wolery et al., 1992) have identified two additional procedures that have been used to achieve transfer of stimulus control: (a) antecedent prompt and test and (b) antecedent prompt and fade.

The antecedent prompt and test strategy has been used most widely with students experiencing mild to moderate disabilities and preschoolers from economically disadvantaged environments (Wolery et al., 1988), but has occasionally been applied in programs for persons with moderate and severe disabilities (e.g., Zane, Walls, & Thvedt, 1981). To use the procedure, the controlling prompt is presented simultaneously with the natural cue for a specified number of trials or sessions. Test trials then follow training trials immediately or at some later time in order to "assess transfer

of stimulus control from the controlling prompt used during instructional trials to the natural discriminative stimulus" (Schuster & Griffen, 1993, p. 300). The prompt is not provided on test trials, but reinforcers and correction procedures may be provided.

A recent variation of the antecedent prompt and test procedure has been referred to as the simultaneous prompting procedure (Schuster & Griffen, 1993; Schuster, Griffen, & Wolery, 1992). When simultaneous prompting is employed, instructors should take care to ensure that the prompt used does, in fact, exert control in order to minimize error responding. In addition, test trials are always presented immediately prior to instruction. In other antecedent prompt and test applications, those trials can occur at any time, but have typically been provided immediately after training trials (Schuster & Griffen, 1993).

The success of antecedent prompt and test methods rests on findings obtained during time delay investigations that "the moment of transfer of stimulus control for some individuals with some tasks using time delay procedures occurs before the delay trials are implemented" (Schuster et al., 1992, p. 307). In other words, under certain circumstances, transfer of stimulus control appears to be obtained during trials in which the natural cue and the prompt are simultaneously presented. Where such transfer is not obtained or is not complete, it is possible that the abrupt and total elimination of prompts during test trials could dramatically reduce the effectiveness and efficiency of the prompt and test procedures. Wolery and colleagues (1988) have warned that the amount of assistance provided by antecedent prompt and test strategies may not be sufficient to meet the needs of some students with severe disabilities.

The antecedent prompt and fade strategy provides a means by which prompted trials may be systematically removed across instructional sessions in a manner that should preserve a relatively high frequency of correct responding within those sessions for learners who may not benefit from antecedent prompt and test methods. Initially, students are provided with the opportunity to respond following the simultaneous presentation of prompt and natural cue. Fading is then accomplished in trials that follow in one of two ways. The first method is similar to most-to-least prompting in that prompt types may be changed (physical to gestural, etc.), the nature of the prompt may be modified within a given sensory dimension (full physical assistance to partial physical assistance, etc.), or the locus of prompts may be changed (hand to wrist, etc.) across trials. Unlike most-to-least prompting, however, criteria for fading assistance are not specified; rather, changes are made based on teacher judgment of whether the learner is "ready" for a reduction in assistance (Wolery et al., 1992).

In the second method, the controlling prompt is decreased in frequency. Billingsley (1987), for example, demonstrated the successful application of an antecedent prompt and fade strategy for teaching a pupil with autism and severe intellectual deficits to initiate gestural requests for food. In order to transfer stimulus control from physical prompts to natural cues, instruction began with one session of 15 trials in which the prompt and natural cue were simultaneously presented. The number of prompted trials was then reduced across instructional sessions and the number of unprompted trials was increased.

Comparative Utility and Recommendations for Fading Assistance

Since the early 1980s, a substantial number of investigations have compared effects of various prompt fading methods. Demchak (1990) identified 17 studies designed to compare major systems for fading teacher assistance, and additional research has been reported since publication of that article (e.g., Doyle, Wolery, Gast, Ault, & Wiley, 1990; Schuster et al., 1992). Unfortunately, interpretations of the findings of existing research are complicated by important differences across studies. Some investigations, for example, employed subsequent prompts (i.e., prompts used as corrections) during application of a given procedure, whereas others used antecedent prompts in a variation of the same general procedure; some assessed the type of assistance required and used that type, but others simply began with physical assistance; some employed discrete responses and others employed chained responses; some used "laboratory tasks" (e.g., two-choice discriminations) and others used functional skills (e.g., setting a table). In addition, considerable variability existed in degree of disability and age of study participants.

Given the differences noted above, research-based recommendations regarding the comparative value of various systems must be accepted with caution. With that in mind, however, findings to date seem to suggest that the most desirable outcomes are associated with the use of prompt fading systems that minimize errors in the presence of natural cues.[2] For students with severe disabilities, such systems are likely to include time delay, decreasing assistance methods that employ antecedent prompts, graduated guidance, and (perhaps) antecedent prompt and fade.

In choosing among approaches that produce low frequencies of error responding, most teachers will probably find the principle of parsimony (Etzel & LeBlanc, 1979) to be of value. As suggested by that principle, educators "should seek the least complex but still effective procedure for changing behavior" (Etzel & LeBlanc, 1979, p. 362).

Some teachers, then, might choose to use constant rather than progressive time delay because it is less complex to implement, and because it has not been found to be less effective or efficient than progressive time delay (e.g., Ault et al., 1988). Likewise, it could be considered advisable to avoid the use of graduated guidance in most situations due to difficulties in making decisions regarding increases or decreases in assistance and the potential resistance that may be encountered on the part of learners.

Future investigations that compare methods to achieve transfer of stimulus control should be encouraged. It is important to recognize, however, that very little research exists regarding specific practices associated with each method that are likely to yield the most beneficial results. Useful knowledge regarding effectiveness and/or efficiency might, therefore, result from examinations of topics such as performance criteria for changing prompts, the interval between natural cues and prompts, the effects of presenting and fading multiple forms of assistance, and the appearance of collateral behaviors. This type of research could contribute substantially to the value of future comparative investigations by increasing the probability that comparisons would be between the strongest forms of two or more methods, rather than between forms that differ in strength relative to other variations of the methods under scrutiny (see Ault et al., 1989).

Fading Teacher Assistance in Inclusive Settings

The technology available for fading teacher assistance requires a level of ongoing, systematic attention to the performance of individual students that may not be customary in many general education programs. Recent demonstrations, however, suggest not only that response-prompt fading systems may be effectively used in such programs, but that these systems can be capably managed even in elementary school settings by typically developing peers when sufficient levels of support are provided.

Wolery, Werts, Snyder, and Caldwell (1994) found that a constant time delay procedure could be used successfully by peer tutors in elementary school programs to teach their partner students with substantial disabilities to read sight words or recognize words that were incorrectly spelled. It was also found that the peer tutors could implement the time delay procedure with a high level of procedural accuracy when they were (a) given training prior to the initiation of tutoring sessions and (b) provided with written scripts to fol-

---

[2]Because recognizing and correcting errors is necessary for successful adaptations to natural settings, programs should be implemented to instruct learners in those skills (see Demchak, 1990).

low. In addition, the classroom teachers involved felt that the students benefited from high levels of positive contact that resulted from the low-error, constant time delay technique. The area in which peers experienced the most difficulty in applying time delay was in providing the correct delay interval. Fortunately, it has been found that the procedure is quite forgiving in that respect (Wilbers & Wolery, 1991). As Wolery and colleagues (1994) noted, "if the delay interval is too long on some trials, too short on other trials, and correctly implemented on still other trials, children's learning is not likely to be affected" (p. 432). In contrast, a failure to provide the prompt when needed can have a substantial negative impact on the outcomes of constant time delay (Holcombe, Wolery, & Snyder, 1994). Tutors observed by Wolery and colleagues (1994), however, implemented that aspect of the procedure with a high degree of fidelity.

In another demonstration, Hunt and colleagues (1994) explored skill acquisition by three second graders with severe to profound intellectual challenges and multiple disabilities when instructional support was provided by typically developing peers in the context of cooperative learning groups. Skills identified for acquisition by the peers in the groups were related to mathematics concepts, whereas those specified for each of the three target pupils included communication and motor skills prescribed by their Individualized Education Programs. The peers received training in the instructional process, as well as ongoing reminders and feedback that were gradually faded. Elements of instruction employed by the peers included the provision of cues designed to set the occasion for responding, individually determined prompts delivered as corrections, reinforcement for correct responding, and fading of prompts across sessions in a decreasing assistance format.

It was found that the peers could accurately implement the instructional procedures and that their instruction was effective in teaching the children with disabilities to independently perform the desired skills. In addition, it was observed that the typically developing children both increased their knowledge significantly in the targeted academic areas and performed in those areas as well as members of a control group in the classroom that did not include a pupil with severe disabilities.

Investigations such as those cited above do not indicate that the competent and effective use of prompt fading techniques can be accomplished without significant teacher involvement. Even when procedures are delivered by peers, teachers, or others with adequate expertise will need to plan, train the peers, perhaps collect data (depending on the skill level of the typically developing students), and make decisions regarding program changes. Current findings, however, do suggest that systematic methods to apply and fade response prompts can be integrated into general education structures in ways that do not constitute an undue burden and do not produce a negative impact on typically developing students (see also illustrations provided by Macdonald & York, 1989). In addition, a survey of a group of special education professionals in 20 states (Billingsley & Kelley, 1994) indicated that a large majority of the respondents felt that the use of such methods should not result in stigmatizing outcomes when applied in inclusive programs. Whether or not various instructional strategies that require considerable, individualized instructor contact do, in fact, produce stigmatizing effects remains a question to be answered by future investigation.

Although methods designed to achieve transfer of stimulus control can make a substantial contribution to the development of independent behavior by students with moderate to profound intellectual disabilities, a word of caution is in order. Response prompts require the presence of a teacher or other program manager. It is, therefore, possible that student behavior will come under the control of the presence of the individual who provided the prompts. In that event, the instructor may successfully fade assistance and erroneously conclude that the student is capable of independent performance. Unfortunately, performance may be reserved for those times when the instructor is in the vicinity.

If truly independent performance is desired, student behavior should always be assessed in the absence of those who provided instruction (unless such individuals will usually be present when the behavior is required) and in new, appropriate, nontraining situations (see White, 1988). Should assessments reveal that the instructor has become a controlling stimulus, his or her presence should be systematically faded, for example, by gradually increasing the distance from the student (Billingsley et al., 1994). Also, during program implementation, instruction could be provided by several persons to decrease the probability that dependence on the presence of any given individual would develop.

Conclusion

The knowledge base regarding the application of response prompts, and methods for the transfer of control of instructed behaviors from those prompts to natural cues, is considerable. As indicated by information contained in this chapter, there are many excellent descriptions of major prompt fading systems, examples of variations, demonstrations of successful application, and a number of guidelines for selecting an appropriate method. Typically, however, investigations or applications of the technology have focused on the effectiveness and efficiency of a particular method (or methods) in achieving transfer of stimulus control for skills within traditional curricular areas, such as academic or "functional" (e.g., reading, self-care, vocational) skills. Although such a focus has been of considerable value, it has recently been recognized that outcomes for students with disabilities should be viewed in a broader context that is particularly relevant within inclusive environments (Billingsley, Gallucci, Peck, Schwartz, & Staub, 1996; Schwartz, Staub, Gallucci, & Peck, 1995).

On the basis of their research findings, Schwartz and colleagues (1995) suggested that important school outcomes for individuals with disabilities accrue within at least three broad and overlapping domains of which development—the domain that includes the academic and functional outcomes most often associated with educational programs—is only one. The other two domains are membership and social relationships. Membership is considered "the sense of 'belongingness' which children with disabilities may experience in a variety of formal and informal contexts in inclusive schools" (p. 99) and "nondisabled children engaging in behaviors which suggest that they view children with disabilities as belonging to the group" (p. 99). Social relationships include outcomes related to "the characteristics and extent of personal relationships between children with disabilities and their peers" (p. 100).

In developing, selecting, or modifying methods by which persons with disabilities can learn to behave independently, educators would do well to consider the application of those methods to behaviors that could be important within nontraditional domains. Educators could, for example, apply prompting and fading systems to instruction designed specifically to promote group membership. Such instruction might involve skills associated with playing a part in a school play, participating in a cooperative learning group, playing games at recess, and so forth. Similarly, instructors could give increased attention to the enhancement of behaviors that are likely to advance social relationships, such as "hanging out" without direct adult supervision, helping other children, or soliciting assistance from peers when needed. On the other hand, it would be of value to consider the impact that particular methods, or particular modes of administration, might have on outcomes across multiple domains.

Older, typically developing students, for example, are probably apt to receive less physical assistance from adults than are younger children. For secondary-level students, therefore, the frequent use of prompt fading methods that involve reducing assistance solely within the physical dimension might yield desirable developmental outcomes, but simultaneously result in stigmatizing effects that would increase difficulties in establishing group membership or social relationships. It is also possible that employing peers rather than adults to administer and fade prompts in some instructional arrangements (e.g., cooperative learning) could produce high levels of positive interactions that would facilitate group membership and the formation of social relationships (see Wolery et al., 1994).

Several of the previously mentioned considerations remain to be subjected to research scrutiny. The paucity of research, however, should not prevent educators from being sensitive to the variety of outcomes that may contribute to the quality of life for their students or from being aware of the potential positive and negative effects that instructional methods could have on these outcomes. Ultimately, effective practices in the transfer of stimulus control should be conceptualized as those that not only promote independent and efficient performance but do so in a manner that permits or promotes behavioral changes that are most valued in inclusive schools and communities.

Acknowledgment

The development of this chapter was supported in part by U.S. Department of Education Field-Initiated Research Grant H023C20212. However, the opinions expressed herein do not necessarily reflect the position or policy of the U.S. Department of Education, and no official endorsement by the Department should be inferred.

QUESTIONS

1. What are response prompts and why is it important to fade them?

2. Why is it important to consider learner errors when selecting a prompt fading method?

3. What prompt fading methods seem most abrupt in the manner by which they attempt to achieve transfer of stimulus control?

4. Although many studies comparing the effectiveness and efficiency of prompt fading systems have been conducted, it is suggested in this chapter that difficulties exist in deriving firm recommendations for practice from that body of research. Why?

5. Presume you are collaborating with a general education teacher to provide effective instruction in an inclusive educational program. What information would you share with that teacher regarding the application and fading of response prompts?

References

Ault, M. J., Gast, D. L., & Wolery, M. (1988). Comparison of progressive and constant time-delay procedures in teaching community-sign word reading. *American Journal on Mental Retardation, 93,* 44–56.

Ault, M. J., Wolery, M., Doyle, P. M., & Gast, D. L. (1989). Review of comparative studies in the instruction of students with moderate and severe handicaps. *Exceptional Children, 55,* 346–356.

Bellamy, G. T., Horner, R. H., & Inman, D. P. (1979). *Vocational habilitation of severely retarded adults.* Baltimore: University Park Press.

Bereiter, C., & Engelmann, S. (1966). *Teaching disadvantaged children in the preschool.* Englewood Cliffs, NJ: Prentice-Hall.

Bijou, S. W. (1981). Behavioral teaching of young handicapped children: Problems of application and implementation. In S. W. Bijou & R. Ruiz (Eds.), *Behavior modification: Contributions to education* (pp. 97–110). Hillsdale, NJ: Erlbaum.

Billingsley, F. F. (1987). A probe intermix procedure for fading response prompts. *Behavioral Disorders, 12,* 111–116.

Billingsley, F. F., Gallucci, C., Peck, C. A., Schwartz, I. S., & Staub, D. (1996). "But those kids can't even *do* math": An alternative conceptualization of outcomes for inclusive education. *Special Education Leadership Review, 3,* 43–55.

Billingsley, F. F., & Kelley, B. (1994). An examination of the acceptability of instructional practices for students with severe disabilities in general education settings. *Journal of the Association for Persons with Severe Handicaps, 19,* 75–83.

Billingsley, F. F., Liberty, K. A., & White, O. R. (1994). The technology of instruction. In E. C. Cipani & F. Spooner (Eds.), *Curricular and instructional approaches for persons with severe disabilities* (pp. 81–116). Needham Heights, MA: Allyn & Bacon.

Billingsley, F. F., & Romer, L. T. (1983). Response prompting and the transfer of stimulus control: Methods, research, and a conceptual framework. *Journal of the Association for the Severely Handicapped, 8,* 3–12.

Browder, D. M., & Snell, M. E. (1993). Functional academics. In M. E. Snell (Ed.), *Instruction of students with severe disabilities* (4th ed., pp. 442–479). New York: Merrill.

Carr, E. G., & Durand, V. M. (1985). Reducing behavior problems through functional communication training. *Journal of Applied Behavior Analysis, 18,* 111–126.

Charlop, M. H., & Walsh, M. E. (1986). Increasing autistic children's spontaneous verbalizations of affection: An assessment of time delay and peer modeling procedures. *Journal of Applied Behavior Analysis, 19,* 307–314.

Cipani, E., Augustine, A., & Blomgren, E. (1982). Teaching profoundly retarded adults to ascend stairs safely. *Education and Training of the Mentally Retarded, 17,* 51–54.

Csapo, M. (1981). Comparison of two prompting procedures to increase response fluency among severely handicapped learners. *Journal of the Association for the Severely Handicapped, 6*(1), 39–47.

Demchak, M. A. (1990). Response prompting and fading methods: A review. *American Journal on Mental Retardation, 94,* 603–615.

Doyle, P. M., Wolery, M., Gast, D. L., Ault, M. J., & Wiley, K. (1990). Comparison of constant time delay and the system of least prompts in teaching preschoolers with developmental delays. *Research in Developmental Disabilities, 11,* 1–22.

Etzel, B. C., & LeBlanc, J. M. (1979). The simplest treatment alternative: Appropriate instructional control and errorless learning procedures for the difficult-to-teach child. *Journal of Autism and Developmental Disorders, 9,* 361–382.

Falvey, M., Brown, L., Lyon, S., Baumgart, D., & Schroeder, J. (1980). Strategies for using cues and correction procedures. In W. Sailor, B. Wilcox, & L. Brown (Eds.), *Methods of instruction for severely handicapped students* (pp. 109–133). Baltimore: Brookes.

Farmer, J. A., Gast, D. L., Wolery, M., & Winterling, V. (1991). Small group instruction for students with severe handicaps: A study of observational learning. *Education and Training in Mental Retardation, 26,* 190–201.

Foxx, R. M. (1982). *Increasing behaviors of severely retarded and autistic persons.* Champaign, IL: Research Press.

Foxx, R. M., & Azrin, N. H. (1973). *Toilet training the retarded: A rapid program for day and nighttime independent toileting.* Champaign, IL: Research Press.

Gast, D. L., Wolery, M., Ault, J. M., Doyle, P. M., & Alig, C. (1988). *How to use time delay.* Lexington: University of Kentucky, Department of Special Education.

Giangreco, M. F. (1983). Teaching basic photography skills to a severely handicapped young adult using simulated materials. *Journal of the Association for the Severely Handicapped, 8*(1), 43–49.

Godby, S., Gast, D. L., & Wolery, M. (1987). A comparison of time delay and system of least prompts in teaching object identification. *Research in Developmental Disabilities, 8,* 282–306.

Hall, M. G., Schuster, J. W., Wolery, M., Gast, D. L., & Doyle, P. M. (1992). Teaching chained skills in a non-school setting using a divided half instructional format. *Journal of Behavioral Education, 2,* 257–279.

Handen, B. L., & Zane, T. (1987). Delayed prompting: A review of procedural variations and results. *Research in Developmental Disabilities, 8,* 307–330.

Holcombe, A., Wolery, M., & Snyder, E. (1994). Effects of two levels of procedural fidelity with constant time delay on children's learning. *Journal of Behavioral Education, 4,* 49–73.

Horner, R. H. (1988, May). Functional analysis in applied settings. In A. J. Cuvo (Chair), *Behavior analysis of community referenced skills: Issues in promoting and transferring stimulus control.* Symposium conducted at the 14th annual convention of the Association for Behavior Analysis, Philadelphia.

Hourcade, J. J. (1988). Effectiveness of gestural and physical guidance prompts as a function of type of task. *Education and Training in Mental Retardation, 23,* 38–42.

Hunt, P., Staub, D., Alwell, M., & Goetz, L. (1994). Achievement by all students within the context of cooperative learning groups. *Journal of the Association for Persons with Severe Disabilities, 19,* 290–301.

Kleinert, H. L., & Gast, D. L. (1982). Teaching a multihandicapped adult manual signs using a constant time delay procedure. *Journal of the Association for the Severely Handicapped, 6*(4), 25–32.

Koegel, R. L., & Egel, A. L. (1979). Motivating autistic children. *Journal of Abnormal Psychology, 88,* 418–426.

Koury, M., & Browder, D. M. (1986). The use of delay to teach sight words by peer tutors classified as moderately mentally retarded. *Education and Training of the Mentally Retarded, 21,* 252–258.

Lent, J. R. (1974). *How to do MORE: A manual of basic teaching strategy.* Bellevue, WA: Edmark.

Luyben, P. D., Funk, D. M., Morgan, J. K., Clark, K. A., & Delulio, D. W. (1986). Team sports for the severely retarded: Training a side-of-the-foot soccer pass using a maximum-to-minimum prompt reduction strategy. *Journal of Applied Behavior Analysis, 19,* 431–436.

Macdonald, C., & York, J. (1989). Instruction in regular education classes for students with severe disabilities: Assessment, objectives, and instructional programs. In J. York, T. Vandercook, C. Macdonald, & S. Wolff (Eds.), *Strategies for full inclusion* (pp. 83–116). Minneapolis: Institute on Community Integration, University of Minnesota.

McDonnell, J. (1987). The effects of time delay and increasing prompt hierarchy strategies on the acquisition of purchasing skills to students with moderate handicaps. *Journal of the Association for Persons with Severe Handicaps, 12,* 227–236.

McDonnell, J., & Ferguson, B. (1989). A comparison of time delay and decreasing prompt hierarchy strategies in teaching banking skills to students with moderate handicaps. *Journal of Applied Behavior Analysis, 22,* 85–91.

Miller, U. C., & Test, D. W. (1989). A comparison of constant time delay and most-to-least prompting in teaching laundry skills to students with moderate retardation. *Education and Training in Mental Retardation, 24,* 363–370.

Moran, D. M. (1994). *A comparison of the effects of fading within and across response prompt stimuli on the skill acquisition of students with severe disabilities.* Unpublished doctoral dissertation, University of Washington, Seattle.

Mosk, M. D., & Bucher, B. (1984). Prompting and stimulus shaping procedures for teaching visual-motor skills to retarded children. *Journal of Applied Behavior Analysis, 17,* 23–34.

Neel, R. S., & Billingsley, F. F. (1989). *IMPACT: A functional curriculum handbook for students with moderate to severe disabilities.* Baltimore: Brookes.

Schoen, S. F. (1986). Assistance procedures to facilitate the transfer of stimulus control: Review and analysis. *Education and Training of the Mentally Retarded, 21,* 62–74.

Schoen, S. F. (1989). Teacher students with handicaps to learn through observation. *Teaching Exceptional Children, 22*(1), 18–21.

Schoen, S. F., Lentz, F. E., & Suppa, R. J. (1988). An examination of two prompt fading procedures and opportunities to observe in teaching handicapped preschoolers self-help skills. *Journal of the Division for Early Childhood, 12,* 349–358.

Schuster, J. W, & Griffen, A. K. (1990). Using time delay with task analyses. *Teaching Exceptional Children, 22*(4), 49–53.

Schuster, J. W., & Griffen, A. K. (1993). Teaching a chained task with a simultaneous prompting procedure. *Journal of Behavioral Education, 3,* 299–315.

Schuster, J. W., Griffen, A. K., & Wolery, M. (1992). Comparison of simultaneous prompting and constant time delay procedures in teaching sight words to elementary students with moderate mental retardation. *Journal of Behavioral Education, 2,* 305–325.

Schwartz, I. S., Staub, D., Gallucci, C., & Peck, C. A. (1995). Blending qualitative and behavior analytic research methods to evaluate outcomes in inclusive schools. *Journal of Behavioral Education, 5,* 93–106.

Snell, M. E. (1982). Analysis of time delay procedures in teaching daily living skills to retarded adults. *Analysis and Intervention in Developmental Disabilities, 2,* 139–155.

Snell, M. E., & Zirpoli, T. J. (1987). Intervention strategies. M. E. Snell (Ed.), *Systematic instruction of persons with severe handicaps* (3rd ed., pp. 110–149). Columbus, OH: Merrill.

Steege, M. W., Wacker, D. P., & McMahon, C. M. (1987). Evaluation of the effectiveness and efficiency of two stimulus prompt strategies with severely handicapped students. *Journal of Applied Behavior Analysis, 20,* 293–299.

Sternberg, L., McNerney, C., & Pegnatore, L. (1985). Developing co-active imitative behaviors with profoundly mentally handicapped students. *Education and Training of the Mentally Retarded, 20,* 260–267.

Terrace, H. S. (1963). Errorless transfer of a discrimination across two continua. *Journal of the Experimental Analysis of Behavior, 6,* 223–232.

Venn, M. L., Wolery, M., Werts, M. G., Morris, A., DeCesare, L. D., & Cuffs, M. S. (1993). Embedding instruction in art activities to teach preschoolers with disabilities to imitate their peers. *Early Childhood Research Quarterly, 8,* 277–294.

Walls, R. T., Haught, P., & Dowler, D. L. (1982). Moments of transfer of stimulus control in practical assembly tasks by mentally retarded adults. *American Journal of Mental Deficiency, 87,* 309–315.

Weeks, M., & Gaylord-Ross, R. (1981). Task difficulty and aberrant behavior in severely handicapped students. *Journal of Applied Behavior Analysis, 14,* 449–463.

White, O. (1988). Probing skill use. In N. Haring (Ed.), *Generalization for students with severe handicaps: Strategies and solutions* (pp. 131–141). Seattle: University of Washington Press.

Wilbers, J. S., & Wolery, M. (1991, May). *Effects of high and low procedural fidelity during the delay interval of constant time delay.* Paper presented at the Annual Conference of the Association for Behavior Analysis, Atlanta, GA.

Wolery, M., Ault, M. J., & Doyle, P. M. (1992). *Teaching students with moderate to severe disabilities: Use of response prompting strategies.* New York: Longman.

Wolery, M., Bailey, D. B., & Sugai, G. M. (1988). *Effective teaching: Principles and procedures of applied behavior analysis with exceptional students.* Needham Heights, MA: Allyn & Bacon.

Wolery, M., & Gast, D. L. (1984). Effective and efficient procedures for the transfer of stimulus control. *Topics in Early Childhood Education, 4,* 52–77.

Wolery, M., Werts, M. G., Snyder, B. S., & Caldwell, N. K. (1994). Efficacy of constant time delay implemented by peer tutors in general education classrooms. *Journal of Behavioral Education, 4,* 415–436.

Wuerch, B. B., & Voeltz, L. M. (1982). *Longitudinal leisure skills for severely handicapped learners: The Ho'onanea curriculum component.* Baltimore: Brookes.

Zane, T., Walls, R. T., & Thvedt, J. E. (1981). Prompting and fading guidance procedures: Their effect on chaining and whole task teaching strategies. *Education and Training in Mental Retardation, 16,* 125–135.

Individual Needs of Students

SECTION IV

Best Practices

The best practice literature clearly points out that the individual needs of the student must be addressed at all levels. This starts with the development of Individualized Family Service Plans, Individualized Education Programs, and Individualized Transition Plans, which are based on the specific needs of the individual. Instructional and treatment programs should follow from this plan and also reflect the needs of the individual being served. Such programs should not be limited by the resources available or by the needs of the larger group being served. Finally, if the needs of the student are to be met, then there must be periodic review and revision of the Individualized Education Program.

Needs should be determined by appropriate assessment (see Section II) and should be evaluated and reviewed regularly (see Section V). Specific curriculum, effective instructional practices, and meeting the individual needs of students are closely related.

This Section of the Book

Section IV addresses practices that meet students' individual needs. Much like specific curricular and effective instructional approaches, meeting the individual needs of students requires teaching skills essential for both present and future functioning. Often such skills are adaptations or approaches specific to an individual student with developmental disabilities.

Multiculturalism as it relates to developmental disabilities is discussed in Chapter 14. Chapter 15 provides a discussion of how to facilitate friendships and other relationships. For students who have low social and functional skills, the facilitation of such relationships is essential. Chapter 16 offers a discussion of choice making by students. Such abilities lead to what is termed self-determination. The use of assistive technology may allow students to access environments, make academic gains, develop friendships, and make decisions on an independent basis. Chapter 17 presents the considerations for usage of technology. The section concludes with Chapter 18, a discussion of transition planning for students to enable smooth and effective moves to new settings.

Multicultural Practice in Mental Retardation and Developmental Disabilities

CHAPTER 14

Scott Sparks

Learning Outcomes

After reading this chapter, you should be able to

■ Distinguish between particularistic and pluralistic approaches to multiculturalism.

■ Identify several ways of overcoming language barriers in the educational setting.

■ Identify several methods for dealing with cultural conflict.

■ State the sequential nature of becoming committed to multiculturalism.

■ State that multiculturalism is more a process than a set of "ethnic" facts.

TERMS[1]

The following terms are important for the understanding of this chapter:

Biases: The exercise of discrimination toward a protected class (e.g., minorities, women); problems with tests or procedures that discriminate unfairly against minority groups in a culture because of their content, vocabulary, or other culturally determined expectations.

Bilingualism: The capacity for using two languages, usually with differing levels of skill. The greatest degree of bilingualism is the ability to speak, read, and write in two languages with the same proficiency as native speakers of each language.

Commitment: In this chapter, the multicultural organization that is genuinely committed to diverse representation of our society. It is sensitive to maintaining an open, supportive, and responsive environment; is working toward and purposefully includes elements of diverse cultures; and is authentic in its response to issues confronting it.

Cultural assimilation: Adherence to the dominant culture's sociocultural traditions and values; usually a prerequisite to social acceptability and access to political structure.

Cultural expectations: For example, the role of the child speaking to an adult may vary from an expectation of silence to a communication of respect to a belief that silence communicates defiance, depending on the cultural expectations.

Limited English proficiency: Limited ability to read, write, or speak English. Many individuals who are limited English proficient are those not born in the United States; those whose native language is not English; those from environments in which English is not the dominant language; or American Indian and Alaskan natives who come from environments in which a non-English language has significantly influenced their proficiency in English (Bilingual Education Act of 1984).

Prejudice: An irrational attitude of hostility directed against an individual, a group, a race, or their supposed characteristics. It is an attitude and, as such, is learned rather than innate behavior.

Respect: To regard and relate to with honor and consideration.

Sensitivity: Awareness and responsiveness of the behaviors, feelings, and motives of others (including cultural differences).

---

[1]See Appendix 14A for additional definitions.

Introduction

The world is rapidly changing and extremely diverse. One can travel across the United States, for example, and confront a plentitude of cultural differences. Educators are increasingly recognizing the challenges and benefits of this tremendous variety of beliefs and values. For students with developmental disabilities or mental retardation, responsive, multicultural educational environments are critical for the appropriate growth of both the learners and their educators. Learning in a multiculturally sensitive manner, from the perspectives of both the learner and the educator, is the focus of this chapter.

An understanding of students' developmental disabilities and cultural differences by others—that is, by school staff, fellow students, and classroom personnel—is necessary before meaningful multicultural education can occur. In a 1994 interview, Takaki (cited in Aronson, 1994) noted that, in order for people to get along and resolve problems, they must first learn more about one another. Takaki further noted that there are two types of multiculturalism: particularistic and pluralistic. The particularistic approach emphasizes the study of a specific people, whereas the pluralistic view emphasizes an examination of a broad range of ethnic and racial groups that characterize the people of a society. The latter approach is the preferred method in that focusing study on only one group can easily lead to separatism and racist attitudes, which in Takaki's view must be overcome before the American dream can become a promise. Students with developmental disabilities are being included more and more in typical educational settings with students of varied cultures and ability levels; therefore, the emphasis of this chapter is based on pluralistic views.

It should be noted that several other viewpoints regarding what is termed multicultural education exist among educators. Banks and Banks (1993) identified the following:

1. *Human relations approach*—Teaching of positive feelings and promotion of group identity and pride for students of color.

2. *Single-group studies*—Research into the characteristics of a particular group of people.

3. *Multicultural education*—Accommodation of various cultural learning styles within the curriculum.

The effective educator will become familiar with a wide variety of thought about multicultural education so that he or she can make informed decisions that are in the best interests of students who are culturally, linguistically, or developmentally different.

Students from culturally different backgrounds are many and widespread. Baruth and Manning (1992) reviewed the 1980 census data for four selected groups (Native Americans, African Americans, Asian Americans and Pacific Islanders, and Hispanic Americans) and their respective subgroups, and found that approximately 54.3 million people were represented in their selected sample. Undoubtedly these numbers have risen dramatically in the years since the 1980 census. Further, the migration of people from culturally different backgrounds into the United States is widespread and continues at a rapid pace.

Respecting diversity, a common theme throughout this chapter, is an essential component of multicultural practice. Grossman (1995) noted that, to increase respect and reduce prejudice, educators must "teach students that all people have similar needs, desires, and problems, but have different ways of satisfying and solving them" (p. 106). Anderson (1991) stated that respect is critical to achieve cultural sensitivity. By including aspects of students' culture in the curriculum, respect can be built and prejudice reduced. A number of curricular adaptations are presented in this chapter for use with students who have developmental disabilities or mental retardation. These adaptations focus on multicultural education as an ongoing part of the curriculum and not as a "special theme" phenomenon, such as the birthday of a famous person from a particular ethnic group. This respect for diversity is intended to benefit students who have disabilities as well, since society often considers these students to be a part of their own "handicapped culture." Special educators have long been aware that to promote acceptance of students with developmental disabilities, they must first educate the communities in positive ways about people with disabilities.

This awareness phase of multiculturalism is mentioned repeatedly in the literature as being an absolute first step in any multicultural program. (This issue is discussed more fully in the final section of this chapter.) However, research findings suggest that, before one can appreciate another's culture, one must first understand and appreciate one's own cultural beliefs and values (Abt-Perkins & Gomez, 1993; Lynch & Hanson, 1992; Grossman, 1995; York, 1991).

Does cultural identification have an impact on learning style? Certainly, students with cognitive disabilities exhibit their own individual learning styles, but how much can be attributed to their cultural affiliation? Diaz (1992) pointed out that cultural experiences can have an effect on a student's learning style and should be considered within a multicultural curriculum. However, he noted that, although certain characteristics can be attributed to culture, the educator must be careful not to stereotype all persons within a culture simply because they belong to that particular cultural group. Learning about individual cultures is a place to start the necessary cultural understanding, and Diaz provided several excellent insights into African American, American Indian, Asian American, and Hispanic American cultures regarding learning styles. By focusing on the specific ethnic group(s) with which one works, a culturally tailored curriculum can be developed. If, for instance, the teacher is aware that a particular child from a specific culture learns more by a verbal than a visual method, the teacher can make modifications to meet this need and, thus, maximize learning potential. The reader is encouraged to identify the specific cultural groups and to find out as much cultural information as appropriate. Contacting local ethnic social groups is an excellent way to gather important cultural information. Gilliland and Reyhner (1988) stated that the auditory teaching approach of the standard school curriculum may work well for urban students who are not Native American, but that Native American students are often highly visual learners due to their cultural upbringing and need a modification in the curriculum that embraces visual learners equally. This variation of learning style is only one of countless culturally related differences within a wide variety of cultural groups.

The terminology or jargon of multicultural education is critical for educators to know and use in a multicultural curriculum. Appendix 14.A lists many common terms used in this area. Professionals must become aware of these terms in order to interpret research and better serve students in a multiculturally sensitive manner. Language is a critical issue and must be considered in developing a multicultural curriculum.

Language Issues

One of the most obvious issues in multicultural education is modifying instruction for students who speak a primary language other than the one spoken by the larger society. In the United States, students are often expected to live up to unrealistic expectations of English competence, as are their parents when school personnel need to contact them. Language is also an issue at Individualized Education Program (IEP) meetings, where complete understanding is critical to developing an appropriate plan. Two primary language issues are discussed in this chapter: dealing with and preventing language barriers and incorporating language differences into the existing curriculum.

Overcoming Language Barriers

Perhaps the first thing that an educator can do to help overcome language barriers is to believe that language and dialectal differences represent a strength in any society. With this attitude, the teacher is less likely to devalue a person's language heritage in the classroom (Adger, Wolfram, & Detwyler, 1993). In classrooms that serve students with developmental disabilities, it is very important to help students preserve the language of their family and primary culture, thereby helping to assure a lifelong support structure. Grossman (1995) cited research suggesting that instructing students in their native language while they learn English as a

second language will help them adjust more quickly to the U.S. school system.

Another method of intervention to overcome language barriers is to use interpreters and translators. Fradd and Wilen (1990) defined interpreters as people who translate orally and translators as people who produce a written translation of what has been communicated. They further pointed out that, due to a paucity of bilingual professionals, alternatives such as using family members or volunteers to interpret must often be used. This is a less than perfect solution as these people are not trained professionals, which can have negative results (Lynch & Hanson, 1992). Due to today's recognition of civil rights, it is very common to see interpreters for individuals who are deaf and hard of hearing at public functions. It seems logical that the same type of service would be available to students with developmental disabilities who speak a different language, as well as their families, when interacting with educational agencies. In assessment practice, language translation has been mandated since the early 1970s. However, as Lynch and Hanson (1992) pointed out, many tests are not available in bilingual editions and one cannot assume that direct translation leads to appropriate assessment of nonbilingual tests. Other ways of gathering information, such as interviews, are very language directed and often require the services of interpreters and/or translators.

Fradd and Wilen (1990) suggested the following three entry-level requirements for interpreters and translators: (a) general English language and numeral literacy, as well as an understanding of general U.S. culture; (b) proficiency in a second language and understanding of the culture of the people who speak that language; and (c) a general knowledge and understanding of the institutions in which limited English-proficient students and families may need language assistance.

The issue of too few bilingual professionals is a very serious impediment to providing for the educational needs of students with developmental disabilities. For example, a common service for students with limited English proficiency is speech. However, a 1994 survey of teachers conducted by Roseberry-McKibbin and Eicholtz found that the most common type of speech treatment for students with limited English proficiency was language, but that 90% of the 1,145 respondents could not speak a second language and 76% had no coursework in working with students with limited English proficiency. Clearly, higher education must take a more active role in including bilingualism in educational preparation programs. Students with limited English proficiency, whether or not they are receiving special education services, are currently at a clear disadvantage due to this lack of professional expertise.

The simplest step a professional can take to build rapport with and gain trust of students and parents with language differences is to make a sincere attempt to learn as much as possible about their culture. In this way, the professional can determine cultural norms and taboos (Thomas & Grimes, 1990). Thomas and Grimes (1990) offered the following suggestions to help the professional become comfortable with people of different cultures: (a) learn as much language of the family as is needed to build rapport; (b) take courses in cross-cultural issues; (c) if possible, visit the countries from which the students derive; (d) visit their homes, eat their native foods, and live in their community; (e) read fiction and nonfiction about the different ethnic groups; (f) accompany a minority family to the welfare office, local hospital, or housing authority and experience first hand the way they are treated; and (g) try to live for a week on the salary of a single parent with a student who has a disability. Although these ideas were written for school psychologists, they are equally applicable to any professional who works with students and families who speak different languages from the predominant culture.

Language and Curriculum

Within the context of the curriculum, language can be a useful tool to infuse multiculturalism into the classroom routine. Students who have mental retardation and other developmental disabilities may feel alienated because of poor English skills and may not be able to keep up academically or socially. The task of the educator, in this case, is to help these students develop competence that peers can see and appreciate. One of the most obvious methods to use in this situation is to have each student with limited English proficiency demonstrate his or her strength in native language skills. Reading a book in another language will no doubt impress peers, and speaking fluently in the student's native tongue may also have this effect. The student with limited English proficiency might also take part in helping other students learn words and phrases in his or her language. The educator can develop activities about the student's home country to help develop understanding and ultimately acceptance. Through activities such as these, peers are more likely to model behavior and accept the new student. Roseberry-McKibben (1994) cited research to support the notion that students with limited English proficiency must practice English with English-speaking peers in order to develop English language skills most efficiently. This sharing of language results in the much-needed practice in linguistic and social skills. The educator should allow for a language-rich environment wherein both English and other languages are spoken frequently and with encouragement.

The educator must also be aware of language differences between students from different cultures. The languages of some cultures reflect respect for authority and being quiet, whereas others employ active and sometimes assertive inquiry. The professional must be aware of these communication differences when planning the curriculum for an individual class.

The timeline for a student with a cognitive disability who speaks another language to learn English like a native speaker must be realistically established. Banks and Banks (1993) noted that a typically developing student with limited English proficiency requires 5 to 7 years to "reach native-like control of the English language in order to perform well on academic tasks" (p. 229). An important implication of this timeline is the need for bilingual education. Banks and Banks (1993) suggested that at least 50% of academic instruction should be in the student's native tongue so that the student will be able to stay up with the cognitive challenges of the curriculum until English usage is appropriate for total academic instruction. According to Baruth and Manning (1992), the number of students with limited English proficiency has increased over the past decade and will continue to grow beyond the 1990s. Clearly, a plan to serve these students is needed.

By building language into the curriculum, the educator is sending a message that the language of every student is important and should be preserved. The culturally sensitive educator will identify and build on each learner's strengths and interests (Franklin, 1992). Grossman (1995) pointed out that "rejecting students' native languages can alienate students and lead them to develop poor self-concepts" (p. 187). It should be noted, however, that very few preservice training programs for teachers include a significant knowledge base in bilingualism or English as a second language.

Respect for Cultural Values

As stated previously, respecting the cultural values of others is an integral aspect of becoming culturally sensitive. The professional who works with people who have developmental disabilities must be culturally sensitive, especially when one considers the disproportionate number of minority students who receive special education services. This section explores the concept of working with culturally different persons, including students, families, and professional colleagues. Best practice ideas are presented in the area of cultural sensitivity and developmental disabilities.

Working with Culturally Different Persons

When interacting with others from culturally different backgrounds, professionals must take care not to stereotype based on ethnicity or other cultural factors. For example, Klein (1995) pointed out several stereotypical misconceptions about people from the culture known as Appalachian. Although the term Appalachian does not represent an ethnic cultural group, it does represent a wide range of behavior among people who identify with Appalachian culture. People from Appalachia are often referred to as Hillbillies and poor whites, and it is commonly held that they inbreed and produce a large number of offspring with serious disabilities. These myths about people from Appalachia have one thing in common: They have mostly negative connotations. Every cultural group is a target for misconceptions, and the overwhelming result of these stereotypes is negative. An open mind and a positive attitude are two things the effective professional should have prior to working with anyone from a culturally different lifestyle. Starting out on a positive note increases the probability of shared meaning and appropriate outcomes.

Developing an accurate understanding of any culture requires some effort and an understanding that one person cannot know everything about all the individual cultures represented in the world, or even in the United States. It is recommended, therefore, that the educator limit study to those people with whom he or she is most likely to come in contact, both in professional and private activities. This "localization" of multiculturalism serves to make it less daunting a task and ultimately a more meaningful experience. As noted in the beginning of this chapter, a pluralistic viewpoint implies development of central ideas and attitudes through multicultural learning. Although this chapter encourages a pluralistic approach, it is inevitable that some particularistic (group- or individual-specific) information must be obtained to effectively interact with individuals who are culturally different from the educator. This mixing of the two types of multiculturalism leads to a professional who is culturally sensitive in both familiar and unfamiliar cultural situations. Baruth and Manning (1992) offered the following five ideas to assist the professional in developing understanding of culturally diverse learners:

1. Read textbooks, journal articles, and other written material on cultural diversity and teaching/learning in multicultural settings.

2. Request information from organizations that disseminate objective information and promote the various cultures.

3. Meet on a first-hand basis culturally diverse learners and their families (perhaps in their homes) to gain a better understanding of what it means to be a culturally different learner.

4. Attend conferences that focus on cultural diversity and working with students and adolescents from the various cultures.

5. Read about cultural diversity in books and magazines that are written primarily for students and adolescents. (p. 163)

A somewhat outdated but still very useful series of reading lists on specific cultural populations and bilingualism was compiled in 1986 under the general title of *Communication Disorders in Multicultural Populations* by the American Speech-Language-Hearing Association's Committee on the Status of Racial Minorities.[2] Again, it is important to regard such information in general terms to help avoid unnecessary stereotyping. As pointed out by Diaz (1992), "effective multicultural education requires that values analysis, institutional and attitudinal reform, and social action accompany the acquisition of factual knowledge" (p. 40).

Along a more pluralistic vein is the way that professionals communicate with people from culturally different backgrounds. The language one uses to refer to an ethnic group, for instance, is clearly indicative of a particular cultural bias. Likewise, the body language that a professional uses in working with culturally different people can give away cultural bias. These language biases can be presented in very subtle ways, and often the professional is unaware of projecting cultural bias. However, to the person who is culturally different, whether developmentally disabled or not, language signals often are very clear and obvious. Lynch and Hanson (1992) suggested that communication effectiveness is improved when the professional does the following:

1. Respects individuals from other cultures,

2. Makes continued and sincere attempts to understand the world from others' points of view,

3. Is open to new learning,

4. Is flexible,

5. Has a sense of humor,

6. Tolerates ambiguity well,

7. Approaches others with a desire to learn. (pp. 51–52)

The self-awareness that the above ideas imply is completely consistent with the widely held notion that the first step to becoming culturally sensitive is to understand one's own culture (Abt-Perkins & Gomez, 1993). By thinking of oneself in cultural terms, a person develops sensitivity to a variety of cultural issues, such as family heritage, beliefs, and values. Culture is not limited to ethnic groups; rather, it is inherent in every individual.

As part of self-awareness, racial biases should also be explored. Hopson and Hopson's (1992) Racial Attitude Assessment Procedure (RAP) was developed to assist people to become aware of their own racial attitudes and biases. The idea of this questionnaire is not to achieve a numerical score, but rather to write down certain beliefs and values in order to provoke cultural thought. The following are the first 10 items on the questionnaire:

1. Black people are _____.

2. White people are _____.

---

[2]The reader may contact this organization by writing to 10801 Rockville Pike, Rockville, MD 20852.

3. I like Black people who _____.

4. I don't like Black people who _____.

5. In school Black people _____.

6. In school White people _____.

7. My greatest fear of Black people _____.

8. My greatest fear of White people _____.

9. The thing I have most in common with White people is _____.

10. The thing I have most in common with Black people is _____. (Hopson & Hopson, 1992, pp. 22–23)

Although the statements are directed toward African American and Caucasian people, any cultural affiliation can be substituted. The educator should know that Hopson and Hopson intended their questionnaire to be done within a family to help family members develop cultural understandings, so some questions (e.g., 18 and 19 on parental attitudes on a number of variables, such as child rearing) should probably be omitted when assessing individuals outside family groups. If one intends to use these family-sensitive questions with students or other groups, caution should be taken regarding issues of confidentiality and privacy. Further, in keeping with good values clarification requirements, any person has the option of rejecting self-disclosure. However, the information derived from this questionnaire might prove valuable in infusing multiculturalism into everyday interactions.

Individuals with developmental disabilities are often viewed in U.S. society as being part of a "handicapped culture." Indeed, this cultural identity also should be dealt with in multicultural education (Baruth & Manning, 1992). Within a multicultural perspective, the disability is accepted as a part of the normalcy of the individual. By embracing the concept of "normal" from an individual rather than a group perspective, being normal is the everyday experience of each person. It is difficult for people to define normal from a group perspective. One approach that has proven effective is to ask a group of people who among them is normal and see what reaction is forthcoming. By defining a developmental disability as a part of a person's normal culture, there would seem to be a greater likelihood of acceptance by others.

Cultural Conflict

Given the hundreds of cultures that exist in the United States, it should come as no surprise that cultural conflict arises. Cheng (1987) pointed out that, when two or more cultures come into contact with one another, conflicts may arise. Cheng further stated that results of cultural conflicts can be either negative or positive:

Negative Conflict Results

1. culture shock

2. marginality (a feeling of isolation one has when one remains on the margins of two cultures)

3. bicultural confusion

4. behaviors such as fighting, drinking, disrespect

Positive Conflict Results

1. contrast and comparison

2. innovation and change

3. new strategies for survival

4. behaviors that arise from a clear understanding of cultural values and from active rather than passive participation in cultural interaction (pp. 5–6)

Certain cultural beliefs may come into conflict with law in the United States. For example, female vaginal mutilation for certain African rituals would be illegal in the United States. When this type of conflict occurs, the minority culture must either change or accept the consequences of continued cultural practice. Of course, this raises the legitimate concern about who makes such cultural decisions and how they are made. The educator who works with students with developmental disabilities should be aware of such legal conflicts and seek positive solutions rather than treat traditional cultural practices with disrespect. Often, people with developmental disabilities have been the target of health practices, such as sterilization, that U.S. society would find unacceptable for persons without disabilities. In working against such practices, people may feel disrespect for their traditional cultural experiences and begin to see their own experience from a negative viewpoint. The purpose of multicultural education is not to become a good judge of another's culture, but to gain understanding from another's perspective. Although conflicting values should be dealt with in the classroom so that students will be able to make a cultural choice with full understanding of the consequences, effective educators mute personal judgments.

Although one frequently hears of conflict between cultural groups living near one another and experiencing cultural friction, conflict also occurs when a person first arrives in a new country. Wei, as cited in Cheng (1987), identified three general areas of conflict that refugee students may face upon arrival in the United States: emotional, cultural-social, and educational. A great deal of "culture shock" occurs when a person leaves his or her country of origin to live in a foreign country. The person faces many language barriers and everyday problems. Also, the educational system must loom menacingly to the young person from another country. Without adaptations to the U.S. system of education, too many of these culturally different students seeking an appropriate education find their way into special education programs.

Working with Culturally Different Families

Many issues surrounding working with parents and family members are covered in other chapters in this text (see Chapters 23 and 24), but a few points about culturally different families should be made at this point. Educators in the United States who work with students who have developmental disabilities are, by law, involved with parents through the IEP process. Working with families who are culturally different requires a clear understanding of their cultural values and beliefs and, often, a good deal of cultural sensitivity. Nevertheless, as Harry, Torguson, Katkavich, and Guerrero (1993) pointed out, very few higher education institutions train education preprofessionals in working with culturally different families.

An important consideration when working with culturally different families is how to avoid making unfounded generalizations based on their perceived involvement in their children's education. Grossman (1995) pointed out that some migrant Hispanic students miss a great deal of school, and school professionals often jump to the conclusion that Hispanic Americans in general devalue education. Although the economic realities of being a migrant worker seem obvious, these overgeneralizations are frequently made of poor, culturally different families. Many families cannot take the time to attend meetings or come to parent–teacher nights due to survival considerations. In rural areas, distance alone represents a major barrier when the school may be 20 miles away.

Another common belief among special educators serving students with developmental disabilities is that they have an obligation to train or educate parents in issues of both education and parenting (Harry, 1992). This represents a lack of respect for diverse parenting styles and is not appropriate in a culturally sensitive relationship. To assume that someone needs parenting education is egocentric and an invasion of privacy. Instead, the effective professional should learn from individual families. Roach (1994) stated that it is important to listen to what family members say about their cultural values and gain insight and trust before giving advice about private lives. Home visits can be an excellent way to develop trust and gain the needed cultural insight into a family.

A Multicultural Training Package

Much has been said in this chapter about the lack of training for professionals in multicultural education. In 1991, the standing committee on Multicultural and Ethnic Concerns of the Ohio Federation Council for Exceptional Students (OFCEC) developed a multicultural training package for both preservice and inservice special education professionals (Lockwood, Ford, Sparks, & Allen, 1991). The package titled *Culture: Differences? Diversity!* utilizes a trainer-of-trainers model to allow for rapid dissemination. The training package is a result of several years of study by the committee members who developed the package (Lockwood et al., 1991).[3]

The design of *Culture: Differences? Diversity!* allows for tailoring to specific cultural groups and in fact recommends that the package be used in a localized fashion; that is, those cultural groups that are served in the immediate geographic area should be the focus for training. Preservice programs may have to globalize the training somewhat, but as stated earlier in this chapter, it is practically impossible to become culturally knowledgeable of the hundreds of cultures found in schools. By localizing multicultural training, the professional does not feel as overwhelmed and sees an immediate relevance to what is being presented. *Culture: Differences? Diversity!* has a pluralistic viewpoint in that it embraces the notion of developing positive, general attitudes toward culturally different persons, while having at the same time a particularistic aspect wherein specific cultural groups within a local geographic area are identified and studied. The training package focuses on serving learners who have developmental disabilities by helping professionals become culturally sensitive and therefore better able to meet diverse needs.

Culture: Differences? Diversity! trainings have two parts: Part A is designed to develop an awareness mindset, and Part B is designed to provide in-depth exploration related to the designated topics to be infused with multicultural concepts. This is important because educators' values and attitudes have a direct impact on the design and implementation of learning environments and services for culturally and linguistically diverse learners, as well as interactions with their families. Prior to conducting the training, the trainer should

1. have actively participated in at least one structured multicultural training program,

2. be familiar and comfortable with a multicultural frame of reference and concepts as discussed in the package,

3. have completed independent research and readings in the area of cultural diversity,

4. have knowledge of multicultural resources and references (written and human), and

---

[3]The *Culture: Differences? Diversity!* training package is available free of charge by contacting Rosa Lockwood, Division of Special Education, 933 High Street, Worthington, OH 43085-2650. An accompanying training video is also available for a nominal fee.

5. familiarize himself or herself with the local cultural groups included in schools of training participants.

The training consists of exploration activities in five component areas that serve as the foundation for *Culture: Differences? Diversity!* These five component areas are as follows (Lockwood et al., 1991):

1. Acquiring cultural awareness of culturally and linguistically diverse groups, as well as gaining knowledge about one's own culture.

2. Understanding cultural differences that learners bring to the educational environment (different values and belief systems) that will allow them to respond differently from each other and also the teachers they may have. Educators must be aware of and understand the differences, identify the many similarities among cultures, and begin to respect the right to be different.

3. Appreciating the diversity of culturally and linguistically diverse learners and their families and being culturally sensitive. Educators have a responsibility to identify what is important to individual groups and demonstrate respect as they, the educators, work with them in the learning environment.

4. Valuing diversity, which begins with self-valuing and discovering what and how individuals feel about themselves. Self-examining individual value systems and attitudes is a prerequisite for understanding the role that self-knowledge plays in self-valuing. Educators who demonstrate a clear self-identity of whom they are culturally can assist culturally and linguistically diverse learners with this important need, with the end result being improved self-esteem.

5. Being committed to appropriately educating culturally and linguistically diverse learners. Commitment is a genuine response to address the unique educational needs of these learners and being motivated to provide quality education and services to and for them.

Each component area is progressive in nature and builds upon the previous one so that one must start with awareness and end with commitment. This progression of cultural exploration cannot be changed and is a crucial part of *Culture: Differences? Diversity!* Ideally, the training is done over a 2-day period and focuses primarily on the awareness component, with the understanding that trainees will complete the other four areas on their own because the timeline for moving from awareness to commitment is extremely variable for each individual. *Culture: Differences? Diversity!* can be used without the formal training due to the extensive directions included, but it is most effectively used in conjunction with the training.

The videotape is a visual support for *Culture: Differences? Diversity!* It addresses definitions to facilitate initial discussions, lists nine characteristics identified as existing across all cultural groups, and has several vignettes of educators in different school settings sharing their experiences with culturally and linguistically diverse learners and their parents. The nine characteristics identified as existing across all cultural groups are family systems, roles and responsibilities, student rearing, communication, religious beliefs, lifestyles, health practices, learning styles, and parental attitude about education.

There are extremes in response to a disability by individual groups, from complete acceptance to nonacceptance. Some typical responses or feelings expressed about a disability may be "The disability is fate," "It is my/our fault," or "It is our responsibility." Culturally and linguistically diverse parents and family members can also share feelings of shame and/or embarrassment. Individual families may not seek assistance for their children and can be reluctant to accept assistance when it is offered. *Culture: Differences? Diversity!* attempts to bring these issues to the forefront for discussion purposes during training. The training stresses that multiculturalism is a process of understanding and tolerance and not a set of facts about a group of people.

Summary and Conclusion

Respecting cultural values different from one's own is a hallmark in multicultural education in both typical and special education settings. Respecting different values from one's own can be difficult, but pays tremendous dividends in understanding and appreciating diversity. Respect and sincere listening skills are attributes that can lead to trust and effective multicultural educational practice.

Multicultural education for people who have developmental disabilities including mental retardation is important, but it is critical for those professionals who serve them in educational settings. As Aronson (1994) noted regarding whether one approaches such instruction from a pluralistic or particularistic perspective, learning more about one another's cultural identity and values is the key to successful multicultural programs. Development of this cultural sensitivity will lead to a world with fewer children who grow up to be racists and more appreciation of cultural diversity.

People with disabilities are frequently seen as having their own handicapped culture. Educators must dispel misconceptions about these students in order to serve them appropriately. For instance, a specific person's disability has an impact on his or her learning style, but that person's primary culture may have an even greater impact. To focus on the disability alone serves to devalue the cultural aspects of a person's life. Effective educators of students with developmental disabilities choose a holistic perspective when developing curricula. These educators learn to serve and understand the whole person and not merely a student's disability.

The issue of individual normalcy should be embraced by every special educator.

Modifying instruction to accommodate linguistically diverse students is crucial for their academic success. By incorporating language differences into the curriculum, the effective educator can help foster understanding among students. Further, by being aware of one's own language, the educator can recognize and appreciate the linguistically different student. Word selection can demonstrate acceptance or rejection, and a multitude of emotional feelings in between. By using interpreters and translators, common misunderstandings can be avoided. By advocating bilingual education, linguistically diverse students have a chance to succeed academically and socially. When bilingual instruction is unavailable, English as a Second Language instruction is preferable to having little or no language accommodation whatsoever.

There is a lack of adequate multicultural preservice training programs. *Culture: Differences? Diversity!* is one program that aims at the higher education community and serves as a resource for inservice educators as well. This package emphasizes five stepwise components that lead to a commitment to quality multicultural education for students with developmental disabilities. Trained professionals are in demand in multicultural education, and higher education must answer the call to deliver such training. Finally, it must be noted that multicultural sensitivity is the result of a process and does not happen without some effort. One must study cultural issues, become familiar with culturally different individuals and groups within one's local geographic region, and develop a positive awareness for one's own culture. To effectively and appropriately serve students with developmental disabilities, the educator must become a learner and embrace the positive concepts of multiculturalism.

 ## QUESTIONS

1. Explain the difference in multicultural perspective between the particularistic and pluralistic viewpoints.

2. *Culture: Differences? Diversity!* is a training package designed for what group of professionals?

3. List three things the teacher can do to enhance the education of students with limited English proficiency.

4. The RAP technique assesses what characteristic?

5. Discuss three ways that cultural conflict can arise.

Appendix 14A
Cultural Terminology Defined[4]

Acculturation: The influence of intercultural contact between different cultural groups on the cultural patterns of one or both groups.

Active listening: Total attention to the speaker and sensitivity to what is being communicated at the verbal and nonverbal levels; being attuned to underlying messages, that is, to what is not being directly expressed.

Ancestors: Closely related people with common blood group genes.

Appreciating: Evaluating the worth, value, or significance of something.

Attitudes: "Culture as a convenient label for knowledge, skills, and attitudes that are learned and passed on from one generation to the next. Accordingly, this transmission of culture occurs in a physical environment in which certain places, times, and stimuli have acquired special meanings" (Rosa Lockwood, personal communication, September 1994).

Barrier: Something that acts to hinder or restrict.

Bicultural: Equal assimilation within one individual of the symbols, linguistic traits, communication styles, values, and attitudes of two cultures.

Cooperative learning: Groups of mixed ability working on a common task. All students in each group must have some responsibility for mastering the material. The group can succeed in reaching its goal only if everyone in the group learns the information or completes the task.

Cultural characteristics: The symbolic, ideational, and intangible aspects that distinguish human societies from one another.

Cultural experience: The behavior patterns and attitudes specific to a given social group.

Curriculum: An organized framework that delineates the content students will learn, the process through which they achieve the identified curricular goals, what teachers do to help them achieve these goals, and the context in which teaching and learning occur.

Dialect: Any given variety of language shared by a group of speakers. These varieties typically correspond to other differences between groups, such as ethnicity, religion, geographic location, social class, or age.

Disability: A physical or mental impairment that substantially limits a person in some major life activity (e.g., walking, talking, breathing, working); a person may also have a record of such a physical or mental impairment or is regarded as having such an impairment and, although it does not limit him or her in any major life activity, if the person is discriminated against, then he or she is defined as having a disability.

Diversity: The fact or quality of being different.

ESL: English as a second language; English instruction in the classroom or in special pull-out classes until English proficiency is achieved; the field of teaching English to speakers of other languages. Three major areas: (a) integrating students' cultural experiences and background into meaningful language learning, (b) teaching structures and vocabulary relevant to students' learning experiences, and (c) applying techniques from second language learning to subject matter presented in English.

Ethnocentric: The belief that one's cultural ways are not only valid and superior to those of others but also universally applicable in evaluating and judging human behavior.

Exceptional learner: A learner who deviates from the average or normal learner in (a) mental characteristics, (b) sensory abilities, (c) neuromotor or physical characteristics, (d) social behavior, or (e) communication abilities, or a learner who requires a modification of school practices or special educational services to develop to maximum capacity.

Expectations: The ways of thinking, behaving, and communicating that are required or anticipated of individuals within specific environments, based on values of the environment (e.g., school).

Generalizations: Ethnocentric perceptions about other cultures based on a little knowledge; nonethnocentric perceptions about other cultures based on a lot of knowledge.

Group identity: The way in which members of a group perceive themselves and are perceived by others; derives from cultural patterns such as values, behaviors, beliefs, language, a sense of history, and ethnicity (defined on the basis of national origin, religion, and/or race).

Home language: Verbal and nonverbal communication, along with the unspoken rules governing discourse that are used in the home environment; may be discontinuous with the language used in the school setting due to cultural differences.

Interactive patterns: Verbal and nonverbal interactions that include eye contact, body stance, facial expressions, social space, and paralanguage (i.e., voice quality, verbal expression, nonverbal sounds) and the messages that these patterns send, intentionally or

---

[4]See Terms at beginning of chapter for additional definitions.

not. Cultural codes define the range of patterns and attach a value to them, such as appropriate, inappropriate, or unacceptable.

Interpersonal skills: The ability to initiate, develop, and maintain effective, fulfilling relationships with other people.

Language differences: Basic verbal and nonverbal behavioral variations between groups of people, as influenced by physical, social, and cultural separation.

Language disorder: Difficulty or inability to master the various language systems and their rules of application, morphology, phonology, syntax, semantics, and pragmatics, which then interferes with communication.

Learning environments: Conditions prepared by educators that allow the children freedom to interact with materials, peers, and the teachers who understand the children's learning need for space, materials, and time to play in an atmosphere of trust and respect.

Lifestyle: A way of life or style of living that reflects the attitudes or values of an individual or group.

Linguistic style: A distinctive manner of language expression and speech system that begins in early childhood and to a large extent remains throughout life. Linguistic style is inextricably linked to culture.

Misconception: A mistaken view, opinion, or belief.

Monocultural: Reflective view that there is only one reality, generally that of the dominant group and exclusive of the viewpoint of many other cultures; the main philosophy of the U.S. education system today.

Motivation: Promoting, stimulating, or impeding in one-to-one or small-group relationships.

Needs: Deficiencies or requirements that people seek to fulfill personal well-being. Behavior is motivated toward goals to satisfy deficiency needs (survival, safety, belonging, self-esteem) and being needs (intellectual achievement; aesthetic appreciation; self-actualization, which is another term for the realization of personal potential). Multicultural needs include seeking personal fulfillment across varying components of diverse regional, ethnic, and religious teachings within a larger society.

Nonverbal Behaviors: Physical or gestural communications or actions and body language that do not use oral language. Functions of nonverbal communication include relaying messages, augmenting verbal communication, contradicting verbal communication, or replacing verbal communication. Features include body build, body odor, hair, dress, kinetics, proxemics, facial expressions, eye contact, and paralanguage. Often both the physical features and their interpretations are influenced by cultural backgrounds.

Oral language: Communication through speech, usually the most efficient mode of communicating. Components include phonology, morphology, syntax, fluency, semantics, and pragmatics.

Overt behaviors: An individual's actions that are observable to others; termed by behaviorists as "overt" to distinguish them from behaviors that are not observable but that can be recorded or registered by various instruments (electroencephalographs, blood pressure gauges, lie detectors, etc.).

Parental involvement: Advocating for the best quality of life for one's children.

Pluralism: The maintenance of a culturally distinct identity by each diverse group that coexists within society; degree of cultural differences that are fostered and encouraged by society.

Pragmatics: The use of language in the context in which it occurs; deals with the relationships among language, perception, and cognition. Examples include knowing what to say, to whom, when, how, and under what circumstances.

Roots: A person or family as the source of offspring or descendants.

Self-actualization: The human necessity to develop one's full potential; the need to strive to become the most effective human being possible.

Self-concept: A person's perception of self that forms through social interaction with others and is a result of how the person perceives the responses of others toward him or her; it serves to guide or influence a person's behavior. Consists of a person's judgments and attitudes about his or her behavior, abilities, and even appearance; it is the person's answer to the question "Who am I?"

Self-esteem: Personal views of physical self, moral-ethical self, personal self, family self, and social self, which evolve from one's subjective evaluation of others' appraisals of oneself.

Significant others: Important people in a child's life who provide role models for sex-role identification, attitudes, values, and beliefs; models for social learning and sources for a child's social identity.

Similarities: Ways in which two or more things (in this case cultures) are alike in substance or structure.

Stereotypes: Ways of patterning that allow people to make shortcuts in their thinking. The principal menace of stereotyping is that it does not allow the communicator to see the other person singly, as a unique individual.

Strengths: Attributes or characteristics that are valued within a group and that help to define the group.

Teaching style: In this chapter, the techniques used by the teacher to serve as a vital catalyst in addressing and challenging distorted prejudices and stereotypes; facilitating recognition, understanding, and appreciation of cultural diversity; and reflecting, supporting, and affirming the identities, experiences, and concerns of all ethnic groups.

Tolerance: The capacity to bear something, although it may be at times unpleasant. Tolerance of differences means that one endures, but not necessarily embraces, them.

Values: Abstract, generalized principles of behavior to which members of society attach a high worth or regard. Individuals acquire their values during socialization. They are one of the most important elements of cultures and microcultures that distinguish one group from another. They influence behavior and also how people perceive their environments.

Variables: Characteristics that may assume different values. The six major variables of culture are (a) values and behavioral styles; (b) languages and dialects; (c) nonverbal communication; (d) cultural cognitiveness; (e) perspectives, world views, and frames of reference; and (f) identification.

Whole language: Speaking, listening, reading, and writing as users interact with life. Whole language evolves as a process based on children's individual interests, born out of their daily experiences and fostered by their play.

References

Abt-Perkins, D., & Gomez, M. L. (1993). A good place to begin: Examining our personal perspectives. *Language Arts, 70,* 193–202.

Adger, C. T., Wolfram, W., & Detwyler, J. (1993). Language differences: A new approach for special educators. *Teaching Exceptional Children, 26*(1), 44–47.

American Speech-Language-Hearing Association. (1986). *Communication disorders in multicultural populations.* Rockville, MD: Author.

Anderson, N. B. (1991). Understanding cultural diversity. *American Journal of Speech-Language Pathology, 1*(1), 9–10.

Aronson, D. (1994). Reflections from a different mirror. *Teaching Tolerance,* pp. 11–15.

Banks, J. A., & Banks, C. A. (1993). *Multicultural education: Issues and perspectives* (2nd ed.). Needham Heights, MA: Allyn & Bacon.

Baruth, L. G., & Manning, M. L. (1992). *Multicultural education of children and adolescents.* Needham Heights, MA: Allyn & Bacon.

Cheng, L. L. (1987). *Assessing Asian language performance: Guidelines for evaluating limited-English-proficient students.* Rockville, MD: Aspen.

Diaz, C. (1992). *Multicultural education for the 21st century.* Washington, DC: National Education Association.

Fradd, S. H., & Wilen, D. K. (1990). Using interpreters and translators to meet the needs of handicapped language minority students and their families. *National Clearinghouse for Bilingual Education, 4,* 1–23.

Franklin, M. E. (1992). Culturally sensitive instructional practices for African-Americans. *Exceptional Children, 59,* 115–122.

Gilliland, H., & Reyhner, J. (1988). *Teaching the native American.* Dubuque, IA: Kendall/Hunt.

Grossman, H. (1995). *Special education in a diverse society.* Needham Heights, MA: Allyn & Bacon.

Harry, B. (1992). Restructuring the participation of African-American parents in special education. *Exceptional Children, 59*(2), 123–131.

Harry, B., Torguson, C., Katkavich, J., & Guerrero, M. (1993). Crossing social class and cultural barriers in working with families: Implications for teacher training. *Teaching Exceptional Children, 26*(1), 48–51.

Hopson, D. P., & Hopson, D. S. (1992). *Different and wonderful: Raising black children in a race-conscious society.* New York: Simon and Schuster.

Klein, H. A. (1995). Urban Appalachian children in northern schools: A study in diversity. *Young Children, 50*(3), 10–16.

Lockwood, R., Ford, B. A., Sparks, S. S., & Allen, A. (Eds.). (1991). *Culture: Differences? Diversity!* (Available from the Ohio Federation Council for Exceptional Children, c/o Rosa Lockwood, Ohio Department of Education, Division of Special Education, 933 High St., Worthington, OH 43085)

Lynch, E. W., & Hanson, M. J. (1992). *Developing cross-cultural competence: A guide for working with young children and their families.* Baltimore: Brookes.

Roach, D. P. (1994). My grandma's house: Reaching out to underserved families of children and youth with neurobiological, emotional or behavioral differences. *Focal Point, 5*(11), 21–23.

Roseberry-McKibben, C. (1994). Assessment and intervention for children with limited English proficiency and language disorders. *American Journal of Speech-Language Pathology, 3*(3), 77–88.

Roseberry-McKibbin, C. A., & Eicholtz, G. E. (1994). Serving children with limited English proficiency in the schools: A national survey. *Language, Speech, and Hearing Services in Schools, 25*(3), 156–164.

Thomas, A., & Grimes, J. (1990). *Best practices in school psychology—II.* Washington, DC: National Association of School Psychologists.

York, S. (1991). *Roots and wings: Affirming culture in early childhood programs.* St. Paul, MN: Toys 'n Things Press.

Facilitating Friendships and Social Relationships Between Students with Severe Disabilities and Their Peers

CHAPTER 15

MaryAnn Demchak

Learning Outcomes

After reading this chapter, you should be able to

■ Identify the importance of interactions and friendships between students with and without disabilities.

■ Identify various types of relationships and interactions that can occur between students with and without disabilities.

■ Identify and be able to implement general strategies that are appropriate for facilitating interactions for students of preschool through high school ages.

■ Identify and be able to implement a circle of friends activity to facilitate friendships between students with and without disabilities.

TERMS

The following terms are important for the understanding of this chapter:

Alternative communication: Methods of communicating that *replace* verbal communication (e.g., communication boards, wallets, or books; electronic communication devices).

Augmentative communication: Those strategies that *supplement* verbal communication skills.

Circle of friends: Structured activity completed with students without disabilities to discuss the importance of friendships and relationships in their lives and to generate ideas regarding ways in which they can be friends with peers who have disabilities.

Students with severe disabilities: Individuals who traditionally have been labeled as moderately, severely, or profoundly mentally retarded; those who require extensive, ongoing supports in more than one major life area.

Introduction

Developing friendships and social relationships with others is important for any individual. Friendships and social relationships serve various purposes and provide numerous benefits to all individuals. Friendships at all ages are typically mutually reciprocal relationships in that friends provide information, emotional support, companionship, and so forth, to one another. Individuals who form friendships with one another frequently come together as a result of common interests or concerns (Zetlin & Murtaugh, 1988). Additionally, friendships typically extend beyond family members to include other individuals. For example, these relationships provide young children with the benefit of learning to interact with individuals outside of their immediate families (Zetlin & Murtaugh, 1988).

Unfortunately, individuals with disabilities, especially severe disabilities, frequently have fewer friends and fewer interactions with peers than do individuals without disabilities. Typically, individuals with severe disabilities do not have friendships that extend beyond their immediate families and staff who are paid to be in their lives. However, friendships between individuals with severe disabilities and individuals without disabilities are possible and can be beneficial to both groups. Peck, Donaldson, and Pezzoli (1990) found that adolescents without disabilities benefited in a number of ways, including improved self-concept, greater understanding of diversity, greater tolerance of others, and growth in the social-cognitive area. These teenagers also reported that they enjoyed their friendships with peers with severe disabilities and thought these relationships were relaxed and accepting.

Friendships for students with severe disabilities are viewed as important by parents and teachers. Parents of students with moderate, severe, or profound disabilities reported that they thought some of the school week should be spent on helping their children to develop friendships and social relationships (Hamre-Nietupski, 1993). Friendships were particularly important to parents of younger children. Additionally, both regular education teachers (Hamre-Nietupski, Hendrickson, Nietupski, & Shokoshi-Yekta, 1994) and special education teachers (Hamre-Nietupski, Hendrickson, Nietupski, & Sasso, 1993) of students with moderate, severe, or profound disabilities indicated that they believe friendships for these students are not only possible but can, as well as should, be facilitated. Both groups of teachers also thought they should have a role in implementing strategies for facilitating friendships between students with severe disabilities and students without disabilities.

The purpose of this chapter is to provide parents, teachers, and others with strategies that they can use to facilitate the development of social relationships and friendships between students with severe disabilities and students without disabilities. Individuals with severe disabilities are those who have traditionally been labeled as moderately, severely, or profoundly mentally retarded. These individuals require extensive, ongoing supports in more than one major life area (e.g., mobility, communication, self-care, community living, employment) to participate in integrated community settings ("Definition," 1991). This chapter presents general strategies that are appropriate for students of preschool through high school ages.

Strategies for Facilitating Friendships and Social Interactions and Relationships

For interactions to occur between students with severe disabilities and peers without disabilities, and ultimately to have friendships or meaningful social relationships develop, it is frequently necessary for parents and teachers to facilitate interactions between these two groups of students. It is insufficient simply to have students with severe disabilities physically placed in classrooms with their nondisabled peers. It is likely that individuals with and without disabilities will need ideas for ways in which to interact with one another. Additionally, students both with and without disabilities will

likely require and benefit from direct instruction regarding interactions with one another. Although professionals cannot promise that actual friendships will occur, providing opportunities for positive interactions may be a first step in development of friendships.

The first step in facilitating interactions between students with and without disabilities is to provide opportunities that help to bring students together. That is, students with severe disabilities need to have regular, meaningful contact with their peers without disabilities. Thus, an important initial step is for students with severe disabilities to attend school with their nondisabled peers. However, it is necessary to move beyond simply being in the same building as other students to having regular contact with peers. Therefore, it is necessary for students with severe disabilities to participate in meaningful ways in regular education classes and activities with their nondisabled peers. If students with severe disabilities do not have regular social contacts with their nondisabled peers, it is unlikely that the students with severe disabilities will be accepted by their peers. Such contacts are necessary for an individual to gain acceptance by members of a community (Kennedy, Horner, & Newton, 1989).

When including students with severe disabilities in general education classrooms, natural proportions should be maintained. Thus, the number of students with severe disabilities included in any one class should not exceed that which would naturally occur given the number of students in the classroom. Effective practices also dictate that one teacher should not be identified as "the inclusion teacher" and all students with severe disabilities placed with that teacher. Rather, students with severe disabilities should be placed in various classes as appropriate for their chronological ages. The following strategies are based on the assumption that students with severe disabilities have meaningful, daily contacts with their nondisabled peers.

Facilitating Interactions

Simply having students with and without disabilities in close proximity to one another is a necessary first step, but it is insufficient for developing relationships and friendships. It is frequently necessary for teachers or teacher assistants to encourage students to interact with one another in a variety of situations. Brown and colleagues (1989) suggested 11 social relationships that can be facilitated between students with severe disabilities and students without disabilities in school settings: (a) peer tutor; (b) eating companion; (c) art, home economics, industrial arts, music, or physical education companion; (d) regular class companion; (e) at-school companion; (f) friend; (g) extracurricular companion; (h) after-school project companion; (i) after-school companion; (j) travel companion; and (k) neighbor.

Encouraging various relationships such as those listed leads to involving students without disabilities with their peers with severe disabilities in ways that move beyond helping interactions. Teachers frequently arrange for nondisabled peers to act as tutors or helpers for students with severe disabilities. Such a helping role is only one way in which students might interact with one another. Teachers should encourage students to interact in such a way that at times it is the student with severe disabilities who is helping other students. For example, in cooperative learning activities the student with severe disabilities could be assigned a role and/or materials that are vital to completion of the group's task. It is also beneficial to encourage students to "hang out" with one another, play together at recess, eat lunch together, work on school projects together, attend school functions together, and interact with one another in other ways the students choose. Although friends help or assist each other in various ways as part of that friendship, that role is only one aspect of the relationship. Similarly, friendships between students with and without disabilities should extend beyond helping relationships.

Facilitating Positive Attitudes

The manner in which the adults (e.g., teacher, teacher assistants) in the setting interact with students with severe disabilities will likely influence the way in which nondisabled peers interact with the students with disabilities. The teacher should demonstrate acceptance of and positive interactions with the student. Students will frequently imitate the behaviors that they see modeled by their teachers or other adults in the setting. Thus, if the teacher and teacher assistants are positive in their interactions with students with severe disabilities, the classmates are more likely to be positive in their interactions. In modeling appropriate interactions, the teacher should avoid use of language that is too juvenile for the student's chronological age when talking to the student with disabilities. Using language or interaction styles that are too juvenile can contribute to peers and others "babying" the student with severe disabilities or encourage the view that the student is less competent than he or she is.

The adults involved with the students with severe disabilities should facilitate presenting the students to others in a positive manner. For example, teachers can have the student share, independently or through adaptations, his or her special interests or talents with the class. This strategy allows others to see the student with disabilities as a competent individual and helps students to see areas of common interest. As previously mentioned, common interests are frequently a basis for the development of friendships. Young (e.g., preschool and elementary school) children may be encouraged to share common interests during group time or routine class activities. Older students may be encouraged to share information about interests during times that students typically interact socially. For example, sharing may occur before school or at lunch time. With both younger and older students, information regarding interests may be shared either verbally or nonverbally (e.g., prerecorded messages on alternative communication devices, photographs). Assisting students to view each other positively and as competent individuals can contribute to positive interactions.

Accommodations and Adaptations

Practitioners should make accommodations or adaptations in the environment to involve students with severe disabilities in meaningful ways in classroom activities. One specific, simple strategy is to avoid seating students with disabilities on the periphery of activities or on the outside of the class. Teachers may rationalize that such seating allows an aide, support teacher, peer tutor, or other person to provide assistance with minimum disruption to the class. Unfortunately, seating students with disabilities on the edge of the class may also lessen their involvement with peers during various class activities.

Adaptations also may be needed in the classroom activities, instructions, and materials for the students with severe disabilities to be involved in meaningful ways. Collaboration between special and regular education teachers is essential for development and implementation of adaptations. The professionals and paraprofessionals involved with the student should meet regularly to review class activities to determine appropriate modifications or supports that will increase involvement of students with severe disabilities. At the same time, the team must ensure that the educational needs of students with severe disabilities, as well as students without disabilities, are being met. Providing adaptations and supports assists peers in the environment to view students with severe disabilities as contributing members of the class and as competent. Subsequently, increased interactions may happen as a result of enhanced participation in classroom activities.

Teaching About Diversity and Friendships

Teachers can use the classroom curriculum to teach about diversity, equality, and friendships. Discussions about disabilities can be one part of a curriculum that focuses on diversity in general. Frequent class discussions that emphasize friendships and belonging can assist all students in becoming more aware of the importance of friendships and how they may encourage friendships with one another. In some instances, the classroom teacher may encourage dialogue focusing on facilitation of friendships for new students (with or without disabilities) (e.g., welcoming committees). In other cases, the classroom teacher might determine that it is necessary to facilitate specific discussions regarding concerns, fears, and questions that may arise pertaining to friendships or interactions with students with severe disabilities (e.g., how to respond when behavior problems occur, how to communicate with a peer who is nonverbal). The teacher can ask peers to help in planning strategies to facilitate friendships and interactions. For example, in a discussion with a fourth-grade class on how to involve a student with severe disabilities in recess activities, the peers provided suggestions on how rules of recess games could be modified, ideas for toys and activities that could be brought from home that would encourage interactions, and suggestions for peer buddies.

Collaborative problem solving that involves peers can lead to strategies that adults might never consider. For example, Bishop and Jubala (1994) described peers without disabilities who decided to wear their "special equipment" (e.g., orthodontic retainers, soccer shin-guards) as a means of encouraging a student with disabilities to wear his hearing aids. This strategy highlighted to everyone in the class that all individuals, with and without disabilities, have differences. Such an approach can help to facilitate a greater acceptance and understanding of such differences.

Cooperative Learning Activities

A frequent recommendation to encourage interactions between students with disabilities and peers without disabilities is for classroom teachers to use cooperative learning activities (Hamre-Nietupski et al., 1993; Hamre-Nietupski et al., 1994). Cooperative learning methodologies encourage collaboration among students and foster an expectation that students with severe disabilities will also participate in class activities with their nondisabled peers. Cooperative learning activities can lead to increased interactions between students with and without disabilities, which may extend beyond those classroom activities. The teacher should give the students with severe disabilities valued roles in cooperative learning groups and other class activities to demonstrate their strengths and competence.

Teaching Friendship Skills

In some instances it may be necessary to teach friendship skills directly to students with severe disabilities, as well as to students without disabilities. Students should be taught conflict resolution skills as well as how to share and provide support to one another (Stainback, Stainback, & Wilkinson, 1992). Specific skills may also need to be taught in regard to communication and social skills (e.g., greetings, conversation skills, turn taking, game playing skills). If students with severe disabilities use augmentative or alternative communication devices or strategies, then their peers need to be taught how to interact with the students using alternative

communication. Teaching all students the skills required to play games may also contribute to the development of social relationships (Taylor, Asher, & Williams, 1987). Classroom teachers may need to provide encouragement to all students, with and without disabilities, to display the targeted skills and to praise students for using the skills.

Nondisabled peers may find it particularly challenging to respond to inappropriate social behaviors (Peck et al., 1990). Therefore, peers may need to be taught specific strategies for responding to such behaviors. Peck and colleagues (1990) suggested that nondisabled peers may need to be taught how to provide clear feedback to peers who do not react to social cues indicating disapproval or discomfort. In some instances, peers may need to be taught specific strategies for dealing with problem behaviors (e.g., how to redirect a student, how to prompt alternative behaviors). Additionally, adults in the setting should respond to challenging behaviors in a manner that teaches peers positive social or coping skills. Thus, positive behavior management strategies are encouraged to increase the likelihood that peers will use positive means of interacting when inappropriate behaviors occur. The adults become positive role models for the nondisabled peers in regard to responding to problem behaviors. Teaching specific interaction skills to students with and without disabilities may assist students in feeling more comfortable in their interactions, which can lead to more frequent as well as different types of interactions.

Circles of Friends

Sometimes a more intense approach for facilitating friendships is necessary. Circles of friends is an activity completed with students without disabilities to discuss the importance of friendships and relationships in their lives and to generate ideas for ways in which they can be friends with peers who have disabilities. The ensuing steps are followed when implementing the circles of friends process (O'Brien & Forest, 1989):

1. Discuss the importance of friendships and relationships in everyone's lives.

2. Provide students with four concentric circles and ask them to identify the important relationships in their lives. After completing each circle, ask students to share their responses if they are willing.

   a. In the inner circle, ask them to put the names of those individuals to whom they are closest (e.g., those they love the most, those with whom they share their secrets).

   b. In the second circle, ask them to list those people they really like, but not quite as much as those in the first circle (i.e., those with whom they do *not* share their secrets).

c. In the third circle, ask them to identify those individuals with whom they like to do things because of the groups to which they belong (e.g., sports teams, clubs, dance groups, scouts).

d. In the fourth, or outermost, circle, ask them to list those people who are paid to be in their lives (e.g., doctor, dentist, teachers, coaches).

e. After discussing the circles of several volunteers, show the class the circles of an individual who has very few relationships (e.g., only family members in the inner circle, perhaps no one in Circles 2 and 3, and numerous service providers in Circle 4).

f. Ask the students to discuss (1) how they would feel and (2) how they would act if their circles looked like those of someone with few relationships. List their responses on chart paper so that a record is made of their reactions.

g. Explain to the class that the circles of a classmate with a severe disability may not look very different from that of the hypothetical individual with few relationships. Ask them what they could do to change that situation. Again, log their responses on chart paper so that a record of possible strategies exists to provide ideas to the circle.

h. Ask the class if there is anyone who would like to become part of circles of the classmate with a disability. Be sure that they know that not everyone must do so. List the names of those who are interested.

3. Hold regular meetings with this classmate's newly developed circle of friends on a weekly basis to help them to brainstorm ways of interacting and being friends. The student with a severe disability should be involved in these ongoing meetings and have input regarding the suggested strategies since that person is the focus of the circle. It may be necessary for various communication approaches to be used to ensure this participation (e.g., augmentative or alternative communication).

For some students, completing a circle of friends activity may be an important first step for encouraging interactions between students with and without disabilities. As previously mentioned, it is important that relationships move beyond being only helping relationships. Therefore, the adult who is acting as the facilitator for a circle of friends should encourage the group to develop strategies that focus on other interactions in addition to helping the student with disabilities. It is essential to remember that a circle of friends is an ongoing process that requires follow through. That is, an adult will continue to meet with the circle of friends on a regular basis to facilitate problem solving and to review ongoing activities. A circle of friends will not be effective if completed as a one-time activity intended as a quick fix. However, when completed correctly and facilitated as an ongoing process, a circle of friends can be effective in facilitating the development of friendships (Falvey, Forest, Pearpoint, & Rosenberg, 1994).

Conclusion

Implementing strategies such as those discussed in this chapter can encourage students with and without disabilities to interact with one another. Facilitating opportunities for interactions and encouraging positive social relationships can be the first steps to the development of meaningful friendships that are important for everyone. Encouraging friendships should be a shared responsibility with families. Further, many of the strategies suggested in this chapter can also be used by families to encourage relationships to develop in settings outside of school such as community activities, child care settings, and typical after-school activities (e.g., playing or hanging out with neighbors and/or classmates).

Throughout this process, one should remember that various types of friendships exist. There can be a range from acquaintances who are interacted with only briefly (e.g., passing in the hall) to intense relationships in which a great deal of time, both in school and out of school, is spent together. Friendships change over time for everyone; a friend this year may not be next year due to changes in circumstances. In some instances (e.g., with young children), it may even seem that friendships change from week to week. Additionally, the number of friends that any individual has varies a great deal. Some individuals will have several close friends, whereas others will have only one or two close friends. It is also essential to remember that friendships are typically based on personal preference and cannot be forced. The strategies discussed in this chapter are meant to foster an environment in which it will be more likely that friendships develop.

QUESTIONS

1. Why is it important for students with severe disabilities to have friendships with others their age?

2. What are examples of the various relationships that can be facilitated between students with and without disabilities?

3. What are examples of general strategies that can be implemented to facilitate the likelihood of friendships between students with and without disabilities?

4. What are the steps involved in implementing circles of friends?

5. Why is it important to provide ongoing support to any circles of friends formed to provide support to students with severe disabilities?

References

Bishop, K., & Jubala, K. (1994). By June, given shared experiences, integrated classes, and equal opportunities, Jamie will have a friend. *Teaching Exceptional Children, 27*(1), 36–40.

Brown, L., Long, E., Udvari-Solner, A., Davis, L., VanDeventer, P., Ahlgren, C., Johnston, F., Gruenewald, L., & Jorgensen, J. (1989). The home school: Why students with severe intellectual disabilities must attend the schools of their brothers, sisters, friends, and neighbors. *Journal of the Association for Persons with Severe Handicaps, 14*, 1–7.

Definition of the people TASH serves. (1991). In L. H. Meyer, C. A. Peck, & L. Brown (Eds.), *Critical issues in the lives of people with severe disabilities* (p. 19). Baltimore: Brookes.

Falvey, M. A., Forest, M., Pearpoint, J., & Rosenberg, R. L. (1994). Building connections. In J. S. Thousand, R. A. Villa, & A. I. Nevin (Eds.), *Creativity and collaborative learning: A practical guide to empowering students and teachers* (pp. 347–368). Baltimore: Brookes.

Hamre-Nietupski, S. (1993). How much time should be spent on skill acquisition and friendship development? Preferences of parents of students with moderate and severe/profound disabilities. *Education and Training in Mental Retardation, 28*, 220–231.

Hamre-Nietupski, S., Hendrickson, J., Nietupski, J., & Sasso, G. (1993). Perceptions of teachers of students with moderate, severe, or profound disabilities on facilitating friendships with nondisabled peers. *Education and Training in Mental Retardation, 28*, 111–127.

Hamre-Nietupski, S., Hendrickson, J., Nietupski, J., & Shokoshi-Yekta, M. (1994). Regular educators' perceptions of facilitating friendships of students with moderate, severe, or profound disabilities with nondisabled peers. *Education and Training in Mental Retardation and Developmental Disabilities, 29*, 102–117.

Kennedy, C. H., Horner, R. H., & Newton, J. S. (1989). Social contacts of adults with severe disabilities living in the community: A descriptive analysis of relationship patterns. *Journal of the Association for Persons with Severe Handicaps, 14*, 190–196.

O'Brien, J., & Forest, M. (1989). *Action for inclusion: How to improve schools by welcoming children with special needs into regular classrooms.* Toronto: Inclusion Press.

Peck, C. A., Donaldson, J., & Pezzoli, M. (1990). Some benefits nonhandicapped adolescents perceive for themselves from their social relationships with peers who have severe handicaps. *Journal of the Association for Persons with Severe Handicaps, 15*, 241–249.

Stainback, W., Stainback, S., & Wilkinson, A. (1992). Encouraging peer supports and friendships. *Teaching Exceptional Children, 24*(2), 6–11.

Taylor, A. R., Asher, S. R., & Williams, G. A. (1987). The social adaptation of mainstreamed mildly retarded children. *Child Development, 58*, 1321–1334.

Zetlin, A. G., & Murtaugh, M. (1988). Friendship patterns of mildly learning handicapped and nonhandicapped high school students. *American Journal on Mental Retardation, 92*, 447–454.

Self-Determination for Children and Youth with Developmental Disabilities

CHAPTER 16

Michael L. Wehmeyer, James E. Martin, and Deanna J. Sands

Learning Outcomes

After reading this chapter, you should be able to

- Understand the construct "self-determination" as an educational outcome.

- Identify why self-determination is an educational outcome that warrants attention.

- Identify and use existing best and effective practices in promoting self-determination for students in early intervention and elementary school programs.

- Identify and use existing best and effective practices in promoting self-determination for students in secondary education programs.

TERMS

The following terms are important for the understanding of this chapter:

Autonomy: A complex process that involves emotional separation from parents, development of a sense of personal control over one's life, establishment of a personal value system, and the ability to execute behavioral tasks needed in adulthood.

Causal agent: An individual who makes or causes things to happen in his or her life. Causal agency implies that actions were purposeful or performed to achieve an end.

Psychological empowerment: The beliefs (a) that one has control over circumstances that are important in one's life; (b) that one possesses the requisite skills to achieve desired outcomes; and (c) that, if one chooses to apply these skills, the anticipated positive outcomes will result.

Self-determination: Acting as the primary causal agent in one's life and making choices and decisions regarding one's quality of life free from undue external influence or interference.

Self-realized behavior: Using a comprehensive, and reasonably accurate, knowledge of oneself and one's strengths and limitations to act in such a manner as to capitalize on this knowledge.

Self-regulated behavior: A complex response system that enables individuals to examine their environments and their repertoires of responses for coping with those environments to make decisions about how to act, to act, to evaluate the desirability of the outcomes of the action, and to revise their plans as necessary (Whitman, 1990, p. 373).

Introduction

Although achieving consensus on the "ultimate" goal of education may be impossible, few educators would disagree with the statement that one viable goal of education is to "produce responsible, self-sufficient citizens who possess the self-esteem, initiative, skills and wisdom to continue individual growth and pursue knowledge" (Sarason, 1990, p. 163).

This goal is as relevant to and important for students with developmental disabilities as for their peers without disabilities. Educational practices that lead to such outcomes benefit all children and youth, but particularly students with mental retardation and developmental disabilities, for whom self-sufficiency, independence, and autonomy remain desired but not frequently achieved outcomes.

There is a growing emphasis on self-determination as an important outcome of the educational process to enable students with developmental disabilities to achieve self-sufficiency and independence. Halloran (1993) called self-determination "the ultimate goal of education" (p. 214) for learners with disabilities. However, students with developmental disabilities too often become adults who are not self-determined because of (a) inaccurate assumptions on the part of family members and professionals that children and youth with developmental disabilities cannot achieve self-determination; (b) the lack of opportunities to access environments that provide the experiences necessary to acquire skills and attitudes conducive to self-determination; and (c) individual limitations imposed by cognitive and physical impairments in the number, complexity, and generalization of skills learned. Successful educators play a pivotal role in addressing each of these barriers and, consequently, promoting self-determination for students with developmental disabilities (Wehmeyer, 1992a). Halloran (1993) suggested that achieving the goal of self-determination would require a purposeful strategy that is carefully implemented. This chapter provides an overview of educational practices that can be used to implement such a strategy.

What Is Self-Determination?

Self-Determination as a Human Right

From its earliest application to people with disabilities, self-determination has meant access to basic civil and human rights. Through the independent living and disability rights movement, people with disabilities have emphasized the importance of choice and control if they are to achieve integration and independence (Ward, 1996). The educational importance of self-determination has emerged from this emphasis, and it is important that such efforts to promote self-determination retain a focus on individual empowerment. Nirje (1972) argued that achieving self-determination for people with disabilities is more than merely a pedagogical effort. A person can learn all the skills needed to be self-determined, but until he or she has the opportunity to exercise them, the person will not achieve self-determination.

Many people with developmental disabilities have too few opportunities to experience choice and control in their lives (Stancliffe & Wehmeyer, 1995; Wehmeyer, Kelchner, & Richards, 1995; Wehmeyer & Metzler, 1995). Effective educational practice to promote self-determination should emphasize learning opportunities in conjunction with efforts to provide greater opportunities and experiences. However, approaching self-determination as a civil right provides only a portion of the impetus needed to achieve this outcome. A civil rights emphasis leads to legislative and societal changes supporting self-determination, but to take advantage of such opportunities, students need adequate skills and abilities.

Self-Determination as a Motivational Construct

A second conceptualization of self-determination is as a motivational construct. Deci and Ryan (1985) argued that humans are intrinsically motivated to learn, undertake challenges, solve problems, and engage in activities in which the primary motivator is an internal, organismic need for competence and self-determination. Self-determination is defined as "the capacity to choose and have those choices be the determinants of one's actions" (p. 38). Deci and Ryan (1985) proposed that self-determination is an innate propensity leading individuals to engage in behaviors that are interesting and internally reinforcing. Much of the research in this area has examined the effects of external reinforcers on the internal motivation of students, and the application of this research to educational settings has provided practical suggestions for enhancing motivation in the classroom (Deci & Chandler, 1986).

Self-Determination as an Educational Outcome

Federal initiatives supporting research and demonstration projects to promote self-determination for youth with disabilities have resulted in assessments, curricular materials, and procedures that address self-determination as an educational outcome for youth with disabilities. These efforts have drawn from definitional, theoretical, and philosophical frameworks emphasized in the civil rights and motivational conceptualizations of self-determination. However, because of the specific focus on promoting self-determination for students with disabilities through the educational process, efforts resulting from this initiative have been more pedagogical, thus constituting a third perspective of self-determination: as an educational outcome.

If educators are to develop and evaluate interventions and instructional models to promote self-determination, it is important that this outcome be specifically defined. Wehmeyer (1992a; 1996) defined self-determination as an educational outcome and identified individuals as self-determined based on characteristics of their behavior. Within this framework, self-determination refers to "acting as the primary causal agent in one's life and making choices and decisions regarding one's quality of life free from undue external influence or interference" (Wehmeyer, 1996, p. 18). Self-determined behavior refers to actions reflecting four essential characteristics: (a) the person acted autonomously; (b) the behavior(s) were self-regulated; (c) the person initiated and responded to the event(s) in a "psychologically empowered" manner; and, (d) the person acted in a self-realizing manner (Wehmeyer, 1996). People who consistently engage in such actions can be described as self-determined, where this refers to a dispositional characteristic (consistent across time and context) of that person.

Self-determined people are causal agents in their own lives. They are autonomous, self-regulating, psychologically empowered, and self-realizing individuals, and their actions reflect these essential characteristics. Behavior is autonomous when it is based on the preferences, interests, and abilities of the individual. Autonomous functioning implies that one acted independently, without undue or excessive interference, but recognizes that individuals are interdependent and act with the influence of others in most activities. Self-regulated behavior describes a constellation of actions that "enable individuals to examine their environments and their repertoires of responses for coping with those environments to make decisions about how to act, to act, to evaluate the desirability of the outcomes of the action, and to revise their plans as necessary" (Whitman, 1990, p. 353). The final two essential characteristics reflect the importance of taking into account not only individual skills, but individuals' perceptions about themselves and their environments. When people act based on the belief that they have control (or causality) over situations, can perform behaviors that will influence outcomes important to them, and believe that such actions will produce the desired outcomes, they are acting in a psychologically empowered manner (Zimmerman, 1990).

People who are self-determined act on the basis of a comprehensive, reasonably accurate understanding of their abilities and limitations. They have a "realistic" self-awareness of their capacities and use this self-knowledge to reach goals and priorities and to influence their quality of life. Wehmeyer (1996) suggested that "these four essential characteristics interact to define a behavioral or dispositional characteristic that is qualitatively different from each element individually. Self-determined behavior is qualitatively different from autonomous, self-regulated, psychologically empowered, and self-realized behaviors when they are viewed outside of the combined framework" (p. 19).

These essential characteristics appear when individuals acquire a set of skills and beliefs, referred to subsequently as component elements of self-determination. These component elements are (a) choice making, (b) decision making, (c) problem solving, (d) goal setting and attainment, (e) self-observation skills, (f) self-evaluation skills, (g) self-reinforcement skills, (h) internal locus of control, (i) positive attributions of efficacy and outcome expectancy, (j) self-awareness, and (k) self-knowledge. Each component element has a developmental course, and instructional emphasis on the various elements will differ according to students' ages

and abilities (Doll, Sands, Wehmeyer, & Palmer, 1996). In essence, however, best and effective instructional practices to promote self-determination will target these component elements across the student's educational career.

Why Focus on Self-Determination?

Why should educators devote increasingly scarce classroom time promoting positive perceptions of control and efficacy, teaching choice making, or working on a problem-solving strategy? There are several reasons: (a) federal policy in education mandates student involvement in educational planning and decision making; (b) research suggests that students with disabilities experience limited opportunities for choice and decision making in the classroom (e.g., Houghton, Bronicki, & Guess, 1987); and (c) adult outcomes for youth with disabilities are less positive than anticipated.

Increased Student Involvement in Educational Planning and Decision Making

The Individuals with Disabilities Education Act of 1990 (IDEA) includes requirements mandating transition-related services for students ages 16 and over who are receiving special education services. In addition, the law requires that such services be based on individual student preferences and abilities. Within the context of the U.S. Department of Education's emphasis on self-determination, this mandate should not be interpreted narrowly, as simply requiring the assessment of student preferences or interests. Instead, students need to be involved in all aspects of the educational process, including planning meetings and educational decision-making activities (Wehmeyer & Ward, 1995).

Many students with disabilities are left out of the educational planning process, from goal development to placement and instructional decision making (Van Reusen & Bos, 1990, 1994). Before the passage of the Education for all Handicapped Children Act of 1975 (EHA; P.L. 94-142), placement and curricular decisions were usually made by school psychologists or other school personnel (Gillespie & Turnbull, 1983). EHA requires that family members be included in the planning process and allows for the participation of students in planning meetings "when appropriate." Unfortunately, as Gillespie and Turnbull (1983) pointed out, little effort was expended to determine just when "whenever appropriate" was, and most students were either uninvolved in the process or involved only peripherally.

However, the limited involvement by students in educational planning does not reflect findings from a number of areas that would support active involvement as a means of improving educational and adult outcomes (Wehmeyer & Ward, 1995). There is increasing evidence that students who are involved in the planning, decision making, and implementation of their educational programs, including making choices about activities based on their preferences, experience more positive educational outcomes than peers who do not (Koestner, Ryan, Bernieri, & Holt, 1984; Schunk, 1985; Swann & Pittman, 1977; Wang & Stiles, 1976). These studies show that students who make choices and set goals for their education are more motivated to engage in educationally valuable activities and achieve more positive outcomes.

Opportunities for Choice and Decision Making in the Classroom

Wehmeyer (1992a) suggested that "the need to structure the special education classroom to meet educational, behavioral and administrative requirements may result in an environment promoting dependence and limiting choice and decision-making opportunities" (p. 302). Deci and Chandler (1986) pointed out that promoting self-determination is not equivalent to letting go of all reins and giving into chaos. Students need direction, structure, and supervision to perform at their optimal levels. In many cases, however, it can be the student who provides that direction and structure.

The existing literature suggests that students with developmental disabilities have few opportunities to experience control and choice. Houghton et al. (1987) found that school personnel responded at low rates to students' expressions of preferences during the school day. By and large, students with developmental disabilities believe themselves to lack control in their lives. They do not believe they have the competencies needed to influence outcomes in their lives, and when they do believe as much, they do not believe that if they were to act to take greater control, this outcome would result (Wehmeyer, 1994a). These beliefs, emerging after years of having others control and structure their lives, affects student performance and outcomes. For example, Wehmeyer (1994b) found that such perceptions were barriers to career decision making for adolescents with disabilities. Thus, a second reason to address self-determination is to provide impetus for making the educational setting a place where children and youth experience opportunities to make choices and participate in decisions that will enable them to assume greater control and responsibility of their lives as adults.

Adult Outcomes for Children and Youth with Disabilities

Education is, increasingly, an outcome-oriented enterprise. IDEA requires that students be provided outcome-oriented transition services, and outcome-based education has become a prevalent approach to education for all children. Research shows that, for children and youth with developmental disabilities, adult outcomes, including employment, community living arrangements, and social integration and inclusion, are less positive than previously anticipated (Wagner et al., 1991). Studies that examine outcomes for students graduating from special education indicate that, despite gains since the implementation of EHA, the adult experiences of these youth are still less than positive (Chadsey-Rusch, Rusch, & O'Reilly, 1991; Wagner et al., 1991).

It is easy to be defensive about these findings. However, the message is not that our educational efforts have failed, but instead that there are some effective instructional models and approaches that work well to achieve positive adult outcomes. Educators need to identify and implement proven best and effective practices and identify additional models and activities that will result in more positive outcomes for youth with developmental disabilities. Addressing self-determination is one such step. If educators are to move up to the next level of effectiveness, it will be by devoting educational resources to achieving this outcome and enabling learners with developmental disabilities to become self-determined.

The Early-Childhood and Elementary Years: Building Blocks for Self-Determination

The Development of Self-Determination

Self-determination emerges as children and adolescents develop the attitudes and abilities identified as component elements, including choice-making, decision-making, and problem-solving abilities; goal-setting and attainment skills; self-observation, self-evaluation, and self-reinforcement skills; an internal locus of control; positive attributions of efficacy and outcome expectancy; a realistic, positive self-awareness; and a comprehensive self-knowledge. Each element has a unique developmental course, spanning early, middle, and late childhood and sometimes extending into adolescence and adulthood (Doll et al., 1996). Professionals should view self-determination not only as a secondary education or transition issue, but as a lifespan issue. If youth with disabilities are to leave school as self-determined adults, instructional emphasis must begin in the early childhood and elementary years.

Although there is no comprehensive description of the development of self-determination, the developmental courses of many of the component elements have been described (Doll et al., 1996; Wehmeyer, 1996). A complete treatment of these various developmental pathways is beyond the scope of this chapter, but one example may help illustrate our contention. Preschool children can make reasonably accurate predictions about their success on a task and have the foundation for effective self-evaluation and self-awareness skills (Butler, 1990). However, at that age level children attribute successful outcomes to the amount of effort they put into an activity, essentially ignoring the contribution of ability or luck to positive outcomes. As they mature, children begin to distinguish between outcomes attributable to effort, ability, or circumstances. By middle elementary grades, students' spontaneous self-evaluations are stable across time and settings, consider all three variables that account for success, are relatively accurate, and have become appropriate foundations upon which other skills, such as self-advocacy, can be built (Dweck & Elliott, 1983; Renick & Harter, 1989).

For self-determination to emerge, early childhood and elementary school educators must support the development of the previously identified component elements. To accomplish this, teachers need to consciously structure learning environments to support self-determination, use methodologies and provide instructional activities conducive to this end, and involve families in the educational process.

The environment in which a child lives, learns, and plays is a critical factor in becoming an independent, self-determined adult (Brotherson, Cook, Cunconan-Lahr, & Wehmeyer, 1995; Cook, Brotherson, Weigel-Garrey, & Mize, 1996; Keating, 1990). Many of the component elements of self-determination emerge within the context of adult–child and child–child relationships. Both parents and professionals have frequent opportunities to constrain or encourage children in their attempts to become more independent (Paris & Winograd, 1990). Adults can provide the scaffolding that ensures that adult–child and child–child interactions foster the development of component elements of self-determination. Teachers should structure environments to provide young children the opportunity to make choices from multiple options, identify preferences and abilities, provide exposure to age-appropriate problem-solving opportunities, and foster a sense of worth and confidence.

For many children with disabilities, the single most important aspect of environments that support the development of self-determined behaviors may be opportunity— that is, opportunity to learn and to practice skills of self-determination (Brotherson et al., 1995). Although it is important to focus instructional efforts on promoting skills that children need to possess to be self-determined, it is equally important to structure learning environments to provide children with the opportunity to use their skills and to experience choice and control.

School environments provide multiple contexts in which to achieve this agenda. Preschool children can be provided opportunities to make choices, participate in decisions, and be involved in individual and group problem-solving activities, within already scheduled snack, free time, work time, and housecleaning activities (Erwin, 1994). Likewise, young children can develop skills related to self-regulation by being given the chance to have some say in daily classroom activities and structure. The preschool years are critical for the development of self-awareness. Classroom activities should provide children the opportunity to experience success and to engage in activities in which they excel.

Initial efforts at the preschool level to support the development of self-determination can be extended and refined during the elementary school years. Emphasis should be placed on helping students to apply their newly acquired, though still emerging, understanding of their own unique abilities, preferences, and learning needs to their benefit. Students in the elementary grades will be better able to participate in problem solving and daily planning and decision-making activities. Students can be provided experiences that allow them to have a voice in and enable them to learn to manage their physical environments, set academic and social goals and objectives, choose curriculum activities, evaluate the effectiveness of their learning and social strategies and habits, and participate in decisions that affect their academic and social lives. For students with disabilities, the Individualized Education Program (IEP) planning process offers a unique forum to experience choice and control. Children in elementary school should participate in such meetings and be encouraged to contribute. This sets the stage for later years when, as adolescents, they will begin to actively plan for their own futures.

Thus, Nirje (1972) was not entirely correct when he stated that self-determination is not achieved solely by pedagogic activities. His point was that self-determination could not be achieved simply by teaching people to make decisions or solve problems. However, as illustrated above, effective pedagogy involves more than instructional activities. Effective teachers are attuned to the development of young children and structure learning environments to support this development.

Curricular and Instructional Practices To Support Self-Determination

Teacher recognition of the importance of skills related to self-determination, as well as the associated management of the classroom, curriculum, and instructional practices to foster those skills, is a critical component to the emergence of self-determination. Children need to be taught, exposed to role models, and actively engaged in learning experiences that provide them the skills to (a) access resources; (b) communicate preferences; (c) set realistic, achievable goals; (d) plan and manage time; (e) identify and solve problems; (f) advocate for their own instructional and curriculum adaptations and modifications; and (g) understand their own internal learning and social needs and styles (Wehmeyer, 1992a, 1992b). A synthesis of the literature regarding the developmental course of related capacities and skills suggests that teachers promote student self-determination when they provide the following:

1. Opportunities to communicate preferences; set realistic, achievable goals; and plan and participate in meaningful decisions about and evaluations of their instructional and curricular interventions, adaptations, and modifications (Garner, 1987; Nelson-LeGall, Kratzer, Jones, & DeCooke, 1990).

2. Direct training in the use of appropriate cognitive (including metacognitive) strategies; explicit, directive feedback regarding the usefulness and effectiveness of their strategy use; and reminders or cues to use strategies (Cornoldi, Gobbo, & Mazzoni, 1991; Ghatala, 1986).

3. Opportunities to apply fixed, precise mastery standards as opposed to normative standards (how well one did in relation to peers) by which to self-evaluate and judge task performances (Butler, 1990; Stowitschek, Ghezzi, & Safely, 1987).

4. Opportunities to learn from successes and failures and from experiences that promote positive self-perceptions of independence, dignity, self-worth, and value (Guess, Benson, & Siegal-Causey, 1985; Higgins, 1989; Renick & Harter, 1989; Spekman, Herman, & Vogel, 1993).

5. Direct instruction in communication skills and problem-solving techniques using meaningful, real-life situations to provide opportunities to (a) understand the perspectives of others, (b) generate multiple solutions, (c) reflect on likely consequences, and (d) use and evaluate solutions (Kendall, 1984; Moore, 1979).

Family and Caregiver Supports to Self-Determination

Best practice dictates that families and caregivers be involved in the education of students with disabilities (Wehmeyer & Davis, 1995). Families and caregivers are critical to the development of self-determination, and early childhood and elementary school professionals need to work closely with the students' homes to achieve this outcome. Turnbull and Turnbull (1996) suggested that certain family features can serve to facilitate or impede an individual's development of self-determined behaviors. Broadly, these features include (a) family characteristics, such as cultural values, beliefs, and expectations, and coping styles; (b) family interactions, such as role expectations, relationships, cohesion, and adaptability; (c) family functions, including economic, daily care, recreation, socialization, affective, educational–vocational, and self-definition needs; and (d) family life-span issues (including developmental stages of family interactions and functions over time; transitions or changes in family charac-

teristics, composition, cohesion, and function). Perhaps the most fundamental considerations that Turnbull and Turnbull (1996) put forth is that not all families value the goal of self-determination for their sons or daughters (with or without disabilities) and that any attempt to intervene on behalf of an offspring to facilitate self-determination "will most likely meet with success when supports and services foster a balance in the functioning of family life" (p. 197).

Given this backdrop, there are certain things that families and caregivers can do to facilitate young children's attitudes and skills of self-determination beginning in preschool and extending into the elementary school years. According to the National Association for the Education of Young Children, the following parenting and caregiver practices support the development of prosocial skills that ultimately influence abilities for self-determination (Bredekamp, 1987, p. 47):

1. Provision of affection and support, comforting children when they cry and reassuring them when they are fearful.

2. Support for children's developing independence, helping when needed, but allowing them to do what they are capable of doing and what they want to do for themselves.

3. Consideration of each child as a unique person with individual patterns and timing for skill development.

4. Provision of activities, interactions, and feedback to develop children's positive self-esteem and positive feelings toward learning.

5. Provision of opportunities to develop social skills such as cooperating, helping, negotiating and talking with persons with whom they are involved in interpersonal problems.

6. Facilitating the development of self-control through positive guidance techniques such as modeling expected behaviors, redirecting children to more acceptable activities, and setting clear limits.

7. Promote perseverance, industry, and independence by providing stimulating, motivating activities; encouraging individual choices; allowing as much time as is needed for children to complete their work; and ensuring private time with close friends and loved ones.

8. Setting clear limits in a positive manner and involving children in establishing rules and in problem-solving.

If the outcome that all children with disabilities leave school as self-determined young adults is to be achieved, educators must begin by providing instructional activities and environments that promote the development of component elements of self-determination while children are in early childhood and elementary school programs. This will require attention not only to school activities and structure, but to the establishment of partnerships with students' families.

The Secondary Years: Transition and Autonomy

Developmental psychologists have identified the process of autonomy as one of the most important accomplishments of adolescence (Damon, 1983). Autonomy refers to the movement from childhood, where an individual is primarily dependent on significant others for protection, structure, and direction in life, to adulthood, where that individual assumes primary responsibility for his or her own life. The parallel educational emphasis to prepare youth with disabilities for the movement to adulthood is the transition process.

Self-determination is one of the most important transition outcomes. Although self-determination is an outcome that emerges based on lifelong learning experiences, adolescence is an important time for its emergence (Ward, 1988). Reflecting this importance, recent self-determination efforts have focused on the adolescent years and the school-to-adult life transition process.

Promoting Self-Determination in Secondary Settings

A series of federally funded projects have developed and made available materials to promote self-determination for youth with disabilities. Most of these projects share related themes and have considerable overlap, promoting a core set of skills leading students to be self-determined. They have used as a common starting point the conceptualization of self-determination forwarded by Ward (1988). He considered self-determination to be both the attitudes that lead people to define goals for themselves and their ability to achieve those goals. Many of these applied efforts benefitted from a foundation built by the Adaptability Model, which itself is a merging of previous approaches into a unified whole.

The Adaptability Model (Mithaug, Martin, & Agran, 1987) operationalizes parental beliefs that secondary instruction "should assist the student to become more independent in understanding what he or she needs and wants, how to set personal goals . . . and to select action plans that will lead to desired outcomes" (Mithaug, Horiuchi, & McNulty, 1987, p. 59). More than anything, the Adaptability Model identifies strategies to teach students to manage their lives. To do this, the Adaptability Model borrows extensively from literature on problem solving, self-management, and self-

regulation (Agran & Martin, 1987; Bandura, 1986; Kanfer & Goldstein, 1986; Martin, Burger, Elias-Burger, & Mithaug, 1988; Mithaug, 1993).

The following are the instructional units of the Adaptability Model:

1. *Decision making.* During the decision-making unit, students identify their needs, interests, and abilities; consider alternatives; and then select their goal.

2. *Independent performance.* Students show independent performance by following through on their action plan. They perform tasks independently by using learning or self-management strategies. These include self-instructional and other antecedent procedures (picture cues, written prompts, verbal labeling).

3. *Self-evaluation.* While working on their tasks, students self-evaluate by monitoring and recording performance outcomes, and then comparing their results with goals and performance objectives set during decision making. In classroom and work situations, their self-evaluations usually focus on being on time, task selections, productivity, accuracy, and earnings. Students adjust by using their self-evaluations to decide what to do next time.

3. *Adjustments.* Adjustments are the essential component of the Adaptability Model in that they connect future actions with past performance. Before beginning another task or project, students review feedback from previous adjustment decisions and select goals, plans, and performance objectives accordingly.

The Adaptability Model was the first to put the different components of self-determined learning into a cohesive structure, and many of the federally funded self-determination projects have incorporated and expanded components of this model in their activities.

Instructional Materials To Teach Self-Determination

As indicated, the U.S. Department of Education's Office of Special Education and Rehabilitation Services has funded numerous self-determination assessment and curriculum demonstration projects. The activities conducted by these projects provide a comprehensive overview of best and promising practices in the area of self-determination in secondary schools.

A Career Education Approach to Self-Determination

Career education is defined by Kokaska and Brolin (1985) as the "process of systematically coordinating all school, family and community components together to facilitate each individual's potential for economic, social, and personal fulfillment and participation in productive work activities that benefit the individual or others" (p. 43). Career education emphasizes instructional activities that prepare students to assume a variety of adult roles, includes a substantial experiential component, and focuses on the development of life skills.

Wehmeyer (1995) utilized the *Life Centered Career Education* curriculum (Brolin, 1993) to promote self-determination skills in four instructional domain areas: self-awareness, self-confidence, choice and decision making, and goal attainment behavior. Table 16.1 provides a list of lesson objectives by instructional domains. Each lesson objective is achieved using activities that move through three stages of career development for each instructional area: (a) career awareness, (b) career exploration, and (c) career preparation. The materials include more than 350 lessons estimated at over 400 hours of instruction and are intended to be implemented when the student enters junior high or middle school and continued throughout the student's secondary education experience.

Promoting Self-Determination Through the Arts

Project PARTnership teaches self-determination by providing "opportunities for self-discovery, creativity, self-concept building, skill development, and social integration" (Harris & McKinney, 1993, p. 5). The curriculum is designed to be infused into existing coursework, although the activities could be done as an independent course or as an extracurricular activity. Students become involved in visual arts, dance, creative writing, music, and photography. A basic knowledge of art education techniques is required to complete several of the lessons. In an accompanying video, various artists who have disabilities described how they became self-determined and the role their artistic endeavors played in developing their self-determination. The materials are designed primarily for students with mild to moderate learning difficulties.

Parent, Student, and Peer Groups To Teach Self-Determination

Hoffman and Field (1995) developed a self-determination curriculum titled Steps to Self-Determination. Parents, the adolescent with a disability, and nondisabled peers meet in

Table 16.1
Instructional Domains and Correlated LCCE Competency Area[a]
Lesson Objectives Used To Promote Self-Determination

Instructional Domain	LCCE Competency Area	Lesson Objectives
Self-awareness	Achieving self-awareness	Identify physical and psychological needs
		Identify interests and abilities
		Identify emotions
		Demonstrate knowledge of physical self
		Awareness of how behavior affects others
Self-confidence	Acquiring self-confidence	Express feelings of self-worth
		Describe others' perception of self
		Accept and give praise
		Accept and give criticism
		Develop confidence in oneself
Choice and decision making	Making adequate decisions	Locate and utilize sources of assistance
		Anticipate consequences
		Develop and evaluate alternatives
Goal attainment	Achieving independence	Strive toward self-actualization
		Demonstrate self-organization
		Recognize nature of a problem
		Develop goal seeking behavior

[a]LCCE = Life Centered Career Education (Brolin, 1993).

after-school group sessions. The lessons use modeling, cooperative and experiential learning, lecture, and discussions. Participants complete an hour-long orientation session, a 6-hour workshop, and 16 classroom-based lessons. Table 16.2 lists the curriculum content. The package includes assessment tools, objectives, preparation guidelines, lesson plans, overhead and handout masters, and teacher information. The materials are designed primarily for students with mild to moderate learning and behavioral difficulties.

Self-Advocacy Groups To Teach Self-Determination

Self-advocacy groups are consumer-run organizations designed to provide a means for self and system advocacy and socialization for people with mental retardation and developmental disabilities (Wehmeyer & Berkobien, 1996). People First is a self-advocacy organization that exists in many states. People First of Tennessee has produced a curriculum to promote self-determination by forming integrated People First groups for high school students (People First, 1995). The Tennessee project recruited student leaders to participate in monthly after-school group meetings. The curriculum teaches group members about disability awareness, self-advocacy, and ways to become included in the social life of their school.

Emphasizing Cultural Uniqueness To Teach Self-Determination

Wehmeyer (1992a, 1996) suggested that people who act in a self-determined manner do so without "undue interference and influence" and that self-determined behavior cannot be defined by specific types of behaviors. This reflects the interdependence of most individuals on others in their lives, and respects the fact that different cultures have differing norms for participation. What one culture views as self-determining may be interpreted in a very different manner in another culture. This is true between cultures, races, and even families. Thus, what one family may view as an acceptable level of influence for decision making may be seen by another family as interference. Teachers must be aware of students' cultural heritages and families' values in order to implement educational practices to support self-determination. This, in turn, can be accomplished only if teachers have established an effective parent–teacher partnership (Wehmeyer & Davis, 1995).

Ludi and Martin (1995) developed a curriculum that addresses the unique needs of learners from different cultures, particularly students of Hispanic and Native American descent. These materials, titled *The Road to Personal Freedom: Self-Determination*, provide instructional activities in eight units: Introduction to Self-Determination; Expanding Student Roles; Communication Styles; Disability and Accommodations; Family, Friends, and Support; Rights and Responsibilities; Future Planning; and Celebration of Self.

Table 16.2
Content of Steps to Self-Determination Curriculum

Sessions	Content
Orientation Session	Overview of curriculum, planning for workshops
	Introduction to self-determination
Workshop Sessions	Getting to know each other
	Overview of curriculum
	Self-awareness
	Self-acceptance
	Rights and responsibilities
	Accessing support from families and friends
	Supporting the self-determination of others
Classroom Sessions	
Session 1	Dreaming to open possibilities
Session 2	What is important to me?
Session 3	Creating options for long-term goals
Session 4	Setting long-term goals
Session 5	Steps to short-term goals
Session 6	Planning steps to reach short-term goals
Session 7	Planning activities to reach short-term goals
Session 8	Taking the first step (risk taking)
Session 9	Creative barrier breaking
Session 10	Group problem solving
Session 11	Role models: disability and self-determination
Session 12	Assertive communication I
Session 13	Assertive communication II
Session 14	Negotiation
Session 15	Conflict resolution
Session 16	Where do we go from here?

This curriculum focuses on building skills in communication, self-understanding, pride, creative thinking, problem solving, goal setting, self-advocacy, and persistence.

Student Involvement in the Educational Planning and Decision-Making Process

Curricular efforts are important, but as was emphasized in our previous discussion of self-determination in the elementary years, students must have the opportunity to experience choice and control. The educational planning and decision-making process is an excellent place to provide students with disabilities with such opportunities. There are several programs that target student involvement in this process.

ChoiceMaker Self-Determination Transition Curriculum and Program

The ChoiceMaker program provides materials to assist students to master crucial self-determination skills through learning the leadership skills to manage their own IEP process. The ChoiceMaker Self-Determination Transition Curriculum (Martin & Huber-Marshall, 1995) consists of three sections: Choosing Goals, Expressing Goals, and Taking Action, and includes an assessment.

The *ChoiceMaker Self-Determination Assessment* (Martin & Huber-Marshall, 1994) is a criterion-referenced self-determination transition assessment tool that matches exactly with the curriculum objectives. Across each curriculum objective, the teacher rates the student's skill level and determines the opportunities the student has to perform each objective. A graphic summary profile is prepared comparing the student's skills to opportunities at school across the three curriculum sections. This assessment is useful to document student and program achievement over time.

The *Choosing Employment Goals* (Huber-Marshall, Martin, Maxson, & Jerman, 1995) lessons enable students to learn the necessary skills and personal information needed to articulate their interests, skills, limits, and goals across one or more self-selected transition areas. The lessons and materials take students through a series of systematic school and community-based experiences across different transition areas. Worksheets keyed to students' experiences assist them to match their skills, limits, and preferences to community opportunities.

With *The Self-Directed IEP* (Martin, Huber-Marshall, & Maxson, 1993, 1994), students learn the leadership skills necessary to manage their IEP meeting and publicly disclose their interests, skills, limits, and goals gleaned from the Choosing Goals lessons. Rather than be passive participants at their IEP meetings, students learn to lead their meeting to the greatest extent of their ability, eagerness, and desire. The lessons teach students 11 steps for leading their own staffing.

The *Taking Action* (Huber-Marshall, Martin, & Maxson, 1995) materials enable students to learn how to break their long-range goals into specific goals that can be accomplished in a week. Students learn how they will attain their goals by deciding: (a) a standard for goal performance; (b) a means to get performance feedback; (c) what motivates them to do it; (d) the strategies they will use; (e) needed supports; and (f) schedules. Rather than having teachers, parents, or support staff tell students what to do, when to do it, and how they did, students assume these responsibilities. Of course,

this requires a learning process that fades teacher instruction as students learn the crucial skills.

Group Action Planning

Turnbull, Anderson, Seaton, Turnbull, and Dinas (1996) developed the Group Action Planning procedure to teach youth with severe mental retardation and developmental disabilities how to become involved in their educational planning. Students, family members, professionals, and others complete a process to identify goals, resources, and obstacles to achieving desired outcomes. Using this information, the student with a disability, supported by the group, formulates action plans across eight areas of daily life: domestic, transportation, employment, financial, recreational, social relationships, behavioral, and community participation.

Whose Future Is It Anyway?

Wehmeyer and Kelchner (1997) developed a student-directed transition planning program for youth with mild cognitive disabilities. The materials provide students the opportunity to acquire the knowledge and confidence to take part in their transition planning process as equal partners. Students complete a series of 36 sessions, each about an hour long, to gain information in six areas: self- and disability awareness; decision making; community resources; development and evaluation of goals and objectives; effective communication in small group settings; and the dynamics of meetings. Each session provides students something they can apply directly to their transition planning meeting. Students learn how to make decisions; give informed consent; identify, write, and track goals; identify community resources; and group problem solve.

Noncurricular Considerations To Teach Self-Determination

Mentoring

Several projects have used mentoring as a means to teach self-determination. The National Center for Disability Services, for instance, matched students with a disability to successful adults who had a similar disability. These adult mentors, who interacted directly with their paired students, provided a model of success in the community. Project Empower, conducted by the Prince George's (Maryland) Private Industry Council, also linked youth with disabilities to successful adults with a similar disabling condition and combined these experiences with community-based experiences at employment and living sites. This project paved a link between the schools and the local Independent Living Center to identify role models and provide an outlet for further resources and support.

Work and Community Experiences

An often used component of the model self-determination projects is work and other community experiences. The Family Resource Center on Disabilities in Chicago has field-tested a process called *MAINROADS to Self-Determination* (Family Resource, 1994) to provide students with disabilities opportunities to explore options in postsecondary education, employment, housing, transportation, recreation and leisure, and policy-making by using frequent community-based learning experiences. The focus of MAINROADS (Family Resource, 1994) is to provide hands-on exploration and experiences that assist students to make informed, independent decisions. The experiential component is coupled with training and educational activities, access to a variety of resources, and individual consultations on transition-related issues to achieve this end.

Other Noncurricular Strategies

Other strategies have been employed and should be part of a comprehensive strategy to promote self-determination. Powers (1993) described a process incorporating such strategies employed by Project TAKE CHARGE in New Hampshire. Powers emphasizes providing teens with the tools to manage barriers, such as goal setting and problem solving, while supporting independence and self-confidence. Project TAKE CHARGE uses team building and partnership opportunities to build networking skills, negotiation, and self-advocacy. The MAINROADS project in Chicago includes opportunities to learn public speaking, journalism, and photography skills as a boost to self-confidence.

Conclusion

The programs and procedures described in this chapter represent the types of practices that Halloran (1993) referred to when stating the need for a purposeful strategy to promote self-determination as an educational outcome for youth with mental retardation and developmental disabilities. If educators implement practices similar to these, they will take the next step toward ensuring quality outcomes for all students exiting school. Emphasis in self-determination is particularly important in light of the movement toward inclusive education for learners with disabilities and the educational reform movement. These two movements stress individual choice, motivation, and student involvement. Federally funded projects have worked with students with disabilities to promote self-determination in more restrictive settings, and it is important for all students with disabilities to be provided educational opportunities leading to self-determination wherever they receive their education. Regardless, if students are to succeed in inclusive settings, as well as in the mainstream of adult community life, they need to be self-determined.

 QUESTIONS

1. What is self-determination?

2. Why is it important that educators promote self-determination for learners with mental retardation and developmental disabilities?

3. What environmental factors, including family and home variables, contribute to the development and acquisition of self-determination for learners with mental retardation and developmental disabilities?

4. What curricular and instructional practices promote self-determination for learners with mental retardation and developmental disabilities?

5. What noncurricular and methodological strategies promote self-determination for learners with mental retardation and developmental disabilities?

References

Agran, M., & Martin, J. E. (1987). Applying a technology of self-control in community environments for individuals who are mentally retarded. In M. Hersen, R. M. Eisler, & P. M. Miller (Eds.), *Progress in behavior modification* (pp. 108–151). Newbury Park, CA: Sage.

Bandura, A. (1986). *Social foundations of thought and action: A social cognitive theory.* Englewood Cliffs, NJ: Prentice-Hall.

Bredekamp, S. (1987). *Developmentally appropriate practice in early childhood programs servicing children from birth through age 8.* Washington, DC: National Association for the Education of Young Children.

Brolin, D. E. (1993). *Life Centered Career Education: A competency based approach.* Reston, VA: Council for Exceptional Children.

Brotherson, M. J., Cook, C. C., Cunconan-Lahr, R., & Wehmeyer, M. L. (1995). Policy supporting self-determination in the environments of persons with disabilities. *Education and Training in Mental Retardation and Developmental Disabilities, 30,* 3–14.

Butler, R. (1990). The effects of mastery and competitive conditions on self-assessment at different ages. *Child Development, 61,* 201–210.

Chadsey-Rusch, J., Rusch, F., & O'Reilly, M. F. (1991). Transition from school to integrated communities. *Remedial and Special Education, 12,* 23–33.

Cook, C. C., Brotherson, M. J., Weigel-Garrey, C., & Mize, I. (1996). Homes to support self-determination for children. In D. J. Sands & M. L. Wehmeyer (Eds.), *Self-determination across the life span: Independence and choice for people with disabilities* (pp. 91–110). Baltimore: Brookes.

Cornoldi, C., Gobbo, C., & Mazzoni, G. (1991). On metamemory–memory relationships: Strategy availability and training. *International Journal of Behavior Development, 14,* 101–121.

Damon, W. (1983). *Social and personality development.* New York: Norton.

Deci, E. L., & Chandler, C. L. (1986). The importance of motivation for the future of the LD field. *Journal of Learning Disabilities, 19,* 587–594.

Deci, E. L., & Ryan, R. M. (1985). *Intrinsic motivation and self-determination in human behavior.* New York: Plenum.

Doll, E., Sands, D. J., Wehmeyer, M. L., & Palmer, S. (1996). Promoting the development and acquisition of self-determined behavior. In D. J. Sands & M. L. Wehmeyer (Eds.), *Self-determination across the life span: Independence and choice for people with disabilities* (pp. 65–90). Baltimore: Brookes.

Dweck, C. S., & Elliott, E. S. (1983). Achievement motivation. In P. H. Mussen (Series Ed.) & E. M. Hetherington (Vol. Ed.), *Handbook of child psychology: Vol. 3. Socialization, personality, and social development* (4th ed., pp. 643–691). New York: Wiley.

Erwin, E. (1994). Promoting democracy in early childhood education. *The Association for Persons with Severe Handicaps Newsletter, 4,* 19–21.

Family Resource Center on Disabilities. (1994). *MAINROADS to self-determination.* Chicago: Family Resource Center on Disabilities.

Garner, R. (1987). *Metacognition and reading comprehension.* Norwood, NJ: Ablex.

Ghatala, E. S. (1986). Strategy-monitoring training enables young learners to select effective strategies. *Educational Psychologist, 21,* 43–54.

Gillespie, E. B., & Turnbull, A. P. (1983). It's my IEP! Involving students in the planning process. *Teaching Exceptional Children, 16,* 27–29.

Guess, D., Benson, H., & Siegal-Causey, E. (1985). Concepts and issues related to choice-making and autonomy among persons with severe disabilities. *Journal of the Association for Persons with Severe Handicaps, 10,* 79–86.

Halloran, W. D. (1993). Transition services requirement: Issues, implications, challenge. In R. C. Eaves & P. J. McLaughlin (Eds.), *Recent advances in special education and rehabilitation* (pp. 210–224). Boston: Andover Medical.

Harris, C. D., & McKinney, D. D. (1993). *Project PARTnership: Instructional kit.* Washington, DC: VSA Educational Services.

Higgins, E. T. (1989). Continuities and discontinuities in self-regulatory and self-evaluative processes: A developmental theory relating self and affect. *Journal of Personality, 57,* 407–444.

Hoffman, A., & Field, S. (1995). Promoting self-determination through effective curriculum development. *Intervention in School and Clinic, 30,* 134–141.

Houghton, J., Bronicki, G. J. B., & Guess, D. (1987). Opportunities to express preferences and make choices among students with severe disabilities in classroom settings. *The Journal of the Association for Persons with Severe Handicaps, 12,* 18–27.

Huber-Marshall, L., Martin, J. E., & Maxson, L. L. (1995). *Taking Action.* Colorado Springs: University of Colorado, Special Education Program.

Huber-Marshall, L., Martin, J. E., Maxson, L. L., & Jerman, P. (1995). *Choosing Employment Goals.* Colorado Springs: University of Colorado, Special Education Program.

Individuals with Disabilities Education Act of 1990, 20 U.S.C. § 1400 *et seq.*

Kanfer, F. H., & Goldstein, A. P. (1986). *Helping people change: A textbook of methods* (3rd ed.). New York: Pergamon Press.

Keating, D. P. (1990). Adolescent thinking. In S. Feldman & G. Elliott (Eds.), *At the threshold: The developing adolescent.* Cambridge, MA: Harvard University Press.

Kendall, P. C. (1984). Social cognition and problem-solving: A developmental and child-clinical interface. In B. Gholson & T. L. Rosenthal (Eds.), *Applications of cognitive developmental theory* (pp. 115–147). New York: Academic Press.

Koestner, R., Ryan, R. M., Bernieri, F., & Holt, K. (1984). The effects of controlling versus informational limit-setting styles on children's intrinsic motivation and creativity. *Journal of Personality, 52,* 233–248.

Kokaska, C. J., & Brolin, D. E. (1985). *Career education for handicapped individuals* (2nd ed.). Columbus, OH: Charles E. Merrill.

Ludi, D., & Martin, L. (1995). The road to personal freedom: Self-determination. *Intervention in School and Clinic, 30,* 164–169.

Martin, J. E., Burger, D. L., Elias-Burger, S., & Mithaug, D. E. (1988). Applications of self-control strategies to facilitate independence in vocational and instructional settings. In N. Bray (Ed.), *International review of research in mental retardation* (pp. 155–193). San Diego: Academic Press.

Martin, J. E., & Huber-Marshall, L. (1994). *ChoiceMaker Self-Determination Assessment.* Colorado Springs: University of Colorado, Special Education Program.

Martin, J. E., & Huber-Marshall, L. (1995). ChoiceMaker: A comprehensive self-determination transition program. *Intervention in School and Clinic, 30,* 147–156.

Martin, J. E., Huber-Marshall, L., & Maxson, L. L. (1993). Transition policy: Infusing self-determination and self-advocacy into transition programs. *Career Development of Exceptional Individuals, 16,* 53–61.

Martin, J. E., Huber-Marshall, L., & Maxson, L. L. (1994). *The Self-Directed IEP.* Colorado Springs: University of Colorado, Special Education Program.

Mithaug, D. E. (1993). *Self-regulation theory: How optimal adjustment maximizes gain.* Westport, CT: Praeger.

Mithaug, D. E., Horiuchi, C. N., & McNulty, B. A. (1987). *Parent reports on the transitions of students graduating from Colorado special education programs in 1978 and 1979.* Denver: Colorado Department of Education.

Mithaug, D. E., Martin, J. E., & Agran, M. (1987). Adaptability instruction: The goal of transitional programming. *Exceptional Children, 53,* 500–505.

Moore, S. G. (1979). Social cognition: Knowing about others. *Young Children, 34*(3), 54–61.

Nelson-LeGall, S., Kratzer, L., Jones, E., & DeCooke, P. (1990). Children's self-assessment of performance and task-related help seeking. *Journal of Experimental Child Psychology, 49*, 245–263.

Nirje, B. (1972). The right to self-determination. In W. Wolfensberger (Ed.), *Normalization* (pp. 176–193). Toronto: National Institute on Mental Retardation.

Paris, S. G., & Winograd, P. (1990). Promoting metacognition and motivation of exceptional children. *Remedial and Special Education, 11*, 7–15.

People First of Tennessee. (1995). *Learning for life*. Santa Barbara, CA: James Stanfield.

Powers, L. E. (1993). Promoting adolescent independence and self-determination. *Family Centered Care Network, 10*(4), 1.

Renick, M. J., & Harter, S. (1989). Impact of social comparisons on the developing self-perceptions of learning disabled students. *Journal of Educational Psychology, 81*, 631–638.

Sarason, S. B. (1990). *The predictable failure of educational reform: Can we change course before it's too late?* San Francisco: Jossey-Bass.

Schunk, D. H. (1985). Participation in goal setting: Effects on self-efficacy and skills of learning-disabled children. *The Journal of Special Education, 19*, 307–316.

Spekman, N. J., Herman, K. L., & Vogel, S. A. (1993). Risk and resilience in individuals with learning disabilities: A challenge to the field. *Learning Disabilities Research and Practice, 8*, 59–65.

Stancliffe, R., & Wehmeyer, M. L. (1995). To choose or not to choose: Variability in the availability of choice to adults with mental retardation. *The Journal of Vocational Rehabilitation, 5*, 319–328.

Stowitschek, J. J., Ghezzi, P. M., & Safely, K. N. (1987). "I'd rather do it myself": Self-evaluation and correction of handwriting. *Education and Treatment of Children, 10*, 209–224.

Swann, W. B., & Pittman, T. S. (1977). Initiating play activity of children: The moderating influence of verbal cues on intrinsic motivation. *Child Development, 48*, 1128–1132.

Turnbull, A. P., Anderson, E. L., Seaton, K. A., Turnbull, H. R., & Dinas, P. A. (1996). Enhancing self-determination through Group Action Planning: A holistic emphasis. In D. Sands & M. L. Wehmeyer (Eds.), *Self-determination through the life span: Independence and choice for people with disabilities* (pp. 237–256). Baltimore: Brookes.

Turnbull, A. P., & Turnbull, H. R. (1996). An analysis of self-determination within a family systems perspective: Balancing the family mobile. In L. Powers (Ed.), *On the road to autonomy: Building self-competence among youth with disabilities* (pp. 195–220). Baltimore: Brookes.

Van Reusen, A. K., & Bos, C. S. (1990). I PLAN: Helping students communicate in planning conferences. *Teaching Exceptional Children, 22*(4), 30–32.

Van Reusen, A. K., & Bos, C. S. (1994). Facilitating student participation in Individualized Education Programs through motivation strategy instruction. *Exceptional Children, 60*, 466–475.

Wagner, M., Newman, L., D'Amico, R., Jay, E. D., Butler-Nalin, P., Marder, C., & Cox, R. (1991). *The first comprehensive report from the national longitudinal transition study of special education students*. Menlo Park, CA: SRI International.

Wang, M. C., & Stiles, B. (1976). An investigation of children's concept of self-responsibility for their school learning. *American Educational Research Journal, 13*, 159–179.

Ward, M. J. (1988). The many facets of self-determination. *NICHCY Transition Summary: National Information Center for Children and Youth with Disabilities, 5*, 2–3.

Ward, M. J. (1996). Coming of age in the age of self-determination: A historical perspective of self-determination. In D. Sands & M. L. Wehmeyer (Eds.), *Self-determination through the lifespan: Theory to practice*. Baltimore: Brookes.

Wehmeyer, M. L. (1992a). Self-determination and the education of students with mental retardation. *Education and Training in Mental Retardation, 27*, 302–314.

Wehmeyer, M. L. (1992b). Self-determination: Critical skills for outcome oriented transition services. *Journal of the Association of Vocational and Special Needs Education, 15*, 3–7.

Wehmeyer, M. L. (1994a). Perceptions of self-determination and psychological empowerment of adolescents with mental retardation. *Education and Training in Mental Retardation and Developmental Disability, 29*, 9–21.

Wehmeyer, M. L. (1994b). Perceptual and psychological factors in career decision-making of adolescents with and without cognitive disabilities. *Career Development for Exceptional Individuals, 16*, 135–146.

Wehmeyer, M. L. (1995). A career education approach: Self-determination for youth with mild cognitive disabilities. *Intervention in School and Clinic, 30*, 157–163.

Wehmeyer, M. L. (1996). Self-determination as an educational outcome: How does it relate to the educational needs of children and youth? In D. J. Sands & M. L. Wehmeyer (Eds.), *Self-determination across the life span: Independence and choice for people with disabilities* (pp. 17–36). Baltimore: Brookes.

Wehmeyer, M. L., & Berkobien, R. (1996). The legacy of self-advocacy: People with cognitive disabilities as leaders in their communities. In G. Dybwad & H. Bersani (Eds.), *New voices: Self-advocacy by people with disabilities* (pp. 245–257). Cambridge, MA: Brookline Books.

Wehmeyer, M. L., & Davis, S. (1995). Family involvement. In D. E. Brolin (Ed.), *Career education: A functional life skills approach* (pp. 91–116). Columbus, OH: Merrill/Prentice-Hall.

Wehmeyer, M. L., & Kelchner, K. (1997). *Whose future is it anyway? A student-directed transition planning program*. Boston: Women's Educational Equity Act Publishing Center.

Wehmeyer, M. L., Kelchner, K., & Richards, S. (1995). Environmental and intraindividual correlates to self-determination for adults with mental retardation. *The Journal of Vocational Rehabilitation*.

Assistive Technology Effective Practices for Students with Mental Retardation and Developmental Disabilities

CHAPTER 17

Howard P. Parette, Jr.

Learning Outcomes

After reading this chapter, you should be able to

- Define assistive technology and assistive technology services.

- Identify characteristics of high- and low-tech assistive technology devices.

- Identify considerations in selecting appropriate assistive technology.

- Identify child, technology, school, cultural, and family issues that should be considered in the process of selecting appropriate assistive technology.

- Describe how the IEP can be used as a mechanism for acquiring assistive technology.

- Describe strategies for using community resources to acquire assistive technology.

TERMS

The following terms are important for the understanding of this chapter:

Assistive technology: Generic term that includes both assistive technology devices and assistive technology services.

Assistive technology device: Any tool that can help a student to effectively perform tasks or lead a more functional life.

Assistive technology service: Any service that supports the effective use of an assistive technology device.

High-tech device: Assistive technology device that is generally more expensive or sophisticated, or that requires considerable training to use effectively.

Low-tech device: Assistive technology device that is generally inexpensive and simple in design, and requires little or no training to use effectively.

Technology abandonment: A process characterized by acquisition and initial use of an assistive technology device, followed by a decision not to continue use of the device.

Introduction

Assistive technology includes a range of items, pieces of equipment, and product systems that may be used to increase, maintain, and improve the functional abilities of children with disabilities [Individuals with Disabilities Education Act of 1990 (IDEA; P.L. 101-476)]. They may be acquired commercially off the shelf, modified, or customized [20 U.S.C. § 1401(a)(25)]. This broad definition of assistive technology recognizes that virtually *any* tool that people use on a daily

basis has the *potential* to help students with disabilities in various aspects of their daily lives. This includes enhancement of human functioning in inter- and intrapersonal relationships (Browning, White, Nave, & Zembrowsky-Barkin, 1986; Gaylord-Ross, Haring, Breen, & Pitts-Conway, 1984; Lewis, 1993), sensory abilities (Burgstahler, 1994; Hawkins, 1990), cognitive capabilities (Ager, 1986; Male, 1994; Rotheray, Sewell, & Morton, 1986), communication (Baumgart, Johnson, & Helmstetter, 1990; Beukelman, Yorkston, & Dowden, 1985; Boothroyd, 1987), motor performance (Butler,

Okamoto, & McKey, 1983; Carey & Sale, 1994; Haring, McCormick, & Haring, 1994), self-maintenance (Horner, Sprague, O'Brien, & Heathfield, 1990), leisure (Lewis, 1993; Sutin, 1990), and productivity (Lewis, 1993; Male, 1994; Vanderheiden, 1985).

The types of assistive technology used by students who have mental retardation and developmental disabilities are frequently the same as those used by children and adults without disabilities (Nalty & Kochany, 1991). For example, a flexible drinking straw used by persons without disabilities may be viewed as a convenience for drinking purposes. For a student with a physical disability who cannot grasp and tilt a cup to drink from it, the straw facilitates a functional daily living skill (i.e., drinking from a cup) with little or no assistance from others. A hand-held remote control is viewed by most people as a convenient technology allowing access to a television or VCR from across the room. It is viewed as an alternative to walking to the television set or VCR and making a selection manually. For students with disabilities, a remote control device could be a necessity, that is, the only means of accessing and interacting with modern conveniences. In general, then, assistive technology is a life necessity for many individuals (Williams, 1991).

Assistive technology devices used by students with mental retardation and developmental disabilities can be grouped into the following categories: (a) augmentative and alternative communication (AAC) devices, (b) adaptive toys, (c) positioning equipment, (d) independent living devices, (e) leisure–recreation equipment, (f) microcomputers and information technologies, (g) environmental access devices, (h) assistive listening devices, (i) mobility devices, and (j) visual aids. Effective professionals should not view assistive technology in any of these categories as an educational outcome. Instead, it should be seen as a means for students to achieve independence and success in functional activities (Church & Glennen, 1992a; Levin & Scherfenberg, 1987; Nalty & Kochany, 1991).

High-Tech Versus Low-Tech Assistive Technology

Parents, teachers, and other professionals often conceptualize assistive technology narrowly by thinking of computer applications, powered wheelchairs, electronic AAC devices that use speech, and other sophisticated devices. However, a wide range of assistive technology devices is available to students with mental retardation and developmental disabilities that vary in (a) cost, (b) flexibility of use, (c) durability, (d) training requirements that enable the student and others to use the device, (e) sophistication, (f) transportability, and (g) maintenance requirements. Thus, assistive technology devices may be distinguished from one another as being high tech or low tech in design (Behrmann & Lahm, 1994; Glennen, 1992; Inge & Shepherd, 1995).

High-tech devices tend to be complex and sophisticated, are expensive to acquire and maintain, and may involve considerable effort by the student to learn to operate (Glennen, 1992; Nalty & Kochany, 1991; PSI International, 1985). Low-tech devices are generally inexpensive, simple in design, and require little training to learn to use (Inge & Shepherd, 1995; Mann & Lane, 1995). Examples of both high- and low-tech devices are listed in Table 17.1.

Interestingly, studies have shown that the average cost of assistive technology devices needed for school-age students with disabilities is not as high as many would be inclined to believe. Parette and VanBiervliet (1990b) surveyed primary caregivers of students with disabilities ages 6 to 21 and found that 30% of these students used devices that cost less than $100, whereas another 15% used assistive technologies that

Table 17.1

Examples of Low- and High-Tech Devices

Low-Tech Devices	High-Tech Devices
Adaptive switches to allow access to battery-operated toys, electrical systems, or electronic systems	Computers for educational tasks, recreation, communication, and environmental control
Call systems, such as buzzers, or loop tapes to communicate short messages	Augmentative and alternative communication devices that use synthetic or digitized speech
Communication boards, notebooks, or folders to communicate a wider variety of messages	Powered mobility devices to enable independent movement about the environment
Activity frames or objects stabilized by Velcro™, Dycem®, elastic, and other materials	Environmental control systems that use infrared, radio frequency, ultrasound, or alternating current (AC) power line control scheme
Adapted books to facilitate participation in story time or reading	
Adapted eating utensils to enable more effective self-feeding	Advanced switches, such as those that detect eye or muscle movements
Jigs, elongated levers for on–off switches, and other adaptations to allow gross or fine motor control, designed for specific work tasks and needs	Modified or alternative keyboards and other computer adaptations
	Braille printers and text-to-speech devices to enable access to information
Tactile enhancement, such as using raised lines on pictures or to label clothes	Computerized visual amplification systems
Talking, lighted, or enlarged clocks and calculators to optimize use of these devices	Powered lifts and transfer systems

cost between $100 and $500. Similar findings have been reported by primary caregivers of younger children ages birth to 5 years (Parette & VanBiervliet, 1991f). However, within specific assistive technology device categories, greater costs may be expected. For example, costs for AAC devices can range from $100 to $8,000, averaging approximately $2,400 for children ages birth to 3 years (Sibert, 1992). The issue of funding for devices for children with disabilities remains a primary issue for most states (Angelo, Jones, & Kokoska, 1995; Morris & Golinker, 1991; Neath, 1993; Parette & VanBiervliet, 1990b, 1991a) and is addressed later in this chapter.

The effective practice of employing assistive technology to meet the needs of students with disabilities should involve consideration of any available technology in the search for the most appropriate possible solution (Langton, 1990). Applying assistive technology devices to solve problems involves matching individual student needs with the potential benefits possible, with less emphasis placed on the design of the device (low vs. high tech). Numerous excellent resources provide detailed descriptions of the various types of assistive technology devices useful with students who have mental retardation and developmental disabilities (e.g., Beukelman et al., 1985; Bigge, 1982; Burkhart, 1980, 1982; Church & Glennen, 1992b; Glennen & DeCoste, 1997; Goosens & Crain, 1986; Judge & Parette, in press; Levin & Scherfenberg, 1987; Male, 1994; Mann & Lane, 1995; Musselwhite, 1986; Ray & Warden, 1995; Wright & Nomura, 1985).

Assistive Technology Services

Because IDEA identifies assistive technology as a service that can be provided to students with mental retardation and developmental disabilities, schools have responsibility for ensuring the delivery of devices and equipment to these students in special education settings. However, the provision of appropriate assistive technology devices cannot occur in the absence of additional services. Assistive technology services are defined as "any service that directly assists an individual with a disability in the selection, acquisition, or use of an assistive technology device" [20 U.S.C. § 1401(26)]. Such services include (a) evaluations of the technology needs of children, including functional evaluations of students in their customary environments; (b) purchasing, leasing, or providing for the acquisition of devices and equipment; (c) selecting, designing, fitting, customizing, adapting, applying, retaining, repairing, or replacing devices and equipment; (d) coordinating and using other therapies, interventions, or services with assistive technology devices; (e) training or technical assistance for a student with a disability and families, when appropriate; and (f) training or technical assistance for professionals, employers, or others who provide services to, employ, or are involved in the major life activities of students with disabilities [20 U.S.C.

§ 1401(26)]. Assistive technology devices and services may be made available if required as part of the student's (a) special education [34 C.F.R. § 300.17], (b) related services [34 C.F.R. § 300.16], or (c) supplementary aids and services [34 C.F.R. § 300.550(b)(2)]. (*Note:* The generic term *assistive technology* is used throughout the remainder of this chapter to refer to both devices and services when appropriate.)

Unfortunately, assistive technology devices have frequently been provided to students with mental retardation and developmental disabilities without ensuring that assistive technology services are in place before, during, and after acquisition of devices and equipment. Assistive technology services are critical if technology abandonment is to be avoided (Batavia, Dillard, & Phillips, n.d.; Batavia & Hammer, 1989; Dillard, 1989; Galvin, n.d. a, n.d. b). Technology abandonment is a pattern characterized by (a) provision of the device subsequent to an evaluation or personal selection process; (b) use of the device followed by recognition that it fails to meet the needs of the user even after attempted modification; (c) continued use of the device, remaining dissatisfied with it until it is no longer usable, or abandoning the device at an early stage; and (d) choosing another device that more appropriately meets needs not met by the previous device, but often failing to meet other needs (Batavia & Hammer, 1990; Batavia et al., n.d.). Examples of technology abandonment have been reported frequently (LeBlanc, 1982; Lifchez, Leiser, Pendleton, & Davis, 1983; Scherer & McKee, 1989; Zola, 1982).

Many special education personnel are aware of unused assistive technology devices that occupy the corners, closets, and storage rooms of classrooms in their respective school districts. To avoid technology abandonment, professionals must ensure that appropriate assistive technology is identified for students. The issue of selecting appropriate assistive technology for persons with mental retardation and developmental disabilities is addressed in greater depth in subsequent sections of this chapter.

Adversarial Relationships

The increasingly expanded possibilities of assistive technology to help students with disabilities in school settings will require educational and related services personnel to reconceptualize the scope of instructional opportunities for these students. In the past, many instructional activities requiring assistive technology may have been viewed by administrative personnel to be impractical due to cost constraints or the degree of the student's disability (Cavalier, 1989; Cohen, 1989; Mendelsohn, 1989; National Information Center for Children and Youth with Disabilities, 1991). The language of IDEA clearly mandates the delivery of assistive technology when it can help students with mental retardation and developmental disabilities to benefit from educational services.

Unfortunately, effective teachers are sometimes placed in adversarial positions when developing Individualized Education Progams (IEPs) due to school administrative personnel concerns regarding costs for assistive technology (Parette, 1994a, 1994b; Parette, Murdick, & Gartin, 1996; Ray & Warden, 1995). Such concerns can be minimized if informed team decision making takes place in the development of a student's IEP (Button, 1991; Galvin, Ross, & Phillips, n.d.; Levin & Scherfenberg, 1987; Parette, Hourcade, & Van-Biervliet, 1993). Similarly, assistive technology devices will become more attainable as the costs of producing them decline (Esposito & Campbell, 1987; Ray & Warden, 1995). With decreases in the costs associated with assistive technology devices, which can help students benefit from special education (Aldinger, Warger, & Eavy, 1995; Carey & Sale, 1994), a wider variety of devices and equipment may be provided with greater frequency. For example, in recent years public schools have increasingly invested fiscal resources in computers for students with disabilities due to declining costs (Lewis, 1993; Male, 1994; Ray & Warden, 1995).

Considerations in Selecting Appropriate Assistive Technology

Selection of assistive technology for students with mental retardation and developmental disabilities may seem to be a challenging task to many professionals. A philosophical foundation that embraces specific ethical principles should be the backdrop for all decisions that are made (see Figure 17.1). The following section presents a discussion of the philosophical foundation that should guide the assistive technology decision-making process. It is followed by sections that describe (a) the assistive technology team, (b) issues related to selecting appropriate technology for students, (c) the relationship between the IEP and assistive technology, (d) assistive technology and IEP goals and objectives, (e) assistive technology as supplementary aids and services, and (f) funding.

The Philosophical Foundation

When participating in team processes that result in the selection of assistive technology for students with mental retardation and developmental disabilities, efforts must be made to select and apply technology in a manner that acknowledges and promotes individual dignity and the opportunity for personal choice (Cavalier, 1988; Guess, Benson, & Siegel-Causey, 1985; Holder-Brown & Parette, 1992; Parette & Van-Biervliet, 1990b; Pfrommer, 1984; Wolfensberger, 1972). To achieve this goal, effective team members should consider a range of factors, as described in the following subsections.

Maintenance of a Student Focus

Effective team members should remember that assistive technology is not an end in itself (Galvin et al., n.d.; Levin & Scherfenberg, 1987; Mann & Lane, 1995), but is a means to provide increased experiences, opportunities, and inde-

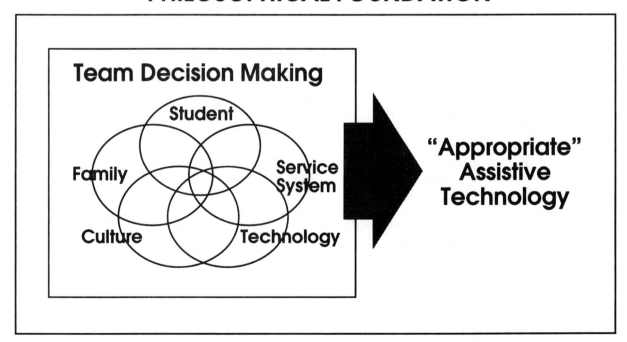

Figure 17.1. Effective team foundation for appropriate assistive technology decision making.

pendence for students. Assistive technology should generally facilitate changes in the student's behavior that are observable and have social validity (Evans & Meyer, 1985; Snell & Browder, 1986).

Limited Knowledge of the Technology

All reasonable assistive technology options, including human and environmental factors, should be explored before a decision is made. This is best accomplished using a variation of the IEP multidisciplinary team (Church & Glennen, 1992a; Parette et al., 1993; Ray & Warden, 1995) composed of individuals representing many disciplines (see Figure 17.2). Each discipline's knowledge base can be used to increase the probability that the most appropriate assistive technology will be identified for a particular student.

Developmental Relevance

Rigorous standards of developmental appropriateness applied to educational strategies and materials (Galvin, n.d. a; Hasselbring & Goin, 1992; Male, 1994; Polloway, Patton, Smith, & Roderique, 1991) must also be applied to assistive technology. Any device or service considered should be linked to anticipated educational outcomes and functional

activities, and promote long-term increased independence for the student.

Self-Perception and the Perception of Others

Assistive technology should not unnecessarily draw attention to student disabilities (Enders & Hall, 1990; Morris, 1991; Parette, Brotherson, Hoge, & Hostetler, 1996). In some instances, this may mean giving more consideration to assistive technology that will be accepted by others in the student's environment as opposed to a device or service that results in greater independence or functionality.

Dignity of Choice

Students and parents have rights and responsibilities to participate in educational planning processes and can share information and expertise regarding their activities, goals, and the environments in which they live (Dunst, Trivette, & Deal, 1988; McGonigel, Woodruff, & Roszmann-Millican, 1994; Rosin, Whitehead, Tuchman, Jesian, & Begun, 1993). Effective participation in assistive technology decision making does not mean presenting the student and parents with a particular option and asking for their consent. It implies sharing information about the strengths and weaknesses of

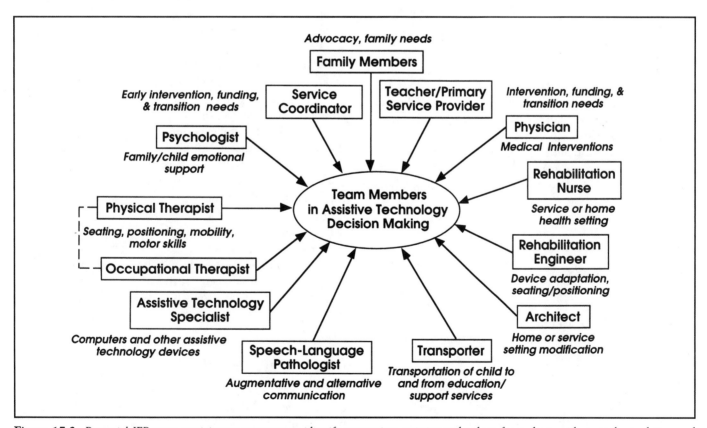

Figure 17.2. Potential IEP team participants necessary to identify appropriate assistive technology for students with mental retardation and developmental disabilities. From "Assistive Technology Decision Making Strategies," by S. L. Judge and H. P. Parette, in press, in *Assistive Technology for Young Children with Disabilities*, by S. L. Lesar and H. P. Parette (Eds.), Cambridge, MA: Brookline. Copyright 1997 by Howard Parette. Reprinted with permission.

all the *alternatives*, and then encouraging and facilitating active family participation in the creation of a plan.

Charity

Historically, children with disabilities have been viewed as being the responsibility of society (Cavalier, 1987; Gartner, Lipsky, & Turnbull, 1991; Holder-Brown & Parette, 1992; Wolfensberger, 1969), resulting in the widespread perception that they should be grateful for the charity (or services) they receive. Consequently, any assistive technology prescribed might be viewed as being better than nothing for a student. Decisions regarding assistive technology should be based primarily on the student's need for that technology in order to participate in an appropriate special education program, rather than mere availability of specific devices, equipment, and services.

Limitations Imposed on the Technology

The limits imposed on a student by any assistive technology will always be present until a more advanced or effective technology is available (Mann & Lane, 1995). Some technology by design will have certain limitations, and additional limitations may be imposed by the educational environment (e.g., policies that assistive technology devices are the property of the school and should not be used in the home setting).

Individual Rights and Social Equity

Current constraints in funding allocated for implementation of IDEA may result in administrative reluctance to provide expensive assistive technology to students with disabilities (Mendelsohn, 1989; Rothstein, 1995). Cost factors must be considered against the full range of assistive technology that might be appropriate to meet a student's educational goals (Batavia et al., n.d.; Galvin, n.d. a, n.d. b; Nalty & Kochany, 1991).

The Assistive Technology Team

Within the public schools, the design and application of adaptations and technological devices is usually accomplished through a multidisciplinary IEP team (Langton, 1990; Mann & Lane, 1995; Parette et al., 1993; Ray & Warden, 1995). Participants may include occupational therapists, physical therapists, speech–language pathologists, special and regular education teachers, and parents. Other professionals may also be required to participate (see Figure 17.2). Part of the assignment of the team is to assure that all dimensions of the student's present levels of performance are considered. This team approach is most effective when persons having expertise in instructional programming, including assistive technology and its applications, work cooperatively with the student, family members, and professionals who are involved in day-to-day instruction.

Special education teachers who participate on the team may be called upon to assume important decision-making responsibilities, though often they may lack adequate training and/or experience with assistive technology and its applications. When teachers are not prepared for the responsibility of selecting devices for students and using them in classroom settings, they may rely too heavily on the judgment of other professionals (e.g., the occupational therapist, physical therapist, speech–language pathologist). These professionals may see the student's needs from a very different (and more limited) perspective than does the teacher. Effective team members have the responsibility of becoming informed decision makers, thus ensuring that assistive technology is *appropriate* for the student.

Selection of Appropriate Technology

It is important for effective team members to develop a philosophical base upon which decisions will be made when selecting appropriate technology for children with disabilities. Issues that should drive the formulation of a philosophical foundation have previously been discussed. It is also important to remember that appropriateness takes on several dimensions. The language of IDEA is designed to address student needs related to learning and/or development, including the need to (a) acquire basic self-help skills, (b) have appropriate adaptive equipment, (c) develop appropriate social interaction skills, (d) acquire basic prevocational skills, and (e) receive therapy services. In each of these areas, assistive technology can play a critical role in assuring the provision of appropriate learning experiences for students with disabilities in public school settings.

From a more traditional perspective, an assistive device is appropriate when its application meets one of three criteria. First, it should be related to specific and clearly defined goals, which result in greater independence for the student. Second, it should be compatible with practical constraints, such as the available resources or amount of training required for the student and the teacher to use the technology. Third, it should result in the student's achieving desirable and sufficient outcomes (Office of Technology Assessment, 1982).

Determining the Fit

To most effectively match assistive technology with any given student, the teacher and other team members must keep in mind five parallel considerations: (a) characteristics of the student, (b) technology features, (c) school issues, (d) cultural factors, and (e) family needs (Parette, Brotherson, Hourcade, & Bradley, 1996; VanBiervliet, Parette, &

Bradley, 1991). Each of these areas is discussed in the following subsections.

Student Characteristics

The characteristics of the student are of the utmost importance, and must be given primary consideration (Parette & VanBiervliet, 1990b). Specific student characteristics are discussed in the following subsections.

Performance Levels. Determination of a student's current capabilities in various developmental areas provides a foundation for determining future goals that can be achieved using assistive technology (e.g., sitting without support, using two hands to perform certain academic tasks, dressing independently, communicating with others in the classroom). Assistive technology devices place varying cognitive demands on students to use them efficiently (e.g., use of a software program that requires one key depression vs. one that requires many keystrokes). The greater the sophistication, or use requirements, of the assistive technology device, the greater the cognitive demands placed on the student. Of particular importance are the social interaction and cooperative learning demands placed on the student. For example, if a student has not learned social communication and cooperative turn-taking skills, great difficulty may be experienced in appropriately using devices in contexts where these skills are required. Similarly, some devices may be easily damaged and may not be appropriate for students who have poor adaptive behavior skills and have a tendency to be destructive with devices. In such instances, specific device features should be given greater attention (e.g., durability, safety characteristics). The presence of a sensory disability also has a direct influence on the types of assistive technology considered for the student. For example, a student with a visual impairment needs devices that do not require vision for effective use, whereas students with hearing disabilities may not benefit from sound features of some devices.

Age. Assistive technology devices should be selected that are developmentally appropriate for a student's chronological level. For example, a battery-operated toy designed for a 3-year-old child typically would not be appropriate for a 15-year-old student in the classroom.

Gender. Effective team members should consider the appropriateness of devices based on features that might make them appropriate for use by males and females. For example, a pink device might not be the best choice for a male student, particularly in an inclusive educational setting in which the student frequently interacts with male peers. Failure to consider gender during assistive technology selection could result in technology abandonment by the student.

Current Devices Used, Past Experiences, and Preferences. Assistive technology that is currently used at home, but not at school, and devices previously used at school should be considered by effective team members. Family participants, as well as teachers and other school personnel who have worked with the student previously, may have valuable information regarding past successes in using or making modifications to specific devices (Parette et al., 1993; Scherer & McKee, 1989; Zola, 1982). Student preferences for assistive technology should be given primary consideration because such preferences are frequently based on past successful experiences. Questions that might be asked by team members that address student characteristics are presented in Table 17.2.

Academic and Vocational Aspirations. Effective team members should anticipate the child's future academic and vocational needs (e.g., developing word processing skills vs. concentration on handwriting) when making decisions about assistive technology for students with disabilities. This is particularly important for older students who are entering transition programs. Team members should also recognize that passage of the Americans with Disabilities Act of 1990 (P.L. 101-336) has resulted in greater employment opportunities for persons with mental retardation and developmental disabilities nationally.

Student Desire for Independence. Assistive technology has the potential to enhance the functional abilities of students with disabilities, resulting in greater independence. Students who have a sense of inner direction, or the motivation to exercise control over their environment, will have needs for different types of assistive technology than their peers who have less motivation. However, desire for independence may be significantly influenced by cultural factors, which are discussed later in this chapter.

Physical Location of the Student. Geographic and environmental factors may suggest specific assistive technology that may be appropriate for a student (Parette & VanBiervliet, 1990b). For example, if independent mobility in the community is deemed important, consideration might be given to the accessibility of sidewalks and other public areas prior to providing a student with a powered wheelchair. Many public buildings and private businesses remain inaccessible, demonstrating that full implementation of the Americans with Disabilities Act of 1990 has not occurred.

Student Training Needs. Some assistive technology, particularly devices that are more sophisticated or unfamiliar to students, will require varying amounts of training to be used effectively (Galvin, n.d. a, n.d. b; Parette & VanBiervliet, 1990b). This is particularly true for students who have motor, cognitive, social, behavioral, or sensory disabilities (Glennen, 1992).

Changes Over Time. Many of the student considerations noted above may change over time due to peer influences,

Table 17.2
Examples of Questions Relating to Student, Technology, School, and Family Issues

Student Issues

What specific strengths and needs does the student have in academic, social, behavioral, motor, recreational, and vocational areas?

How can assistive technology assist the student in any of these areas?

How will the student's gender and age influence the selection of a particular device?

What are the student's preferences for a device?

What are the student's past experiences in using specific devices?

What are the student's academic and vocational goals?

Technology Issues

What technologies are available to assist the student in identified areas of need?

What are the features of the device that can assist the student? Strengths? Limitations?

What is the cost of the device (advertised and hidden)?

How dependable is the device? How long can it be used before repair is necessary?

How easily can the device be repaired? How long will the student be without the device during repair, and what device alternatives are available in the interim? Is a loaner device available from the manufacturer during repair?

How easily can the device be transported across environments?

Can the device be used with other devices (e.g., computers), or does it perform only one task?

Is the device available for trial usage by the student?

Is the device easy to be maintained by the child, teacher, and family?

Is the device comfortable and safe (e.g., no sharp edges, safe from electrical shock)?

How easily can the device be assembled? Can it be adapted or modified?

School Issues

What resources are available to purchase the device?

What outside resources are available to assist in purchasing the device?

If the student needs the device in both school and home, how will the device be protected from theft and damage?

How will the student transport the device to and from school (or where services are provided)?

What training will be required for the student, teacher, and family members to use the device?

Is family- and student-friendly training provided?

Cultural Issues

Has the family clearly communicated concerns, needs, and goals about the student?

Are the family's and student's daily routines identified? Would the family and student like a support group to convey information or training regarding assistive technology devices?

Would the family prefer a community leader or liaison to convey information regarding assistive technology devices?

Are family expectations of the assistive technology assessment process clearly understood?

Does the family understand issues related to funding and ownership of the assistive technology device?

Have the various settings where the child might use assistive technology devices, and resulting demands and consequences of device usage there, been identified?

Do families want to use devices in community settings?

Are the family expectations of the assistive technology device clearly understood prior to purchase?

Family Issues

What preferences does the family have for a device?

In what family activities will the device be used?

What changes in family routines will result following introduction of the device?

Will the device affect family interaction patterns? Increase levels of stress?

Does the family have time to attend training on the use of the device?

From *Assistive Technology and Disabilities: A Guide for Parents and Students*, by H. P. Parette and A. VanBiervliet, 1990. Little Rock: University of Arkansas at Little Rock Press. Copyright 1990 by University of Arkansas at Little Rock Press. Reprinted with permission.

family and academic experiences, and other factors. As a student has more experiences with assistive technology (and subsequent failures and successes), periodic changes in student preferences may be exhibited, requiring the IEP team to examine new assistive technology solutions to most effectively meet student needs.

Technology Characteristics

Once relevant characteristics of the student have been identified and considered, the features of assistive technology devices being considered for the student may be addressed (Batavia & Hammer, 1990). Goals for the use of devices should emerge as a result of the assessment of student needs, desires, and capabilities. Specific factors that should be considered are noted in the following subsections.

Range and Availability of Technologies. Often many assistive technology devices may be appropriate to help students with mental retardation and developmental disabilities benefit from special education programming.[1] Effective IEP team members should consider as many devices as possible that might potentially help the student achieve identified goals. Catalogues from vendors should be examined and, if appropriate, vendor representatives may be contacted to provide demonstrations and hands-on opportunities with devices. This will allow team members to effectively ask questions regarding specific device features that can assist in decision making (e.g., How much memory does it have? What is its repair record? Is a loaner available if it has to be sent to your facility for more than a few weeks?). Team members should also make inquiries regarding the availability of assistive devices. Devices purchased from manufacturers may not always be in stock and/or require lengthy periods of time to manufacture, resulting in lengthy delays in delivery.

Ability to Enhance Levels of Performance. Once a student's performance levels are known by the IEP team, long-term goals and objectives naturally emerge from this information through team decision making (Polloway & Patton, 1993). Although many assistive technology devices are designed to perform targeted functions, other devices may have multiple uses across tasks and settings. For example, a Dycem® placemat designed to prevent a plate from sliding across a wheelchair lapboard during mealtime could also be used during academic activities to prevent undesired movement of manipulatives. Sometimes devices are accompanied by product manuals that provide documentation regarding device functions and limitations. If documentation is not available, effective IEP team members may need to directly examine devices being considered. If necessary, inquiries may be made to the manufacturer or to students with disabilities who have used the device in the past. Information obtained from previous users is especially important, because they sometimes report problems that have been unnoticed by vendors.

Real Cost. The cost of technology is frequently identified as a primary barrier to acquiring technology for students with disabilities (Parker et al., 1990; Uslan, 1992). The initial and ongoing costs of the technology are also frequent concerns expressed by school administrative personnel (Cavalier, 1989; Galvin & Toonstra, n.d.; Office of Technology Assessment, 1982). Of particular importance to the IEP team is the real cost of the device, including costs associated with assembling, special batteries, parts, maintenance requirements, and additional assistive devices that are required to operate the device being considered. If these hidden expenses are explored initially, they may be written into the child's IEP as an assistive technology service, and the school will be responsible for paying for the expenses.

Ease of Use. The simplicity of operation of an assistive technology device is an important consideration. Often schools purchase complex devices that require tremendous training time investments by both teachers and students. This can result in reluctance on the part of teachers to learn how to use such devices. Similarly, if the cognitive or motoric demands of the device exceed the student's performance levels, the student may be resistant to using the device, resulting in technology abandonment (Batavia et al., n.d.; Phillips, n.d.).

Comfort. Careful thought must be given to the physical demands placed on the student to operate or use any assistive technology device, and the level of comfort experienced by the student during use. Some devices may be used with great ease and comfort, whereas others can be used only for short periods before the user becomes tired. For example, some students with physical disabilities may have limited range of motion in their upper extremities and have great difficulty using their fingers to operate some technologies without discomfort.

Dependability. When resources are expended for assistive devices, a major concern is whether the product is dependable. This issue includes the extent to which (a) device performance matches manufacturer claims and (b) the device meets the needs of students (Galvin, n.d. a, n.d. b). Effective IEP team members must examine the ability of devices to

---

[1] Information regarding assistive device technology product comparisons has been compiled in a series of documents by the Request Rehabilitation Engineering Center at the National Rehabilitation Hospital, Washington, D.C. The Alliance for Technology Access (ATA) Centers and state projects funded under the Technology-Related Assistance for Individuals with Disabilities Act of 1988 may also be contacted for product information. Information regarding each of these sources is currently housed on the National Rehabilitation Information Center (NARIC) database (800/346-2742; email http://www.cais.com/naric).

provide performance or evaluation data necessary for the documentation of student progress. Certain technologies, especially computer-based devices, readily lend themselves to objective, behavioral record-keeping strategies (Lewis, 1993; Male, 1994; Simonson & Thompson, 1994). If information regarding the device dependability is not available, team members may contact persons with disabilities who have used the device and obtain feedback regarding the user's perspective.

Transportability. It is also important that team members consider the transportability of a particular device (Batavia & Hammer, 1990; Parette & VanBiervliet, 1990b). Sometimes bulky or heavy devices are chosen for students who may not have the strength to carry them around in the environment (Carey & Sale, 1994). This places responsibility on adults working with the student to ensure the availability of the assistive technology device for academic tasks. Smaller devices may be cumbersome for a child to transport, requiring a special case, satchel, or bag.

Longevity and Durability. Because fiscal resources are often limited, it may be desirable to choose assistive technology devices that have utility for a number of years. Some assistive devices must be handled carefully and cannot be subjected to even moderate abuse (e.g., drooling, spills, being dropped), whereas other devices are specifically designed to resist very rugged use by students. Product manuals should be examined for information regarding longevity and durability; if unavailable, direct contact with the manufacturer may be helpful.

Adaptability. Because many technologies will be used for a long period of time, adaptability to meet the changing needs of children over time must be carefully considered (Galvin & Toonstra, n.d.; Parette & VanBiervliet, 1990b; Phillips, n.d.). Devices that may be used across many educationally related tasks may be preferable to, and more cost effective than, those that perform only one function. However, some devices are designed to perform a specific function and cannot be adapted. For example, an augmentative and alternative communication (AAC) device having expandable memory (thus allowing new vocabulary to be added over time) might be more desirable than an AAC device with limited vocabulary capabilities that could be used for only 1 year. Before an assistive technology device is purchased, effective IEP team members might weigh potential modifications needed for the device over time against available fiscal and human resources (e.g., school personnel, community volunteers) necessary to make needed modifications.

Compatibility with Other Devices. Related to hidden costs is the extent to which a device being considered can be used with other assistive technology. Wheelchairs, for example, are usually designed so that other devices can be easily added on; other types of technology may not be so easily modified (Parette & VanBiervliet, 1990b). Team members should give thought to both the student's present and future needs when examining the ability of the technology to be used with other devices.

Opportunity for Hands-on Experience. Effective team members should attempt to ensure that the student has an opportunity to use an assistive technology device prior to purchase (Galvin & Toonstra, n.d.; Governor's Task Force on Technology and Disabilities, 1987; Parette, 1991; Parette & VanBiervliet, 1990b). Many vendors allow a trial usage period prior to billing, and many will provide demonstrations on request. For example, computer software vendors typically allow a 30-day examination period before billing the school.

Safety Features. Effective IEP members cannot assume that all assistive technology devices are safe for use with all students with disabilities, and specific device features should be carefully examined. For example, a small device that could be easily placed in a student's mouth and swallowed might not be appropriate for students having a tendency to mouth objects. Some devices may have sharp edges that could injure a student during a fall or handling. Other devices might cause electrical shock if placed in water.

Repair Considerations. Because some assistive devices require lengthy or frequent repair intervals (Batavia & Hammer, 1990; Parette & VanBiervliet, 1990b; Phillips, n.d.), effective team members should request information from vendors about product testing, reliability, and repair records. Persons in the community who use devices that are being considered should be contacted to obtain a user perspective regarding repair issues. Team members should also ask vendors whether the student will have a backup or "loaner" device provided by the manufacturer while the device is being repaired and whether a warranty is available. If a warranty is not available, team members may identify (a) local shops or companies that can provide parts or repair damaged devices or (b) students, parents, and school personnel who might have the tools and skills to repair assistive technology devices.

School Issues

The third area of concern that must be addressed by the IEP team includes factors directly related to the school. Several key issues are typically of great concern to many school districts, and are discussed in the following subsections.

Cost. The reality of limited funding presents a major challenge to the IEP team, and underscores the effective practice of identifying appropriate technologies for students. Often, inexpensive assistive devices or those that can be modified, customized, or made by the school (using available resources) at minimal cost are appropriate for many students

(Parette & VanBiervliet, 1990b). However, this in no way circumvents the responsibility of the school to purchase an expensive device that is identified as the only means to assist a student to benefit from special education. Team members may consider leasing as an alternative to purchasing expensive devices, thus minimizing hidden expenses (ApparaTek, Inc., n.d.; Hofmann, 1994; Parnes, 1988). Another effective practice solution is to use community resources as an alternative funding source when severe fiscal resource limitations are present. This process is discussed in greater detail later in the section titled Use of Community Resources.

Outside-School Usage of Devices.

Sometimes devices are used only in the school environment, and the student is not allowed to take them home (Parette & VanBiervliet, 1990b; Prentke Romich Co., 1989). If family members feel that it is important for a device to be used at home, or if teachers feel that certain skills taught in school must be practiced in the home, IEP objectives should be written to address this need. For example, an AAC device used by a student to communicate with peers at school might also be used to discuss homework problems with the student's parents, or to practice spelling and grammar skills.

Protection from Theft and Damage.

If a decision is made to allow a child to take a device home, liability issues related to theft or damage should be considered (Parette & VanBiervliet, 1990b). Although many school systems have insurance policies that cover school property while it remains on school premises, these policies may not cover devices once students take them home. An examination of the existing school policy should be made to determine whether devices are covered under such circumstances; if not, it may be that a rider could be negotiated between the school and insurer to replace or repair the student's device in the event of theft or damage.

School Personnel Training Needs.

Effective IEP team members should not ignore the necessity of training personnel how to use assistive technology devices efficiently (Parette, 1991; VanBiervliet & Parette, 1989). Whereas many assistive devices can easily be used without training, more sophisticated devices (e.g., keyboard emulators, nondedicated speech devices, environmental control systems) may require considerable staff training commitments. Training is an assistive technology service that can be written into the IEP (see the later section titled The IEP and Assistive Technology).

Transportation.

Sometimes IEP members must consider whether an assistive device chosen for the student can be transported to and from the school (Parette, 1991; Parette & VanBiervliet, 1990a). Some assistive devices, such as powered wheelchairs, require the removal of seats to create additional space, and installation of wheelchair locks and ramps on transportation vehicles.

Cultural Factors

When team members consider assistive technology devices for children with disabilities, they must be sensitive to important cultural issues that are too frequently overlooked (Hourcade, Parette, & Huer, in press). Specific questions that may be asked by the team are noted in Figure 17.2. Families and teachers may have very different perceptions and values, based in part on the differing cultural backgrounds they bring to the IEP table. This issue is particularly significant to team members, given the continuing overrepresentation of students from minority racial and cultural backgrounds (see, e.g., Ysseldyke, Algozzine, & Thurlow, 1992). Individuals from non–European American cultural backgrounds may see the world quite differently. In such cases the quality of the special educational services provided to both students and family members may be impaired when interventions are provided that do not take into account variations in perceptions and values (Hanson, 1992; Hetzroni & Harris, 1996; Parette, in press; Soto, Huer, & Taylor, in press; Trivelli, 1994).

A variety of issues relevant to special education have been found to differ systematically across cultures in America. These include (a) perceptions of disability held by family members (Groce & Zola, 1993), (b) attitudes toward the education system (Harry, Allen, & McLaughlin, 1995), (c) priorities regarding services deemed important for the child and family (Soto et al., in press), (d) ideas regarding the importance and process of childcare (Anderson & Fenichel, 1989; Ogbu, 1987), and (e) the extent to which life circumstances are viewed as being overwhelming (Rosado, 1994).

Recognition of culture-specific differences in how these issues are perceived is critical when considering the possible use of assistive technology devices (Hourcade et al., in press). In the excitement over the possibilities these technologies may offer to students with disabilities, team members may fail to consider that their perceptions of the advantages and disadvantages of these devices may be quite different from the perceptions of the families of these students (Parette, 1997, in press). A number of resources discuss the impact of cultural issues on assistive technology decision making (see e.g., Parette, 1996; Parette, in press; Soto et al., in press; Vitaliti & Bourland, 1995). In general, three primary concerns are often reflected in conversations held with family members across cultural groups: (a) emphasis on independence and self-sufficiency, (b) sensitivity to changes in family routines, and (c) needs for information (Hourcade et al., in press). Each of these is discussed in the following sections.

Emphasis on Independence and Self-Sufficiency.

Teachers must realize that the European American values of independence and self-sufficiency are not values shared by family members from all cultures. Some cultures—for example, Asian and Native American cultures—are more *collectivist* in nature (Hyun & Fowler, 1995; Nguyen, 1995). Often in these cultures children are viewed less as individuals in their own right, and more as parts of the family and community. A certain degree of dependence on the family throughout life is expected and valued. Thus, the typical special education goal of increased independence that an assistive technology device might help a student achieve may not be seen as important to these families. Professionals must have an understanding of the cultural value systems of family members before making assumptions that all families want their children with disabilities to be independent in their respective communities (Parette, Brotherson, Hoge, & Hostetler, 1996).

Extent to Which Families Desire To Be Seen as Being Different. Closely related to collectivism is the desire of many families from different cultures to be accepted in community and other settings, and to avoid being perceived as being different from others (Parette, Brotherson, Hoge, & Hostetler, 1996). For example, some families in the African American community may prefer not to have attention drawn to their children in social settings when using assistive technology devices (Parette, Brotherson, Hoge, & Hostetler, 1996; Smith-Lewis, 1992). An assistive device that is obtrusive and does just this may be an inappropriate choice for some children (Hourcade et al., in press).

Needs for Information. Many families from all cultures express ongoing needs for information regarding assistive technology devices (Parette, Brotherson, Hoge, & Hostetler, 1996). Special educators might be careful not to let their own cultural backgrounds filter the information they share with families (Hourcade et al., in press). For example, many professionals from European American cultural backgrounds may automatically assume that mothers desire information regarding how assistive technology devices may be used for socialization purposes and in community settings, and that fathers are more interested in repair, maintenance, and programming (Angelo, Kokoska, & Jones, 1996). However, as with many other generalizations, such an assumption may be invalid for family members from non-European American backgrounds.

The manner in which information is shared with family members from differing cultural backgrounds should also be considered (Parette, Brotherson, Hoge, & Hostetler, 1996; Parette, in press). Family members from certain cultural backgrounds may mistrust European American school personnel. In such cases, having a representative from a community support system (e.g., a church or community action group) at the IEP meeting can help resolve communication problems. It is often helpful to ask community resource or support personnel who are from the same cultural backgrounds of families to assist team members by providing information regarding assistive technology devices to families, and learning their needs. Families may prefer the use of support groups for the delivery of information from other family members and children who use assistive technology devices. Such support groups provide a mechanism for the delivery of information from persons who have confronted specific problems related to assistive technology devices (e.g., training concerns, funding, working with professionals). Use of interpreters may also need to be considered by team members to clearly communicate with family members and to understand their concerns and needs during assistive technology decision making (Lynch, 1992; Roseberry-McKibbin, 1995).

Family Issues

For full implementation of Part B of IDEA to occur, an equitable system of service delivery must be developed nationally. As previously discussed, the system can be influenced by many factors: parental preference, student characteristics, financial resources, ethnicity, student age, geographic location, professional preference, and service availability (Sontag & Schacht, 1993).

IEP team decisions regarding assistive technology are generally made after student, technology, and school factors have been considered (Angelo, 1997; Parette, 1994a; Parette, VanBiervliet, & Bradley, 1994). School personnel may have a tendency to focus on how assistive technology can help a student in the classroom and other educational settings (e.g., shopping trips to the grocery store). Family members, on the other hand, often want devices that can be used both at school and at home. For example, an augmentative and alternative communication device may be purchased by the school if it can help a student to communicate in the classroom. Family members may need to be prepared to show IEP team members how assistive technology that helps the student at home will also help the child to benefit from special education services.

In a national study of states funded under the Technology-Related Assistance for Individuals with Disabilities Act of 1988 (P.L. 100-407), Parette (1995) found that less consideration is given to family issues than to technology, child, and service system factors during assistive technology assessment and prescriptive processes. An effective practice is for IEP team members to develop an approach that recognizes and considers family issues, because parents and family members do not always share the same concerns or preferences for assistive technology as school personnel (Angelo, 1997; Beukelman & Mirenda, 1993). Specific family issues are discussed in the following subsections.

Changes in Activities, Routines, and Resources. If service plan implementation is to be effective, family values, routines, and resources should be considered by IEP members (Angelo, 1997; Brinker, Seifer, & Sameroff, 1994; Caldwell, Sirvis, Todaro, & Accouloumre, 1991; Condry, 1989; Gallimore, Weisner, Bernheimer, Guthrie, & Nihira, 1993; Parette & Angelo, in press). This is particularly important when devices are identified for use both at school and in the home. Higher levels of stress may occur if (a) increased caregiving demands are placed on families (Haddad, 1992; Harris, 1988; McNaughton, 1990; Murphy, 1988), (b) great amounts of time are required for family members to provide school-recommended interventions (Brotherson & Goldstein, 1992), and (c) specific assistive devices are provided that require family time and resource commitments (Allaire, Gressard, Blackman, & Hostler, 1991; Angelo, 1997; Angelo et al., 1995; Brotherson, Oakland, Secrist-Mertz, Litchfield, & Larson, 1995; Culp, Ambrosi, Berniger, & Mitchell, 1986; McNaughton, 1990; Parette, 1994a). Specific questions should be posed to family members (see Table 17.2) in an effort to understand how an assistive technology device might affect the family. Such sensitivity will reflect respect for the family and may encourage greater family participation in the child's educational program.

Effect on Interaction Patterns. When assistive devices are introduced in the home setting, unexpected outcomes sometimes result. For example, if a mother has to spend large amounts of time learning how to use a sophisticated device, less time could be available for routine household tasks and interaction with other family members. The resulting heightened levels of stress among all family members could culminate in a range of family difficulties (e.g., arguments, decrease in communication among family members, resentments). When the IEP team is aware that introduction of an assistive technology device might require certain changes in family routines, probing questions should be asked: "If we allow Johnny to take his AAC device home, will you be able to come to school a day a week during the first few weeks of school to learn how to use the device? If so, will this affect your family in some important way? What will your spouse think? Will your children understand?" Such questions can provide valuable insights into the potential impact of assistive technology on the family.

Independence. IEP team members should view the provision of an assistive device from the perspective of potentially increased student independence. As noted previously under cultural issues, many family members may not desire increased levels of independence for the student. For team members concerned about the impact of assistive technology, this issue includes consideration of improvement in the student's living condition, ability to perform important tasks in the classroom and other environmental settings, and ability to be independent. If the device does not facilitate improvement in these areas, a different assistive technology may need to be considered by the team.

Linkages Among Domains

In the process of identifying appropriate assistive technology for any student with a disability, team members should incorporate examination of the linkages among the five domains, as depicted in Figure 17.3 (VanBiervliet et al., 1991). Predicting the nature of changes expected in specified domains, and timelines relating to the appearance of anticipated outcomes, is especially helpful (Parette, Brotherson, Hourcade, & Bradley, 1996). Face-to-face discussions with family members are important to identify specific issues for each domain and timelines relating to the appearance of anticipated outcomes. For example, if an expensive AAC device is provided to a student, it would be important to project the length of time required for the student and others to use the device in functional settings (Parette & Brotherson, 1996). This would simultaneously require that thought be given to (a) the nature, extent, and timing of training that would be required for family members, the student, and others in the community, and (b) the impact of the training requirements on changes in family routines. This may mean that professionals would work with families across multiple domains to obtain baseline information. Family members could also be questioned regarding their perceptions of the impact of assistive devices (e.g, "What do you think will happen if . . . ?" or "How will this device get from home to school?" or "What will it cost for you to modify this at home?"). Brainstorming questions can result in useful information for planning overall family support services. Otherwise, the planning that is conducted may be more hopeful than helpful and not based on the diversity and realities of family life (Parette & Brotherson, 1996).

The IEP and Assistive Technology

Inclusion of assistive technology in a student's IEP should be considered on a case-by-case basis by effective IEP team members (RESNA Technical Assistance Project, 1992). Assistive technology may be included (a) as part of the student's annual goals or short-term objectives; (b) in a list of specific accommodations needed for the student to function in the least restrictive environment; and (c) as a related service necessary for the student to benefit from special education (e.g., receiving training in the use of a specific assistive technology device). The school district has a responsibility to provide assistive technology at no cost to the student and family once a determination is made that it is needed either at school or in the home for the student to receive a free and appropriate public education (RESNA Technical Assistance Project, 1992, 1994).

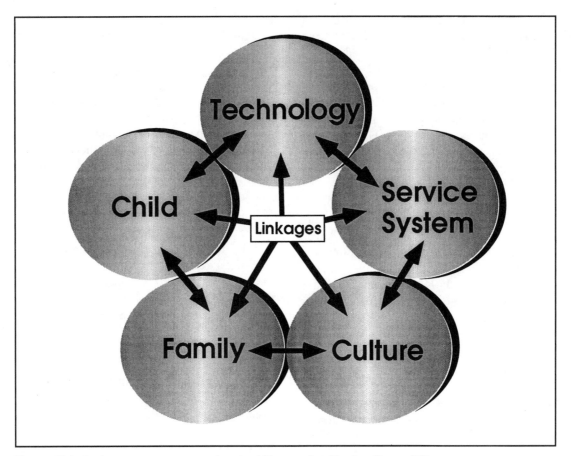

Figure 17.3. Linkages among issue areas that should be considered by the effective IEP team.

Assistive Technology and IEP Goals and Objectives

The IEP must clearly state how the use of assistive technology will help a student attain educational goals (RESNA Technical Assistance Project, 1992, 1994). The annual goals should reflect *critical features* of an assistive device determined to be important for the student. For example, if the student has a physical disability and requires a switch to operate a device, this means of access should be stated in the goal. If a student requires a powered mobility device to move in the environment, this also should be specified. It is not necessary that a particular product marketed by a company be identified. Effective IEP team members should examine a range of appropriate alternatives that might meet the student's needs, and select the most effective assistive technology after a careful consideration of student, technology, school, and family issues.

Objectives developed as measurable intermediate steps between the present level of educational performance and the annual goals can include the use of specific assistive technology that will be part of the conditions under which some skill will be acquired. For example, an annual goal might read, "Using direct selection of icons presented on an electronic AAC device, Jesse will express 10 sentences to communicate personal needs to others with 80% accuracy." Objectives leading to this goal might include preliminary exploration of the use of an AAC speech device that uses synthesized speech; trials to learn use of the device through the sequencing of words or icons on the display panel of the device; drill and practice in creating utterances to communicate the student's needs in targeted situations; and increasing the length, complexity, and number of utterances.

Another type of goal may address a skill that is necessary for using assistive technology (RESNA Technical Assistance Project, 1992, 1994). For example, an annual goal might read, "Using a computer keyboard, Susan will type 10 words per minute with no errors over 10 or more consecutive trials." In this case, the student might spend a year learning basic keyboarding skills with the goal of achieving at least 10 words per minute with complete accuracy. For a young student who experiences some fine motor difficulties, this goal would be challenging, but it might be achievable in a year's time. Objectives leading to this goal might involve preliminary exploration of the keyboard, gradual introduction of the letters and numbers on the keyboard, practice to build speed and accuracy, and eventually timed trials until 10 consecutive trials could be achieved with no errors at a rate of 12 words per minute or better (RESNA Technical Assistance Project, 1992, 1994).

Assistive Technology as Supplementary Aids and Services

Supplementary aids and services, or modifications to the regular class program, must be included in a student's IEP goals and objectives. Assistive technology can be a form of a supplementary aid or service needed to facilitate a student's education in the least restrictive environment and to perform educational and social tasks (RESNA Technical Assistance Project, 1992, 1994). Assistive technology is necessary as a supplementary aid if its presence (along with other necessary aids) supports the student sufficiently to maintain his or her class placement, and its absence requires the student's removal to a more restrictive setting. For example, if a student with multiple or physical disabilities can make independent, educational progress on IEP goals and objectives in the regular classroom with the use of a computer and an AAC device, and cannot make such progress in that setting without the devices, then those devices are determined to be necessary supplementary aids (RESNA Technical Assistance Project, 1992, 1994).

Funding for Assistive Technology

Other funding streams for assistive technology devices have been discussed in the professional literature (Morris & Golinker, 1991; Parette, Hofmann, & VanBiervliet, 1994; Prentke Romich Co., 1989; REquest, 1992; RESNA Technical Assistance Project, 1992; United Cerebral Palsy Association, 1991; Wallace, 1995). These include such sources as Medicaid, private insurance, private businesses, and community organizations. Assistive technology curricula have also been developed to assist educators, family members, and professionals in identifying appropriate technologies for students with disabilities and securing funding for devices (Parette & VanBiervliet, 1990b, 1991a–e). These curricula have been modified by several states funded under the Technology-Related Assistance for Individuals with Disabilities Act of 1988, for training persons with disabilities, family members, and professionals in assistive technology service delivery issues.

The effective IEP team may make informal inquiries in the community to determine if organizations might be receptive to collaboration with the school in securing assistive technology devices for students. Members of civic organizations can be questioned about (a) past community service projects, (b) current efforts to develop service projects, or (c) the availability of special funds, scholarships, or monetary rewards for members of the community. Businesses in the private sector may have an established history of collaboration with the school to fund various projects. This is particularly true of larger corporations that may employ persons with disabilities in their workforces. Also, new businesses not yet firmly established may have expressed a willingness or desire to become more visible in the community.

Of primary importance during this information gathering phase is the identification of any goals held by the civic group or business that might be linked to the student's need for, and use of, assistive technology. A shared vision of outcomes for the student, present or future, provides a justification for collaboration. If possible, the effective team should link usage of the assistive technology to long-term outcomes, including (a) development of work-related skills that increase the potential for inclusion in and contributions to the community and (b) increased independence.

Conclusion

Information regarding the availability and usefulness of assistive technologies for students with mental retardation and developmental disabilities may be expected to increase in the years ahead. To be more effective members of IEP teams, special educators, family members, and other professionals will increasingly be called on to develop new competencies relating to assistive technology. Such competencies may include (a) increasing the knowledge bases of individual team members regarding the range, use, and maintenance of various assistive technology devices and (b) developing more effective skills in examining the range of factors that may affect the selection of appropriate assistive technology. By basing assistive technology decisions on sound ethical principles and careful consideration of student, technology, school, cultural, and family factors, IEP team members can effectively ensure that all students with disabilities achieve maximal levels of learning and independence.

Coinciding with the increased awareness and availability of assistive technology, school personnel are faced with balancing limited fiscal resources against the potential of increased requests for assistive technology to meet the needs of students. Effective IEP team members may play an important role in assisting the school to secure needed resources in the community through collaboration with civic organizations and businesses.

QUESTIONS

1. Describe the difference between low- and high-tech devices that can be used with students having mental retardation and developmental disabilities. What are important considerations in determining whether a device is low or high tech?

2. Discuss key components of a philosophical foundation that underpins the provision of assistive technology devices and services to students with mental retardation and developmental disabilities.

3. As a member of an IEP team that must make decisions about appropriate assistive technology devices and services for a student, four domains must be simultaneously considered. Identify three considerations related to assistive technology service delivery for each of the following domains: (a) student, (b) device, (c) service system, (d) culture, and (e) family.

4. How is the IEP used to provide students with appropriate assistive technology devices and services? Provide several examples.

5. In what instances should community resources be used to acquire assistive technology devices and services for students? What are some considerations in obtaining these outside resources?

References

Ager, A. K. (1986). The role of microcomputers in teaching mentally retarded individuals. In J. Berg (Ed.), *Science and service in mental retardation* (pp. 224–231). London: Methuen.

Aldinger, L. E., Warger, C. L., & Eavy, P. W. (1995). Expert systems software in special education. *Teaching Exceptional Children, 27*(2), 58–62.

Allaire, J. H., Gressard, R. P., Blackman, J. A., & Hostler, S. L. (1991). Children with severe speech impairments: Caregiver survey of AAC use. *Augmentative and Alternative Communication, 7*, 248–255.

Americans with Disabilities Act of 1990, 42 U.S.C. § 12101 *et seq.*

Anderson, P. P., & Fenichel, E. S. (1989). *Serving culturally diverse families of infants and toddlers with disabilities.* Arlington, VA: National Center for Clinical Infant Programs.

Angelo, D. H. (1997). AAC in the family and home. In S. L. Glennen & D. C. DeCoste (Eds.), *Handbook of augmentative and alternative communication* (pp. 523–541). San Diego: Singular.

Angelo, D. H., Jones, S. D., & Kokoska, S. M. (1995). A family perspective on augmentative and alternative communication: Families of young children. *Augmentative and Alternative Communication, 11*, 193–201.

Angelo, D. H., Kokoska, S. M., & Jones, S. D. (1996). Family perspective on augmentative and alternative communication: Families of adolescents and young adults. *Augmentative and Alternative Communication, 12*, 13–20.

ApparaTek, Inc. (n.d.). *Lease financing of assistive technology.* Northbrook, IL: Author.

Batavia, A. I., Dillard, D., & Phillips, B. (n.d.). *How to avoid technology abandonment.* Washington, DC: REquest Rehabilitation Engineering Center, National Rehabilitation Hospital.

Batavia, A. I., & Hammer, G. (1989). Consumer criteria for evaluating assistive devices: Implications for technology transfer. In J. J. Presperin (Ed.), *Proceedings of the 12th Annual Conference of the Rehabilitation Engineering Society of North America* (pp. 194–195). Washington, DC: RESNA Press.

Batavia, A. I., & Hammer, G. S. (1990). Toward the development of consumer-based criteria for the evaluation of assistive devices. *Journal of Rehabilitation Research and Development, 27*, 425–436.

Baumgart, D., Johnson, J., & Helmstetter, E. (1990). *Augmentative and alternative communication systems for persons with moderate and severe disabilities.* Baltimore: Brookes.

Behrmann, M. M., & Lahm, E. A. (1994). Computer applications in early childhood special education. In J. L. Wright & D. D. Shade (Eds.), *Computer applications in early childhood special education* (pp. 105–120). Washington, DC: National Association for the Education of Young Children.

Beukelman, D. R., & Mirenda, P. (1993). *Augmentative and alternative communication: Management of severe communication disorders in children and adults.* Baltimore: Brookes.

Beukelman, D. R., Yorkston, K. M., & Dowden, P. A. (1985). *Communication augmentation: A casebook of clinical management.* San Diego: College-Hill.

Bigge, J. (Ed.). (1982). *Teaching individuals with physical and multiple disabilities* (2nd ed.). Columbus, OH: Merrill.

Boothroyd, A. (1987). Technology and science in the management of deafness. *American Annals of the Deaf, 132*, 326–329.

Brinker, R. P., Seifer, R., & Sameroff, A. J. (1994). Relations among maternal stress, cognitive development, and early intervention in middle- and low-SES infants with developmental disabilities. *American Journal on Mental Retardation, 98*, 463–480.

Brotherson, M. J., & Goldstein, B. (1992). Time as a resource and constraint for parents of young children with disabilities: Implication for early intervention services. *Topics in Early Childhood Special Education, 12*, 508–527.

Brotherson, M. J., Oakland, M. J., Secrist-Mertz, C., Litchfield, R., & Larson, K. (1995). Quality of life issues and families who make the decision to use a feeding tube for their child. *The Association for Persons with Severe Handicaps, 20*, 202–212.

Browning, P., White, W. A. T., Nave, G., & Zembrowsky-Barkin, P. (1986). Interactive video in the classroom: A field study. *Education and Training of the Mentally Retarded, 21*, 85–92.

Burgstahler, S. (1994). Focus on technology. In N. G. Haring, L. McCormick, & T. G. Haring (Eds.), *Exceptional children and youth: An introduction to special education* (pp. 58–61). New York: Merrill.

Burkhart, L. (1980). *Homemade battery powered toys and educational devices for severely handicapped children.* College Park, MD: Author.

Burkhart, L. (1982). *More homemade battery powered devices for severely handicapped children with suggested activities.* College Park, MD: Author.

Butler, C., Okamoto, G., & McKey, T. (1983). Powered mobility for very young disabled children. *Developmental Medicine and Child Neurology, 25,* 472–474.

Button, C. (1991). Fast facts on individualized education programs. *A.T. Quarterly, 2*(5), 5–6.

Caldwell, T. H., Sirvis, B., Todaro, A. W., & Accouloumre, D. S. (1991). *Special health care in the school.* Reston, VA: Council for Exceptional Children.

Carey, D. M., & Sale, P. (1994). Notebook computers increase communication. *Teaching Exceptional Children, 27*(1), 52–69.

Cavalier, A. (1987). The application of technology in the classroom and workplace: Unvoiced premises and ethical issues. In A. Gartner & T. Joe (Eds.), *Images of the disabled/disabling images* (pp. 129–141). New York: Praeger.

Cavalier, A. (1988). *Technology assistance: Devices, techniques, and services for people with cognitive impairments. Testimony to the Select Subcommittee on Education of the Committee on Education and Labor of the U.S. House of Representatives.* Arlington, TX: Association for Retarded Citizens.

Cavalier, A. (1989, May). *Ethical issues related to technology.* Paper presented to the Pre-conference for the Association for Retarded Citizens/ Arkansas 1989 Annual Conference, Little Rock.

Church, G., & Glennen, S. (1992a). Assistive technology program development. In G. Church & S. Glennen (Eds.), *The handbook of assistive technology* (p. 1–26). San Diego: Singular.

Church, G., & Glennen, S. (1992b). *The handbook of assistive technology.* San Diego: Singular.

Cohen, C. (1989, March). *Funding streams for assistive technology.* Paper presented to the Technology Access for Arkansans, DeGray Lodge Retreat, Arkadelphia.

Culp, D. M., Ambrosi, D. M., Berniger, T. M., & Mitchell, J. O. (1986). Augmentative and alternative communication aid use—A followup study. *Augmentative and Alternative Communication, 2,* 19–24.

Dillard, D. (1989). *National study on abandonment of technology: 1989 Annual Report on the National Rehabilitation Hospital's Rehabilitation Engineering Center's Evaluation of Assistive Technology* (Cooperative Agreement No. H:33E0016). Washington, DC: National Institute on Disability and Rehabilitation Research.

Dunst, C., Trivette, C., & Deal, A. (1988). *Enabling and empowering families: Principles and guidelines for practice.* Cambridge, MA: Brookline.

Enders, A., & Hall, M. (1990). Evaluating the technology. In *Assistive technology sourcebook* (pp. 102–121). Washington, DC: RESNA Press.

Esposito, L., & Campbell, P. H. (1987). Computers and severely and physically handicapped individuals. In J. D. Lindsey (Ed.), *Computers and exceptional individuals* (pp. 105–124). Columbus, OH: Merrill.

Evans, I., & Meyer, L. (1985). *An educative approach to behavior problems: A practical decision model for interventions with severely handicapped learners.* Baltimore: Brookes.

Gallimore, R., Weisner, T. S., Bernheimer, L. P., Guthrie, D., & Nihira, K. (1993). Family responses to young children with developmental delays: Accommodation activity in ecological and cultural context. *American Journal on Mental Retardation, 98,* 185–206.

Galvin, J. C. (n.d. a). *Evaluation of assistive technology.* Washington, DC: REquest Rehabilitation Engineering Center, National Rehabilitation Hospital.

Galvin, J. C. (n.d. b). *User evaluation of assistive technology.* Washington, DC: REquest Rehabilitation Engineering Center, National Rehabilitation Hospital.

Galvin, J., & Toonstra, M. (n.d.). *Adjusting technology to meet your needs.* Washington, DC: REquest Rehabilitation Engineering Center, National Rehabilitation Hospital.

Galvin, J., Ross, D., & Phillips, B. (n.d.). *Meeting user needs through assistive technology.* Washington, DC: REquest Rehabilitation Engineering Center, National Rehabilitation Hospital.

Gartner, A., Lipsky, D. K., & Turnbull, A. P. (1991). *Supporting families with a child with a disability: An international outlook.* Baltimore: Brookes.

Gaylord-Ross, R., Haring, T. G., Breen, C., & Pitts-Conway, V. (1984). The training and generalization of social interaction skills with autistic youth. *Journal of Applied Behavior Analysis, 17,* 229–247.

Glennen, S. (1992). Augmentative and alternative communication. In G. Church & S. Glennen (Eds.), *The handbook of assistive technology* (pp. 93–122). San Diego: Singular.

Glennen, S. L., & DeCoste, D. C. (Eds.). (1997). *Handbook of augmentative and alternative communication.* San Diego: Singular.

Goosens, C., & Crain, S. (1986). *Augmentative communication intervention resource.* Wauconda, IL: Don Johnston Developmental Equipment.

Governor's Task Force on Technology and Disabilities. (1987). *A final report of the Task Force on Technology and Disabilities.* Albany: State of New York.

Groce, N. E., & Zola, I. K. (1993). Multiculturalism, chronic illness, and disability. *Pediatrics, 91,* 1048–1055.

Guess, D., Benson, H., & Siegel-Causey, E. (1985). Behavior control and education of severely handicapped students: Who's doing what to whom? And why? In D. Bricker & J. Filler (Eds.), *Severe mental retardation: From theory to practice* (pp. 230–244). Reston, VA: Council for Exceptional Children.

Haddad, A. (1992). The long-term implications of caring for a ventilator-dependent child at home. *Home Healthcare Nurse, 10,* 10–11, 57.

Hanson, M. J. (1992). Ethnic, cultural, and language diversity in intervention settings. In E. W. Lynch & M. J. Hanson (Eds.), *Developing cross-cultural competence: A guide for working with young children and their families* (pp. 3–19). Baltimore: Brookes.

Haring, N. G., McCormick, L., & Haring, T. G. (Eds.). (1994). *Exceptional children and youth* (6th ed.). New York: Merrill.

Harris, P. (1988). Sometimes pediatric home care doesn't work. *American Journal of Nursing, 88,* 851–854.

Harry, B., Allen, N., & McLaughlin, M. (1995). Communication versus compliance: African-American parents' involvement in special education. *Exceptional Children, 61,* 364–377.

Hasselbring, T. S., & Goin, L. I. (1992). Integrated technology and media. In E. A. Polloway & J. R. Patton (Eds.), *Strategies for teaching learners with special needs* (pp. 145–162). New York: Merrill.

Hawkins, D. B. (1990). Amplification in the classroom. In J. Davis (Ed.), *Our forgotten children: Hard-of-hearing pupils in the schools* (pp. 39–47). Bethesda, MD: Self Help for Hard of Hearing People.

Hetzroni, O. E., & Harris, O. L. (1996). Cultural aspects in the development of AAC users. *Augmentative and Alternative Communication, 12,* 52–58.

Hofmann, A. C. (1994). *The many faces of funding.* Mill Valley, CA: Phonic Ear.

Holder-Brown, L., & Parette, H. P. (1992). Children with disabilities who use assistive technology: Ethical considerations. *Young Children, 47,* 73–77.

Horner, R. H., Sprague, J. R., O'Brien, M., & Heathfield, L. T. (1990). The role of response efficiency in the reduction of problem behaviors through functional equivalence training. *Journal of the Association for Persons with Severe Handicaps, 15,* 91–97.

Hourcade, J. J., Parette, H. P., & Huer, M. B. (in press). Family and cultural considerations in assistive technology assessment. *Teaching Exceptional Children.*

Hyun, J. K., & Fowler, S. A. (1995). Respect, cultural sensitivity, and communication. *Teaching Exceptional Children, 28*(1), 25–28.

Individuals with Disabilities Education Act of 1990, 20 U.S.C. § 12101 *et seq.*

Inge, K. J., & Shepherd, J. (1995). Assistive technology applications and strategies for school system personnel. In K. F. Flippo, K. J. Inge, & J. M. Barcus (Eds.), *Assistive technology: A resource for school, work, and community* (pp. 133–166). Baltimore: Brookes.

Judge, S. L., & Parette, H. P. (in press). Assistive technology decision making strategies. In S. L. Lesar & H. P. Parette (Eds.), *Assistive technology for young children with disabilities.* Cambridge, MA: Brookline.

Langton, A. J. (1990). Delivering assistive technology services: Challenges and realities. In A. T. Langton, R. W. Parker, L. W. Trachtman, & V. Augustine (Eds.), *Proceedings of the Southeast Regional Symposium on Assistive Technology* (pp. 1–9). Columbia, SC: Center for Rehabilitation Technology Services.

LeBlanc, M. A. (1982). Rehabilitation technology linkages. In M. R. Redden & V. W. Stern (Eds.), *Technology for independent living* (pp. 59–61). Washington, DC: American Association for the Advancement of Science.

Levin, J., & Scherfenberg, L. (1987). *Selection and use of simple technology in home, school, work, and community settings.* Minneapolis: ABLENET.

Lewis, R. B. (1993). *Special education technology: Classroom applications.* Pacific Grove, CA: Brooks/Cole.

Lifchez, R., Leiser, L., Pendleton, H. M., & Davis, C. (1983). Technology for the living environment. In M. R. Redden & V. W. Stern (Eds.), *Technology for independent living* (pp. 83–92). Washington, DC: American Association for the Advancement of Science.

Lynch, E. W. (1992). From culture shock to culture learning. In E. W. Lynch & M. J. Hanson (Eds.), *Developing cross-cultural competence: A guide for working with young children and their families* (pp. 19–59). Baltimore: Brookes.

Male, M. (1994). *Technology for inclusion: Meeting the special needs of all students* (2nd ed.). Needham Heights, MA: Allyn & Bacon.

Mann, W. C., & Lane, J. P. (1995). *Assistive technology for persons with disabilities: The role of occupational therapy* (2nd ed.). Rockville, MD: American Occupational Therapy Association.

McGonigel, M. J., Woodruff, G., & Roszmann-Millican, M. (1994). The transdisciplinary team: A model for family-centered early intervention. In M. J. McGonigel, R. K. Kaufmann, & B. H. Johnson (Eds.), *Guidelines and recommended practices for the individualized family service plan* (2nd ed., pp. 95–131). Bethesda, MD: Association for the Care of Children's Health.

McNaughton, S. (1990). Gaining the most from AAC's growing years. *Augmentative and Alternative Communication, 6*(1), 2–14.

Mendelsohn, S. (1989, March). *Payment issues and options in the utilization of assistive technology.* Paper presented to the National Workshop on Implementing Technology Utilization, Washington, DC.

Morris, M. (1991). *Part 1: A road map to funding resources. Assistive technology: A funding workbook.* Washington, DC: RESNA Press.

Morris, M., & Golinker, L. (1991). *Assistive technology: A funding workbook.* Washington, DC: RESNA Press.

Murphy, K. E. (1988). *Psychosocial model of discharge and home care planning.* Chicago: Division of Services for Crippled Children, University of Illinois at Chicago.

Musselwhite, C. (1986). *Adaptive play for special needs children: Strategies to enhance communication and learning.* San Diego: College-Hill.

Nalty, L., & Kochany, L. (1991, Winter). Enabling technology for persons with mental retardation. *Spectrum,* pp. 1–2, 4.

National Information Center for Children and Youth with Disabilities. (1991). Related services for school-aged children with disabilities. *NICHCY News Digest, 1,* 1–25.

Neath, J. F. (1993). *Consumer and professional technology needs: Report from the 1992 survey.* Fayetteville: Arkansas Research and Training Center in Vocational Rehabilitation.

Nguyen, T. (1995). Outreach and service delivery to the Southeast Asian population. In L. Vitale & E. Bourland (Eds.), *Project Reaching Out—Proceedings of the Forum on Human Diversity* (pp. 50–58). Arlington, VA: RESNA.

Office of Technology Assessment. (1982). *Technology and handicapped people.* Washington, DC: U.S. Government Printing Office.

Ogbu, J. (1987). Cultural influences on plasticity in human development. In J. J. Gallagher & C. T. Ramey (Eds.), *The malleability of children* (pp. 155–169). Baltimore: Brookes.

Parette, H. P. (1991). The importance of technology in the education and training of persons with mental retardation. *Education and Training in Mental Retardation, 26,* 165–178.

Parette, H. P. (1994a). Assessing the influence of augmentative and alternative communication (AAC) devices on families of young children with disabilities. *Perceptual and Motor Skills, 78,* 1361–1362.

Parette, H. P. (1994b, April). *Bringing community resources together: Practical strategies for obtaining assistive technology for young children with disabilities.* Paper presented to the Arkansas Federation of the Council for Exceptional Children, Division for Early Childhood Spring Conference, Little Rock.

Parette, H. P. (1995). Augmentative and alternative communication (AAC) assessment and prescriptive practices for young children with disabilities: Preliminary examination of state practices. *Technology and Disability, 4,* 215–231.

Parette, H. P. (1996, April). *Augmentative and alternative communication device decision-making strategies for IEP teams.* (ERIC Document Reproduction Service No. ED 394 223)

Parette, H. P. (1997, April). *Collaboration, diversity, and augmentative and alternative communication: Issues and practitioner strategies.* Paper presented at the Council for Exceptional Children Annual Convention, Salt Lake City, UT.

Parette, H. P. (in press). Cultural issues and family-centered assistive technology decision making. In S. L. Judge & H. P. Parette (Eds.), *Assistive technology for young children with disabilities: A guide to providing family-centered services.* Cambridge, MA: Brookline.

Parette, H. P., & Angelo, D. H. (in press). Impact of assistive technology devices on families. In S. L. Judge & H. P. Parette (Eds.), *Assistive technology for young children with disabilities.* Cambridge, MA: Brookline.

Parette, H. P., & Brotherson, M. J. (1996). Family participation in assistive technology assessment for young children with disabilities. *Education and Training in Mental Retardation and Developmental Disabilities, 31,* 29–43.

Parette, H. P., Brotherson, M. J., Hoge, D. R., & Hostetler, S. A. (1996, December). *Family-centered augmentative and alternative communication issues: Implications across cultures.* Paper presented at the International Early Childhood Conference on Children with Special Needs, Phoenix, AZ.

Parette, H. P., Brotherson, M. J., Hourcade, J. J., & Bradley, R. H. (1996). Family-centered assistive technology assessment. *Intervention in school and clinic, 32*, 104–112.

Parette, H. P., Hourcade, J. J., & VanBiervliet, A. (1993). Selection of appropriate technology for children with disabilities. *Teaching Exceptional Children, 23*, 18–22.

Parette, H. P., Murdick, N. L., & Gartin, B. (1996). Mini-grant to the rescue! Using community resources to obtain assistive technology devices for children with disabilities. *Teaching Exceptional Children, 28*(2), 20–23.

Parette, H. P., & VanBiervliet, A. (1990a). *Assistive technology and disabilities: A guide for parents and students.* Little Rock: University of Arkansas at Little Rock Press. (ERIC Document Reproduction Service No. ED 364 026)

Parette, H. P., & VanBiervliet, A. (1990b). A prospective inquiry of the technology needs and practices of school-age children with disabilities. *Journal of Special Education Technology, 10*, 198–206.

Parette, H. P., & VanBiervliet, A. (1991a). *Assistive technology curriculum for Arkansans with disabilities.* Little Rock: University of Arkansas at Little Rock Press. (ERIC Document Reproduction Service No. ED 324 886)

Parette, H. P., & VanBiervliet, A. (1991b). *Assistive technology curriculum for parents of Arkansans with disabilities.* Little Rock: University of Arkansas at Little Rock Press. (ERIC Document Reproduction Service No. ED 324 885)

Parette, H. P., & VanBiervliet, A. (1991c). *Assistive technology curriculum: A module of inservice for professionals [and] instructor's supplement.* Little Rock: University of Arkansas at Little Rock Press. (ERIC Document Reproduction Service No. ED 324 887)

Parette, H. P., & VanBiervliet, A. (1991d). *Assistive technology curriculum: A module of instruction for students in Arkansas colleges and universities [and] instructor's supplement.* Little Rock: University of Arkansas at Little Rock Press. (ERIC Document Reproduction Service No. ED 324 884)

Parette, H. P., & VanBiervliet, A. (1991e). *Assistive technology guide for young children with disabilities.* Little Rock, AR: University of Arkansas at Little Rock Press. (ERIC Document Reproduction Service, No. ED 324 888)

Parette, H. P., & VanBiervliet, A. (1991f). Rehabilitation technology issues for infants and young children with disabilities: A preliminary examination. *Journal of Rehabilitation, 57*, 27–36.

Parette, H. P., & VanBiervliet, A. (1995). *Culture, families, and augmentative and alternative communication (AAC) impact: A multimedia instructional program for related services personnel and family members.* Grant funded by the U.S. Department of Education, Office of Special Education and Rehabilitative Services, Office of Special Education Programs Special Projects (No. H029K50072).

Parette, H. P., VanBiervliet, A., & Bradley, R. H. (1994). Impact of augmentative and alternative communication (AAC) devices on family functioning: An examination of current state assessment and prescription practices. In American Association on Mental Retardation (Ed.), *Abstracts of the 118th Annual Meeting of the American Association on Mental Retardation* (p. 125). Washington, DC: American Association on Mental Retardation.

Parker, S., Buckley, W., Truesdell, A., Riggio, M., Collins, M., & Boardman, B. (1990). Barriers to the use of assistive technology with children: A survey. *Journal of Vision Impairment and Blindness, 84*, 532–533.

Parnes, P. (1988). *Funding and service delivery of augmentative and alternative communication devices in Ontario, Canada: Status and issues.* Washington, DC: RESNA Press.

Pfrommer, M. C. (1984). Utilization of technology: Consumer perspective. In *Discovery '84: Technology for disabled persons. Conference papers* (pp. 237–242). Menomonie, WI: Stout Vocational Rehabilitation Center.

Phillips, B. (n.d.). *Technology abandonment: From the consumer point of view.* Washington, DC: REquest Rehabilitation Engineering Center, National Rehabilitation Hospital.

Polloway, E. A., & Patton, J. R. (1993). *Strategies for teaching learners with special needs* (5th ed.). New York: Merrill.

Polloway, E. A., Patton, J. R., Smith, J. D., & Roderique, T. W. (1991). Issues in program design for elementary students with mild retardation: Emphasis on curriculum development. *Education and Training in Mental Retardation, 26*, 142–150.

Prentke Romich Co. (1989). *How to obtain funding for augmentative devices.* Wooster, OH: Author.

PSI International, Inc. (1985). *Low-cost technology* (Rehab Brief, Vol. 8, No. 1). Falls Church, VA: Author.

Ray, J., & Warden, M. K. (1995). *Technology, computers and the special needs learner.* Albany, NY: Delmar.

REquest. (1992). *An annotated bibliography on funding for technology.* Washington, DC: Rehabilitation Engineering Center, National Rehabilitation Hospital.

RESNA Technical Assistance Project. (1992). *Assistive technology and the individual education program.* Washington, DC: RESNA Press.

RESNA Technical Assistance Project. (1994). Technology and the individualized education program: A primer for parents and professionals. *Technology and Disability, 3*, 100–108.

Rosado, L. R. (1994). Promoting partnerships with minority parents: A revolution in today's school restructuring efforts. *The Journal of Educational Issues of Language Minority Students, 14*, 241–254.

Roseberry-McKibbin, C. (1995). *Multicultural students with special language needs.* Oceanside, CA: Academic Communication Associates.

Rosin, P., Whitehead, A., Tuchman, L., Jesian, G., & Begun, A. (1993). *Partnerships in early intervention: A training guide on family-centered care, team building, and service coordination.* Madison: Waisman Center, University of Wisconsin–Madison.

Rotheray, D. R., Sewell, D. F., & Morton, J. R. (1986). The design of educational software for children with severe learning difficulties. *Programmed Learning and Educational Technology, 23*, 119–123.

Rothstein, L. F. (1995). *Special education law* (2nd ed.). New York: Longman.

Scherer, M. J., & McKee, B. G. (1989). But will the assistive technology device be used? In J. J. Presperin (Ed.), *Proceedings of the 12th Annual Conference of the Rehabilitation Engineering Society of North America* (pp. 356–357). Washington, DC: RESNA Press.

Sibert, R. I. (1992). *Assistive technology cost estimate for the Part H program of Delaware.* Wilmington: Center for Applied Science and Engineering in Education, University of Delaware.

Simonson, M. R., & Thompson, A. (1994). *Educational computing foundations* (2nd ed.). New York: Merrill.

Smith-Lewis, M. (1992). *What is mental retardation? Perceptions from the African American community.* Unpublished manuscript, Hunter College, New York.

Snell, M., & Browder, D. (1986). Community-referenced instruction: Research and issues. *Journal of the Association for Persons with Severe Handicaps, 11*, 1–11.

Sontag, J. C., & Schacht, R. (1993). Family diversity and patterns of service utilization in early intervention. *Journal of Early Intervention, 17,* 431–444.

Soto, G., Huer, M. B., & Taylor, O. (in press). Multicultural issues in augmentative and alternative communication. In L. L. Lloyd, D. H. Fuller, & H. H. Arvidson (Eds.), *Augmentative and alternative communication.* Needham Heights, MA: Allyn & Bacon.

Sutin, J. (1990). Accessing the muse: Music technology and the handicapped user. *Closing the Gap, 9*(2), 12–15.

Technology-Related Assistance for Individuals with Disabilities Act of 1988, 29 U.S.C. § 2210 *et seq.*

Trivelli, L. U. (1994). The impact of human and multicultural diversity on assistive technology outreach and services. *NARIC Quarterly, 4*(3), 1, 6–8.

United Cerebral Palsy Association. (1991). *National Council on Disability study of the financing of assistive technology for people with disabilities.* Washington, DC: Author.

Uslan, M. M. (1992). Barriers to acquiring assistive technology: Cost and lack of information. *Journal of Vision Impairment and Blindness, 86,* 402–407.

VanBiervliet, A., & Parette, H. P. (1989). *Consumer and professional technology needs: An exploratory investigation of Arkansans with disabilities.* Unpublished manuscript.

VanBiervliet, A., Parette, H. P., & Bradley, R. H. (1991). Infants with disabilities and their families: A conceptual model for technology assessment. In J. J. Presperin (Ed.), *13th Annual RESNA National Conference Proceedings* (pp. 219–221). Washington, DC: RESNA Press.

Vanderheiden, G. C. (1985). Promises and concerns of technological intervention for children with disabilities. In Health Resources and Services Administration, *Developmental handicaps: Prevention and treatment III. A cooperative project between University Affiliated Facilities and state MCH/CC programs* (pp. 23–50). Rockville, MD: Office for Maternal and Child Health Services.

Vitaliti, L. T., & Bourland, E. (Eds.). (1995). *Project Reaching Out: Proceedings of the Forum on Human Diversity.* Arlington, VA: RESNA.

Wallace, J. F. (1995). Creative financing of assistive technology. In K. F. Flippo, K. J. Inge, & J. M. Barcus (Eds.), *Assistive technology: A resource for school, work, and community* (pp. 245–268). Baltimore: Brookes.

Williams, R. R. (1991). Assistive technology and people with disabilities: Separating fact from fiction. *A.T. Quarterly, 2*(5), 6–7.

Wolfensberger, W. (1969). The origin and nature of our institutional models. In R. Kugel & W. Wolfensberger (Eds.), *Changing patterns in residential services for the mentally retarded* (pp. 59–171). Washington, DC: President's Committee on Mental Retardation.

Wolfensberger, W. (1972). *The principle of normalization in human services.* Downsview, Toronto: National Institute on Mental Retardation.

Wright, C., & Nomura, M. (1985). *From toys to computers: Access for the physically disabled child.* San Jose, CA: Authors.

Ysseldyke, J. E., Algozzine, B., & Thurlow, M. L. (1992). *Critical issues in special education* (2nd ed.). Boston: Houghton Mifflin.

Zola, I. (1982). Involving consumers in the rehabilitation process: Easier said than done. In M. R. Redden & V. W. Stern (Eds.), *Technology for independent living* (pp. 112–120). Washington, DC: American Association for the Advancement of Science.

Transition Practices for Students with Mental Retardation and Developmental Disabilities

CHAPTER 18

James M. Brown, Dianne Berkell Zager, Pat Brown, and Linda Price

Learning Outcomes

After reading this chapter, you should be able to

■ Identify the transition service components related to futures-based planning, outcomes-oriented secondary program options, and community linkages.

■ Describe key school-to-work opportunities issues.

■ Describe the phases of students' development that result from participating in service learning interventions.

TERMS

The following terms are important for the understanding of this chapter:

Accommodation teams: Cooperating groups of educators with differing points of view, insights, and skills that are brought together to develop and implement viable, effective strategies designed to enhance students' transition-related outcomes.

Futures-based planning: The use of functional vocational evaluation strategies, in combination with specific training focused on self-determination.

Service learning: A teaching–learning method that connects community service experiences with academic learning, personal growth, and civic responsibility.

Transition services: A coordinated set of activities for a student, designated within an outcome-oriented process, which promotes movement from school to postschool activities, including postsecondary education, vocational training, integrated employment (including supported employment), continuing and adult education, adult services, and independent living or participation.

Introduction

Preparing students with mental retardation and developmental disabilities for the transition from school to work is a primary goal and a major challenge for special educators. Although this area has received much attention during the past decade, successful transitions for the majority of persons with developmental disabilities have yet to be attained (Dragan, 1994; Johnson, Thompson, & Matuszac, 1990). With the passage of the Education for All Handicapped Children Act of 1975 (P.L. 94-142), it was hoped that access to publicly funded education would ensure effective programs and equitable outcomes for students with disabilities. However, despite the legislation, students leaving special education do not enjoy the same success as their nondisabled peers (Weh-

man, 1992). In fact, fewer than 15% of the students with disabilities who complete school earn above the minimum wage (Edgar, 1987), and, according to Hasazi et al. (1985), only 21% of persons with mental retardation are employed full time.

Policies aimed at facilitating the transition of students with disabilities from school to the adult world have evolved in an attempt to focus attention on issues of equity as well as access. First mentioned in the Education of the Handicapped Act Amendments of 1983, dialogue about transition gained impetus in 1984, when Madelyn Will, then the director of the Office of Special Education and Rehabilitative Services (OSERS), wrote *OSERS Programming for the Transition of Youth with Disabilities: Bridges from School to Working Life*. This publication described transition as a movement from school to work for students with special needs.

Will (1984) stated that transition occurs at the point of graduation and continues into the first years of adult life. Although some students do not require any additional special support and are able to independently access typical community supports, many others require some type of assistance, such as services from the Division of Vocational Rehabilitation or ongoing job coaching. Halpern (1985) extended Will's definition of transition, by pointing out that transition programs that address only employment are insufficient; access to community recreational facilities and residential services is equally important The discussion continued when Wehman, Kregel, Barcus, and Schalock (1986) defined transition as an extended process of planning for the adult life of individuals with disabilities.

In 1990 President Bush signed the Individuals with Disabilities Education Act (IDEA; P.L. 101-476). IDEA mandates the provision of transition services for students in special education who are 16 years of age and older. It defines transition services as "a coordinated set of activities for a student, designated within an outcome-oriented process, which promotes movement from school to post-school activities, including postsecondary education, vocational training, integrated employment (including supported employment), continuing and adult education, adult services, independent living or community participation" (34 C.F.R. § 300.18). IDEA also states that "students will take an active role in developing, revising and reviewing their IEP [Individualized Education Program]" (O'Leary, 1992, p. 9).

As mandated by IDEA, transition services often begin as early as age 14 but must be implemented by age 16. Transition plans include descriptions of transition-related support services and, when appropriate, identify interagency responsibilities and linkages that are to be implemented before each student leaves school (Dragan, 1994). Schools are responsible for coordinating services that will assist students with developmental disabilities to become employed and/or to obtain further education. Since 1990 legislation in several areas has emphasized the importance of transition services for students with disabilities. The Carl D. Perkins Vocational and Applied Technology Education Act of 1990 provides federal funds for program improvement in vocational education, including support services to students with special needs. The Americans with Disabilities Act (ADA) of 1990 ensures persons with disabilities, including students, equal access to employment, transportation, public accommodations, and telecommunications. The 1992 reauthorization of the Rehabilitation Act of 1973 has adopted the definition of transition used in IDEA and requires state rehabilitation agencies to establish policies and procedures to facilitate the transition of youth with disabilities from school to the rehabilitation service system. The Job Training Partnership Act, reauthorized in 1992, notes that programs receiving Job Training Partnership Act funds should help youth cope with problems that inhibit their ability to make successful transitions from school to settings related to work, apprenticeship, the military, or postsecondary education and training. Finally, the School-to-Work Opportunities Act of 1993 addresses the transition of all students, including students with disabilities, by directing educators to provide school-based learning, work-based learning, and activities developed to integrate classroom instruction with on-the-job training.

Effective Transition Service Components

Recent transition legislation, with its emphasis on student-centered planning and consideration of outcomes for adult living, focuses on issues concerning quality of life (Halpern, 1993). Effective transition services, as supported by the federal legislation, begin with the student and include three components: futures-based planning, outcome-oriented secondary program options, and community linkages.

Futures-Based Planning

Regardless of the level of severity of disability, futures-based planning by students, parents, school staff, and community adult service providers must begin at least by the time the student reaches age 16. This planning addresses the interests and aptitudes of the student, interests of the parents, and available options in the school and the community. Planning should be outcome based with linkages to existing community resources. Student-centered futures-based planning consists of a functional vocational evaluation, as well as specific training in self-determination. Functional vocational evaluation is an ongoing process, resulting in an individualized and coordinated set of activities contained in each student's IEP that leads to anticipated postschool outcomes. Students, families, school personnel, and adult service providers participate in functional vocational evaluations, providing valuable information regarding each student's interests, aptitudes, and preparation opportunities within the school and in the community. Informal assessments, such as teacher observations, student interest surveys, and student self-evaluations, may be used together with formal assessment instruments to gather vocational information. This information, compiled into a personal profile of the student, includes the student's interests and preferences, functional life skills, academic skills, learning ability and style, communication skills, physical strengths and limitations, work experiences, and leisure and recreational activities.

Training in self-determination provides opportunities for choice, encourages student control, and focuses on outcomes. Self-determination is "the attitudes, abilities and skills that lead people to define goals for themselves and to take the initiative to reach these goals" (Ward, 1988). Students with mental retardation and developmental disabilities benefit from direct instruction in self-determination. Several curricula are available to facilitate students' learning about their own preferences, self-regulation, and self-management.

Furney, Carlson, Lisi, and Yuan (1993) developed *Speak Up for Yourself and Your Future* to assist students of middle- and high school-ages in assessing individual skills and developing goals through self-advocacy skills. The *Self-Directed IEP* (Martin, Marshall, Maxson, & Jerman, 1993) teaches self-determination and self-advocacy skills by training students with disabilities to participate in IEP conferences. Self-determination involves recognition of student preferences, sometimes manifested nonverbally, as well as opportunities to engage in decision making (Wehmeyer, 1992). *The McGill Action Planning System (MAPS)* (Vandercook, York, & Forest, 1989) and *It's Never Too Early, It's Never Too Late* (Mount, Beeman, & Ducharme, 1988) offer insight into empowering students, particularly those with significant disabilities, to participate in decision making.

Outcome-Oriented Secondary Program Options

Researchers (e.g., Edgar, 1987) have suggested that changes in curriculum are necessary if students are to attain a meaningful improvement in postschool adjustment. Outcome-based secondary program options focus on interests and aptitudes of students and offer functional curricula, preparing them for success in their anticipated postschool environment. Functional assessment helps educators target appropriate postschool outcomes, and, when incorporated into instructional programming, functional curriculum allows students to attain these outcomes.

Most students with mental retardation and developmental disabilities have the ability, with appropriate community-based training and supports, to enter competitive or supported employment after completing high school. Community-based instruction enhances social skills, work-related behaviors, and job-specific skills. Programs for students in community-based apprenticeship options include instruction and activities from three areas: academics, vocational training, and social skills. Vocational training begins with systematic exposure to occupations. Students with developmental disabilities benefit from community-based training based on functional vocational evaluations and transition plans. Age-appropriate social skills also can be enhanced through school clubs, extracurricular activities, community groups, service groups, volunteer experiences in the community, and development of lifelong recreational pursuits (Inge & Wehman, 1993; Wilcox & Bellamy, 1987).

Students with mental retardation and developmental disabilities often require ongoing support in the workplace and in their homes in order to enjoy a successful adulthood. Program options that prepare students for supported employment and adult living include functional academics, community-based instruction, and the facilitation of community and adult service linkages. Functional academics focus on reading and writing, money handling, time management, and self-care, which consists of food preparation, hygiene, safety, and health (Inge & Wehman, 1993; Wilcox & Bellamy, 1987).

Vocational training includes school-based work experiences in varied job clusters and training formats, such as enclaves, individual supported jobs, and mobile work crews. The determination of how much time students will spend in regular classrooms, special education environments, and community settings generally depends on several factors, including chronological age, ability level, work setting and job characteristics, supervision requirements, transportation schedules, budgetary issues, and the prevailing philosophy and practices in schools. Participation in extracurricular activities and infusion of social skills training in natural environments, in and outside of school, increase the likelihood of successful integration into the adult community.

Community-based job training for students of high school age includes experiences in varied job clusters and training formats. Secondary programs should address (a) recreation and leisure, including extracurricular activities (activities to be done alone and with friends); (b) general community functioning, such as travel, safety, shopping, and eating out; and (c) social skills, communication skills (including choice in technique and symbol systems), and motor skills taught in integrated settings (Inge & Wehman, 1993; Wilcox & Bellamy, 1987).

Evaluating Outcome-Oriented Secondary Programs

Evaluation of programs to ensure quality is an ongoing process, with self-evaluation by the teacher and school district personnel being essential for controlled systemic change. The Center for Change in Transition Services in Washington State has developed quality indicators for each of the four outcome-based secondary school options. In this transition model, quality indicators are divided into three elements: futures-based planning, secondary program, and community linkages. Table 18.1 lists indicators for community-based apprenticeships and for preparing students for supported employment options.

School-to-Work Opportunities Issues

The School-to-Work Opportunities Act of 1993 (P.L. 103-239) represents a federal initiative designed to promote

Table 18.1

Outcome Oriented Program Options: Quality Indicators

Community-Based Apprenticeship	Preparing Students for Supported Employment
Futures-Based Planning	
Functional vocational evaluation	Functional vocational evaluation
Team planning: student, parents, school staff, adult service providers	Team planning: student, parents, school staff, adult service providers
Student centered	Student centered
Self-determination training developed for student	Self-determination training developed for student
Secondary Program	
Citizenship skills	Community referenced
Basic skill level appropriate with anticipated postschool outcome	Functional
Systematic occupational awareness training	Chronologically age appropriate
Community vocational activities: Job Club, job shadowing, mini-internships, summer employment, supervised work exploration	Job training in real work settings at a variety of sites
Social skills training	Students interact with peers of varying ability
Self-advocacy	Addresses employment, community living, recreation, leisure activities
	Addresses appropriate work behaviors
	Employers and co-workers are involved in the student's support on the job
Community Linkages	
Appropriate ongoing support is in place prior to leaving school	Appropriate ongoing support is in place prior to leaving school
Follow-up data on graduates are collected	Follow-up data on graduates are collected
Functioning interagency team is in place	Functioning interagency team is in place
Functioning community inclusion team is in place	Functioning community inclusion team is in place

development of statewide systems that will provide comprehensive mechanisms to facilitate students' education and employment transitions. A variety of existing and emerging programs provides the foundation upon which transition-enhancement efforts will be based. These efforts include Tech Prep, youth apprenticeship, cooperative education, and career academy programs. For these programs to successfully create a comprehensive system focused on transition from school to work, significant changes in relationships between education and work settings are needed (Gugerty, 1994).

Current levels of demands to improve educational programs to prepare persons for careers have never been so great. Recent legislation has given programs at the local level the autonomy needed to develop programs that can effectively address the unique needs of their local communities. According to Brustein and Mahler (1994), this legislative initiative encourages educators to "build on what is working, fix or modify what is not, and to eliminate programs that are not adequate for tomorrow's challenges" (p. 16). An essential element of school-to-work programs involves partnerships between academic and vocational, secondary and postsecondary, and business and education communities. For persons with mental retardation and developmental disabilities to be adequately accommodated by programs supported by this initiative, special educators and vocational educators need to become well informed about the related legislation and to collaborate effectively. The following discussion examines recent legislation and its implications for collaborative efforts.

Coping with Federal and State Initiatives

Gugerty (1994) noted the need to effectively integrate federal and state legislative initiatives into a conceptually sound system for students with disabilities. Such efforts have been made more complex as Goals 2000: Educate America Act of 1994 (P.L. 103-227) and the School-to-Work Opportunities Act of 1993 have been coupled with existing legislation, such as the Individuals with Disabilities Education Act of 1990 and the Perkins Act. Gugerty suggested that the directives of these multiple legislative mandates can be addressed more effectively when the following issues are considered:

- *Student's perspective:* Educators should contemplate how students will be impacted by new initiatives and programs. Quality programs should be developed and implemented with appropriate support mechanisms, which will enable all students to attain skills needed for integration into their communities.

- *Organization's perspective:* Changes are needed to achieve and maintain equity and quality for the full spectrum of students. This includes changes related to organizational structure, staffing, curriculum, and interagency partnerships.

- *Legal obligations:* Legislative initiatives typically include mandates for service provision. These mandates address (a) services to be provided, (b) individuals responsible for service provision, (c) eligible recipients of services, (d) duration and extent of services, and (e) performance monitoring and evaluation criteria.

- *Funding:* Identification of funds available to support and maintain mandated programs, as well as knowledge of how to obtain funding, is a prerequisite for program development.

- *Staff perspective:* It is essential that staff roles and responsibilities be clearly delineated. For example, program developers should determine (a) who is responsible for which services, (b) what training is needed in order for staff to become capable of carrying out their responsibilities, and (c) with whom staff will need to collaborate in order to attain quality standards for all students.

- *Potential barriers:* Finally, how can potential barriers be corrected, circumvented, and/or compensated? Barriers frequently include problems related to legal, organizational, budgetary, and staff issues.

Inclusion of Students with Mental Retardation and Developmental Disabilities in School-to-Work Programs

To meet the diverse needs of individuals with disabilities, career preparation programs should include three key components (Gugerty, 1994). The first component includes work-based learning to take advantage of the assumption that students learn best by "doing." Connections between education and work settings help make educational programs relevant and motivational. Second, school-to-work systems should provide school-based learning focused, when feasible, on Goals 2000's standards. Third, systems should connect schools and work settings, as well as match students with appropriate employers. In addition, the provision of technical assistance helps employers to integrate students with developmental disabilities into their work environments.

Gugerty (1994) suggested that school-to-work programs be evaluated by examining the extent to which they address the following:

1. Outreach and publicity efforts.
2. Student assessment procedures and outcomes.
3. Strategies to provide career exploration and career counseling services.
4. Interagency articulation, coordination agreements, and collaborative procedures.
5. Coordination of activities instructors and support staff.

6. Strategies to provide on-going support to instructional activities.
7. Modification of instructional materials and strategies, as needed and appropriate for the full range of students in programs.
8. Meaningful involvement of members of business and industry in program development and implementation efforts.
9. Integration of vocational curricula into academic curricula and integration of academic curricula into vocational curricula.
10. Modification of program prerequisites and completion requirements.
11. Strategies to meaningfully measure students' performance.
12. Procedures for evaluating the program, as well as collecting and analyzing meaningful outcome data related to students in the program. (p. 9)

The Transition Component of IEPs

A review of the literature by Rojewski (1992) examined numerous researchers' attempts to identify key components of successful transition programs. Although the following list is not claimed to be exhaustive, Rojewski concluded that it does present essential transition program elements:

1. Individualized transition planning: Longitudinal transition planning leads to successful community integration. Transition planning as a component of the IEP should be reviewed annually, beginning at entrance into high school, and should address vocational goals, as well as those for independent living.

2. Integration within mainstreamed settings: Placement options vary depending on individual student needs, but may include secondary and/or postsecondary education settings, the work site, or the community-based settings.

3. Paid work experience: Students need to acquire work history prior to completing high school. While some transition programs incorporate volunteer or unpaid vocational placements, most emphasize the need to provide paid experiences in integrated work settings. Students receiving paid work experience are more likely to be employed following the completion of high school than those not receiving it.

4. Active family involvement: A network of family and friends can provide added support required by students with developmental disabilities.

5. Coordination of data and services: Active cooperation between educators and adult service providers, critical to the success of the transition process, can be increased through collaborative agreements to share information and resources.

6. Job-seeking and placement: In addition to direct job placement, instruction on how to locate and obtain employment is necessary because it is often necessary to change jobs during one's working years.

7. Follow-up and follow-along: Emphasis is placed on student follow-up and follow-along to provide additional support to students and to help educators understand the impact of secondary programming changes on transition outcomes. (p. 137)

Dragan (1994) stated that the success of transition instruction can be enhanced by contributions from students, parents, teachers, and other service providers. Transition components of IEPs should be comprehensive, identify who will be responsible for what activities and when they are to be implemented, and acknowledge the challenges associated with accomplishing transition goals and activities.

To coordinate services and establish a multidisciplinary planning system, transition plans are discussed in depth prior to and during the IEP meeting. This ensures that students' academic and vocational training are adequately related, and avoids isolating transition programs from the existing educational curricula. Model plans include skills to function at home, on the job, and in the community. Guidelines and criteria for the evaluation of transition plans need to be clearly described. Gillet (1987) listed requirements of transition plans:

1. Competencies to be acquired for areas of independent living, personal/social, and vocational areas.

2. Behaviors considered to be most important for independent living and competitive employment.

3. Services needed to achieve outcomes prior to graduation.

4. Activities prioritized to reach the stated outcomes.

5. Options for future residence and employment.

6. Services needed to follow through on post-secondary recommendations for further training, work placement, and community living.

7. Names of persons and appropriate agencies and businesses that will cooperate in the plan.

8. Timelines to achieve the outcomes and provide the recommended services. (pp. 118–119)

Community Linkages: Effective Interagency Collaboration

Effective transition planning requires a complex set of coordinated activities and services that can best be designed and delivered through a collaborative interagency effort. IDEA acknowledges the need for transition activities to reach outside the secondary education program and requires educators to develop the necessary linkages with postsecondary edu-

cation, vocational rehabilitation, competitive or sheltered employment, and independent living or other adult services. According to S. E. Brown and Johnson (1993), these linkages must be documented in IEPs.

Interagency transition councils within the community often serve as linkages between schools and providers of adult services. Public school personnel have historically provided the leadership for the formation of transition councils. Interaction of professionals at transition council meetings has facilitated working relationships between schools and community agencies through (a) communication and the exchange of information, (b) mutually planned service coordination, and (c) shared funding resources. Representatives from education, government, businesses, families, and community areas participate on transition councils. Composition of transition councils varies as determined by the particular needs of different communities. Some possible representatives may include representatives from education, case workers from adult services, business representatives, and community members.

Students with disabilities and their families are often isolated members of the community. One strategy to reduce isolation, being developed at the Center for Change in Transition Services in Washington State, is the formation of community inclusion groups. The membership of the community inclusion group consists of people who have a vested interest in students with disabilities, not those paid to work with the students. Membership consists of advocacy groups, social clubs, service groups, churches, private employers, families, and school district staff. The school provides information on resources that students will need in the future, and the community inclusion group works to make the community more accessible. The group may address such issues as transportation, independent living, community access, financial planning, recreation and leisure, and employment options.

Examples of successful community transition councils exist throughout the United States. In 1985, the Minnesota Legislature created the Interagency Office on Transition Services. This agency has assisted in the development of local transition councils. Each of these local councils develops a scope of work designed to meet the needs of its particular community. Some examples of their activities include (a) developing a single transition document to be used across agencies, (b) conducting needs assessments, (c) developing curricula to teach self-advocacy, and (d) developing a network of trained educators to facilitate transition issues (Hunt, 1994).

The Center for Change in Transition Services is helping local communities develop transition councils. To evaluate the effectiveness of transition councils, the Center has established quality indicators. The quality of a transition council is determined by evaluating five areas: (a) group composition, (b) postschool linkages, (c) group process, (d) group activity, and (e) the collection of follow-up data. Composition of the council must be representative of the community and include a cross-section of the previously listed members. When establishing postschool linkages, councils need to develop interagency agreements between group members to define the structure of the working relationship among participants. The council members work together to develop a vision statement, and to implement strategies that will facilitate change for students with developmental disabilities. Finally, each council should collect follow-up data on students who exit high school programs and evaluate this information to determine the effectiveness of the council.

Parental Involvement

When anticipating and experiencing changes associated with transition, every person in the family, not only the individual with disabilities, is faced with adjustments and may be in need of some type of support. As questions arise about transition from school to work, parents require information on such issues as eligibility criteria, procedures for obtaining vocational rehabilitation services, and access to community resources and facilities. Facing the new challenges inherent in the transition process can create stress and anxiety in families. Active involvement and partnership of family members with teachers and adult service providers are key factors in family adjustment, as well as in successful adult outcomes (Benz & Halpern, 1987). Parental involvement is essential at each level of transition planning (Everson & Moon, 1987) and includes futures-based planning, academic programming, and community linkages. School districts' responsibilities to parents include providing information when developing transition plans, as well as providing training for parents on the transition services available from adult services and in the local community. Parents can provide input into futures-based planning by participating in conferences, completing questionnaires and observations, and actively participating in the IEP process. School personnel need to recognize the validity and importance of the information that parents offer concerning their children. Turnbull and Summers (1985) noted that school district staff would benefit from viewing parents as responsible decision makers who have much valuable information to offer for transition planning.

Effective Interagency Collaboration: In-School and In-Community Accommodation Teams

Students with mental retardation and developmental disabilities exhibit a wide range of behavioral characteristics and learning styles. These students often require special accommodations to maximize the chances of successfully attaining their educational and community integration goals (J. M. Brown, Bohns, & Gardner, 1990). Many programs have developed guidelines that help educators develop curricula based on the learning needs of individual students (Brolin, 1982; Rusch & Mithaug, 1980). J. M. Brown et al. (1990) described an educational institution where instructors needed (a) improved abilities to teach academic skills to a wider range of students; (b) increased knowledge of, and sensitivity to, a wide variety of differences unique to students with disabilities; and (c) greater understanding of students' multidimensional needs. The Minnesota Department of Education (1994) recommended that planning teams designed to enhance the effectiveness of students' transition efforts should include the following representatives: (a) mandatory—administrator or designee, regular education teacher, and a special education teacher and (b) recommended—the student, one or both of the student's parents or guardians, a member of the assessment team, related service providers, and representatives of nonschool agencies that may be involved in the provision of services (e.g., vocational rehabilitation, health care, residential services, employment services, leisure and recreation, postsecondary education). Such teams can be very successful at coping with the transition needs of students as they exit from school and enter the workplace. A more intensive approach is often needed to accommodate the ongoing educational needs of students with severe disabilities as they participate in a wide range of programs within a school. The model in-school accommodation teams described in the following paragraphs have proven to be an effective mechanism for enabling educational staff to work together in facilitating the transition from school to work for students with mental retardation and developmental disabilities.

Northeast Metropolitan Technical College, White Bear Lake, Minnesota, has created cooperative groups that were called accommodation teams. Each accommodation team consisted of a vocational counselor, an instructor, and a support services specialist. These teams focused on the unique learning needs of specific students, including students with severe developmental disabilities, and developed possible solutions for those students' problems. The team approach was used to bring together educators with differing points of view, insights, and skills to address the needs of each student. Their common goal was to develop and implement viable, effective strategies to enhance students' transition outcomes. The concepts used by that educational institution provide the basis for the following recommendations.

While developing the accommodation team model, an institution should provide staff development efforts to teach team members to effectively coordinate their respective skills and to collectively focus on students, from the initial steps in the enrollment process until program completion and job placement. Initially, training for team members consists of a series of specially designed courses or workshops. These training activities serve to provide participating staff members with a common perspective regarding the following:

1. Students with mental retardation and developmental disabilities and the nature of their unique learning needs and strengths

2. Legal, ethical, and societal issues impacting students with disabilities

3. Specific strategies designed to enhance instructional accommodations for students with disabilities

Ideally, a substantial proportion of an agency's personnel should participate in professional staff development efforts. Participants may include teachers, support services staff, and administrators, in order to promote an across-the-board increase in awareness of disability and transition-related issues. Because funding and logistical limitations preclude including all staff members in these training activities, a train-the-trainer approach can be used. Training activities for team members include a heavy emphasis on strategies for integrating students with developmental disabilities into the workforce, as well as strategies to accommodate students as they participate in training programs within the community. Goals should be focused on formulating instructional strategies that incorporate appropriate academic skills into instructional activities and materials. For example, if students will be required to ride a bus to work, then instruction in how to read bus signs should be included in the curriculum. When properly implemented, team strategies can help educators effectively identify the unique characteristics and needs of students and determine how their accommodations can be delivered in a transdisciplinary manner (i.e., related service providers work together with one professional serving as case manager).

The Preparation of Students with Disabilities for Postschool Employment: Follow-Up Programming After Secondary School

Summers (1992) suggested that a variety of new concepts are emerging that will empower persons with moderate and severe disabilities, and their family members, to make decisions to help them live productive, meaningful lives in their adult communities. The new concepts have been labeled with a variety of names, such as family-centered services, person-centered services, family empowerment, consumer empowerment, family-driver assessments, and self-determination. Each of these concepts assumes that people with disabilities are capable of participating in decisions regarding their own fates and that they, and their families, should be empowered to facilitate their own resources, rather than depending on being managed by community-based service providers. As youth with developmental disabilities make the transition

into work settings, they and their families need to play greater roles as partners with professional educators, as they jointly plan and prepare for these youth to prepare for their lives as adults.

This trend is especially important when considering efforts to assist individuals with mental retardation and developmental disabilities to enter employment. Ehrsten and Vreeberg Izzo (1988) reported that youth who are unable to find employment tend to soon lose the job-related skills acquired during their prior training programs. An estimated $12,000 per person is spent each year by government support programs that provide Supplemental Security Income (SSI), health care, housing, and food stamps to individuals who have the potential to be employed. These programs often diminish individuals' levels of self-empowerment and create situations in which persons who want to work often find it hard to do so because existing societal mechanisms are not designed to support their return to work settings. Wehman (1992) reported that cost–benefit analyses conducted among programs for persons with mental retardation found that effective employment-related programming offset costs and led to greater productivity in work settings. This productivity resulted in more taxes paid, reduced levels of public services needed, and increased levels of personal satisfaction.

Wehman (1992) also noted that research has shown that special educators can have a substantial effect on students' educational experiences. Educators are capable of "(a) improving the graduation rate of students in special education programs, (b) increasing social and interpersonal skills, (c) assuring that all students have basic functional skills, and (d) decreasing disruptive or negative behaviors, at least in school settings" (p. 69). The progression from school to the adult community should be viewed as a sequence of events that is planned well in advance.

After students leave school and begin jobs, their support needs and the resources to address those needs change substantially. Ehrsten and Vreeberg Izzo (1988) described a three-phase model for guiding transition program efforts to enhance the integration of persons with disabilities into the workforce. The model's components are described in the following subsections.

Preparation Phase

Provide school-based assessment and training that (a) focuses on analysis of individuals' interests, abilities, and special learning identified in their IEPs; (b) provides vocational training in multiple settings, such as classrooms, vocational laboratories, and community work sites; (c) arranges for community service providers to collect information about each person's abilities and needs to identify the appropriate adult support service providers; (d) matches individuals' interests and abilities to potential job sites; (e) arranges necessary modifications and accommodations for each individual; and (f) involves appropriate community support agencies' case managers, job coaches, and other specialists, as needed and appropriate.

On-the-Job Training Phase

Provide work site orientation and on-the-job training to (a) orient employees to work sites; (b) orient and train regular staff to effectively assist the new employee; (c) provide on-the-job training to the employee; (d) use co-workers as supervisors and job coaches, as necessary; and (e) use agency personnel to help train each employee, if necessary.

Integration Phase

Gradually diminish daily support and provide follow-along services to employees: (a) emphasize integration of employees into the workplace as they become capable of working independently on their jobs, (b) use selected co-workers to help assist and supervise employees with disabilities, and (c) gradually fade out the use of agency personnel so that they are subsequently used only for consultation on an as-needed basis.

Service Learning: Community Service Within the Curriculum

Wagner (1990) reported that service activities in community settings can enhance both the personal and the intellectual development of students. Clearly, such potentially powerful and effective learning experiences should be considered for inclusion of students with developmental disabilities in transition programs. Students with severe disabilities are typically perceived only as being persons in need of assistance and seldom are viewed as being capable of providing assistance and supporting positive changes within their communities. Service learning provides a mechanism through which students can improve their levels of self-esteem and interact with their communities with a sense of dignity. This is a powerful tool for transition programs to help students change from feeling like victims of services to being beneficiaries (Institutional Development and Economic Affairs Service, n.d.).

Preparing for, performing, and reflecting on service experiences benefit students personally, socially, and intellectually. Community service can help students overcome potential fears related to being in community settings, encourage them to practice social skills, expose them to job-related skills, raise their self-esteem, and identify their talents and interests. In social terms, service learning helps students see themselves as role models, increases their awareness of the needs of others, gives them a new perspective on their personal abilities and limitations, and enhances their interpersonal and communications skills. Service learn-

ing provides learning opportunities in integrated situations, expands students' knowledge base, and increases their incentive to attain functional goals. Finally, performing service activities allows participants to be viewed positively by the rest of the school population and by the community at large, helping to reshape society's view of individuals with disabilities as capable, contributing members of society (Institutional Development and Economic Affairs Service, n.d.). The service learning model, depicted in Table 18.2, was proposed by Delve, Mintz, and Stewart (1990) and includes phases of students' development that result from participating in service learning interventions.

The Institutional Development and Economic Affairs Service (n.d., pp. 22–23) reported that service learning activities can be matched to the needs of many categories of

Table 18.2
Phases of Students' Development Resulting from Participation in Service Learning Interventions

Intervention Phase

Mode: Refers to whether the student participates in service learning individually or as a member of a group.

Setting: Characterized by the student's relationship to the client population.

Indirect: Students are physically distant from the service site and the populations served.

Nondirect: Students are actually in the environment of the population being served, but not in direct contact with them.

Direct: Students are face-to-face with the service population at the service site or in other settings.

Commitment Phase

Frequency: Refers to how often students engage in an activity.

Duration: Specifies the long-term and short-term nature of the commitment, as well as where commitments are found (e.g., in student groups, service activities, service sites).

Behavior Phase

Needs: Refer to the motivations that students have for engaging in service learning activities.

Outcomes: Describes possible effects that will emerge after the service learning activities have been completed.

Balance Phase

Challenges: Describes the tension-inducing stimuli that must be introduced for development to occur during a student's period of equilibrium.

Supports: Factors that empower individuals to act on the challenges that they encounter.

students with disabilities by focusing on four types of adaptations. First, materials or equipment can be modified in ways that allow students with more significant learning deficits to participate. Second, procedures and rules can be modified or simplified to facilitate students' participation. Third, activities can be broken down into smaller steps through task analysis, or the sequence of steps can be rearranged to eliminate some difficulties. Fourth, simplified versions of activities can be created that allow students to participate in activities that would otherwise be inaccessible to them.

Review of Key School-to-Work Opportunities Issues

Clearly, the School-to-Work Opportunities Act of 1993 has had a substantial impact on many states' efforts to develop or improve their statewide systems for facilitating all students' education and employment transitions. However, Gugerty (1994) noted that initiatives at both the federal and state levels have yet to integrate conceptually systems for individuals with developmental disabilities. Gugerty also identified 12 factors that should be used to evaluate school-to-work systems in regard to accommodating students with developmental disabilities. Other important issues that should be addressed include (a) transition components of IEPs, (b) the use of community linkages to enhance the effectiveness of interagency collaboration, (c) active involvement and participation by family members, (d) innovative and effective use of educators in accommodations teams, (e) the extension of transition services into postschool programs that support integration into the adult community, and (f) the integration of community-based service activities into curricula in order to improve the levels of self-esteem and dignity of students with developmental disabilities as they interact with their communities (Institutional Development and Economic Affairs Service, n.d.; Wagner, 1990).

Summary

Since the legislative initiative that began with the Education for All Handicapped Children Act in 1975, and continuing through the School-to-Work Opportunities Act of 1993 and ongoing legislative efforts to revise the Individuals with Disabilities Education Act of 1990, publicly funded education programs have been asked to enhance the educational and adult living processes and outcomes of persons with disabilities. Unfortunately, too many students who participate in special education programs still do not succeed at levels approaching the levels attained by their peers without disabilities (Wehman, 1992). As an increasing number of separate legislative initiatives seek to address this problem, the task of implementing multiple laws more effectively has

become more complex and challenging. Gugerty (1994) suggested that the following issues should be addressed in order to cope with this complexity:

1. Student's perspective
2. Organization's perspective
3. Legal obligations
4. Funding
5. Staff perspective
6. Potential barriers

School-to-work programs should be designed with the intent of addressing the unique educational needs of all learners, including those with disabilities. These career-oriented educational programs are most effective for persons with disabilities when they address the following issues: (a) an emphasis on work-based learning that helps students learn by doing, (b) an emphasis on school-based learning that focuses on Goals 2000's priorities, and (c) the connection of school-based and work-based learning experiences in ways that match students with appropriate potential employers and career opportunities (Gugerty, 1994).

Instructional offerings related to transition enhancement are likely to be enhanced if approached as a collaborative effort by students, parents, teachers, and other appropriate service providers. In addition, the transition components of IEPs should be comprehensive, clearly specify who is responsible for each component, specify associated timelines, and identify potential areas of difficulty. Effective transition-enhancing efforts implement well-designed collaborative efforts that typically require cooperative interagency strategies. These groups should function as accommodation teams focused on the intensive procedures often required to address the ongoing educational needs of students with developmental disabilities as they interact with a wide variety of educational programs and services. These efforts to function effectively as teams of educators and service providers often draw upon skills and knowledge that are far different from those typically required to teach in regular classroom settings. Therefore, professional development strategies for collaborative team members should be offered that emphasize (a) integrating students with disabilities into the workforce, (b) developing and implementing training accommodations for students within community settings, (c) designing follow-up programs appropriate for students after they have left school and entered adult communities, and (d) developing and adapting service learning programs based in community settings in order to improve the personal and intellectual development of students.

None of these recommended strategies and priorities requires cutting-edge technological breakthroughs in order to be implemented successfully. What is required, however, is that existing concepts and practices be adapted and/or applied in new and challenging ways. Persons addressing the unique educational needs of persons with development disabilities are encouraged to creatively apply the strategies and ideas discussed in this chapter in order to improve the school-to-work transition processes and outcomes of students with disabilities.

QUESTIONS

1. Describe futures-based planning and explain how it might be applied in a transition program for students with developmental disabilities.

2. Describe the key federal legislation mentioned in this chapter that affects transition programs for students with developmental disabilities.

3. Select two issues related to school-to-work opportunities and describe the implications they have for efforts to implement transition programs for students with developmental disabilities.

4. What is service learning and why does it have potential innovative uses within transition programs for students with developmental disabilities?

References

Americans with Disabilities Act of 1990, 42 U.S.C. § 12101 *et seq.*

Benz, M. R., & Halpern, A. S. (1987). Transition services for secondary students with mild disabilities: A statewide perspective. *Exceptional Children, 53,* 507–514.

Brolin, D. (1982). *Vocational preparation of persons with handicaps* (2nd ed.). Columbus, OH: Merrill.

Brown, J. M., Bohns, C., & Gardner, H. (1990). Facilitating the integration of academic skills into postsecondary vocational education programs. *The Journal for the Career Development of Exceptional Individuals, 13*(1), 35–40.

Brown, S. E., & Johnson, K. L. (1993, February–March). The impact of recent federal legislation on life after special education. *Focus: A Review of Special Education and the Law,* pp. 1–7.

Brustein, M., & Mahler, M. (1994). *The School-to-Work Opportunities Act overview.* Alexandria, VA: American Vocational Association.

Delve, C. I., Mintz, S. D., & Stewart, G. M. (1990). Promoting values development through community service: A design. *New Directions for Community Services, 50,* 7–29.

Dragan, E. F. (1994, November). Transition planning: What schools need to know. *Today, 1*(7), 1–14.

Edgar, E. (1987). Secondary programs in special education: Are many of them justifiable? *Exceptional Children, 53,* 555–561.

Education for All Handicapped Children Act of 1975, 20 U.S.C. § 1400 *et seq.*

Education of the Handicapped Act Amendments of 1983, 20 U.S.C. § 1400 *et seq.*

Ehrsten, E. E., & Vreeberg Izzo, M. (1988). Special needs youth and adults need a helping hand. *Journal of Career Education, 15*(1), 53–64.

Everson, J. M., & Moon, M. S. (1987). Transition service for young adults with severe disabilities: Defining professional and parental roles and responsibilities. *Journal of the Association for Persons with Severe Handicaps, 12,* 87–95.

Furney, K., Carlson, M., Lisi, D., & Yuan, S. (1993). *Speak up for yourself and your future.* Burlington: Enabling Futures Project.

Gillet, P. K. (1987). Transition: A special education perspective. In R. N. Ianacone & R. A. Stodden (Eds.), *Transition issues and directions.* Reston, VA: The Council for Exceptional Children, Division on Mental Retardation.

Gugerty, J. J. (1994, November). From the editor. *Tech Prep Advocate, 2*(1), 9.

Halpern, A. S. (1985). Transition: A look at the foundation. *Exceptional Children, 51,* 497–486.

Halpern, A. S. (1993). Quality of life as a conceptual framework for evaluating transition outcomes. *Exceptional Children, 59,* 486–498.

Hasazi, S. B., Gordon, L., Roe, C. A., Hull, M., Finck, K., & Salembier, G. (1985). A statewide follow-up on post high school employment and residential status of students labeled "mentally retarded." *Education and Training of the Mentally Retarded, 20,* 222–234.

Hunt, P. (1994). *Transition in Minnesota: What's working.* Minneapolis: Transition Technical Assistance Project.

Individuals with Disabilities Education Act of 1990, 20 U.S.C. § 1400 *et seq.*

Inge, K., & Wehman, P. (1993). *Designing community-based vocational programs for students with severe disabilities.* Richmond, VA: Vocational Options Project.

Institutional Development and Economic Affairs Service, Inc. (n.d.). *A sense of pride: Establishing a Fox Fire adapted model of experientially based career education for handicapped youth.* (Final report). Netherland, CO: Author.

Johnson, D. R., Thompson, S. J., & Matuszak, P. (1990). *Interagency planning for transition in Minnesota.* Minneapolis: Institute on Community Integration, University of Minnesota.

Martin, J. E., Marshall, L. H., Maxson, L., & Jerman, P. (1993). *Self-directed IEP.* Colorado Springs: University of Colorado Center for Educational Research.

Mount, B., Beeman, P., & Ducharme, G. (1988). *It's never too early, it's never too late: A booklet about personal futures planning.* St. Paul: Minnesota Governor's Planning Council of Developmental Disabilities.

Minnesota Department of Education. (1994). *Making the transition team work.* St. Paul: Author.

O'Leary, E. (1992). *Infusing transition into the IEP: A synopsis of the final regulations*. Unpublished paper.

Rehabilitation Act of 1973, 29 U.S.C. § 701 *et seq*.

Rehabilitation Act Amendments of 1992, 106 Stat. 4344, as codified at 29 U.S.C. § 701 *et seq*.

Rojewski, J. W. (1992). Key components of model transition services for students with learning disabilities. *Learning Disability Quarterly, 15*, 135–150.

Rusch, F., & Mithaug, D. (1980). *Vocational training for mentally retarded adults: A behavior analytic approach*. Champaign, IL: Research Press.

School-to-Work Opportunities Act of 1993, 20 U.S.C. § 6101 *et seq*.

Summers, J. A. (1992). Decision making in the 90s: A new paradigm for family, professional, and consumer roles. *Impact, 5*(2), 2–3, 20.

Turnbull, A. P., & Summers, J. (1985). *From parent involvement to family support: Evolution to revolution*. Paper presented at the Down Syndrome State of the Art Conference, Boston.

Vandercook, T., York, J., & Forest, M. (1989). The McGill Action Planning System (MAPS): A strategy for building the vision. *Journal of the Association for Persons with Severe Handicaps, 14*, 205–215.

Wagner, J. (1990). Beyond curricula: Helping students construct knowledge through teaching and research. *Community Service as Values Education, 50*, 43–53.

Ward, M. J. (1988). The many facets of self-determination. *NICHY*, (5), 2–3.

Wehman, P. (1992). *Life beyond the classroom: Transition strategies for young people with disabilities*. Baltimore: Brookes.

Wehman, P., Kregel, J., Barcus, J., & Schalock, R. (1986). Vocational transition for students with developmental disabilities. In W. E. Kiernan & J. A. Stark (Eds.), *Pathways to employment for adults with developmental disabilities*. Baltimore: Brookes.

Wehmeyer, M. L. (1992). Self-determination and the education of students with mental retardation. *Education and Training in Mental Retardation, 27*, 302–314.

Wilcox, B., & Bellamy, G. T. (1987). *The activities catalog: An alternative curriculum for youth and adults with severe disabilities*. Baltimore: Brookes.

Will, M. (1984). *OSERS programming for the transition of youth with disabilities: Bridges from school to working life*. Washington, DC: Office of Special Education and Rehabilitative Services.

Systematic and Data-Based Instruction and Management

SECTION V

Best Practices

It is clearly a best practice to base ongoing instruction on observable progress and to modify instruction based on data supporting the lack of progress. This implies the use of systematic data collection, visually displayed, which leads to evaluation of data and discussion as to whether the student is progressing.

Several effective systems have been developed and validated for individuals with developmental disabilities. The general components of these systems are similar; however, the specific practices and approaches are quite varied. Systematic monitoring of students with developmental disabilities has not received much attention by teachers in general education programs; however, thinking related to this area continues to evolve.

The management and improvement of a student's behavior also rest on systematic interventions. Modification of behavior is an instructional activity that, to be effective, must be developed, monitored, and modified using the same approaches as academic and other instructional approaches. Numerous effective and promising practices, which are systematic and data based, exist in the area of behavior management.

This Section of the Book

Section V begins with an overview of data-based measurement and evaluation, in Chapter 19. This discussion contains both effective and promising practices that can be employed to evaluate change in students with developmental disabilities. The chapters that follow discuss specific approaches to behavioral management and change based on concepts presented in Chapter 19. Chapters 20 and 21 provide practices for managing classrooms and reducing challenging and inappropriate behaviors, respectively.

Data-Based Measurement and Evaluation

CHAPTER 19

Christine A. Macfarlane

Learning Outcomes

After reading this chapter, you should be able to

- Describe various strategies for collecting learner performance data.

- Select and design an appropriate graphic display of learner performance data.

- Discuss the key components of data-based decision making.

- Describe applications of technology for measurement and evaluation.

TERMS

The following terms are important for the understanding of this chapter:

Acquisition stage of learning: The initial stage of learning, where direct instruction procedures are most effective.

Algorithm: A mathematical or logical sequence for completing a task.

Content analysis: A method for identifying similar themes, patterns, and/or trends among measures that are not quantitative.

Datum: A singular data point.

Equal interval graph: An arithmetic chart in which the distance between each of the number lines and each of the time lines is the same.

Expert system: A computer program incorporating aspects of artificial intelligence that has been designed to emulate the human decision making needed in order to solve a real-world problem.

Fluency building stage of learning: The stage at which a learner can perform a task accurately but not proficiently; emphasis should be placed on appropriate practice.

Instructional data: Information gathered about learner performance in an instructional environment that may include cues, reinforcement, or feedback.

Learning pictures: Pictures that are formed when learning lines are drawn on a standard celeration chart for fair pairs.

Mean score: The average score.

Minimum celeration line: The least amount of positive change a learner can make as evidenced by a trend line.

Natural cue: A stimulus (e.g., sight, sound, smell) that occurs within the environment and serves as a prompt or cue to perform a task or routine.

Portfolio: A collection of permanent products that documents learner progress over time.

Probe: A test situation to gather information about learner performance in the natural environment without artificial cues, reinforcers, or feedback typically found in instructional settings.

Proficiency stage of learning: Refers to fluent level of performance believed to be necessary for maintenance and generalization.

(continues)

Reinforcer: In accordance with the operant behavioral paradigm, a consequence that follows the occurrence of a behavior and increases the likelihood that the behavior will recur under the same circumstances.

Scale anchor: A descriptive word used to define the points on a rating scale.

Standard celeration chart: A semi-logarithmic chart that accurately displays frequency of behavior in terms of rate of learning.

Introduction

Regardless of level of disability, age of learner, or type of disability, effective teachers collect data (i.e., monitor learner performance) and analyze that data to assist with instructional decision making (Browder, 1991; Cooper, 1981; Fuchs, Fuchs, & Hamlett, 1993). The type of data collected, the intensity of data collection, and the subsequent decisions may change, but the need for measurement and evaluation does not. Educators must not guesstimate progress or make decisions based on hunches. Instead, they must use sound evidence to document progress and support instructional changes (Young, West, & Macfarlane, 1994).

Measurement

Establishing Baseline Performance

A learner's Individualized Education Program (IEP) contains annual goals and short-term objectives that build on strengths and remediate weaknesses identified by the learner's present level of educational performance. The present level of performance is determined through assessment practices discussed in Chapter 5. Annual goals provide the framework for long-term (i.e., yearly) planning. Short-term objectives divide goals into sequential or concurrent instructional phases. However, objectives are too broad to guide daily instruction. Instead, a series of instructional objectives (i.e., skill analysis) provides a systematic plan to guide the actual implementation of instruction. Before instruction can begin, information must be gathered to document or select (a) the instructional starting point (i.e., baseline performance), (b) the prompt level, (c) materials, (d) reinforcers, and (e) other essential facts. Determining baseline performance verifies whether the learner cannot perform the target skill and has the necessary prerequisite skills, and provides a basis from which to judge future performance. For students with more severe disabilities, this form of ongoing instructional assessment will likely follow a teacher-made protocol. Whether formal or informal, commercial or teacher made, this form of instructional assessment must follow the assessment guidelines identified in Chapter 5. (Figures 5.5 and 5.7 are examples of completed ongoing assessments used to gather baseline data.)

Probes

In a test or probe situation, the teacher documents how well the learner performs outside the instructional setting or without instruction, that is, the effect of natural cues and reinforcers on learner performance. A probe may be conducted to determine baseline performance, current performance, generalization, maintenance, or simply what the learner can do in the natural environment. A probe may consist of a single opportunity or multiple opportunities. With a single-opportunity probe, the probe is over as soon as the learner makes an error; therefore, learner performance more closely matches what the learner can do in the natural setting (Brown & Snell, 1993). However, once an error occurs and testing stops, no other information is gathered even though the learner may be able to complete later steps or additional problems. Performance during a multiple-opportunity probe generally approximates data collected during instruction because the probe continues after an error occurs. The teacher steps in and intervenes long enough to get the learner past the obstacle. Although less indicative of performance under natural conditions in which assistance would not be available, a multiple-opportunity probe may provide more information than a single-opportunity probe and indicate subtle gains in ability. Both types of probes may reflect effective practice depending on the professional's needs.

Often, teachers probe learner performance immediately following instruction. Such a probe tests only the immediate effects of instruction. Probes delayed for a significant time interval after instruction are better indicators of retention because they measure long-term effects.

Instruction

For learners with severe disabilities, it may be important to collect data during instruction. Instructional data are collected as instruction occurs and reflect the variables used to stimulate a response. The effect of prompts, cues or stimuli, error correction procedures, and reinforcers can be accurately judged when the teacher has a record of assistance needed or used and correct and error responses that occurred during instruction. Although a teacher may rely solely on probe data for decision making, it would be inappropriate to rely only on instructional data for decision making. Instead, the best decisions result from a combination of probe and instructional data.

Data Collection

Once the decision has been made to collect probe and/or instructional data, the next question is how often to collect data. The answer depends on the amount of information needed to make accurate decisions. In most instances instructional data or learner performance data must be gathered daily. Probes should be conducted at least weekly. Generalization or maintenance probes can be done less frequently. Farlow and Snell (1989) found that teachers of learners with severe disabilities could make accurate decisions about positive learner progress with one datum per week. However, if problems occurred, then a minimum of 3 days' data per week was needed for accurate decision making. Given once-a-week data collection, it would take 3 weeks for a teacher to identify a potential problem. Research indicates the prudent answer is to collect data a minimum of three times weekly.

Permanent Products

The most common method for documenting learner progress is to rely on permanent products for data collection (Cooper, 1981). Probe sheets, such as the example given in Figure 5.8 in Chapter 5, provide a concise picture of learner performance. Worksheets and other written products (e.g., spelling tests, business letters) are also examples of permanent products. Probes may be untimed or timed. When conducting a timed probe, the teacher must maintain consistency. If the time-based outcome is duration (e.g., length of time needed to fill out a job application), a reliable definition must be established for when to start the timing (e.g, when the person picks up pen) and when to stop the timing (e.g., when the person reaches the end and puts down pen). The person doing the timing maintains consistency by starting and stopping the timing exactly as defined. If the time-based outcome is rate or frequency (e.g., number of multiplication facts per minute), data are more consistent when timings are all the same length (e.g., 1 minute). Data from longer timings when compared with data from shorter timings may paint a less accurate picture of learner performance because of fatigue. Also, in any timed probe, the number of opportunities to respond must exceed the number of responses expected if the timed probe is to accurately measure learner performance.

Nonacademic products, such as items produced on an assembly line, a sewn-on button, or a batch of chocolate chip cookies (although consumable), are also examples of permanent products. Once the task is completed, it is possible to count items, examine the item for errors, and/or rate the quality of the item. Portfolios are a collection of permanent products over time. The contents of a portfolio may highlight various skills, represent the learner's best efforts, or provide ongoing snapshots of the learner's work during an instructional year. Videotapes and audiotapes recording the learner's behavior are also considered permanent products and may become part of a portfolio or be used to observe the learner at a more convenient time.

Behavioral Observation

Although permanent products can be stored, rated after the fact, and accumulated, many skills can be assessed only as they happen. In those cases, behavioral observation is the data-collection tool of choice. The teacher or other classroom personnel may conduct observations while working with the learner, or an observer may watch at a distance from the learner and instructor. Traditional observation tools include stopwatches, data-collection sheets, and clipboards. However, when instruction occurs outside the classroom in a natural setting, traditional methods of data collection should be replaced with less obtrusive methods (Browder, 1991). Data-collection sheets may be hidden inside checkbook covers, magazines, or newspapers, or be reduced in size and coded on small cards. Rather than paper-and-pencil tally marks, data can be recorded by transferring coins from one pocket to another or by using a golf counter.

Unobtrusive data collection within the community can be aided by current technology. For example, in modern grocery stores there is no need to collect data on purchasing groceries. The cash register receipt will contain an itemized list of the products bought, the amount tendered, and the time the person checked out. The teacher need only record the time the learner entered the store or began shopping. Later, a comparison can be made between planned purchases and items on the receipt. Reasons for discrepancies can be noted (e.g., store was out of item) and anecdotal information can be recorded. Careful planning eliminates the "training mission" look, and still provides for accurate and valuable information.

Event Frequency Recording

Young and colleagues (1994) recommended event frequency recording as a teacher's first choice for data collection. With this method "the observer counts each occurrence of the behavior during a predefined time period" (p. 63). The target behavior must occur at moderate to low rates so that the observer can count it; it must have an easily observed beginning and end; and each response should take approximately the same amount of time to perform. Examples of such events include the number of bites eaten; the number of peer contacts on the playground; and recitation of personal information, the alphabet, or rote numbers. Use of a standard timing period allows the observer to translate the numerical score to number or count per minute (i.e., rate). Just as calculators have made math accessible to many learners with disabilities, computers can assist teachers with this type of data collection. Ferguson and Fuchs (1991) found that, when computers were used to score spelling tests in conjunction with computer-based measurement, scores were more accurate and stable.

Discrete Categorization Recording

Discrete categorization can be used to measure (a) behavior that occurs or does not occur, is correct or incorrect, or is satisfactory or unsatisfactory; (b) steps in a task analysis; and (c) components on a checklist. In some instances discrete categorization is used when the outcome of an entire task must be judged as correct or incorrect (e.g., total task). For example, when placing a telephone call, the person must dial the entire number correctly or it is wrong. When putting on shoes, the right shoe must match the right foot and the left shoe must match the left foot. A child either smiles or does not smile. In each case learner performance can be judged only as yes or no, correct or incorrect, performed or not performed.

Although not a perfect dichotomy, scoring of task analyses also fits into this paradigm, especially if it is important to know whether the learner can perform the entire task independently. Coffee, for example, cannot be made with 95% accuracy. The only error may have occurred on the step that involves putting the coffee in the filter. Even though all the other steps were performed correctly, the coffee is not made.

The exception occurs when the learner is in the acquisition stage of learning. Initially, performance could vary on each step of the task analysis. Because the desired outcome is independent behavior, it may be very important to measure levels of assistance (i.e., prompts) during instruction. Often, teachers or other observers score the level of prompt needed on each step of the task analysis (e.g., V = verbal, M = model, P = physical). Knowing that a verbal prompt to put the coffee in the filter resulted in a correct response can translate into "performed 19 of 20 steps independently" or "performed at a level of 95% independence."

Prompt levels also can be translated into a numerical score (i.e., percentage) by assigning a number to each prompt level. For example (see Figure 5.5 in Chapter 5), independent behavior is scored 4, behavior requiring a verbal prompt 3, the use of a model 2, and a physical prompt 1. Given a nine-step task analysis, a total of 36 points would accrue if independent behavior occurred at each step. Prompted behavior on any step would result in a total score of less than 36. The number of points received would then be divided by the total points possible (i.e., 36) to determine percentage of independent behavior. This method detects small changes in learner performance.

Time-Based Measures

Duration recording consists of timing the target behavior from the moment it begins until it stops. Some behaviors occur so rapidly that, even though they are discrete, single behaviors, it would be difficult to isolate an individual behavior. For example, when a learner engages in conversation, it might be difficult for the teacher to count the number of spoken words, but it would be easy to time the length of the conversation. Other target skills need to be completed quickly to demonstrate proficiency (e.g., dressing) or should be completed within a reasonable time (e.g., laundry). Timings can be continuous (e.g., time on task) or discontinuous (e.g., total time on task during a class period).

Latency recording is appropriate to use when proficiency can be demonstrated by how quickly a learner begins to respond once the stimulus is given. In a social situation, when one person is greeted by another (e.g., "Hi, how are you?"), a quick response (e.g., "Fine. How are you?") acknowledges the greeter and suggests interest. When asked a question, a prompt answer denotes competency. If the anticipated latency is short, then the observer can simply count (e.g., "one thousand one, one thousand two"). However, if the latency is going to be longer than 5 seconds, the behavior should be timed using a stopwatch or a watch with a second hand.

Interval recording methods, although not as precise, are excellent tools for estimating the occurrence of behavior (Young et al., 1994). Momentary time sampling is the method most often used by classroom teachers when an independent observer is not available. Observations occur on a predetermined schedule (e.g., every 5 minutes). The teacher checks briefly to see whether the target behavior is occurring. Whole interval and partial interval recording methods rely on an independent observer to obtain accurate results. These methods work well for high-rate behaviors that may not have an easily discernible beginning or end. The observer can simultaneously collect data on time and number of behaviors. Also, an interval method is effective when observing more than one person or behavior at a time (e.g., children on a playground). For either method, the observation period is divided into an equal number of discrete time periods. Intervals as short as 5 seconds or as long as 5 minutes can be used. Often a "behavioral" interval (e.g., 10 seconds) is followed by a "scoring" interval (e.g., 5 seconds). When using the whole interval recording method, the target behavior must occur during the entire interval. In an observation using a partial interval recording method, the interval is scored if the behavior occurs at any time during the interval.

Qualitative Ratings

For many behaviors, proficiency cannot be measured numerically. Instead, target behaviors must be judged as acceptable or unacceptable or rated on a scale (e.g., the Likert scale) from low to high. In many instances, decision making would be enhanced by a combination of numerical data and qualitative data. For example, writing can be evaluated by looking at the correctness of letter formation and adherence to standard rules of English; however, the content also must be considered. A person may follow a recipe correctly, but the results may not be palatable. Frequently, the success of peer interactions or adult–learner interactions depends on subjective evaluation. The most important information is whether the adult or peer is satisfied with the learner's performance. The learner may have smiled, but did the smile seem real or was it artificial?

Ratings can also be very helpful. Voice quality during conversation can be rated from *very unacceptable* (e.g., 1) to *very acceptable* (e.g., 5), with *average* performance in the middle (e.g., 3). Most rating scales range from 4 to 11 points unless administered orally (Weller & Romney, 1988). With oral ratings, 2- to 4-point scales are more common. The scale anchor should reflect an image of the target behavior. For example, if a learner is rating daily class performance, the scale might begin with a *really bad day* and end with a *super day*. Much like scores generated with the discrete categorization recording method, rating scores can be averaged or divided by the total number possible.

Anecdotal Recording

Another method for gathering qualitative information is to note anecdotal information that occurs during instruction. Perhaps the child seemed tired or was agitated. Later, if data appear variable, written comments might help explain a change in behavior. Furthermore, written comments can be shared with interested personnel and the teacher does not have to rely on personal memory. Interviews, informal observations, unstructured situations, and community-based instruction may necessitate recording field notes. In any of these scenarios, the observer takes notes during the observation or records information as soon afterward as possible. Hand-held tape recorders and computers can make this task much easier (Pfaffenberger, 1988).

Naturalistic Observation

Gathering simultaneous information on ecological variables and learner behavior is perhaps one of the most difficult observational tasks. Most teachers can record a running account of what happens and code the events as antecedents (i.e., behavioral triggers), behaviors, or consequences for one student. This type of observation is particularly important in conducting a functional analysis. However, when the focus of the observation expands to more than one student, it becomes very difficult to accurately note all the events. Sophisticated paper-and-pencil coding systems and computer programs have been developed to systematize the process, but they are generally used during formal research studies. If professionals find themselves in a situation where they must engage in naturalistic observation, they may want to record a videotape as a backup. Reviewing the videotape at a later time would allow them to fill in their notes and concentrate on the task. Distractions would be reduced and the videotape could be stopped as needed.

Behavioral States

For learners with profound disabilities, the most effective strategy may be to collect data on biobehavioral states, that is, periods of time defined by levels of arousal (Richards & Sternberg, 1994). When an individual is in a "state of calm, alert arousal," there is more chance for interactions with environmental stimuli (p. 64). It is also important to determine the learner's orienting responses (i.e., responses to inanimate or animate visual and/or auditory stimuli). After determining the status of the learner's arousal state and orienting responses, effective and efficient programming and staffing decisions can be made. Although the research is limited, this method appears to have a great deal of merit and should be particularly beneficial for professionals in early intervention programs.

Self-Management

Collecting data when learners manage their own behavior presents a unique challenge. To begin with, teachers need to teach the learner how to accurately rate behavior. Initially, reinforcement is given for correctly identifying behavior (positive or negative) and matching the teacher's perception and rating of the learner's behavior. Later, the learner independently assesses and records his or her own behavior. Young learners or students with more severe disabilities may use pictorial representations (e.g., smiling face, frowning face) to judge and rate behavior. School-aged learners with mild disabilities can usually rate their behavior on a numerical Likert scale (e.g., 1 = *rotten behavior*, 3 = *average behavior*, 5 = *excellent behavior*). In vocational settings, learners may collect data on the quality of their work and/or the rate at which they work. Although somewhat time consuming to initiate, self-management is an effective tool for promoting learner independence.

Observational Reliability

Regardless of the data-collection method or combination of methods used, the teacher or observer must ensure that the data are reliable. The importance of establishing observational reliability cannot be overlooked. Ultimately, the decisions made will only be as good as the data collected. As time and staffing patterns permit, it is wise to conduct simultaneous observations to determine interobserver agreement. Event frequency recording can be interrated by dividing the smaller frequency by the larger frequency and multiplying by 100 to obtain percentage of agreement. Time-based methods are done in a similar manner. The shorter time is divided by the longer time and multiplied by 100. For interval methods of recording, the number of agreements is divided by the number of agreements plus disagreements and multiplied by 100. This yields percentage of agreement.

Evaluation

Graphing and Charting

It has been said that a picture is worth a thousand words. When it comes to the analysis of learner performance data, no truer words have been written. A graph summarizes the data into a concise format that supports efficient and effective interpretation (Fuchs & Fuchs, 1987; Grigg, Snell, & Lloyd, 1989).

Equal Interval Graphs

The most common format for presenting a visual picture is an equal interval graph (see Figure 19.1). Bar or column graphs and line graphs are the most popular styles. Although fairly easy to construct, most equal interval graphs are not standardized. Graphs vary tremendously due to the wide variety of graph paper and computerized graphing programs available. Lines on a graph can range from 4 to 10 per inch. As a result, either axis scale can be adjusted to emphasize data in a certain way or to present data in a skewed manner. Although computerized graphing programs provide a standard format, the amplitude (i.e., range) of the data will also affect the size and presentation of the graph. Furthermore, if teachers want a hard copy for decision making, filing, or sending home to parents, they must print a new graph each time data are entered.

Standard Celeration Chart

The standard celeration chart or standard behavior chart was developed by Lindsley (1964) as part of precision teaching. The use of the six-cycle, semi-logarithmic chart eliminated problems associated with sharing and interpreting nonstandard graphs among professionals. Detailed explanations were no longer needed to familiarize others with the content and display of the graph. Haring, Liberty, and White (1980) provided a detailed explanation of the standard celeration chart and its charting conventions. Figure 19.2 contains an example of data displayed on a standard celeration chart. Although the chart is difficult for novices and untrained people to use, the standard procedures do present data in a consistent manner. Also, the use of logarithmic number lines creates trend lines that are accurate in predicting future behavior.

Calendars

Although not a formal graph, a calendar does offer a simple format for visual analysis. An overall picture of good days and bad days or satisfactory or unsatisfactory performance can be depicted by means of special markings, stickers, or facial expressions (e.g., smiling face). A calendar works particularly well with young learners or in conjunction with a self-management project.

Scatterplots

A scatterplot is a tool for visually displaying behavioral patterns. Besides recording the occurrence of the behavior, the time is also noted. Toilet training and problem behaviors are ideal examples. Noting dry pants versus wet pants in 15-minute increments across 30 days can lead to the development of a toilet training schedule. Likewise, a visual display of the time frames when a problem behavior occurs can help to predict when the behavior will recur and assist in analyzing the functions of behavior (e.g., consistent problem behavior 30 minutes prior to lunch time may indicate hunger).

Experimental Designs

Historically, the use of various experimental designs (e.g., multiple baseline, reversal, alternating treatments) to monitor instructional effects and assist in analysis has played a tremendous role in applied behavior analysis. The extensive knowledge base concerning persons with developmental disabilities would not exist without single-subject research. For the most part, though, classroom teachers have shied away from implementing formal research studies. However, when research is both necessary and justified to document reduction of problem behavior, determine the most appropriate instructional strategy, or select an intervention tool, then effective teachers use experimental designs. Kazdin's (1982) book is a complete reference on the selection and use of single-subject research designs. Another resource, *The Single Subject Research Advisor* (Blackhurst, Schuster, Ault, & Doyle, 1994), is a computer expert system designed to assist researchers in selecting and using an appropriate single-subject experimental research design to answer questions in

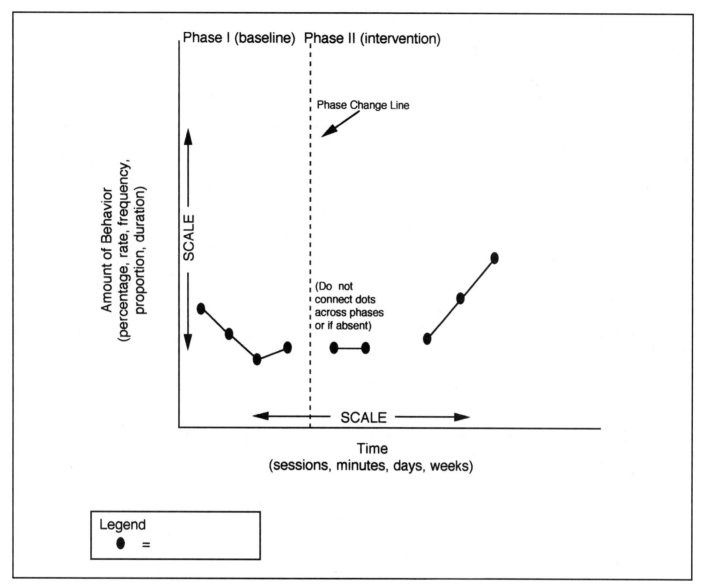

Figure 19.1. Components of a typical equal interval graph.

special education, psychology, and related fields. Computers also can be used to improve data collection and analysis during research studies (Repp, Karsh, Van Acker, Felce, & Harman, 1989). Software programs are available to assist the teacher or observer in gathering data with a laptop computer. Once trained, most observers can enter far more data than they could by hand and the computer facilitates collecting extremely precise time-based data and its evaluation.

Qualitative Evaluation

Recently, the focus of evaluation has broadened from a strictly quantitative approach to include qualitative evaluation as well. However, rather than relying on hunches or nondocumented sources of information, effective qualitative evaluation is based on information collected in a standardized manner. Qualitative data present a composite picture of

the learner that numbers alone cannot document. Few formal systems exist to guide this process. For research studies, results can be analyzed by means of a content analysis to identify common factors. Although not as formal, educators should examine qualitative data for common threads and try to identify patterns or commonalities. Also, behavior can be judged or rated by an outside reviewer.

Data-Based Decision Making

The outcome of data analysis depends on two things: (a) the accuracy of the information (i.e., data) and (b) the skill of the evaluator. Even more important, however, is the realization that unless decision making takes place, measurement serves no purpose. Teachers must realize that feedback helps them "to shape their own behavior and become more responsive to the individual needs of each pupil" (White,

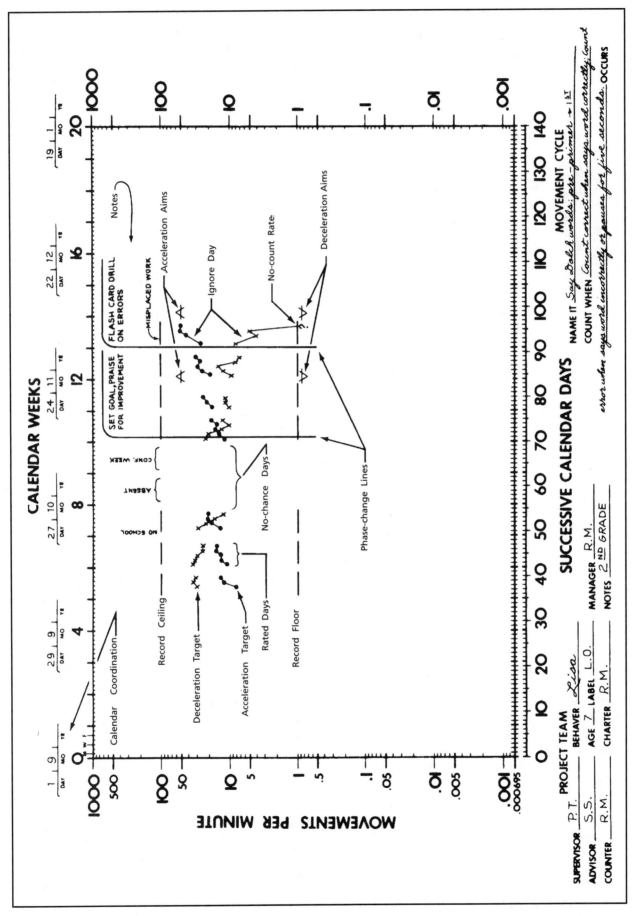

Figure 19.2. An example of a standard celeration chart. From *Exceptional Teaching* (p. 90), by O. R. White and N. G. Haring, 1980, Columbus, OH: Merrill. Copyright 1980 by Charles E. Merrill. Reprinted with permission.

1984, p. 31). Data-based decision making can take place with as little as 3 days' worth of data and must never be postponed beyond 10 days. Table 19.1 contains a checklist to guide data-based decision making. Decisions can be based on a visual analysis of graphed or charted data or analysis of raw data.

The first step in data analysis is to calculate an overall score based on the data collected. Depending on the type of data gathered, the teacher will determine (a) accuracy by comparing correct performance with errors, (b) fluency by evaluating time, (c) level of independence by reviewing number and types of prompts, (d) frequency by counting the number of occurrences per time unit, and/or (e) level of satisfaction by studying ratings and subjective evaluations. Given a simple data pattern (Browder, 1991) or aim line, the teacher can first check to see whether the learner has met the criterion. If so, the learner can move on to the next instructional objective. If not, analysis continues and becomes more complex.

If data have been graphed or charted, the trend line(s) or slope must be determined next. A trend line to compare learner performance from the first datum to the last datum in the review period can be generated by (a) simply connecting the data points, (b) drawing a line of "best fit," or (c) drawing a line of progress (see Figure 19.3). The evaluator notes the direction of the trend line. Is it going up (i.e., accelerating), flat (i.e., staying the same), or going down (i.e., decelerating)? It is also important to note the amount of change (i.e., magnitude) and to determine if it is acceptable (Young et al., 1994). Precision teachers judge acceptability against a minimum celeration line (see White & Haring, 1980). Teachers using curriculum-based measurement analyze at least 8 days of data by noting the criterion for mastery, drawing a line of best fit, and comparing it with the goal line (i.e., line drawn from initial performance to mastery level at end of year) (Fuchs & Fuchs, 1990). Browder (1991) suggested comparing the mean score from the previous evaluation period with the mean score from the current evaluation period. The difference from one period to the next should reflect at least a 5% change. At any rate, the object is to compare performance level from lowest to highest and note the degree of change.

If data were not graphed, raw data can be examined for error patterns. Errors that consistently occur at the beginning of instruction may indicate that relearning is taking place each time, whereas errors at the end of instruction might suggest that the learner is bored or tired. The occurrence of random errors usually indicates guessing (Fredericks et al., 1975). Other consistent error patterns suggest that the learner's behavior is maintained by a faulty algorithm; that is, the learner probably never acquired the correct response. Instead, the learner developed an incorrect paradigm (i.e., rules) or was inadvertently reinforced for the wrong answer.

When a trend line or line of best fit cannot be drawn, the data are considered highly variable and, therefore, too inconsistent for analysis. However, if a hypothesis can be developed to explain why the learner's behavior is erratic (e.g., effect of frequent seizures), then decisions can still be made. Even when a trend line can be drawn, the data may still be too variable for accurate decision making (Young et al., 1994). One strategy for determining variability is to draw a parallel line above and below the original line (see Figure 19.3, Strategy B). Data points that fall outside the envelope would be considered too variable. If this amounts to only one or two data points, then discard the extreme outliers and recalculate the trend line. Browder (1991) found that variability was often difficult to judge and, if present,

Table 19.1
Checklist for Data-Based Decision Making

1. Score the assessment.
   a. If corrects and errors have been recorded, determine accuracy.
   b. If time has been recorded, determine fluency.
   c. If level of prompt has been recorded, determine independence.
   d. If number of occurrences has been recorded, determine frequency.
   e. If qualitative rating has been recorded, determine satisfaction.

2. Determine if the learner has met the criterion for the current instructional, short-term, or long-term objective. If yes, move to Step 7.

3. Determine trend or slope of lines or data pattern.
   a. Draw a line of "best fit."
   b. Is it accelerating (i.e., going up, getting better)?
   c. Is it flat (i.e., staying the same)?
   d. Is it decelerating (i.e., going down, getting worse)?

4. Look for unacceptable variability in the data.
   a. Discard extreme outlyers and recalculate line of best fit.
   b. Note possible explanations for variability.

5. Determine learning picture.
   a. Is it an improving picture (i.e., making progress)?
   b. Is it a maintaining picture (i.e., flat, no progress)?
   c. Is it a worsening picture (i.e., deteriorating)?

6. Determine stage of learning.
   a. Is the learner in acquisition?
   b. Is the learner in fluency building?
   c. Is the learner in generalization?
   d. Is the learner in maintenance?

7. Make decision.
   a. If learner has met criterion, change instruction to the next instructional objective.
   b. If learner is making acceptable progress, do not change instructional program.
   c. If learner is making unacceptable progress (i.e., too slow, not enough), modify instructional program slightly.
   d. If learner is not making progress, modify instructional program.
   e. If learner is deteriorating, modify instructional program considerably.

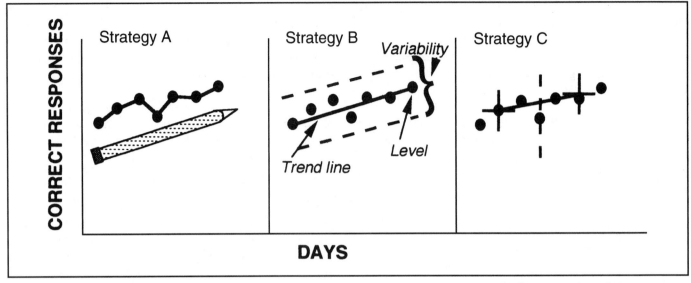

Figure 19.3. A series of strategies for determining the change in trend. With Strategy A, one connects the data points. A quick way to estimate trend is to position a pencil so that it covers as many data points as possible. Strategy B shows a line of "best fit" with an envelope drawn around it to determine variability. A line of progress using the midday, midrate method is depicted in Strategy C.

not necessary to consider because other factors (e.g., lower mean, decreasing trend line) would be sufficient for decision making. If possible, though, it is advantageous to note possible explanations for variability to further enhance decision making.

The most accurate decisions will result from analyzing a complete learning picture, that is, a trend line that reflects correct performance and a trend line that reflects error performance. A learning picture is either (a) improving (i.e., making progress), (b) maintaining (i.e., flat, no progress), or (c) worsening (i.e., deteriorating). Figure 19.4 contains examples of common learning pictures. An improving learning picture suggests that instruction is appropriate and should

continue as is. A change is necessary only when the learner has reached criterion. If the learner is making unacceptable progress (i.e., too slow, not enough), the instructional or motivational program should be modified slightly. When the learner is not making any progress, as evidenced by a maintaining learning picture, moderate changes in instruction, motivation, or practice are indicated. However, a worsening learning picture indicates that the learner's performance is deteriorating. Major instructional or motivational (i.e., reinforcement) changes must take place immediately.

Determining the appropriate instructional or motivational change depends on stage of learning. Generally, learners in the acquisition stage of learning perform at less than

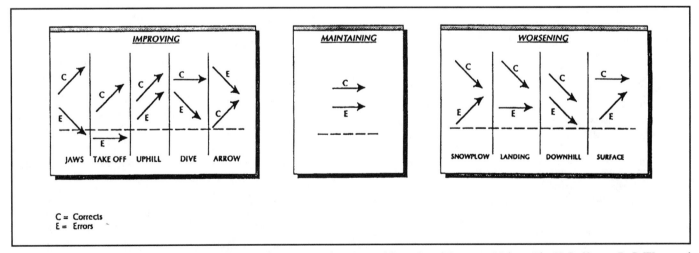

Figure 19.4. Learning pictures. From "Program Development, Evaluation, and Data-Based Decision Making," by K. R. Young, R. P. West, and C. A. Macfarlane, 1994, in *Curricular and Instructional Approaches for Persons with Severe Disabilities* (p. 72), by E. C. Cipanie and F. Spooner (Eds.), Needham Heights, MA: Allyn & Bacon. Copyright 1994 by Allyn & Bacon. Reprinted with permission.

one third of the criterion. During fluency building, performance level ranges from one third of criterion to criterion with an accuracy greater than 70%. When performance reaches or exceeds criterion, then the learner enters the generalization and maintenance stages of learning (Young et al., 1994). Learners in the acquisition stage of learning will benefit most from changes in instruction. The teacher may want to modify or add directions, prompts (e.g., verbal cues, modeling, physical assistance, graduated guidance), permanent prompts, and/or materials. Stronger reinforcement may be called for, along with the use of error correction procedures. In the fluency-building stage of learning, the teacher will want to consider motivational strategies that emphasize performing the skill faster and with less assistance. It may be necessary to manipulate consequences, change instructions, or increase drill and practice. During the generalization and maintenance stages of learning (i.e., proficiency), decisions will focus on strategies to expand and extend a learner's performance beyond the original instructional objective.

To standardize instructional decision making and make it more reliable, several models based on empirically derived guidelines have been developed. Haring et al. (1980) initially developed guidelines for teachers using precision teaching techniques. Later, Liberty, Haring, White, and Billingsley (1988) extended those guidelines to include decision rules for promoting generalization. Because many teachers do not use precision teaching, Browder, Liberty, Heller, and D'Huyvetters (1986) modified the original guidelines to evaluate data plotted on equal interval graphs. Further research led to the Lehigh model (Browder, Demchak, Heller, & King, 1989). Despite the demonstrated success of these models to track progress and guide instruction, many teachers fail to evaluate data on a consistent basis because of time constraints. Some teachers, burdened by the complexity of providing a variety of instruction to too many learners, may find little time for decision making.

The need to apply decision rules in an efficient and consistent manner has led to the development of computer programs to assist teachers. In addition to storing and graphing data, early programs provided limited monitoring and data analysis. The *Data-Based Program Modification* software (Fuchs, Deno, & Mirkin, 1983) supported teachers using curriculum-based measurement. *AIMSTAR: A Data Management and Decision-Making System* (Hasselbring & Hamlett, 1983) offered a similar program. However, computer-generated advice, such as decision rule guidelines, was very basic. Teachers continued to struggle to determine appropriate changes when given generic decisions (e.g., "improve moti-

vation"). Often, novice teachers could not identify appropriate specific strategies for implementing such advice.

AC-CEL (West, Young, West, Johnson, & Freston, 1985) incorporates the tenets of precision teaching with an expanded set of decision rules. This program assists teachers in monitoring and analyzing the performance of learners working on high-rate academic behaviors. Further research at Utah State University led to the development of two expert systems, *Classroom Advisor* (Macfarlane, Young, Weeks, Kemblowski, & Blair, 1990) and *DECEL* (Young, Kemblowski, Blair, & Macfarlane, 1992). In addition to generating decisions based on trend lines, performance level, learning picture, and stage of learning (see Figure 19.5), *Classroom Advisor* was programmed with expertise to help teachers solve problems with instruction and motivation. For example, if the initial decision indicates a motivation problem, *Classroom Advisor* engages the teacher in a "dialogue" (e.g., "Did you recently change the reinforcer?") to ascertain the underlying cause. Figure 19.6 contains a sample dialogue. *DECEL*, as mentioned in an earlier section, was developed to guide teachers through the complex decision-making process needed to conduct functional analyses and develop nonaversive behavioral interventions. See Figure 19.7 for a sample report from *DECEL*. These highly sophisticated systems augment and extend teacher expertise.

Summary

The process of gathering sound educational information is one of the top priorities of effective professionals. Learners with disabilities have the right to a free and appropriate education. An appropriate education can occur only when measurement becomes an integral part of a learner's program and unlocks the key to instruction. Professionals who measure learner performance and engage in data-based decision making deliver the best possible instruction, ensure accountability, and implement best practices.

Acknowledgement

The author wishes to thank Emily A. Johnson for her generous support in helping to edit earlier versions of this manuscript; Alan Hilton for his support and direction as co-editor; and K. Richard Young for his support as friend, colleague, and mentor in learning, teaching, researching, and writing about measurement and evaluation.

(*text continues on page 253*)

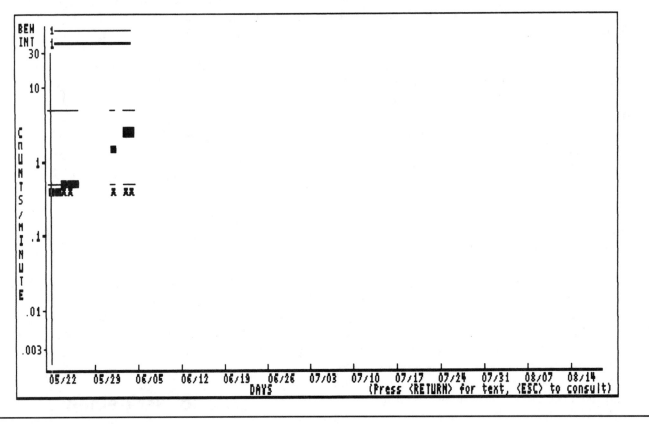

Figure 19.5. An example of advice given by *Classroom Advisor* (Macfarlane et al., 1990) following an 8-day analysis of student performance data.

```
>>> Is the reinforcer effective?   (Y/N)

          YES

>>> Could the learner be satiated on the current reinforcer?   (Y/N)

          NO

>>> Is the reinforcer functional?  (Y/N)

          YES

>>> Is an effective reinforcer available?   (Y/N)

          YES

>>> Does the instructor deliver the reinforcer immediately?   (Y/N)

          NO
```

Reinforcer Advice
Deliver the reinforcer immediately after the learner makes a correct response. 8 User supplied confidence: 100
Press any key to continue

Figure 19.6. A sample dialogue between the user and *Classroom Advisor* (Macfarlane et al., 1990).

```
--------------------------------------------------------------
                           KATHY
                BEHAVIOR ASSESSMENT SUMMARY REPORT
                 Head motion            05/25/1994
--------------------------------------------------------------
Target record created: 04/18/1994

General type of problem behavior: Stereotypic/habitual behaviors
Specific problem behaviors:
        Perseveration
Consultation-based hypothesis of behavior function:
        Escape/Avoidance
        Material reinforcement
        Sensory stimulation
        Attention/Assistance
Data-based hypothesis of behavior function:
        29%     Escape/Avoidance
         6%     Material reinforcement
        57%     Sensory stimulation
         9%     Attention/Assistance
Communicative intent(s) of behaviors:

This target HAS been screened for instructional factors.

This target HAS been screened for environmental factors.

This target HAS been screened for  medical factors.

Factors which appear to maintain the problem behaviors:
```

Antecedent	Correlation
Easy task	32%
Task trans	27%
End task	18%
Demands	14%
Correction	5%

Consequence	Correlation
Sens stim	91%
Simpl corr	5%
Redirect	5%

Situation	Rate
Conversation	1/hr

Person	Rate
Dudley	1/hr
Lindsay	2/hr

Figure 19.7. An example of a report generated by *DECEL* (Young et al., 1992).

QUESTIONS

1. Describe a situation in which it would be appropriate to collect time-based data.

2. What are the differences between an equal interval chart and the standard behavior chart?

3. What are the advantages to graphing data?

4. Why should an effective teacher use data for decision making rather than depending on hunches?

5. How can technology assist the teacher in the data collection and decision-making process?

References

Blackhurst, A. E., Schuster, J. W., Ault, M. J., & Doyle, P. M. (1994). *The single subject research advisor* [Computer program]. Lexington: University of Kentucky, Department of Special Education.

Browder, D. M. (1991). *Assessment of individuals with severe disabilities: An applied behavior approach to life skills assessment* (2nd ed.). Baltimore: Brookes.

Browder, D. M., Demchak, M., Heller, M., & King, D. (1989). An in vivo evaluation of the use of data-based rules to guide instructional decisions. *Journal of the Association for Persons with Severe Handicaps, 14,* 234–240.

Browder, D., Liberty, K., Heller, M., & D'Huyvetters, K. (1986). Self-management by teachers: Improving instructional decision-making. *Professional School Psychology, 1,* 165–175.

Brown, F., & Snell, M. (1993). Measurement, analysis, and evaluation. In M. E. Snell (Ed.), *Instruction of students with severe disabilities* (4th ed., pp. 152–183). New York: Merrill.

Cooper, J. O. (1981). *Measuring behavior* (2nd ed.). Columbus, OH: Merrill.

Farlow, L. J., & Snell, M. E. (1989). Teacher use of student performance data to make instructional decisions: Practices in programs for students with moderate to profound disabilities. *Journal of the Association for Persons with Severe Handicaps, 14,* 13–22.

Ferguson, C. L., Jr., & Fuchs, L. S. (1991). Scoring accuracy within curriculum-based measurement: A comparison of teachers and microcomputer applications. *Journal of Special Education Technology, 11,* 26–32.

Fredericks, H. D. B., Baldwin, V. L., Moore, W., Templeman, V. P., Grove, D., Moore, M., Gage, M. A., Blair, L., Alrick, G., Wadlow, M., Fruin, C., Bunse, C., Makohon, L., Samples, B., Moses, C., Rogers, G., & Toews, J. (1975). *A data based classroom for the moderately and severely handicapped.* Monmouth, OR: Instructional Development Corp.

Fuchs, L. S., Deno, S. L., & Mirkin, P. K. (1983). Data-based program modification: A continuous evaluation system with computer software to facilitate implementation. *Journal of Special Education Technology, 6*(2), 50–57.

Fuchs, L. S., & Fuchs, D. (1987). The relation between methods of graphing student performance data and achievement: A meta-analysis. *Journal of Special Education Technology, 8*(3), 5–13.

Fuchs, L. S., & Fuchs, D. (1990). Traditional academic assessment: An overview. In R. A. Gable & J. M. Hendrickson (Eds.), *Assessing students with special needs: A sourcebook for analyzing and correcting errors in academics* (pp. 1–13). New York: Longman.

Fuchs, L. S., Fuchs, D., & Hamlett, C. L. (1993). Technological advances linking the assessment of students' academic proficiency to instructional planning. *Journal of Special Education Technology, 12,* 49–62.

Grigg, N. C., Snell, M. E., & Lloyd, B. (1989). Visual analysis of student evaluation data: A qualitative analysis of teacher decision making. *Journal of the Association for Persons with Severe Handicaps, 14,* 23–32.

Haring, N., Liberty, K., & White, O. (1980). Rules for data-based decisions in instructional programs: Current research and instructional implications. In W. Sailor, B. Wilcox, & L. Brown (Eds.), *Methods of instruction for severely handicapped learners* (pp. 159–192). Baltimore: Brookes.

Hasselbring, T. S., & Hamlett, C. L. (1983). *AIMSTAR: A data management and decision-making program* [Computer program]. Portland, OR: ASIEP Education Co.

Kazdin, A. E. (1982). *Single-case research designs: Methods for clinical and applied settings.* New York: Oxford University Press.

Liberty, K. A., Haring, N. G., White, O. R., & Billingsley, F. F. (1988). A technology for the future: Decision rules for generalization. *Education and Training in Mental Retardation, 23,* 315–326.

Lindsley, O. R. (1964). Direct measurement and prosthesis of retarded behavior. *Journal of Education, 147,* 62–81.

Macfarlane, C. A., Young, K. R., Weeks, R. A., Kemblowski, E. J., & Blair, M. E. (1990). *Classroom advisor* [Computer program]. Logan: Department of Special Education, Utah State University.

Pfaffenberger, B. (1988). *Microcomputer applications in qualitative research.* Newberry Park, CA: Sage.

Repp, A. C., Karsh, K. G., Van Acker, R., Felce, D., & Harman, M. (1989). A computer-based system for collecting and analyzing observational data. *Journal of Special Education Technology, 9,* 207–217.

Richards, S., & Sternberg, L. (1994). Assessing levels of state and arousal. In L. Sternberg (Ed.), *Individuals with profound disabilities: Instructional and assistive strategies* (pp. 61–87). Austin, TX: PRO-ED.

Weller, S. C., & Romney, A. K. (1988). *Systematic data collection.* Newberry Park, CA: Sage.

West, R. P., Young, K. R., West, W. J., Johnson, J. I., & Freston, C. W. (1985). *AC-CEL* [Computer program]. Logan, UT: AC-CEL Enterprises.

White, O. R. (1984). Performance-based decisions: When and what to change. In R. P. West & K. R. Young (Eds.), *Precision teaching: Instructional decision making, curriculum and management, and research: Proceedings from the National Precision Teaching Conference* (pp. 30–61). Logan, UT: Utah State University, Department of Special Education.

White, O. R., & Haring, N. G. (1980). *Exceptional teaching.* Columbus, OH: Merrill.

Young, K. R., Kemblowski, E. J., Blair, M. E., & Macfarlane, C. A. (1992). *DECEL* [Computer program]. Logan: Department of Special Education, Utah State University.

Young, K. R., West, R. P., & Macfarlane, C. A. (1994). Program development, evaluation, and data-based decision making. In E. C. Cipanie & F. Spooner (Eds.), *Curricular and instructional approaches for persons with severe disabilities* (pp. 50–80). Needham Heights, MA: Allyn & Bacon.

Classroom Management: Promising and Effective Practices for Students with Developmental Disabilities

CHAPTER 20

Deborah Huntington

Learning Outcomes

After reading this chapter, you should be able to

■ List four questions that should be considered when selecting an appropriate intervention for a problem behavior.

■ Identify the elements of contingency contracting.

■ Describe how to assess the social validity of a problem behavior.

■ Design a level system that you could implement in your present teaching situation.

TERMS

The following terms are important for the understanding of this chapter:

Contingency contracting: The mutual negotiation between instructor and student regarding the amount of student behavior required to earn specific reward(s).

Positive reinforcer: A preferred consequence that is received following the performance of a behavior and that leads to an increase in the performance of that behavior.

Level system: A system of token economies within which a student who meets behavioral requirements can prog-

ress from an intrusive environment to a range of less intrusive environments.

Token economy: The use of tokens as an interim reinforcer, when a student meets the behavioral requirement for specific reward(s); the tokens are later exchanged for backup reinforcer(s).

Social validation: Observing the target behavior in other students to assess the occurrence of the behavior in a particular student.

Introduction

Although increasing numbers of students with developmental disabilities are being served in inclusive settings, regular elementary and secondary teachers report that they have received little preparation for inclusion in their preservice teacher education programs (Aksamit, 1990; Phillips, Allred, Brulle, & Shank, 1990). One of their major concerns about inclusive education is classroom management. Preliminary research suggests that neither inclusion nor any other option on the continuum of services is inherently successful for students with developmental disabilities without the provision of predetermined interventions designed to address individual student needs (Altman & Kanagawa, 1994).

Successful teachers use classroom management techniques based on systematic instruction. Systematic instruction provides a structure for determining behaviors in need of change and designing behavior management interventions empirically validated for individuals with developmental disabilities. Specifically, this approach focuses on changing significant observable behaviors that are clearly defined. Through systematically manipulating environmental factors, such as the instructional setting, for example, targeted responses are changed, shaped, increased, or decreased.

Direct observations and measurement provide means for documenting functional relationships between change in the target behavior and a specific behavioral intervention. This chapter provides an overview of general classroom management practices and their application to individuals with developmental disabilities. However, because it does not provide a comprehensive review of applied behavioral analysis, the reader may wish to read the books by Alberto and Troutman (1990) and Cooper, Heron, and Heward (1987).

Behavioral interventions are based on principles that have been demonstrated and empirically validated with both animal and human subjects. Behavioral responses can be altered by manipulating antecedent stimuli (e.g., the learning environment, the assigned task) or by manipulating consequences (e.g., teacher praise, free time). The antecedent sets the occasion for a specific response to occur, whereas the consequence alters the probability that the behavior will increase or decrease in the future (Cooper et al., 1987).

The first step in analyzing behavior is to conduct a functional analysis, whereby antecedent–response–consequence patterns are studied through direct observation. Decision models have been developed to systematically analyze the aberrant behavior of persons with severe disabilities (Evans & Meyer, 1985; Gaylord-Ross, 1980; Meyer & Evans, 1989). The general flow of these models is as follows: first, assess whether the problem behavior is severe enough to warrant intervention; second, determine ecological or curricular factors that may set the occasion for the behavior; and third, determine consequences that may reinforce the unwanted response. This general approach is addressed in the following discussion of behavior management techniques for students with developmental disabilities in classroom settings.

Students with developmental disabilities may exhibit many challenging behavior problems in school, work, and home environments. Although these behaviors may seem overwhelming to some teachers, they can often be managed through nonintrusive procedures, such as providing a predictable, consistent environment; assigning functional tasks that are realistic; providing natural consequences; and matching instruction to a student's level of functioning. When behavior problems persist despite a consistent classroom environment and well-matched curricular demands, more intrusive interventions may be needed. To determine which type of intervention would be most appropriate, a number of questions must be answered:

1. Is the challenging behavior truly a problem when viewed in the context of peers and other individuals in the natural environment?

2. Does the behavior occur across settings and with different teachers, adults, or students?

3. Does the behavior impede functional progress or social skills development?

4. Is the frequency, intensity, or duration of the behavior sufficient to warrant more intrusive measures?

These questions can be answered by defining the behavior and then systematically observing and measuring it through direct observation. The student should be observed in multiple settings to determine if the problem is context specific. For example, Mary is reportedly too talkative during third-period language arts and sixth-period math. Through observation it is determined that this problem is context specific in that she sits next to Kelly in only these two of her classes.

It is also vital to obtain measures for social comparison. Expectation and student behaviors may vary greatly within different environments and subenvironments. Social validation measures can be obtained through collecting direct observation data on the behavior of interest as exhibited by three "typical" individuals. For example, data collected during direct observation indicates that Karen, Paul, and Tiffany, normally achieving students, were off task 39% of the time during second-period art class. This data will be compared with data collected on a student with intellectual disabilities in the same setting at the same time.

After following these guidelines and conducting a medical examination to rule out interfering physical conditions, it may be decided that more intrusive interventions are warranted. It is essential that the least intrusive interventions (e.g., linking rule following to teacher praises) be implemented and evaluated prior to using more intrusive interventions (e.g., withholding privileges). In the next section, intervention options are described, beginning with less intrusive measures and moving to more intrusive yet functionally desirable intervention options.

Interventions

Consistent, Structured Environment

Many potential behavior problems can be prevented or minimized by providing a predictable, consistent, structured environment. It is unrealistic and unfair to expect students to maintain specific behavioral standards when the standards are unknown, unclear, or always changing. Successful practice has shown that behavioral expectations should be clearly stated through explicit classroom rules. Rules should be stated in a positive (e.g., "Raise your hand to speak") rather than a negative (e.g., "Don't talk out") manner. Although an instructor could devise a list of 20 or more rules to cover potential problems, rules should be kept to a minimum. Having five rules or fewer is considered an effective practice. Finally, rules should be posted, taught, and then reviewed frequently. Feedback provided by teachers in the form of specific praise for rule following is considered an effective practice.

Research based on naturalistic observations of teacher–pupil interactions reveals that teachers are inclined to provide more negative than positive feedback to students (Strain, Lambert, Kerr, Stagg, & Lenkner, 1983; Thomas, Presland, Grant, & Glynn, 1978; White, 1975). In addition, Strain and colleagues (1983) found that the general level of teacher feedback, both negative and positive, is remarkably low, and that positive feedback is often misplaced. For example, teachers sometimes praise an entire class that includes noncompliant students. It is possible that group praise provides inadvertent positive reinforcement for certain students' inappropriate behavior. Successful teachers use a four-to-one ratio of positive interactions to corrective interactions.

Students with developmental disabilities as a group have difficulty with organization. Specific environmental arrangements can facilitate student organization. For example, on a job site, students may enter the building, put away lunch and personal belongings in a locker room, use the restroom, and then clock in. Advance organizers can be provided to prepare students for key points in a discussion and to ready students for changes in routines or schedules (Bos & Vaughn, 1988; Darch & Gersten, 1986; Lenz, Alley, & Schumaker, 1987). Written and/or pictorial schedules assist students in dealing with transition, a task difficult for many individuals, as well as changes in routines or schedules. Through structure, routines, and advance organizers, numerous types of difficulties can be preempted. Direct instruction should be used to teach students routines prior to implementation.

Positive-Consequence Environmental Interventions

For some students, a predictable routine, enforced classroom rules, and consistent, contingent teacher praise for appropriate behavior are not enough to sustain acceptable behavior. For students who present problem behaviors, more intrusive interventions, such as positive reinforcement, contingency contracting, token economies, or specific level systems, may be necessary. The following subsections provide discussions of these approaches. The section on interventions ends with negative-consequence environmental interventions, which are more intrusive.

Positive Reinforcement

A stimulus or event that is administered contingently following a behavior is termed a positive reinforcer if the future occurrence of the behavior increases (Ayllon & Azrin, 1968; Cooper et al., 1987; Kelley & Stokes, 1982). For example, if a student receives free time contingent upon completing mathematical word problems with a certain level of accuracy, the likelihood that future completion of problems will increase if free time is a positive reinforcer for the student.

All reinforcers are either primary (unlearned or unconditioned) or secondary (learned or conditioned). Primary reinforcers include universal or automatic reinforcers to which all people respond. If an individual is hungry, thirsty, or cold, primary reinforcers would be food, drink, and warmth, respectively. Through their association with primary reinforcers, secondary reinforcers develop their reinforcing value. Secondary reinforcers commonly used in school-based settings include task completion, grades, attention, approval, favorite activities, and tokens. Secondary reinforcers commonly available in community settings include task completion, a positive employee evaluation, personal or group recognition through an announcement or visual display, earning a pay raise, time off, and a T-shirt or food for perfect attendance and/or productivity. When using contingency contracting, token economies, and level systems, interim reinforcers (e.g., check marks, stars) are generally earned, accumulated, and then exchanged for backup reinforcers.

Ideally, reinforcers should be age appropriate, natural, and context appropriate. For example, providing time to learn a leisure activity, such as playing a new card game, should be considered more context and age appropriate for an 11th grader than earning a brownie for staying on task. An effective teacher has two specific goals for students related to reinforcement given. First, the instructor seeks to provide more reinforcement options for students. Second, the teacher attempts to replace primary and/or age-inappropriate reinforcers with naturally occurring age-appropriate reinforcers.

Reinforcers must be assessed individually for students (Ayllon & Azrin, 1968). Free time may be a reinforcer for some students but not for others. Potential reinforcers may be determined by simply asking students what they prefer, by interviewing parents and/or caregivers, or by observing what activities seem enjoyable. Green and associates (1988) found that systematic assessment of student preferences is a likely, but not certain, source of reinforcers for individuals with profound disabilities. The only way to determine whether a potential reinforcer will actually work for any particular student is to try it and observe future behavior.

Contingency Contracts

A contingency contract is a written agreement that clearly specifies a contingent relationship between specific behaviors and access to a specified reward. According to Cooper and colleagues (1987), a contingency contract is not merely a simple positive reinforcement contingency, but rather it represents a complex intervention package of related positive and negative reinforcement contingencies.

Contingency contracting involves mutual negotiation between the student and the teacher regarding the amount of student behavior required to earn specific rewards. According to Kelley and Stokes (1982), contingency contracting provides students with opportunities for self-management (i.e., setting and achieving goals). The contract includes the task (i.e., who, what, when, criteria), the reward (specifically stated), and a place to record the progress (which may serve as an interim reinforcer) toward the goal or reward. For example, a teacher and a student may stipulate that, after each consecutive 5-day period during which the student remembers to wear deodorant, he will earn a video pass.

Kelley and Stokes (1982) evaluated the effects of a student–teacher contracting system on the academic productivity of disadvantaged high school dropouts in a vocational setting. Students were paid for the correct completion of an agreed-upon number of academic tasks. The teacher met weekly with each student to negotiate a contract specifying daily and weekly goals for the number of items to be completed. Students earned more money each day they reached their goals. Students also were rewarded for weekly goal achievement in that they were reinforced when they completed work missed when absent or assignments they had not completed for a daily grade. The initial goal was 10% above current level of productivity. Examination of the single-subject design data indicated upward trends during contracting phases for each of the seven participants. Social validity was established by interviewing students to determine consumer satisfaction. Students reported a preference for contracting because they knew exactly how much work they had to accomplish each day and could not be reprimanded for wasting time after they had completed their work.

Token Economies

Token economies have been widely used as an effective behavior management technique with individuals in home, educational, and rehabilitation settings (Cooper et al., 1987; Kazdin, 1982; McLaughlin & Malaby, 1977). A number of researchers have demonstrated the effectiveness of token economies for improving both academic and social behaviors of students with mild disabilities (McLaughlin & Malaby, 1977; Pavchinski, Evans, & Bostow, 1989; Robinson, Newby, & Ganzell, 1981). Tokens have been used in combination with praise as reinforcers to modify a wide variety of behaviors in students with moderate and severe intellectual disabilities (Kazdin & Bootzin, 1972; Snell & Zipoli, 1987). Tokens are given contingent upon behaviors and, in turn, are exchanged for the "purchase" of a backup primary or secondary reinforcer.

Successful teachers select the manner in which initial training in implementing a token economy is conducted depending on the functioning level of the learners. For students with mild disabilities, the initial training may be min-

imal. Three steps are often sufficient. First, an example of the system is given. The instructor might show a token to a student and tell the student that he or she can earn it by performing the specified behavior. The teacher then explains that, as the student continues the behavior, he or she can earn more tokens. During the specified time period, the student can exchange the tokens to earn specified items. The items may be listed on a schedule or displayed on a table with the number of tokens needed for purchase. The instructor then explains that the student can spend only tokens earned, but that it is possible to accumulate tokens until enough have been earned to purchase a more expensive item. The second step is to model the procedure for token delivery. For example, the instructor directs the student to perform the target behavior. Immediately after the occurrence of the behavior, the teacher praises the student (e.g., "Sue, you set up the display correctly!") and delivers the token. The third step is to model the procedure for the token exchange. Learners should be shown the items for purchase. All students will already have one token that was received during the modeling of token delivery. During modeling, it is critical that the instructor provide several items with the value of one token each to enable the student to exchange his or her token for an item. (The price of these items may be increased later.) Each student should make an actual exchange during this experience.

During ongoing token reinforcement, several procedures should be followed for the effective use of reinforcement. Tokens should be dispensed contingently and immediately after the occurrence of the desired behavior. Procedures for the delivery and exchange of tokens should be clear and followed consistently. The program should emphasize increasing desirable behaviors through token delivery rather than decreasing undesirable behaviors through token response cost.

It is recommended that the teacher take part in the token economy. The instructor may pinpoint a behavior of his or her own to be increased, and could then model how to keep track of tokens earned, how to save tokens, and how to act when one does not get a token. For example, if Mr. Jones has a goal of developing healthy eating habits, he may reward himself with a token every time he chooses a healthy lunch.

After 2 to 3 weeks, a revision in the token economy may be needed. Students should evaluate the schedule of exchange, the backup items available, and desirable behaviors to be targeted. If some individuals have rarely earned tokens, their target behavior should be analyzed to determine whether a simpler response or a prerequisite skill would be a more appropriate goal. For individuals who have always earned the maximum possible tokens, the instructor should consider increasing the complexity of the target behavior.

According to Kazdin (1982), token economies can be viewed as economic systems, in which "token-earning behaviors represent income or wages; back up events represent expenditures, and accumulated tokens can be viewed as savings" (p. 433). In light of this analogy, teachers must be cognizant of the relative effects of altering the rate of token economy, cost of backup reinforcers, and number of tokens that can be accumulated in savings. The primary goal of motivating individuals to earn tokens by following rules can be maintained though adding potent, novel backup reinforcers and by altering the rate of exchange.

As token economies are extrinsic to the student, effective teachers should have a plan to withdraw the system yet maintain improved student behavior through less intrusive means. According to Cooper and colleagues (1987), this can be accomplished through the following procedures. First, the token presentation should always be paired with verbal praise to increase the reinforcing effect of the social approval and to serve to maintain behaviors after token withdrawal. Second, the number of responses needed to earn tokens should be gradually increased. Third, the length of time per day the token economy is in effect should be gradually decreased. Fourth, the activities and privileges that serve as backup reinforcers should reflect items that are in place in the natural situation. Fifth, the prices of the more desirable items should be gradually increased while the prices on less desirable items should be kept low. Sixth, the physical evidence of the token should be gradually faded. For example, the teacher can move from poker chips, to slips of paper, to tally marks, to tallies kept by the teacher and announced at the end of the day. Finally, the tokens should be faded completely.

Level Systems

Level systems provide a framework that allows the student to progress from a more to a least intrusive setting (LaNunziata, Hunt, & Cooper, 1984). In general, level systems list specific behavioral expectations, requirements, and privileges for the student at each level, and standards for moving up or down the levels. Lower levels involve more teacher control and fewer behavioral privileges for the students than do upper levels. As students move up through the levels, the behavioral expectations and privileges change, moving from external teacher control to internal self-management.

For example, LaNunziata and associates (1984) proposed a four-level system in which each student begins at Level 1, where tokens are given approximately every 15 minutes. Every morning and afternoon each student is allowed to rent games, materials, or activity privileges for a 15-minute free period. When a student reaches the criterion (e.g., 85% academic success for 10 consecutive school days with no major rule infraction), he or she moves up to Level 2. At Level 2, students have a card on which they may receive a check every 30 minutes. The check marks are exchanged at the end of the day for classroom privileges for the following day. In addition, Level 1 privileges are free for students at Level 2.

After maintaining performance for 10 consecutive school days, the student is advanced to Level 3. Students make contracts for each morning and afternoon period. At the end of each session, the teacher reviews the contract to determine whether the contract has been met. Students meeting criterion receive schoolwide privileges, such as library passes, study hall passes, passes to attend other classes of interest, or other appropriate privileges involving increased responsibility. Level 1 and Level 2 privileges are free for students at Level 3. Following 10 successful days at Level 3, students are advanced to Level 4, where weekly report cards are used to determine whether goals have been met. In Level 4, special responsibilities are encouraged, such as school patrol, tutoring others, and monitoring the cafeteria.

Negative-Consequence Environmental Interventions

For some students, positive-consequence environmental interventions do not provide enough support to maintain acceptable behavior. A successful teacher provides a consistent structured environment for all students and implements positive-consequence environmental interventions before considering the use of negative-consequence environmental interventions. In this section, more intrusive interventions, such as planned ignoring and response cost procedures, are presented.

Planned Ignoring

In planned ignoring, when an inappropriate behavior occurs, social reinforcers such as attention, physical contact, or verbal interaction are briefly removed (Cooper et al., 1987; Kerr & Nelson, 1983). Planned ignoring can be systematically implemented by looking away from the individual, remaining quiet, and/or refraining from any interaction whatsoever for a specific period of time. Planned ignoring can be conducted by an individual, such as an instructor, or by a group, such as in peer-mediated time-out (Kerr & Nelson, 1983). For example, suppose that during a lunch break, peers are discussing a baseball game and an individual interjects a comment about a TV cartoon character. Peer-mediated time-out is practiced when the group breaks off eye contact and does not respond to the verbalization in any way until the individual's comments are more consistent with the group's discussion. At that point, eye contact is made and verbal interaction is resumed.

Response Cost

Often token economies and level systems incorporate negative consequences or response cost procedures when students break rules or exhibit undesirable behaviors. The negative consequence usually entails the student's losing previously earned tokens or moving down to a more restrictive level in a level system. Response cost is a form of punishment and should be considered only if less intrusive positive procedures are found to be ineffective in curbing disruptive behavior with few differential effects (Cooper et al., 1987; Iwarta & Bailey, 1974; Kaufman & O'Leary, 1972). Therefore, it is recommended that, when response cost is used, it should be paired with some type of reinforcement component (Cooper et al., 1987).

Typically, when an economy is structured around response cost alone, tokens, markers, or visible marks on the board are given to students at the beginning of a period and then taken away as rule infractions occur. Although this type of procedure has been effective in managing the behavior of students with mild disabilities (Salend & Lamb, 1986), it seems to focus more on rule infractions than on rule-following behaviors. Furthermore, students are more likely to perceive the system as punitive. Imagine working in a system in which your salary is paid in advance, but you are fined for missing deadlines. Contrast how you would feel if, instead, you are given bonuses for meeting deadlines. For this reason, when cost response procedures are implemented, they should be closely monitored.

Assertive discipline (Cantor, 1976), a behavior change system once adopted wholesale by many school districts, is often practiced solely as a response cost system. Typically, when students break classroom rules, their names are written on the chalkboard and check marks are added for any additional rule violations. Preset negative consequences, such as a loss of a privilege or a visit to an administrator, are linked to the system. The frequently punitive nature of the implementation of this system and a lack of empirical support has led to recent criticism of assertive discipline (Evans, Evans, Gable, & Kelhem, 1991; Gartrell, 1987).

Summary

The dramatic increase in the number of students with developmental disabilities being served in inclusive settings has resulted in tremendous interest in ways to manage classrooms that include these students. The research-based approaches presented in this chapter can be successfully implemented in an inclusive setting. Classroom management procedures presented in this chapter include a consistent, structured environment; positive-consequence environmental interventions; and negative-consequence environmental interventions. These approaches can be used on an individual or a group basis. Often an instructor may choose to incorporate one or more approaches into a group management plan, while individual plans may be written on a case-by-case basis, considering the physical, social, emotional, and academic needs of specific students. The systematic application of these and other approaches leads to the effective management of individuals and groups.

 QUESTIONS

1. Discuss the considerations in planning a management system for the classroom.

2. What role does reinforcement play in management of behavior?

3. Discuss how you would establish an environment that would assist a teacher to be more effective.

4. How would a teacher decide when to use negative consequences?

References

Aksamit, D. L. (1990). Practicing teachers' perceptions of their preservice preparation for mainstreaming. *Teacher Education and Special Education, 13*, 21–28.

Alberto, P. A., & Troutman, A. C. (1990). *Applied behavior analysis for teachers* (3rd ed.). Columbus, OH: Merrill.

Altman, R., & Kanagawa, L. (1994). Academic and social engagement of young children with developmental disabilities in integrated and nonintegrated settings. *Education and Training in Mental Retardation and Developmental Disabilities, 29*, 184–193.

Ayllon, T., & Azrin, N. H. (1968). Reinforcer sampling: Technique for increasing the behavior of mental patients. *Journal of Applied Behavior Analysis, 1*, 13–20.

Bos, C. S., & Vaughn, S. (1988). *Strategies for teaching students with learning and behavior problems*. Needham Heights, MA: Allyn & Bacon.

Cantor, L. (1976). *Assertive discipline: A take charge approach for today's educators*. Los Angeles: Lee Cantor and Associates.

Cooper, J. O., Heron, T. E., & Heward, W. L. (1987). *Applied behavioral analysis*. Columbus, OH: Merrill.

Darch, C., & Gersten, R. (1986). Direction-setting activities for reading comprehension: A comparison of two approaches. *Learning Disability Quarterly, 9*, 235–243.

Evans, I. M., Evans, S. S., Gable, R. A., & Kelhem, M. A. (1991). Assertive discipline and behavioral disorders: Is this a marriage made in heaven? *Beyond Behavior, 2,* 13–16.

Evans, I. M., & Meyer, L. H. (1985). *An educative approach to behavior problems: A practical decision model for interventions with severely handicapped learners.* Baltimore: Brookes.

Gartrell, D. (1987). Assertive discipline: Unhealthy for children and other living things. *Young Children, 12*(2), 10–11.

Gaylord-Ross, R. (1980). A decision model for the treatment of aberrant behavior in applied settings. In W. Sailor, B. Wilcox, & L. Brown (Eds.), *Methods of instruction for severely handicapped students* (pp. 135–158). Baltimore: Brookes.

Green, C. W., Reid, D. H., White, L. K., Halford, R. C., Brittain, D. P., & Gardner, S. M. (1988). Identifying reinforcers for persons with profound handicaps: Staff opinion versus systematic assessment of preferences. *Journal of Applied Behavior Analysis, 21*(1), 21–43.

Iwarta, B. A., & Bailey, J. S. (1974). Reward versus cost token systems: An analysis of the effects on students and teacher. *Journal of Applied Behavior Analysis, 7,* 567–576.

Kaufman, K. F., & O'Leary, K. D. (1972). Reward, cost, and self-evaluation procedures for disruptive adolescents in a psychiatric hospital school. *Journal of Applied Behavior Analysis, 5,* 293–309.

Kazdin, A. E. (1982). The token economy: A decade later. *Journal of Applied Behavior Analysis, 15,* 431–445.

Kazdin, A. E., & Bootzin, R. R. (1972). The token economy: An evaluative review. *Journal of Applied Behavior Analysis, 5,* 343–372.

Kelley, M. L., & Stokes, T. F. (1982). Contingency contracting with disadvantaged youth: Improving classroom performance. *Journal of Applied Behavior Analysis, 15,* 447–454.

Kerr, M. M., & Nelson, C. M. (1983). *Strategies for managing behavior problems in the classroom.* Columbus, OH: Merrill.

LaNunziata, I. J., Hunt, K. P., & Cooper, J. O. (1984). Suggestions for phasing out token economy systems in primary and intermediate grades. *Techniques, 1,* 151–156.

Lenz, B. K., Alley, G. R., & Schumaker, J. B. (1987). Activating the inactive learner: Advance organizers in the secondary classroom. *Learning Disability Quarterly, 10,* 53–67.

McLaughlin, T. F., & Malaby, J. E. (1977). The comparative effects of token reinforcement with and without a response cost contingency with special education children. *Educational Research Quarterly, 2,* 1–41.

Meyer, L. H., & Evans, I. M. (1989). *Non-aversive intervention for behavior problems: A manual for home and community.* Baltimore: Brookes.

Pavchinski, P., Evans, J. H., & Bostow, D. E. (1989). Increasing word recognition and math ability in a severely learning-disabled student with token reinforcers. *Psychology in the Schools, 26,* 397–410.

Phillips, W. L., Allred, L., Brulle, A. R., & Shank, K. S. (1990). The Regular Education Initiative: The will and skill of regular educators. *Teacher Education and Special Education, 34,* 182–185.

Robinson, P. W., Newby, T. J., & Ganzell, S. L. (1981). A token economy for a class of underachieving hyperactive children. *Journal of Applied Behavior Analysis, 14,* 307–315.

Salend, S. J., & Lamb, E. A. (1986). Effectiveness of a group-managed interdependent contingency system. *Learning Disability Quarterly, 9,* 268–273.

Snell, M. E., & Zirpoli, T. J. (1987). Functional academics. In M. E. Snell (Ed.), *Systematic instruction of persons with severe handicaps* (3rd ed., pp. 110–150). New York: Macmillan.

Strain, P. S., Lambert, D. L., Kerr, M. M., Stagg, V., & Lenkner, D. A. (1983). Naturalistic assessment of children's compliance to teacher's requests and consequences for compliance. *Journal of Applied Behavior Analysis, 16,* 243–249.

Thomas, J. D., Presland, I. E., Grant, M. D., & Glynn, T. L. (1978). Natural rates of teacher approval and disapproval in grade-7 classrooms. *Journal for Applied Behavior Analysis, 11,* 91–94.

White, M. A. (1975). Natural rates of teacher approval and disapproval in the classroom. *Journal of Applied Behavior Analysis, 8,* 367–372.

Reducing Challenging Behaviors in Learners with Developmental Disabilities Through the Modification of Instructional Practices

CHAPTER 21

John J. Wheeler

Learning Outcomes

After reading this chapter, you should be able to

- Identify the functions of challenging behavior often exhibited by children with developmental disabilities.

- Describe the purpose of functional assessment and the components that comprise the functional assessment process;

- Understand how environmental and instructional variables can serve as causal factors for challenging behavior in learners.

- Identify best and effective teaching practices for modifying the physical environment to promote positive behavior in learners.

- Identify best and effective teaching practices for modifying instructional practices to promote positive behavior in learners.

TERMS

The following terms are important for the understanding of this chapter:

Functional assessment: A method used to determine what specific factors influence the occurrence of challenging behavior in learners.

Functions of challenging behavior: The purpose (or function) that the challenging behavior serves for the learner.

Instructional and environmental modifications: Any modifications made by the teacher to instruction or to the classroom environment that are aimed at specifically promoting positive behavior and reducing or minimizing the occurrence of challenging behavior in an individual learner or group of learners.

Introduction

A common concern voiced by classroom teachers and other direct care staff who provide instruction to learners with developmental disabilities is how to effectively deal with the occurrence of challenging behavior. Often the level of frustration voiced by teachers and direct care staff is enhanced by many factors, including limited supports within the school system and limited training and understanding of the factors that may influence these behaviors in learners (Axelrod, Moyer, & Berry, 1990). The challenging forms of behaviors of learners with developmental disabilities may be directly related to a variety of factors acting alone or in combination. These factors can be related to the physical health of the learner, such as illness, effects of medication, and hunger (Carr, 1977; Mace, Lalli, & Pinter-Lalli, 1991); environmental factors, such as temperature, lighting, seating arrangements, overcrowding, and noise levels within the classroom; and instructional variables, such as lack of learner choice in selecting activities, lack of predictability or routine, inappropriate levels of teacher assistance, length of activities, relevance of activities, and difficulty level of activities. It is essential that teachers and direct care staff recognize and understand how external variables influence behavior in their students and that often these behaviors are directly related to the physical environment and/or curriculum and instruction.

The purpose of this chapter is to identify effective practices that classroom teachers and other direct care staff can use to assess challenging behaviors displayed by learners with developmental disabilities, and how to modify environmental and instructional variables so that these behaviors can be prevented or minimized. Emphasis is given to the presentation of effective instructional practices that can assist teachers and direct care staff in implementing such interventions.

Functions of Challenging Behavior

For learners with developmental disabilities, the occurrence of challenging behavior can often be linked to attempts to communicate (Durand, 1990; Hummel & Prizant, 1993). It is not uncommon for these individuals to experience communication skills deficits, and frequently their responses represent attempts to communicate anger, frustration, boredom, pain, and sadness (Carr & Durand, 1985; Reichle & Johnson, 1993). Challenging behavior exhibited by learners with developmental disabilities also occurs in part due to the absence of alternative, more acceptable forms of behavior in the skill repertoires of these individuals and the insensitivity of the environments in which and professionals with whom these students participate (Durand, 1990). Taking these factors into consideration, challenging behaviors serve a function or purpose. It is important that teachers and direct care staff realize the dynamics of the interrelationships between the limited skill repertoire of the learner, insensitivity of the environment to the needs of the learner, and subsequent demands and expectations placed on the learner by the teacher.

Functional Assessment

The method recognized as the best and effective practice in the assessment of challenging behavior is referred to as functional assessment. Functional assessment is defined by Reichle and Wacker (1993) as "a process used to define the variables that influence the occurrence of challenging behaviors, and to use these variables to construct effective behavioral support plans" (p. xiv). Functional assessment within classroom and other instructional settings typically involves structured interview, scatter-plot analysis, and narrative recording.

Structured Interview

The structured interview consists of a systematic set of questions aimed at operationally defining the target behavior in clear and precise terms that can be observed and measured. The structured interview also attempts to obtain an estimate of (a) the frequency with which the target behavior occurs and (b) the probable causal factors of the behavior. An example of a structured interview is in Figure 21.1.

Scatter-Plot Analysis

Scatter-plot analysis (Touchette, MacDonald, & Langer, 1985) involves the collection of frequency counts on the target behavior across the day, usually in designated time periods of 15 to 20 minutes. It is a very easy and user-friendly method to use. The teacher or staff member notes each occurrence of the target behavior in the designated box for the time slot in which the behavior occurred. By using such a method, the teacher or staff person can determine if there is a pattern of high frequencies of behavior, as indicated by high numbers of occurrences within specific time slots. After determining the time period(s) and day(s) in which the highest frequencies of behavior occur, the teacher must ask several important questions: Does the behavior occur consistently over a number of days? Does the occurrence of the behavior coincide with specific activities during specific time periods? The teacher can then more easily examine the daily schedule and pinpoint activities that coincide with these high rates of behavior. Figure 21.2 is an example of a scatter-plot data sheet.

Narrative Recording

Upon obtaining information from the scatter-plot analysis and determining the periods during the day when the target behaviors occur most frequently, narrative recording can assist the teacher to more closely scrutinize the events that surround the behavior. Narrative recording focuses attention on identifying the specific antecedents that seem to precipitate the target behavior and the consequences that follow these occurrences. This method is also referred to as Antecedent–Behavior–Consequence (ABC) recording. Attention should be given to identifying whether a relationship exists between specific environmental and instructional factors as antecedents. Figure 21.3 is an example of a narrative recording sheet.

Putting It in Perspective

Once the functions or purposes of target behaviors have been determined, and the patterns associated with their occurrence and probable causal factors have been identified, the teacher is ready to develop an intervention plan. The use of functional assessment procedures to determine development of an intervention can be viewed as a proactive form of intervention. Unlike traditional behavior management approaches, which often emphasize the role of consequence events and the manipulation of consequences through token reward systems, response cost programs, time-out, and often the introduction of more intrusive procedures such as corporal punishment (Evans & Richardson, 1995) to manage problem behaviors, the use of functional assessment places emphasis on determining the underlying causes of these

Student's Name: _____

Date: _____

Person Completing this Questionnaire: _____

1. Describe the target behavior in clear and precise terms.

2. What events typically coincide with the target behavior?

3. What typically happens after the behavior occurs?

4. Are there times of day when the target behavior is more likely to occur?

5. What is the communicative intent of the target behavior?

6. What intervention methods have been used in the past?

7. Have any of these methods been successful?

8. Are there medical–health reasons that could account for the target behavior?

9. Does the student have a predictable classroom routine or schedule?

10. What activities does the student enjoy or prefer?

Figure 21.1. Sample structured interview format.

Name: _____   Behavior: _____

	Monday	Tuesday	Wednesday	Thursday	Friday
8:00–8:15					
8:15–8:30					
8:30–8:45					
8:45–9:00					
9:00–9:15					
9:15–9:30					
9:30–9:45					
9:45–10:00					
10:00–10:15					
10:15–10:30					
10:30–10:45					
10:45–11:00					
11:00–11:15					
11:15–11:30					
11:30–11:45					
11:45–12:00					
12:00–12:15					
12:15–12:30					
12:30–12:45					
12:45–1:00					
1:00–1:15					
1:15–1:30					
1:30–1:45					
1:45–2:00					
2:00–2:15					
2:15–2:30					

Figure 21.2. Sample scatter-plot data recording form.

Name of Student: _____ Date: _____

Time Observed: _____ to _____

Class Period: _____

Antecedent	Behavior	Consequence(s)

Figure 21.3. Sample narrative recording form.

behaviors, and the teaching of positive, alternative forms of behavior from the outset.

The reliance on more punitive forms of behavior management represents a philosophy aimed at the rapid reduction or suppression of these behaviors with little or no emphasis being given to teaching appropriate forms of behavior (Durand, 1990). The use of more intrusive procedures such as corporal punishment can be very damaging to an individual's self-esteem and create avoidance behaviors if used repeatedly over time. In short, it exemplifies the notion of treating the symptoms and not the cause. The use of corporal punishment does little to ensure that the learner will acquire and develop appropriate alternative behaviors. It simply punishes those behaviors that are found to be intolerable without concern for cause and no attention given to active intervention.

As stated previously, the occurrence of challenging behaviors is often directly related to instructional variables. Munk and Repp (1994), in a review of the literature, determined that seven categories of instructional variables were associated with the occurrence of challenging behavior in students with developmental disabilities as reported in the studies reviewed. These seven variables included (a) student choice of task, (b) task variation, (c) pace of instruction, (d) high-probability tasks, (e) partial versus whole-task training, (f) task difficulty, and (g) multielement package. Studies by Dunlap and colleagues (1994) and Foster-Johnson, Ferro, and Dunlap (1994) support the relationship between instructional and curricular content and the occurrence of challenging behavior in students with (a) emotional and behavioral disorders and (b) mental retardation, respectively. In the following section, attention is devoted to how teachers and direct care staff can modify environmental and instructional variables once the functional assessment process has been completed and evidence exists that points to a causal relationship between these variables and the occurrence of challenging behavior.

Classroom and Instructional Modifications

Gold (1980) proclaimed "that a lack of learning in any particular situation should first be interpreted as a result of inappropriate or insufficient use of teaching strategy, rather than an inability on the part of the learner" (p. 3). This statement illustrates a philosophy that should be extended to include how teachers view the teaching and learning process in all learners, not merely learners with developmental disabilities. If teachers do not give adequate levels of attention to assessment issues, such as a student's learning history, development (in the case of young children), strengths, disability level, and level of individual supports needed, before developing and implementing instructional programs, they are at best approximating in their attempts to provide meaningful instruction to the students whom they teach. Many classroom and instructional modifications can be made once the teacher has determined a plausible function for the target behavior and a relationship between high rates of the target behavior and classroom or instructional activities.

Classroom Modifications

Teachers have been instructed for many years in how features of the classroom environment can influence learning. Challenging behavior can result due to lighting, seating arrangements, poor positioning for students who use wheelchairs or other adaptive equipment during their school day, room temperature, inappropriate amount of sensory stimulation, and overcrowding or density. Some specific classroom modifications aimed at supporting the diverse learning needs of students with developmental disabilities and minimizing the occurrence of challenging behavior include the physical arrangement and the classroom schedule.

Physical Arrangement

The teacher should attempt to provide as much organization and structure within the classroom as possible. The preschool or elementary classroom should include individual seating assignments, as well as areas for working individually and cooperatively in small groups, such as learning centers for academic, motor, music, and play activities. The classroom could be modified given the diverse and individual student characteristics. Similar modifications could be used in a secondary program, within either an inclusive setting or a self-contained classroom setting. Modifications are especially important for preschool and elementary-aged children. Paths for traveling in and about the classroom should be defined and clearly indicated (Stainback, Stainback, & Froyen, 1987). Classroom arrangement can assist in reducing potential problem behavior by providing students with consistent and clear cues as to where in the classroom certain activities are done. The teacher should be aware that the need many children have for physical structure in the classroom will vary according to age, developmental level, cognitive disability level, receptive and expressive communication skill levels, and individual learning style.

Classroom materials should be well organized for each student, based on individual learning needs and educational objectives, as well as for group activities. Materials should be stored in individual work areas or on storage shelves. Students should be instructed in organizational strategies that are appropriate for them in terms of locating specific materials and replacing materials upon completion of activities.

Classroom Schedule

One of the most basic and fundamental components of a successful classroom is the schedule. The teacher must develop a classroom schedule that will reinforce a pattern of consistency in the classroom setting for all students. This level of consistency must also be adhered to and reinforced by teacher aides, related service professionals, and classroom volunteers. Use of a classroom schedule will reinforce daily routines for students to follow and will make events and activities within the classroom more predictable. Table 21.1 is a schedule for a typical elementary classroom.

A classroom schedule is also vitally important to a special education teacher in a secondary special education program. Typically, teachers in these settings must not only serve in the role of teacher but also coordinate many other activities, including community-based instruction, community-based work experiences, job programs, and so forth. Table 21.2 illustrates what a classroom schedule might look like for a secondary special education program.

Instructional Modifications

In addition to modifying the physical environment of the classroom, teachers can also employ a variety of instructional modifications to promote optimal performance in individual students and reinforce desirable classroom behavior. DeLuke and Knoblock (1987) identified nine areas related to instruction that teachers could define for each student as a means of developing optimal instructional arrangements for each student: (a) learning style, (b) successful teaching/ response formats, (c) cognitive level/skills, (d) language/ communication skills, (e) rate of learning, (f) favorite or preferred activities, (g) effective reinforcers, (h) ability to function with peers, and (i) classroom structure/climate. By taking such variables into consideration for each student, the teacher develops a profile for each student in a class and the circumstances that will promote and enhance learning.

Specific strategies that teachers can use in their instruction of students with developmental disabilities to promote learning and often minimize the occurrence of challenging behavior are described in the following subsections.

Allowing Students To Choose Activities

Allowing students to choose their activities has been validated as an effective instructional practice in several studies with students with developmental disabilities and emotional–behavioral disorders (Dunlap et al., 1994; Foster-Johnson et al., 1994; Newton, Horner, & Ard, 1993). These investigations have used a variety of methods to determine students' choices, including the use of menus, demonstrated preference for activities or materials through student manip-

Table 21.1

Sample Schedule for Inclusionary Elementary Classroom

8:00–8:10	Transition from Bus/Toileting/Handwashing
8:10–8:20	Group Time "Greetings" "Calendar" Review Class Schedule
8:20–8:45	Individual Seat Work
8:45–9:45	Small Reading Groups Rotated with Individual Learning Centers with Modifications for Select Students
9:45–10:15	Music or Physical Education Integrated Physical Therapy on P.E. days
10:15–10:45	Group Instruction (Math), Followed by Individual Work with Modifications for Select Students
10:45–10:50	Restroom Transition Before Lunch
10:50–11:20	Lunch
11:20–11:30	Transition from Lunch to Classroom/Toileting and Handwashing Program with Select Students
11:30–11:50	Story Time (Teacher Reads Aloud to Students)
11:50–12:00	Transition to Next Activity
12:00–12:20	Individual Work (Language Arts) Integrated Speech–Language Therapy
12:20–12:50	Recess
12:50–1:20	Cooperative Learning Group Activities
1:20–2:00	Learning Centers (Science) with Modifications for Select Students
2:00–2:30	Arts/Crafts/Snack
2:30–2:45	Clean-up/Transition Work on Toileting and Handwashing Program with Select Students
2:50	Exit School

ulation, and degree of resistance to having materials removed. Problem behaviors were reduced and levels of task engagement increased when students were afforded greater opportunities for choice making in their daily routines. Teachers should attempt to offer more opportunities for choice into daily routines for students. Allowing students to have input into their own educational programs can contribute to self-determination and promote the likelihood of positive forms of behavior.

Table 21.2

Sample Schedule for Secondary Transition Classroom
for Students with Developmental Disabilities

8:00–8:15	Arrive School/Transition from Bus to Classroom
8:15–8:45	Home Room/Review Class and Individual Schedules
8:45–9:15	(Jason, Susan, Robert, Matt) Clean Cafeteria (Sam, Leland, Billy) Functional Reading
9:15–9:45	Group Morning Snack/Preparation and Cleanup
9:45–10:00	Self-Help Skills Training Program Brushing Teeth, Toileting, and Handwashing Programs
10:00–10:50	(Susan, Matt, Billy) Chorus (Jason, Robert, Sam, Leland) Physical Education (Integrated with typical peers)
10:50–11:00	Transition Back to Transition Classroom
11:00–11:50	(Jason, Susan, Robert, Matt) Functional Reading (Sam, Leland, Billy) Functional Math * Develop grocery store list * Budgeting using calculator
11:50–12:00	Transition to Lunch
12:00–12:30	Lunch (with typical peers)
12:30–12:45	Transition Back to Transition Classroom Self-Help Skills Training Program Brushing Teeth, Toileting, and Handwashing
12:45–1:00	Review Afternoon Schedule
1:00–1:50	(Jason, Susan) Integrated for Math
1:00–2:50	(Sam, Leland, Billy) Community Grocery Shopping (Robert, Matt) Purchasing "Dollar More" * Teacher/Teacher Aide
1:50	(Jason, Susan) Transported to Community-Based Jobs with Job Coaches at Job Sites
2:50–3:00	(Sam, Leland, Billy, Robert, Matt) * Return to School and Leave School for Home

Alternating Preferred and Unpreferred Activities

One method that can promote completion of unpreferred activities is to intersperse them with preferred activities throughout the student's daily schedule. Alternating activities can promote completion of less preferred tasks and serve as a built-in functional reinforcer within the schedule. If a student is aware that he or she will be able to participate next in a preferred activity, it will enhance the ability to tolerate and complete a less preferred activity. Foster-Johnson and colleagues (1994) have validated this method for reducing challenging behavior in students with developmental disabilities.

Teaching Students To Use a Schedule

An individual schedule should be developed for each student to help him or her understand the sequence of activities for the day. Teaching students to use individual schedules will promote independence in the student, reduce the student's dependence on teacher cues, and provide the student with concrete visual cues that will assist the student in discriminating what is expected in terms of performance. Mesibov, Schopler, and Hearsey (1994) recommended that schedules take on different forms depending on the developmental level of the child. They advocate that schedules (a) be developed based on students' individual needs and (b) consist of either objects, pictures, symbols, or a written form (i.e., a concrete-to-abstract continuum). For learners who are young, do not read, or have more severe disabilities, a schedule may take the form of objects or pictures. For learners who read, are older, and have mild or moderate disabilities, a schedule might use symbols or words. Mesibov and colleagues (1994) have used this system effectively with learners with autism, and others have examined the use of visual prompt systems with learners with mental retardation to assist in completion of work tasks (Wacker & Berg, 1984) and in teaching cooking skills (Johnson & Cuvo, 1981).

Matching the Level of Instruction to the Student

Students with developmental disabilities often experience frustration when confronted with tasks that are too difficult and that do not match their level of ability, resulting in challenging behavior. To prevent this from occurring, the teacher must determine the level of instruction appropriate for the student. This can be determined, for example, through a task analysis to determine the specific skills required to complete a task and assessment of the student's ability to perform each skill. Other forms of curriculum-based assessment can be used to determine a student's current level of functioning. If the teacher has doubts, it is better to start at a level that ensures the student's success and then proceed gradually to increased levels of difficulty. The teacher should also consider each student and his or her unique and diverse learning style. For example, if the student has moderate or severe levels of cognitive disability coupled with severe receptive language skills deficits, the student may respond best to instruction that is limited in terms of the number of verbal instructions, and that uses modeling, gestures, physical prompts, and built-in visual prompts. When developing instructional programs for students with developmental disabilities, one should always consider the individual's levels of receptive and expressive communication. Durand (1990) referred to this as determining the student's input and output modes. Translated to instruction, this implies that the teacher should predefine how instruction will be primarily delivered to the student (verbal prompts, gestural or other visual prompts, and/or verbal prompts paired with physical assistance). This often involves a series of trial-and-error approaches during the initial stages of instruction and takes into account the student's past learning history and the methods that have been most and least successful.

Delivering Clear and Consistent Instructional Cues

Teachers must attempt to use clear and consistent instructional cues to enhance the likelihood of successful performance of students with developmental disabilities. Once the instructional cues have been determined for teaching a specific task to a learner, they should be adhered to as closely as possible by all persons involved in teaching the student. Consistency will reinforce correct response patterns on the part of the learner and minimize confusion, errors, and levels of frustration. Individual learners, given their diverse learning styles and characteristics, need cues that are directed to their abilities and needs. It is advisable to build in cues that will promote independent performance as an ultimate goal. Independent performance by some students, however, requires a self-management format, which could involve the use of picture task analyses for completing a task, checklists, and various other devices to elicit student performance without teacher assistance.

Determining the Appropriate Length of Activities

The length of activities can often provoke problematic behavior in students with developmental disabilities. Time spent on activities should be determined by the student's age, developmental appropriateness, and functioning level. Shorter periods of time should be allotted for activities for young children and for students with severe levels of disability when attention spans and internal states are concerns. The teacher should use preinstructions or cues to communicate to the student the performance expectations and time allotted for the task prior to initiating the task.

Determining Reinforcers

The teacher should determine the activities and reinforcers most preferred by the student. If possible these should be built into the student's daily routine and integrated if possible throughout the day. Keeping reinforcement functional is preferable to introducing artificial reinforcers (Durand, 1990).

Varying Activities

Based on a review of relevant literature, Munk and Repp (1994) identified task variation as a major instructional variable related to lowering rates of challenging behavior in students with developmental disabilities. Teachers should plan varying activities across the day to prevent student boredom and frustration.

Making Tasks Functional and Relevant to the Student

The functionality and relevance of tasks can greatly influence the behavior of some students. If tasks are directed around student interests and strengths, student behavior may be positively influenced. If students perceive that there is little relevance to the tasks in which they are engaged, the risks of problematic behavior and task disengagement are greater.

Planning for Transitions

Facilitating effective and smooth transitions between activities is often a challenging task for the teacher. If transitions are not well planned, they can contribute to problematic behavior. Suggestions for facilitating smooth and effective transitions include preinstructing students with appropriate cues to announce the transition and teacher expectations during the transition. The teacher should also prepare in advance for potential trouble spots, structure transitions, and maintain consistency across transitions. The routine for transitions should be kept as similar as possible throughout the day.

Summary

The main purpose of this chapter has been to provide an overview of effective instructional practices for reducing challenging behavior in students with developmental disabilities. The intent of this chapter is not to imply that classroom and instructional factors always serve to provoke challenging behaviors in students; however, these variables above all others are most applicable to the classroom teacher or direct care staff person and can be readily modified in most cases to promote positive behavioral outcomes for students. It is important for teachers and staff to understand the importance and interconnectedness of assessment and intervention.

Development of instructional programs should take into consideration variables that are specific to the individual student, including student strengths, learning style, level of instruction needed, and optimal learning conditions needed. Teachers and other staff members need to realize that they are facilitators of learning, and that student behaviors often are directly related to the instructional activities and methods employed. Students with developmental disabilities represent a diverse group of learners and, therefore, require the use of a variety of effective instructional practices to facilitate optimal learning outcomes.

Many of the behaviors encountered in the classroom can be minimized, and possibly prevented, if attention is given to the information presented in this chapter. The methods described represent best and effective, student-centered practices and illustrate an "active teaching" philosophy. The use of these methods will not replace all forms of intervention for challenging behavior in all students; however, they represent approaches that should be explored and exhausted before more intrusive procedures are even considered.

QUESTIONS

1. Describe the purpose of functional assessment in determining the function(s) of challenging behavior and the causal factors associated with the target behavior.

2. Identify and describe the typical components of a functional assessment.

3. What is the relationship between classroom and instructional variables and the occurrence of problematic behavior in some students with developmental disabilities?

4. Identify best and effective practices for modifying the classroom environment to promote positive behavior in students.

5. Describe some suggested methods identified as effective practices that teachers can use to modify instruction to promote positive behavior in students.

References

Axelrod, S., Moyer, L., & Berry, B. (1990). Why teachers do not use behavior modification procedures. *Journal of Educational and Psychological Consultation, 1,* 309–320.

Carr, E. G. (1977). The motivation of self-injurious behavior: A review of some hypotheses. *Psychological Bulletin, 84,* 800–816.

Carr, E. G., & Durand, V. M. (1985). The social-communication basis of severe behavior problems in children. In S. Reiss & R. R. Bootzin (Eds.), *Theoretical issues in behavior therapy* (pp. 219–254). New York: Academic Press.

DeLuke, S. V., & Knoblock, P. (1987). Teacher behavior as preventive discipline. *Teaching Exceptional Children, 16,* 18–24.

Dunlap, G., DePerczel, M., Clarke, S., Wilson, D., Wright, S., White, R., & Gomez, A. (1994). Choice making to promote adaptive behavior for students with emotional and behavioral challenges. *Journal of Applied Behavior Analysis, 27,* 505–518.

Durand, V. M. (1990). *Severe behavior problems: A functional communication training approach.* New York: Guilford Press.

Evans, E. D., & Richardson, R. C. (1995). Corporal punishment: What teachers should know. *Teaching Exceptional Children, 27,* 33–36.

Foster-Johnson, L., Ferro, J., & Dunlap, G. (1994). Preferred curricular activities and reduced problem behaviors in students with intellectual disabilities. *Journal of Applied Behavior Analysis, 27,* 493–504.

Gold, M. (1980). *Did I say that?* Champaign, IL: Research Press.

Hummel, L. J., & Prizant, B. M. (1993). A socioemotional perspective for understanding social difficulties of school-age children with language disorders. *Language, Speech, and Hearing Services in Schools, 24,* 216–224.

Johnson, B., & Cuvo, A. (1981). Teaching mentally retarded students to cook. *Behavior Modification, 5,* 187–202.

Mace, F. C., Lalli, J. S., & Pinter-Lalli, E. (1991). Functional analysis and treatment of aberrant behavior. *Research in Developmental Disabilities, 12,* 155–180.

Mesibov, G. B., Schopler, E., & Hearsey, K. A. (1994). Structured teaching. In E. Schopler & G. B. Mesibov (Eds.), *Behavioral issues in autism* (pp. 195–207). New York: Plenum Press.

Munk, D. D., & Repp, A. C. (1994). The relationship between instructional variables and problem behavior: A review. *Exceptional Children, 60,* 390–401.

Newton, J. S., Horner, R. H., & Ard, W. R. (1993). Validating predicted activity preferences of individuals with severe disabilities. *Journal of Applied Behavior Analysis, 26,* 239–245.

Reichle, J., & Johnson, S. S. (1993). Replacing challenging behavior: The role of communication intervention. *Topics in Language Disorders, 13,* 61–76.

Reichle, J., & Wacker, D. P. (1993). *Communicative alternatives to challenging behavior: Integrating functional assessment and intervention strategies.* Baltimore: Brookes.

Stainback, W., Stainback, S., & Froyen, L. (1987). Structuring the classroom to prevent disruptive behavior. *Teaching Exceptional Children, 16,* 12–16.

Touchette, P. E., MacDonald, R. F., & Langer, S. (1985). A scatter plot for identifying stimulus control of problem behavior. *Journal of Applied Behavior Analysis, 18,* 343–351.

Wacker, D. P., & Berg, W. K. (1984). Training adolescents with severe handicaps to set up job tasks independently using picture prompts. *Analysis and Intervention in Developmental Disabilities, 4,* 353–366.

Family Involvement and Community Attitudes

SECTION VI

Best Practices

Literature and practice has come to accept that parent and family involvement is a best practice in the field of developmental disabilities. The word involvement takes on varied meaning for different families, but the opportunity for such involvement is essential to the education and training of the person with developmental disabilities. This involvement must not be limited to the development of the Individualized Education Program or other legal requirements, but also must extend into nonmandated practices.

The foundation of such practices rests on (a) the understanding of the impact of having a child with a disability on a family and (b) the recognition of both the needs and the strengths that such families have. Effective professionals provide families meaningful access to information, training, and participation in the system.

The role of the family whose children with developmental disabilities are included in the general education classrooms has not been fully defined. Further, the roles and responsibilities of professionals in such settings are not clear. However, the attitudes of all professionals and members of the community are critical to the present and future success of individuals with developmental disabilities.

This Section of the Book

Section VI provides, in Chapter 22, a model for understanding parents and families based on the critical factors that influence their functioning and interaction with professionals. This discussion provides a set of promising practices that gives professionals the understanding to move toward empowering families, as discussed in Chapter 23, so that they become partners with professionals. Empowerment is the step that goes beyond understanding families to allowing them to participate in the educational process. The final chapter of this section, Chapter 24, focuses on changing attitudes of professionals and community members.

Lack of involvement and empowerment of families and inappropriate attitudes toward individuals are all barriers to the success of students and adults with developmental disabilities. Each of the chapters in Section VI addresses promising practices that, upon implementation, would lead to breaking barriers.

A Multidimensional Model for Understanding and Working with Parents and Families

CHAPTER 22

Alan Hilton

Learning Outcomes

After reading this chapter, you should be able to

■ Understand the uniqueness of parents and families of children with developmental disabilities.

■ Explain the critical factors that impact parents and families of children with developmental disabilities.

■ Define the role of the professional in working with families of children who have developmental disabilities.

TERMS

The following terms are important for the understanding of this chapter:

Coping: The actions people take to avoid or reduce stressful events in their lives.

Grieving process: A set of unique yet anticipated reactions to parenting a child with developmental disabilities.

Personal strengths: The knowledge, skills, experiences, and attitudes that are internal to a parent and family members that help in coping.

Stress: Reactions to life's pressures, demands, and/or crises that result in a pattern of physiological and psychological reactions.

Support systems: The groups or individuals within the family or community who help parents cope.

Introduction

There is little debate about the importance and potential benefits of involving families in the education of students with disabilities. Family involvement has been consistently and continually mentioned in the discussions of best practices for students with developmental disabilities (Bates, Renzaglia, & Wehman, 1981; Bellamy & Wilcox, 1980; Hilton, Faught, & Hagan, 1984; Snell, 1988; Williams, Fox, Thousand, & Fox, 1990). Families should have the opportunity to play a role in virtually all aspects of the education of students with disabilities, but for this to take place educators must work directly with parents. In some cases, however, teachers find such collaboration a difficult task (Hilton & Henderson, 1993). Parents present wide variance in their reactions to the identification of a child as having a disability (Blacher, 1984; Mary, 1990; Mullins, 1987); handling of the stress of parenting (Hanline, 1991); personal needs

(Harris & McHale, 1989) and philosophies (Erin, Rudin, & Njoroge, 1991; Frey, Greenberg, & Fewell, 1989); reactions to and dealings with professionals (Roos, 1978; Wilgosh, Waggoner, & Adams, 1988); methods of coping and use of other personal strengths (Frey et al., 1989; Meyer & Bailey, 1993); and use of support systems. This variance makes each parent and family unique in how they discuss their experiences (Blacher, 1984; Mary, 1990; Mullins, 1987) and how they interact with the educational community. These differences often make it difficult for professionals to understand the needs of families and to work effectively with parents (Spidel, 1995). Allen and Affleck (1985) suggested that this uniqueness requires professionals to deal with each parent individually, in what might be viewed as a "tabla raza" approach.

Although dealing with families without a framework or model for understanding may be quite attractive, it is not the most effective approach from the standpoint of efficient use of time for parents or professionals. Further, if such an approach is used in a time-limited relationship, such as that typical of parent–teacher interactions, this approach leaves open the possible omission of important issues. Although models that explain family coping (Knafl & Deatrick, 1987) and grief (Kubler-Ross, 1969) have been put forth for use when dealing with families, these models do not form an integrated tool that will help the professional (and the parent) understand the multidimensional nature of the needs of the family. Meyer and Bailey (1993) urged professionals to take a comprehensive view of the child and the family, considering both the strengths and the limitations that are present. This approach encourages the recognition of family strengths, individuality, and coping abilities.

The purposes of this chapter are to define the influences that impact family members' interactions with professionals and to provide a framework for understanding parents. This framework or model is presented graphically to further understanding.

Critical Factors Influencing Parent and Family Functioning

The goal of parents and families of children with disabilities to function successfully seems to be essential to the progress and ultimate success of the child in school and life. This goal is often referred to as coping or adjustment. Patterson and McCubbin (1983) identified three patterns of parent coping that apply to families of children with developmental disabilities. These are maintaining family integration, cooperation, and optimism; developing and maintaining social support, self-esteem, and physiological stability; and understanding the condition or syndrome. Parents are able to achieve these goals by using their personal strengths and support systems.

Another approach to understanding families of children who have disabilities has been to examine parents' coping strategies. Coping is directly related to how stress is dealt with. Researchers have not looked at how to cope with the child, but at how the parent copes with the stress associated with the identification of and the living with a child with disabilities. Lazarus and Folkman (1984) argued that personal resources impact coping with stress. They proposed five categories of coping resources: social networks, problem-solving skills, general and specific beliefs, utilitarian resources, and health/energy/morale. Later research found that these categories interrelate and interact (e.g., Dunst, Trivette, & Cross, 1986; Frey et al., 1989) and that stress must be included in any multidimensional model for understanding parents with disabilities (Frey et al., 1989). The role of the influential factors is briefly examined in the following subsections.

Personal Strengths

According to Friedrich, Wilturner, and Cohen (1985), parents' ways of coping with stress and the emotional reactions related to having children with developmental disabilities has a relationship with the parents' abilities to assess the sources of stress and mobilize personal strengths and other resources. Parents' personal strengths play a major role in the development of family strengths. Psychological well-being (Lambie & Daniels-Mohring, 1993) and capacity to interact with the outside world (Imber-Black, 1986) have been identified as essential for parents in order to develop and maintain contact with needed support systems. Ronnau and Poertner (1993) pointed out that more and more professionals are recognizing the importance of identifying strengths as a prominent component of helping parents and families. This approach opposes the more traditional outlook of examining only weaknesses. Potential family strengths can be categorized in the following manner: family structure and interaction; culture and ethnicity; family development and change; and family functions. Personal strengths may be viewed as the inner knowledge, skills, experiences, attitudes, and beliefs with which an individual enters the parenting process. Each of these potential strength areas can play a positive or a negative role in the coping process. For example, depending on the parents' religious and cultural values, they may view a child with developmental disabilities as a gift or a punishment (Knafl & Deatrick, 1987; Mary, 1990).

Garber (1992) discussed a variety of personal strengths that help parents cope. These include good physical health, problem-solving skills, and positive perception. Karpel (1986) identified a slightly different list of essential personal resources: self-respect, protectiveness, tolerance, affection, flexibility, hope, and family pride. Each of these characteristics is influenced by other factors. For example, good physical health requires proper food intake, limited or no intake of alcohol and drugs, exercise, and so forth.

One of the key aspects of a family's ability to cope with the stress and feelings of loss associated with having a child with disabilities involves the strengths possessed by each individual family member. As pointed out by Meyer and Bailey (1993), coping is a multifaceted concept and varies from parent to parent. For example, Newman (1980) found two primary styles of coping, both of which were effective for specific parents: (a) becoming a committed part of a team attempting to solve problems presented by the child and (b) becoming distant and opting out of the process.

Economic stability is a critical issue influenced by both parents whether or not they reside together. A personal strength is the ability to contribute to the family's economic status (Paul, Porter, & Falk, 1993). Associated with income is the ability to attain health insurance, which is often essential to the family with a child who has disabilities. Higher income families also can obtain respite care, other external supports, and out-of-home activities for the children (Stoneman, Brody, Davis, Crapps, & Malone, 1991) at levels not available to poorer families.

Self-perceived competence as a parent is an important personal strength. Mothers who have increased perceived competence in the experience of parenting a child with developmental disabilities often experience less stress and fewer bouts with self-doubt and guilt. However, these perceptions may change with the development of the child (Haldey & Hanzlik, 1990). Related to this concept are the cultural values of the parent and the family. Smith (1993) pointed out that some cultures view disabilities as ordained by fate, providing the parent with the goal of attaining harmony with nature. A parent possessing cultural values such as these does not experience the same emotional reactions and causes of stress as parents who view disabilities differently.

Parents can improve their personal strengths through training and personal growth activities (e.g., reading). Using personal strengths enables a parent to access supports available in the family and the community. Such strengths are critical to reducing stress and effective parenting.

Support Systems

Another issue that differentiates parents' ability to cope with the challenges of raising a child with disabilities is their ability to develop and maintain support systems. The level of family adjustment often reflects the support received from relatives and the use of available community services (Jaffe, 1991). The ability to use support systems may be limited by personal strengths (e.g., poor communication skills, distrust of strangers); however, the use of available support systems may make up for these limitations.

Mothers and fathers within the same family often have different needs for support (Beckman, 1991). Mothers tend to report higher needs than fathers for support systems (Simeonsson & Simeonsson, 1993). However, support in general—specifically respite care—has been shown to be essential for families with children who have developmental disabilities (Rimmerman, 1989). Mothers often need respite and special relief (Garber, 1992). Support can come from the family or the community. Relief can come from individuals or groups trained to help people who need support, or from less formal sources.

Family Resources

The immediate family is often considered a key to the individual parent's coping ability. Spouses and the child's siblings can play important supportive roles. It has been found that siblings vary greatly from child to child and family to family in their reactions and the support they offer (Powell

& Ogle, 1985). Today single-parent status does not necessarily constitute a dysfunctional family (Thomas, 1993); however, it may result in family disorganization, role confusion, and reduced available financial resources. (Lambie & Daniels-Mohring, 1993).

The extended family also can be of value in providing support. Smith (1993) pointed out that, in some cultures, extended and multiple families live in one household and collaborate in caregiving and parenting functions. However, in some cases the extended family may have rejected the child with disabilities (Smith, 1993).

Each family member sometimes provides support and at other times provides a measure of stress to the family. Siblings, for example, often provide support for the parent in child-rearing or supervision activities (Stoneman et al., 1991); however, during adolescence, these same siblings often experience feelings of grief that can add stress to the family. Beyond the additional demands placed on the family, the child with disabilities often plays a positive role in the family. Many parents have reported that the presence of a child with developmental disabilities strengthens the family unit (Hanline, 1991; Spidel, 1995), and others have felt that the child improved their quality of life (Hanline, 1991).

A number of variables must be addressed in attempting to understand the needs of the family. Thomas (1993) indicated that, to understand African American families (and probably all families), these variables include socioeconomic status, family structure, and personal support. Gartner, Lipsky, and Turnbull (1991) found that cultural, ethnic, and socioeconomic backgrounds affect interactions among family members and society. Tashima (1981) found that Asian families tend to underutilize mental health services. Such cultural factors may result in reduced levels of support and increased stress on the parent.

The variability in familial support is as wide as the structures of families today. Cultures view the family in different manners. In the Chinese and other Asian cultures, the family is a tightly knit group that is clearly separate from the rest of the community. The tight kinship relationships are such that crisis is handled by the immediate and extended family. Chinese families with children with disabilities tend to look inward to the family rather than outward for community resources (Wang, 1993). Similarly, kinship has a historical importance within the African American culture. However, in the African American culture, extended families tend to go beyond the traditional to include nonblood extended families, which also provide support (Thomas, 1993).

Financial stability can affect the need for family support by individual parents (Bush & Peters, 1979; Gartner et al., 1991; Paul et al., 1993). Employment also may reduce the need to deal with additional professional and social service agencies, because the ability to gain medical treatment for the child and respite care often are related to employment.

Community Resources

Beyond the family, numerous potential community-based resources exist from which parents of a child with developmental disabilities may gain support. Kazak and Wilcox (1984) found that parental subsystems comprising friends, day-care providers, babysitters, and professionals provided essential assistance and support to these parents.

Webb-Mitchell (1993) pointed out the importance that religion and the religious community can play in supporting the family with a child who has disabilities. In some cultures, such as the African American, the church is a major source of social support (Thomas, 1993). Further, the church often serves as crisis support, acts as a surrogate family when needed, provides role models for siblings, and conveys feelings of hope and the capacity to survive (Boyd-Franklin, 1989).

Donovan (1988) found that human service professionals and formal programs play a critical role in successful maternal adaption to a child with disabilities, and this support was reported to be especially important during the child's adolescence. Simeonsson and Simeonsson (1993) pointed out that parents' needs vary at different times in a family's development. Professionals are useful to the family to ensure that information and services are accessible. Seeking external assistance from professionals and others has been reported as a critical coping skill (Nadler, Lewinstein, & Rahav, 1991). Most family resource programs have their roots in parent information and educational systems (Paul et al., 1993). Increasingly, programs are moving toward family-centered approaches. Beyond this, the provision of professional respite care has been shown to reduce maternal stress. Respite was found to be especially effective when families also took advantage of other support services, such as family counseling and training (Rimmerman, 1989).

One area often overlooked by the traditional professional community is that of alternative medicine and healers. These professionals can provide an important source of support within some minority communities (Smith, 1993).

Differences in perceptions of the usefulness of professionals are affected by cultural values. For example, Sontag and Schacht (1994) found that Anglo parents, more often than Hispanic and American Indian parents, felt that professionals did not listen to them. On the other hand, the authors found that Hispanic and American Indian parents reported greater need to receive information about how to obtain services than did Anglo parents. It is also critical for professionals to understand what the family hopes to achieve and develop a trusting relationship based on these goals (Winton & Bailey, 1993). If this does not occur, parents reduce the use of valuable resources.

Professionals who assess the strengths of parents and the family are better able to effectively work with the family. This is achieved by assessing the family characteristics, culture and ethnicity, interactions within the family, family life cycle, and the needs of the family members (Ronnau & Poertner, 1993).

Other Parents and Disability Groups

Parents and families of children with disabilities often find support and direction from other parents of children with developmental disabilities (Mayer, 1994). Although American Indian and Hispanic parents apparently are less likely to provide this type of support than Anglo parents (Sontag & Schacht, 1994), all families may be able to find some level of support from other parents.

Extensions of parents helping parents are groups formed for the specific purpose of helping parents of children with disabilities. These groups may be formal or informal. Examples include local chapters of the Arc and the National Society for Autistic Children.

Stress

Although all parents and families experience stress during the parenting process, increased stress has been associated with having a child with disabilities within a family (Beckman, 1991; Guralnick & Bricker, 1987; Jaffe, 1991; Meyer & Bailey, 1993). Stress by itself does not cause families to be dysfunctional, and a family with a child with disabilities should not be viewed as a family with a deficit (Donovan, 1988; Garber, 1992). However, increased stress should be understood as normal in the life of the parent of a child with developmental disabilities and as being present at every stage of the family's life cycle (Lambie & Daniels-Mohring, 1993). Parents' use of interpersonal and intrapersonal resources works to buffer stress (Friedrich et al., 1985).

Stress seems to occur from a variety of sources. Some sources include those associated with extensive amounts of time spent on daily care and/or long or intense medical care needs (Beckman & Pokorni, 1988; McDonald, Kysela, & Reddon, 1988; Spidel, 1995), increased parental responsibilities (Waggoner & Wilgosh, 1990), increased financial responsibilities (McDonald et al., 1987), dealing with health care and educational professionals (Kroth, 1987; Meyer & Bailey, 1993; Turnbull, 1983; Waggoner & Wilgosh, 1990), loss of control of decision making (Harrison, 1983; Meyer & Bailey, 1993), social network contradictions (Lambie & Daniels-Mohring, 1993), cultural demands and confusions (Lambie & Daniels-Mohring, 1993), unmet needs or lack of services (Garber, 1992; Mayer, 1994), transitions and critical events (Hanline, 1991; Lambie & Daniels-Mohring, 1993), the deficits of the individual child (Donovan, 1988; Lambie & Daniels-Mohring, 1993), and the demands of other family members (Lambie & Daniels-Mohring, 1993).

Dyson and Fewell (1986) found that parents of children with developmental disabilities who are able to increase social support experienced reduced levels of stress. Rimmerman (1989) pointed out that families receiving respite care experienced significant reductions in levels of stress and burnout. Stress seems to have more impact when support systems are reduced. For example, Salisbury (1987) found that single mothers experienced increased stress due to reduced support in the family. Mothers of preterm babies who experienced elevated levels of stress were found to have less support than mothers who experienced lower levels of stress (Beckman, Pokorni, Maza, & Blazer-Martin, 1987; Intagliata & Doyle, 1984). Further, mothers and fathers reported differences in their perceptions of the amount and type of stress they experienced (Beckman, 1991).

The area of parent–professional interactions is especially important as a source of parental stress. Professionals may not always view family involvement with the importance as they do direct intervention with the child (Hilton & Henderson, 1993; Smith, 1993). This may lead to resistance and lack of effort on the part of professionals to provide needed information and support, which in turn may increase parental stress and even hostility. Other issues may also add to parental stress, including a professional's lack of knowledge, respect, and/or appreciation for family values and cultural differences (Smith, 1993). On the other hand, attempting to help parents who do not perceive the need for help may increase the levels of stress (Affleck, Tennen, Rowe, Roscher, & Walker, 1989; Meyer & Bailey, 1993). Paul et al. (1993) pointed out the importance of professionals being sensitive to the feelings of the family. To be successful, professionals need to recognize unique family values, explain information in an understandable manner, make the complex technical vocabulary understandable, and attempt to affirm parents' value systems. Otherwise, families often experience added levels of stress. Expectations of the school professionals may run counter to cultural and behavioral expectations of parents of minority students, thus causing friction (Ogbu, 1985).

The results of this stress may include changes in family relationships (McDonald et al., 1987), emotional problems for the parent (Gowen, Johnson-Martin, Goldman, & Appelbaum, 1989; Nadler et al., 1991), poor communication and possible conflict with professionals (Gargiulo & Graves, 1991; Hancock, Wilgosh, & McDonald, 1990), changes in belief systems (Erin et al., 1991), and a sense of loss of competence and/or self-esteem (Hanline, 1991). All of these results may have a negative impact on the child with developmental disabilities.

Stress has been found to affect different family members in varying manners (e.g., Beckman, 1991; Goldberg, Marcovitch, MacGregor & Lojklasedk, 1986; Jaffe, 1991). Typically, however, stress does not lead to distressed or dysfunctional families (Beckman, 1991) or have an adverse impact on individual family members (Beavers, Hampson, Hulgus, & Beavers, 1986). A parent's or family's ability to handle stress is also impacted by the number of stressful events or challenges that occur at once. Resources for coping may become depleted, limiting the parent's or family's ability to handle additional change or stressful events (McCubbin & Patterson, 1981). Personal strengths (coping resources and styles) and support systems often mediate the effects of stress (Frey et al., 1989).

Reactions/Grieving

The identification of a child as having a developmental disability can be a traumatic event to parents. Often parents' lives are changed from that point on (Gowen et al., 1989). These changes may be significant. It has been pointed out that having a child with disabilities often has significant financial and emotional impacts (Meyer and Bailey, 1993; Mullins, 1987). Although parents are clearly not a homogeneous group, studies have continually identified patterns of reactions that occur at the birth or identification of a child with disabilities (Blacher, 1984; Simeonsson & Simeonsson, 1993). These feelings relate to grieving or loss of the "perfect child" (Solnit & Stark, 1961) and/or the loss of dreams (Gargiulo, 1985). Olshansky (1962) characterized this process as the "chronic sorrow syndrome." Jaffe (1991), like others, pointed out that parents experience feelings of guilt, anger, disappointment, withdrawal, sadness, and denial early in the process, and later depression, helplessness, ambivalence, and burden. These feelings and added responsibilities continue for a lifetime (Hanline, 1991; Olshansky, 1962; Spidel, 1995). Such feelings of loss occur regardless of children's ages at identification of the disabilities and across levels of severity of the disabilities (Barsch, 1968; Featherstone, 1981). It does appear, however, that the intensity of the reactions may vary depending on the child's age and severity level (Gargiulo, 1985; Mandell & Fiscus, 1981; Mullins, 1987). The severity of the child's condition may increase the level of stress parents experience (Donovan, 1988).

Specific factors noted in the literature seem to influence parental reactions (see Blacher, 1984, for a summary). These include socioeconomic status, support services, physician attitude and procedures, presence of other children and spouse in the home, prior information, cultural and ethnic values, availability of support systems, religion, other handicapped children in the family, and family functioning (Blacher, 1984; Lambie & Daniels-Mohring, 1993; Mary, 1990). Most of these factors are discussed in the earlier section of this chapter on personal strengths.

Early work with parents of children with disabilities focused on the grieving process. Kubler-Ross' (1969) work has become the basis for the currently accepted model used to explain parental reactions and overt behavior toward professionals. Kubler-Ross provided a five-stage model in which an individual worked from denial through anger, bargaining, and depression until reaching acceptance. Most discussions published since use somewhat different language to explain the stages of grief, but many authors have merely expanded on the original stages proposed by Kubler-Ross (1969). For example, Gargiulo (1985) proposed a model with 10 stages organized into three phases. Like other explanations of grieving, the parent(s) work through stages until they can accept or resolve the grief. Allen and Affleck (1985) pointed out that these stages are temporally sequenced steps that parents go through.

The basic concepts of Kubler-Ross' (1969) model are used pervasively in the training of special educators, counselors, and health care professionals (e.g., Spidel, 1995). These individuals in turn use the model to help parents to understand what they are experiencing. The model incorporates the following assumptions: parents go through all stages; parents move from one stage to another in a sequential pattern; this sequential movement is an orderly process; the parents' goal, often with the guidance of the professional, is to reach acceptance and get on with their lives; failure to progress at a reasonable rate or to get past a stage indicates a problem in the parent's life or that one specific feeling has not been resolved; and these feelings of grief are somewhat abnormal, destructive to the family, and need resolution (Anderson, 1971; Blacher, 1984; Bryant, 1971; Gallagher, 1956). These assumptions tend to flavor both the parents' and the professionals' view of the grieving process. Often the nature and direction of the interventions sought by parents and/or selected by professionals are based on these assumptions.

Weaknesses in the present models used for understanding grieving have been identified in the literature (i.e., Allen & Affleck, 1985; Blacher, 1984; Featherstone, 1981; Mary, 1990). Allen and Affleck (1985) pointed out a number of weaknesses with the stage model, including its inability to handle the variety, intensity, and direction of change that parents report. Further, many of the assumptions of the models, stated above, actually are unproven based on parental reports and interviews (i.e., Blacher, 1984; Featherstone, 1981; Mullins, 1987). The literature is clear that parents go through the process at different rates, they sometimes return to specific feelings, these feelings return during times of stress, feelings of loss go on for the life of the parents, and acceptance is never completely reached (Blacher, 1984; Mullins, 1987; Searl, 1978). Currently used models have difficulty in explaining such differences (Blacher, 1984; Mary, 1990) and do not provide for the effects of social and support relationships in modifying the adjustment of families (Allen & Affleck, 1985; Frey et al., 1989).

Multidimensional Model for Understanding Parents

The criticisms of the current models lent direction for the construction of a new model, which has been shown to be effective in gaining understanding and working effectively with parents and families of students with developmental disabilities. As discussed previously, individual parents of children with disabilities experience different feelings at different times (see Blacher, 1984), enter the process with differing feelings and abilities to cope, continue to experience feelings of grief or loss for extensive periods of time, and express that these feelings return during periods of stress (see Turnbull & Turnbull, 1985, for examples; Mullins, 1987, for a discussion). Taking these factors into consideration, it seems difficult to explain parental grieving using a linear stages model having a beginning and an end. Although some individuals go through specific stages and ultimately reach resolution, this model does not match or explain what parents as a group actually experience.

The model presented in this chapter is multidimensional in nature; individual in orientation; flexible enough to handle the criticisms of other models, which in part were noted earlier; and functional in that it organizes interventions and approaches used by professionals.

A Graphic View

Instead of a linear stages model, the one proposed here views the process of understanding parents as being circular in nature. One way to represent this graphically is by using concentric circles.[1] The inner circle represents the individual parent's understandings, skills, and strengths, including personality factors such as personal philosophy about disabilities, internal ability to handle stress, and feelings concerning personal control. These factors are influenced by previous experiences such as exposure to persons with disabilities, religion, upbringing, and education. The size of this inner circle is determined by the level or extent at which these factors are in place within the individual.

On the outer circle, the parent's feelings associated with loss are located. These feelings form a circle or ring that is accessible to the individual. The variety of feelings available (i.e., experienced) is limited only by the individual. The literature is robust with the most commonly experienced feelings. For the purpose of continuity of this discussion, the

---

[1]The use of concentric circles has evolved out of practice and is only one manner to present the model. Other circular representations have been used, and some parents feel more comfortable with other forms to express their experience. One alternative is a bicycle wheel with the hub being the personal strengths and the tire area being the emotional reactions. Another is a solar system with the personal strengths being the sun and the emotions being the planets in their orbits. The method of representing the dimensions of the model are less important than the concepts presented. A graphic representation is often helpful to both parents and professionals to gain clearer communication.

majority of feelings offered in Gargiulo's (1985) work are included. Because resolution is never reached, this feeling is omitted, whereas adaptation and adjustment are not placed on the circumference of the outer circle but are goals for the parent, which are discussed later.

Initial Identification

It is important to recognize that individual parents possess a set of skills, understandings, and strengths that are in place at the time their child is identified as having a disability. In terms of the model, this is the center circle. The emotions or feelings brought on by identification of a child as having a disability are displayed on the outer circle. At the initial identification of the child as having a disability, the outer circle is relatively small in diameter. The visual representation of this state is provided in Figure 22.1.

The feelings that are determined by the parent's personal emotional makeup are close to each other and to the center circle. Each of the feelings is readily accessible. In fact, parents often report that they are deluged with emotion. This occurs in some cases to the extent of causing the individual to be inhibited from action. The period of time that such an emotional impact lasts varies based on a number of factors determined in part by past experience, starting probably in early childhood, and the person's current state of mental and physical health (Rowitz, 1989). Also included are support provided from professionals, support groups, peers, and family members; improved strategies to cope with stress; the obtaining of information and understanding concerning the child's condition and prognosis; understanding of the personal feelings the parent is experiencing; and a number of aspects relating to the stability of the current environment, including personal health, siblings, the effect of grieving on other family members, and so on.

The Coping/Adaptation Process

As these aspects of a parent's life come into play, access to the feelings related to loss becomes less rapid. In terms of the

model, the circle's circumference becomes larger. It then takes longer for a person to access the feelings. The circle shown in Figure 22.2 represents such a state.

With time, the development of support systems, the use of personal strengths, and the growth of understanding by the parent, the outside circle continues to expand. More and more a parent is able to adapt, order, and systematize his or her life.

The diameter of the circle varies, depending on what experience, support, and understanding parents have obtained and their personalities. Examples of such support and understanding include grandparents providing babysitting, or a state agency providing respite care, or the gathering of information concerning the etiology of the child's disability. Although the importance of such support and understanding has been well recognized (Allen & Affleck, 1985; Hanline, 1991), such factors have not been incorporated into earlier models. The diameter of the outside circle will change depending upon how the person is adapting to the feeling associated with loss and the reduction or addition of stress.

The Impact of Stress

As discussed, parents of children with disabilities, like all parents, experience stressful feelings related to family, employment, health, and financial difficulties (Gallagher, Beckman, & Cross, 1983; Gowen et al., 1989). Additionally, however, they feel stress relating to parenting a child with disabilities, including increased demands from providing care, finding child care, and conflicts with professionals (Gallagher et al., 1983). Stress from the environment plays a definite role as a parent experiences the grieving process. It has been noted that there are predictable periodic times of stress that occur within families containing children with developmental disabilities (Flynt & Wood, 1989). In relation to the model, stress enhances an individual's access to feelings. This effect seems to be manifested in two manners. The first is that stress can undo many of the effects of support, understanding, and adjustment. In this case, for a period of time,

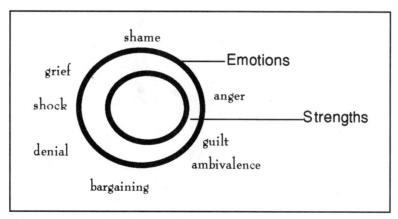

Figure 22.1. Initial identification.

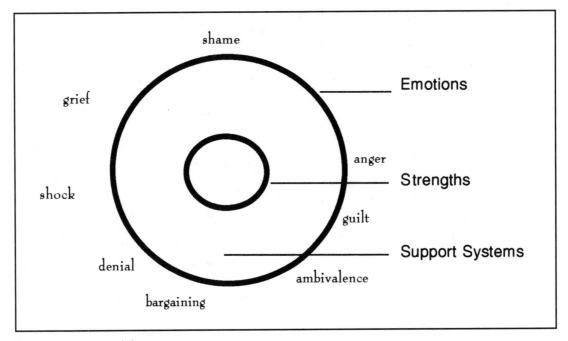

Figure 22.2. Coping/adaptation.

the parent returns to a state in which a variety of feelings, such as lack of control, emotional instability, and emotional devastation, rapidly enter his or her life. Usually this state of emotional deluge is transient and the parent returns to a state of emotional stability similar to that prior to the onset of the stress. In other words, support systems and the individual coping skills reduce the impact of the stress. In terms of the model, the circle returns to a state similar to Figure 22.1.

The second manner in which a parent may be affected by stress is that the inner circle becomes offset within the outer circle. That is, the parent under stress gravitates toward a certain feeling or groups of feelings. A prime example is the parent who, under stress, becomes angry over a variety of activities, such as the Individualized Education Program process and relations with school personnel, for a period of time. Figure 22.3 demonstrates the movement of the inner circle toward one side of the outer circle, indicating that the

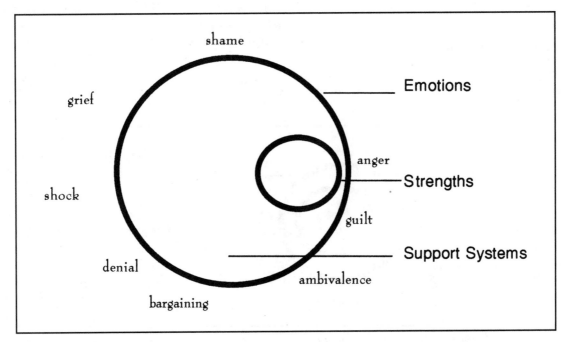

Figure 22.3. The impact of stress.

feelings located on that side of the circle are more accessible to the parent.

Individual professionals and/or specific settings may cause unusual stress for a parent, causing the parent to focus on one set of feelings when dealing with that person or in that place. When a parent's feelings are off center, special steps, which may include seeking professional assistance, may be necessary to help the parent return to a more centered set of feelings. Sometimes parents choose to remain in this state for periods of time. Gradually, however, support systems and the passage of time help remove or lessen the impact of stress. The parent then moves back to a more centered state. An example might be found at the time of the child's transition from the safety of elementary school to the unknowns of middle school. Feelings of fear may become very accessible until questions and concerns are resolved. The exact feelings will vary depending on the parent's personality and background.

Assumptions of the Multidimensional Model

A set of assumptions, which differ from those of the linear models, follow from the acceptance of this multidimensional model. A basic understanding that the model is based on and demonstrates is that grieving is an ongoing process. Parents and family members experience feelings related to grief and loss, often for long periods of time, and sometimes for a lifetime. Grieving is not only a healthy process but a totally normal process through which all parents of children with developmental disabilities go. The extent to which it affects their lives varies based primarily on the unique individual factors that make up the components of the model when applied to the individual parent.

Grieving is not a static process. Stress, time, knowledge, and support systems all play roles in causing change in an individual parent's grieving experience. Understanding that grieving is ongoing and nonstatic in nature leads to the recognition that varying levels and types of professional intervention are appropriate. Intervention has to be focused based on the needs of the parent as the parent perceives those needs, not as the professional views them. The measure of appropriateness varies, depending on parent strengths and weaknesses and environmental stress.

Parental grieving and coping are not defined by the model. Instead, the model is completed for an individual based on the identifiable components in that individual's life. Effective professionals working with parents should present the concepts and discuss with the parents or family members their personal strengths, support systems, and feelings. Using parental input, the model can then be filled in based on the individual. Ongoing interaction between professionals and families should include focusing on the changes that have taken place over time. The professional must be careful not to judge change or lack of change, but use that

sort of information to help the direction of support that the parent may choose.

Professionals who accept the assumptions on which this model is based must also recognize the implications of the model to their roles. Their roles then become the following:

1. Facilitating the family's understanding of grieving, stress, support systems, and personal strengths.

2. Helping parents and family members to recognize that the interaction of stress and emotional actions in a grieving process is normal and healthy.

3. Assisting parents and family members to realize that the grieving process is an ongoing and changing process.

4. Empowering parents to act independently.

5. Developing and providing training to families concerning the components of the model.

6. Facilitating parents' interactions with other families and appropriate professionals.

7. Resisting taking on roles that are beyond the responsibility and training of the professional (e.g., a teacher acting as a family counselor).

8. Helping families understand that each family member presents a unique set of needs based on his or her personal strengths, support systems, and emotional reactions to stress.

9. Recognizing that with some parents or family members and at some times other professionals may interact more effectively.

By keeping these role definitions and limitations in mind, the professional can effectively understand and work with parents and families of children with developmental disabilities.

Summary

A multidimensional model has been presented that has been an effective tool for understanding and working with parents and families. This model differs in several respects from the traditional models used to explain what parents of students with developmental disabilities experience. First, it is not linear but circular in representation. Second, it requires consideration of the parent's strengths and support systems along with the impact of stress on the emotional reactions associated with parenting a child with developmental disabilities. Third, it is a fluid model in that its representation changes depending on the realities of the individual parent at a specific time.

For professionals to work effectively with parents and families of children with developmental disabilities, it is essential that they recognize the uniqueness of these parents. Effective professionals investigate and develop an understanding of parents in the areas of personal strengths, support systems, emotional reactions, and stress. After this understanding is developed for the family members involved, the effective professional assumes a role as a parent educator and a facilitator. The ultimate goal is to empower parents to work toward the goals of achieving the best for the family and the student with disabilities.

QUESTIONS

1. What role does stress play in relation to the emotional reactions of parents and family members of children with developmental disabilities?

2. What information is necessary to clearly understand a parent, and how would you go about gaining that information?

3. What role should the educator play and what should be the educator's limits when working with a parent and a family of a child with developmental disabilities?

4. What are the components of the multidimensional model presented, and how do they interrelate?

5. Develop a graphic representation of your reaction to a loss. What would this representation look like and what areas would you need to work on to help you cope with this loss?

References

Affleck, G., Tennen, H., Rowe, J., Roscher, B., & Walker, L. (1989). Effects of formal support on mothers' adaptation to the hospital-to-home transition of high-risk infants: The benefits and cost of helping. *Child Development, 60,* 488–501.

Allen, D. A., & Affleck, G. (1985). Are we stereotyping parents? A postscript to Blacher. *Mental Retardation, 23,* 200–202.

Anderson, K. (1971). The "shopping" behavior of parents of mentally retarded children: The professional person's role. *Mental Retardation, 9,* 3–5.

Barsch, R. (1968). *The parent of the handicapped child: The study of child-rearing practices.* Springfield, IL: Thomas.

Bates, P., Renzaglia, A., & Wehman, P. (1981). Characteristics of appropriate education for severely and profoundly handicapped students. *Education and Training of the Mentally Retarded, 4,* 142–149.

Beavers, J., Hampson, R. B., Hulgus, Y. F., & Beavers, W. R. (1986). Coping in families with a retarded child. *Family Process, 25,* 365–378.

Beckman, P. J. (1991). Comparison of mothers' and fathers' perceptions of the effect of young children with and without disabilities. *American Journal on Mental Retardation, 95,* 585–595.

Beckman, P. J., & Pokorni, J. C. (1988). A longitudinal study of families of preterm infants: Changes in stress and support over the first two years. *Journal of Special Education, 22,* 55–65.

Beckman, P. J., Pokorni, J. L., Maza, E. A., & Blazer-Martin, L. (1987). A longitudinal study of stress and support in families of preterm and full-term infants. *Journal of the Division of Early Childhood, 11*(1), 2–9.

Bellamy, G. T., & Wilcox, B. (1980). Secondary education for severely handicapped students: Guidelines for quality services. In B. Wilcox & A. Thompson (Eds.), *Critical issues in educating autistic children and youth.* Washington, DC: U.S. Department of Education.

Blacher, J. (1984). Sequential stages of parental adjustment to the birth of a child with handicaps: Fact or artifact? *Mental Retardation, 22,* 55–68.

Boyd-Franklin, N. (1989). *Black families in therapy: A multisystems approach.* New York: Guilford Press.

Bryant, J. (1971). Parent–child relationships: Their effect on rehabilitation. *Journal of Learning Disabilities, 4,* 325–329.

Bush, N. A., & Peters, D. A. (1979). *Parental development in first time mothers of handicapped, at-risk, and normal children: Final report.* Washington, DC: Department of Health, Education, and Welfare.

Donovan, A. M. (1988). Family stress and ways of coping with adolescents who have handicaps: Maternal perceptions. *American Journal on Mental Retardation, 92,* 501–509.

Dunst, C. J., Trivette, C. M., & Cross, A. H. (1986). Roles and support networks of mothers of handicapped children. In R. R. Fewell & P. F. Vadasy (Eds.), *Families of handicapped children: Needs and supports across the life-span* (pp. 167–192). Austin, TX: PRO-ED.

Dyson, L., & Fewell, R. R. (1986). Stress and adaptation in parents of young handicapped and nonhandicapped children: A comparative study. *Journal of the Division for Early Childhood, 10,* 25–34.

Erin, J. N., Rudin, D., & Njoroge, M. (1991). Religious beliefs of parents of children with visual impairments. *Journal of Visual Impairments and Blindness, 85,* 157–162.

Featherstone, H. (1981). *A difference in the family: Life with a disabled child.* New York: Basic Books.

Flynt, S. W. & Wood, T. A. (1989). Stress and coping of mothers of children with moderate mental retardation. *American Journal on Mental Retardation, 94,* 278–283.

Frey, K. S., Greenberg, M. T., & Fewell, R. R. (1989). Stress and coping among parents of handicapped children: A multidimensional approach. *American Journal on Mental Retardation, 94*(3), 240–249.

Friedrich, W. N., Wilturner, L. T., & Cohen, D. S. (1985). Coping resources and parenting mentally retarded children. *American Journal of Mental Retardation, 90,* 130–139.

Gallagher, J. (1956). Rejecting parents? *Exceptional Children, 22,* 273–276.

Gallagher, J. J., Beckman, R., & Cross, A. H. (1983). Families of handicapped children: Sources of stress and its amelioration. *Exceptional Children, 56,* 10–20.

Garber, M. (1992). Helping families with developmentally delayed children: POP as a model of parental involvement. In L. Kaplan (Ed.), *Education and the family* (pp. 41–53). Needham Heights, MA: Allyn & Bacon.

Gargiulo, R. M. (1985). *Working with parents of exceptional children.* Boston: Houghton Mifflin.

Gargiulo, R. M., & Graves, S. B. (1991). Parental feelings. *Childhood Education, 67,* 176–178.

Gartner, A., Lipsky, D. K., & Turnbull, A. (1991). *Supporting families with a child with a disability: An international outlook.* Baltimore: Brookes.

Goldberg, S., Marcovitch, S., MacGregor, D., & Lojklasedk, M. (1986). Family response to developmentally delayed preschoolers: Etiology and the father's role. *American Journal of Mental Deficiency, 90,* 610–617.

Gowen, J. W., Johnson-Martin, N., Goldman, B. D., & Appelbaum, M. (1989). *American Journal on Mental Retardation, 94,* 259–271.

Guralnick, M. H., & Bricker, D. (1987). The effectiveness of early intervention for children with cognitive and general developmental delays. In M. H. Guralnick & F. C. Bennett (Eds.), *The effectiveness of early intervention for at-risk and handicapped children* (pp. 115–173). Toronto: Academic Press.

Haldey, M. B., & Hanzlik, J. R. (1990). A comparison of perceived competence in child-rearing between mothers of children with Down syndrome and mothers of children without delays. *Education and Training in Mental Retardation, 25,* 132–141.

Hancock, K., Wilgosh, L., & McDonald, L., (1990). Parenting a visually impaired child: The mother's perspective. *Journal of Visual Impairment and Blindness, 84,* 411–413.

Hanline, M. F. (1991). Transitions and critical events in the family life cycle: Implications for providing support to families of children with disabilities. *Psychology in the Schools, 28,* 53–59.

Harris, V. S., & McHale, S. M. (1989). Family life problems, daily caregiving activities, and psychological well-being of mothers of mentally retarded children. *American Journal on Mental Retardation, 94,* 231–239.

Harrison, H. (1983). *The premature baby book: A parent's guide to coping and caring in the first years.* New York: St. Martin's Press.

Hilton, A., Faught, K. K., & Hagan, M. (1984). A yardstick for special education. *Principal, 64*(2), 34–36.

Hilton, A., & Henderson, C. J. (1993). Parent involvement: A best practice or forgotten practice? *Education and Training in Mental Retardation, 28,* 199–211.

Imber-Black, E. (1986). Toward a resource model in systemic family therapy. In M. Karpel (Ed.), *Family resources: The hidden partner in family therapy* (pp. 148–174). New York: Guilford Press.

Intagliata, J., & Doyle, N. (1984). Enhancing social support for parents of developmentally disabled children: Training in interpersonal problem solving skills. *Mental Retardation, 22*(1), 4–11.

Jaffe, M. L. (1991). *Understanding parenting.* Dubuque, IA: W. C. Brown.

Karpel, M. (Ed.). (1986). *Family resources: The hidden partner in family therapy.* New York: Guilford Press.

Kazak, A. E., & Wilcox, B. (1984). The structure and function of social support networks in families with handicapped children. *American Journal of Community Psychology, 12,* 645–661.

Knafl, K. A., & Deatrick, J. A. (1987). Conceptualizing family response to a child's chronic illness or disability. *Family Relations, 36,* 300–304.

Kroth, R. (1987). Mixed or missed messages between parents and professionals. *Volta Review, 89,* 1–10.

Kubler-Ross, E. (1969). *On death and dying.* New York: Macmillan.

Lambie, R., & Daniels-Mohring, D. (1993). *Family systems within educational contexts: Understanding students with special needs.* Denver: Love.

Lazarus, R. S., & Folkman, S. (1984). *Stress, appraisal and coping.* New York: Springer.

Mandell, C. J., & Fiscus, E. (1981). *Understanding exceptional people.* St. Paul, MN: West.

Mary, N. (1990). Reactions of black, Hispanic, and white mothers to having a child with handicaps. *Mental Retardation, 28,* 1–5.

Mayer, J. A. (1994). From rage to reform: What parents say about advocacy. *Exceptional Parent, 24,* 49–51.

McCubbin, H. I., & Patterson, J. M. (1981). *Family stress and adaptation: A double ABCX model of family behavior.* Paper presented at the National Council on Family Relations, Milwaukee. (ERIC Document Reproduction Service No. ED 310676)

McDonald, L., Kysela, G. M., & Reddon, J. (1987, May). *Stress and supports to families with a handicapped child.* Paper presented at Alternative Futures for the Education of Students with Severe Disabilities, Edmonton, Canada. (ERIC Document Reproduction Service No. ED 310 578)

Meyer, E. C., & Bailey, D. B. (1993). Family-centered care in early intervention: Community and hospital settings. In J. L. Paul & R. J. Simeonson (Eds.), *Children with special needs: Family, culture, and society* (2nd ed., pp. 181–209). Fort Worth, TX: Harcourt Brace Jovanovich.

Mullins, J. B. (1987). Authentic voices from parents of exceptional children. *Family Relations, 36,* 30–33.

Nadler, A., Lewinstein, E., & Rahav, G. (1991). Acceptance of mental retardation and help-seeking by mothers and fathers of children with mental retardation. *Mental Retardation, 29,* 17–23.

Newman, L. F. (1980). Parents' perceptions of low birthweight infants. *Pediatrician, 9,* 182–190.

Ogbu, J. (1985). A cultural ecology of competence among inner-city blacks. In M. Spencer, G. Brookins, & W. Allen (Eds.), *Beginnings: The social and affective development of black children* (pp. 45–66). Hillsdale, NJ: Erlbaum.

Olshansky, S. (1962). Chronic sorrow: A response to having a mentally defective child. *Social Casework, 43,* 190–194.

Patterson, J. M., & McCubbin, H. I. (1983). Chronic illness: Family stress and coping. In C. Figley & H. McCubbin (Eds.), *Stress and the family: Vol. 2. Coping with catastrophe* (pp. 21–36). New York: Brunner/Mazel.

Paul, J. L., Porter, P. B., & Falk, G. D. (1993). Families of children with disabling conditions. In J. L. Paul & R. J. Simeonson (Eds.), *Children with special needs: Family, culture, and society* (2nd ed., pp. 3–24). Fort Worth, TX: Harcourt Brace Jovanovich.

Powell, T. H., & Ogle, P. A. (1985). *Brothers and sisters: A special part of exceptional families.* Baltimore: Brookes.

Rimmerman, A. (1989). Provision of respite care for children with developmental disabilities: Changes in maternal coping and stress over time. *Mental Retardation, 27,* 99–102.

Ronnau, J., & Poertner, J. (1993). Identification and use of strengths: A family system approach. *Children Today, 22*(2), 20–23.

Roos, P. (1978). Parents of mentally retarded children—Misunderstood and mistreated. In A. Turnbull & H. Turnbull (Eds.), *Parents speak out* (pp. 13–27). Columbus, OH: Merrill.

Rowitz, L. (1989). Editorial: Trends in mental retardation in the 1990's. *Mental Retardation, 27,* iii–iv.

Salisbury, C. (1987). Stressors of parents with young handicapped and nonhandicapped children. *Journal of the Division for Early Childhood, 11,* 154–160.

Searl, S. (1978). I'll never do that! *Exceptional Parent, 5,* 6–10.

Simeonsson, R. J., & Simeonsson, N. E. (1993). Children, families, and disability: Psychological dimensions. In J. L. Paul & R. J. Simeonsson (Eds.), *Children with special needs: Family, culture, and society* (2nd ed., pp. 25–50). Fort Worth, TX: Harcourt Brace Jovanovich.

Smith, C. (1993). Cultural sensitivity in working with children and families. In J. L. Paul & R. J. Simeonsson (Eds.), *Children with special needs: Family, culture, and society* (2nd ed., pp. 113–121). Fort Worth, TX: Harcourt Brace Jovanovich.

Snell, M. E. (1988). Curriculum and methodology for individuals with severe disabilities. *Education and Training in Mental Retardation, 23,* 302–314.

Solnit, A., & Stark, M. (1961). Mourning the birth of a defective child. *Psychoanalytic Study of the Child, 16,* 523–537.

Sontag, J. C., & Schacht, R. (1994). An ethnic comparison of parent participation and information needs in early intervention. *Exceptional Children, 60,* 422–433.

Spidel, J. (1995). Working with parents of the exceptional child. In E. H. Berger (Ed.), *Parents as partners in education* (4th ed.). Columbus, OH: Merrill.

Stoneman, Z., Brody, G. H., Davis, C. H., Crapps, J. M., & Malone, D. M. (1991). Ascribed role relations between children with mental retardation and their younger siblings. *American Journal on Mental Retardation, 95,* 537–550.

Tashima, N. (1981). Asian Americans in psychiatric systems. In D. Claerbaut (Ed.), *New directions in ethnic studies: Minorities in America* (pp. 95–106). Saratoga, CA: Century Twenty One.

Thomas, D. D. (1993). Minorities in North America: African-American families. In J. L. Paul & R. J. Simeonsson (Eds.), *Children with special needs: Family, culture, and society* (2nd ed., pp. 122–138). Fort Worth, TX: Harcourt Brace Jovanovich.

Turnbull, A. (1983). Parent–professional interactions. In M. Snell (Ed.), *Systematic instruction of moderately and severely handicapped* (2nd ed., pp. 18–43). Columbus, OH: Merrill.

Turnbull, H. R., & Turnbull, A. P. (1985). *Parents speak out: Then and now.* Columbus, OH: Merrill.

Waggoner, K., & Wilgosh, L. (1990). Concerns of families of children with learning disabilities. *Journal of Learning Disabilities, 23,* 97–98, 113.

Wang, T. M. (1993). Families in Asian cultures: Taiwan as a case example. In J. L. Paul & R. J. Simeonsson (Eds.), *Children with special needs: Family, culture, and society* (2nd ed., pp. 165–178) Fort Worth, TX: Harcourt Brace Jovanovich.

Webb-Mitchell, B. (1993). Hope in despair: The importance of religious stories for families with children with disabilities. In J. L. Paul & R. J. Simeonsson (Eds.), *Children with special needs: Family, culture, and society* (2nd ed., pp. 97–110). Fort Worth, TX: Harcourt Brace Jovanovich.

Wilgosh, L., Waggoner, K., & Adams, B. (1988). Parent views on education and daily living concerns for children with mental handicaps. *Australia and New Zealand Journal of Developmental Disabilities, 14,* 255–259.

Williams, W., Fox, T. J., Thousand, J., & Fox, W. (1990). Level of acceptance and implementation of best practices in the education of students with severe handicaps in Vermont. *Education and Training in Mental Retardation, 25,* 120–131.

Winton, P. J., & Bailey, D. (1993). Communication with families: Examining practices and facilitating change. In J. L. Paul & R. J. Simeonsson (Eds.), *Children with special needs: Family, culture, and society* (2nd ed., pp. 165–178). Fort Worth, TX: Harcourt Brace Jovanovich.

Empowering Family Members To Work as Partners with Professionals

CHAPTER 23

Ann Horwath

Learning Outcomes

After reading this chapter, you should be able to

■ Recognize inclusion of families in all planning for children with disabilities as best practice for all professionals.

■ Identify the family unit for every child with a disability.

■ Use strategies to include families as partners in planning for children with disabilities.

TERMS

The following terms are important for the understanding of this chapter:

Family: Those significant persons in the child's life who interact with and support the child on a daily basis.

Family driven: Considering family issues and needs as the foci of planning, implementation, and evaluation of activities for children with disabilities.

Partnership: Collaborative efforts that strengthen the end product and help to achieve the best results for the child and family.

Introduction

Participation by families in the planning for their children with disabilities has long been recognized as being paramount to successful outcomes for the children. The challenge is to involve families in the planning process, but professionals often do not have effective strategies to get the families to participate (O'Connor, 1992). Too often the planning process reflects the values of professionals rather than being centered on realistic outcomes for the individual with disabilities and those people that most impact his life, the family (Turnbull & Turnbull, 1990). Planning for children with disabilities needs to be family centered as the family is the first line of ongoing support for the child (Turnbull, 1988). Families must be empowered to actively participate and buy in to the planning process for their child. Without empowerment, families may leave the decision making to the judgments of professionals. Families need to be empowered to become actively involved (Cornell, n.d.).

This chapter focuses on effective strategies for professionals to create partnerships while empowering families through collaboration with professionals. Included are methods of defining the family, strategies for meetings with families, understanding the family support continuum, and empowering family members through partnership to be involved in all planning for the child. Two examples of family–professional partnership approaches are presented.

Defining the Family

Defining the family unit for a child with disabilities is an important first step in developing a partnership with a family. A realistic definition of family is those significant persons in the child's life who interact with and support the child on a daily basis. Therefore, a family unit can include birth parents, stepparents, foster parents, guardians, siblings, relatives, friends of the individual and family, and any other significant persons in the life of the child with a disability (e.g., a roommate, nanny). A family may comprise one person or any number of people supporting the child. What is important in defining family is the interactions of the people with the child, which is not limited to a relative or a legalized person such as a legal guardian. Determining the family for a given individual takes time and involvement. Time spent in determining the family unit will impact the child with disabilities and reap benefits later in the planning process and be reflected in the outcomes (Turnbull, 1988).

Strategies for Professional–Family Meetings

The next step in the process of building partnerships between professionals and family members is getting the family members to actively participate in planning for the child. Professionals and family members must be brought together. The term *meeting* may be threatening to families as it indicates a formalized setting that may not be familiar or comfortable. Organizing a *get-together* to talk more informally at a location that helps put a family at ease may take this first encounter out of the school building. Meeting at a school puts the discussion into a more professional arena. The family home, a neighborhood church, library, community meeting room, or restaurant may be more comfortable for the family and enable them to express themselves more freely (Turnbull & Turnbull, 1990).

Sometimes even a planned get-together is not the answer. Creativity may be necessary. For example, a teacher had tried everything to get a family to meet to design the Individualized Education Program (IEP). The child played on the junior varsity football team and the parents and siblings always went to the games. The teacher sat next to the family at games and talked informally until the teacher had enough information from the family and the teacher had discussed enough about what was happening and could happen with their son in school that an IEP could be written. Once the teacher told the family that the plan was outlined, meeting briefly to formalize the plan was not a problem.

Even if the setting is friendly, it still may be difficult to get a family involved. Families may avoid participation with professionals for a number of reasons. Encounters with professionals in the past may have left negative feelings toward all professionals. Professionals may be overwhelming to families if efforts are not made to help the families understand the terminology used. Some professionals tell family members to read a form or document and sign if they agree; however, the family member may not understand medical or educational terms used or may be illiterate. Being asked to affix a signature to a document that is not understood can be embarrassing and lead to a lack of desire to interact with professionals in the future (O'Connor, 1992). Interactions with professionals may also bring up negative feelings for family members who have had to deal with professionals in times of stress, such as medical emergencies, school disciplinary problems, or crisis situations. Although a professional cannot always know the background when a family hesitates to interact with professionals, every creative effort must be made to involve families. One approach is to ask the family when and where they would like to meet. Another is to serve refreshments to make a meeting more relaxed.

Understanding and Facilitating the Family Support Continuum

The family must be empowered to take an active role in planning for the child with disabilities. This empowerment can take place by utilizing the current circumstances and status of the family and child and by not trying to rectify situations that have occurred in the past. To empower families to take an active role in planning for their child, there must be a sense of where the family is in terms of support for their child. A look at family support along a continuum may help determine how to build a strategy to empower the family. Following are some levels of family involvement:

1. Survival of family unit

2. Preparing child to participate in school

3. Participation in events at child's school

4. Becoming active in planning for child

5. Becoming an advocate and seeking services for child

6. Participation in activities that involve families

7. Participating in activities that impact persons with disabilities

8. Becoming proactive for persons with disabilities

9. Becoming a professional in the field of disabilities

Each of these levels is briefly explained below. Examples of activities to involve families, along with the role of the professional, are included.

Survival of Family Unit

The planning process for a family must be very basic and may include the accessing of adequate housing and the purchasing of essentials of life, such as food, electricity, and heat. Family support at this level may involve keeping the family unit together and working with agencies to secure financial and medical supports. Planning might focus on goals for the family to send the child with disabilities to school healthy and adequately clothed.

Preparing Child To Participate in School

When a family unit is more active in anticipating their child's needs, short-term goals that can easily be measured will help get the family involved in planning for their child. For example, the family can be involved by helping the child arrive at school on time, prepared for the school day, and providing excused absences for health reasons. Communication to reinforce the family's efforts should be established.

Participation in Events at Child's School

The family should be encouraged to attend meetings that pertain to the child, including parent–teacher and general school meetings, as well as planning (e.g., IEP) meetings for their child. A family involved at this level can become more empowered to take an active role in planning for their child. The professional should work at building a relationship through ongoing communication with the family, which will help the family members feel comfortable expressing the needs of the child and family. Helping the family see tangible outcomes of their planning will help make short-term goals more meaningful and build a stronger family–professional relationship. Short-term goals to determine if what the child learns in school is generalized into home and community life can provide reinforcement. Communication between the school and family can track these short-term goals. Reinforcement of the family's efforts to participate is important to encourage the family to continue involvement with the child. For example, one parent reported to the teacher involved that the child was demonstrating at home one of the IEP goals of the physical therapy intervention at school: alternating feet to walk up stairs. This reinforced the parent as an active participant in monitoring an IEP goal being carried into the natural environment of the child from the school setting.

Becoming Active in Planning for Child

When the family unit asks questions and contributes actively in planning for the child, emphasis should be placed on shared responsibility of planning for the child with family members as equal partners with the professional. These family members can be encouraged to attend family-centered trainings and conferences and to join family-centered organizations. Partnering these family members with professionals and other members from more experienced families can encourage them to participate. Many organizations offer informational trainings, conferences, and seminars for professionals in the field of disabilities. A family member may not feel comfortable attending such a formalized session for the first time, but by being linked with a partner may become empowered to attend. The professional's role in this partnership may include inviting a family member to attend, arranging funds for any fees, providing transportation, and being a supportive partner at the event.

Becoming an Advocate and Seeking Services for Child

When a family has been empowered to participate to a greater degree in planning for the child, they can become the child's case manager of services. Once the family can articulate the needs of the child, they can work with professionals in partnership to seek those services and interventions that work best for their child in school, at home, and in the community. One parent shocked a teacher by initiating a meeting at the school prior to the IEP meeting. The teacher felt threatened and that he must be doing something wrong. The parent assumed the role of making the meeting comfortable for the teacher and began the development of a partnership to plan for the child.

Participation in Activities that Involve Families

Family members may participate and take lead roles in activities that benefit other families. School activities could include parent–teacher functions, informational meetings, fairs, and fundraisers. Family members can be invited to participate with professionals in the planning and implementation of activities at the school and in the community. This will help to make the activities more friendly for families. These family members can also be instrumental in bringing other families to participate in activities. Utilizing a family member to call other family members and invite them to an activity or meeting can encourage reticent family members to attend.

Participating in Activities that Impact Others

A family unit that includes a member or members who go beyond planning for their own child and demonstrate leadership skills may partner with other families as advocates and help others become more involved in the planning for their children. In many meeting situations, professional members greatly outnumber family members and the child with disabilities. Professionals should encourage families to network with each other. A family may participate more actively at a meeting, such as for an IEP, if it is attended also by a networking family member with whom the family has built a relationship.

Becoming Proactive for Persons with Disabilities

When family members become active participants in organizations that plan for, advocate for, and implement services for persons with disabilities on local, statewide, national, and international levels, they are excellent role models for other families. Family members who partner with professionals in the field of disabilities can help them become more inclusive of families in planning for persons with disabilities. An effective professional should seek out these family members to assist in activities relating to all planning for persons with disabilities within systems and agencies. Partnerships between these family members and professionals can give a reality base to planning and be powerful alliances for systems change. For example, a family member initiated change within a system when she organized the other family members in her child's class to advocate for a classroom aide. The teacher had been turned down numerous times by the administration to add a position for an aide, but the families were able to move the administration to secure money to hire an aide.

Becoming a Professional in the Field of Disabilities

Family members often are most influential in providing avenues for systems change while working within the system. A family member of a child with disabilities has a great amount of credibility in the profession. Partnerships between professionals who are family members of children with disabilities can impact families and professionals at all levels that provide for systems change, including training of professionals and legislation.

This overview of a family support continuum places no value in being at any one point along the continuum over another. Some family members do become more proactive and move to greater involvement with the child and the system. Some families never become more involved or, because of changes that adversely affect the family unit, may back away from a greater level of involvement. At any level of involvement, the family is the constant in the child's life and with encouragement will be able to be active in planning for the child with disabilities. Families are not generic and each family unit is unique. It is critical to use each family's needs and strengths in planning for the child. When the family is at the center of all planning for the child, the outcomes for the child with disabilities will be greater.

Creating Partnerships

For professionals and families to plan for the child, partnerships need to be developed (Olson, 1990). One example of family–professional partnerships was the development and implementation of a graduate-level course bringing together professionals and family members as partners in learning and planning for youth with disabilities transitioning out of high school (Horwath, 1993). Family members are often included in university courses as guest speakers and panelists, but are rarely class participants unless they are university students. Professionals and family members training together at the university level demonstrates a new partnership model for instruction. This partnership model was reinforced by bringing together a parent and a professional as co-instructors for the course.

The first challenge of this partnership course was to solicit the involvement of family members as participants. Because the course was offered through the college of continuing education, family members did not have to go through the university admission process. Monies were secured through a grant from the U.S. Department of Education, Office of Special Education Programs, to provide instructors' fees, which were divided between the instructors. Also, stipends were provided for family members as incentives to complete the course. The stipend money allowed the tuition fees to be paid plus some extra money that could be used for transportation, child care, and other expenses. The small amount of stipend money, however, did not cover the total cost for a family that needed to pay a childcare provider.

As they reviewed various issues for youth with disabilities, the professionals and family members were able to get a perspective of the issues from each other's point of view. With both professionals and family members as class participants, an us-versus-them situation was avoided and participants worked collaboratively to discuss issues and problem solve together. What emerged was a strong sense by the participants that "the collaborative efforts of partnership strengthen the end product and that partnerships help to achieve the best results for the student and his/her family" (Horwath, 1993, p. 17). The following are statements developed from class discussions between family members and professionals that exemplify commitment to collaboration:

1. Mutual trust and respect between family members and professionals is very important.
2. Professionals must be totally convinced of the importance of involvement of family members.
3. Burnout is a possibility for both professionals and family members and all benefit from support.
4. Do not generalize, all professional and family members are not the same.
5. Every family member has the right to participate in planning for their child.
6. Family members must live with the outcome of the planning for the child.
7. Language should not be a barrier to communication, time must be spent to facilitate/understand. (p. 17)

From the collaborative activities presented throughout the course emerged some value statements. These values exemplify best practice for professionals and families to work together in partnership. Some of the value statements from the course participants are as follows:

1. To establish that all participants be included and involved in all activities.
2. To empower all participants to freely express ideas.
3. To respect each participant's views.
4. To foster a safe environment for sharing ideas in the classroom.
5. To honor the diversity of opinions of class participants.
6. To promote partnerships between professionals and family members.
7. To support individual choices and risk taking to enable participants to develop partnerships.
8. To celebrate the diversity of individual class participants (p. 15).

Empowerment of Families Through Collaboration with Professionals

Including families in planning too often means that professionals give suggestions and present ideas in an authoritative manner and then ask family members to contribute. Families must be able to contribute from the beginning in all planning for the child. Families are the major force in the implementation of the planning and share in the outcomes for the child with disabilities, often for the lifetime of the child (Turnbull, 1988). In a true sense, the family is the key professional. The family unit lives with the child with disabilities and, by virtue of the amount of time spent interacting with the child, needs to play the major role. The challenge to the professionals is to illicit the information necessary by empowering the family to recognize their importance in planning. Then all the professionals and family member "professionals" can work collaboratively in planning for the child with disabilities (Horwath, 1993).

For professionals to be successful, collaboration must be preceded by relationship building for all parties to "buy into" the planning. Relationships cannot be built through one or two formalized meetings. Relationships must be nurtured through increased contact that is not necessarily on a one-to-one basis (Turnbull & Turnbull, 1990). Groupings bringing professionals and family members together can take many forms, including discussion groups to deal with issues for a number of families and children with disabilities; choosing and hearing a guest speaker on issues of interest to the group; or providing ongoing support through discussion,

networking, and planning. For example, a group of family members and professionals can take on tasks such as fund raising to get monies to enable family members to attend seminars, workshops, and conferences. On a more personal one-to-one level, relationships can be nurtured through informal meetings, such as at lunch time in the school cafeteria, through phone calls, or via notes. An important element in relationship building is continuing communication (Turnbull & Turnbull, 1990).

Relationships can lead to empowerment of professionals and family members to build partnerships for collaboration. Through the commitment of the Hawaii University Affiliated Program, a four-phase process was developed to empower families to participate in all levels of this agency's activities (Stodden & Horwath, 1993). This process can be utilized by any group to empower families to work in partnership with professionals. This is a family-driven process. Family driven is defined as follows: "To see family issues and needs as the foci of planning, implementation and evaluation of activities" (Stodden & Horwath, 1993, p. 4) for children with disabilities.

Three principles must be accepted to institute a family-driven process:

1. Realize that family members are the experts on their children.
2. Empower family members to take the lead on activities that produce outcomes for persons with disabilities and their families.
3. Utilize family issues and needs as the motivating factor in an activity. (Stodden & Horwath, 1993, p. 4)

The first phase of the process is to empower family members to take the lead by bringing them together to network, express their ideas, and define their needs and issues. Consideration is given to their schedules, needs such as transportation and childcare, and most important establishment of an investment to the process. Families can be recruited for this process only by someone who has a relationship with them. To get family members to buy into the process, they must believe that their needs and issues will be heard and that there is an opportunity to interact with professionals to plan outcomes based on the input of families.

Once families invest and begin the process, family member leaders and facilitators can organize the families into working groups. The purpose of these groups is to develop a framework based on the issues and needs of families, laying the groundwork for partnerships with professionals. Some examples of family issues that were developed by families participating in this process are:

1. We're competent families first.
2. Help families see their normalcy, strengths, and weaknesses.

3. Respect a family's reality and values.

4. Focus on the abilities of the family as a whole.

5. Families are "wholistic." Every player is significant.

6. Give families tools, information, means to support the family and to exchange information with professionals, community, and other families.

7. Dreams and visions bring us to our highest potential.

8. Aspire toward a quality of life that utilizes everyone's strengths—differences are okay.

9. Develop a unique design tailored toward each individual family.

10. If professionals understand the qualities of "family" they automatically become partners for effective change.

11. Empathy and understanding evoke self-reflection for professionals (Stodden & Horwath, 1993, p. 55).

With the empowerment developed by bringing families together to determine their issues and needs, the family members then can assume leadership roles in the next phase of the process, which is interfacing with the professionals. Utilizing specialists in group facilitation, the family members and professionals begin to form working groups to discuss how the families' issues and needs can be integrated into the planning and implementation of programs and services for persons with disabilities.

Once the process of involving families in planning is begun, there must be continued commitment to nurture the partnerships. Collaboration with families adds a reality base to all planning for children with disabilities. Families do expect outcomes and to be a part of those outcomes. Some successful outcomes for the families who participated in the restructuring of the Hawaii University Affiliated Program (UAP) were as follows:

1. Three family member participants have been hired by the Hawaii UAP as staff members.

2. Two interagency agreements between Hawaii UAP and family driven organizations have been signed.

3. Positions specifically for family members have been written into grant applications.

4. Family members have been involved in the development of a statewide curriculum for training direct care providers.

5. Two new family members have been included on the Hawaii UAP advisory committee.

6. Family members have been included as presenters in numerous courses presented by Hawaii UAP staff.

7. Family members have been included as guest speakers and panelists at trainings, workshops and inservices conducted by Hawaii UAP.

8. Family members have been included in reviewing products disseminated by Hawaii UAP. (Stodden & Horwath, 1993, p. 27)

Summary

Best practice mandates the inclusion of families in all planning for their child with disabilities. Family members must be empowered by professionals to participate. The family provides continuity in the child's life and must be convinced of the importance of their role as an active participant in planning. An effective professional must understand that time needs to be spent with the family members to define the family unit and continue communication to build partnerships. Meeting once a year will not build partnerships between families and professionals. Partnerships between families and professionals utilize the strengths of all participants and enhance successful outcomes for the child. Effective professionals will work to develop strategies to involve all families in planning for their child with disabilities.

 ## QUESTIONS

1. How can the family unit be identified?

2. State some reasons families need to be partners in planning for their child with disabilities.

3. List some elements for successful partnerships between families and professionals.

4. Describe family driven.

5. List some activities in which family and professional collaboration would enhance planning for children with disabilities.

References

Cornell Empowerment Project. (n.d.). *Empowerment through family support*. Ithaca, NY: Cornell University.

Horwath, A. (1993). *Family–professional partnerships through training*. Honolulu: Hawaii University Affiliated Program.

O'Connor, S. (1992). Supporting families: What they want versus what they get. *OSERS News in Print, 5*(1), 7–11.

Olson, L. (1990, April 4). Parents as partners. *Education Week*, pp. 17–24.

Stodden, R., & Horwath, A. (1993). *Integrating a family focus within a University Affiliated Program*. Honolulu: Hawaii University Affiliated Program.

Turnbull, A. (1988). The challenge of providing comprehensive support to families. *Education and Training in Mental Retardation, 23*(4), 261–272.

Turnbull, A. P., & Turnbull, H. R. (1990). *Families, professionals and exceptionality: A special partnership* (2nd ed.). Columbus, OH: Merrill.

Attitudes About Individuals with Developmental Disabilities

CHAPTER 24

Ravic Ringlaben and Dale Dahmen-Jones

Learning Outcomes

After reading this chapter, you should be able to

- Describe the function of attitude as a barrier to full participation in society by persons with disabilities.

- Identify and describe some of the major negative attitudes held toward persons with disabilities.

- Compare and contrast the medical model and the social-political model for viewing persons with disabilities.

- Discuss the major attitudinal environments and the negative attitudes toward persons with disabilities that affect service delivery in those environments.

- Identify and discuss the major strategies for promoting positive attitudes toward persons with disabilities.

Introduction

The appropriate inclusion of persons with disabilities, particularly persons with developmental disabilities, is a focus of this text. However, in previous chapters, little discussion has been presented relating to attitudes about persons with developmental disabilities. Perhaps a typical assumption is that professionals, as well as individuals without disabilities, have the "proper" attitudes concerning people with disabilities. The purpose of this chapter is to review literature pertaining to attitudes concerning persons with developmental disabilities and to provide some suggestions for improving those attitudes.

Currently, almost 50 million Americans have disabilities (R. M. Donaldson, Helmstetter, Donaldson, & West, 1994). This astonishing number makes persons with disabilities the largest minority group in the United States. Disability knows no boundaries with regard to race, creed, color, national origin, sex, age, religion, economic status, sexual preference, and so forth.

As with other minority groups, persons with disabilities, and their advocates, have had to "fight" to receive the same rights as other individuals (Gliedman & Roth, 1980; Lynch & Thomas, 1994). "Changes in the relations between disabled and able-bodied persons are often brought about through a political process" (Stubbins, 1988, p. 22). Two main thrusts of this process have been legislation and litiga-

tion, which have expanded the access for individuals with disabilities to increase their participation in society and determined that individuals with disabilities "have the same needs, desires, and goals for themselves as do all other Americans" (Gerry & Mirsky, 1992, p. 341). Unfortunately, "while many legal rights have been acquired by citizens with disabilities in the last twenty years, much needs to be done in advocating for the enforcement of existing legislation" (Kilbury, Benshoff, & Rubin, 1992, p. 9).

Once individuals with disabilities receive access to an environment, how are they treated? What are the attitudes of persons without disabilities in those environments? What are some of the assumptions (biases, stereotypes) held by persons without disabilities? What are some of the social and educational policies that evolve from legislation and litigation that perpetuate continued segregation of persons with disabilities in U.S. society?

Assumptions, Biases, and Stereotypes

It is well recognized that environmental and social policy variables affect participation in society of individuals with disabilities (Kilbury et al., 1992; Lynch & Thomas, 1994). Many persons with disabilities believe that the greatest barrier to their full participation in society is not their disability or the inaccessible environments, but rather the biased attitudes of, prejudices of, and inappropriate treatment by persons without disabilities (Berry & Jones, 1991; Buscaglia, 1983; R. M. Donaldson et al., 1994; Fine & Asch, 1988; Kilbury et al., 1992; Larson, 1986; Rittenhouse, Johnson, Overton, Freeman, & Jaussi, 1991). However, attitudes of the public are a critical component of the environment with which persons with disabilities must continually contend (Hahn, 1987). "Negative social attitudes toward people with disabilities are most likely expressed in terms of exclusion from, or lack of access to, social roles, activities and facilities" (Westbrook, Legge, & Pennay, 1993, p. 617). Bogdan and Biklen (1977) used the term "handicapism" and defined it as "a set of assumptions that promote the differential and unequal treatment of people because of apparent or assumed physical, mental or behavioral difference" (p. 14).

People with disabilities should not only be given access to all facets of society but be treated with dignity and respect. Almost half a century ago, Barker (1948) wrote that the primary accommodation for persons with disabilities "must involve changes in the values of the physically normal" (p. 37). More recently, McCarthy (1988) suggested that "*accommodation is an attitude* that allows for the full expression of human talent. It does so either by removing whatever barriers (attitudinal, physical, procedural) interfere with accomplishing a goal or by providing whatever assistance or support is needed to bring someone to the level where goals can be approached by standard or alternative means. Accordingly, accommodation should be thought of as a right by which to obtain equal opportunity to participate, not as a special privilege" (p. 258).

Historically, persons with disabilities, especially those labeled as having developmental disabilities, have been considered "not quite whole" because they did not meet the criteria of physical attractiveness or functional independence. People with disabilities produce anxiety in persons without disabilities (Hahn, 1988). People without disabilities often reflect on the following questions when meeting or coming into contact with people with disabilities: How could they lead a satisfactory life? How could they ever really find true happiness? Therefore, people with disabilities were and continue to be treated differently, and are devalued, socially stigmatized, and placed in subordinate roles that produce unequal status (Fine & Asch, 1988; Makas, 1988).

Individuals complete a sequential process when coming into contact with a person with a disability. This process involves perception, attitude–belief, emotion, and behavior. Hence, one's belief or attitude about individuals with disabilities influences one's behavior. "The perception we have about a handicap allows us to believe as we might have learned and to act the way we have been taught to act; and that is that persons with disabilities tend to be viewed as inferior to those without disabilities" (Lessen, 1991, p. 31). If one believes people with disabilities are "in-valid" or that

all people with disabilities are handicapped ("cap-in-hand"), one's behavior will reflect that attitude or belief. Members of society, as a whole, and educational or service delivery professionals specifically, need to reflect on their particular attitudes and beliefs, decisions, and policies that may facilitate or harm the integration and participation of people with disabilities in the educational, social, political, and economic mainstream. Correcting negative beliefs and attitudes that are held toward people with disabilities must take place if people with disabilities are to participate effectively in society (R. M. Donaldson et al., 1994.) This "change toward acceptance is a long and difficult process. We need to get over our irrational fears and replace them with thoughts and actions that are based on reason and facts" (Lessen, 1991, p. 36).

Service Delivery Philosophy

The manner in which services are provided to people with disabilities is often influenced by philosophy. Over time, service philosophies have varied and do vary based on the beliefs and attitudes about persons with disabilities. Two of the major service philosophies are described below.

Historically, the medical model has focused on the limitations and functional impairments of a disability (Hahn, 1988). Disability is something that needs to be fixed, like any other illness. The individual is a victim of the disability. "The concept of victim is entwined with the concept of environment–person interaction and implies helplessness, fate and being at mercy with the environment" (Lynch & Thomas, 1994, p. 9). In fact, much of the literature about people with disabilities indicates that people without disabilities still believe that people with disabilities "are sick or that their disabilities are contagious" (Murray-Seegert, 1989, p. 107). People with disabilities need to be made more normal. A service delivery philosophy based on the medical model focuses on changing the person with a disability. When the individual with a disability is confronted with a problem, it is assumed that the impairment is the cause of the problem (Fine & Asch, 1988; Lynch & Thomas, 1994). The individual is devalued, and placed in a role that is subordinate or unequal (Makas, 1988). Expectations are developed based on failure. Different is abnormal.

A social–political service delivery model focuses on the limitations and functional impairments of the environment. The environment is the disability (Hahn, 1987). This philosophy includes the concept of people with disabilities as "an oppressed minority group" that needs to be afforded the same rights as other citizens and can also be referred to as a minority–civil rights model. The person with a disability is a multidimensional individual, with the disability being only one of the dimensions. This philosophy differs from the medical model in that, rather than concentrating on the origin of the disability, it focuses on changing the environment to assist the person with the disability to function as effectively and naturally as possible. It also empowers the individual to grow and mature in positive directions (Lynch & Thomas, 1994). Expectations are developed based on success. Different is normal. According to Brotherson, Cook, Cunman-Lahr, and Wehmeyer (1995), "Modifying the physical environment to promote choice and self-determination serves two broad purposes. First, modifications of the physical environment have a direct impact on children with disabilities by permitting greater access to home, school and community settings. . . . A second and more subtle and less well-recognized purpose is that increased accessibility affects the attitudes of persons with and without disabilities" (p. 4).

This cure-versus-care model dispute is an issue of continued debate in delivering services to individuals with disabilities, and continues to impact attitudes.

Important Attitudinal Environments

Any philosophy of service delivery is perpetuated one person at a time. There seem to be a number of "environments" in which service delivery philosophy is perhaps more important than in others. In this section of this chapter, a selected number of these environments are described, including suggestions for attitude improvement.

Education

The educational service delivery system has gone through many changes during the last 25 years. At one time, school was for those individuals who could benefit from being there. Education for students with disabilities was nonexistent, or at best limited. With the initiation of litigation and legislation in the 1970s on behalf of students with disabilities, the educational system became more accessible. The educational service delivery philosophy has evolved from one that believed that students with disabilities should be educated primarily in segregated settings, to one in which students with disabilities were to be "mainstreamed" and to spend at least part of the day with "normal" peers, to one that supports the full-time education and inclusion of students with disabilities in general education classes. In 1980, Gliedman and Roth described this new vision of the education of students with disabilities: "It is to bring the handicapped child into the mainstream of childhood. It is to end his exclusion from social experiences appropriate to children his age. It is to provide him with an education that no longer reinforces—however inadvertently—society's traditional misconceptions and stereotypes about the abilities of handicapped individuals. It is . . . to improve education by break-

ing down the barriers of prejudice and misunderstanding that have excluded the handicapped from the mainstream of American life for so long" (p. 218).

In fact, Putnam, Spiegel, and Bruininks (1995) believe that, by the year 2000, "the opportunity for a child to attend a local public school (one that the child would have attended if s/he were not disabled) will be seen as a fundamental right, no matter how severe the child's disability" (p. 567).

General Education Teachers

It has been documented that the attitudes and expectations that teachers hold toward students with disabilities will directly impact their behavior and thus affect the manner in which their students are educated (Brady, Linehan, Campbell, & Neilson, 1992; Ringlaben & Price, 1981; Smith, Polloway, Patton, & Dowdy, 1995). Positive attitudes and expectations tend to produce positive educational experiences for students with disabilities, whereas negative attitudes and expectations tend to produce negative experiences. It appears that the development of attitudes, including that of teacher attitudes, is influenced by several factors, including knowledge, experiences, and support (Hannah, 1988).

The knowledge about students with disabilities that teachers bring to the classroom was likely acquired during their educational process. This knowledge could have been acquired by information provided in the family, friends, local schools, and the community. Information received during college years and the teacher training program is also very important. If the information provided in these environments was that individuals with disabilities are sick, hopeless, or less than whole, then that person who became a teacher may very well perpetuate these beliefs. However, if information shared portrayed individuals with disabilities as people first and provided facts that emphasized similarities rather than differences, the teacher may treat students with disabilities in a manner that evokes dignity and respect.

Past experience and knowledge also lend much to the development of attitudes and educational programs. That is, because of past educational practice, teachers with approximately more than 20 years of teaching experience may not have had contact with peers with disabilities when they were attending school. However, university students currently in teacher training programs and teachers with fewer than 20 years of teaching experience probably have experienced contact with peers with disabilities.

There has been a call to have teacher preparation programs for general educators include more information about and experiences with students with disabilities. "The reality is that today's teachers must be prepared to teach all kinds of students, including those who present special needs in classrooms" (Smith et al., 1995, p. 4). Traditionally, general educators receive a significant amount of information through one course devoted to principles and practices in educating students with special needs. This course may be the first and only formal professional exposure to information and experiences concerning children with disabilities (Fox & Rotatori, 1986). However, even this one component of a teacher education program can produce positive attitudes in future teachers, according to a review of the literature reported by Hannah (1988). It also should be noted that the texts and materials for this kind of course tend to follow a disability labeling format that emphasizes differences and the failure of the educational system, and may perpetuate "segregated thinking." It is suggested that this type of course be structured to emphasize similarities between children; provide information about changing the environment as opposed to changing the student with a disability; provide knowledge about working as a team member; and utilize direct, structured, successful experiences with students with disabilities (Carrigan, 1994; Eichinger, Rizzo, & Sirotnik, 1991). It is also important that teacher education students, as well as those students in other "helping" professional preparation programs, reflect upon why they have chosen to enter their particular profession. Wanting to help others is certainly an admirable desire; however, it can be interpreted as doing for others rather than teaching skills and building confidence in students to help themselves (Lynch & Thomas, 1994). For example, Asch (1989) reported that "disabled students and parents . . . complain that adapting or accommodating to a disability all too often results in lowered expectations and patronization" (p. 189).

Once on the job, if general educators are to become committed to the concept of integrating and including students with disabilities, they will need to understand the purpose of this philosophy, receive additional knowledge and training that meets their individual needs, and be provided with professional supports that foster the philosophy (Janney, Snell, Beers, & Raynes, 1995a; Wolery, Werts, Caldwell, Snyder, & Lisowski, 1995). It has been discovered that general education teachers go through a process of transformation when they are introduced to and have experiences with the inclusion philosophy (Giangreco, Dennis, & Cloninger, 1993). Teachers get their "rewards" by being successful with students and are concerned that they might not be able to "reach or teach" students with disabilities. Therefore, teachers often initially are hesitant and resistant. However, as their knowledge and skills to have successful experiences with students with disabilities are developed, and as they receive specific supports, they move to a spirit of cooperation and support that enhances the educational experiences of students with disabilities through a collaborative service delivery system (Janney, Snell, Beers, & Raynes, 1995b). This change is described by Giangreco and colleagues (1993): "Transformations were gradual and progressive rather than discrete and abrupt. Teachers described an emerging recognition that their initial expectations regarding the student with disabilities were based on unsubstantiated assumptions. Teachers . . . came to the realization they could be successful and that including was not as difficult as they had originally imagined. . . . They developed a willingness to (a) interact with the student, (b) learn skills needed to teach the student, and (c) change their attitude toward the student" (p. 365).

Special Education Teachers

The knowledge and experiences that assist in preparing special education professionals have a significant impact on their attitudes about including students with disabilities in the general school environment. Traditionally, special education teacher training has been delivered apart from general education with the exception of several basic courses, such as those on the history of U.S. schools and educational psychology. With the shift of philosophy, special educators need to be trained with an emphasis that includes a recognition of the interpersonal and peer relation needs of students with disabilities. In reflecting on the field of special education, Murray-Seegert (1989) indicated that the "field's traditional emphasis on the intrapersonal aspects of disability is accompanied by lack of inquiry into the interpersonal aspects of disability. And, in general, the more severe the disability experienced (especially if mental retardation is involved), the less likely it is that interpersonal behavior will be described. . . . Not only do the most severely disabled individuals have the capacity to develop peer relations, but these relations make the difference between surviving in the community and returning to closed institutions" (p. 12).

The special educator's role emphasis is also shifting to one of being a support person not only to students but to other professionals. The job also requires the development of appropriate communication skills, the ability to work as an effective team member, and the ability to work as a co-teacher within the general education classroom. According to Black and Meyer (1992), "special education teachers are in a unique position to advocate for their students' rights, needs and potential and to have an impact on the attitudes of others" (p. 472). General education teachers have reported that they prefer special education support professionals who engage in at least four practices: (a) a shared framework and goals for inclusion, (b) physical presence (many general education teachers have felt alone in the inclusion of students with disabilities), (c) a validation of effective practices by the general educator, and (d) moral support and a spirit of teamwork (Giangreco et al., 1993).

Students Without Disabilities

It seems that attitudes about students with disabilities is also related to what students know and have experienced (Salend, 1994). It is natural for "children to go up to persons with disabilities and talk to them. It is when someone drags them away that children begin to believe something is wrong" (Weisman, 1986, p. 66). As Gleason (1991) pointed out, this type of experience can develop negative attitudes and stereotypic thinking, which ultimately can develop into prejudice, discrimination, and lowered expectations. Researchers have emphasized that earlier positive experiences and social contact between children with and without disabilities promote more positive attitudes. Additionally, information about the abilities and positive qualities of children with disabilities, even in the early stages of education, can help to limit later negative attitudes (Kishi & Meyer, 1994; Morrison & Ursprung, 1987).

Reportedly, most students without disabilities who have had experience in integration and inclusion programs support the inclusion of students with disabilities, even when those students have severe disabilities (York, Vandercook, MacDonald, Heise-Neff, & Caughney, 1992). Importantly, it is not merely that students without disabilities "put up with" students with disabilities. A growing body of empirical literature supports the conclusion that integration and inclusion experiences seem to benefit students without disabilities in at least several ways (Biklen, Corrigan, & Quick, 1989; R. M. Donaldson et al., 1994; Helmstetter, Peck, & Giangreco, 1994; Murray-Seegert, 1989; Staub & Peck, 1995; Staub, Schwartz, Gallucci, & Peck, 1994): students (a) learn patience, including reduced fears of others who are different; (b) feel good in helping others and successfully meeting a challenge (improved self-concept); (c) gain future benefits in learning how to get along with others who are different; and (d) develop warm and caring friendships based on common interests. "As a friend to a child with severe disabilities, a peer without disabilities may be able to elicit socially appropriate behavior, and, further, may be able to reinforce uniquely such positive social behavior" (Grenot-Scheyer, 1994, p. 260).

In a review of the literature, as well as in their own study, Helmstetter and associates (1994) concluded, "The expanding literature of the outcomes of integration for students without disabilities suggests that a powerful means for addressing these issues exists potentially in every school in which a student with significant disabilities is enrolled. Far from simply *helping* those with disabilities, the practice of integrating students with highly diverse physical, developmental, and behavioral characteristics may turn out to be "best practice" for *all* the students involved" (p. 275). It appears from this review of the literature that (a) the attitudes of students without disabilities can be influenced positively, (b) students without disabilities benefit from educational programs that include peers with disabilities, and (c) students without disabilities can have a positive effect on peers with disabilities.

Professionals and parents may be concerned about the "perceived" negative effects of inclusion on students without disabilities. Because educators may believe that including students with disabilities in the regular classroom is "harmful" to students without disabilities, it is important that they receive information such as that provided by Staub and Peck (1995), which indicated that students without disabilities involved in "inclusion classrooms" (a) did not decline in academic progress, (b) did not lose significant teacher time and attention, and (c) did not learn undesirable behavior from students with disabilities. Sharpe, York, and Knight (1994) studied the effects of inclusion on students without disabilities in classrooms where students were and were not included and found no significant differences between the groups.

Students with Disabilities

A disability, by and of itself, may not automatically produce negative attitudes. Some literature seems to suggest a relationship between the characteristics or "topography" of the disability and negative reactions and attitudes. Westbrook and colleagues (1993) described "that less visible disabilities . . . are those which are accepted and that visible disabilities, disabilities involving mental functioning or disabilities for which the person is seen as morally responsible are those most stigmatized" (p. 617). It appears that "those disabilities we cannot see or which are difficult to understand evoke less compassionate responses in us" (Lessen, 1991, p. 32). Students with disabilities may have a limited number of friends "because others view them in terms of their differences, instead of interests and needs they have in common with many nondisabled persons" (R. M. Donaldson et al., 1994, p. 233).

Students with and without disabilities may have little contact with each other in the home or community. Therefore, "the public school classroom has particular importance as a context for the development of relationships between groups of children who have little contact outside the school setting" (Salisbury, Gallucci, Palombaro, & Peck, 1995, p. 126). This is where all students, if permitted to do so, can discover "common ground" and learn that others who seem different may in actuality be very similar. Weinberg (1988) suggested that all students will view disability "as a difficulty that imposes limits and problems in much the same way that other facets of life impose difficulties. Life has elements of a struggle for everyone, and the struggle of the disabled person is not so different. . . . Disability is a problem and a difficulty, but it is not the only one" (p. 153).

Students with disabilities can learn and apply appropriate skills maximally in a "normalized" environment such as the general education classroom (Haring, 1991), especially when interactive and interpersonal skill strategies, such as cooperative learning groups, are utilized (Hunt, Staub, Alwell, & Goetz, 1994). The classroom must stay as normal as possible so that student differences are minimized and accommodated in the least intrusive manner. It is imperative that teachers reflect on the appropriateness of accommodations, at the very least, because of the following: "The student with a disability deserves to master skills for as much independence as possible, and providing aides or even assigning students as guides, wheelchair pushers, and writers of assignments may needlessly thwart development of self-sufficiency or discourage typical interactions with classmates and adults" (Asch, 1989, p. 187).

According to R. M. Donaldson and associates (1994), "interaction between students with and without disabilities is perhaps the most effective approach to increased understanding of individual differences, creation of new friendships, and greater inclusion of students with moderate or severe disabilities in the life of the school" (p. 236). In a detailed ethnographic study, Murray-Seegert (1989) discovered that "the more severely impaired students . . . were observed to be involved in the same wide range of social relations as the students with more moderate impairments" (p. 140).

Interpersonal Relationships

It may be that the ability to build and maintain interpersonal relationships is the most salient predictor of the successful transition from school to adult environments for individuals with disabilities, or for any individual (Strully & Strully, 1992). Interpersonal relationships, although difficult at times for all of us, present a different set of situations and circumstances for individuals with disabilities (Lessen, 1991). These relationships will happen more often and be more successful if teachers structure situations for these students to interact (Abery & Fahnestock, 1994; Baker, Wang, & Walberg, 1994; J. Donaldson, 1980; File & Buzzelli, 1991; Gliedman & Roth, 1980; Helmstetter et al., 1994; McGookey, 1992; Murray-Seegert, 1989; Smith et al., 1995). This may be extremely important because merely having students in the same educational environment, by itself, may not be effective (McGee & Paradis, 1993; Sale & Carey, 1995; Schnorr, 1990). An attitude of administrators, teachers, and peers "that expects disabled students to participate and perform on a par with non-disabled students communicates an important message . . . : that regardless of physical characteristics and disabilities, students are more similar than different" (Asch, 1989, p. 191). Murray-Seegert (1989) reported from her study, "The fact that severely disabled students were not isolated in their self-contained classrooms, but were present in so many school and community areas, had a positive influence on their access to intergroup relations. The special education teachers promoted proximity by scheduling as much instruction as possible outside the special education classrooms, by using common facilities at the same time as regular students, and by making sure that their students participated in special school events" (p. 119).

Students with and without disabilities can enjoy mutual friendships. In fact, positive characteristics in the area of social skills, even for a student with a disability, may have much greater impact in developing friendships. Interestingly, in a study by Grenot-Schuyer (1994), "characteristics such as developmental level and receptive language ability did not differentiate friends from acquaintances" (p. 259). Green, Schleien, Mactavish, and Benepe (1995) discovered that nondisabled friends of persons with mental retardation were attracted to the friendship not only for altruistic reasons, but for discovered similarities such as (a) common interests, (b) compatible skill levels in activities, and (c) appropriate social skills. Today, individuals with developmental disabilities and "mental retardation are living among, working, playing and interacting with their peers without disabilities. Friendships between adults with and without mental retardation may be the key to ensuring that transitions from segregated services to community environments are successful" (Green et al., 1995, p. 92).

Because "teacher behavior, classroom climate, and instructional practices may differently affect the development and maintenance of friendships in inclusive classrooms" (Staub et al., 1994, p. 324), teachers should attempt to provide experiences for all students with disabilities, even severe disabilities, that promote developing friendships with students without disabilities. Asch (1989) described the following, which might be crucial practices in facilitating these friendships:

1. the amount of integration;
2. the expectation that the disabled student meet class norms of participation, behavior, and cooperation;
3. creation of situations where the disabled student must interact in projects with non-disabled classmates and can make a positive contribution;
4. assertiveness on the part of parents when children are young to create opportunities for children to play with others outside of school;
5. similar assertiveness by the disabled student to create opportunities if others do not initiate them;
6. equipping disabled students with skills to function as independently as possible in the widest range of activities; and,
7. an accessible environment for communication, mobility and transportation. (pp. 196–197)

In a more recent study, Salisbury and colleagues (1995) discovered a number of groups of strategies that appeared effective for teachers to use to foster the development of interpersonal relationships between students with and without disabilities. These included (a) actively facilitating social interactions (cooperative grouping, collaborative problem solving, peer tutoring and classroom roles, and time and opportunities for interaction), (b) valuing insights and contributions of students, (c) building community in the classroom, (d) modeling acceptance, and (e) building and administrative support.

Employment

One of the main purposes of education is to prepare an individual for an occupation and employment. For an individual with a disability, the prospect of gainful employment is much different from that for an individual without a disability. It is well documented that individuals with disabilities, when compared with the rest of the population, are significantly more often unemployed and underemployed (McCarthy, 1988; Shapiro, 1993). In fact, "problems of poverty, unemployment and underemployment, and associated social isolation are, in part, attributable to a denial of basic civil rights to citizens with disabilities" (Kilbury et al., 1992, p. 6). Even in terms of language used in the business sector, "disability . . . refers exclusively to those physical or health conditions that limit an individual's ability to work" (Gliedman & Roth, 1980, p. 275) and perhaps has perpetuated the practice of not fairly evaluating the skills of a person with a disability, which then has led to employment discrimination.

Matkin (1983) and Funk (1987) described some of the "unfounded" perceptions of employers toward workers with disabilities: (a) increased costs are a barrier to hiring disabled workers, especially when architectural changes are believed by the employer to be necessary; (b) insurance rates for employees will increase when disabled workers are hired; (c) attendance among disabled workers will be substandard, job turnover will be higher, and productivity will be negatively affected; and (d) the disabled employee will be less flexible in the ability to perform a variety of jobs, thereby increasing the associated manpower needs (costs) of the employer.

It seems that the business sector is following a process similar to that of the educational sector and that employers are going through a transformation of attitudes and beliefs similar to that of general education teachers and students without disabilities. Efforts to facilitate the acceptance of people with disabilities into the workplace will apparently be facilitated by improving the attitudes of employers and co-workers and altering the workplace environment.

Employers

Just as general educators who support inclusion efforts in the school often have had previous positive experiences with students with disabilities, employers and co-workers who have had previous positive experiences with employees with disabilities have a positive attitude about employing and working with an individual with a disability (Levy, Jessop, &, Rimmerman, 1992). Kilbury et al. (1992) predicts that "the integration into the workplace of citizens with disabilities as a result of the passage of the Americans with Disabilities Act should allow the predominantly nondisabled workforce a chance to modify their attitudes towards this minority group" (pp. 8–9).

Perhaps the business sector has reached a time of readiness to accept persons with disabilities as equal members of the work community as education is accepting students with disabilities as equal members of the school community. In a survey of employment executives of the Fortune 500 listing at the time, Levy and associates (1992) found the attitudes "quite favorable to employment of persons with disabilities, even severe disabilities both in terms of its advantages for the individual and lack of disadvantages for others in the work setting" (p. 71). Similarly, Black and Meyer (1992) concluded that "persons in the business community can adjust their existing conceptions of work and productivity to allow for the . . . intensive supports necessary for employment participation by persons with very severe disabilities" (p. 472).

Employees/Co-Workers Without Disabilities

Just as students without disabilities need appropriate information about and positive experiences with students with disabilities, so does the co-worker of a person with disabilities, with experience being the most likely of the two. Employers can provide "interventions" of knowledge and experience to employees without disabilities to enhance positive attitude change rather than expecting or assuming that the employee with the disability will do all the changing (Chadsey-Rusch & Heal, 1995). These experiences, as in the general classroom, should be structured and "normal" and suggest that "experience with persons with disabilities in the work context is associated with positive attitudes . . . and suggest that it is positive contact around work itself that determines attitudes towards employability and that attitudes toward persons with disabilities in general are also similarly affected by such work contact" (Levy et al., 1992, p. 73).

Hagner, Cotton, Goodall, and Nisbet (1992) reported that, after having experiences with co-workers with disabilities, even those who are involved in supportive employment situations, co-workers appeared to treat co-workers with disabilities "as full-fledged members of the work group and supported them in whatever way was required, as they would do for anyone else, without calculating who received or gave more. Support was perceived as mutual, even when it might appear one-sided to an outsider" (p. 253).

Employees with Disabilities

Certainly any education and training program for students with disabilities will focus on successful skill development.

However, successful transition to the work environment should also include, when appropriate, "effective social skills training . . . to enhance the social competence of students" (O'Reilly & Glynn, 1995, p. 187). As students with disabilities become adults and/or employees with disabilities, they must display appropriate interpersonal skills for increased acceptance by co-workers and job fulfillment (Abery & Fahnestock, 1994). Besides these skills, employees with disabilities may often be placed in the role of "educator" about their particular disability.

Health Care

Although not all individuals with disabilities will have contact with the health care system, many who do are likely to discover accompanying negative attitudes. As Falconer (1982) described, "When illness or injury occurs, most individuals are rapidly reduced to a childlike dependent status. Those who fully recover return to adult status; the denigrating experience of disability soon becomes a distant nightmare. Those who fail to recover are forced to participate in a medical system which values health, beauty and physical perfection. The disabled are the failures of medical care, to be hidden away, experimented on, kept-alive, allowed to live in society only as second-class citizens" (p. 137).

One main area for concern for persons with disabilities regarding the health care environment is that of choice where "more health care decisions are made by more people, the decisions have more and far ranging consequences, and the disabled are less involved in the decision-making process" (Falconer, 1982, p. 140). In reflecting on her experiences with the health system and the fact that health care professionals get little if any training about people with disabilities, Saxton (1984) reflected, "In all my hospital experiences, the saddest part was always the same. All those people trying so hard to help me. . . . All of them hoping for me to get better and do well, all wanting to be kind and useful, all feeling how important helping me was. Yet never did anyone of them ask what it was like for me. They never asked me if I wanted their help" (p. 133).

Media

Because knowledge is a major contributing factor to the attitudes that individuals have toward individuals with disabilities, and the majority of citizens receive most of their information through the media, then the attitudes the media perpetuates about individuals with disabilities are extremely important (Schleifer & Klein, 1984). Today, people with disabilities appear in all forms of media, from the Sunday advertisement inserts, to comic strips, to being the main characters in television shows, specials, and films. An important question is whether the disability featured is only one dimension or the *main* dimension of the character.

Several authors believe the media in particular contributes to society's negative attitudes (Biklen, 1987; Longmore, 1987; Shapiro, 1993). Norden (1994) wrote, "the movie industry has perpetuated stereotypes over the years . . . so durable and pervasive that they have become mainstream society's perception of disabled people" (p. 3). Attitudes are affected by the use of language in the media, such as "victim," "suffered," "afflicted," "crippled," and "confined." Several categories of negative stereotypes are often perpetuated through the media, including (a) the cap-in-hand/tin-cup image (pleading for help); (b) telethon poster child, when the disability is the focus and the person gets lost; (c) superhero (i.e., "supercrip"), where the focus on "overcoming" the disability has devalued a legitimate claim to fame; and (d) the grisly image of a "fate worse than death" (the terrible accident, illness, condition with which the viewer or reader could never cope). Commenting further on the media, Lynch and Thomas (1994) wrote, "The concept of a person with a disability as "victim" is embedded in the public press and everyday conversations of the general public. . . . The search for sympathy for "victims" of disease and disability is big business. However, the message promoted does not emphasize a potential for independence or the individuality of each person. . . . People with disabilities are characterized either as victims, or as inspirational figures who overcame their disability by some miracle" (p. 8).

Conversely, the media in general and the broadcast industry specifically can be important sources of accurate information. In one review of research, Byrd and Elliott (1988) pointed out that "accurate depiction of disability may positively influence attitudes of viewers toward persons with disabilities. These results imply that the mass media can play a role in the formulation of informed, positive attitudes among the public by depicting accurate characterizations of persons with disabilities" (p. 89).

A Review of Suggestions for Improving Attitudes

Although several suggestions have been discussed or implied in this chapter, the following is a brief but important list of the major effective practices in improving attitudes toward people with disabilities, as mentioned by a number of authors (Asch, 1989; J. Donaldson, 1980; File & Buzzelli, 1991; Horne, 1988; Jorgensen, 1992; Murray-Seegert, 1989):

1. Provide accurate information about disabilities that promotes them not as deficits, but as a normal part and variation within humanity.

2. Implement a behavior change component. Do not simply talk about people with disabilities; get involved with repeated interactions, both directly

and indirectly, with people with disabilities, in situations that are cooperative and co-equal.

3. Emphasize affective education, as well as information.

4. Locate the interventions where they belong: in program and building accessibility; the attitudes of teachers and employers; and so forth.

5. Consider using disability simulations to analyze the dynamics of prejudice in group discussions.

6. Expose the inappropriate portrayal of disabilities in the media, social policies, and practices.

Summary

The purpose of this chapter has been to review the effects that positive and negative attitudes have on persons with disabilities. The impact that service delivery philosophy has toward attitudes has also been addressed. The chapter has examined some of the major "attitude environments" that involve persons with and without disabilities and presented some strategies that promote positive attitudes toward persons with disabilities.

 QUESTIONS

1. What are the main factors that produce negative attitudes toward individuals with disabilities?

2. What are some specific strategies that are effective in producing positive attitudes toward persons with disabilities by general and special education teachers?

3. What are some specific strategies that are effective in producing positive attitudes toward students with disabilities by students without disabilities?

4. What are some specific strategies that are effective in producing positive attitudes toward persons with disabilities by employers and co-workers?

5. What may be the main concern of persons with disabilities about the health care system?

6. What effect does the media have in producing attitudes toward individuals with disabilities?

7. What components would be included in a "positive attitude curriculum" toward individuals with disabilities?

References

Abery, B. H., & Fahnestock, M. (1994). Enhancing the social inclusion of persons with developmental disabilities. In M. F. Hayden & B. H. Abery (Eds.), *Challenges for a service system in transition: Ensuring quality community experiences for persons with developmental disabilities* (pp. 83–119). Baltimore: Brookes.

Asch, A. (1989). Has the law made a difference? What some disabled students have to say. In D. Lipsky & A. Gartner (Eds.), *Beyond separate education: Quality education for all* (pp. 181–205). Baltimore: Brookes.

Baker, E. T., Wang, M. C., & Walberg, H. J. (1994). The effects of inclusion on learning. *Educational Leadership, 52*(4), 33–35.

Barker, R. G. (1948). The social psychology of physical disability. *Journal of Social Issues, 4*(4), 28–37.

Berry, J. O., & Jones, W. H. (1991). Situational and dispositional components of reactions toward persons with disabilities. *The Journal of Social Psychology, 131,* 673–684.

Biklen, D. (1987). Framed: Print journalism's treatment of disability issues. In A. Gartner & T. Joe (Eds.), *Images of the disabled, disabling images* (pp. 79–95). New York: Praeger.

Biklen, D., Corrigan, C., & Quick, D. (1989). Beyond obligation: Students' relations with each other in integrated classes. In D. Lipsky & A. Gartner (Eds.), *Beyond separate education: Quality education for all* (pp. 207–221). Baltimore: Brookes.

Black, J., & Meyer, L. H. (1992). But . . . is it really work? Social validity of employment training for persons with very severe disabilities. *American Journal on Mental Retardation, 96,* 463–474.

Bogdan, R., & Biklen, D. (1977). Handicapism. *Social Policy, 7*(5), 14–19.

Brady, M. P., Linehan, S. A., Campbell, P. C., & Neilson, W. L. (1992). Too high, too low, too young: An ethnography of teachers' curriculum and instruction decisions for students with severe disabilities. *Education and Training in Mental Retardation, 27,* 354–366.

Brotherson, M. J., Cook, C. C., Cunman-Lahr, R., & Wehmeyer, M. L. (1995). Policy supporting self-determination in the environments of children with disabilities. *Education and Training in Mental Retardation and Developmental Disabilities, 30,* 3–13.

Buscaglia, L. (1983). *The disabled and their parents: A counseling challenge* (rev. ed.). New York: Holt, Rinehart and Winston.

Byrd, E. K., & Elliott, T. R. (1988). Media and disability: A discussion of research. In H. E. Yuker (Ed.), *Attitudes toward persons with disabilities* (pp. 82–95). New York: Springer.

Carrigan, J. (1994). Attitudes about persons with disabilities: A pilot program. *Art Education, 47,* 16–21.

Chadsey-Rusch, J., & Heal, L. W. (1995). Building consensus from transition experts on social integration outcomes and interventions. *Exceptional Children, 62,* 165–187.

Donaldson, J. (1980). Changing attitudes toward handicapped persons: A review and analysis of research. *Exceptional Children, 46,* 504–514.

Donaldson, R. M., Helmstetter, E., Donaldson, J., & West, R. (1994). Influencing high school students' attitudes toward and interactions with peers with disabilities. *Social Education, 58,* 233–237.

Eichinger, J., Rizzo, T. L., & Sirotnik, B. (1991). Changing attitudes toward people with disabilities. *Teacher Education and Special Education, 14,* 121–126.

Falconer, J. (1982). Health care delivery: Problems for the disabled. In M. G. Eisenberg, C. Griggins, & R. J. Duval (Eds.), *Disabled people as second-class citizens* (pp. 137–151). New York: Springer.

File, N. K., & Buzzelli, C. A. (1991). Gaining respect and understanding: Helping children learn about disabilities. *Day Care and Early Education, 18,* 39–40.

Fine, M., & Asch, A. (1988). Disability beyond stigma: Social interaction, discrimination, and activism. *Journal of Social Issues, 44,* 3–21.

Fox, R., & Rotatori, A. F. (1986). Changing undergraduate attitudes towards the developmentally disabled through volunteering. *College Student Journal, 20,* 162–167.

Funk, R. (1987). Disability rights: From caste to class in the context of civil rights. In A. Gartner & T. Joe (Eds.), *Images of the disabled, disabling images* (pp. 7–30). New York: Praeger.

Gerry, M. H., & Mirsky, A. J. (1992). Guiding principles for public policy on natural supports. In J. Nesbit (Ed.), *Natural supports in school, at work, and in the community for people with severe disabilities* (pp. 341–346). Baltimore: Brookes.

Giangreco, M. F., Dennis, R. E., & Cloninger, C. J. (1993). "I've counted Jon": Transformational experiences of teachers educating students with disabilities. *Exceptional Children, 59,* 359–372.

Gleason, J. J. (1991). Multicultural and exceptional student education: Separate but equal? *Preventing School Failure, 36,* 47–49.

Gliedman, J., & Roth, W. (1980). *The unexpected minority: Handicapped children in America.* New York: Harcourt Brace Jovanovich.

Green, F. P., Schleien, S. J., Mactavish, J., & Benepe, S. (1995). Nondisabled adults' perceptions of relationships in the early stages of arranged partnerships with peers with mental retardation. *Education and Training in Mental Retardation and Developmental Disabilities, 30,* 91–108.

Grenot-Scheyer, M. (1994). The nature of interactions between students with severe disabilities and their friends and acquaintances without disabilities. *The Journal of the Association for Persons with Severe Handicaps, 19,* 253–262.

Hagner, D. C., Cotton, P., Goodall, S., & Nisbet, J. (1992). The perspectives of supportive coworkers: Nothing special. In J. Nesbit (Ed.), *Natural supports in school, at work, and in the community for people with severe disabilities* (pp. 241–256). Baltimore: Brookes.

Hahn, H. (1987). Civil rights for disabled Americans: The foundation of a political agenda. In A. Gartner & T. Joe (Eds.), *Images of the disabled, disabling images* (pp. 181–203). New York: Praeger.

Hahn, H. (1988). The politics of physical differences: Disability and discrimination. *Journal of Social Issues, 44,* 39–47.

Hannah, M. E. (1988). Teacher attitudes toward children with disabilities: An ecological analysis. In H. E. Yuker (Ed.), *Attitudes toward persons with disabilities* (pp. 154–170). New York: Springer.

Haring, T. G. (1991). Social relationships. In L. Meyers, C. Peck, & L. Brown (Eds.), *Critical issues in the lives of people with severe disabilities* (pp. 195–218). Baltimore: Brookes.

Helmstetter, E., Peck, C. A., & Giangreco, M. F. (1994). Outcomes of interactions with peers with moderate or severe disabilities: A statewide survey of high school students. *The Journal of the Association for Persons with Severe Handicaps, 19,* 263–276.

Horne, M. D. (1988). Modifying peer attitudes toward the handicapped: Procedures and research issues. In H. E. Yuker (Ed.), *Attitudes toward persons with disabilities* (pp. 203–222). New York: Springer.

Hunt, P., Staub, D., Alwell, M., & Goetz, L. (1994). Achievement by all students within the context of cooperative learning groups. *The Journal of the Association for Persons with Severe Handicaps, 19,* 290–301.

Janney, R. E., Snell, M., Beers, M. K., & Raynes, M. (1995a). Integrating students with moderate and severe disabilities: Classroom teachers' beliefs and attitudes about implementing an educational change. *Educational Administration Quarterly, 31,* 86–114.

Janney, R. E., Snell, M., Beers, M. K., & Raynes, M. (1995b). Integrating students with moderate and severe disabilities into general education classes. *Exceptional Children, 61,* 425–439.

Jorgensen, C. M. (1992). Natural supports in inclusive schools: Curricular and teaching strategies. In J. Nesbit (Ed.), *Natural supports in school, at work, and in the community for people with severe disabilities* (pp. 179–215). Baltimore: Brookes.

Kilbury, R. F., Benshoff, J. J., & Rubin, S. E. (1992). The interaction of legislation, public attitudes, and access to opportunities for persons with disabilities. *Journal of Rehabilitation, 58*(4), 6–9.

Kishi, G. S., & Meyer, L. H. (1994). What children report and remember: A six-year follow-up of the effects of social contact between peers with and without severe disabilities. *The Journal of the Association for Persons with Severe Handicaps, 19,* 277–289.

Larson, D. A. (1986). What disabilities are protected under the Rehabilitation Act of 1973? *Labor Law Journal, 137,* 752–766.

Lessen, E. (1991). On being different. In S. Schwartz (Ed.), *Exceptional people: A guide for understanding* (pp. 29–49). New York: McGraw-Hill.

Levy, J. M., Jessop, D. J., & Rimmerman, A. (1992). Attitudes of Fortune 500 corporate executives toward the employability of persons with severe disabilities: A national study. *Mental Retardation, 30,* 67–75.

Longmore, P. K. (1987). Screening stereotypes: Images of disabled people in television and motion pictures. In A. Gartner & T. Joe (Eds.), *Images of the disabled, disabling images* (pp. 65–78). New York: Praeger.

Lynch, R. T., & Thomas, K. R. (1994). People with disabilities as victims: Changing an ill-advised paradigm. *Journal of Rehabilitation, 60*(1), 8–11.

Makas, E. (1988). Positive attitudes toward disabled people: Disabled and nondisabled persons' perspectives. *Journal of Social Issues, 44,* 49–61.

Matkin, R. E. (1983). Educating employers to hire disabled workers. *Journal of Rehabilitation, 49*(3), 60–63.

McCarthy, H. (1988). Attitudes that affect employment opportunities for persons with disabilities. In H. E. Yuker (Ed.), *Attitudes toward persons with disabilities* (pp. 246–261). New York: Springer.

McGee, G. G., & Paradis, T. (1993). Free effects of integration on levels of autistic behavior. *Topics in Early Childhood Special Education, 13,* 57–67.

McGookey, K. (1992). Drama, disability and your classroom. *Teaching Exceptional Children, 24*(2), 12–14.

Morrison, J. M., & Ursprung, A. W. (1987). Children's attitudes toward people with disabilities: A review of the literature. *Journal of Rehabilitation, 53,* 45–49.

Murray-Seegert, C. (1989). *Nasty girls, thugs, and humans like us: Social relations between severely disabled and nondisabled students in high school.* Baltimore: Brookes.

Norden, M. F. (1994). *The cinema of isolation: A history of physical disability in the movies.* New Brunswick, NJ: Rutgers University Press.

O'Reilly, M. F., & Glynn, D. (1995). Using a process social skills training approach with adolescents with mild intellectual disabilities in a high school setting. *Education and Training in Mental Retardation and Developmental Disabilities, 30*, 187–198.

Putnam, J. W., Spiegel, A. N., & Bruininks, R. H. (1995). Future direction in education and inclusion of students with disabilities: A delphi investigation. *Exceptional Children, 61*, 553–576.

Ringlaben, R. P., & Price, J. R. (1981). Regular classroom teachers' perceptions of mainstreaming effects. *Exceptional Children, 47*, 302–304.

Rittenhouse, R. K., Johnson, C., Overton, B., Freeman, S., & Jaussi, K. (1991). The black and deaf movements in America since 1960: Parallelism and an agenda for the future. *American Annals of the Deaf, 136*, 392–400.

Sale, P., & Carey, D. M. (1995). The sociometric status of students with disabilities in a full-inclusion school. *Exceptional Children, 62*, 6–19.

Salend, S. J. (1994). Strategies for assessing attitudes toward individuals with disabilities. *The School Counselor, 41*, 338–342.

Salisbury, C. L., Gallucci, C., Palombaro, M. M., & Peck, C. A. (1995). Strategies that promote social relations among elementary students with and without severe disabilities. *Exceptional Children, 62*, 125–137.

Saxton, M. (1984). The something that happened before I was born. In A. Brightman (Ed.), *Ordinary moments: The disabled experience* (pp. 127–140). Baltimore: University Park Press.

Schleifer, M. J., & Klein, S. D. (1984). Media and attitudes towards people with disabilities. *Exceptional Parent, 14*(2), 15.

Schnorr, R. F. (1990). Peter? He comes and he goes. First graders' perspectives on a part-time mainstream student. *The Journal of the Association for Persons with Severe Handicaps, 19*, 231–240.

Shapiro, J. P. (1993). *No pity: People with disabilities forging a new civil rights movement.* New York: Times Books.

Sharpe, M. N., York, J. L., & Knight, J. (1994). Effects of inclusion on the academic performance of classmates without disabilities. *Remedial and Special Education, 15*, 281–287.

Smith, T. E. C., Polloway, E. A., Patton, J. R., & Dowdy, C. A. (1995). *Teaching students with special needs in inclusive settings.* Needham Heights, MA: Allyn & Bacon.

Staub, D., & Peck, C. A. (1995). What are the outcomes for nondisabled students? *Educational Leadership, 52*(4), 36–40.

Staub, D., Schwartz, I. S., Gallucci, C., & Peck, C. A. (1994). Four portraits of friendship at an inclusive school. *The Journal of the Association for Persons with Severe Handicaps, 19*, 314–325.

Strully, J. L., & Strully, C. F. (1992). The struggle toward inclusion and the fulfillment of friendship. In J. Nesbit (Ed.), *Natural supports in school, at work, and in the community for people with severe disabilities* (pp. 165–177). Baltimore: Brookes.

Stubbins, J. (1988). The politics of disability. In H. E. Yuker (Ed.), *Attitudes toward persons with disabilities* (pp. 21–32). New York: Springer.

Weinberg, N. (1988). Another perspective: Attitudes of people with disabilities. In H. E. Yuker (Ed.), *Attitudes toward persons with disabilities* (pp. 141–153). New York: Springer.

Weisman, J. (1986). Who wouldn't want me. In F. Weiner (Ed.), *No apologies* (pp. 66–67). New York: St. Martin's Press.

Westbrook, M. T., Legge, V., & Pennay, M. (1993). Attitudes towards people with disabilities in a multicultural society. *Social Science & Medicine, 36*, 615–623.

Wolery, M., Werts, M. G., Caldwell, N. K., Snyder, E. D., and Lisowski, L. (1995). Experienced teachers' perceptions of resources and support for inclusion. *Education and Training in Mental Retardation and Developmental Disabilities, 30*, 15–26.

York, J., Vandercook, T., MacDonald, C., Heise-Neff, C., & Caughney, E. (1992). Feedback about integrating middle-school students with severe disabilities in general education classes. *Exceptional Children, 58*, 244–258.

Appropriate Services
and Other Practices

SECTION VII

Best Practices

The best practices literature on educating students with developmental disabilities has long held that services encompassed by the broad meaning of the term therapy must be integrated, whenever possible, into the teaching environments. This approach allows teachers to learn specialized techniques often not taught to educators and to learn therapy routines, thus expanding the ability to offer specialized treatment to students at times when therapists are not present. Further, such an approach allows the therapist to work with more than one student at a time, thus increasing the engaged time of students.

Education and treatment of students with disabilities must often be done by teams of professionals if growth is going to be made by the student. These teams work not only with the student but with other environmental (i.e., home and community) factors that affect the individual's life.

The current trend toward fully including students with developmental disabilities in general education classrooms leads to an emphasis on the roles of all professionals, but especially those of the classroom teacher and the paraeducator. The inclusion trend demonstrates that education and services for individuals with developmental disabilities are in an ongoing state of refinement and modification.

This Section of the Book

Section VII concludes the book with three chapters: Chapter 25 on the need to define the role of the paraeducator, Chapter 26 on the changes in the roles and strategies for creating inclusive schools, and Chapter 27 on methods for achieving change within social service and educational systems. The common thread that runs through these chapters is the pressure placed on systems by the inclusion movement. If students with developmental disabilities are to be successful in educational settings, changes must occur in how and by whom services are delivered. Beyond this the service systems for children and adults with developmental disabilities must be changed. Some of the promising practices to meet these ends are included in this concluding section of the book.

The Roles and Responsibilities of Paraeducators Who Serve Students with Developmental Disabilities

CHAPTER 25

Anna Lou Pickett and Kent Gerlach

Learning Outcomes

After reading this chapter, you should be able to

- Describe currently recognized distinctions in roles and duties of school professionals and paraeducators.

- Describe the differences in the responsibilities of principals, teachers, and other school professionals for effectively integrating paraeducators into educational teams.

- Describe the core competencies required by all paraeducators employed in inclusive classrooms and other education programs serving children and youth with disabilities.

- Describe specific additional competencies required by paraeducators employed in (a) home visitor and center-based programs for infants and young children, (b) inclusive classrooms serving school-age students, and (c) vocational and transition training programs.

- Define policy questions and issues connected with paraeducator roles, preparation, and supervision that require the attention of different constituencies.

TERMS

The following term is important for the understanding of this chapter:

Paraeducator (paraprofessional, aide, assistant, or technician): Personnel (a) who either instructs or provides related services to children or youth and their parents, and (b) who works under the direction of teachers and other professional practitioners who are responsible for determining educational needs for individual and groups of students, designing and implementing programs and services, and assessing the impact on student performance and progress.

Introduction

Paraeducators have become important contributors nationwide to programs serving children with disabilities. Not only do they serve as members of instructional teams in inclusive general education classrooms or other special education programs, but they work as physical, occupational, and communication disorder assistants. They are health assistants and speech–language pathology assistants, and increasingly, local school districts are employing them to work in early childhood and vocational training and transitional programs for students with disabilities.

The paraeducator, as a member of the instructional team, assists and enables the teacher to fulfill the functions of a classroom manager. The paraeducator performs both administrative and instructional duties that complement and support the teacher's programmatic and management functions. Paraeducators are still referred to as teacher aides in many districts. Other titles include instructional assistant, educational assistant, paraprofessional, instructional aide, teaching assistant, educational technician, or transition trainer.

The roles and responsibilities of paraprofessionals, like those of their professional colleagues, have become more complex and demanding since paraprofessionals were introduced into classrooms as teacher aides more than 40 years ago. In today's schools and other educational settings, they work alongside teachers or other professional practitioners as technicians "who are more aptly described as *paraeducators*, just as their counterparts in law and medicine are designated as paralegals and paramedics" (Pickett, 1989).

Although many reasons exist for employing paraeducators, the primary and in essence the paramount reason is to improve the quality of education and related services for children, youth, and their parents. To ensure that the presence of paraeducators on service delivery teams does indeed increase the quality of education programs, policies and infrastructures designed to improve their deployment, management, preparation, and retention must be incorporated in state and local regulatory and administrative procedures. Distinctions in the roles of teachers and paraeducators in differentiated staffing arrangements must be delineated. Similarities and differences in the roles of paraeducators working in various programs and settings must be defined. Skills needed to work in different programs and levels of paraeducator positions must be identified and training needs determined. Comprehensive opportunities for training and career development must be provided, and standards and systems to certify that paraeducators have the skills they require must be established (Pickett, 1996; Pickett, Vasa, & Steckelberg, 1993).

To help teachers successfully meet current and emerging challenges and to expand the availability of services designed to meet the needs of all children and youth, policy makers have turned to paraeducators to support teachers' programmatic and administrative functions in classrooms and other educational settings. Programs include (a) inclusive general and special education programs serving students who have developmental, physical, sensory, and learning disabilities and challenging behaviors; (b) vocational and occupational work experience programs, including supported employment programs for students with disabilities; (c) transitional training programs to prepare students with developmental disabilities to live independently or with support in their communities; (d) physical and occupational therapy and speech–language pathology programs; and (e) early intervention and preschool programs serving children with and without disabilities (Blalock, 1991; Pickett, 1996).

Addressing these needs must be undertaken collaboratively. State departments of education, local education agencies, institutions of higher education, unions, and professional organizations must all be actively engaged in developing and maintaining policies, standards, and infrastructures that will enhance the status, increase the productivity, and improve the management of paraeducators. One example of this that helps frame the discussion that follows is the Position Statement of the Board of Directors of the Mental Retardation and Developmental Disabilities Division (MRDD) of the

Council for Exceptional Children (CEC). That statement is found in Appendix 25A at the end of this chapter.

Information in this chapter is divided into two parts. The first part, Integrating Paraeducators into Service Delivery Teams, is concerned with the emerging roles of paraeducators in differentiated staffing arrangements, role distinctions among principals and teachers in the supervision and management of paraeducators, and the knowledge and skills required by teachers to work effectively with paraeducators. The purpose of the second part, Developing Training and Other Infrastructures, is to provide policy makers and administrators with information they can build on to identify skills and knowledge that paraeducators need to work in different education programs and settings and to develop and maintain comprehensive systems of professional development for paraeducators.

Integrating Paraeducators into Service Delivery Teams

Paraeducators in Differentiated Staffing Arrangements

The delivery of instructional and related services to children and youth with developmental disabilities requires different levels of staff with different levels of skills. Differential staffing identifies the distinction in roles and duties and recognizes the hierarchy of skills required by different personnel in different disciplines, including teachers, physical and occupational therapists, speech–language pathologists, and paraeducators. The move to differentiated staffing in various educational settings has had a profound impact on the roles of paraeducators. While they still perform clerical tasks and monitor students in lunchrooms and study halls, on buses and playgrounds, paraeducators also work alongside teachers as active participants in all components of the instructional process.

In some cases school professionals and paraeducators may perform some tasks that overlap. It is, however, the professional staff member who is the team leader, decision maker, interpreter of data, identifier of instructional and related service goals, organizer of learning experiences, and evaluator of educational outcomes (Pickett & Gerlach, 1997; Snodgrass, 1991).

Duties for instructional paraeducators include instructing individual and small groups of students, documenting data about student performance, administering and scoring standardized tests, conducting prescribed reading and math programs, implementing teacher-designed behavior management behavior programs and disciplinary procedures, and preparing instructional materials (Blalock, 1991; Lyons, 1995;

Passaro, Pickett, Latham, & HongBo, 1994; Pickett, Faison, & Formanek, 1993; Pickett, Vasa, & Steckelberg, 1993).

Although paraeducators support and extend program and administrative functions of professional practitioners in many ways, placing them in a classroom and other educational settings is not necessarily a panacea. In fact, problems can be created if their duties are not clearly defined and communicated to them, if lines of authority are not delineated, if their work is not effectively supervised, if their on-the-job performance is not systematically evaluated, and if they are not prepared to carry out their assigned tasks.

Management and Supervision of Paraeducators

Principals, teachers, and related services personnel have individual and shared responsibility for integrating paraeducators into the educational team. The specific responsibilities of supervisory personnel are described below.

Principals are responsible for ensuring that teachers and paraeducators understand the distinction in their roles and are aware of district policies connected with the management and supervision of paraeducators, and for scheduling opportunities for teachers and paraeducators to meet regularly for on-the-job training and planning. In addition, principals should develop, in concert with teachers, criteria and instruments for assessing the performance of and conducting annual performance reviews of paraeducators. Other roles of the principal could include assisting members of the instructional team to resolve interpersonal or other problems that may occur in the classroom and serving as an advocate for the roles and contributions of paraeducators in the delivery of education and related services (Pickett & Gerlach, 1997).

Teachers or related services personnel are responsible for planning and assigning tasks to be performed by paraeducators on a daily, weekly, or periodic basis; directing and monitoring the day-to-day work of paraeducators; providing orientation and on-the-job training for paraeducators; providing regular feedback about on-the-job performance of paraeducators; serving as an advocate for the roles and contributions of paraeducators in the delivery of education and related services; and serving as a professional role model for paraeducators working with children, youth, their parents, and staff (French & Pickett, 1996; Pickett, Vasa, & Steckelberg, 1993).

Effective practice has demonstrated that, to carry out these management and administrative functions, teachers must be prepared to integrate, direct, and provide on-the-job coaching for paraeducators. French and Pickett (1996) pointed out the skills they require:

1. A knowledge of district policies with regard to the employment, roles and duties, placement, and evaluation of paraeducators;

2. An ability to plan, assign, and schedule specific duties for paraeducators based on a knowledge of their previous experience, level of training, and demonstrated competency to perform a task;

3. An ability to direct and monitor the day-to-day work of the paraeducator;

4. An ability to delegate appropriate tasks to paraeducators;

5. An ability to use effective communication and problem-solving techniques to reduce interpersonal or other problems that may occur in the classroom;

6. An ability to objectively and systematically determine the strengths and weaknesses of paraeducators assigned to the classroom; and

7. An ability to plan and provide structured on-the-job coaching sessions based on the identified training needs of the paraeducators.

Developing Training Programs and Other Infrastructures

Despite increased reliance on paraeducators and increased emphasis on the instructional nature of their jobs, most state departments of education, local education agencies, and other education provider agencies do not have administrative policies or regulatory procedures that set standards for the employment, training, and management of paraeducators. For the most part, where guidelines and systems do exist, they often have not been revised or updated since the late 1960s or early 1970s when paraeducators were first included in the workforce. The most critical issues connected with employment, training, and management of paraeducators that confront policy makers, administrators, and personnel developers in state departments of education, local education agencies, and institutions of higher education are summarized in the following paragraphs.

Although the vast majority of paraeducators spend most of their time providing instructional and other direct services to children, youth, and/or their parents, job descriptions have not been changed to reflect these more complex duties. (Pickett, 1996). The value of job descriptions that clearly delineate the roles and responsibilities of paraeducators cannot be overstated. Effective, well-constructed job descriptions will provide administrators, personnel developers, and teachers with information they can use to (a) identify skills and knowledge that paraeducators require to perform their duties, (b) determine experiential and education requirements for specific paraeducator positions, (c) establish criteria for advancement to other paraeducator positions, and (d) set standards for evaluating the performance of paraeducators.

Training for paraeducators, when it is available, is often highly parochial, is not competency based, and is rarely part of a comprehensive system of career development that includes (a) systematic on-the-job training, (b) structured inservice training, and (c) access to flexible postsecondary education that enables paraeducators to earn academic credit and degrees while they continue to work. Additionally, few states have credentialing systems or other mechanisms linked to competency-based training to certify that paraeducators have the skills they require to work in different levels of paraeducator positions (Pickett, 1996).

Finally, in addition to their programmatic and administrative functions, teachers and other professional practitioners are increasingly becoming more responsible for directing the work of paraeducators. For the most part, teachers are not prepared at either the undergraduate or the graduate level to work effectively with paraeducators or to assess the potential for even greater utilization of paraeducators as one method of freeing professional staff to plan and deliver individualized educational programs, confer with parents and colleagues, try broader ranges of instructional strategies, evaluate student progress, and achieve other educational outcomes (French & Pickett, 1996; Lindeman & Beegle, 1988). Effective practice dictates that these issues be addressed.

Initiating and maintaining comprehensive systems of training, career development, and credentialing or other mechanisms linked to training are not easy tasks. One key for effectively focusing attention on issues that surround the preparation and management of paraeducators is to establish partnerships representing provider agencies; 2- and 4-year programs in institutions of higher education; and unions and professional organizations with responsibility for or interest in improving the management, preparation and retention of skilled paraeducators (Pickett & Gerlach, 1997).

A competency-based core curriculum designed to prepare paraeducators to work with children and youth with disabilities in inclusive classrooms and communities has been developed by the National Resource Center for Paraprofessionals in Education and Related Services at the City University of New York. The curriculum and instructional materials were developed and pilot tested nationwide in different geographic and demographic areas. Participants in the pilot testing included community colleges, local school districts, Head Start and other early childhood programs, and agencies providing transitional and supported employment services to students with developmental disabilities.

Developed in 1993 through a grant from the Office of Special Education Programs, the suggested competency-based core curriculum is designed to prepare paraeducators to work with children and youth with disabilities in inclusive education and community-based programs. Three sets of instructional modules that comprise the program are preparing paraeducators to work in (a) center and home visitor programs for infants and young children with disabilities ages birth to 5, (b) inclusive general and special education programs serving school-age students, and (c) transitional services and supported employment programs.

The content in the core curriculum recognizes the similarities in the competencies that paraeducators require to work in various educational and related services. The content in the individual training programs stresses specific skills that paraeducators must have to work with children and youth of different ages who have different ability levels and educational needs. The goals of the training are designed to prepare all paraeducators to

1. Understand the value of inclusive education for children and youth with disabilities.

2. Understand the rights of children and youth with disabilities and their parents.

3. Respect diversity in cultural heritage, lifestyles, and value systems among children, youth, and their families.

4. Understand the distinctions in the roles and duties of professional personnel and paraeducators.

5. Communicate effectively with team members, children and youth, parents, and other people with whom they come into contact on the job.

6. Practice ethical and professional standards of conduct.

7. Participate effectively in different phases of the instructional process.

8. Assist children and youth with disabilities to build self-esteem and interpersonal skills that will help them avoid isolation in different educational and living environments.

9. Follow emergency, health, and safety procedures established by the agency.

The following subsections contain competencies required by all paraeducators, regardless of the program area in which they work, and specific competencies for paraeducators employed in different programs.

Core Competencies for All Paraeducators

To work in education and related services programs for children and youth with special needs, paraeducators must demonstrate the following (Pickett, Faison, & Formanek, 1993; Pickett, Faison, Formanek, & Semrau, 1993; Pickett, Faison, Formanek, & Woods, 1993):

1. An understanding of the value of serving children and youth with disabilities and other special needs in integrated settings.

2. An understanding of differentiated staffing patterns and the distinctions among the roles and responsibilities of professional and paraprofessional personnel.

3. An ability to communicate with colleagues, follow instructions, and use problem-solving and other skills that will enable them to work as effective members of the instructional team.

4. A knowledge of the legal and human rights of children and youth with special needs and their families.

5. A sensitivity to diversity in cultural heritage, lifestyles, and value systems among children, youth, and families they serve.

6. A knowledge of human development and milestones typically achieved at different ages, and risk factors that may prohibit or impede typical development.

7. An ability to motivate and assist children and youth with special needs to (a) build self-esteem, (b) develop interpersonal skills that will help avoid isolation in different learning and living environments, and (c) strengthen skills to become more independent by monitoring and controlling their behavior.

8. An ability to follow health, safety, and emergency procedures developed by the employing agency.

9. An ability to use assistive technology and adaptive equipment, and provide special care or physical assistance that infants, children and youth may require (e.g., positioning, transferring, feeding).

Specific Additional Competencies for Paraeducators in Home Visitor and Center-Based Programs for Infants and Young Children

To work in *center-based programs* for young children, paraeducators must demonstrate the following (Pickett, Faison, Formanek, & Semrau, 1993):

1. An ability to use developmentally appropriate instructional intervention for curriculum activities in the areas of cognitive, motor, self-help, social and play, and language development for infants and young children, ages birth to 5 years.

2. An ability to gather and share information about the performance of individual children with professional colleagues.

3. An ability to prepare and use developmentally appropriate materials.

4. An ability to communicate and work effectively with parents and other primary caregivers.

To work in *home visitor programs*, paraeducators must demonstrate the following (Pickett, Faison, Formanek, & Semrau, 1993):

1. An ability to participate as a member of Individualized Family Service Plan (IFSP) teams responsible for

developing service plans and educational objectives for children and their parents.

2. An ability to listen to and communicate with parents in order to gather information that the service delivery team can build on to meet the needs of the child and family.

3. (a) A knowledge of health care providers, social services, education agencies, and other support systems available in the community to assist parents and their child, and (b) an ability to support parents and provide them with the skills and information they require to gain access to these services.

Specific Additional Competencies for Paraeducators Working in Inclusive Classrooms and Programs for Students with Special Needs

To work in inclusive programs, paraeducators must demonstrate the following (Pickett, Faison, & Formanek, 1993):

1. An ability to tutor students in academic subjects and self-help skills using lesson plans and instructional strategies developed by teachers or other school professionals.

2. An ability to (a) gather and maintain data about the performance and behavior of individual students and (b) confer with special and general education practitioners about student schedules, instructional goals, progress, and performance.

3. An ability to use instructional procedures and reinforcement techniques that are developmentally and age appropriate.

4. An ability to operate computers, assistive technology, and adaptive equipment that will enable students with disabilities and other special needs to participate more fully in general education.

Specific Additional Competencies for Paraeducators Working in Vocational and Transitional Training Programs

To work in vocational and transitional programs, paraeducators must demonstrate the following (Pickett, Faison, Formanek, & Woods, 1993):

1. An understanding of the distinctions among different employment models.

2. An ability to participate as a member of the team responsible for transitional planning and vocational assessment for individual students.

3. An ability to participate in preemployment, vocational, or transitional training in classrooms or at off-campus sites.

4. An ability to task-analyze job requirements, sequence the day, observe and record data, and provide training at job sites using appropriate instructional interventions.

5. An ability to motivate students to work.

6. An ability to communicate effectively with employers and employees at work sites, and personnel or members of the public in other transitional learning environments.

7. An ability to modify services based on school and work site regulatory procedures.

8. (a) A knowledge of social, rehabilitation, and support systems that will enable youth to participate fully in the community and (b) an ability to provide students and parents with skills and information they can use to gain access to the services.

To address the competencies described in the previous subsections, policy makers, administrators, faculty in 2- and 4-year personnel preparation programs, unions, and parents need to find more effective ways of utilizing the resources of paraeducators in differentiated staffing arrangements; set standards for their employment, preparation, and supervision; and establish infrastructures that will assure the availability of opportunities for professional development. Pickett and Gerlach (1997) identified questions and issues that require the attention of various constituencies:

1. What barriers to or support for the development of standards and systems to improve the performance, management, and preparation of paraeducators exist in our state?

2. How do federal mandates and funding, state reimbursement, or collective bargaining agreements influence the employment and training of paraeducators in our state?

3. Should roles and duties for paraeducators be prescribed by the State Department of Education or another administrative agency?

4. Should our state have a credentialing system or another mechanism for ensuring that paraeducators have the skills required to carry out their duties? If one currently exists, does it need to be revised?

5. What is or should be the role of state and local agencies, 2- and 4-year institutions of higher education, professional organizations representing different disciplines, unions, and other stakeholders in setting standards for paraeducator utilization, professional development, credentialing, and management?

6. How can we strengthen linkages among the various partners?

Summary

This chapter has discussed several issues and questions that need to be addressed at local and state levels concerning the role of paraeducators working with children and youth who have developmental disabilities. Paraeducators should be supported as team members responsible for assisting in the delivery of education and related services. To address the previously listed questions and to achieve effective practice, policy makers, teachers, paraeducators, and personnel developers need to join forces to establish more effective systems and practices for supervising paraeducators and setting standards for the employment and preparation of paraeducators.

 QUESTIONS

1. What are the distinctions between teacher and paraeducator roles?

2. What are the responsibilities of principals in developing and supporting effective teacher and paraeducator teams?

3. What knowledge and skills are required by teachers to supervise and provide on-the-job coaching for paraeducators?

4. What core competencies are required by all paraeducators? What additional skills are required to work in a specific program or education setting?

5. Why is it important for state departments of education, local education agencies, institutions of higher education, and other stakeholders to cooperate in defining appropriate paraeducator roles; setting standards for their training, professional development, and supervision; and establishing infrastructures that enhance the skills and performance of paraeducators? How can these networks be established and sustained?

Appendix 25A
The Board of Directors–CEC MRDD
Position Statement on the Employment, Preparation, and Management of Paraeducators (Paraprofessionals) and Support Staff

As school districts move to include young children and school-aged students with developmental disabilities in general education programs, paraeducators and other support personnel are increasingly being asked to assume extended roles which are closely related to the functions of teachers, therapists, and other direct service professionals. Inclusion has, at times, blurred issues concerning supervision, training, placement and roles of these personnel. Despite the growing reliance on paraeducators in more complex and demanding roles, little attention is being paid to the employment, preparation and management of paraeducators (paraprofessionals) and support staff. Moreover, for the most part teachers and other professionals are typically not prepared at either the undergraduate or graduate levels to direct, and work effectively with, paraeducators.

It is the position of the Board of Directors of the Division on Mental Retardation and Developmental Disabilities that paraeducators and other support staff can be valuable human resources in providing education, vocational/transitional, therapeutic and other related services to children and youth with developmental disabilities and their parents. Further, paraeducators and other support staff must perform educational functions adjunct to the primary role of a teacher, therapist or other specialist who is licensed/credentialed/endorsed within the guidelines set by the state in which they are employed. Decisions concerning the placement and use of paraeducators and other support staff must be based on the needs of students with disabilities.

To ensure effective and appropriate teacher and administrative support for paraeducators in the delivery of education and related services in various settings, the Board calls on states, local districts, institutions of higher education and professional organizations to work together to develop standards, guidelines and advisory boards that address:

1. Role distinctions among teachers, therapists or other credentialed, licensed specialists and paraeducators working in a variety of programs and settings;

2. Strategies for structured, systematic management, supervision and evaluation of paraeducators;

3. Legal and ethical responsibilities for paraeducators working in a variety of positions;

4. Job descriptions that contain the skills (and constraints) required by paraeducators to perform their assigned tasks;

5. Opportunities for pre-service training, inservice training, and professional development combined with career advancement opportunities for paraeducators and other support staff;

6. Preparation of teachers, therapists and other specialists to manage and supervise paraeducators and other support staff. (cited in Hilton & Gerlach, 1997)

References

Blalock, G. (1991). Paraprofessionals: Critical team members in our special education programs. *Intervention in School and Clinic, 26,* 200–214.

French, N. K., & Pickett, A. L. (1996). *The utilization of paraprofessionals in special education: Issues for teacher educators.* Manuscript submitted for publication.

Hilton, A., & Gerlach, K. (1997). Employment, preparation and management of paraeducators: Challenges to appropriate service for students with developmental disabilities. *Education and Training in Mental Retardation and Developmental Disabilities, 32*(2), 71–76.

Lindeman, D. P., & Beegle, G. P. (1988). In brief: Pre-service training of the classroom paraprofessional: A national survey. *Teacher Education and Special Education, 11*(4), 183–186.

Lyons, D. (1995). *Training for special education-funded paraprofessionals.* Federal Way: Washington Education Association.

Passaro, P., Pickett, A. L., Latham, G., & HongBo, W. (1994). The training and support needs of paraeducators in rural special education settings. *Rural Special Education Quarterly, 13*(4), 3–9.

Pickett, A. L. (1989). *Restructuring the schools: The role of paraprofessionals.* Washington, DC: Institute for Policy Studies, National Governors' Association.

Pickett, A. L. (1996). *A state of the art report on paraeducators in education and related services.* New York: National Resource Center for Paraprofessionals in Education and Related Services, City University of New York.

Pickett, A.L., Faison, K., & Formanek, J. (1993) *A core curriculum and training program for paraeducators working in inclusive classrooms for school age students.* New York: National Resource Center for Paraeducators in Education and Related Services, City University of New York.

Pickett, A. L., Faison, K., Formanek, J., & Semrau, B. (1993). *A core curriculum and training program for paraeducators working in early childhood programs.* New York: National Resource Center for Paraeducators in Education and Related Services, City University of New York.

Pickett, A. L., Faison, K., Formanek, J., & Woods, J. (1993). *A core curriculum and training program for paraeducators working in transitional and supported employment programs.* New York: National Resource Center for Paraeducators in Education and Related Services, City University of New York.

Pickett, A. L., & Gerlach, K. (Eds.). (1997). *Supervising paraeducators in school settings: A team approach.* Austin, TX: PRO-ED.

Pickett, A. L., Vasa, S. F., & Steckelberg, A. L. (1993). *Using paraeducators effectively* (Fastback No. 358). Bloomington, IN: Phi Delta Kappa Foundation.

Snodgrass, A. S. (1991). *Actual and preferred practices of employment placement, supervision and evaluation of teacher aides in Idaho school districts.* Unpublished doctoral dissertation, University of Idaho, Moscow.

Creating Inclusive Schools: Changing Roles and Strategies

CHAPTER 26

Darlene E. Perner and Gordon L. Porter

Learning Outcomes

After reading this chapter, you should be able to

■ Describe what is meant by inclusive education for students with disabilities.

■ Describe actions that school administrators can take to support the development and operation of inclusive programs.

■ Describe actions that can be taken by teachers to facilitate the inclusion of students with disabilities into their classrooms.

■ Describe the role of the consulting teacher in supporting classroom teachers with inclusion.

■ Describe the concept of multi-level instruction and how it can be used to support the inclusion of students with disabilities in regular classes.

TERMS

The following terms are important for the understanding of this chapter:

Consulting teacher: A teacher assigned to provide regular class teachers with professional support and assistance in dealing with the issues and challenges of teaching a class that includes students with varying learning strengths and needs; usually implies provision of collegial and collaborate support. Other terms sometimes used for this role include method and resource teacher and integration or inclusion facilitator.

Inclusion: A high level of involvement of students with disabilities in regular classes, including significant participation in classroom activities and experiences.

Integration: The early steps to move students with disabilities from segregated classes and schools, to classroom and school placements in which they are with their peers who do not have disabilities.

Multi-level instruction: An approach to classroom instruction and curriculum organization that emphasizes provision of appropriate learning opportunities for students with varying levels of academic skill through the same "core lesson." This approach suggests consideration by teachers of the (a) underlying concept of the lesson, (b) method of presentation by the teacher, (c) method of practice by the student, and (d) method of evaluation.

Introduction

The educational program and school placement of students with developmental disabilities have been long-time concerns of special educators. Even though they might not always be in agreement on every issue, educators and parents have worked together to improve the education, supports, and services for these students.

Over the past decade, numerous inclusive education programs have been implemented throughout the United States (National Center on Educational Restructuring and Inclusion, 1994) and Canada (Crawford & Porter, 1992). Many factors have been identified to facilitate integration and improve educational programming of all students in inclusive environments (CEC Working Forum on Inclusive Schools, 1994; Crawford & Porter, 1992; National Center on Educational Restructuring and Inclusion, 1994; Perner, 1991; Sapon-Shevin, 1994; Stainback & Stainback, 1989). For example, the CEC Working Forum on Inclusive Schools (1994) described 12 features that characterize inclusive schools: sense of community, leadership, high standards, collaboration and cooperation, changing roles and responsibilities, array of services, partnership with parents, flexible learning environments, strategies based on research, new forms of accountability, access, and continuing professional development. The National Center on Educational Restructuring and Inclusion (1994) identified seven factors for successful inclusion: visionary leadership, collaboration, refocused use of assessment, supports for staff and students, funding, effective parental involvement, and models and classroom practices that support inclusion.

Providing appropriate services and effective supports to students with developmental disabilities is of primary concern to special educators. Many practitioners and researchers have stressed the importance of supporting classroom teachers in integrated and inclusive settings (Crawford & Porter, 1992; Perner, 1991, 1993; Porter & Richler, 1991). O'Neil (1994) asked Sapon-Shevin to define inclusion: "The vision of inclusion is that all children would be served in their neighborhood schools in *regular classrooms* with children their own age. The idea is that these schools would be restructured so that they are supportive, nurturing communities that really meet the needs of all the children within them: rich in resources and support for both students and teachers" (p. 7).

In this chapter, strategies for developing and implementing inclusive education for students with developmental disabilities are described. The focus is on providing various types of support to classroom teachers involved in inclusive education and strategies to assist these teachers. The supports and strategies identified are directed to both school administrators and to teachers. Also included is a description of two specific support models. They are the consulting teacher model and multi-level instruction.

Inclusion and Students with Developmental Disabilities

The discourse over the utility of inclusion for students who have been labeled developmentally disabled takes two forms. It is asserted that for those students with significant disabilities, functional life skills cannot be taught in regular education classes where the emphasis is primarily on academic learning. For students with mild disabilities, the fear is that they will be "lost" in the regular classroom and that the extra supports that had been provided in special education classes will be squeezed out of the system in the interests of cost cutting and fiscal restraint. Although these concerns are legitimate, there have been many documented experiences in

which barriers have been overcome by the implementation of a sound inclusive program (Crawford & Porter, 1992).

In the case of students with significant developmental disabilities, direct and indirect supports have continued to be available and new strategies have been developed to ensure that the students benefit from classroom activities and interactions. Systematic planning has been used to help meet the unique needs of students in the context of the regular classroom. Life skills can be taught and reinforced at times when they are connected to their function. For example, toileting skills can be dealt with when the child needs to go to the toilet, with a paraprofessional providing support and instruction at the same time. A student can be taught money skills during lunch or recess time when the student buys food or a treat at the school cafeteria or canteen.

The situation for students with mild disabilities is somewhat different because individual needs are more difficult for the classroom teacher to determine. Some degree of collaborative assistance is helpful to classroom teachers in adequately addressing these students' needs. The literature (Dunn, 1968; Lieberman, 1984; Reynolds, Wang, & Walberg, 1987) supports regular class placement for students with mild disabilities, while ensuring that teachers have direct assistance from paraprofessionals in their classrooms and from other experienced, supportive professionals. It is apparent that consultative personnel need to be available to regular education teachers so that teachers can provide direct service to students with developmental disabilities in their classrooms (Crawford & Porter, 1992; Perner, 1993; Schloss, 1992).

Effective school and classroom strategies and practices that support the creation of successful inclusive schools are described in this chapter. They are not the only things needed to ensure successful inclusion of students, but they are among the most critical. The following discussion on vision and beliefs helps to set the framework for these strategies and practices.

Vision and Beliefs

Accomplishing significant change in any organization rich in history and practices requires a major focus on the process of change itself. Keilty (1994) and Sarason (1982) described the immutable nature of school organization and practice in public school settings and how difficult it is to bring about change. Fullan and Steigelbauer (1991) added a great deal to the discussion of how change in education can be understood and achieved.

As cited in Porter and Richler (1991), Fullan suggested that change in special education is particularly complex because of the issues involved and that highly skilled leadership is required to meet this challenge. He noted that "the solutions to inclusion are not easily achieved. It is complex both in the nature and degree of change required to identify and implement solutions that work. Given what change requires—persistence, coordination, follow-up, conflict resolution, and the like—leadership at all levels is required" (p. ii). In this context, it is clear that integrating students in regular classes or creating inclusive schools requires strong leadership based on a well-defined vision of the value of integration or inclusion. It is essential that the shared beliefs and principles of a school team are well articulated and communicated both internally and externally.

In her review of research on inclusion, Zeph (1994) identified six values commonly associated with developing successful inclusion models and establishing a sense of school community: respect for diversity, recognition of gifts and talents for all, ability to listen and understand before trying to be understood, spirit of cooperation, desire and ability to collaborate, and ability to establish a positive climate.

Each individual school needs to develop its unique statement of beliefs that will help to facilitate a "sense of community" within the school. Some schools (e.g., in Vermont and New Brunswick, Canada) have been able to frame their beliefs based on provincial or state legislation and/or policies. For example, the Department of Education in the Province of New Brunswick, in conjunction with school districts, has developed a set of beliefs and principles that are considered to be the foundation of an inclusive education policy. Schools and school districts can use these as a basis for their own statements. They are as follows:

1. All children can learn.
2. All children attend age-appropriate regular classrooms in their local schools.
3. All children receive appropriate educational programs.
4. All children receive a curriculum relevant to their needs.
5. All children participate in co-curricular and extra-curricular activities.
6. All children benefit from cooperation among home, school and community. (Province of New Brunswick, 1994, p. 1)

Support Strategies: School Administrators and Teachers

Policy guidelines for inclusion at the province or state level, as well as at the school district level, can be a significant advantage for those striving to change school and classroom practices. In the end, however, it is the leadership provided in the individual school that will determine the extent to which the vision of inclusion will become a reality. Although it may be possible to achieve change in school practice through the efforts of parents, teachers, and the community, the principal is the person in position to contribute the most

leadership in this effort. This is consistent with the assertions that a positive educational environment is needed and that the school principal is the key to achieving "a sense of community" among parents, students, teachers, and others (CEC Working Forum on Inclusive Schools, 1994).

Through effective leadership, principals have been able to implement inclusive educational practices even when a school board or district has not established a philosophy or policy on integration or inclusion (Crawford & Porter, 1992). Crawford and Porter (1992) identified a number of elements that are crucial to visionary leadership:

1. a positive view about the value of education to students with disabilities;
2. an optimistic view of the capacity of teachers and schools to change and to accommodate the needs of all learners;
3. confidence that practices evolve and that everyone benefits from the move toward inclusive education. (pp. 35–36)

There are numerous means by which principals and teachers can facilitate the inclusion of students with developmental disabilities. In the following subsections, a number of strategies are identified and described based on feedback from principals and teachers who have had successful experiences with students with disabilities, particularly those students with developmental disabilities, in the regular classroom (Perner, 1991, 1993). These teachers and principals have developed ways to implement inclusion and make it successful in their own situations. They have enhanced their skills using a variety of sources, such as attending workshops, reading books and articles, visiting inclusive education classrooms, taking courses, sharing with colleagues, and having practical experiences.

School Administrators

In this section, some strategies to facilitate inclusive practices are described. Both teachers and principals identified these practices of school administrators as being most helpful to them with the integration and inclusion of students with disabilities (Perner, 1991). As reported in this study, principals should make a commitment; enhance teacher expectations; utilize strengths and provide support systems; provide scheduled preparation time; meet with teachers; establish school-based teams; provide time for visitations, observations, and sharing sessions; allow for transitional planning; support the consulting teacher; and recognize success and promote public awareness.

Make a Commitment

Because the principal is seen as the leader of the school, it is imperative that the commitment to integration and inclusion be reflected in the school administrator's behavior. As stated by principals who were interviewed about integration by the California Research Institute (1989), "the importance of [school] building leadership [is] characterized by: . . . unwavering commitment" (p. 1). Schools that have progressed the farthest in the change process are the ones in which the school administrators (principal and vice principal) have a commitment to inclusion. As stated by one group of teachers, "The success of integration in these schools is based on school administrators who planned, promoted, implemented and rewarded" their school staff (Perner, 1991, p. 157).

Enhance Teacher Expectations and Attitudes

In some cases educators feel that teacher expectations of and attitudes toward their students with disabilities need to be enhanced. This appears to be particularly true for teachers of high school students. To help alleviate confusion and develop realistic expectations, effective practice dictates that the school administrator should be responsible to ensure that all classroom teachers are involved in the initial planning sessions for integrating students with disabilities. Although junior and senior high school programs involve many teachers and meetings require juggling a number of schedules or hiring substitute teachers, involvement in early meetings allows teachers to know in advance what is expected of them and their students. Our intent is not to diminish the importance of having all teachers meet for subsequent planning, but to stress that the initial meeting helps the teachers and students from becoming overwhelmed and frustrated from vague and unclear expectations and goals. Teachers need to be involved right from the beginning.

School administrators do not always agree on how to get all of their staff involved in the inclusion process. For many, it may be a question of the principal's administrative style. Some principals think that, initially, they should allow their staff to volunteer to integrate students with disabilities into their classrooms. Provided with many opportunities for sharing, observing, and in-service training, the other teachers will get involved naturally. It is felt that this process gives teachers time to allay their initial fears.

Other principals feel that all teachers on staff should be responsible for integrating students with disabilities right from the beginning. In these schools, students are automatically placed in their age-appropriate class. Through direct experience with ongoing in-service and supports, the teachers become less fearful and consequently change their attitudes.

Utilize Strengths and Provide Support Systems

Often, it is the responsibility of the school administrator to expand the use of school resources when integrating students with disabilities. For example, a teacher who uses cooperative learning strategies may be the ideal person to help other teachers integrate students along with the consulting teacher. A teacher of physical education or activity-based science may feel comfortable in helping other teachers to adapt curriculum so that students with disabilities can participate in class instruction. The school administrator should be flexible and creative in using within-school resources.

Also, school administrators should advocate at the district level for support personnel and resources needed to effectively prepare and enhance the skills of school staff. These should include consulting teachers and paraprofessionals along with professional development resources. The principals should facilitate in-school supports, such as volunteer programs, peer support groups, and resource centers.

Provide Scheduled Preparation Time

Principals who plan for and are able to schedule additional preparation time for their teachers are supported by their staff. This can be done in a variety of ways and seems to depend on the individual principal and the school district's mode of operation. For example, one principal developed an extensive inclusion plan and presented it as a school improvement project. She requested additional substitute teacher days for the staff so that the classroom and consulting teachers could meet on a regular basis during the school day. They used this time for planning and preparing adaptive lessons and materials. In another school, the principal permitted the teachers involved in integration to schedule physical education, art, and music at the times they requested. One teacher in this school chose to have art, music, and physical education "back to back" so that she could have at least one long, uninterrupted preparation period per week. Another teacher in this school requested the special classes at the end of the day so that she could continue her preparation right after school.

In another school the principal allowed his staff to brainstorm ideas for giving extra preparation time for a teacher with a newly integrated student with significant developmental disabilities. The teachers decided that their colleague could be released from lunch and recess duty so she would have additional preparation time. The principal also taught this teacher's class one period every 2 weeks to provide time for her to collaborate with the consulting teacher. A popular strategy is for the school administrators and the consulting teachers to substitute teach for a period while the classroom teachers use that time to meet with their own consulting teacher or to plan for the class.

Meet with Teachers

Many teachers feel supported by principals when discussion time, either formal or informal, is scheduled on a regular basis or at the teacher's request. One of the main needs teachers have is for the principal to listen to them in an open-minded way and to interact in a manner that supports teachers' innovative ideas or new approaches to difficult situations. Principals who provide caring and authentic support through personal interest and encouragement using the above approaches do much to support and empower classroom teachers.

Establish School-Based Teams

School-based teams are consistently recommended as being helpful for teachers involved in inclusion (e.g., CEC Working Forum on Inclusive Schools, 1994; Chalfant, Pysh, & Moultrie, 1979; Porter, 1994; Porter, Wilson, Kelly, & den Otter, 1991; Thousand, Fox, Reid, Godek, & Williams, 1986). Each team may vary significantly in membership, format, and function. However, frequent use of collaborative and problem-solving teams has led to successful inclusion programs. Although the most frequent and effective use of teams is to help generate specific strategies for particular classroom and instructional situations, practices may vary depending on the needs of the school and staff members involved. Team members also may help a teacher prepare and plan for the inclusion of a student with developmental disabilities or may assist in establishing a student's Individualized Education Program.

Some administrators feel that it is important for the principal to be involved on the school-based team during the formative years, perhaps even acting as chairperson. Once a team is running smoothly, the principal may remain a member but not necessarily act as chairperson. Some school administrators have included teachers who are not supportive of inclusion as members of the team. When a staff member has become part of an active group responsible for developing strategies and supporting teacher colleagues, attitudes and behaviors have changed positively.

School administrators who have established school-based teams emphasize the importance of the team meeting schedule. The recommendation is that, if possible, team meetings should be scheduled during the school day rather than before or after school. As well, reasonable time limits should be established, agreed upon, and adhered to for these meetings. As one administrator stated, "People appreciate knowing that the [Teacher Assistance Team] TAT [problem solving session] will end on time and usually are not opposed to staying after school if they have participated in making the decision about the meeting time" (Perner, 1991, p. 166).

Provide Time for Visitations, Observations, and Sharing Sessions

Effective practice demonstrates that school administrators should facilitate teachers and other staff to visit and observe the classes of teachers who have experience in integrating students with disabilities. This may be in the teacher's own school or in another school. The principal should arrange the visitations, look for feedback and follow-up, and assist the teacher in drawing constructive strategies from the experience. In many communities principals are in a position to use their networks of contact among schools to benefit their teachers and students.

In addition to sharing through visits, principals can use regular staff meetings to share a successful inclusion experience from a specific classroom. Some principals have successfully achieved this by scheduling special "pot luck" breakfasts or lunches where staff can combine a meal and sharing. One principal found more time for teachers to share experiences and problem solve by putting all school announcements in a flyer to be read before a staff meeting. Once essential questions about the announcements were answered at the meeting, the staff could then concentrate on talk about teaching.

Allow for Transitional Planning

Transitional planning is seen as an important strategy in the inclusion process. It should begin before a student with disabilities enters school or, once the student is in school, at the end of the school year. The principal should ensure that a process for this planning is in place. Release time needs to be arranged so the teachers receiving a student with disabilities will have adequate time to observe the student in class, meet with the parents, and discuss the student's needs with the current teacher(s). Likewise, the current teacher(s) will need time to prepare the receiving teacher(s). This may include observing the receiving teacher in the classroom environment, meeting with the teacher, and following up on observations and meetings once the student has been in the receiving teacher's class.

This type of planning becomes crucial when a student is entering a new school (e.g., middle or high school). The principals of both schools need to facilitate cooperation among teachers to make transitional planning run smoothly and effectively.

Support the Consulting Teacher

A key factor in making many inclusion programs successful is a consulting teacher model. This model has been used successfully in several Canadian school districts (Crawford & Porter, 1992). This approach is described in more detail in the later section titled The Special Educator as Consulting Teacher. It is appropriate to note here, however, that the consulting teacher needs the support of the principal in implementing inclusion in the school.

Initially, the consulting teacher may need to assist the regular class teacher in a variety of ways. To do this effectively, planning time needs to be scheduled. The principal can help by arranging for teachers to be released for specific periods of time to collaborate with the consulting teacher. As teachers become more experienced in teaching students with disabilities in the regular class, the consulting teacher should need less direct assistance from school administrators.

Many principals emphasize the importance of selecting consulting teachers who can assume a leadership role and effectively collaborate with staff and parents. Because administrators have numerous responsibilities within their school, they tend to rely on the expertise of the consulting teacher. Once inclusion is under way, principals feel that the consulting teacher plays a major role in facilitating the inclusion of students. The role of the school administrators then is to provide support when needed.

Recognize Success and Promote Public Awareness

It is important for school administrators to promote inclusion by ensuring that the positive experiences are shared with staff, parents, and the community at large. In addition to parent meetings, school bulletins, and other internal means, the local media—including newspapers, radio, and television—can be used. Principals can thus see that the work of effective teachers is recognized. Successes also need to be shared with school board members and district administrators because their support can be critical to any school program.

Several schools have made short videos showing how students with disabilities are included in their schools and classes. Other schools, once they have gained experience with integration, have volunteered to have other teachers visit, observe, and discuss the program with their staff. Some principals have encouraged teachers involved with inclusion to attend conferences and workshops and, when possible, participate as presenters. Teachers feel complimented when their principals ask them to share their experiences with others within and outside of the school environment.

Teachers

This section focuses on specific suggestions for the classroom teacher involved in the process of integrating students with disabilities into regular classrooms. They are based on feedback from teachers who have had that experience (Perner, 1991, 1993). These suggestions are that teachers make a commitment; visit integrated classes; meet the student, parents, and current teacher; become directly involved; accept responsibility; determine realistic expectations; accept assistance; participate in professional development; share experiences and problem solve; and enhance parent support.

Make a Commitment

For some teachers, making a commitment to inclusion requires overcoming fears and prejudices and changing attitudes about students with disabilities. To have a better understanding of inclusion, it may be helpful to spend time talking to parents and other teachers who have had experience with students with disabilities. This kind of information sharing can help allay the fears that are a natural part of

inexperience. Meeting a student with disabilities can also make a difference in attitudes and the commitment to provide instruction. These kinds of actions can diminish fear and give the teacher more confidence by knowing what to expect in different situations.

Changing attitudes may be helped by other types of input, such as visiting classes where students are successfully integrated, reading articles and books, and perhaps viewing videotapes on integration. One administrator said he finally understood the possibilities for integration after reading an article about curriculum adaptations. He realized that many of the strategies suggested in the article were ones he often used with students in his sixth-grade class and felt he could apply these techniques as well with students who have disabilities. A teacher stated that he had a better understanding of parents' reasons for wanting integration after he viewed a television documentary on the subject. He indicated that, even though he had been informed in a professional way about integration, he was more deeply affected by the personal nature of the documentary about families and school inclusion. Watching this program made the teacher feel more motivated and committed to the success of the integration effort in his school.

Teachers may have different opportunities to prepare for their first experience with integration but they can still make a commitment. For many teachers, it was having an attitude of just trying it and doing their best.

Visit Integrated Classes

For teachers, a beneficial professional development activity is to visit classes in which students are integrated. Initially, these visitations may have to take place outside of one's own school or school district. As more and more schools include students with disabilities in regular classrooms, the need to visit outside of the home school district diminishes greatly. Teachers not only gain knowledge from these visitations, but also appreciate being given the opportunity to visit on a school day and learn from their colleagues. With the gradual movement to inclusion, more classes are accessible for visitations and for learning. The availability of various integrated and inclusive settings allows teachers with no integration experience to observe in classrooms close to home where educational and social conditions are similar to their own.

One example of this involved two special education teachers who were asked to integrate several students with developmental disabilities, who were being educated in a segregated class, and were being moved into regular classes. The teachers were skeptical but willing to visit another school where students with similar needs were integrated already. Arrangements were completed, and the two special education teachers visited the other school and observed a sixth-grade integrated class. They observed classroom practices, met the classroom teacher and consulting teacher, and were able to see the practical day-to-day possibilities for integrating the students in their own school. The information and strategies gleaned from their visit helped them initiate the integration process for their own students.

Meet the Student, Parents, and Teacher

Before the start of the school year, it is helpful for the receiving teacher to meet the student and parents. It is also helpful to meet the current teacher and to visit the student's class if possible. In some school districts substitute teacher days are allocated to allow time for the receiving teacher(s) to visit, observe, meet, and consult with the child's current teacher(s) prior to integrating the student for the first time. This not only helps to allay teachers' fears but gives them an opportunity to learn from one another and more adequately prepare for the arrival of students with disabilities.

Become Directly Involved

Direct involvement with the inclusion process has been identified by classroom teachers as a primary factor in changing their attitudes and feelings about the matter. When a student with disabilities is actually in the class, teachers are provided with a new learning experience from which positive outcomes can flow.

To ensure the full benefit of direct experience, support personnel should provide the teacher with time for planning, consultation, and in-service training. Time might also be provided for the teacher to work individually with the student with disabilities so the personal level of knowledge of the child's strengths and needs is clear. Teachers who have had experience with inclusive education encourage their peers to "get involved and try" but also to accept that it is all right to make mistakes as you go along. Many teachers have noted that they learned a great deal because they were allowed to try different ways of integrating students.

Accept Responsibility

Although the responsibility for student success in learning is one shared by all the members of a school staff, the classroom teacher must accept ownership for the learning of the student with disabilities included in the class. The classroom teacher should be in charge and make decisions regarding the education of the student with disabilities, just like the teacher does for all other students in the class. Accepting this ownership does not mean the teacher should feel alone in the inclusion process. The teacher should still have the active involvement and support of the school principal and the consulting teacher. In instances where the consulting teacher is the former special class teacher, the importance of clearly transferring responsibility is even more critical. It is easy to simply continue to defer to the expert special education teacher. This practice tends to erect what may be an unintended barrier to making a student with disabilities a fully included member of the class. This does not detract from the importance of collaboration between the classroom teacher and the consulting teacher. As the classroom teacher gains experience and is provided with support, however, accepting responsibility for the child's program will increase.

Determine Realistic Expectations

Teachers who are asked to have a student with disabilities included in their classrooms often have initial expectations that are too high. Consequently, these teachers become very frustrated because their students with disabilities are unable to perform like the other students. When the students do not perform at an expected level, teachers may conclude that they are not doing enough for their students with disabilities. Therefore, it is important to involve the classroom teachers right from the beginning in all phases of planning. With background information and assistance in setting realistic goals, the classroom teacher will have a better understanding of what to expect.

Once the student is in the regular class and the classroom teacher has had time to observe and work with the student, it is helpful for the classroom teacher to collaborate with the consulting teacher to establish appropriate goals and outcomes. For example, they might want to seek answers to the following questions: What will be expected of the student? What will be expected of each teacher (i.e., classroom teacher and consulting teacher)? The collaborative discussion of these matters will help ensure that realistic expectations are part of the process and thus benefit both the teacher and the student.

Accept Assistance

In some schools, the teachers who initially volunteer to have students with disabilities integrated into their classes are so dedicated and committed that they can be described as "super teachers." They try extremely hard to keep things going and hesitate to ask for help, even when there is a clear need for it. They are accustomed to working independently and may consider asking for help and assistance as a sign of failure or inadequacy. These teachers may not be sure how to make use of the support available from the consulting teacher or others in a position to assist them.

Over time, these teachers realize that they do not have to do it all alone. There are legitimate reasons to seek support from colleagues who will listen and help them resolve difficult situations. Many teachers identify their principal as being someone who will listen to them and offer assistance. In some cases, the principal may teach their class so that they can have an extra period for planning. The consulting teacher may help in the same way, as well as provide additional resource materials and assist in adapting the curriculum. In some situations, the consulting teacher teaches the class while the regular class teacher works closely with a student who has developmental disabilities. Once classroom teachers accept assistance from other school staff, they realize how important it is to create a collaborative climate. A positive educational environment facilitates successful integration and inclusion.

Participate in Professional Development

Most school districts and schools provide a variety of opportunities for teacher in-service experiences, such as workshops, visitations, and consultations. Teachers, however, should maintain responsibility for some of their own professional development. Teachers, for example, may request in-service training on specific topics or instructional strategies. They may propose that this be made available at the school or district level or they may request support to attend sessions outside the district. Teachers choose a variety of activities, including taking university courses, reading articles and books, viewing videotapes, or making school visitations. Many teachers, in turn, share this information with other staff members in their school or district. One approach is to form a study group that meets once a month after school at which the members help each other through self-selected in-service training, sharing, and problem solving.

As stated previously, there are many ways for teachers to develop professionally. Most of the educators involved in inclusion programs place the greatest value on sharing and problem-solving sessions, and school visitations. School-based in-service training is considered extremely effective because the specific needs of teachers can be assessed and addressed.

Over time, school-based in-service training changes from sessions dealing with attitudes and access to learning about effective planning and instructional techniques. Many of these strategies help teachers to meet individual needs and objectives of students with developmental disabilities while facilitating their participation in regular class instruction and activities. For example, a team assessment process used to identify individual strengths, needs, and objectives, and to plan for instruction within the regular class is *The McGill Action Planning System* (Lusthaus & Forest, 1987; Vandercook, York, & Forest, 1989). The Scheduling Matrix (Giangreco, Cloninger, & Salce Iverson, 1993) was developed to help teachers to include individual learning objectives within the context of the regular class curriculum. Many techniques are used to assist teachers to organize instruction and to adapt and enhance curriculum for all students, such as Multi-level Instruction (Campbell, Campbell, Collicott, Perner, & Stone, 1988; Collicott, 1991; Schulz & Turnbull, 1984), Cooperative Learning (Johnson & Johnson, 1986), Curriculum-Based Collaboration (Nolet & Tindal, 1994), and the School-wide Enrichment Model (Renzulli, 1994).

One benefit of inclusion programs is that they generate staff development strategies that apply to teaching all students more effectively. Teachers indicate that they have expanded and enhanced their instruction by using new strategies that are related to effective inclusive practices.

Share Experiences and Problem Solve

Throughout the process of integration, sharing and problem-solving sessions help educators to make changes and experience the benefits of integration. Teachers and principals who have had both successful and unsuccessful experiences should share these with their colleagues. Successful experiences help to allay the fears of teachers and school administrators who are new to implementing integration. Situations that are not going well are discussed and analyzed so that solutions, or at least better alternatives, can be found.

One of the most beneficial aspects of inclusion is that it encourages school staff to develop ways to collaborate on problem solving. As noted above in the section dealing with administrators, teachers involved with inclusion need the help of their peers to generate the diversity of solutions required for individual or unique situations. These problem-solving sessions or team meetings provide teachers and school administrators with the opportunity to choose and implement solutions that best meet their own needs. Teachers must create their own solutions to problematic situations. There are no preset approaches that will exactly fit the situation. As one elementary teacher stated, "For us, teaming has avoided many problems—everyone participates in problem solving—from teachers, to the student(s), to the principal" (Perner, 1993, p. 12).

In one district, consulting teachers are given extensive training in how to conduct problem-solving meetings (Porter et al., 1991). In fact, the approach proved of such interest to educators in other settings that they obtained a grant to demonstrate the factors considered essential in operating school teams to support inclusion (Porter, 1994). School-based teams are one systematic way for teachers and school administrators to share and problem solve.

Enhance Parent Support

In any circumstance, the active participation and support of parents enhances the prospect for successful outcomes for students. In integration and inclusion programs, parents are seen as primary supports in the change process. There is widespread agreement that effective parent–teacher communication is an important component in making inclusion work. To develop a strong working relationship with parents, teachers need to involve parents in meaningful ways in their children's education program. This facilitates parents to be more involved in decision making and to be participating members of the planning team. Also, many parents welcome the opportunity to be members of problem-solving teams and provide a distinct perspective to the situation at issue.

Parents should be invited to visit and observe in the class, especially when the child is perceived to be acting differently at home or at school. This can help eliminate possible conflict between home and school over student performance levels. An extremely useful procedure to help parents get involved, resolve conflicts, and make decisions is *The McGill Action Planning System* (Lusthaus & Forest, 1987; Vandercook et al., 1989). Although this system has been used extensively by teachers to help plan inclusive programs for students with developmental disabilities, the application of the process for students with mild disabilities has been successfully used and could be utilized more systematically with positive results.

The Special Educator as Consulting Teacher

An inclusive educational program, by definition, mandates a different role for school-based special education staff. Special education class teachers and resource teachers no longer provide or provide reduced levels of direct instructional service to students who are now part of the regular class. Several models for a new role have evolved in individual schools and school districts, depending on how the transition to inclusion has been handled. Team teaching and co-teaching approaches have been developed and have been seen as successful (CEC Working Forum on Inclusive Schools, 1994; National Center on Educational Restructuring and Inclusion, 1994). The approach described in this section is less oriented toward direct instruction than other approaches. It is a school-based collaborative consultation model, which is termed the consulting teacher model in this chapter, but which has been described elsewhere as the method and resource teacher model (Porter, 1991). Among the consulting teacher's functions are the following: program planning and development, program implementation, assessment and prescriptive services, program monitoring, communication and liaison, and instruction.

In an inclusive school, the consulting teacher acts as a collaborative consultant to the regular classroom teacher. The consulting teacher is responsible for assisting the classroom teacher in developing strategies and activities so that students with disabilities can be effectively included in the regular class. Consulting teachers do a number of things during the course of a school day to support teachers and, thus, students. However, behind each activity, two key functions can be distinguished. First, the consulting teacher assists in elaborating pertinent questions about student learning and instructional practices that effect the learning of all stu-

dents. In practical terms this might be helping to define the instructional issue (or problem) perceived by the teacher. By asking key questions, the consulting teacher helps the classroom teacher focus on the critical instructional issues and variables at work in the class. Second, the consulting teacher helps the teacher to solve identified classroom problems, or stated another way, to work out the most promising alternatives for more effective instruction.

Time Use

One district that was concerned with monitoring the way consulting teachers use their time had them complete a time-use log over 2 consecutive work days. The teachers recorded their major activities for each 15-minute time period while they were at school. These records were used for analysis of their actual work activities (Porter, 1991). The results of this analysis appear in Table 26.1.

The significant change in role for the consulting teacher in an inclusive system is made clear in the information presented in Table 26.1. Special education teachers spend almost all their time providing direct care and instruction to students with disabilities. Even resource room teachers spend most of their time providing small-group or individual instruction to students with learning difficulties. It is interesting to note that consulting teachers in this district spend only 8% of their time on pull-out instruction. They devote their time to collaborating with regular classroom teachers rather than replacing them by providing direct instruction.

A common theme emerged from the comments of the consulting teachers who participated in this survey. Most indicated that it is necessary to visit the classroom frequently so they can observe student participation in the instructional process and assess student behavior in an authentic manner.

Providing Support to Teachers and Students

Most consulting teachers in the district discussed in the previous section identified numerous qualities a person should have to be successful at this job. They reported that consulting teachers must be optimistic, confident, and persistent, and have a positive approach. They must be able to accept people for whom they are and show genuine concern for the student. Being diplomatic, flexible, observant, creative, and innovative are also considered assets of consulting teachers. Problem solving, keeping things in perspective, knowing about the education system, and pushing for change are reported to be key qualities as well.

Consulting teachers must not be seen as experts who take over responsibility for student learning from the classroom teacher. A challenge for the consulting teacher is to find workable solutions to problems (which are welcomed

Table 26.1
Major Activities of Consulting Teachers

Activity	Description	Percentage
Collaboration	Collaborating with teachers, teachers' assistants, other consulting teachers, parents, principal, and consulting professionals, such as psychologists and therapists. Done by phone calls or formal and informal meetings.	31%
Instructional Support	Providing direct instruction to the whole class so regular teachers can work with the individual student; developing student programs; monitoring and observing individual students or small groups in the regular classroom; evaluating and assisting with classroom management; developing strategies concerning student behavior; providing individual guidance; meeting with students or student groups.	29%
Teacher Support	Responding to referrals; completing assessments; planning; developing Individualized Education Programs; preparing materials for instruction.	20%
Direct Instruction	Pulling students out for instruction in the resource room; assisting students who required extra help; providing individual attention.	8%
Other	Engaging in all the other teacher activities, such as professional development, staff meetings, and supervision duty.	12%

by the teacher) that occur in the class. Consulting teachers who have extensive classroom teaching experience and are regarded by peers as able classroom teachers have the greatest success in this position (Porter, 1991). Most consulting teachers stated that having regular class teaching experience was essential to their role in support of inclusion. Regular teaching experience gives them credibility with other teachers.

Consulting teachers work with students, teachers, administrators, and parents and, thus, they need to be willing to adjust their plans to others' needs even if they have a plan for the day already established. They must work to sustain positive expectations for students with disabilities even when other staff members find their own enthusiasm waning. Classroom teachers who are teaching students with disabilities for the first time need support from someone with an optimistic and positive perspective. The fact is that regular class teachers can and will respond positively to the challenge. The consulting teacher can help ensure this outcome by maintaining support for the teacher throughout the process of finding a resolution to a problem.

One aspect of the consulting teacher role is the requirement for ongoing collaboration with other teachers. This is a new responsibility for most special educators. It is also a new experience for the regular classroom teacher. As a result, a different set of skills, much more tied to working effectively with other adults, not children, becomes critical to achieving success. In fact, teachers as a whole do not have a lot of experience sharing responsibility and decision making. Thus, good communication skills, as well as sound instructional knowledge and experience, are required of a consulting teacher.

Other areas of strength needed are sound organizational skills, facilitation skills, the ability to complete appropriate assessments, and skills in writing individualized programs. A commitment to inclusive education is also essential. Finally, consulting teachers should be committed to ongoing personal development in both knowledge and skills.

School districts committed to successful outcomes ensure that consulting teachers participate in training on a regular basis. Some districts schedule a meeting of consulting teachers for one-half day every second week, whereas others meet 1 day per month. Consulting teachers suggest that this time is an important support to them in fulfilling their role. It allows for exchange with peers, sharing successful strategies, and developing a sense of continuity and collaboration. This type of staff development also permits instruction in new techniques and skills, new materials, and new methods. The ongoing sessions help keep the consulting teachers' morale up and help them deal with the frustrations of the job. Working together, they are able to keep their goals and vision clear and develop a sense of teamwork and collegiality in their new role.

Strategies for the Collaborative Role

Experienced consulting teachers consistently note the need to support regular class teachers but to avoid being drawn into providing "easy" answers to the teachers' problems. The regular class teacher should take ownership of both the problem and the plan to deal with it.

Because a major part of the role is visiting classes, maintaining a thoroughly professional and confidential approach to these experiences is required. Teachers need to know the purpose of a visit and how the information will be used.

Finally, the consulting teacher needs to be a good listener and facilitator, and often that means more emphasis on encouragement and confirming the value of the teacher's efforts than on suggesting new practices or approaches. The consulting teacher can help the classroom teacher select an appropriate strategy, but it is the teacher who will implement it in the classroom.

The constant search for effective ways to work with regular classroom teachers in support of inclusive education is the major challenge of consulting teachers. The consulting teacher must find ways to work as an effective collaborator and problem solver with each individual teacher. Open communication is necessary if the relationship is to work.

Instructional Innovation: Multi-level Instruction

Once inclusion is well under way, and teachers are beyond the stage of acceptance and attitude change; emphasis moves from achieving integrated placements to creating inclusive classroom and school environments for students with disabilities. An inclusive classroom should provide learning opportunities for all students that are age appropriate and meaningful. A class consisting of 20 to 30 students is an obvious challenge for the teacher trying to achieve the goal of inclusion for students with disabilities.

One of the essential questions in determining how to proceed is to decide how to organize instruction. One option is to attempt to teach students on an individualized basis; another is to teach by using instructional groups. A third alternative, one that has been viewed as effective in achieving the goals of inclusion, has been for the teacher to establish one key concept and then find ways for each student to participate in the lesson and activities in a meaningful way. By doing so, appropriate learning opportunities can be provided to all the students.

This last approach was determined as a realistic option, and the concept of multi-level instruction was identified and developed (Campbell et al., 1988; Collicott, 1991; Schulz & Turnbull, 1984). A number of other instructional strategies and techniques logically compliment this approach and provide teachers with the means to achieve success. Some of these techniques include cooperative learning, whole-language instruction, activity-based learning, and authentic assessment. In the following subsection, the key elements in multi-level instruction are described.

The Multi-level Instruction Process

Multi-level instruction is a planning strategy that has been adapted by Collicott and Stone (Campbell et al., 1988; Collicott, 1991) from the works of Schulz and Turnbull (1984). The process helps teachers to plan and implement one lesson to accommodate all students and encourages each student to participate at his or her own level in shared class activities. This strategy is particularly useful for including students with developmental disabilities because it focuses on developing concepts by using content as a means for teaching specific skills, rather than teaching the content as an end in itself (Campbell et al., 1988).

To develop a unit or lesson, the teacher needs to identify the objective(s) of the planned instruction. The teacher also should be able to include numerous teaching techniques to accommodate the various levels of ability within any one class. According to Collicott (1991), the teacher should consider student learning styles and preferences; involve students in lessons through questioning aimed at different levels; adapt expectations for some students (e.g., include different objectives and outcomes); allow for various levels of participation; give students a choice in methods of practice and in how they will demonstrate understanding of the concept being taught; be aware that each method is of equivalent value; and evaluate students based on their individual differences.

Multi-level instruction is a four-step planning process for developing instructional lessons and units. It consists of the following:

1. Identifying the underlying concepts to be taught;
2. Determining the method of presentation;
3. Establishing the method of practice and performance; and
4. Deciding on the method of evaluation. (Campbell et al., 1988, pp. 17–18)

Underlying Concept

The first step in the multi-level instruction process is for the teacher to identify what concepts are going to be taught. The objectives for students will differ, but the lesson concept should be a shared one. "For example, the study of the novel or short story is not taught for the sake of the content, but is undertaken in order to understand the concepts of plot, character development, setting and atmosphere" (Campbell et al., 1988, pp. 17–18).

Method of Presentation and Method of Practice and Performance

In the next two steps of the multi-level instruction process, the teacher determines the method of presentation and method of practice and performance. The teacher identifies various ways to present or include the concepts or skills to be taught and for students to practice or use these concepts or skills.

In both of these phases, the teacher considers the use of different presentation and performance modes. For example, as cited in Schulz and Turnbull (1984), Smith and Bentley identified input and output modes, which include a selection of activities categorized under headings such as view, read, make/construct, and solve (see pp. 107–108). Wood (1992) provided a list of activities under modes categorized as expository, inquiry, demonstration, and activity.

In selecting (a) presentation and (b) practice and performance methods, teachers also should consider variations in questioning techniques and thinking skills (e.g., using Bloom's, 1956, cognitive domain), student learning styles (e.g., visual, auditory, and/or tactile; seating and lighting; independent or group work), and level of student participation (e.g., partial or total). For example, some students may do parts of an assignment, whereas others may be expected to complete the entire task. Some students may work alone, and others may be paired.

Many instructional methods are planned and used so that students have some choices in how they are going to show their understanding of a concept or their acquisition of a skill. For example, if the novel is being studied and the concept of setting is being taught, then both methods of presentation and of practice and performance might include the following: Draw or find a picture to depict a described setting; briefly describe a setting of a television program or rock video; and design a new setting for a favorite television show.

Method of Evaluation

The fourth step in the multi-level instruction process is to determine whether students have learned the concept(s) or skill(s) being taught. The teacher identifies a variety of evaluation techniques in order to allow for individual abilities and differences. For example, evaluation assignments to determine students' understanding of the concept of setting in a story might include completing an oral presentation, constructing a diorama, or creating an illustration. Consistent with the former step, the teacher should allow for a variety of ways to evaluate students' preferences of presentation style. By giving students choices in their preferred mode of performance, the teacher allows each student the best opportunity to demonstrate understanding of the concept.

Summary

Teachers who have used multi-level instruction have found it an effective strategy to provide for the educational needs of students with disabilities. It has proven a practical and realistic way for classroom teachers to accommodate to the requirements of an inclusive education program (Collicott, 1991; Perner, 1993). However, the most compelling factor in using this kind of approach is that it has the potential to improve the quality of instruction for all students.

Conclusion

In this chapter, the importance of establishing a vision and set of values for integrated or inclusive education has been discussed. Policy and leadership dimensions, as well as the expanding role of school administrators and teachers, have been described. Strategies have been identified to help both school administrators and classroom teachers initiate and maintain integrated and inclusive education.

Two specific models that provide support to classroom teachers have been defined, with examples of how they work. First, the consulting teacher model was described. It sets out one way in which teachers can be supported in developing practical strategies and activities for their classrooms. Second, the multi-level instructional approach, which provides a framework for planning and implementing classroom instruction, was discussed.

The need for a creative and responsive school environment, where collaboration among teachers leads to effective problem solving and shared learning, has been described. The need for developing a school climate where this kind of collaboration is part of the school culture was presented. Innovative school and classroom practices are required if public education is to serve all students, including those with disabilities, in an effective way. Through participation and learning in the regular classroom, students with disabilities will have the opportunity to take their place as contributing citizens of communities.

QUESTIONS

1. Create a vision statement reinforced by some belief statements for a school that is developing an inclusive education model.

2. Describe what a school principal can do to facilitate inclusive education practices. What do you feel is the most important action? Why?

3. Describe what teachers can do to facilitate inclusive education practices in their school. What do you feel is the most important action? Why?

4. What are some of the characteristics that a consulting teacher in an inclusive education school should possess? What do you feel is the most important characteristic? Why?

5. In planning a regular class lesson which will include students with disabilities, what are some factors that a teacher should consider when making adaptions to his lesson?

References

Bloom, B. S. (Ed.). (1956). *Taxonomy of educational objectives: The classification of educational goals. Handbook I: Cognitive domain.* New York: Longman.

California Research Institute. (1989). What makes integration work? *Strategies . . . A part of the TASH dissemination project, 1,* 1.

Campbell, C., Campbell, S., Collicott, J., Perner, D., & Stone, J. (1988). Adapting regular class curriculum for integrated special needs students. *Education New Brunswick Journal, 3,* 17–20.

CEC Working Forum on Inclusive Schools. (1994). *Creating schools for all our students: What twelve schools have to say.* Reston, VA: Council for Exceptional Children (CEC).

Chalfant, J., Pysh, M., & Moultrie, R. (1979). Teacher assistant teams: A model for within-building problem solving. *Learning Disabilities Quarterly, 2,* 85–96.

Collicott, J. (1991). Implementing multi-level instruction: Strategies for classroom teachers. In G. Porter & D. Richler (Eds.), *Changing Canadian schools* (pp. 191–218). North York, Ontario: The Roeher Institute.

Crawford, C., & Porter, G. L. (1992). *How it happens: A look at inclusive educational practice in Canada for children and youth with disabilities.* North York, Ontario: The Roeher Institute.

Dunn, L. (1968). Special education for the mildly retarded—Is much of it justifiable? *Exceptional Children, 35*(1), 5–22.

Fullan, M. G., & Steigelbauer, S. (1991). *The new meaning of educational change.* New York: Teacher's College Press.

Giangreco, M., Cloninger, C., & Salce Iverson, V. (1993). *Choosing options and accommodations for children: A guide to planning inclusive education.* Baltimore: Brookes.

Johnson, D., & Johnson, R. (1986). Mainstreaming and cooperative learning strategies. *Exceptional Children, 52,* 553–561.

Keilty, G. C. (1994, August). *Turning the corner: Effective strategies for educational change.* Paper presented at the Excellence and Equity in Education International Conference, Toronto.

Lieberman, L. (1984). *Preventing special education for those who don't need it.* Newton, MA: Gloworm.

Lusthaus, E., & Forest, M. (1987). The kaleidoscope: A challenge to the cascade. In M. Forest (Ed.), *More education integration* (pp. 1–17). North York, Ontario: The Roeher Institute.

National Center on Educational Restructuring and Inclusion. (1994). National survey on inclusive education. *NCERI Bulletin, 1.*

Nolet, V., & Tindal, G. (1994). Curriculum-based collaboration. *Focus on Exceptional Children, 27*(3), 1–12.

O'Neil, J. (1994). Can inclusion work? A conversation with Jim Kauffman and Mara Sapon-Shevin. *Educational Leadership, 52*(4), 7–11.

Perner, D. (1991). Leading the way: The role of school administrators in integration. In G. Porter & D. Richler (Eds.), *Changing Canadian schools* (pp. 155–171). North York, Ontario: The Roeher Institute.

Perner, D. (1993, December). *All students attend regular classes in neighbourhood schools: A case study of three schools in Woodstock, New Brunswick, Canada.* Research report for Organisation for Economic Co-operation and Development/Centre for Educational Research and Innovation International Conference on Active Life for Disabled Youth— Integration in the School Project. Vaals, The Netherlands.

Porter, G. L. (1991). The method and resource teacher: A collaborative consultant model. In G. Porter & D. Richler (Eds.), *Changing Canadian schools* (pp. 107–154). North York, Ontario: The Roeher Institute.

Porter, G. L. (Executive Producer). (1994). *Teachers helping teachers: Problem solving teams that work* (Video and Manual). Toronto, Ontario: The Roeher Institute and School District No. 12, New Brunswick.

Porter, G. L., & Richler, D. (Eds.). (1991). *Changing Canadian schools: Perspectives on disability and inclusion.* North York, Ontario: The Roeher Institute.

Porter, G. L., Wilson, M., Kelly, B., & den Otter, J. (1991). Problem solving teams: A thirty-minute peer-helping model. In G. Porter & D. Richler (Eds.), *Changing Canadian schools* (pp. 219–238). North York, Ontario: The Roeher Institute.

Province of New Brunswick. (1994). *Best practices for inclusion.* Fredericton, NB: Student Services Branch, Department of Education.

Renzulli, J. (1994). Teachers as talent scouts. *Educational Leadership, 52*(4), 75–81.

Reynolds, M. C., Wang, M. C., & Walberg, H. J. (1987). The necessary restructuring of special and general education. *Exceptional Children, 53,* 391–398.

Sapon-Shevin, M. (1994). Why gifted students belong in inclusive schools. *Educational Leadership, 52*(4), 64–67.

Sarason, S. B. (1982). *The culture of school and the problem of change* (Revised ed.). Needham Heights, MA: Allyn & Bacon.

Schloss, P. (1992). Mainstreaming revisited. *The Elementary School Journal, 92,* 233–244.

Schulz, J., & Turnbull, A. (1984). *Mainstreaming handicapped students: A guide for classroom teachers*. Needham Heights, MA: Allyn & Bacon.

Stainback, W., & Stainback, S. (1989). Practical organizational strategies. In W. Stainback, S. Stainback, & M. Forest (Eds.), *Educating all students in the mainstream of regular education* (pp. 71–87). Baltimore: Brookes.

Thousand, J., Fox, T., Reid, R., Godek, J., & Williams, W. (1986). *The homecoming model: Educating students who present intensive educational challenges within regular education environments* (Monograph No. 7-1, pp. 33–37). Burlington: University of Vermont, Center for Developmental Disabilities.

Vandercook, T., York, J., & Forest, M. (1989). The McGill Action Planning System (MAPS): A strategy for building the vision. *The Journal of the Association for Persons with Severe Handicaps, 14*, 205–215.

Wood, J. (1992). *Adapting instruction for mainstreamed and at-risk students* (2nd ed.). Toronto: Maxwell MacMillan Canada.

Zeph, L. (1994, August). *Assessing the quality of education in inclusive schools: Research and rationale*. Paper presented at the Excellence and Equity in Education International Conference, Toronto.

Effective Practice for Generating Outcomes of Significance: The Complexities of Transformational Change

CHAPTER 27

Garnett J. Smith, Patricia J. Edelen-Smith, and Robert A. Stodden

Students begin their schooling, and educators enter their profession, eager to learn, to absorb, to "grow up," to make a difference, to feel worthy and accepted, not passively to await a future but to reach for it. Rarely does it work out for them as they hoped. And if we do not face up to those disappointments, I am forced to this prediction: the maxim that says the more things change, the more they remain the same will be invalidated. Things will get worse.

(Sarason, 1993, p. xiv)

Learning Outcomes

After reading this chapter, you should be able to

- Explain why external federal, state, and local mandates, initiatives, and legal directives have had so little impact upon achieving outcomes of significance for individuals with developmental disabilities at the school and community level.

- Define the premise upon which adhocracy organizations and learning organizations are based.

- List four factors that should be considered by planning and improvement teams, partnerships, or other organizations attempting to engage in transformational change.

- Delineate six effective practice elements or variables necessary to generate and sustain core transformational reform.

- Specify how transformational change develops out of the interaction within and between (a) actionable knowledge, (b) behavioral change, and (c) critical mass.

TERMS

The following terms are important for the understanding of this chapter:

Actionable knowledge: A comprehensive understanding of theories, practical methods, and tools that generate new ways of thinking and have the power to transform the way the planning partners conduct their work.

Adhocracy organization: An organization operating within a dynamic environment where the norm is to engage in divergent thinking aimed at innovation, rather than convergent thinking aimed at problem prevention or compliance.

Design-down principle: One of the key principles of outcome-oriented planning; it directs that program and

service planning start with the preferred outcome and proceed back to an instructional starting point.

External monitoring systems: Systems that promote the hierarchy of authority through (a) responsibility specification; (b) rules, regulations, and standard operating procedures; and (c) an impersonal view of people functioning in a subordinate capacity.

Ideal vision: A collective portrait of a preferred future that the planning partners choose to create for tomorrow's citizens with developmental disabilities.

Learning organization: An organization skilled at creating, acquiring, and transferring knowledge, and at modifying its behavior to reflect new knowledge and insights.

(continues)

Outcomes of significance: Exhibitions of learning that have major influence and function in facilitating the access of individuals with developmental disabilities to the benefits of society.

Systems planning: A comprehensive albeit subjective process concerned with examining over time the interrelationships between programs, practices, services, and other forces for individuals with developmental disabilities.

Team: A finite number of people with complementary skills committed to a common vision and purpose, set of performance goals, and plan of action for which they hold themselves accountable.

Transformational change: Fundamental alterations in the appearance, configuration, or nature of existing educational, vocational, and community roles and infrastructures.

Introduction

If Special Education Is the Solution, What Is the Problem?

Educational, social, and/or vocational success—providing individuals with developmental and other disabilities with the skills, knowledge, attitudes, and abilities to be self-sufficient, self-reliant, competent, caring, and mutually interdependent adults—is more than writing measurable objectives for Individualized Education Programs (IEPs) (Edelen-Smith, 1995). It encompasses more than the introduction of new and tougher mandates, proclamations, and edicts to improve life role outcomes. The future educational, vocational, and/or social successes of students in special education programs ultimately depend upon the educational planning partners—individuals or teams of individuals with a direct interest in planning for the long-term functioning, competence, and success of persons with developmental disabilities (Spady, 1994)—who develop an ideal vision of tomorrow for individuals with disabilities and then, using the design-down principle outlined in the Individuals with Disabilities Education Act of 1990, identify and initiate the necessary contributions these education planning partners (schools, community support agencies, parents, employers, and individuals with disabilities) will make in order to achieve that preferred future (Kaufman, 1995). This chapter describes an effective school–university–community training practice that the Hawaii University Affiliated Program for Developmental Disabilities has used to enlist and support teams of educational, vocational, family, and community planning partners to improve the adult outcomes of individuals with developmental disabilities.

It has been 20 years since P.L. 94-142, the Education for All Handicapped Children Act of 1975, was signed into law. During those 20 years, a multitude of companion initiatives, legislative mandates, court orders, and other external directives have been imposed upon state education agencies, local education agencies, and institutions of higher education in an attempt to mechanistically reform and improve programs and services for children and youth with disabilities.

A 1994 special report on school reform produced by the SouthEastern Regional Vision for Education (SERVE), a federally funded laboratory to improve educational outcomes, pessimistically noted that one problem with mechanistic interventions is that most mandated reforms have not worked, or at best have not worked as well as policy makers had hoped. Despite all the good intentions and activities of external reformers and the billions of special education tax dollars that have flowed into the public schools, the educational, social, and vocational outcomes of U.S. students with disabilities continue to be little better now than they were in 1975 (DeStefano & Wagner, 1993; Edgar & Polloway, 1994; Johnson et al., 1993; Kohler, 1993; Smith & Edelen-Smith, 1990; Stodden & Leake, 1994).

Until the late 1980s, special education reform and improvement efforts basically involved doing more of the same with what already existed: more federal and state control of special education programs and services, more procedures to facilitate the micromanagement of IEPs, and more "carrots" or "sticks" that were wielded by federal and state "overseers" to entice or to threaten educational practitioners. The result of this "more of the same" reform, said William Raspberry (cited in SERVE, 1994), columnist for the *Washington Post*, was that the educational tidal wave of change expected from reform efforts has resulted in nothing more than a public policy whirlpool. He lamented that nothing substantive has come from all of this contradictory activity except to instill new levels of skepticism among the various educational partners expected to accomplish the reform.

Surprisingly, the recurring patterns of confusion, inflexibility, and stifling regulated conformity that follow external improvement and reform efforts may not be the greatest barriers to general, vocational, and special education improvement and reform (Goodlad, 1991; SERVE, 1994). The project director of the Public School Forum of North Carolina contended that the fundamental reason why general, vocational, and special education reform and improvement efforts have had so little relevant effect on programs and services has been the reluctance of educational planners, policy makers, special needs advocates, and other educational planning partners at national, state, and local levels to "deal with the messiness" of true special education reform and improvement (Campbell, 1995). It has been the failure of these educational planning partners to acknowledge the fact that reform and improvement cannot be instituted through fiat but must evolve out of the process of building a shared vision. This vision encompasses outcomes of significance for individuals with disabilities to which the educational planning partners, operating throughout the special education system and beyond, choose to align (Astuto, Clark, Read, McGree, & Fernandez, 1994; Beane, 1995; Senge, Roberts, Ross, Smith, & Kleiner, 1994; Spady & Marshall, 1991). "Caring is not enough. Passing new and ambitious laws is not enough. . . . We must stop selecting single-variable/single-issue responses to address our concerns. We must *change*: revitalize our schools and our resolve, rethink our goals and purposes, and restructure our [special] education system so that it works smarter—more effectively and efficiently" (Kaufman, 1995, p. 4).

Cultivating Planning and Improvement Partnerships, Commitment, and Competence through Organizational Change

Outcome-oriented system and structure reform that is dynamic enough to transform the adult and community accomplishments of individuals with developmental disabilities requires a fundamental change in the "roles, rules, and relationships that influence how people work and interact" (Newmann, 1993, p. 12). These new and innovative systems and structures need to be convincing enough and powerful enough to persuade a loosely knit group of interdependent, cross-functional professionals, family members, agency caregivers, and other educational planning partners to rethink their habits and culture, their practices, and their beliefs about special education systems, processes, and outcomes. These systems and structures must be dynamic enough to provide the educational planning partners with experiences (both practice and authentic) that produce transformational growth. This growth goes beyond small improvements on the edge of practice. These systems and structures must deal with basic special education change at its core (Edelen-Smith, 1995; Evans, 1993; Mintzberg, 1994; Senge et al., 1994; Stodden & Leake, 1994). Unfortunately, there are no clear step-by-step models or formulas when it comes to pro-

ducing transformational change. However, it is clear that school-by-school transformational special education reform and improvement "demands a new kind of education and new forms of school organization" (Darling-Hammond, 1993, p. 753). Senge (1990) and his associates (Senge et al., 1994) referred to this new organizational form as "the learning organization." Skrtic (1991) and Mintzberg (1994) called this new form of school organization an "adhocracy organization." Regardless of the name, these organizational forms are "premised on the principle of *innovation* rather than standardization . . . a problem-solving organization configured to invent new programs. It is the organizational form that configures itself around work that is so ambiguous and uncertain that neither the programs nor the knowledge and skills for doing it are known" (Skrtic, 1991, p. 182).

How Do We Get to Transformational Change?

Albert Shanker (1990), president of the American Federation of Teachers, delineated four lessons that have been gleaned from the experience of organizations (schools, agencies, businesses) attempting to inspire transformational change in their overall vision, goals, habits, and culture.

First, "nothing changes if the people in the organization do not change" (Shanker, 1990, p. 101), and "people" change requires a great deal of internal and external training and assistance to achieve it. Without essential training and assistance, an interdependent consortium of professionals, family members, agency service providers, and other educational and community partners will rarely, if ever, produce and sustain the extraordinary effort actually needed to transform new knowledge and practice into existing programs and services. This assistance is explicitly expressed in the form of a "trust covenant" that unequivocally conveys to the educational planning partners that they will have continual access to training, support, and resources of significance.

Second, transformational change is a highly volatile experience. Creating transformational opportunities for professionals, family members, agency personnel, individuals with developmental disabilities, and other educational and community partners is a high-risk activity that generally results in a certain amount of chaos and confusion. These diverse associations of educational and community partners "need to expect this, and they need to know also that they will make mistakes as they begin new activities and new ways of doing things" (Shanker, 1990, p. 101). Each school site, team, or educational planning partner needs to be assured that it will be supported to the maximum extent possible in the decisions made and the actions taken (given they do not violate federal, state, and local law), even if these decisions and actions should later prove to be faulty or ineffective. "They need to learn and they will learn by doing" (Shanker, 1990, p. 101).

Third, the purging of "old ways" requires sacrifice. Decisions that require sacrifice must be carefully thought out as to their "systemic" implications. When the old ways have not worked well or seem detrimental to the achievement of outcomes of significance for individuals with disabilities, removing them means taking away the familiar. Therefore, the removal of any existing practices, procedures, or programs should always be undertaken with great caution. Reform and improvement changes that can be made within current structures and resources should be reviewed and considered before making changes that require major adaptations in current structures and resources (Smull, 1995).

Fourth, as new roles and responsibilities develop within and across institutions of higher education, state education agencies, and local education agencies, all the educational planning partners must be provided access to information, research data, and technical assistance that can assist them in effectively functioning in areas of knowledge new to them (i.e., strategic thinking, follow-up and follow-along data, redesigned adult agency roles and responsibilities, and menus of "effective practices" that have demonstrably contributed to outcomes of significance for individuals with disabilities). Information, research data, and technical assistance provide the operational knowledge base and "how-to" procedures for reform.

The Details of Practice and the Hawaii University Affiliated Program

Garvin (1993) criticized most authors who write about learning organizations or transformational improvement and reform for their penchant to focus on "high philosophy and grand themes, sweeping metaphors rather than the gritty details of practice" (p. 79). Since 1991, the Hawaii University Affiliated Program for Developmental Disabilities (Hawaii UAP) at the University of Hawaii has been involved in the "details of practice" involving the formation, training, and support of 41 cross-functional institutions of higher education/professional/community educational planning and improvement teams from California, Hawaii, Minnesota, Ohio, and Florida nationally, and from American Samoa and the Republic of the Marshall Islands in the Pacific Basin. The explicit purpose for formulating these Hawaii UAP planning and improvement team partnerships has been to improve the capability and capacity for critical professional, family, agency, and community planning partners to produce systemic improvements within local programs and services that directly impact the adult and community lives of individuals with developmental disabilities.

These Hawaii UAP planning and improvement team partnerships are designed to be highly dynamic and interactive systems. They have repeatedly demonstrated their utilitarian worth in linking "insider" (local practitioner and consumer) experience and knowledge to "outsider" (institutions of higher education and state education agencies) effective practices for achieving transformational improvement and change in the adult and community outcomes of individuals with disabilities. Each of the participant teams involved in the partnership voluntarily has dedicated itself to the "core" transformation of existing special education and agency programs and services in a persistent bid to induce outcomes of significance for individuals with developmental disabilities in adult and community settings (Hawaii UAP, 1994). (For further descriptions, see Smith, Bisconer, van Geldern, & Rhuman, 1994; Smith & Edelen-Smith, 1993; Smith, Edelen-Smith, & Stodden, 1995; Smith & Stodden, 1994; Smith, Stodden, & Edelen-Smith, 1994; Stodden, 1991; Stodden & Leake, 1994.) Figure 27.1 depicts the three-stage model process that the Hawaii UAP uses to "support educational planning teams, agencies, individual service providers, and consumer and family organizations to improve services, supports, and outcomes in Hawaii, the Pacific Region, and nationally" (Hawaii UAP, 1994, p. 19). This process model reflects a systems change orientation specifically designed to generate and sustain the development of learning organization teams within and across six fundamental elements identified as being critical to the installation of core transformational reform (Astuto et al., 1994; Evans, 1993; Fullan, 1993a; Garvin, 1993; Kaufman, 1995; Maeroff, 1993; Senge, 1990; Senge et al., 1994). The model reflects these six elements:

1. It recognizes that transformational change is a long-term process which necessitates the provision of actionable knowledge and support infrastructures (plans, processes, and procedures), which in turn will generate the needed dynamism to alter the individual and collective behavior of the educational planning partners and their team organizations.

2. It supports the development of "critical mass" properties, defined as "situations in which a process becomes self-sustaining after some threshold point . . . the point when one accepted social paradigm no longer makes sense and is replaced by another (Aburdene & Naisbitt, 1992, pp. xvi–xvii).

3. It recognizes that the process of transformational reform needs to begin where it makes the most sense, in the planning and improvement partners' own schools and communities, working in tandem with the external agencies and community support systems that serve those schools and communities.

4. It supports the opinion that transformational reform cannot be mandated or externally installed. Rather, it evolves from a clear collaborative preferred vision of tomorrow for individuals with developmental

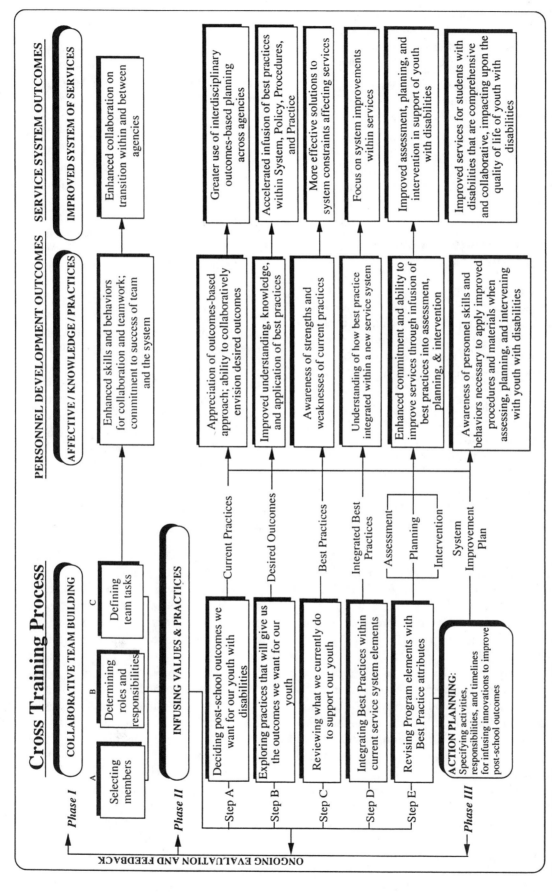

Figure 27.1. The Hawaii University Affiliated Program cross-training framework for integrating stakeholder development and system improvement outcomes.

disabilities and the identification of the design-down contributions that special education systems, programs, services, and the educational planning partners choose to make in order to reach that vision.

5. It acknowledges the importance of building "critical friend" networks of technical experts who help planning and improvement partners in their work.

6. It emphasizes the necessity of providing the planning and improvement partners with opportunities, both practice and authentic, to work and network with a wide range of professional, family, and community colleagues over time.

Actionable Knowledge, Behavioral Change, and Critical Mass

"Two Chinese characters represent the word 'learning.' The first character means to study . . . or to accumulate knowledge. The second character means to practice constantly" (Senge et al., 1994, p. 49). The Chinese view of learning begins with a simple truth: new ideas (actionable knowledge) are essential if learning is to take place. Sometimes these ideas are created spontaneously, sometimes they are communicated by professional and consumer specialists in-the-know, and sometimes they arrive via institutions of higher learning "critical-friend" partners. Although these ideas can serve as the trigger for core transformational improvement and change, ideas alone will never create a learning organization. If ideas are to become realities through transformational reform, education professionals, parents, agency personnel, individuals with disabilities, and other educational and community partners must have an accompanying opportunity to practice using their ideas in a process of systemic special education program and service renovation within their local communities (Garvin, 1993).

Organizational learning is a developmental process that can usually be attributed to three interactive phases (Dobyns & Crawford-Mason, 1994; Garvin, 1993; Senge et al., 1994; Tapscott & Caston, 1993) (see Figure 27.2). The first phase is cognitive. In this phase, professional, family, agency, and other community planning partners are exposed to new ideas (actionable knowledge) to expand their awareness of and to begin the process of thinking differently about themselves and the role(s) that they and their planning partners play in the process of improving existing special education program and service systems.

The second phase is behavioral. Professional, family, and community planning partners are given the opportunity to internalize their actionable knowledge both in practice ("formal" courses and training sessions) and in the reality of their community settings (on-site planning teams). The consequence of this accumulated knowledge and ongoing practice (learning) is that the planning teams choose to alter

their individual and collective behavior to achieve improved outcomes and options—preferred futures—for individuals with disabilities in their communities.

The third phase is transformational improvement. Transformational improvement includes those quantitative and qualitative improvements in professional support and development, systems and communities, and services and supports that emerge from interactions between Steps 1 and 2.

A number of researchers (Aburdene & Naisbitt, 1992; Fullan, 1993a; Gleick, 1987; Horgan, 1995) have commented on the resemblance of transformational change in social systems to transformational change in physical or chemical systems, particularly in regard to the notion of "critical mass." Complex systems or organizations, be they human or molecular, tend to remain fairly constant even while being acted upon by external and internal events or forces, that is, until they reach a decisive—although indeterminate—point of interconnectedness or involvement known as critical mass. Critical mass initiates a chain reaction that shifts the system, organization, or team out of entrenched practices, products, and beliefs and into a new plane of operation. When critical mass occurs, planning partners persistently apply actionable knowledge within their collaborative networks and introduce core transformational variations into their educational, vocational, and community programs and services for individuals with developmental disabilities. Column 3 in Figure 27.2 depicts examples of some potential transformational outcomes.

Involvement of the Planning and Improvement Partners

Astuto et al. (1994) noted that the solutions to the problem of authentic special education improvement and reform are best determined at the local level: one individual, one parent, one teacher, one program, one school, one community. If transformational reform in special education is to occur, the reformers must directly involve planning and improvement partners at the grassroots level. Mintzberg (1994) emphasized that a grassroots planning model is the opposite of prescriptive planning models. Prescriptive planning models typically view the formulation of strategies leading to program and service improvement and reform as being dichotomous to implementation, thus separating thinking from acting. Grassroots planning models turn this prescriptive construct on its head. In the Hawaii UAP model, the implementors—the planning partners who are charged with the responsibility for carrying out strategies—are the same persons who formulate those strategies. Practice has shown that improvement and reform strategies are more likely to lead to outcomes of significance for individuals with developmental disabilities if they are actively generated by those professional, family, agency, and community partners who will be

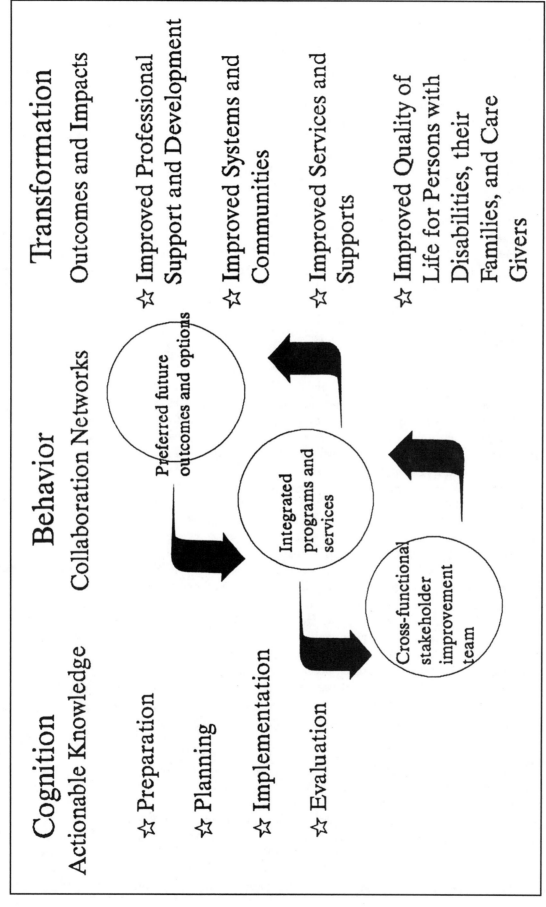

Figure 27.2. The three interactive steps attributed to organization learning: how actionable knowledge and collaborative networks can generate outcomes and impacts of significance.

expected to implement them, thus connecting thinking to action (Cook, 1995; Fullan, 1993a, 1993b; Kaufman, 1995; Siegel & Byrne, 1994).

Collective Vision

The charge of each Hawaii UAP planning team is to create a collective ideal vision of a preferred future for individuals with developmental disabilities. This vision subsequently serves to guide the planning and improvement process. The shared vision articulates for each professional, family, agency, and community partner and their planning team, the transformational ideals and values to which they have committed. Senge et al. (1994) maintained that, without a guiding vision, "there is no passion, no overarching sense of direction or purpose. People ask, 'Why are we doing this?' or 'What's this change in infrastructure all about?'" (Senge et al., 1994, p. 36). With the installation of a guiding collective vision, a diverse group of partners develops a sense of direction: a common orientation point, pulling everyone toward the same preferred future (Senge et al., 1994). (See Figure 27.2, Column 2.)

Maximal movement toward an ideal vision—outcomes of significance for individuals with developmental disabilities—however, cannot be achieved totally by the planning and improvement teams alone. Experience has shown that planning for outcomes of significance is a highly interdependent process. External partners who may be or will be expected to play an active role through the delivery of additional supports and/or resources (e.g., Social Security, Developmental Disabilities Councils, Protection and Advocacy Councils, Vocational Rehabilitation, employers) are inherently involved in the process. If external partners are to deliver needed supports and resources, it is crucial to gain their approval of the plan of action. It is not enough merely to identify these external partners. Each team must be willing to let them become active contributors to the transformational reform and improvement process as well. The importance of securing the involvement and commitment of external educational, social, and/or vocational partners cannot be overstated. Unless these external partners accept the vision and mission of the team, quick fixes and random attacks from dissident partners are likely to derail the whole enterprise (Harvey, 1988; Kaufman, 1995; Smith et al., 1995).

Critical-Friend Associations

Adhocracy "alliances, partnerships, consortia, and collaborations all connote joint agreements and action over a period of time in which all parties learn to work differently and achieve qualitatively different results" (Fullan, 1993b, p. 94). Providing the school, team, or individual planning partners with immediate, long-term access to institution of higher education, state education agency, and local education agency critical-friend support networks has proven to be a constructive procedure for strengthening and preserving delicate newly formed alliances, partnerships, consortia, and joint agreements and for supporting long-term actions (Arends, 1990; Fullan, 1993a; Fullan & Stiegelbauer, 1991; "A Higher Mission," 1994; Joyce, 1990; Smith et al., 1994; Smith & Edelen-Smith, 1993; Smith & Stodden, 1994). The editors of *Education Week* ("A Higher Mission," 1994) define a critical friend as an outside source of consultation, help, and technical assistance whose single purpose is to develop a school-level capacity to support and sustain transformational improvement and reform. Costa and Kallick (1993) referred to critical friends as trusted individuals who ask provocative questions, provide data to be examined from an external viewpoint, and offer an impartial critique of the work of the planning partners and their teams as friends. "A critical friend takes the time to fully understand the context of the work presented and the outcome that the person or group is working toward. The friend is an advocate for the success of that work" (Costa & Kallick, 1993, p. 50).

Expanding upon these descriptions, the Hawaii University Affiliated Program defines a critical-friend network as a "nourishing" consultant association between the team, the Hawaii UAP, and other state education agency and local education agency support programs. Research and effective practice related to special education program and service reform and improvement is showcased for—but not imposed upon—individual planning partners as well as collective teams through these critical-friend associations. In addition, each planning partner and their team is assured of critical-friend partners who have a wide range of experience working in and with other communities, schools, and agencies that are attempting to institute similar reforms and improvements. Each of the 41 participating learning organization teams recognizes that a core objective of the Hawaii UAP is to provide educational planning partners with access to critical-friend expertise, training, and support that is continuous, tolerant of individual and team function, and clearly separate from supervision and evaluation (punitive threat) (Fullan & Stiegelbauer, 1991).

Building Networks Through Practice Sessions that Improve the Real Game

In sports and in the performing arts, two settings where teams consistently enhance their capabilities, players move regularly between a practice field and the real game, between rehearsal and performance. It is impossible to imagine a basketball team learning without practice, or a chamber music ensemble learning without rehearsal. Yet that is what is expected to occur in organizations (partnership teams). People are expected to learn when the costs of failure are high, when personal threat is great, when there is no opportunity to "replay" an important decision, and when there is no way to simplify complexity and shorten time delays so as to better understand the consequences of actions. Is it any wonder that learning in organizations is rare (Senge et al., 1994, p. 35)?

The most important attribute offered to the planning partners and their teams by the Hawaii UAP model process is the opportunity to practice a viable field-tested method for empowering the teams to effect change within the context of their own schools and communities. As Senge et al. (1994) pointed out, nothing is changed if the team partners are given a demonstration of collaborative training in an in-service training session, but then are not allowed to practice that knowledge in the actual educational setting. Likewise, it is futile for the partnership planning teams to become accomplished in the "practice" of constructing a vision of a preferred adult and community future for individuals with developmental disabilities if they are not provided access to new actionable knowledge that assists them in generating movement toward that vision. For this reason, the operational elements of the Hawaii UAP transformational model process are introduced and rehearsed through planning and improvement prior to any of those elements being undertaken or implemented in actual system, program, and/or service settings (Maeroff, 1993; Senge, 1990; Senge et al., 1994; Smith & Stodden, 1994).

The experience of 4 years of working with the partnership planning teams has demonstrated repeatedly the value of simultaneously providing actionable knowledge with useful, relevant practice opportunities for the teams. Generally these practice opportunities have been infused into pertinent courses offered each semester through the University of Hawaii to interested professionals, parents, agency personnel, and other community partners. In particular, these courses have proven to be very popular with education and agency professionals (enrollments of up to 80 individuals) because the courses provide credits that can lead to a higher educational or professional degree, merit pay increase, or promotion. In addition, they are generally provided to invested professional partners without charge as an incentive to remain in the team network, and are scheduled at the convenience of the individuals enrolled in the course (e.g., at a specific school site, or on a Saturday) (Stodden & Leake, 1994). However, one Hawaii UAP practice field format—the Summer Teaming Institute, which is similar in ideology to the Leadership Academies sponsored by the Rockefeller Foundation (see Maeroff, 1993, for a complete review)—has demonstrated its popular and practical value to parents; Developmental Disability council members; employers; general, vocational, and special education teachers; school administrators; agency personnel; and individuals with developmental disabilities who are concerned with improving the adult and community outcomes of individuals with developmental disabilities. A 2-day intensive training and support session held on campus at the University of

Hawaii, the Summer Teaming Institute has provided to more than 500 interested professional, family, and agency partners over the past 4 years, an "environment in which team members can safely take their first steps toward building a team-driven learning organization" (Smith & Stodden, 1994, p. 19). The Summer Teaming Institute provides partner team members the initial opportunity to establish the collaborative networks they will need to use in order to succeed in the real game of attaining a preferred future for individuals with developmental disabilities.

Results

When all is said and done, people judge the value of core transformational improvement and revision by the results. The strategy for building adhocracy or learning organization teams used by the Hawaii UAP is based on the premise that these new, innovative team organizations dramatically will improve the quality of adult and community outcomes for individuals with developmental disabilities as compared with older, more traditional special education organizations (Garvin, 1993; Kaufman, 1995; Senge et al., 1994; Smith & Stodden, 1994). It is evident that the worth of any practice, learning, and/or organizational transformation will be assessed ultimately by the value that each element adds in terms of "how well the real game is played" (Senge et al., 1994; Smith et al., 1994; Smith & Stodden, 1994). The problem with assessment, however, lies in knowing how and when to measure important "real game" results (Senge et al., 1994).

Evaluating outcome-oriented results requires a new mindset. The planning and improvement team partners are encouraged to start viewing results as a formative tool for monitoring transformational movement and change within and across their own schools, programs, or services rather than as unrelated summative data that will be reported to some external overseer. When all the planning partners begin to think of results as something useful to their own evolutionary (formative) development as a team organization, they begin to insist that information be collected, stored, and retrieved in ways that are suited to their program improvement functions (Hoachlander, 1995).

Beginning in Phase 1 (see Figure 27.1), each professional, family, agency, or community partner and their team must be made aware of the value of and need for "patience" because transformational learning and change do not produce tangible evidence of high-impact results (program and service improvement and reform) for a considerable amount of time. " 'You don't pull up the radishes to see how they're growing,' says William O'Brien of the Center for Organizational Learning at MIT; 'Time periods for measurement must be congruent with the gestation period of the learning' " (cited in Senge et al., 1994, p. 45). Although it is easy to assert the principle behind the need for patience, the Hawaii

UAP has found it to be very hard for impatient institutions of higher education, state education agencies, local education agencies, administrators, parent advocacy groups, developmental disability councils, and other external groups to accept.

A second difficulty encountered relative to the assessment of results and outcomes by the partner teams is how to separate quality results from quantity results. During the past 4 years, a multitude of significant quantitative results—benchmarks of physical transformation—have occurred within and across each of the 41 team organizations. These include articulated agreements between secondary vocational education systems and community college vocational education systems; improved assessment and planning interventions that support outcomes of significance for individuals with disabilities; greater use of the Hawaii University Affiliated Program, Developmental Disability council, and Protection and Advocacy networks; among others. However, many of the most important results accomplished by the teams have been qualitative in nature and benchmarks of affective transformation: for example, acceptance of diversity, confidence, genuine caring, determination, and feelings of individual and collective ownership. Finding ways to measure and document the affective growth of team organizations has been a challenge. Chapter length prevents a thorough review of the formative processes and procedures developed by the Hawaii UAP to assess quantity and quality participant and/or team results; however, they have been thoroughly described elsewhere (see Smith et al., 1994; Smith & Stodden, 1994; Stodden & Leake, 1994).

Conclusion

The Chairman of the Coalition of Essential Schools noted that prescriptive directives, such as ordering school systems to improve student performance and outcomes, are analogous to ordering a Model T to drive 60 miles per hour. "You can order all you want, but unless you change the vehicle, right down to how the engine's organized, you're not going to go 60 miles per hour" (O'Neil, 1995a, p. 4). Too many reformers never question the basic assumptions upon which special education program and service systems are organized. People who formulate reform policies without addressing the core organizational system do not understand that reform necessitates a fundamental reshaping of the way special education program and service systems operate. When external policy makers continuously tamper with the hubcaps, or simply add on flashy accessories, the special education vehicle only appears to be changing. At its core it is still a Model T.

The external governance processes and procedures of "command and control" may have been successful in improving and reforming special education program and service systems in the 1970s and 1980s, but they will never be capable of producing the complex systemic transformational changes required to produce outcomes of significance for individuals with disabilities in the 1990s, let alone the 21st century. The days when a centralized authority could determine and dictate what local practitioners needed or should do to improve and reform school outcomes are a thing of the past. As Senge (1990) pointed out, "In an increasingly dynamic, interdependent and unpredictable world, it is simply no longer possible for anyone [or any one group] to 'figure it all out at the top'" (p. 340). If change is to occur, the prescriptive planning model of special education program and service organization where administrators (top) formulate improvement and reform strategies and the practitioner (bottom) implements them must give way to a learning or adhocracy organizational form that has the potential to create new ways and means of thinking and acting at all levels.

Adhocracy or learning organization planning and improvement teams are unique by definition (O'Neil, 1995b; Skrtic, 1991). Because each planning and improvement team needs to reflect its own school and community culture, there can be no universal model or method of implementation. Transformational improvement and reform is a process that requires support and collaboration among all the planning and improvement partners in a particular community: general, vocational, and special education teachers; individuals with developmental disabilities; families; agency personnel; employers; and other relevant partners.

This chapter has described an operational grassroots process capable of generating core transformational change in special education program and service systems through the creation and installation of a learning organization of educational planning teams. The discussion on learning organization teams has moved beyond a discourse of "high philosophy" and "grand themes" and into descriptions of the "details" of practice. The Hawaii University Affiliated Program for Developmental Disabilities has used, and is currently using, this transformational process method to provide technical assistance, training, and support to 41 cross-functional (profession and consumer) planning and improvement partnership teams across the United States and the Pacific Basin. Six elements were identified as being critical to the core transformation of special education systems, programs, and services: (a) actionable knowledge and support infrastructures that support individual and collective behavioral change, (b) the role of critical mass, (c) involvement of all relevant educational planning partners, (d) collective vision, (e) critical-friend associations, and (f) the construction of collaborative networks. Finally, the importance of formative assessment and some inherent difficulties in assessing both quantitative and qualitative results were addressed.

Decades of external monitoring have proven that individuals will comply with outside demands either from fear of punishment or from desire for material rewards. However, compliance rarely results in transformation. Individuals will attempt to transform themselves and their organizations only through their personal commitment. Such commitment evolves from a genuine sense of vision, a dream if you will, of what individuals with developmental disabilities need to know and do in order to assure their right to a "life that makes sense" in the world of today and tomorrow. Genuine transformational or core change cannot be mandated, installed, or imposed. Rather, it emerges through collaboration and through learning by experience. Albert-Gyrgyi maintained that transformational growth is a discovery process that "consists of seeing what everybody has seen and thinking what nobody has thought" (cited in Dobyns & Crawford-Mason, 1994, p. 28). Change comes from the confidence that grows through the efforts of planning and improvement teams in developing plans of action that are capable of generating a preferred future for individuals with developmental disabilities in their schools, their communities, and the world.

QUESTIONS

1. How does a "command and control" construct of program and service reform impede the development of programs and services based on a construct of a "preferred future" for individuals with developmental disabilities?

2. What lessons have been learned through the experience of other schools, agencies, and planning organizations attempting to engage in transformational change?

3. How do prescriptive planning models compare and contrast with grassroots planning models?

4. How do critical-friend associations and practice sessions add value to the planning partners engaged in transforming programs and services for individuals with developmental disabilities?

5. How does the collective creation of a vision based on a preferred future for individuals with developmental disabilities assist educational planning partners to better understand and implement the design-down principle described in the Individuals with Disabilities Education Act of 1990?

References

Aburdene, P., & Naisbitt, J. (1992). *Megatrends for women*. New York: Willard Books.

Arends, R. I. (1990). Connecting the university to the school. In B. Joyce (Ed.), *Changing school culture through staff development*. Alexandria, VA: Association for Supervision and Curriculum Development.

Astuto, T., Clark, D., Read, A., McGree, K., & Fernandez, L. (1994). *Roots of reform: Challenging the assumptions that control change in education*. Bloomington, IN: Phi Delta Kappa Educational Foundation.

Beane, J. A. (Ed.). (1995). *Toward a coherent curriculum* [1995 ASCD Yearbook]. Alexandria, VA: Association for Supervision and Curriculum Development.

Campbell, D. (1995). The Socrates syndrome: Questions that should never be asked. *Phi Delta Kappan, 76*, 467–469.

Cook, A. (1995, March 8). Teachers as team players or, how many heroes does it take to change a school? *Education Week, 14*(24), 30, 40.

Costa, A. L., & Kallick, B. (1993). Through the lens of a critical friend. *Educational Leadership, 51*(2), 49–51.

Darling-Hammond, L. (1993). Reframing the school reform agenda: Developing capacity for school transformation. *Phi Delta Kappan, 74*, 753–761.

DeStefano, L., & Wagner, M. (1993). Outcomes assessment in special education: Implications for decision-making and long-term planning in vocational rehabilitation. *Career Development for Exceptional Individuals, 16*, 147–158.

Dobyns, L., & Crawford-Mason, C. (1994). *Thinking about quality: Progress, wisdom, and the Deming philosophy*. New York: Times Books.

Edelen-Smith, P. J. (1995). Eight elements to guide goal determination for IEPs. *Intervention in School and Clinic, 30*, 297–301.

Edgar, E., & Polloway, E. (1994). Education for adolescents with disabilities: Curriculum and placement issues. *The Journal of Special Education, 27*, 438–452.

Education for All Handicapped Children Act of 1975, 20 U.S.C. § 1400 et seq.

Evans, R. (1993). The human face of reform. *Educational Leadership, 51*(1), 19–23.

Fullan, M. (1993a). *Change forces: Probing the depths of educational reform*. Bristol, PA: Falmer Press.

Fullan, M. (1993b). Innovation, reform, and restructuring strategies. In G. Cawelti (Ed.), *Challenges and achievements in American education* (pp. 116–133). Alexandria, VA: Association for Supervision and Curriculum Development.

Fullan, M., & Stiegelbauer, S. (1991). *The new meaning of educational change*. New York: Teachers College Press.

Garvin, D. A. (1993). Building a learning organization. *Harvard Business Review, 71*(4), 78–91.

Gleick, J. (1987). *Chaos: Making a new science*. New York: Penguin.

Goodlad, J. I. (1991). Why we need a complete redesign of teacher education. *Educational Leadership, 49*(3), 4–10.

Harvey, J. B. (1988). *The Abilene paradox and other meditations of management*. San Diego: University Associates.

Hawaii University Affiliated Program for Developmental Disabilities. (1994). *Executive Summary Report*. Honolulu: Author.

A higher mission? Defining the role of colleges and universities in K–12 reform. (1994, April 13). *Education Week* (special report addition: Alliance for learning: Enlisting higher education in the quest for better schools), pp. 17–23.

Hoachlander, G. (1995). What the numbers really mean. *Vocational Education Journal, 70*(3), 20–23, 50.

Horgan, J. (1995). From complexity to perplexity. *Scientific American, 272*(6), 104–109.

Individuals with Disabilities Education Act of 1990, 20 U.S.C. § 1400 *et seq.*

Johnson, D., Thompson, S., Sinclair, M., Krantz, G., Evelo, S., Stolte, K., & Thompson, J. (1993). Considerations in the design of follow-up and follow-along systems for improving transition programs and services. *Career Development for Exceptional Individuals, 16*, 225–238.

Joyce, B. (1990). Prologue. In B. Joyce (Ed.), *Changing school culture through staff development* (pp. xv–xviii). Alexandria, VA: Association for Supervision and Curriculum Development.

Kaufman, R. (1995). *Mapping educational success* (Revised). Newbury Park, CA: Corwin Press.

Kohler, P. D. (1993). Best practice in transition: Substantiated or implied? *Career Development for Exceptional Individuals, 16*, 107–121.

Maeroff, G. I. (1993). *Team building for school change: Equipping teachers for new roles*. New York: Teachers College Press.

Mintzberg, H. (1994). *The rise and fall of strategic planning*. New York: Free Press.

Newmann, F. M. (1993). Beyond common sense in educational restructuring: The issue of content and linkage. *Educational Researcher, 22*(2), 4–13, 22.

O'Neil, J. (1995a). On lasting school reform: A conversation with Ted Sizer. *Educational Leadership, 52*(5), 4–9.

O'Neil, J. (1995b). On schools as learning organizations: A conversation with Peter Senge. *Educational Leadership, 52*(7), 20–23.

Sarason, S. (1993). *The case for change: Rethinking the preparation of educators*. San Francisco: Jossey-Bass.

Senge, P. M. (1990). *The fifth discipline: The art and practice of the learning organization*. New York: Doubleday-Currency.

Senge, P., Roberts, C., Ross, R., Smith, B., & Kleiner, A. (1994). *The fifth discipline fieldbook: Strategies and tools for building a learning organization*. New York: Doubleday-Currency.

Shanker, A. (1990). Staff development and the restructured school. In B. Joyce (Ed.), *Changing school culture through staff development*, Alexandria, VA: Association for Supervision and Curriculum Development.

Siegel, P., & Byrne, S. (1994). *Using quality to redesign school systems*. San Francisco: Jossey-Bass.

Skrtic, T. M. (1991). *Behind special education: A critical analysis of professional culture and school organization*. Denver: Love.

Smith, G. J., Bisconer, S. W., van Geldern, L., & Rhuman, J. H. (1994, April). *Assessing the value added through transformational staff development: The challenge to evaluate quality*. Paper presented at the 72nd Annual Conference of the Council for Exceptional Children, Denver.

Smith, G. J., & Edelen-Smith, P. J. (1990). A commencement based model of secondary education and training in mild mental retardation. *Education and Training in Mental Retardation, 25*, 15–24.

Smith, G. J., & Edelen-Smith, P. J. (1993). Restructuring secondary special education Hawaiian style. *Intervention in School and Clinic, 28*, 248–252, 256.

Smith, G. J., Edelen-Smith, P. J. & Stodden, R. A. (1995). How to avoid the seven pitfalls of systematic planning: A school and community plan for transition. *Teaching Exceptional Children, 27*(4), 42–47.

Smith, G. J., & Stodden, R. A. (1994). Restructuring vocational special needs education through interdisciplinary team effort: Local motion in the Pacific Basin. *Journal for Vocational Special Needs Education, 16*(3), 16–23.

Smith, G. J., Stodden, R. A., & Edelen-Smith, P. J. (1994). Restructuring and improving transition services through school–university collaboration. *Educational Perspectives, 28*(2), 21–24.

Smull, M. W. (1995). After the plan. *AAMR News and Notes, 8*(4), 5, 8.

SouthEastern Regional Vision for Education. (1994). *Overcoming barriers to school reform in the southeast*. Greensboro, NC: Author.

Spady, W. G. (1994). *Outcome-based education: Critical issues and answers*. Arlington, VA: American Association of School Administrators.

Spady, W. G., & Marshall, K. J. (1991). Beyond traditional outcome-based education. *Educational Leadership, 49*(2), 67–72.

Stodden, R. A. (1991). *Career/vocational preparation for students with disabilities: A program improvement guide*. Tallahassee: Florida State Department of Education.

Stodden, R. A., & Leake, D. W. (1994). Getting to the core of transition: A re-assessment of old wine in new bottles. *Career Development for Exceptional Individuals, 17*(1), 65–76.

Tapscott, D., & Caston, A. (1993). *Paradigm shift: The new promise of information technology*. New York: McGraw-Hill.

Author Index

Subject Index